D0906558

NATIONAL SECURITY
AND
INTERNATIONAL STABILITY

Written under the auspices of the Center for International and Strategic Affairs, University of California, Los Angeles.

A list of other center publications appears at the end of this book.

National Security and International Stability

Edited by

Bernard Brodie
Michael D. Intriligator
Roman Kolkowicz
Center for International and Strategic Affairs
University of California, Los Angeles

  Oelgeschlager, Gunn & Hain,
Publishers, Inc.
Cambridge, Massachusetts

International Standard Book Number: 0-89946-172-7

Library of Congress Catalog Card Number: 82-18913

Printed in the U.S.A.

Library of Congress Cataloging in Publication Data

Main entry under title:

National security and international stability.

Includes index.
1. National security—Addresses, Essays, lectures.
2. Strategic forces—Addresses, essays, lectures.
3. World politics—1945-   —Addresses, essays,
lectures.   4. International relations—Addresses, essays,
lectures.   I. Brodie, Bernard, 1910-   .   II. Intriligator, Michael D. III. Kolkowicz, Roman.
UA10.5.N28   1983   355'.033'0046   82-18913

ISBN 0-89946-172-7

CONTENTS

Part I   **Introduction**

Chapter 1   Introduction: National Security and   1
                    International Stability   *Roman Kolkowicz*,
                    University of California, Los Angeles and
                    Michael D. Intriligator, University of California,
                    Los Angeles

Part II   **Substantive and Analytic Treatment of Broader
                    Issues**

Chapter 2   The Development of Nuclear Strategy   5
                    Bernard Brodie, University of California, Los
                    Angeles
Chapter 3   On Fighting a Nuclear War   *Michael E.*   23
                    Howard, Oxford University
Chapter 4   The Role of Strategic Concepts and Doctrine in   37
                    U.S. Strategic Nuclear Force Development
                    Desmond Ball, Australian National University

Chapter 5   Changing Attitudes Toward Deterrence   *Henry*   65
             Trofimenko, Institute of the USA and Canada,
             Soviet Academy of Sciences

Chapter 6   The Operational Level of War   *Edward N.*   111
             Luttwak, Georgetown University

Chapter 7   Deterrence and Perception   *Robert Jervis*,   131
             Columbia University

Chapter 8   Revolutions in Warfare: An Earlier Generation   157
             of Interpreters   *Peter Paret*, Stanford
             University

Chapter 9   On Strategic Suprise   *Klaus Knorr*, Princeton   171
             University

Chapter 10   Toward a Soviet—American Crisis Prevention   189
             Regime: History and Prospects   *Alexander L.*
             George, Stanford University

Chapter 11   The Terrorist Use of Nuclear Weapons   209
             Thomas C. Schelling, Harvard University

Chapter 12   Nuclear Proliferation   *George H. Quester*,   227
             University of Maryland

Chapter 13   Nuclear Proliferation and the Probability of   257
             Nuclear war   *Michael D. Intriligator*,
             University of California, Los Angeles and
             Dagobert L. Brito, Tulane University

Chapter 14   Military Strategy and Political Interests: The   273
             Soviet Union and the United States   *Roman*
             Kolkowicz, University of California, Los Angeles

Part III   **Case Studies**

Chapter 15   American Perceptions and Strategic Options in   301
             the Korean War   *Robert R. Simmons*,
             University of Guelph

Chapter 16   The H-Bomb Decisions: Were They Inevitable?   327
             Barton J. Bernstein, Stanford University

Chapter 17   On Memories, Interests, and Foreign Policy: 357
             Vietnam   *Michael Nacht*, Harvard University

Chapter 18   The ABM Debate   *George Rathjens*,   379
             Massachusetts Institute of Technology

Chapter 19   MIRV   *Herbert F. York* and *G. Allen Greb*,   407
             University of California, San Diego

Index   429
About the Editors   439

Chapter 1

Introduction: National Security and International Stability

Roman Kolkowicz
and
Michael D. Intriligator

Strategic nuclear studies are barely three decades old, and yet one already perceives a sense of intellectual decline and theoretical exhaustion within the community of strategic analysts. One reads nostalgic recollections of a "golden age" of strategic thought: there seems to be general agreement about its starting point, and "all are agreed that the golden age has passed."[1] The lore of contemporary strategic study perceives the beginning of the strategic renaissance to coincide in the mid-1950s with the publication of W. W. Kaufmann's *Military Policy and National Security*,[2] and Henry Kissinger's *Nuclear Weapons and Foreign Policy*,[3] and then to sharply decline in the mid-1960s after the publication of T. C. Schelling's *Arms and Influence*[4] and K. Knorr's *On the Uses of Military Power in the Nuclear Age*.[5] The archetypal nuclear strategist of this "golden age" was not difficult to recognize, according to a recent study of "The Evolution of Strategic Thinking":

He was an American; a civilian; basically an 'academic', operating from a university or a well-funded research institute, but moving relatively freely between this base and government; and with a commitment to peace and stability through a combination of deterrence, arms control, and crisis management. This was the dominant group in the golden age (and since); they were the most productive, the most read, the most fashionable, and they were considered the most congenial by the policy makers.[6]

The nascent revisionist literature on strategic studies in the United States has offered some harsh indictments against the strategic founders and their successors: "In 1961 the promise was high. The civilian strategists came to Washington to assume an influential role in the new administration. Yet in 1971 it is fair to say that their performance had not lived up to their promise. And that's putting it mildly."[7]

The basic problems with the theories of these civilian strategists were, according to their critics:

the dominance of the economic conflict model: the assumption that international conflict can be analyzed in terms of rational, strategic men was "useful in the development of strategic theory, but it has proven fatal to the relevance of theorists who have shifted from model-bulding to prescription."

the transition from prophet to courtier: strategic theorists entered the corridors of power and "the United States has been living off its strategic theoretical capital" ever since.

the bureaucratization of strategic art and science: the attempt to free strategy from the excessive controls of the military patron, and to thus encourage participation by academics in the development of strategy has spawned many think tanks. However, think tanks, the middle ground between academe and government as exemplified by the Rand Corporation, began to manifest dual loyalty and, according to the critics, tended to produce "both irrelevant policy advice and poor scholarship."[8]

Critical assaults on the strategic community did not, however, affect the output of its practitioners. Far from entering a steep decline, strategic and defense analysis, at least in terms of the sheer volume of published work and contract research, became a growth industry. Moreover, the critics were taken to task by defenders such as Hedley Bull, who thought the criticism highly unfair because it "called into question the validity of their methods, their utility to society, and even their integrity of purpose" and who found some of this criticism "of so scurrilous a nature as not to deserve a reply."[9]

The present volume is, in a sense, an outgrowth of these reassessments and debates in the strategic community. The three editors, having all at one time or another worked at the Rand Corporation, served as consultants to various parts of the government, testified before congressional committees on defense and strategic issues, and having subsequently joined the faculty of the University of California, had more than a passing interest in the state of strategic studies in the United States. The concern with the perceived intellectual exhaustion in the strategic community motivated one of them (Kolkowicz) to begin research on the roles and influence of defense intellectuals in the Soviet Union and the United States. A first tentative assessment was presented to a Harvard seminar in 1968 and was subsequently published in 1972.[10] With the formation of the Center for International and Strategic Affairs (CISA) at UCLA, under a grant from the Ford Foundation, there were many opportunities to consider these issues at various meetings and seminars. And, as members of CISA, it became possible for the editors to pursue this sort of analysis on a more sustained basis. Roman Kolkowicz therefore asked Bernard Brodie and Michael Intriligator to consider jointly editing a volume of essays that would reassess the theoretical and policy validity of earlier writings on the problems of national security, strategy, and arms control.

During several memorable afternoons and evenings at the hillside home of Bernard Brodie, the editors discussed the content, organization, and thematic thrust of the planned volume, and agreed to invite contributions from several of the most outstanding and pioneering scholars in the field of strategic studies, as well as some younger scholars whose views and perceptions might differ. The contributors were asked to consider the formative ideas, theories, and policy prescriptions of the "golden age" of strategic studies, to reflect upon these ideas and theories from a two- or three-decade long perspective, and then to provide their evaluations and reassessments.

Bernard Brodie's influence on this enterprise was invaluable. A towering figure in the field of strategic studies and a pioneer in the complexities of nuclear strategy who was the first to perceive the revolutionary changes that nuclear weapons would bring to the nature of war and peace, Brodie was greatly concerned, toward the end of his career, with the disarray in the strategic community. Tragically, his enthusiastic participation in the planning of this volume was disrupted by a wasting illness and eventually ended with his death on November 24, 1978.

This volume is intended to reflect Brodie's strongly held views, which are shared by the two other editors, that:

"we need people who will challenge, investigate, and dissect the prevailing dogmas"[11] of our foreign policy, and of strategic studies; it is important for students of strategy to be aware of the "inevitable limitations and imperfections of scientific method in strategic analysis and decisionmaking" particularly with regard to the imperfections of the practitioners, "whose greatest limitation is that they sometimes fail to observe true scientific discipline;" it is necessary to understand that the "most basic issues of strategy often do not lend themselves to scientific analysis . . . because they are laden with value judgements and therefore tend to escape any kind of disciplined thought";[12] and last, but not least, the Clausewitzian admonition on the "need to stress the superior importance of the political side of strategy to the simply technical and technological side"[13] is particularly relevant in the age of nuclear deterrence.

The contributions to this volume reflect the high intellectual standards espoused by Bernard Brodie and thus contribute to the exchange of ideas and to the critical self-assessment necessary for the continued intellectual vitality and policy relevance of the field.

NOTES

1. Ken Booth, "The Evolution of Strategic Thinking," in John Baylis *et al.*, *Contemporary Strategy: Theories and Policies*, Holmes and Meier, New York, 1975, p. 35.
2. William W. Kaufmann, *Military Power and National Security*, Princeton University Press, Princeton, N.J., 1956.
3. H. A. Kissinger, *Nuclear Weapons and Foreign Policy*, Harper and Row, New York, 1957.
4. T. C. Schelling, *Arms and Influence*, Yale University Press, New Haven, Conn., 1966.
5. Klaus Knorr, *On the Uses of Military Power in the Nuclear Age*, Princeton University Press, Princeton, N.J., 1966.
6. Booth, "Strategic Thinking," p. 36.
7. Colin Gray, "What RAND Hath Wrought," *Foreign Policy*, no. 4, Fall 1971.
8. *Ibid.*, see also his "Across the Nuclear Divide—Strategic Studies, Past and Present" in *International Security*, Summer 1977, pp. 24-45; and "Nuclear Strategy: The Case for a Theory of Victory," *International Security*, Summer 1979, pp. 54-86.
9. Hedley Bull, "Strategic Studies and Its Critics," *World Politics*, July 1968, pp. 593-605.
10. Roman Kolkowicz, "Strategic Elites and Politics of Superpower," *Journal of International Affairs*, vol. 26, no. 1 (1972), pp. 40-59.
11. Bernard Brodie, "Why Were We So (Strategically) Wrong?," *Foreign Policy*, Winter 1971-72, pp. 151-162.
12. Bernard Brodie, "The Scientific Strategists" in Robert Gilpin and Christopher Wright, eds., *Scientists and National Policy-Making*, Columbia University Press, New York, 1964, p. 253.
13. Brodie, "Why Were We So (Strategically) Wrong?," p. 161.

Chapter 2

The Development of Nuclear Strategy

Bernard Brodie

At the beginning of the nuclear age, a concept was put forward almost at once which is still the dominant one of nuclear strategy—deterrence. It fell to me, as one of the very few civilians interested in military strategy at the time, to publish the first analytical paper on the military implications of nuclear weapons. It appeared in the autumn of 1945 as an occasional paper of what was then the Yale Institute for International Studies. In expanded form it was included as two chapters in a book published the following year, edited by me under the title *The Absolute Weapon*, and also containing essays on political implications by four of my Yale colleagues.[1]

I would like to cite one brief paragraph from that 1946 book, partly because it has recently been quoted by a number of other writers—usually with approval but in one conspicuous instance with strong disapproval:

Thus, the first and most vital step in any American security program for the age of atomic bombs is to take measures to guarantee to ourselves in case of attack the possibility of retaliation in kind. The writer in making that statement is not for the moment concerned about who will *win* the next war in which atomic bombs are used. Thus far the chief purpose of our military establishment has been to win wars. From now its chief purpose must be to avert them. It can have almost no other useful purpose.[2]

It was obvious then, as now, that this description of deterrence applied mostly to a war with the only other superpower, the Soviet Union, who did not yet have nuclear weapons but was confidently predicted in the same book to be able "to produce them in quantity within a period of five to ten years."[3] (The person who has recently expressed strong disapproval of the above-quoted statement is Professor Richard Pipes of Harvard, in an article published in the July 1977 issue of *Commentary*. I shall postpone consideration of his views to a later point in this paper.)

Let me mention a few more points in that 1946 essay to indicate what any reflective observer of the time would have found more or less self-evident. It stated that among the requirements for deterrence were extraordinary measures of protection for the retaliatory force so that it might survive a surprise attack; that margins of superiority in nuclear weapons or the means of delivering them might count for little or nothing in a crisis as long as each side had reason to fear the huge devastation of its peoples and territories by the other; that while it was possible the world might see another major war in which the nuclear bomb is not used, the shadow of that bomb would nevertheless "so govern the strategic and tactical dispositions of either side as to create a wholly novel form of war"[4]; and that this latter fact had particular implications for the uses of sea power, the classic functions of which depended on an intact home base and the passage of considerable time. It was also observed that while the idea of deterrence per se was certainly nothing new, being as old as the use of physical force; what was distinctively new was the degree to which it was intolerable that it should fail. On the other hand, one could add that "*in no case is the fear of the consequences of atomic bomb attack likely to be low,*"[5] which made it radically different from a past in which governments could, often correctly, anticipate wars that would bring them considerable political benefits while exacting very little in the way of costs.

Since 1946 there has been much useful rumination and writing on nuclear strategy, especially on the nature of deterrence, but the national debates on the subject have revolved mostly around three questions, all of which relate directly to the issue of expenditures. These three questions are: (1) What are the changing physical requirements for the continuing success of deterrence? (2) Just what kinds of wars does nuclear deterrence really deter? and (3) What is the role, if any, for tactical nuclear weapons? Far down the course in terms of the public attention accorded it is a fourth question: If deterrence fails, how do we fight a nuclear war and for what objectives? That last question has been largely neglected by civilian scholars, though lately some old ideas have been revived having to do with what are called limited nuclear options. Otherwise most questions about the actual use of nuclear weapons in war, whether strategic or tactical, have been largely left to the military and its in-house civilian retainers, who had to shoulder responsibility for picking specific targets, especially in the strategic category, and who were expected to give guidance about the kinds and numbers of nuclear weapons required.

In that connection, one must stress a point that certain young historians new to the field have found it difficult to grasp. Virtually all the basic ideas and philosophies about nuclear weapons and their use have been generated by civilians working quite independently of the military, even though some were residing in institutions like the Rand Corporation, which was largely supported by one or another of the services. In these matters the military has been with no significant exceptions, strictly a consumer, naturally showing preference for some ideas over others but hardly affecting the flow of those ideas otherwise. Whatever the reasons, they must include prominently the fact that, to the military man, deterrence comes as the byproduct, not the central theme, of his strategic structure. An philosophy that puts deterrence at the heart of the matter must be uncongenial to him. One military writer significantly speaks of the deterrence-oriented "modernist" as dwelling "in the realm of achieving non-events in a condition where the flow of events is guided, not by his initiatives, but by other minds." And further: "The obvious difficulty with deterrent theory ... is the yielding of the initiative to the adversary," where in the preceding sentence initiative has already been called the sine qua non of success.[6]

I propose in the following to say as much as my limited space permits on each of the four major questions mentioned above. The first concerns the question of how one preserves enough of one's retaliatory force against surprise attack so that the opponent, in anticipation thereof, is deterred. Obviously there is a political dimension to that question, because the need for precautionary measures does vary according to whether or not we think the opponent is straining at the leash to destroy us. There used to be current a notion that if the opponent saw his way clear to destroy us without suffering too much damage in return, that fact alone would impel him to do it. But whether or not that view was ever correct, which I doubt, it is not likely ever to be a feasible option for him. Still, to prepare against *all* possible crises in the future, it is desirable to minimize that proportion of our retaliatory forces which the opponent can have *high confidence* of destroying by a surprise blow and to help keep alive in his mind a full awareness of the penalties for miscalculation.

At the beginning of the nuclear age, the United States had a period of grace when it did not have to worry about the enemy nuclear attack. Conditions changed with the passing years, but the first sharp public reminder that we had an important vulnerability problem came only with the publication early in 1959 of Albert Wohlstetter's widely read article, "The Delicate Balance of Terror."[7] What is not generally known is that this article was precipitated by Wohlstetter's frustration with the air force. For over a year, he had been leading a large research project at Rand Corporation to find the best means of protecting our bomber aircraft. After considering various alternatives, including the "airborne alert" favored by the air force (which was itself second choice to the Douhetian idea of striking at the enemy before he gets off the ground), the project group decided that the most cost-effective defense for bombers against surprise attack was a slightly-below-ground concrete shelter for each aircraft. The air force vehemently rejected this solution, invoking slogans identifying concrete with the Maginot Line and excessive defense-mindness. Wohlstetter's article was thus an appeal to the public, which, by its response, showed both surprise and alarm at the situation he depicted—the more so as his elegant use of the facts and figures lent great persuasiveness to his message.

However, that problem too passed without ever being resolved because the article appeared on the eve of the coming of the intercontinental ballistic missile (ICBM), which lent itself to being put underground without controversy. The Polaris submarine was not far behind. Wohlstetter had been concerned with defending bombers, mostly against bomber attack. We still have bombers as one of the legs of our so-called triad, and now these have to fear enemy missile attack. The air force still has no shelters for these bombers and does not comtemplate any. Obviously, it still relies on their being in the air when the enemy attacks. In fact, on the often-mentioned grounds that they can be sent off early because they are recallable, our bombers are frequently projected as a non-vulnerable retaliatory force. Well, perhaps they are, if one knows just how to read and respond to various types of ambiguous warning. The challenge is to send them off neither too late nor too early.

However, I do agree fully with the belief implicit in the air force position that some kind of political warning will always be available. Attack out of the blue, which is to say without a condition of crisis, is one of those worst-case fantasies that we have to cope with as a starting point, but there are very good reasons why it has never happened, at least in modern times. For comparable reasons, I regard it as so improbable in a nuclear age that it is virtually certain not to happen, which is to say it is not a possibility worth spending much money on.

For similar reasons, I must add before leaving the Wohlstetter article that I could never accept the implications of his title—that the balance of terror between the Soviet Union and the United States ever has been or ever could be "delicate." My reasons have to do mostly with human inhibitions against taking monumental risks or doing things which are universally detested, except under motivations far more compelling than those suggested by Wohlstetter in his article. This point is more relevant today than ever before because of the number and variety of American forces an enemy would need to have a high certitude of destroying in one fell swoop.

The numbers of those forces, incidentally, grew during the 1960s like the British Empire was said to have grown—in a series of fits of absentmindness. There are reasons the number 1,000 was chosen, rather than a lesser number, for our Minuteman missiles, in addition to our 56 Titans. And there are reasons we chose to build forty-one Polaris–Poseidon submarines capable of firing sixteen missiles each, in addition to the 400 plus B-52s we had at the time, not to mention the quick reaction alert forces we have long had in Europe. But whatever those reasons were, they were not a response to Soviet figures. They in fact gave us, or rather continued, an overwhelming superiority, later increased by the application of the MIRV (Multiple Independently Targeted Reentry Vehicle) system to more than half our Minuteman missiles and three-quarters of our submarines. Today we are still far superior in numbers of strategic warheads, and we also have a marked advantage in the important factor of accuracy.

In the mid-1960s the U.S. defense community could look with satisfaction on our immense superiority in retaliatory forces, which appeared also utterly secure by virtue of being, for the most part, either underground or underwater. However, our restless research efforts were already tending to undermine that stable and comfortable situation by pushing to fruition the most incredible advances in ballistic missile accuracy, even without terminal guidance. Those advances resulted mostly from developments in micro-electronics circuitry, which made it feasible to put complex computers aboard missiles and to integrate them wth hypersensitive inertial-guidance gyros. Reliable unclassified estimates put the CEPs of today's American ICBMs at under 300 yards, which is utterly fantastic for an object being hurled some 4,000 miles. When that kind of accuracy is combined with MIRV, the silo-emplaced ICBM begins to be at risk. To be sure, the United States has continued to lead in the developments by a wide margin, and *our* accuracy does not imperil *our* silos, but the long lead times that some systems require make it appear provident, usually, to anticipate the opponent's cancellation of some specific technological advantage of ours.

Meanwhile, new discoveries on the effects of x-rays above the atmosphere had rekindled interest in the development of an anti-ballistic missile (ABM) system. Progress was being made toward the system originally called "Sentinel," which President Richard M. Nixon was to rename "Safeguard," when the developments in missile accuracy seemed suddenly to give it an important purpose. Up to then it had been a system in search of a mission. Inasmuch as most of its advocates admitted that the ABM could not reliably defend cities, interest focused on its use in defending hard-point targets, which is to say missile silos. Then there arose the great ABM controversy, an amazing chapter in our story because of the intense passions engendered among the adversaries. Moreover, unlike certain other controversies, it was not a debate between the informed and the ignorant. There was plenty of technological sophistication on both sides.

My objectivity in this will not, I hope, be utterly compromised if I admit that I could never fully understand the pro-ABM position. It always seemed to me that in the expensive and fixed "Safeguard" mode readied for adoption—and later actually deployed at one site in North Dakota—the ABM could in principle be defeated in a number of ways that were already on the horizon, including hardening the reentry vehicle against the x-rays of the Spartan missile warhead, cheaply multiplying the number of reentry vehicles (RVs) as is done by MIRV, adopting terminal guidance in the RV, or adopting the cruise missile, against which the radar of "Safeguard" would be ineffective.

Now, in retrospect, we can add that it is most questionable whether American ICBMs needed any such protection at the time that "Safeguard," with its complex but fixed technology, was being readied for deployment, or whether they will need it for a long time to come, if ever. Only about 23 percent of U.S. strategic nuclear warheads are carried in ICBMs as compared with about two-thirds for the Soviet Union. Our silos have already been super-hardened. An attack on our ICBMs would involve enormous timing problems for the Soviet Union, especially with most of their ICBMs still of the liquid fuel variety. No one yet knows what kinds of fratricidal problems will arise among RVs detonating near each other within a short space of time. It would be an optimistic Soviet planner who did not count on some 200 or 300 of our ICBMs surviving even a well-concerted attack with much more accurate Soviet missiles than they have today, and that says nothing about the 7,000 to 8,000 warheads in the other two legs of our triad. Surely no sensible opponent would try to eliminate our ICBMs in an initial attack unless he confidently believed that he could, at the same time, eliminate major portions of our other retaliatory forces. One important aspect of the triad, in other words, is that each of the legs helps protect the other two. Besides, how would the Soviets know that we would not launch our ICBMs on tactical warning, or at least *during* an attack which could hardly be simultaneous? In short, the long-term utility of the ABM was at best dubious, but surely it was desirable to avoid deploying a technologically-fixed system well before it could be needed.

Anyway, our Safeguard ABM was effectively cancelled by the SALT I agreements, incidentally demonstrating that the greater utility of arms control agreements lies not in enhancing our security, which is usually beyond their power, but in helping to save both sides from wasteful expenditures.

That brings us to where we are now. The B-1 bomber has effectively been dispatched, but looming over the horizon is the monumentally costly MX missile. Each would be well over twice the weight of the Minuteman III and would carry up to fourteen large nuclear warheads. The cost per missile in a 200 to 250 missile program would be some $100 million. Although the air force is not advocating the MX because of the alleged vulnerability of Minuteman, it seems reasonable to put so costly and powerful a missile into a mobile configuration, though that nearly doubles the cost of the system. Whether we need it in addition to Trident—which expands the operating area of our strategic submarines from about 2.5 million square miles to about 40 million square miles—and the cruise missile, is not going to be determined on any realistic consideration of vulnerability. Rather, protagonists and opponents will take their positions on political grounds, depending on whether they harbor views inclining them toward the Committee on the Present Danger or live on lower levels of anxiety.

This brings me back to some items I had postponed. The question of how much power is enough to deter has always been with us in one form or another, but it is amazing to find it raised anew with intensified vigor now when the number of strategic nuclear warheads in the American arsenal must be at least 9,000 to 10,000. Nevertheless, we have anguished statements like that of Professor Pipes, to whom I referred earlier. Mr. Pipes, professor of Russian history at Harvard University, compels our attention because he was the chairman of that Team B selected in 1976 at the prodding of Major General George Keegan to straighten out the relevant groups at the CIA, whose interpretation of Soviet intentions had apparently been too relaxed for some tastes. His recent *Commentary* article, which bears the title "Why the Soviet Union Thinks It Could Fight and Win a Nuclear War,"[8] was circulated in reprint form by the Committee on the Present Danger, of which Professor Pipes is a charter member, and also by the like-minded National Strategy Information Center.

The "why" in the title of Mr. Pipes' article preempts the prior question *whether* some entity called the Soviet Union thinks as he says it does. The appropriate question is: *who* in the Soviet Union thinks they can fight and win a nuclear war? The article tells us that some Soviet generals think so, with not a single political leader mentioned. One could at this point dismiss the issue by remarking that there are also plenty of U.S. generals who think the United States could fight and win a nuclear war and are even willing to define the word "win," though few of us would be comfortable with that definition. Still, it is interesting to notice what kind of evidence Pipes adduces for his thesis.

A prime piece of evidence for him is that Soviet generals believe that "the basic function of warfare, as defined by Clausewitz, remains premanently valid." He quotes the late Marshal Sokolovskii to that effect, with his own added emphasis: "It is well known that the essential nature of *war as a continuation of politics does not change with changing technology and armament.*"[9]

It is obvious that Professor Pipes reads into that famous dictum of Clausewitz a meaning quite different from that which Clausewitz intended. That might leave open the question what Marshal Sokolovskii intended, except that we know from other portions of his work that Sokolovskii did study Clausewitz, perhaps even with some care. Clausewitz's meaning, which is in fact basic to everything that one thinks about nuclear deterrence, is developed at length in Books I and VIII of his *On War*. In essence it amounts to the idea that war would be only senseless destruction if it were not in pursuit of some valid political objective. It is precisely the fact that one finds it difficult, if not impossible, to find a valid political objective that would justify the destruction inevitable in a strategic nuclear exchange that makes the whole concept of nuclear deterrence credible. In short, far from finding Marshal Sokolovskii's quoted statement ominous, we should all be able to agree with it with a fervent "amen."

 Mr. Pipes takes exception to my 30-year-old statement on the importance of deterring nuclear wars rather than winning them. He does so on the grounds that it has had a generally bad effect on American strategic thinking. I wonder how he would change it? Pipes and his many like-minded associates imply, or some may even state, that the Soviet Union has interests conflicting with ours which its leaders are so unwilling to inhibit or moderate that they are capable of coldly contemplating waging agressive war against us. However, they fall short of telling us what those inexorable interests might be, usually falling back on the old stand-by, "miscalculation." Miscalculation in a crisis is indeed something to be concerned about, but surely such concern should lead to efforts to make deterrence work, not to circumvent it.

General Keegan is one who thinks that the Soviet leaders simply want to eliminate the United States as a superpower rival, and he has some absurd notions about how their allegedly heroic efforts in civil defense have reduced the human casualties they would suffer to a remarkably low level, though it is still reckoned in millions. However, even he admits they would sacrifice virtually all their capital investment above ground, not to mention the amount of fallout they would have to cope with in the environment. Others, including Pipes, point to the 20 to 30 million Russian lives lost during World War II as though the Soviet leaders had had a choice and had willingly offered a sacrifice to entice the Nazis to their destruction.

Mr. Paul Nitze, another charter member of the Committee on the Present Danger, offers us a scenario in which the Soviet Union delivers a surprise attack which does not, to be sure, eliminate more than a portion of our retaliatory forces but which leaves us so inferior that the President, whoever he is, elects to quit the fight before making any reply in kind.[10] Thus, the Soviet Union succeeds in making that otherwise elusive first-strike-with-impunity! An interesting thought, but it would take an exceedingly venturesome and also foolish Soviet leader to *bank* on the President's not retaliating. Even Mr. Nitze is not really sure; he says only that he *believes* the president would not.

But one must ask: even if all their evaluations are correct, what would these people have us *do*? Start a preventive war? Of course not. In the few instances where an attempt at an answer is offered, it seems to run as follows: abandon deterrence strategies in favor of war-winning strategies. But what does that mean? So long as we would not initiate or welcome the outbreak of a war, our basic peacetime strategy would still be that of deterrence. However, a difference is intended. The military has long been fond of saying that the best deterrence force is a war-winning force. Such a statement has certainly not been without meaning in the past, and even in the nuclear age it has some meaning in terms of tactical or theater forces. But when we speak of strategic nuclear exchanges, it is virtually impossible to find a reasonable meaning except in negative terms. That is, we can say what a war-winning force is not, or, to be more precise, what the people who use these phrases seem to mean by them. They mean a force which is definitely not inferior in any one of the several meaningful, or allegedly meaningful, attributes by which rival forces are usually compared.

The United States has about two-thirds the number of ICBMs deployed by the Soviet Union and is substantially inferior in terms of throw weight. Actually, since 1970 the United States has built and deployed more ICBMs than the Soviet Union (550 versus 330). The difference is that our newer ones replaced older types which were retired, while the Soviet Union has kept active nearly all the ICBMs it has ever built—which tells us something about the difference in quality between the two forces. And concerning throw weight, about which so much is heard in some quarters, let us remember that the U.S. military deliberately chose, some two decades ago, to go for smaller ICBMs than the Soviets fancied. There were at least three good reasons for this: first, our people favored the increased readiness that would go with a solid-fuel propellant; second, we knew that our accuracy was much superior to that of the Soviets and likely to remain so for some time; and third, our smaller warheads were really not so very small. We keep forgetting that it was only a 14 KT weapon that devastated Hiroshima.

Whether against hard-point targets or any other kind, our retaliatory force, with its far greater number of warheads and its much better accuracy and readiness, remains today clearly superior to that of the Soviet Union—a "war-winning force" if one insists upon it. And if it remains that today, how about the recent past? Where a Committee on the Present Danger brochure speaks of "the brutal momentum of the massive Soviet strategic arms build-up—a build-up without precedent in history,"[11] it is speaking of something which no student of the American strategic arms build-up in the 1960s could possibly consider unprecedented. Since we are looking so hard for the reason for the Soviet Union build-up, one possibility that ought to be considered is that it was simply triggered by ours, and that it continues to be stimulated by a desire to catch up.

I have left myself too little space to deal properly with the three other questions that I promised to treat, but fortunately two of them—what kinds of wars does nuclear deterrence deter and what is the role for tactical nuclear weapons—are closely related. The question of what nuclear weapons deter hardly arose in the early years of the nuclear age. The dogma of the time was that every modern war is total war, and the only war one seriously thought about was that between the United States and the Soviet Union. This view survived into the first part of the Korean War, which was regarded by the Pentagon as a Soviet ruse to draw us into the western Pacific while they prepared to launch an attack on Europe. Then came the thermonuclear weapon, which caused some people to think about the necessity of separating general war from limited or theater war, and following that came the Eisenhower administration with its somewhat atavistic commitment to massive retaliation. The famous speech by John Foster Dulles of January 1954 caused a strong reaction that finally came into full bloom in 1961 at the advent of the Kennedy administration, with its remarkable Secretary of Defense, Robert S. McNamara.

The idea developed that strategic nuclear power deterred only the use of strategic nuclear power and hardly any other form of violence. In fact, some argued that the existence of strategic nuclear weapons made lesser wars, in which no nuclear weapons were used, more likely, as though the pressure for war was more or less constant and blocking it in one direction made it only more insistent to break out in another. Then we began to hear of nuclear weapons being "decoupled" from diplomacy, for obviously they were not going to be used anyway. The next step was to argue that nuclear weapons must not be used in theater warfare even in Europe, and that the way to avoid their use was to build up our conventional forces—with our allies—so that the threshold for use of tactical nuclear weapons would be raised too high to be breached. Such strong conventional forces, proponents held, made a far better theater deterrence than could any reliance upon tactical nuclear weapons. These ideas were fervently adopted by President Kennedy and Secretary McNamara, and, after some hesitation, by the armed forces, especially the army and navy. After all, large conventional forces meant more of everything, as well as the kind of war that military leaders felt they knew how to fight.

Thus, what some sixteen years ago was a novel and even radical idea has long since become the conventional wisdom, especially in the United States. And, whether a good idea or not, it has cost this country a great deal of money. The massive retaliation idea was, after all, justified mostly on grounds of economy, and the more we departed from it the higher the costs were likely to go.

To save space, and also because the alleged advantages of the conventional build-up policy have had good press and are well known, I shall confine myself to expressing the opposing arguments.

First, one of the strongest reasons consistently advanced by people like Alain Enthoven for doing away with tactical nuclear weapons is their alleged escalatory effect.[12] According to this view, to use one nuclear weapon in the field, however small, is simply to pull the plug on the use of any and all nuclear weapons. One use thus leads quickly and directly to holocaust. It is interesting that our European partners favor the deployment of tactical nuclear weapons for the same reason that so many of our people oppose it. In my opinion, both are wrong. During World War II, there was no problem distinguishing between tactical and strategic bombing and avoiding the latter where it seemed politically desirable to do so. It is not self-evident that the distinction would be more difficult where nuclear weapons are involved, especially if we confine ourselves to much smaller tactical nuclear weapons than many that presently exist—which we should want to do anyway.

Second, the strategic nuclear forces of each superpower *does* inhibit the other from *any* war-like action against it. This was strongly proved during the Cuban missile crisis, when our side—we know—and the other side—we have good reason to guess—each thought it was facing a strategic nuclear war. It is also noteworthy that our people seemed to derive little comfort from the knowledge of having an overwhelming superiority in nuclear arms.[13] It is indeed the fear that escalation is possible, some think probable, that causes the ultimate sanction to have this general deterrent effect, at least between the two superpowers. Granted we need some military power in the theater so the opponent knows he could not make a truly aggressive move there without provoking a war, but it is nevertheless an area where we should be interested in economies.

Actually, our allies have predictably left us no choice in the matter. They simply do not see the Soviet Union as threatening to attack. They have therefore firmly and consistently refused, despite long and continued prodding by our government, to build up to anything like the levels demanded by the conventional war thesis. Thus, we do not presently have, and are not likely to get, a real conventional capability in Europe—one capable of dealing with a deliberate Soviet attack against the West. For that matter, we don't have a good tactical nuclear capability either, but that is much more easily attainable. It would mean mostly changes in doctrine, in training, and in types of weapons, but not large net increases in anything.

Third and most important, we should recognize that inasmuch as all our war plans are predicated upon an act of major Soviet aggression, the choice would not really be ours to make. The Soviets are hardly likely to enter a duel where they leave so critical a choice of weapons up to us. At any rate, we could not assume in advance that they would leave the choice to us. We are presently committed to using tactical nuclear weapons if the Soviets use them first *or if we find ourselves losing without them.* If they were making a deliberate attack, the Soviets would refrain from using them—if they refrained at all—only if they were confident they would quickly overwhelm us without them. It is folly to think we could wait to see. Major adjustments in posture and tactics during a fast-moving battle are not so easily made, especially if one is in the process of being overwhelmed.

The Soviets do not appear to be straining at the leash to pounce upon us in Europe. Quite the contrary. Our investment, therefore, need be only relatively modest there. Yet if we have any substantial force at all it ought to be truly effective as a fighting force and certainly as a deterrent. It is nonsense to hold that a force trained and equipped to fight conventionally—even though it has some essentially unusable nuclear weapons behind it—makes a better deterrent than one of comparable size trained and equipped to fight with nuclear weapons designed exclusively for tactical use. By the latter I mean something like the enhanced radiation bomb, which should have been presented to the public for what it is—a means of making bombs smaller while retaining optimum effectiveness—and which makes an ideal anti-tank weapon.

Finally, a few words on my fourth item—the wartime use of strategic nuclear weapons. Here I shall confine myself to commenting briefly on the special views identified with James R. Schlesinger as former Secretary of Defense, though they are more accurately described as a revival of some old ideas.[14] In the form offered by Schlesinger they have been best described and advanced by an enthusiatic advocate, Benjamin Lambeth.[15] The general idea is to find options outside what is regarded as the straight-jacketed posture of deterrence—waiting supinely to be struck and then attempting to expend our whole nuclear stockpile as rapidly as possible. The alternative suggested by the Schlesinger school is that we should be prepared during a crisis to initiate the use of strategic nuclear weapons, but only a few at a time—perhaps only one or two. The purpose usually mentioned is to show our "determination" or "resolve." In somewhat more hushed tones, another purpose is sometimes whispered, one that immediately calls up references to the "surgical scalpel"—to get the enemy's top command and control apparatus before the few people who are the key to it have a chance to go underground.

Various people have long questioned the wisdom or even the purpose of planning to deliver all our nuclear weapons as rapidly as possible in replying to an attack, for many targets are not time-urgent and most of our own weapons are not directly threatened. The main war goal at the beginning of a strategic nuclear exchange should surely be to terminate it as quickly as possible and with the least amount of damage possible—on both sides. The U.S. military has indeed told us that it takes a different view. According to General George Brown, Chairman of the Joint Chiefs of Staff, "What we are doing now is targeting a war recovery capability."[16] The military's object, in plainer words, is to see to it that, in a strategic nuclear exchange, the Soviet Union will suffer so much greater damage to its industrial plants and population than we do that its recovery would be much more prolonged. Whatever else may be said of this idea, one would have to go back almost to the fate of Carthage to find an historical precedent. In more recent times, the United States has usually put itself to considerable effort and expense to help a defeated enemy recover, normally with the expectation that a vastly changed government in the defeated power will make it adopt an attitude toward the world that is much more congenial with ours. It is incidentally curious, and totally opposed to all the Clausewitzian canons, that so far-reaching a military decision should escape any political input, a situation which no doubt reflects the very low priority that our top political leaders automatically put on war fighting as opposed to deterrence concerns. Nevertheless, one has to acknowledge that targeting "recovery capability" may put some premium on rapid expenditure of one's stockpile.

However, the proposal of the Schlesinger-Lambeth school is not concerned really with the issue of possibly excessive or excessively speedy *retaliation* to an attack upon us. Its central concern is with getting out of the retaliatory bind, with opening American considerations to the possibility of striking first in the hope of winning advantages hitherto disregarded or at least insufficiently considered. The idea of keeping the number of weapons used to a low level does sometimes seem like a mere palliative to the central notion that we should be prepared to initiate the exchange, though of course the idea that weapons be used for mere warning requires that their numbers be kept low. Otherwise the opponent is sure to do what he is all too likely to do anyway— misapprehend our moderately benign intentions.

The Schlesinger–Lambeth school makes much of the advantage of expanding the options of any President during a crisis, a theme which had an especially high rating with Mr. McNamara when he was Secretary of Defense. The notion that it is incontestably good to expand the chief executive's options is rather peculiar inasmuch as it runs directly counter to the basic tenets of constitutional government. A case in point is the long conflict between Congress and President Nixon during the Vietnam War concerning what seemed to be the limitations laid down by the Constitution upon presidential prerogatives and war-making powers. From both the legal and pragmatic view, it is certainly not clear that the national interest lay in expanding the President's options. More recently we saw Congress deny President Gerald Ford the right to send a large quantity of munitions to an obviously collapsing South Vietnamese government, and later deny him the option of intervening in Angola with munitions if not with troops. In both instances President Ford and his Secretary of State complained most bitterly and offered dire warnings of the evils that would befall American interests from such unseemly opposition to their wills. In both instances enough time has passed to suggest that the fears conjured up in those warnings were exaggerated, if not wholly imaginary. In short, the President does not always know best.

The above examples refer to legal limitations upon the power of the executive. However they may affect the national interest in any specific instance, the idea that such limitations should exist is considered absolutely basic to democracy as opposed to dictatorship. Of another character are limitations imposed by the lack of specific physical capabilities such as might have been provided in good time if a different outlook had prevailed. In recent times it has generally been taken for granted that the wider the President's range of physical options, the better. But why this should be so is not altogether clear.

Actually, one notices that the thesis has usually been defended in terms of extending the range of options *downward*, as in the arguments made some years ago that to increase conventional forces is to reduce or remove the pressure upon the President in particular circumstances to use the nuclear option. Unfortunately, when President Kennedy did expand the conventional ground forces for that reason, his successor found himself with the means early in 1965 of sending combat forces to Vietnam without calling up the reserves! His options had been expanded in a way that particularly suited his own nature and outlook, but it is not obvious that the national interest benefited from the result. Naturally, one should not hinge too much on single cases. President Lyndon B. Johnson's conduct does not make a case against having sufficient ground forces. It should, however, cast doubt on the notion that expanding the President's military options is always a good thing. It may be a good thing if we can always be sure of having wise Presidents, but it also throws a heavier burden upon that wisdom, so that any lack of it becomes the more telling. It is an old story that one way of keeping people out of trouble is to deny them the means for getting into it. We put in the President's hands a huge military power because we believe that the country's security demands that we do so, and we are obliged to trust that he will use it wisely. But to expand that power simply for the sake of expanding his options is to go beyond that obligatory trust.

Anyway, if the President did not already have the power to make the kinds of first strikes envisioned in the Schlesinger proposals, which inevitably he does, it would seem a very dubious proposition indeed that we should bestir ourselves to provide it. Certain kinds of weapons, like the cruise missile, may—because of their extreme accuracy—lend themselves particularly well to the kind of "surgical strikes" that, in some people's fantasies, bring victory without cost or even danger, but there had better be other reasons for calling for them than the desire to free the President for conducting such experiments.

In fact, the overwhelming odds are that, when and if the crisis comes, the man occupying the seat of power in the United States will exercise at least the caution of a John F. Kennedy during the Cuban missile crisis, who by his brother's intimate account was appalled by the possibility that any precipitous use of physical power by the United States might unleash the nuclear holocaust.[17] He had firmly decided upon a confrontation and had made his requirements plain to the adversary. There is no reason to suppose that President Kennedy was anything but well above the mean level of courage we might expect in any President finding himself in a comparable situation. Yet we know from his conduct that the last thing he was interested in experimenting with during the crisis was some violent means of proving his resolve.

There may indeed be worse crises than that of October 1962, but during such crises the man who must make the ultimate decisions for the United States will likely be searching desperately for the resolve he is supposed to show and may well be the wiser man for having difficulty in finding it. In short, the notion that, in an extremely tense crisis—which may include an ongoing theater war—there is any useful purpose in firing strategic nuclear weapons, however limited in number, seems vastly to underestimate both the risks to the nation and the burden upon the person who must make the decision. Divorced from consideration of how human beings actually behave in a crisis, it fits Raymond Aron's definition of "strategic fiction," analogous to "science fiction."[18]

Lambeth is simply playing with words when he argues that the Schlesinger proposals introduce flexibility into an area of thinking hitherto marked by extreme rigidity and introduce *strategy*—in the form of choice—where no possibility of strategy existed before. The rigidity lies in the situation, not in the thinking. The difference between war and no war is great enough, but that between strategic thermonuclear war and war as we have known it is certain to be greater still. Any rigidity which keeps us from entering the new horrors or from nibbling at them in hopes that a nibble will clearly be seen as such by the other side, is a salutary rigidity. And we need not worry whether the choices the President is obliged to make during extremely tense situations fit anyone's definition of strategy. The important thing is that they be wise choices under the circumstances.

It is especially curious that the notions discussed above should be advanced by many who continue to oppose the use of tactical nuclear weapons because of their alleged escalatory danger! That danger must be greater by orders of magnitude when the weapon of weapons detonated are, by type and by choice of target, clearly of the strategic variety. Though it could indeed by desirable to condition the people who control our own retaliatory forces not to regard the arrival of one or a few enemy warheads as necessarily the onset of an all-out attack, that kind of conditioning would hardly be dependable even for our own side, and we should certainly not seek to depend upon its existing with suitable firmness on the other.

Finally, a word about what one puts on the line for such proposals. The defense community of the United States is inhabited by people of a wide range of skills and sometimes of considerable imagination. All sorts of notions and propositions are churned out and often presented for consideration with the prefatory words: "It is conceivable that . . ." Such words establish their own truth, for the fact that someone has conceived of whatever proposition follows is enough to establish it as conceivable. Whether it is worth a second thought, however, is another matter. It should undergo a good deal of thought before one begins to spend much money on it. In defense matters sums of money spent on particular proposals can easily become huge.

Schlesinger's original proposal for "limited nuclear options" seems to have been loosely connected to the then new cruise missile, which fortunately has other factors to recommend it. Recently, however, Mr. Colin S. Gray, in a "letter to the editor" in the *New York Times*,[19] opines that since it is now established that the United States will initiate the coming strategic nuclear exchange (concerning which he seems to have no doubt) we should proceed at once to buy the MX missile system. Fortunately, Mr. Gray is not a senior official in the Defense Department, but his considerable writings have brought him attention within the defense community. Just why he considers the MX especially suited for initiating strikes is not clear—the cruise missile has at least the advantage of extreme accuracy—but his readiness to spend billions of dollars to cover a contingency that most of his peers would regard as extremely dubious is a little breathtaking. Surely the chances of his prediction being realized, even if more than infinitesimal, are not so great that we could not make-do, if and when the time came, with vehicles deployed for retaliatory purposes.

In these matters, to be sure, we are dealing fundamentally with conflicting intuitions. No doubt some people's intuitions are better than others, but the superiority of the former, though sometimes definable and explicable, may be difficult to prove. Still, it is deceptively cheap and easy to think up ingenious new possibilities, and the burden of proof must be on those who urge the payment of huge additional premiums for putting their notions into practice.

NOTES

1. Bernard Brodie, ed., *The Absolute Weapon* (New York: Harcourt, Brace, 1946). Coauthors were Frederick S. Dunn, Arnold Wolfers, Percy E. Corbett, and William T. R. Fox.
2. Ibid., p. 76. The Brodie chapters comprise pp. 21–110.
3. Ibid., pp. 63–69.
4. Ibid., p. 83.

5. Ibid., p. 80. Emphasis added.
6. Col. Richard L. Curl, "Strategic Doctrine in the Nuclear Age," *Strategic Review* (Washington, D.C.: U.S. Strategic Institute), Winter 1975, p. 48.
7. *Foreign Affairs*, Vol. 37, No. 2, January 1959, pp. 211–256.
8. *Commentary*, Vol. 64, No. 1, July 1977, pp. 21–34. See also the several "letters to the editor" provoked by this article in the second issue following: *Commentary*, Vol. 64, No. 3, September 1977, pp. 4–26.
9. *Commentary*, July 1977, p. 30.
10. Paul H. Nitze, "Deterring our Deterrent," *Foreign Policy*, No. 25, Winter 1976–77, pp. 195–210.
11. Committee on the Present Danger: "Where We Stand on SALT," July 6, 1977, p. 5.
12. Alain C. Enthoven has for some fifteen years been the outstanding spokesman for this school of thought, which has, however, included such prominent thinkers as Albert Wohlstetter and Thomas C. Schelling. One of Enthoven's most recent articles on the subject was his "U.S. Forces in Europe: How Many? Doing What?" *Foreign Affairs*, April 1975, pp. 512–532.
13. See especially Robert F. Kennedy, *Thirteen Days: A Memoir of the Cuban Missile Crisis*, (New York: W.W. Norton, 1969). It is interesting that at no time in his gripping narrative does Kennedy bring up or mention anyone else's bringing up the very clear American superiority in nuclear arms, from which they might have been expected to derive additional hope of deterring Soviet resort to war. That, of course, does not mean that nobody thought about it.
14. An earlier exposition of similar ideas is found in Klaus Knorr and Thornton Read (eds.), *Limited Strategic War* (New York: Praeger, 1962).
15. Benjamin S. Lambeth, *Selective Nuclear Options in American and Soviet Strategic Policy*, Rand Report R-2034-DDRE, December 1976. Despite my criticisms in the text, I should point out here that Lambeth explicitly disavows belief that circumstances of the future are ever likely to favor American limited first use. He simply wants it adopted as a "standing contingency capability," though his argument endorsing that capability does wax exceedingly enthusiastic. His report indicentally also includes a brilliant analysis of recent Soviet tactical and strategic thinking.
16. Quoted in *The Defense Monitor* (Washington, D.C.: Center for Defense Information), Vol. 6, No. 6, August 1977, p. 2.
17. See above, *Thirteen Days*.
18. Raymond Aron, "The Evolution of Strategic Thought," included in Alastair Buchan (ed.) *Problems of Modern Strategy* (London: Chatto & Windus, 1970), p. 30.
19. *New York Times*, October 19, 1977.

Chapter 3

On Fighting a Nuclear War

Michael E. Howard

Thirty-five years have passed since Bernard Brodie, in the first book that he—or indeed anyone else—wrote about nuclear war, set down these words:

> The first and most vital step in any American security program for the age of atomic bombs is to take measures to guarantee to ourselves in case of attack the possibility of retaliation in kind. The writer in making this statement is not for the moment concerned about who will *win* the next war in which atomic bombs have been used. Thus far the chief purpose of our military establishment has been to win wars. From now on its chief purpose must be to avert them. It can have almost no other useful purpose.[1]

For most of those thirty-five years the truth of this revolutionary doctrine was accepted in the Western world as self-evident, and our whole military posture became based on the concept of deterrence that Brodie had defined so presciently and so early. The fear of nuclear war *as such* was considered sufficient deterrent against the initiation of violence on the scale of the Second World War, and the policy of the United States, its allies, and perhaps also its adversaries was to create a strategic framework which made it not only certain that a nuclear attack would provoke a nuclear response, but likely that an attack with conventional weapons would do so as well. It was agreed almost without a dissenting voice that nuclear wars were "unwinnable." A nuclear exchange on any scale would cause damage of a kind that would make a mockery of the whole concept of "victory."

When Brodie died, that consensus was beginning to disintegrate. In the last article he published, "The Development of Nuclear Strategy," in the Spring 1978 issue of *International Security*, he defended the above passage. While accepting the changes that had occurred both in weapons technology and in the structure of the military balance over the past thirty years, he saw no reason to alter his view. It was necessary to develop and to deploy nuclear weapons in order to deter their use by others. Such weapons, he believed, might perhaps be utilizable on a limited scale in the European theater. But as instruments of policy, as strategic tools in a general war, they could have no utility. Nuclear war was unfightable and unwinnable.

Brodie's belief that a nuclear war could not be "won" did not of course mean that he held no strong views about the optimal deployment and targeting of nuclear weapons, a matter on which his opinion was greatly valued by successive Chiefs of the Air Staff. The maintenance of a credible capacity for nuclear retaliation, and its structuring to create maximum political and psychological effect, was a problem which deeply concerned him throughout his career at Rand Corporation. But what if deterrence failed and these weapons had to be used? What should the political objective of the war be, and how would nuclear devastation help to attain it? How and with whom was a peace to be negotiated? Above all, in what shape would the United States be, after suffering substantial nuclear devastation itself, to negotiate any peace?

Brodie could have asked further questions and no doubt did. What would be the relationship between the Soviet Union and the United States after such a war? What would their position be in an international community that could hardly have emerged intact from a nuclear battle on so global a scale? How could the post-nuclear world environment be seen as an improvement of the pre-war situation, an improvement worth enduring—and inflicting—such unimaginable suffering to attain? It is not surprising that, in his 1978 article, Brodie defined "the main war goal upon the beginning of a strategic nuclear exchange" as being "to terminate it as quickly as possible and with the least amount of damage possible—on both sides."

This phrase was taken up a year later by one of Brodie's keenest critics, Colin Gray, who commented sarcastically:

> Of course the best prospect of all for minimizing (prompt) damage lies in surrendering preemptively. If Bernard Brodie's advice were accepted, the

West would be totally at the mercy of a Soviet Union, which viewed war in a rather more traditional perspective.[2]

By the time that article appeared Brodie was dead, but one can well imagine his sardonic response: "Would the Soviet Union or anyone else view *anything* in a 'traditional perspective' after a nuclear exchange?"

Gray's question does, however, go to the heart of the problem that has led many people in the United States to reject the "conventional wisdom" of Brodie's position as no longer relevant in a new and harsher age: the fear that a posture of nuclear deterrence, however structured, may not be enough to prevent a Soviet Union—that accepts nuclear war as an instrument of policy and has built up a formidable nuclear arsenal—from thinking the unthinkable, accepting the unacceptable, and not only initiating but fighting through a nuclear conflict expecting victory whether the United States wishes to fight or not. And if such a conflict is forced upon the United States, how can this country conduct it effectively unless it also has a positive objective to guide its strategy, other than the mass annihilation of Soviet civilians? Should the United States not also regard nuclear war "in a rather more traditional perspective"?

The criticism of the deterrent posture arises from two linked sources. The first is the development of missile technology: the growing accuracy of guidance systems, the miniaturization of warheads, the increasing capability of target acquisition processes, the whole astounding panoply of scientific development in which the United States has, to the best of my knowledge, in every instance taken the lead, with the Soviet Union, at great cost to its economy, keeping up as best it can. Incidentally, it is curious that a scientific community that was so anguished over its moral responsibility for the development of the first crude nuclear bombs should have ceased to trouble itself over its continuing involvement with weapons systems whose lethality and effectiveness make the weapons that destroyed Hiroshima and Nagasaki look like clumsy toys. Be that as it may, it is the continuous inventiveness of the scientific community—and primarily the Western scientists—that has made the pursuit of a stable nuclear balance and mutually assured *deterrence* (which seems to me the correct explication of that much abused acronym MAD) seem to be the chase for an *ignis fatuus*, a will-o'-the-wisp.

The second ground for criticizing the original concept of deterrence is the widespread belief that the Soviet Union does not share it and never has. The absence from Soviet textbooks of any distinction between a "deterrent" and a "war-fighting" capability; the reiterated statements that nuclear weapons cannot be exempted from the Clausewitzean imperative that military forces have no rationale save as instruments of state policy; the confident Marxist-Leninist predictions of socialism ultimately prevailing over the capitalist adversary whatever weapons

systems or policies he might adopt: does this not make it clear that American attempts to indoctrinate the Soviet Union in strategic concepts quite alien to Soviet ideology and culture have failed? And this perception of the Soviet Union as a society coolly prepared to contemplate the prospect of fighting a nuclear war as an instrument of policy is enhanced by a worst-case analysis of its capacity to do so: its first-strike capacity against U.S. land-based ICBMs; its civil defense program to reduce its own casualties to an "acceptable" level; and a historical experience of suffering which, according to some authorities, enables their leaders to contemplate witout flinching the prospect of frightful damage and casualties running into scores of millions if it enables them to achieve their global objectives.

Arguing with those who hold this view of the Soviet Union is arguing with people whose attitude, like that of committed pacifists, is rooted in a visceral conviction beyond the reach of any rational discourse I can commend. This is evident by their deployment of two arguments in particular. The first is that, since the Soviet Union had suffered some 20 million dead in the Second World War, they might equally contemplate further comparable losses in pursuit of a political objective sufficiently grandiose to warrant such a sacrifice. It is, however, a matter of historical record to what shifts and maneuvers Josef Stalin was reduced in his attempt to *avoid* having to fight that war; and writing as a representative of the British people who lost nearly a million war dead between 1914 and 1918, I suggest that the record also shows that readiness to risk heavy losses in another war does not necessarily increase in direct ratio with the sacrifices one endured in the last.

The second argument maintains that Soviet civil defense measures provide incontrovertible evidence of Soviet intentions to launch a first strike. These arguments are all the more curious in that they are advanced almost simultaneously, and often from the same sources, as the very well-reasoned advocacy of an almost identical United States civil defense program—a program adopted by President Kennedy's administtration and abandoned only in the face of the kind of popular and congressional resistance with which the Soviet leadership does not have to contend. The difference between the development of civil defense in the two countries thus tells one rather more about their respective political structures than about their strategic intentions. Until recently indeed it would not have occurred to anyone outside a tiny group of strategic analysts in this country that civil defense preparations were anything except prudent and proper precautions for a remote but horribly finite possibility. Unfortunately their view is now more widely spread; and those in Europe who have been urging the advisability of taking even minimal precautions for civil defense now find themselves accused by true believers on the Left, as the Russians are accused by true believers on the Right, of planning to precipitate the very catastrophe against which they seek to insure.

The debate about Soviet intentions has been conducted by people so far more expert than myself that I shall not seek to add to it beyond underlining and reinforcing Bernard Brodie's gently understated comment on those who see the build-up of Soviet forces over the past two decades as incontrovertible proof of their aggressive intentions:

> Where the Committee on the Present Danger in one of its brochures speaks of "the brutal momentum of the massive Soviet strategic arms build-up—a build-up without precedent in history," it is speaking of something which no student of the American strategic arms build-up in the sixties could possibly consider unprecedented.[3]

In fact one of the oldest "lessons of history" is that the armaments of an adversary always seem "brutal" and threatening, adjectives that appear tendentious and absurd when applied to our own.

The sad conclusion of this debate is that no amount of argument or evidence will convince a large number of sincere, well-informed, highly intelligent, and, now, very influential people that the Soviet Union is not an implacably aggressive power prepared to use nuclear weapons as an instrument of its policy. But I would argue that the Soviet leadership, and any of their successors within the immediately foreseeable future, are cautious and rather fearful men, increasingly worried about their almost insoluble internal problems, increasingly aware of their isolation in a world in which the growth of Marxist socialism does little to enhance their political power, deeply torn between gratification at the problems besetting the capitalist world economy and alarm at the difficulties those problems are creating within their own empire. Above all, they are conscious of the inadequacy of the simplistic doctrines of Marxits-Leninism, on which they were nurtured, to explain a world far more complex and diverse than either Marx or Lenin ever conceived. Their *Staatspolitik*, that complex web of interests, perceptions, and ideals that Clausewitz believed should determine the use of military power, thus gives them no clearer guidance for use of their armed forces than it gives to us.

The evidence for this view of Soviet motivations seems at least as conclusive as that for the beliefs of, for example, the Committee on the Present Danger, which will no doubt consider this argument as visceral, emotive, and irrational, as I have found all too many of its publications. I would only say in defense of these views that first, they take more into account the complexities of the historic, political, and economic problems of the Soviet Union than do their views; and second, for what it is worth, that they correspond more closely with views held by most

Europeans among whom I move than do those of the Committee on the Present Danger. Naturally, in Europe as elsewhere there is a diversity of views, and there can be few more enthusiastic supporters of Paul Nitze than British Prime Minister Margaret Thatcher. Nonetheless, one finds in Europe a far more relaxed attitude toward the Soviets than one encounters in the United States because, paradoxically, Europeans are less frightened of the Soviets than Americans are. Europeans find it easier to see them as real people with real, and alarming, problems of their own: people of whom we must be constantly wary and whose military power and propensity to use it when they can safely do so, is certainly formidable, but with whom it is possible to do business, in every sense of the word. Europeans certainly do not see them as people who have any interest in, or intention of, deliberately unleashing a nuclear war as an instrument of policy.

And here again I should like to underline, if possible with even greater emphasis, what Bernard Brodie had to say in his article about the Soviet dedication to Clausewitz' theory of the relationship of war to policy. Clausewitz was a subtle, profound, and versatile thinker, and his teaching about the relationship between war and policy was only one of the many insights he provided into the whole phenomenon of war. He wrote:

> War is only a branch of political activity; it is in no sense autonomous . . . [It] cannot be divorced from political life—and whenever this occurs in our thinking about war, the many links that connect the two elements are destroyed, and we are left with something that is pointless and devoid of sense.[4]

Insofar as the Soviets believe this and hammer it into the heads of successive generations of soldiers and politicians, we should admire and imitate them. When they castigate us for ignoring it and for discussing nuclear war *in vacuo*, as we almost invariably do, they are absolutely right, and we should be grateful for their criticism. When I read the flood of scenarios in strategic journals about first-strike capabilities, counterforce or countervailing strategies, flexible response, escalation dominance, and all the rest, I ask myself in bewilderment: this war they are describing, *what is it about*? The defense of Western Europe? Access to the Gulf? The protection of Japan? If so, why is this goal not mentioned, and the strategy related to the progress of the conflict in these regions? But if it is not related to this kind of specific object, what are we talking about? Has not the bulk of American thinking been exactly what Clausewitz described: something that, because it is divorced from any political context, is "pointless and devoid of sense"?

When I made these comments a couple of years ago in a now much-quoted article in *Foreign Affairs*, I was gratified but slightly alarmed by the response. I certainly did not expect my arguments to be cited in support of the thesis that nuclear war is fightable and winnable, and that we should base our strategy on that assumption; I wish to distance myself from that school of thought and explain why I do so.

Undeniably, Soviet theoreticians attempt to fit nuclear weapons into their Clausewitzean framework and maintain that, should nuclear war occur, nuclear weapons should be used to forward overall policy goals and ensure a victory for the armed forces of the Soviet Union. But one only has to state the opposite of this doctrine to accept that it is, in theory, unexceptionable and that it would be difficult for the Soviets to say anything else. The ideological and bureaucratic framework within which this Soviet teaching has evolved has been convincingly described in recent articles by such experts as Raymond Garthoff and Benjamin Lambeth,[5] and I find convincing the formulation propounded by the latter:

> [The Russians] approach their strategic planning with the thoroughly traditional conviction that despite the revolutionary advances in destructive power brought about by modern weapons and delivery systems, the threat of nuclear war persists as a fundamental feature of the international system and obliges the Soviet Union to take every practical measure to prepare for its eventuality ... They appear persuaded that in the nuclear age no less than before, the most reliable way to prevent war is to maintain the appropriate wherewithal to fight and win it should it occur.

Logical as this doctrine may appear, and no doubt necessary for the maintenance both of ideological consistency and of Soviet military morale, our own response, it seems to me, should *not* be to imitate it but to make it clear to the Soviets, within their own Clausewitzean framework, that it simply will not work: that there is no way that the use of strategic nuclear weapons could be a rational instrument of state policy, for them or for anyone else.

This view commands satisfyingly wide consensus, or did until recently. Paul Nitze himself, in his famous plea for a maximalist American defense posture, emphasized that the object of the measures he proposed "would not be to give the United States a war-fighting capability: it would be to deny to the Soviet Union the possibility of a successful war-fighting capability."[6] Another leading thinker of the maximalist school, Colin Gray, also accepts that "one of the essential tasks of the American defense community is to help ensure that in moments of crisis the Soviet general staff cannot brief the Politburo with a plausible theory of military victory."[7] But Gray believes that another task of the defense community is to brief the White House with a plausible theory of military victory, and that is surely a very different matter.

Gray is a Clausewitzean and believes that U.S. strategy should be geared to a positive political object. "Washington," he suggests, "should identify war aims that in the last resort would contemplate the destruction of Soviet political authority and the emergence of a post-war world-order compatible with Western values."[8] For this, it would be necessary to destroy, not the peoples of the Soviet Union in genocidal attacks on cities, but the apparatus of the Soviet state. He identifies the principal assets of the latter as "the political control structure of the highly centralized Communist Party of the Soviet Union (CPSU) and government bureaucracy; the transmission belts of communication from the center to the regions; the instruments of central official coercion (the KGB and armed forces); and the reputation of the Soviet state in the eyes of its citizens." He writes:

> The entire Soviet political and economic system is critically dependent upon central direction from Moscow. If the brain of the Soviet system were destroyed, degraded, or—at a minimum—isolated . . . , what happens to the cohesion, or pace of recovery, of the whole?[9]

There are a number of problems with this scenario. The first problem is one that Gray, quite frankly, admits himself. "Is it sensible," he asks, "to destroy the government of the enemy, thus eliminating the option to negotiating an end to the war?"[10] The answer is no, it is not, unless we believe that out of the midst of this holocaust an alternative organized government would somehow emerge, capable—in spite of the destruction of all internal communications networks—of taking over the affairs of state. The alternative is, presumably, the conquest, occupation, and re-education of the Soviet peoples in "Western values"—an interesting but ambitious project which might be said to require further study.

Second, it is quite unrealistic to assume that such strikes against centers of government and communications could be carried out without massive casualties—numbering scores of millions—among the peoples we would be attempting to "liberate." And if historical experience is any guide, such suffering, inflicted by an alien power, serves only to strengthen social cohesion and make support for the regime, however unpopular it might be, a question literally of physical survival. The strategic bombardment of Germany only intensified the control exercised by the Nazi regime over that unhappy nation. The suffering inflicted on the Russian peoples during the Second World War—those 20 million casualties which, we are asked to believe, only whetted their appetite for starting a Third World War—not only strengthened Stalin's tyranny; it went far to legitimize it. The prospect of any regime in the least compatible with what Gray calls "Western values" emerging from a bloodbath on yet a more horrific scale is, to put it mildly, pretty remote.

Finally, what would be going on here while the U.S. strategic strike forces were conducting their carefully calibrated and controlled nuclear war? I shall leave out of this account the problems of command and control, of maintaining fine-tuning and selective targeting under the kind of nuclear retaliation that is to be expected during such an attack. This is the famous "C³I factor" addressed in President Jimmy Carter's Presidential Directive (PD) No. 59, and some of America's finest technologists are no doubt working on the problem. Even if they do come up with plausible solutions, however, nobody can possibly tell whether, in practice, they will work; and for strategic planners to prepare to fight a nuclear war on the firm assumption that they would work would be criminally irresponsible. Nor do I address the question of what would be happening in Western Europe during such an exchange. Henry Kissinger, in that very curious speech he delivered in Brussels in September 1979, informed his audience that "the secret dream of every European was . . . if there had to be a nuclear war, to have it conducted over their heads by the strategic forces of the United States and the Soviet Union."[11] In fact I have yet to meet an intelligent European who thinks that anything of the kind would be possible, or that Western Europe would, under any circumstances, be omitted from the Soviet targeting plan. Few believe that there would be much left of Europe's highly urbanized, economically tightly integrated and desperately vulnerable societies after even the most controlled and limited strategic nuclear exchange.

But it is the implications for the United States itself that I want to consider. Gray and his colleagues admit that there is a problem here, but they assert that "strategists can claim that an intelligent United States offensive strategy, wedded to homeland defenses, should reduce U.S. casualties to approximately 20 million, which should render U.S. strategic threats more credible."[12] Perhaps they can claim it, in the same way that Glendower could claim, in Shakespear's *Henry IV*, that he could "call spirits from out the vasty deep," to be asked in retrn, "but will they come when you do call for them?" How valid is such a claim—especially since a Soviet leadership in its death throes would have no possible incentive, to limit the damage to 20 million or to any other figure?

But even if it *is* valid, and granted that 20 million is a preferable figure to 180 million, it is not clear to me that Gray has thought through all the implications of his suggestion. Those twenty million *immediate* casualties—and we leave out those dying later from residual radiation— are only the visible tip of an iceberg of destruction and suffering of literally incalculable size. The very careful and sober report by the Congressional Office of Technology Assessment, *The Effects of Nuclear War*, is worth considering. It came to the conclusion:

> The effects of nuclear war that cannot be calculated are at least as important as those for which calculations are attempted. Moreover even these limited calculations are subject to very large uncertainties . . . This is

particularly true for indirect effects such as deaths resulting from injuries and the unavailability of medical care, or for economic damage resulting from disruption and disorganization rather than direct destruction.[13]

As for a small or "limited" attack, the impact of this, points out the report, would be "enormous ... [and] the uncertainties are such that no government could predict with any confidence what the results ... would be, even if there was no further escalation."[14] Certainly the situation in which the survivors of a nuclear attack would find themselves would be unprecedented.

> Natural resources would be destroyed; surviving equipment would be designed to use materials and skills that might no longer exist; and indeed some regions might be almost uninhabitable. Furthermore, prewar patterns of behavior would surely change, though in unpredictable ways.[15]

As for the outcome of the conflict in which this suffering was incurred, a memorandum Brodie wrote for Rand Corporation more than twenty years ago has lost none of its relevance:

> Whether the survivors be many or few, in the midst of a land scarred and ruined beyond all present comprehension, they should not be expected to show much concern for the further pursuit of political-military objectives.[16]

Under such circumstances the prime concern of everyone, American, Russian, European—to say nothing of the rest of the world which is always left out of these scenarios—would be simply to survive in an unimaginably hostile environment. What would become of "Western values" in such a world is anyone's guess. It is my own belief that the political, cultural, and ideological distinctions that separate us from the Soviet Union today would be seen, in comparison with the literally inconceivable contrasts between *any* pre-atomic and *any* post-atomic society, as almost insignificant. Indeed I am afraid that the United States would probably emerge from a nuclear war with a regime which, in its inescapable authoritarianism, would look much more like that which governs the Soviet Union today than the government of the Soviet Union would resemble that of the United States; and this would almost certainly be the case in Western Europe.

Admittedly this is all guesswork. But what is absolutely clear is that to engage in nuclear war, to attempt to use strategic nuclear weapons for "war-fighting," would be to enter the realm of the unknown and the unknowable. What little we do know about it is appalling. Those who believe otherwise, whether they do so—like the Soviet writers—because of the constraints imposed by their ideology and cultural traditions, or— as do some Americans—out of technological hubris, are likely to be proved equally and dreadfully wrong—as wrong as those European strategists who, in 1914, promised their political masters decisive victory before Christmas.

I take issue with Colin Gray in particular, not because I do not admire his work, but simply because he has had the courage to make explicit certain views that are now circulating widely in some circles in the Uniied States and which, unless publicly and firmly countered, might become influential, with catastrophic consequences. I also believe that, if a thinker as intelligent as Gray is unable to provide nuclear strategy with a positive political object, no one else is likely to succeed any better. But this does not mean that Clausewitz' theory has to be abandoned and that nuclear weapons can serve no political purpose. Clausewitz accepted that strategy might have a *negative* object and pointed out that, historically, this had more often than not been the case. This negative object he defined as the ability to make clear to the other side "the improbability of victory . . . [and] its unacceptable cost."[17] In a word, deterrence; or in Gray's own admirable words, to "ensure that in moments of acute crisis the Soviet general staff cannot brief the Politburo with a plausible theory of military victory."[18]

This takes us back to Bernard Brodie's warning that "the first and most vital step in any American security program . . . is to take measures to guarantee to ourselves in case of attack the possibility of retaliation in kind."[19] In principle nothing has changed since then, even though in practice the problem has become enormously more difficult. In particular, Brodie's phrase *"in kind"* has acquired a significance that he could not possibly have anticipated. With the diversification of nuclear delivery systems, deterrence becomes an ever more complex business. Prudent account has to be taken of the contingency that deterrence might fail, in order to provide feasible alternatives between holocaust and surrender. But the object of such "intra-war deterrence" would still be, as Brodie put it, "to terminate 'the strategic exchange' as quickly as possible, with the least amount of damage possible—on both sides," in the interests not just of the United States but of mankind as a whole. Can one doubt that in 1914 rational European statesmen would have cut their losses and made peace at the end of the year if they had not been driven on by popular pressures and delusive expectations of victory? Or that if they had done so, the world would be a rather better place than it is today?

What about Brodie's other pronouncement: "Thus far the chief purpose of our military establishment has been to win wars. From now on its chief purpose must be to avert them"? Does this remain valid? Indeed it does, but there is nothing new about this. It has always been the role of military establishments in peacetime to dissuade their opponents from using force as an instrument of policy—even of *defensive* policy—by making it clear that any such action on their part would be counterproductive, either because they would *lose* in such a war, or because they could gain victory only at an unacceptably high cost. That still seems to be true. And it also seems to be true that such a deterrent posture lacks conviction if one does not have the evident capacity to fight such a war—in particular, to defend the territory which our opponent may wish to occupy.

This is where a "war-fighting capability" comes in: a capability, not to fight through a war to an impossible, mutually destructive "victory"— and let us remember Clausewitz' epigram "in strategy there is no such thing as victory"—but to set a price on victory for our opponent that he cannot possibly afford to pay. And for this we must have the evident will and readiness to defend ourselves and one another; something that can only be made clear by the presence or availability of armed forces capable of fighting for territory—adequately armed, adequately trained, adequately supported, and, in our market economies, adequately paid.

This is the war-fighting capability that acts as the true deterrent to aggression and the only one that is convertible into political influence. There is as little reason to suppose that Soviet nuclear superiority will give them political advantages in the 1980s as the American nuclear superiority lent weight to the foreign policy of the United States in the 1960s. The neighbors of the Soviet Union are primarily impressed by the war-fighting capacity of its conventional forces, and the rest of the world by its growing capacity to project that force beyond its frontiers. Within Europe, the "theater nuclear balance" concerns only a tiny group of specialists. The presence and fighting capability of the United States army and air forces are seen as the real, and highly effective, deterrent to Soviet attack. It is regrettable that the British government should have decided to spend five billion pounds of a very restricted defense budget on a strategic nuclear strike force which can only be at the expense of the conventional forces Britain can contribute to the alliance. Also, however much the Reagan administration may feel it necessary to spend on new strategic nuclear weapons systems to match or overmatch those of the Soviet Union, the effect on America's influence within the international community is likely to be negligible if it is not matched by a comparable and evident capability to defend American interests on the oceans and on the ground with forces capable of fighting.

For the best part of a century the peoples of industrial societies have been applying technological expertise and industrial power, initially to assist, but increasingly to replace, the traditional military skills and virtues on which they formerly relied for the protection of their political integrity. As a result they have been able to attain their objects in war only at the cost of enormous and increasingly disproportionate destruction. With the advent of nuclear weapons, the disproportion becomes insensate. It is politically so much easier, so much less of a social strain, to produce nuclear missiles rather than trained, effective military manpower and to believe that a valid trade-off has somehow been made. It has not. And the more deeply we become committed to this belief, on both sides of the Atlantic, the greater will be the danger that we are trying to avoid: on the one hand, the impossibility of defending the specific areas and interests that are seriously threatened by a potential adversary, and, on the other, the possibility that, in a lethal mixture of hubris and despair, we might one day feel ourselves compelled to initiate a nuclear war. Such a war might or might not achieve its object, but I doubt whether the survivors on either side would care very much.

NOTES

1. Bernard Brodie, ed., *The Absolute Weapon* (New York: Harcourt Brace, 1946), p. 76.
2. Colin Gray, "Nuclear Strategy: The Case for a Theory of Victory," *International Security,* Summer 1979, p. 76.
3. Brodie, "The development of Nuclear Strategy," *International Security,* Spring 1978, p. 75.
4. Carl von Clausewitz, *On War,* (Princeton, N.J.: Princeton University Press, 1976), bk. VIII, Chap. 6B, p. 605.
5. Raymond L. Garthoff, "Mutual Deterrence and Strategic Arms Limitation in Soviet Policy," *International Security,* Summer 1978; and Benjamin S. Lambeth, "The Political Potential of Soviet Equivalence," *International Security,* Fall 1979, p. 27.
6. Paul Nitze, "Deterring our Deterrent," *Foreign Policy,* Winter 1976-1977, p. 210
7. Gray, "Nuclear Strategy," p. 56.
8. Colin Gray and Keith Payne, "Victory Is Possible," *Foreign Policy,* Summer 1980, p. 21.
9. Gray, "Nuclear Strategy," p. 21.
10. Gray and Payne, "Victory Is Possible," p. 24.
11. *Survival,* November-December 1979, p. 266.
12. Gray and Payne, "Victory Is Possible," p. 25.
13. Congressional Office of Technology Assessment, *The Effects of Nuclear War* (London: Croom Helm, 1980), p. 3.
14. Ibid.
15. Ibid.
16. "Implications of Nuclear Weapons on Total War," Rand Corporation Memorandum, July 1957, p. 1118.
17. Clausewitz, *On War,* bk. I, Chap. 2.
18. Ibid.
19. Ibid.

Chapter 4

The Role of Strategic Concepts and Doctrine in U.S. Strategic Nuclear Force Development

Desmond Ball

Despite their extremely different histories, resources, strategic cultures and geopolitical situations, the United States and the Soviet Union have developed and deployed strategic nuclear forces that are, by any general criteria, remarkably similar. At the beginning of the 1980s, both superpowers had more than 2,000 strategic nuclear delivery vehicles (SNDVs), consisting of intercontinental ballistic missiles (ICBMs), submarine-launched ballistic missiles (SLEMs), and long-range strategic bombers, with roughly comparable technologies. There are, of course, some significant differences in the particular characteristics of these respective strategic forces. The U.S. strategic nuclear posture is, according to most indices, rather more balanced than that of the Soviet Union; in comparison with the United States, the Soviet Union has a much greater concentration of resources in the ICBM leg of its triad and a relative disregard for the long-range strategic bomber. Overall, the Soviet strategic force has slightly more than twice the megatonnage of the U.S. force, but this is carried by less than two-thirds the number of warheads (about 6,000 compared to 9,200 as of January 1980) and is generally deliverable with somewhat less accuracy than the U.S. vehicles. The Soviet Union has also deployed sixty-four anti-ballistic missiles (ABMs); while these would have only a very marginal significance against U.S. ballistic missiles, the United States has decided to entirely forego any such deployment. Both the United States and the Soviet Union support their strategic nuclear forces with a roughly similar structure of command, control, and communications (C^3) systems, although the U.S. C^3 capability is perhaps a little more sophisticated. These particular characteristics of the respective strategic force postures, although less significant than the more fundamental similarities, have nevertheless been remarkably persistent—the above observations would have generally pertained equally well had they been made more than a decade ago!

This situation of roughly similar overall force postures, coupled with some quite persistent but more peculiar endogenous characteristics, sits rather uncomfortably with the situation regarding relative U.S. and Soviet strategic doctrines. For most of the period since 1945, those doctrines have been at extreme variance with each other, with the degree of polarity modified only by the volatility of American declaratory policy. Soviet strategic doctrine has, at least until quite recently, reflected a fairly simple extrapolation into the nuclear age of traditional Soviet military thinking. Whereas the development of "the absolute weapon" created a revolution in strategic thinking in the United States after 1945, the atomic bomb was regarded in the Soviet Union as little more than a new, albeit enormously more powerful, piece of ordnance. The notion of deterrence as adumbrated by Bernard Brodie and others in 1946,[1] or the more particular formulation of Mutual Assured Destruction (MAD) expounded by Defense Secretary Robert S. McNamara in the mid-1960s, never attracted any support within the USSR. And there has also been no Soviet interest in strategic concepts that would limit nuclear strikes to particular targets while deliberately avoiding others— such as the "no cities" version of counterforce strategy adopted by the Kennedy/McNamara administration in 1961–1962, or the periodic declarations of U.S. officials to the effect that the respective national leaderships and critical command and control facilities might be regarded as "sanctuaries" in any nuclear exchange. While U.S. strategic doctrines have been characterized as "shifting sands,"[2] Soviet strategic doctrine has exhibited remarkable consistency. In the event of a nuclear war, Soviet strategic forces would be used massively rather than sequentially, and against a wide range of nuclear and conventional military targets, command and control facilities, centers of political and administrative leadership, economic and industrial facilities, power supplies, etc., rather than more selectively; while urban areas would not be attacked in pursuit of some arbitrary minimum level of fatalities, neither would they be avoided if they were located among military, political, or industrial targets.

This so-called war fighting strategy is reflected fairly well in the size and character of the Soviet strategic forces. As Benjamin Lambeth has noted, Soviet military doctrine has played "a major role in Soviet force structure development ... The Soviet force posture ... has shown far more consistency over time than any comparable American effort and has imparted real teeth to Soviet military doctrine in a manner far too systematic to be dismissed as mere happenstance."[3] But if the overall U.S. and Soviet strategic postures are essentially similar, with roughly comparable weapons technologies and types, and if "the strategic concepts that inform Soviet force development and contingency planning are fundamentally different from those of the United States,"[4] then the implication is that American strategic concepts have had little influence on U.S. strategic nuclear force developments!

Strategic analysts are generally—and perhaps quite rightfully— skeptical of conclusions reached on the basis of such simple syllogistic reasoning. The elucidation of Soviet strategic doctrine, given incomplete access to the source materials and the difficulties of penetrating the ideological obfuscation, is necessarily speculative to some degree, providing a basic premise for the syllogism that might not be very secure. And even in the U.S. case, there is rarely a single, clear, and coherent doctrine dominant at any given time. Rather, there is generally a melange of frequently inchoate notions, some of which are invoked to inform policy declarations, or targeting principles, or contingency planning, or a variety of other purposes—and which have an extraordinarily complex relationship with force structure development. In this situation, the precise role of strategic concepts and doctrine in U.S. strategic nuclear force structure development can only be determined on some more empirical bases.

THE BEGINNING OF NUCLEAR STRATEGY

At the outset of the nuclear age, the relationship between strategic concepts and doctrine and U.S. strategic nuclear force development was quite unambiguous. The Manhattan Project and the strikes against Hiroshima and Nagasaki proceeded unencumbered by the musings of any strategists. Rather, the new technology generated a revolution in U.S. strategic thought—as Bernard Brodie observed at the time, the atomic bomb would "so govern the strategic and tactical dispositions of either side as to create a wholly novel form of war."[5]

The central strategic concept that emerged and went essentially unchallenged in the U.S. for three decades—that of *deterrence*—derived from another classic paragraph written by Brodie in 1946:

> Thus, the first and most vital step in any American security program for the age of atomic bombs is to take measures to guarantee to ourselves in case of attack the possibility of retaliation in kind. The writer in making that statement is not for the moment concerned about who will *win* the next war in which atomic bombs are used. Thus far the chief purpose of our military establishment has been to win wars. From now its chief purpose must be to avert them. It can have almost no other useful purpose.

Brodie went on to state that among the requirements for deterrence were extraordinary measures of protection for the retaliatory force so that it might survive a surprise attack, and that margins of superiority in nuclear weapons or the means of delivering them might count for little or nothing in a crisis as long as each side had reason to fear the huge devastation that could be visited on its peoples and territories by the other.

From the point of force structure development, however, these observations begged as many questions as they answered. How large a retaliatory force was needed for viable deterrence? Was the possession of one or a handful of protected atomic bombs sufficient? What levels of assured devastation were required before margins of superiority became meaningless? What precise contingencies did the atomic bomb actually deter? What other defense forces should be procured to complement the atomic elements and provide deterrence across the whole spectrum of possible national security contingencies?

Strategic thinking did not begin to address these questions until the late 1940s. By then the development of U.S. strategic nuclear forces had proceeded a considerable distance—by 1950 the United States had several hundred atomic bombs, and on 31 January that year the administration formally decided to go ahead with the development of the H-bomb. Targeting of the U.S. strategic forces in the late 1940s and early 1950s more reflected the planning and practices of the Eighth and Twentieth Air Forces during the Second World War than any consideration of the requirements of nuclear deterrence.[7]

The first serious attempt to define a comprehensive strategic doctrine that could guide U.S. force structure development occurred in 1950. On 31 January, at the same time he formally approved the development of the H-bomb, President Harry S. Truman issued a directive to the Secretaries of State and Defense "to undertake a reexamination of our objectives in peace and war and of the effect of these objectives on strategic plans, in the light of the probable fission bomb capability and possible thermonuclear bomb capability of the Soviet Union."[8] The subsequent review, generally known as NSC 68, was prepared by a State-Defense Policy Review Group, chaired by Paul H. Nitze, and was completed on 7 April 1950. Four "possible courses of action" were considered by the group: continuation of current policies and programs; isolation; preventive war; and a rapid build-up "of the political, economic, and military strength of the free world." After extended discussion, the first three ideas were rejected: a continuation of current policies would only lead to further deterioration of America's relative military strength as the Soviet nuclear program developed; isolation would deprive the U.S. of the supplementary strength of its allies and hence only enhance the relative position of the Soviet Union; and preventive war would probably be unsuccessful, since it was unlikely that the Soviet Union "would wait for such an attack before launching one of its own." The recommended course of action was therefore a broadly-based and rapid build-up that would include a "substantial increase in expenditures for military purposes." At a meeting on 29 September 1950, the NSC accepted the conclusions of NSC 68 "as a statement of policy to be followed over the next four or five years."[9]

NSC 68 as such, however, had little impact on U.S. Strategic force development. To begin with, as one recent critic has observed, it was "[when] viewed as a call to action rather than policy analysis ... an amazingly incomplete and amateurish study." The discussion of alternative basic national security policies was not at all objective but, rather, addressed "two straw options (isolation and war), one unacceptable choice (continuation of current policies), and the obviously desired solution (a rapid political, economic, and military build-up)." Moreover, the authors of NSC 68 had "deliberately avoided including specific recommendations for program expansion or cost estimates."[10] In any case, the Korean War broke out in June 1950 and NSC 68 passed from the deliberations. The imperatives of the war generated a rapid expansion in U.S. conventional capabilities; the total personnel strength of the U.S. armed forces, for example, went from 1,461,000 in June 1950 to 3,636,000 as at 1 July 1952.[11] The development of the U.S. atomic arsenal also proceeded apace, passing 1,000 bombs in 1952, but without either any strategic guidance or current planning contingency to inform it.

MASSIVE RETALIATION

The formulation of a basic and comprehensive national security policy was regarded by President Dwight D. Eisenhower, who took office on 20 January 1953, as one of the mose urgent and important tasks of his administration. In May 1953, he inaugurated "Operation Solarium," which has been described as "an effort to determine future national security policy in the broadest sense."[12] The product of this study was NSC 162/2, approved by President Eisenhower on 30 October 1953, which laid the foundation for the doctrine of "massive retaliation" announced by Secretary of State John Foster Dulles in his historic address before the Council of Foreign Relations on 12 January 1954:

> The way to deter aggression is for the free community to be willing and able to respond vigorously at places and with means of its own choosing.
>
> Now, so long as our basic concepts in these respects were unclear, our military leaders could not be selective in building our military power.... Before military planning could be changed, the President and his advisers, represented by the National Security Council, had to make some basic policy decisions. This has been done.
>
> And the basic decision was ... to depend primarily upon a great capacity to retaliate instantly by means and at places of our own choosing.[13]

The doctrine of massive retaliation required that the U.S. maintain and be prepared to use effective means to make aggression too costly to be tempting. As such, it made explicit the two essential elements of all deterrence notions—capability and credibility. With respect to capability, the clear guidance provided to the military leaders responsible for "building our military power" was that U.S. forces must be survivable against a Soviet first strike (and hence able to "retaliate"), must be large enough to inflict "massive" devastation, and must be capable of high and continuous alert rates so as to respond "instantly." It was the responsibility of declaratory policy to ensure that the posture was credible, that there was no doubt in the mind of any potential adversary about the American willingness to execute the strategy.

As it happened, there was, in fact, reasonable cause for concern about both the elements of the doctrine. The work of Albert Wohlstetter and others at the Rand Corporation in the early- and mid-1950s showed quite clearly the potential vulnerability of the U.S. strategic forces, even to the much smaller Soviet forces. In 1956 the Strategic Air Command (SAC) had about 1,650 strategic bombers capable of striking the USSR (consisting of some 1,300 B-47s, some 250 B-3s, and about 100 B-52s), while the Soviet Union had fewer than 150 bombers capable of reaching the United States, but almost the entire SAC force was based in peacetime at only thirty lightly-defended bases in the United States, and only another seventy bases overseas were available to it in wartime.[14] Secondly, massive retaliation lacked credibility. Before 1954-1955, the United States could have launched a nuclear attack on the Soviet Union with virtual impunity, but by the time of Dulles' announcement the Soviet Union was developing a capability to deliver bombs on the United States itself. And as this capability increased, massive retaliation became increasingly incredible.

These points formed the substance of vigorous criticism of the doctrine, in response to which Secretary Dulles and other members of the administration made a series of "clarifying" and "explanatory" statements which, as Bernard Brodie pointed out, "amounted virtually to a retraction."[15] However, this backtracking was not reflected in U.S. force structure development. As Brodie also observed,

> If one examines the course actually pursued by national defense policy and military programming over the next several years [i.e. 1954-1959], it was the original speech which stood and not the retractions .... Developments in our military force structure ... were in the direction of increased rather than lessened dependence on massive retaliation.[16];

THE KENNEDY ADMINISTRATION

The Kennedy administration came into office on 20 January 1961 determined to rectify this situation. Both President Kennedy and Defense Secretary McNamara had personal predilections against the inflexibilities they perceived in extant U.S. strategic nuclear policy—as expressed, for example, in Kennedy's criticism during the 1960 presidential campaign that the current U.S. posture provided no choices other than "humiliation or holocaust." In this, they were fully supported by their chosen advisers—in the President's case, military representative General Maxwell Taylor; and in McNamara's case, a highly articulate group of analysts from the Rand Corporation, including William Kaufmann, Alain Enthoven, Charles Hitch, Henry Rowen, and Daniel Ellsberg. Moreover, this group of analysts had unquestioned confidence in the ability of management techniques, such as the planning, programming, and budgeting system (PPBS), systems analysis, and cost-effectiveness studies, to generate force structure designs that precisely reflected the strategic guidance. And the Kennedy administration was perfectly placed in terms of the technological evolution of ICBM and SLBM systems to impose its doctrinal predilections on the U.S. strategic force posture.[17]

When the Kennedy administration took office, the United States was just entering the "missile age"; only about a dozen ICBMs were operational, all of which were slow-reacting, radio-guided, liquid-fuelled, extremely vulnerable Atlas D missiles, and only two FBM submarines had been deployed (with Polaris A-1 missiles). Under Eisenhower, about 1,100 strategic ballistic missiles had been programmed; about 20 percent of these were the first-generation Atlas and Titan ICBMs, later phased out of the missile inventory, and about 10 percent were Mobile Minuteman ICBMs, later withdrawn from the program because of cost and technical problems. Only some 800 missiles were the strategically viable, second-generation Polaris and hard-silo Minuteman missiles. By the time of President Kennedy's assassination, in November 1963, this figure had more than doubled—to over 1,900 strategic ballistic missiles consisting of fifty-four storable liquid-fuelled, large payload Titan II ICBMs, 656 Polaris SLBMs, and 1,200 Minuteman ICBMs (cut back to 1,000 the following year). The decisions of the Kennedy administration essentially determined the size and character of the U.S. strategic missile forces for the next two decades.

Most of these decisions were made in 1961—and principally by the fall of 1961. In a special message to Congress on 28 March, President Kennedy announced the decision to limit the Titan program to 54 Titan IIs and, though it was not explicated, to limit the U.S. strategic missile forces essentially to small, relatively low-payload missiles. The decision to limit the Polaris program to 41 submarines (656 SLEMs), rather than the 45 that the Navy was seeking, was made by Secretary McNamara on 22 September 1961. The FY 1963 defense budget, presented to Congress on 18 January 1962, contained authorization for 800 Minuteman ICBMs and projected a total force through FY 1968 of 1,200. Although the formal decision to limit the number of Minuteman to 1,000 was not made until 5 November 1964, it is believed that Secretary McNamara had personally decided, no later than December 1961, that 1,000 would be sufficient.

The period during which these decisions were being made was one of extraordinary excitement from the point of view of development and refinement of strategic concepts and doctrines. The debate both within and outside the administration was relatively thorough and comprehensive and broached the essential rationales of the strategic forces. At least within the administration there was, from the beginning, a sufficient consensus in the argument to provide some general illumination to force structure issues: the U.S. strategic forces must be capable of more than merely surviving a Soviet first strike and inflicting unacceptable damage on the Soviet urban-industrial system; the delivery vehicles must be sufficiently numerous and accurate to be used against a wide range of counterforce targets, including hardened missile silos; and the command and control systems must be sufficiently survivable and sophisticated to permit a range of alternative retaliatory strikes, including some relatively limited ones. However, the clarification and operationalization of the concepts and the delineation of compatible targeting plans in the Single Integrated Operational Plan (SIOP) was still, at the time the principal missile decisions were made, quite tentative and rudimentary. The progress made in only eight months or so was very impressive, but the work was still more than six months away from completion; it had certainly not proceeded to the point of providing any specific basis for determining the size and character of the U.S. strategic forces.

McNamara's introduction to strategy occurred within the first week after he took office, when William Kaufmann gave him a formal briefing on a series of studies undertaken by the Rand Corporation and the Air Staff during 1959-1960. Those studies pointed to the strategic utility of counterforce strikes that held attacks on cities and population to a minimum. McNamara was an immediate convert to this particular "no cities" version of counterforce strategy and, on 6 March 1961, ordered the preparation of a draft memorandum revising U.S. basic national security policies, including an examination of "the assumptions relating to counterforce strikes." The section on "objectives and general war," the first draft of which was completed by 7 April 1961 and the final draft by mid-May, was prepared by Daniel Ellsberg and stressed the necessity of providing the President with a variety of options in the event of nuclear war. At the same time, the Joint Chiefs of Staff were also ordered to "prepare a Doctrine which, if accepted, would permit controlled response and negotiating pauses in the event of thermonuclear war." This study, prepared by Lt.-Col. Robert P. Lukeman, also argued for strategic flexibility and graduated options. These papers were then embodied in the Department of Defense's *Guidelines for Planning*, later to be included in a draft *Policy Guidance on Plans for Central War*, which in turn became the basis of the 1961 revision of the SIOP.

The SIOP inherited from the Eisenhower administration had contained only one plan under which the United States would launch all its strategic nuclear delivery vehicles (SNDVs) immediately upon the initiation of nuclear war with the Soviet Union. The single National Strategic Target List (NSTL) predominantly included Soviet and satellite cities; no strategic reserves were to be retained and there was no provision for the preservation of command and control capabilities. As Daniel Ellsberg has observed, "If the SIOP [of 1960-1961] were activated, we would have hit every city in the Soviet Union and China in addition to all military targets."[18] Expected Soviet, Chinese, and satellite fatalities were placed by the JCS at 360 to 425 million people.

In place of this single option, a new, more flexible strategic policy was drawn up. For example, China and the satellite countries were separated from the Soviet Union for targeting purposes; Soviet strategic forces were separated from Soviet cities on target lists; strategic reserves were to be held by the United States; U.S. command and control systems were to be protected, to allow "controlled response"; and Soviet command control was to be preserved, at least in the initial stages of any nuclear exchange.

With regard to any nuclear exchange with the Soviet Union, the SIOP was given five options, plus various suboptions, with U.S. attacks to proceed along the following spectrum:

1. Soviet strategic nuclear delivery forces, including missile sites, bomber bases, and submarine tenders.
2. Other elements of Soviet military forces and military resources, located away from cities—for example, air defenses covering U.S. bomber routes.
3. Soviet military forces and military resources near cities.
4. Soviet command control centers and systems.
5. If necessary, all-out urban-industrial attack.

Suboptions included such things as provision for the use of clean or "dirty" bombs, larger or smaller warheads, air- or ground-burst weapons, etc.

Initial work on the revised SIOP, done mainly by Daniel Ellsberg and Frank Trinkl under the direction of Alain Enthoven (all Rand Corporation alumni), was completed by late summer 1961. It was then taken up by Henry Rowen and General Maxwell Taylor and was formalized in the fall of 1961. The JCS studied and approved the strategic change in late 1961, and it was officially adopted in January 1962. To provide the Soviet Union with the option of fighting a "controlled" nuclear war, Moscow was specifically separated from other targets on the NSTL in late 1961. Final approval was given to specific targets, ground-zero areas were marked, and specific bombs and missiles were allocated to the targets—all prepared by the JSTPS—at a meeting between McNamara, his deputy, Roswell J. Gilpatric, and the United States' most senior military officers at SAC headquarters in the last week of June 1962.

The adoption of the no-cities version of counterforce strategy was supported by two strategic developments of the early 1960s. One was the development in 1960-1961 of photographic reconnaissance satellites, which by September 1961 had provided complete photographic coverage of the Soviet Union. Two U.S. satellite programs were involved. The best-known is the air force's satellite and missile observation system (SAMOS), which involved radio transmission of photographs from the satellite to several ground stations around the world. The first of these satellites, SAMOS II, was successfully launched on 31 January 1961; however, the resolution of the photographs obtained in this way was relatively poor. In any case, SAMOS II was only operational for about three weeks, not enough time to fully cover the Soviet Union. The next successful SAMOS was not launched until 22 December 1961. The CIA program was much more important. It launched a series of satellites under the cover of the air force's "Discoverer" biosatellite program. These CIA satellites, using recoverable capsules to retrieve the photographic intelligence and orbiting at lower altitudes, provided much greater resolution. The first of these satellites was launched on 19 August 1960 and recovered the next day; subsequent successful recoveries were made from satellites launched on 12 November 1960, 7 December 1960, 16 June 1961, 7 July 1961, 30 August 1961, and 12 September 1961, by which time the "missile gap" myth of 1958-1961 had finally been laid to rest. The National Intelligence Estimate (NIE) of mid-September 1961 estimated that the Soviet Union had fewer than ten operational ICBMs.

These satellites provided the first fully comprehensive mapping of the Soviet Union—the ICBM and IRBM bases, the submarine ports, air defense sites, army and air force bases, etc.—without which the no-cities version of counterforce strategy could not have been implemented.

The second development was the acknowledged attainment of clear and overwhelming U.S. strategic superiority, which the satellite photographs directly certified. At the end of 1961, when the strategic basis of the 1962 SIOP was completed and accepted by the Joint Chiefs of Staff, the Soviet Union had only four SS-6 ICBMs operational, whereas the U.S. had fifty-four ICBMs and five FBM submarines with eighty Polaris SLBMs. At the end of 1962, the respective figures were thirty Soviet ICBMs against 200 U.S ICBMs and 144 U.S. SLBMs. Moreover, the NIE's of late 1961 and late 1962 projected a U.S. superiority of between 2 to 1 and 4 to 1 by the mid-1960s. A counterforce strike by the United States in the early 1960s could perhaps have fully disarmed the Soviet Union.

Despite these developments, McNamara quickly began to backtrack from his no-cities position. The second draft presidential memorandum (DPM) on strategic forces, for example, prepared in late 1962, represented a distinct retreat from his earlier position. It stated, for example, "we do not want a comprehensive damage limitation posture."

There were several reasons for McNamara's apparent retreat from counterforce and no-cities.

First, within the United States there was much criticism of the first strike implications of the counterforce strategy. As one former McNamara aide is reported to have said: " . . . there could be no such thing as primary retaliation against military targets after an enemy attack. If you're going to shoot at missiles, you're talking about first strike."[19] This question was unnecessarily complicated because of the administration's ambiguity on whether U.S. policy completely ruled out striking first. President Kennedy had said in March 1962, for example, that "Khrushchev must NOT be certain that, where its vital interests are threatened, the United States will never strike first."[20]

A second factor was the Soviet reaction. In their public statements at least, Soviet spokesmen denied the possibility of controlled counterforce warfare. Avowed Soviet strategy was to strike against military targets, governmental and administrative centers, and cities simultaneously and immediately on the outbreak of general hostilities. Whether in fact the Soviets would accept the U.S. strategy was an open question; McNamara himself actually believed that any Soviet nuclear attack on the United States would include major urban areas. In any case, it was argued, while Soviet missiles were few and vulnerable and U.S. force numerically so superior, the Soviet Union could not afford to play "games" of controlled "tit-for-tat" with missiles. And as the Soviet force grew larger and became hardened and dispersed, McNamara believed the destruction of any large number of missiles would be "unfeasible."

A third factor was the unfavorable reaction of West European allies. McNamara had first described the "no-cities" strategy to them at a secret session of NATO in Athens in May 1962; the audience was reportedly incredulous. In June, Secretary of State Dean Rusk made a three-day tour of six Western capitals to explain the new U.S. policy to West Europe's leaders. But he met with frustration; the NATO allies were obviously unwilling to accept the implications of the "no-cities" strategy, especially for small, independent European nuclear capabilities. Not only did the "no-cities" strategy deny the Europeans nuclear independence and fail to consider the different targeting priorities of the European governments; it also raised the specter of separating European security from that of the United States and—by removing the threat to Soviet cities—of removing *pari passu* the deterrent to a Soviet attack on Europe, and even of the possibility of fighting a nuclear war over European territory while leaving the Soviet and U.S. homelands unscathed.

But, most importantly, McNamara decided to withdraw from the "no-cities" policy for bureaucratic reasons. By the time the FY 1964 defense budget was developed in late 1962, it was clear to McNamara that the services, particularly the air force, were using his declared policy of "no-cities" counterforce as a basis for requesting virtually open-ended strategic weapon programs—both more Minuteman missiles and procurement of a force of supersonic reconnaissance-strike (RS-70) bombers. He thus came to place more stress on assured destruction capabilities (although by defining the assured destruction criteria conservatively he could still procure sufficient forces to allow a damage-limiting mission), and in January 1963 he directed William Kaufmann to brief some dozen air force generals to the effect that they were no longer to take the avowed U.S. strategy as a criterion for strategic force proposals. In separating declaratory policy from actual policy, McNamara was, to a large extent, using strategic doctrine as a weapon in the continuous intramural bureaucratic battles over military programs and defense (and service) budgets.

FROM COUNTERFORCE TO ASSURED DESTRUCTION

McNamara did not move immediately to a wholesale acceptance of "assured destruction"; rather, declaratory policy from 1964 through 1966 included both "assured destruction" and "damage limitation" as basic U.S. strategic objectives.

The development of the concept of "damage limitation" was principally the responsibility of General Glenn A. Kent (USAF), who headed a study group initially established by McNamara in the summer of 1962 to undertake a comprehensive analysis of various alternative strategic policies available to the United States and the weapons systems and force levels each implied. The results of a pilot survey were ready in July 1963, and the full study, entitled *Damage Limitation: A Rationale for the Allocation of Resources by the US and USSR*, was published on 21 January 1964.

In a memorandum dated 12 March 1964, McNamara asked for an amplification of the January study and requested "that the Services conduct studies during the next six months that would focus attention on 'damage limitation' and 'assured destruction.'" These studies were integrated by the Weapons System Evaluation Group (WSEG) in a two-volume study known as WSEG No. 79 and formally entitled *Analysis of General Nuclear War Postures for Strategic Offense and Defense Forces*, dated August 1964. The project was formally completed on 8 September 1964 with the preparation of *A Summary Study of Strategic Offense and Defense Forces of the US and USSR*.

The Kent study and the associated analyses formed the basis of McNamara's discussion of U.S. strategic nuclear policy in his FY 1965 and 1966 defense budget statements. In his FY 1965 statement, submitted to Congress in January 1964, McNamara stated: "comprehensive studies of alternative U.S. strategic retaliatory force structures employed in a nuclear exchange with a wide range of possible Soviet forces and under a wide variety of assumptions pertaining to the outbreak of war and United States and Soviet operational factors [have] found that forces in excess of those needed simply to destroy Soviet cities would significantly reduce damage to the United States and Western Europe. And the extent to which damage to ourselves can be reduced depends importantly on the size and the character of our own forces, particularly by the surface-to-surface missiles such as Minuteman that can reach their targets quickly ... While a cities-only strategic retaliatory force would, in our judgment, be dangerously inadequate, a full-first-strike force, as I defined it earlier, is, on the basis of our estimates of the Soviet nuclear strike forces in the fiscal year 1967-69 period, simply unattainable .... Thus, a damage-limiting strategy appears to be the most practical and effective course for us to follow. Such a strategy requires a force considerably larger than would be needed for a limited cities-only strategy. *While there are still some differences of judgment on just how large such a force should be,* there is general agreement that it should be large enough to insure the destruction, singly or in combination of the Soviet Union, Communist China, and the Communist satellites as national societies, under the worst possible circumstances of war outbreak that can reasonably be postulated, and, in addition, to destroy their war-making capability so as to limit, to the extent practicable, damage to this country and to our allies."[21]

The concepts of "assured destruction" and "damage limitation" were described by McNamara in his FY 1966 defense budget statement presented to Congress in February 1965:

> The strategic objectives of our general nuclear war forces are:
> 1. to deter a deliberate nuclear attack upon the United States and its allies by maintaining a clear and convincing capability to inflict unacceptable damage on an attacker, even were that attacker to strike first;
> 2. in the event such a war should nevertheless occur, to limit damage to our populations and industrial capacities.
>
> The first of these capabilities (required to deter potential aggressors) we call 'Assured Destruction', i.e., the capability to destroy the aggressor as a viable society, even after a well planned and executed surprise attack on our forces. The second capability we call 'Damage Limitation', i.e., the capability to reduce the weight of the enemy attack by both offensive and defensive measures and to provide a degree of protection for the population against the effects of nuclear detonations.[22]

However, these studies and resultant concepts and doctrines had little impact on U.S. strategic nuclear force development. For one thing, this elucidation of strategic criteria never proceeded to the point of providing any specific bases for strategic weapons procurement. As McNamara testified in 1964, there were "still some differences of judgment" on what the size of the U.S. missile force should be. The final decision to limit the Minuteman force to 1,000 missiles was formally made by the

Department of Defense on 5 November 1964 and upheld by President Lyndon B. Johnson in a meeting with the Joint Chiefs of Staff, Secretary McNamara, Deputy Secretary Cyrus Vance, and the Director of the Bureau of the Budget, Kermit Gordon, on 22 December 1964. The "damage limitation" project was in hand to inform this decision, but the overwhelming weight of evidence implies that McNamara and his key aides made the actual decision to limit the Minuteman program to 1,000 missiles some years before then, and for quite other reasons. As General Kent himself has stated, the "damage limitation" project provided little more than a rationalization of the predetermined force levels.

In 1965, in fact, McNamara had already moved to substantially downplay the "damage limitation" aspects of avowed U.S. strategic policy, and by 1967 it was all "assured destruction." McNamara gave the first formal definition of "assured destruction" to Congress in his FY 1966 budget statement of 18 February 1965:

> A vital first objective, to be met in full by our strategic nuclear forces, is the capability for Assured Destruction. What kinds and amounts of destruction we would have to be able to inflict in order to provide this (capability) cannot be answered precisely. But, it seems reasonable to assume the destruction of, say, one-quarter to one-third of its population and about two-thirds of its industrial capacity . . . would certainly represent intolerable punishment to any industrialized nation and thus should serve as an effective deterrent.[23]

In considering the relationship between concepts and U.S. force development, there are two especially noteworthy aspects of the conceptual transition from counterforce to "assured destruction" that took place under McNamara's stewardship. The first is that the force procurement requirements of the former, no matter how imprecisely formulated, are obviously much different from those of the latter; indeed, some aspects of the "assured destruction" posture, with its necessary emphasis on urban targeting, are likely to be quite incompatible with those of the extreme "no cities" version of counterforce. On the other hand, the force posture designed in 1961-1962 remained essentially intact at the end of the 1960s.

Second, the criteria on which "assured destruction" was defined did not remain static. In McNamara's FY 1968 budget statement, presented to Congress on 23 January 1967, the required levels of destruction were reduced to "one-fifth to one-fourth of its [the Soviet Union's] population and one-half to two-thirds of its industrial capacity."[24] This reduction in the destruction levels did not represent any philosophical reconsideration of the requirements of viable deterrence; rather, it represented a more accurate reflection of U.S. capabilities against the Soviet urban-industrial target structure.

RECENT DEVELOPMENTS IN U.S. STRATEGIC POLICY AND FORCE STRUCTURE

Current developments in U.S. strategic policy, which can be trace directly back to 1972, are in many respects remarkably similar to those which occurred under Secretary McNamara in 1961-1962—but which he was later to disavow. Again, however, it is difficult to correlate these policy developments with recent developments in the U.S. strategic force structure.

In mid-1972, without public announcement, President Richard M. Nixon named his Assistant for National Security Affairs, Henry Kissinger, to chair a top-level interdepartmental group "to come up with additional nuclear war options." The resultant report, National Security Study Memorandum (NSSM)—169, completed in 1973, recommended that U.S. strategic nuclear employment policy be modified to provide for a wide range of options, including at least some "selective" attacks on Soviet military targets.[25] NSSM—169 led directly to the development of National Security Decision Memorandum (NSDM)—242, signed by President Nixon in early January 1974, which in turn authorized the Secretary of Defense to promulgate the *Policy Guidance for the Employment of Nuclear Weapons* and the associated *Nuclear Weapons Employment Policy* (NUWEP), signed by Secretary James Schlesinger in April 1974. These documents were the basis of changes to both action policy, in terms of the "new" targeting plans given effect in SIOP-5 of 1 January 1976, as well as in declaratory policy, as reflected in the enthusiastic pronouncements by Secretary Schlesinger throughout 1974-1975.

NSDM—242 contained three principal policy components. The one which most engaged public debate, of course, was the reemphasis on the targeting of a wide range of Soviet military forces and installations, from hardened command and control facilities and ICBM silos to airfields and army camps.[26] This reemphasis, however, was much more declaratory than substantive, since the SIOP had—at least since 1962 and including the period when "assured destruction" was avowed policy—contained most of these counterforce targets. The second element of NSDM—242 was the requirement for "escalation control" whereby the National Command Authorities (NCA) should be provided with the ability to execute their selected options in a deliberate and controlled fashion throughout a strategic nuclear exchange. And, third, NSDM—242 introduced the notion of "withholds" or "non-targets," (i.e., things that would be preserved from destruction). Some of these, such as "population per se," have now been exempted absolutely from targeting; others, such as centers of political control, are exempted only for the purposes of intra-war deterrence and intra-war bargaining, and strategic reserve forces are to be maintained to allow their eventual destruction if necessary. Specific quantitative objectives derived from these concepts are set out in NUWEP as guidance to the Joint Strategic Targeting Planning Staff for preparation of the SIOP; most especially, NUWEP requires that the SIOP forces be able to destroy 70 percent of the Soviet industry needed to achieve economic recovery in the event of a large-scale strategic nuclear exchange.[27]

Despite some initial expectation that the administration of President Jimmy Carter and Secretary Harold Brown would move to change U.S. policy back toward something more like "assured destruction," the concepts and doctrines embodied in NSDM—242 were essentially retained, and indeed further refined, through to the present day.[28] The documentary reappraisal of NSDM—242 began with the preparation of Presidential Review Memorandum 10 (PRM-10), signed by President Carter on 18 February 1977, just four weeks after he assumed office. This five-month inter-agency study, supervised by Samuel P. Huntington for the President's national security adviser, was a comprehensive assessment of the Soviet-American global power relationship. This assessment included a study entitled "Military Strategy and Force Posture Review" (prepared largely by the office of the assistant secretary of defense for international security affairs), which considered details of the military balance and alternative military strategies— including strategies for possible nuclear war with the Soviet Union.[29]

PRM-10 was completed in late June 1977 and, with its attendant reports, was considered by a cabinet level group, chaired by Zbigniew Brzezinski, on 7 July. The PRM-10 conclusions were more sanguine and optimistic than most observers had expected. The study assumed the deployment of Trident SLBMs, the Mark 12A warhead on Minuteman ICBMs, the development of cruise missiles, and the continued development of the MX ICBM. Assessing the impact of a major nuclear war between the two superpowers, the study found that, at a minimum, the United States would suffer 140 million fatalities and the Soviet Union 113 million and almost three-quarters of their respective economies would be destroyed. In such a conflict, the report concluded, "neither side could conceivably be described as a winner." The report stated that neither side would have an advantage in launching a limited nuclear attack against the other's land-based ICBM forces, and, in fact, that "whichever side initiates a limited nuclear attack against the ICBM forces of the other side will find itself significantly worse off" in surviving numbers of missiles and missile warheads. The study also found that U.S. anti-submarine warfare (ASW) capability was significantly greater than that of the Soviets and that even after a Soviet missile attack against U.S. air bases, the surviving U.S. bomber force would be larger than that now possessed by the Soviets.[30]

On 24 August 1977, following further intensive review of PRM-10 and the attendant "Military Strategy and Force Posture Review" by NSC officials and the Departments of Defense and State, and extended debate in the Special Coordination Committee (dominated by Brzezinski, Secretary of State Vance, and Secretary of Defense Brown), President Carter issued Presidential Directive 18, entitled "US National Strategy." This directive instructed the Pentagon to review six aspects of U.S. strategic policy: U.S. nuclear targeting; the definition of strategic forces; the continuation of the Triad; U.S. counterforce needs; American civil defense; and U.S. interrelationship with allies at the level of strategic weaponry.[31]

Most important from the viewpoint of action policy, PD-18 reaffirmed the continued use of NSDM—242 in "the absence of further guidance for structuring the U.S. strategic posture."[32] It insisted that the United States maintain the capability to inflict "unacceptable damage" on the Soviet Union even if that nation struck first with nuclear weapons. But it instructed the Pentagon to develop options for limited U.S. nuclear responses. It also directed that a "reserve" of strategic forces be maintained, safe from attack, for use if nuclear war became relatively extended. Finally, it stated that U.S. forces should be strong enough to ensure that a possible nuclear war would end on the most favorable terms possible to the United States.[33]

The "further guidance" called for by PD-18 was provided by a Nuclear Targeting Policy Review (NTPR), an inter-agency study headed by Leon Sloss in the Pentagon. This study identified several targeting issues that were studied further before being incorporated into a new SIOP. Although the SIOP now has some 40,000 designated targets—increased from about 25,000 in 1974 when the Schlesinger doctrine was promulgated—there were no radical changes in the structure of its targeting philosophy.[34]

With respect to the U.S. strategic nuclear force posture, three principal developments took place contemporaneously with these post-1972 policy developments. One was that the number of deliverable warheads in the U.S. strategic nuclear forces was more than doubled, and although the average yield of these warheads decreased substantially, this allowed an increase in the number of certain targets that could be covered in the Soviet Union. The second was the introduction of the Command Data Buffer System, which greatly enhanced the targeting flexibility of the Minuteman III force. And the third was the increasing resources allocated to improving the survivability, endurance, responsiveness, and capacity of U.S. command, control, and communications (C[3]) systems. Each of these related to significant aspects of the conceptual and doctrinal developments of the 1970s, but none of them were, in fact, determined by those developments.

At the beginning of the 1970s, the United States had slightly fewer than 5,000 deliverable warheads, with one on each of the 1,910 ICBMs and SLBMs in the strategic ballistic missile force and about 2,800 bombs and Hound Dog air-to-surface missiles carried on the FB-111 and B-52 bombers. By 1976 this figure had more than doubled, to slightly more than 10,100 deliverable warheads. This was due principally to the deployment of the Minuteman III ICBMs and the Poseidon SLBMs with three and ten MIRVs respectively (which together accounted for 6,610 warheads). This greatly increased the number of conventional military targets (such as airfields, army bases, ports, rail marshalling yards, tank concentrations, etc.) and economic and industrial facilities (such as petroleum refineries, power stations, factories, etc.) that could be attacked by the SIOP forces, as well as enhancing the flexibility with which U.S. planners could approach the Soviet target base. However, the development of MIRVs was essentially a product of the period when "assured destruction" was the ascendant philosophy.

The notion of using a single missile to accurately deliver each of several warheads along separate trajectories was conceived and suggested to the military simultaneously by a number of individuals and groups within the U.S. technical community in 1962-1963, and was accepted within the Department of Defense in 1964. In the fall of that year, decisions were made to proceed with the engineering development of a Mark 12 MIRV system for the Minuteman and a larger version of the Polaris B-3 SLBM (later renamed the Poseidon C-3) that would also carry MIRVs. Although it received some support because of its possible counterforce and warfighting attributes, the determinate strategic consideration within the Pentagon was its utility as a penetration aid in the event of the deployment of a large Soviet ABM system.[35] The first group of ten Minuteman III ICBMs (with the Mark 12 MIRV) became operational in June 1970, about a year later than the original target date. The first patrol of a Poseidon submarine began on 31 March 1971[36]—several years before the doctrinal reassessments began to take effect in the mid-1970s. The great increase in U.S. warheads produced by the deployments of the Minuteman IIIs and, most especially, the Poseidons, posed something of a problem for U.S. military planners: most of these warheads lacked a sufficient yield/accuracy combination to be used against Soviet ICBM silos, and the major Soviet population centers were already covered to the point where additional warheads had little marginal value. The end result was that the great bulk of Soviet targets in the SIOP came to be made up of non-strategic military installations, military and quasimilitary production and R&D facilities, and industrial centers. The broad spectrum of targets described by Secretary Schlesinger in his 1974 policy declarations were much more the consequence of this force development than of any conceptual or doctrinal initiatives. As Dr. William J. Perry was to testify in February 1979, the policy declarations from Secretary Schlesinger to Secretary Brown had no operational impact: "The targeting policy is based on the force we have."[37]

The second important force posture development of this period was that of the Command Data Buffer System (CDBS). In March 1974, Secretary Schlesinger testified that $33 million included in the FY 1975 defense budget "to complete development and to continue procurement of the Command Data Buffer" was the largest single expenditure item related to "the new targeting doctrine."[38] (Quite a revealing observation about the relationship between doctrine and force development!) The CDBS enables crews in Minuteman III launch control centers to retarget the missiles in about twenty minutes by electronic means, a process which previously required the physical insertion of new target tapes into each missile's computers, which took up to thirty-six hours. This new retargeting system greatly enhanced the flexibility and war-fighting capability of the Minuteman III force and jelled nicely with the needs of the so-called Schlesinger doctrine. However, the design of the CDBS had actually evolved during the late 1960s, the program was first announced by Secretary Melvin R. Laird in March 1971,[39] and installation of the CDBS had begun (at the 90th Strategic Missile Wing, Francis E. Warren Air Force Base, Wyoming) in November 1972.[40] The system was, in fact, first proposed as an aid to SAC missile maintenance officers involved in retargeting the ICBMs during the periodic SIOP revisions; it was only much later that its strategic utility was appreciated.

The other significant element of force structure development in the 1970s consisted of an extensive array of measures designed to enhance the endurance, survivability, capabilities, flexibility, and responsiveness of the U.S. command, control, and communications (C^3) and related strategic intelligence systems to the National Command Authorities. The most important particular projects have been the reorganization and modernization of the World Wide Military Command and Control System (WWMCCS); the procurement of Boeing 747 aircraft for the Advanced Airborne National Command Post (AABNCP); development and deployment of the Defense Satellite Communications System (DSCS), the Satellite Data System (SDS), the navy's Fleet Satellite Communications (FLTSATCOM) system, and the air force's satellite Communications (AFSATCOM) system; installation of the MOLINK satellite hotline between Washington and Moscow; and improvements in the U.S. ability to detect and process information concerning enemy

ICBM and SLBM launches. Secretary Schlesinger testified in 1974 that these measures, together with the procurement of the CDBS, constituted the only development efforts required by his "new targeting doctrine."[41] More recently, Dr. Perry has testified that the primary systems acquisition requirement identified in the Nuclear Targeting Policy Review (NTPR) of 1977-1978 was that the C^3 system for the SIOP forces "should have greater endurance than the present system."[42] However, it is very difficult to identify any particular C^3 project that derived from or was affected in any specific way by the policy revisions of the mid- and late-1970s. Most C^3 developments now associated with current strategic policy and doctrine were, in fact, initiated in the late 1960s, during the depths of "assured destruction," when the demands of doctrine on the C^3 system were much simpler. The intensity and complexity of the activity in recent years notwithstanding, the expenditure on strategic C^3 was higher in the 1960s than it ever became in the 1970s.[43] Moreover, these developments derived from a variety of different impulses and were generally subject to little overall coordination; they certainly did not arise, or proceed, as integral parts of any coherent U.S. strategic posture. The single most important milestone in recent U.S. C^3 development is DoD Directive 5100.30, signed by Deputy Defense Secretary David Packard on 2 December 1971. That directive vested overall control of the U.S. armed forces in the National Command Authorities (NCA), which consists "only of the President and the Secrretary of Defense or their duly deputized alternates or successors," and defined the chain of command as being "from the NCA through the Chairman of the Joint Chiefs of Staff [*direct*] to the executing commander." It redefined the principal missions of the WWMCCS to make the system more responsive to the needs of the NCA, and it ordered "a very vigorous ... effort to improve the reliability and survivability of the nation's early-warning, post-attack assessment, and communications capability."[44] An immediate result of this was the Pentagon's request in early January 1972 for a fleet of seven AABNCP aircraft.[45] But DoD Directive 5100.30 was a product, more than anything else, of the communications failures and patent lack of C^3 responsiveness exhibited in the USS Liberty, USS Pueblo and EC-121 spy plane incidents of 8 June 1967, 23 January 1968, and 14 April 1969 respectively. Only as subsequent inquiries progressed did concern develop about the survivability and responsiveness of strategic C^3 systems—but that was still before any substantive revision in U.S. strategic doctrine had begun.

The initiative for satellite developments lay elsewhere: these principally reflected the pull of technological potential. Satellites had been developed in the late 1950s and 1960s for a wide range of early-warning, surveillance, and communications purposes, and as the capabilities of the sensors improved and the number and bandwidths of channels increased it was natural to incorporate the advances in new "requirements." The revolutions in computer processing and microcircuitry offered increasingly broad and attractive menus, and strategic concepts provided no effective criteria for determining how much was enough.

CONCLUSION

The historical record not only provides overwhelming empirical support to the proposition deduced at the outset of this chapter, i.e. that strategic concepts and doctrine have played very little role in U.S. strategic force structure development; it also illumines something of the extent to which the strategic concepts and doctrine are the dependent variable, and of the nature of that particular relationship; and it indicates some principal factors actually involved in force structure development.

Any impact that strategic concepts and doctrine have had on U.S. force structure development has never been direct or sustained. There are, however, two general notions which warrant consideration. First, the sophisticated strategic calculus, largely originating at the Rand Corporation in the 1950s, which argued the necessity for a survivable, second-strike nuclear retaliatory force, was invoked in the decisions of early 1961 to accelerate the Polaris and silo-based Minuteman programs. Second, throughout the 1950s and early 1960s there was a generally accepted assumption, so fundamental to the thinking of both military and civilian strategists that it was frequently unarticulated, to the effect that the United States required a substantial degree of strategic nuclear superiority over the Soviet Union. However, it was never made clear just how this "superiority" was to be measured. By themselves, general principles of "survivability" and "superiority," though they might act as signposts, could not serve as guides to the determination of specific force levels or force characteristics.

At the other extreme, it is possible to find some specific force structure decisions that derived directly from the acceptance and/or declaration of a particular strategic concept or doctrine. Perhaps the clearest examples were the recommendations of the Fletcher Committee, a group of analysts and scientists set up by the Secretary of the Air Force Eugene Zuckert in mid-1961 to review the changes in the Minuteman missile system required by the policy change from "massive retaliation" to "controlled flexible response." Many qualitative improvements effected in the Minuteman II (LGM-30F) missile—the first ten of which were officially declared operational in October 1965—were the direct result of Fletcher Committee recommendations: whereas previous plans allowed the Minuteman force to be launched only in squadrons (of fifty missiles) it was now given a selective, individual launch capability; and whereas the Minuteman IA (LGM-30A) missile could only be programmed with a single target, the LGM-30F was given a target selection capability of eight targets. But examples such as this are very few and far between.

In fact, insofar as there is any identifiable relationship between strategic concepts and doctrine on the one hand and U.S. strategic nuclear force development on the other, it is very much one in which military technology is the determinate variable. With respect to strategic policy, it is easy to establish this in a negative sense. It is obvious, for example, that certain counterforce strategies were impossible to pursue before technology provided the means of locating enemy missile silos and bomber bases and the means of accurately delivering relatively large numbers of high-yield nuclear weapons; hence, little serious thought was given to counterforce strategies before the late 1950s (following the deployment of U-2 reconnaissance aircraft and, from August 1960, surveillance satellites; large numbers of strategic nuclear delivery vehicles; and the H-bomb). And strategies involving controlled and flexible responses were not possible until the development of sophisticated command and control systems, multiple targeting memories, and individual and selective missile launch capabilities. But the positive side of the relationship is more interesting: viz., that what technology permits is frequently adopted as doctrine. This certainly seems to have been the case with some of the more significant elements of the so-called Schlesinger doctrine and, at least partially, the retention of that doctrine by the Carter administration. By 1977, most strategic force requirements of a strategy of controlled, limited, counterforce operations, together with the necessary command and control arrangements, were already in place; unless one were persuaded of their counterproductive arms control impact, there would have been little point in dismantling them and denying oneself the potential options and flexibility they allowed.

This is not to suggest the operation of any pure form of technological determinism. For one thing, it begs the question of where the impetus for technological development derives. There are some instances, such as the development of the H-bomb in the late-1940s and early 1950s and perhaps the pursuit of more accurate ballistic missile guidance systems in the 1960s, where the professional interest of the scientific and technical community was paramount. But this community is only one of the many interested groups that contribute to the decisionmaking process, and it is certainly far from being the most powerful.

In the U.S. weapons acquisition and force development process there is a wide range of quite disparate groups and individuals, each with its own peculiar loyalties, interests, perspectives, and predilections, and each with some semiautonomous power-political base from which it works to promote its respective positions. The most important of these "quasi-sovereignties" is of course the President, but the outcomes are generally shaped less by presidential directives than by adversary processes involving a complex interaction of all the participants[46]—the White House staff (and especially the President's Assistant for National Security Affairs), the Secretary of Defense and his principal civilian assistants, the military chiefs and their respective services, and the Office of Management and Budget (OMB). Studies of the major U.S. force development decisions of the 1950s through the 1970s—the decision to develop the ICBM, the decisions to deploy a long-range strategic ballistic missile force of 1,000 Minuteman ICBMs and 656 SLBMs, and the decision to develop the MIRV—all indicate that the outcomes were, more than anything else, the product of intramural bargaining, negotiation, and compromise between these quasi-sovereignties, with the quality of the arguments and the strategic analysis being decidedly secondary to the political power of respective adversaries.[47]

Strategic concepts and doctrines are themselves not the product of any abstract reflection on national interests. Rather, they are more typically products of the technological and bureaucratic-political environments in which they are developed and advanced. And their role in U.S. nuclear force structure development is as instruments to be employed in the intra-mural bargaining rather than as signposts to illumine that development.

This is not a novel conclusion: the generally expediential and partisan character of American strategic thought was an implicit theme in Bernard Brodie's *Strategy in the Missile Age*, and one to which he returned in his last essay.[48] However, it is one that deserves wider recognition, for it offers hope to those rationalists who might despair at the failure of U.S. strategic force development to reflect the evolution of strategic concepts and doctrines. For if those concepts and doctrines are appreciated for their instrumental value—to be employed in adversary situations ranging from budget discussion through weapons acquisition processes to international arms control negotiations—then strategic analysis in a broader sense will, in the end, come closer to realizing its intended impact—and that will include its impact on U.S. strategic nuclear force development.

NOTES

1. Bernard Brodie (ed.), *The Absolute Weapon: Atomic Power and World Order*, (New York: Harcourt, Brace and Company, 1946).
2. See James R. Schlesinger, "Uses and Abuses of Analysis", in Senate Committee of Government Operations, *Planning, Programming, Budgeting*, (Washington, D.C.: U.S. Government Printing Office, 1970), p. 133.
3. Benjamin S. Lambeth, *The Elements of Soviet Strategic Policy*, The Rand Corporation, P-6389, September 1979.
4. Ibid., p. 4. For further discussion of the differences between U.S. and Soviet strategic thought, see Benjamin S. Lambeth, *Selective Nuclear Options in American and Soviet Strategic Policy*, The Rand Corporation, R-2034-DDRE, December 1976; and Fritz W. Ermarth, "Contrasts in American and Soviet Strategic Thought," *International Security*, Fall 1978, pp. 138-155.
5. Brodie, *The Absolute Weapon*, p. 83.
6. Ibid., p. 76.
7. See Anthony Cave Brown (ed.), *Operation World War III: The Secret American Plan "Dropshot" for War with the Soviet Union*, (London: Arms and Armour Press, 1979).
8. See Samuel F. Wells, "Sounding the Tocsin: NSC 68 and the Soviet Threat," *International Security*, Fall 1979, pp. 124-125.
9. Ibid. pp. 134-138.
10. Ibid., pp. 139.
11. Samuel P. Huntington, *The Common Defense: Strategic Programs in National Politics*, (New York: Columbia University Press, 1961), pp. 59-61.
12. Ibid., p. 73.
13. *New York Times*, 13 January 1954.
14. See A. J. Wohlstetter, F. S. Hoffman, R. J. Lutz, and H. S. Rowen, *Selection and Use of Strategic Air Bases*, The Rand Corporation, R-266, April 1954; and A. J. Wohlstetter, F. S. Hoffman, and H. S. Rowen, *Protecting U.S. Power to Strike Back in the 1950's and 1960's*, The Rand Corporation, R-290, 1 September 1956.
15. Bernard Brodie, *Strategy in the Missile Age*, (Princeton, N.J.: Princeton University Press, 1959), p. 249.
16. Ibid., pp. 249, 263.
17. For a fuller discussion of the developments in strategic nuclear policy during the Kennedy administration, together with detailed documentation, see Desmond Ball, *Politics and Force Levels: The Strategic Missile Program of the Kennedy Administration*, (Berkeley: University of California Press, 1980), chap. 9.
18. *International Herald Tribune*, 9 May 1978.
19. Henry L. Trewhitt, *McNamara: His Ordeal in the Pentagon*, (New York: Harper & Row, 1971), p. 115.
20. *Newsweek*, 9 April 1962, p. 32.
21. Senate Appropriations Committee, *Department of Defense Appropriations, 1965*, pp. 31-32.
22. Senate Armed Services Committee & Senate Appropriations Committee, *Military Procurement Authorizations, fiscal year 1966*, p. 43.
23. *Statement of Secretary of Defense Robert S. McNamara before the House Armed Services Committee on the Fiscal Year 1966-70 Defense Program & 1966 Defense Budget*, 18 February 1965, p. 39.
24. *Statement of Secretary of Defense Robert S. McNamara before a Joint Session of the Senate Armed Services Committee & the Senate Subcommittee on Department of Defense Appropriations on the Fiscal Year 1968-72 Defense Program & 1968 Defense Budget*, 23 January 1967, p. 39.

25. For a fuller discussion of the strategic developments of this period, see Desmond Ball, *Deja Vu: The Return to Counterforce in the Nixon Administration*, California Seminar on Arms Control and Foreign Policy, no. 46, December 1974.

26. See, for example, Senate Foreign Relations Committee, *U.S.-U.S.S.R. Strategic Policies* (Top Secret hearing held on 4 March 1974; sanitized and made public on 4 April 1974).

27. See *Los Angeles Times*, 2 February 1977, p. 1; and House Armed Services Committee, *Hearings on Military Posture and H.R. 1872*, pt. 3, bk 1, February-April 1979, pp. 6-26.

28. See Desmond Ball, *Developments in U.S. Strategic Nuclear Policy Under the Carter Administration*, ACIS Working Paper no. 21, center for International & Strategic Affairs, UCLA, February 1980.

29. See Robert G. Kaiser, "Global Strategy Memo Divides Carter's Staff," *Washington Post*, 7 July 1977; Hedric Smith, "Carter Study Takes More Hopeful View of Strategy of U.S.," *New York Times*, 8 July 1977, p. 1; and Richard Burt, "U.S. Study Asserts Russians Could Not Win Nuclear War," *International Herald Tribune*, 7-8 January 1978.

30. Ibid.

31. *Aviation Week and Space Technology*, 6 March 1978, p. 16.

32. Ibid.

33. Charles Mohr, "Carter Orders Steps to Increase Ability to Meet War Threats," *New York Times*, 26 August 1977, pp. 1, 8.

34. See testimony of Dr. William J. Perry, House Armed Services Committee, *Hearings on Military Posture & H.R. 1872*, pt 3., bk 1., February-April 1979, pp. 10-12.

35. See Ted Greenwood, *Making the MIRV: A Study of Defense Decision Making*, (Cambridge, Mass.: Ballinger Publishing Company, 1975), chap. 2.

36. Ibid., p. 10.

37. House Armed Services Committee, *Hearings on Military Posture & H.R. 1872*, pt. 3, bk. 1, February-April 1979, pp. 24-25.

38. Senate Foreign Relations Committee, *U.S.-U.S.S.R. Strategic Policies*, 4 March 1974, p. 29.

39. *Statement of Secretary of Defense Melvin R. Laird before the House Armed Services Committee on the FY 1972-1976 Defense Program and the 1972 Defense Budget*, 9 March 1971, p. 67.

40. *Development of Strategic Air Command 1946-1976*, Office of the Historian, SAC Headquarters, 21 March 1976, p. 166.

41. Senate Foreign Relations Committee, *U.S.-U.S.S.R. Strategic Policies*, 4 March 1974, p. 29; and *Report of the Secretary of Defense James R. Schlesinger to the Congress on the FY 1975 Defense Budget & FY 1975-1979 Defense Program*, 4 March 1974, pp. 72-77.

42. See testimony of Dr. William J. Perry, Senate Armed Services Committee, *Department of Defense Authorization for Appropriations for Fiscal Year 1980*, pt. 1, pp. 298-299; and House Appropriations Committee, *Department of Defense Appropriations for 1980*, pt. 3, pp. 116-117.

43. *Report of Secretary of Defense Harold Brown to the Congress on the FY 1981 Budget, FY 1982 Authorization Request and FY 1981-1985 Defense Programs*, 29 January 1980, p. 71.

44. *Aviation Week & Space Technology*, 6 March 1972, pp. 12-13.

45. *Aviation Week & Space Technology*, 17 January 1972, p. 11. See also *Statement of Secretary of Defense Melvin R. Laird before the House Armed Services Committee on the FY 1973 Defense Budget & FY 1973-1977 program*, 17 February 1972, p. 73.

46. William T. R. Fox, foreword to Michael H. Armacost, *The Politics of Weapon*

Innovation: The Thor-Jupiter Controversy, (New York: Columbia University Press, 1969), p. vii.

47. See Edmund Beard, *Developing the ICBM: A Study in Bureaucratic Politics*, (New York: Columbia Unversity Press, 1976); Desmond Ball, *Politics & Force Levels: The Strategic Missile Program of the Kennedy Administration*, (Berkeley: University of California Press, 1980); and ted Greenwood, *Making the MIRV: A Study of Defense Decision-Making.* (Cambridge, Mass.: Ballinger Publishing Company, 1975).

48. Bernard Brodie, *The Development of Nuclear Strategy*, ACIS Working Paper no. 11, Center for Arms Control and International Security, UCLA, February 1978.

Chapter 5

Changing Attitudes Toward Deterrence

Henry Trofimenko

GENESIS OF THE CONCEPT

The principle of deterrence is as old as history. It consists of restraining an opponent from a hostile action through the threat of unacceptable retaliation.[1] For deterrence—in its preatomic version—to be effective, one side had to possess visible military superiority. The existence of a great discrepancy in power potential and capability could result in coercion of the weaker side by the stronger one.[2]

Actually, coercion is the ultimate form of deterrence. This is illustrated in the ancient Egyptian myth depicting the struggle for succession between Set and Horus. The war-goddess Neith threatens to bring down the sky unless Horus is made king of Egypt[3]—an attempt at coercion from a position of strength.

In theory, for deterrence to work it is sufficient if the weaker side psychologically acknowledges its inferiority. The actual demonstration of indisputable superiority, however, can increase the deterrent effect. For example, one can say that the U.S. naval superiority in the western Mediterranean, demonstrated in the early nineteenth century by Captain Stephen Decatur, served to deter corsairs of the Barbary Coast from attacking American merchant ships. Another more recent example is the Soviet armed forces' demonstration of obvious superiority when they effectively checked military probes of the Japanese militarists on the Soviet borders and in Mongolia in 1938-1939. This undoubtedly played an important part in the Japanese cabinet's subsequent decision not to wage war against the Soviet Union in the East after Germany invaded the Soviet Union in the West. Instead, Japan chose to start a war against the United States, despite American military superiority, because that superiority remained a thing in itself, did not impress the Japanese as awesome, and therefore had no deterring effect.[4]

In theory, mutual deterrence is also conceivable when the antagonists possess military potential sufficient to rebut each other's military aspirations. But, in the preatomic age, mutual deterrence was never stable because the stakes in warfare were comparatively moderate. In earlier wars the fate of the nation normally did not come into question. Underestimation of the opponent's power and subsequent defeat in a war launched by misjudgment resulted, at the worst, in a change of the ruling dynasty. That is why Napoleon Bonaparte could propose his well-known formula for a military commander: *"On s'engage et puis . . . on voit"* (first one must engage in the battle and then one shall see).

The arrival of the nuclear age at first did not alter the principle of deterrence. That is, the party with the inferior power potential was still discouraged from an attack through the threat of retaliation by the superior military power.[5] However, the quality of the threat changed. In the nuclear age it implied not simply the capacity to overwhelm advancing enemy armies and make them retreat, but also the capacity to devastate the enemy country, to destroy both its population and industry. Another important qualitative change connected with the development of aviation and the subsequent introduction of ballistic missiles was the capacity to inflict massive punishment of this kind not only on the neighbor guilty of aggression but also on another country.

The possibility of punishing not only neighbors but also remote countries existed hypothetically since the emergence of aviation. However, even the most massive use of technically well-developed aviation could not have brought about capitulation of Germany or Japan in World War II without simultaneous land and sea operations. In this sense, the theory of air warfare developed by Giulio Douhet—in vogue on the eve of World War II—was inadequate.[6] This theory postulated that massive aerial bombings of the enemy's vital centers and installations would guarantee a quick and decisive victory for the side that achieved air dominance. But Douhet did not take into account three things: (1) the comparatively low efficiency of air bombings using conventional explosives; (2) the great opportunity to counter air attacks with active air defense and passive civil defense; (3) and the ability of one state to achieve the absolute level of air superiority necessary for victory when confronted with a technologically developed equal who takes technical countermeasures to negate the former's military preparations.[7]

The appearance of nuclear explosives seemed to resurrect the theory expounded by Douhet and his American follower, General Billy Mitchell, and made it possible to view atomic air warfare not only as a means to deter the opponent but also as a means to manipulate the latter's behavior, i.e., to coerce him. Victory over Japan, for example, was primarily achieved on land and on sea through the defeat of the Japanese navy and army in Manchuria (the latter operation carried out by Soviet forces). Nevertheless, many American military commanders, especially the air force generals, perceived the decisive factor in Japan's capitulation to be the United States' use of atomic weapons against Japanese cities, which constituted the final triumph of the Douhet-Mitchell concept. This strategy of air blitzkrieg became the starting point for the American military build-up after World War II.

As far as the essence of postwar strategic theory is concerned, it does not matter whether the United States or the Soviet Union was the first to obtain nuclear weapons. At every given stage of weapons technology, any state that masters it can employ the same set of options, or tactics, within the constraints of the weapon's technical parameters (delivery means included). Yet the fact that nuclear weapons were first deployed by the United States predetermined specific political features of the emerging nuclear strategy, features that bore the stamp of experience, tradition, the geopolitical situation, and general goals of the United States after the war. The cry of nuclear deterrence began as a distinctly American ethnocentric concept. Later on, of course, the principle of nuclear deterrence could be separated from U.S. strategy and treated as a general theoretical tenet of nuclear strategy. Nevertheless, this principle retained the American mark, if only for the fact that the terminology, the semantics of nuclear strategy, was largely created by American theorists—Bernard Brodie, Herman Kahn, and Albert Wohlstetter prominent among them.[8]

AMERICANOCENTRISM OF THE INITIAL DETERRENT CONCEPT

One peculiarity of nuclear deterrence is that this concept did not originate as abstract theory but as a specific underlying principle of U.S. strategy vis-à-vis the Soviet Union. After World War II the United States was in a situation of approximate military parity with the Soviet Union, its main partner in the anti-Hitler coalition.[9] Not satisfied with that parity, which could have been consolidated and subsequently lowered on the basis of international agreements, the United States set out to acquire a position of superior strength.

This intent was clearly stated in various official American documents of that period (top secret then, declassified now) and hardly requires any special corroboration.[10] The American domestic postwar conditions and the atomic monopoly led the nation's leadership to pursue a policy of acquiring superior strength through the accumulation of atomic weapons and their delivery means—first bombers, later missiles. As it was then officially explained, the U.S. leadership needed this position of superior strength to "contain" the Soviet Union.[11]

In the process of formulating this general strategy, a new nuclear concept of deterrence was elaborated. It broke with the traditional meaning of this term and introduced a specific American accent.[12]

If deterrence in its traditional sense (prenuclear and, so to speak, preAmerican) implied prevention of an attack through the threat of unacceptable punishment, the term acquired a wider connotation through American usage in a nuclear context. As a component of American strategy, deterrence was directed against a country that entertained no aggressive intent toward the United States and its allies, was *physically unable* to directly attack the United States with conventional weapons, and was equally unable to initiate a nuclear strike against the United States because it lacked both nuclear weapons and corresponding delivery vehicles (of intercontinental range).[13]

In the absence of a Soviet military threat to the United States, American deterrence of the Soviet Union thus acquired an offensive rather than defensive character.[14] What was being deterred was not the Soviet military threat to the United States, which should have been the case according to the classical concept of deterrence, but a hypothetical Soviet threat to "American security interests," which could mean any set of U.S. foreign policy objectives. The United States, which had unilaterally assumed the role of custodian of the postwar world, began to describe virtually any Soviet foreign policy action that it did not like as "threatening American national interests." Washington presented Moscow's refusal to accept any one-sided U.S. proposal for global or regional postwar arrangement in this way. As put forward by American leadership and American strategists after World War II, deterrence was not designed to present a Soviet attack on the United States (an attack that was not comtemplated by anyone in the Soviet Union and that realistically belonged to the realm of physical impossibility at the time), but to subordinate the Soviet Union to American dictates in the sphere of international relations. This objective is clearly stated in official American documents of the period.[15]

Herman Kahn called this Type II deterrence in contrast to Type I deterrence—"the deterrence of a direct attack".[16] Nowadays this type of deterrence is usually referred to as "extended deterrence." Type II deterrence, as described by Kahn, is of a higher order and aims at deterring "extreme provocations" (whatever the definition) by the threat to escalate immediately to a central U.S.–USSR nuclear exchange.[17] This posture can only be adopted by a country sure of its absolute dominance in such an exchange. Therefore, Kahn specifies that Type II deterrence ought to be based on the U.S. possession of a credible first strike capability; which, in the strategist's jargon, means a strike of such magnitude that it can render the enemy virtually helpless and unable to retaliate.[18] Commenting on this posture, I wrote some time ago that "the deterrence of this type implies not merely the defense of the U.S. territory, but exemplifies the traditional American approach towards deterrence as a method of removing obstacles in the path of furthering the U.S. 'national interests,' of continuing to raise the frontier—that is, as a form of an offensive. With this type of deterrence, the United States intends to ensure, even in the era of approximate nuclear parity, the capability for conducting power politics on a wide scale, including support for military policies of U.S. allies."[19]

The apotheosis of this American interpretation of deterrence was the Dulles strategy of "massive retaliation" that envisaged nuclear punishment of the Soviet Union for any action contrary to U.S. interests. This applied not only to the Soviet Union and its immediate allies, but also to any world event that could undermine the pro-American status quo, whether it were a pronunciamento by leftist officers somewhere in Latin America or a partisan offensive in the Malayan jungle. Thus, deterrence in the Dulles interpretation was a clear attempt to compel the Soviet Union to follow a certain type of behavior imposed by the United States through the threat of superior atomic power and retribution for "wrong behavior."

However, the realization of this theory turned out to be its undoing. Having reached "the conceptual absolute," the strategy of deterrence in its peculiar interpretation by Truman and later by Dulles failed to meet the requirements of world conditions and had to undergo urgent modification.

Soviet acquisition of strategic bombers, intercontinental ballistic missiles and powerful nuclear warheads compelled American strategists to give up the maximal interpretation of deterrence as a means of unilaterally exerting military pressure on the Soviet Union. They were obliged to view deterrence in a more traditional way—as a means of preventing an enemy's attack against American territory proper. The responsibility for implementing this theoretical turnabout fell nominally upon President Kennedy and practically upon his Secretary of Defense, Robert McNamara, who drew upon the ideas of Brodie and Wohlstetter[20] to formulate the policy of "deterrence by the threat of inflicting unacceptable damage in second-strike retaliation."[21]

MCNAMARA'S REFINEMENT OF DETERRENCE AND THE COMING OF THE U.S.–USSR NUCLEAR PARITY

Many of those who write about military subjects evidently fail to see the implications of McNamara's idea of deterrence, which restored the classical, prenuclear meaning to the concept although he used this principle on the nuclear level. Under McNamara the United States abandoned Dulles' notion of using strategic forces to deter "world Communism" or "Soviet scheming." Instead it sought—theoretically—only to prevent a "possible" (possible in the opinion of Washington, but never contemplated by Moscow) Soviet nuclear strike on the United States by the threat of a no less destructive retaliatory second-strike. As with any deterrence strategy, it was necessary to demonstrate to the adversary that the threat was credible and that the United States was both ready and able to implement "unacceptable retaliation" in the event of a nuclear attack. This explains the elaboration of quantitative parameters of nuclear "sufficiency" carried out by Pentagon theorists under Charles Hitch and Alain C. Enthoven in the 1960s.[22]

The nation's leadership also concluded that U.S. regional interests could best be served not through some abstract "deterrence of Communism" but by definite military action on the local level when a nuclear stalemate started to take shape. This led to U.S. intervention in Vietnam and other interventionist overseas operations in the 1960s. (I shall not discuss here whether the involvement in Vietnam served the U.S. national interests. Events answered this in the negative, and the American leadership had to accept this answer.)

I believe that if the American leadership had not gone beyond the needs of the concept of "finite deterrence"—providing the United States with sufficient strategic forces to cause the opponent unacceptable damage through second-strike retaliation—it might have been possible to avoid the next round of the strategic arms race. However, after developing and publicly proclaiming the concept of sufficiency for the deterrence of a strategic nuclear strike against the United States, the

Pentagon theorists and U.S. leaders went further than clearly defined required levels of sufficiency.[23] An excuse was provided by "worst case" planning, which based evaluation of probable capabilities of the other side on the overstated estimates of the trends of its strategic arms build-up. But the real reason for the continued arms race in the United States was the desire of the American leadership to achieve and to refine first-strike capability vis-à-vis the Soviet Union.

Incidentally, one could not help notice that it took twenty years for Mr. McNamara to move from a theoretical exposition of the concept of mutual deterrence by means of both sides upholding credible second-strike capability to a practical advocacy of advisability of such a posture for the United States. In the 1960s none of the U.S. officials was heard speaking about a *mutual* assured destruction (MAD) posture. Such a posture would allow for unacceptable damage to the aggressor in a second, retaliatory strike. It was always only a one-sided assured destruction of the Soviet Union by the United States. True, in order to mollify and deceive the Soviet Union, some American officials occasionally granted the Soviet Union symbolic strategic parity with the United States. But in reality at that time none of the U.S. leaders or strategic theorists doubted for a moment that the United States possessed first-strike disarming capability against the Soviet Union. Mr. McNamara himself frankly acknowledged this in an interview with the Los Angeles Times staff writer Robert Scheer.

"The issue of first-strike is absolutely fundamental,—" said Mr. McNamara."—And I have no doubt that the Soviets thought we were trying to achieve a first-strike capability . . . "

"Read again my memo to President Kennedy (recently declassified - H.T.). It scares me today to even read the damned thing: 'The Air Force has rather supported the development of forces which provide the United States a first-strike capability credible to the Soviet Union by virtue of our ability to limit damage to the United States and our allies to levels acceptable in light of the circumstances and the alternatives available.'"

"What that means is the Air Force supported the development of U.S. forces sufficiently large to destroy so much of the Soviet nuclear force, by a first strike, that there would not be enough left to cause us any concern if they shot at us."[24]

Such were the hopes of the American leaders and strategic planners. They supported the following developments in strategic construction aimed at increasing the counterforce capabilities of the U.S. strategic forces and at providing for increased damage limitation from a Soviet retaliatory strike by its strategic forces crippled by the American attack:

1. development of multiple-charge strategic systems (bombers carrying SRAMs, ICBMs, and SLBMs with MIRVs);
2. special emphasis on endowing these systems with counterforce capability, i.e., the capability to neutralize the opponent's offensive systems with better yield-to-weight ratios of nuclear warheads and their increased accuracy;
3. intensification of damage-limiting measures to decrease the impact of a Soviet retaliatory strike, including the construction of a rather wide network of atomic shelters,[25] and the decision to develop a nationwide ABM system.[26]

Now, twenty years and two cycles of strategic arms build-up later, Mr. McNamara witnessed the justification of his earlier remark that, "It is futile for each of us [the United States and the USSR] to spend $4 billion, $40 billion or $400 billion—and, at the end of all spending, at the end of all the deployment, at the end of all the effort, to be relatively at the same point of balance on the security scale that we are now."[27] He evidently finally came to believe in the practical desirability of the MAD posture for both sides through the invulnerable second-strike capability as really the least evil in a nuclear confrontation. Writing in *Foreign Affairs*, Mr. McNamara and his colleagues McGeorge Bundy, George F. Kennan, and Gerard Smith suggested that the United States officially renounce the first use of nuclear weapons and thus enhance the stability of the Soviet-American strategic balance.

In explaining their reason for such a suggestion, the four authors wrote: "The evolution of essentially equivalent and enormously excessive nuclear weapons systems both in the Soviet Union and in the Atlantic Alliance has aroused new concern about the dangers of all forms of nuclear war. The profusion of these systems, on both sides, has made it more difficult than ever to construct rational plans for any first use of these weapons by anyone."[28]

It stands to reason that if the U.S. posture was always defensive–retaliatory, as we were assured it had been, then today there would be no need for such an appeal and all the ensuing debate. Evidently, it is only now that some segment of the U.S. leadership class has come to embrace the MAD posture as desirable from the point of view of ensuring the country's security. In the 1960s and even in the early 1970s, this posture, though energetically advertised and sold to the "potential opponent" in numerous scholarly American publications, was evidently not considered suitable for the United States. (It does not appeal to the present U.S. administration either.)

In June 1982 the Soviet Union officially renounced the first use of nuclear weapons against any country, nuclear or not. This Soviet step if taken also by the United States and other nuclear countries could really enhance the stability of the global balance and decrease the danger of nuclear war.

But back in the 1960s matters stood differently. The Soviet Union at that time could not accept at face value reassuring statements by McNamara and his colleagues that the United States would not exceed specified optimal levels of sufficiency which, in those times always, were defined and presented only in quantitative terms.[29] Rather, it had to deal with the unusually high rate of U.S. strategic arms build-up and its wide scope.[30]

Under these circumstances, the only realistic strategy that could ensure Soviet security was the assured capability to respond with shattering retaliation. In the 1960s and 1970s, that strategy was translated into reality through Soviet development and deployment of invulnerable submarine-based strategic systems and improvements in the land-based component of strategic forces, including measures to increase its survivability.

As a result, the capability that McNamara initially granted the Soviet Union theoretically became a fact of life. The Soviet Union acquired the actual capability to inflict "unacceptable damage" upon the United States in a retaliatory strike. Thus, mutual deterrence emerged.

The implication of mutual deterrence was to deprive the United States of the chance to pursue a policy of coercion—of diplomatic pressure—toward the Soviet Union. As long as the United States enjoyed strategic superiority over the Soviet Union, it was apt to brandish the nuclear sword to pressure the Soviet Union, being confident its edge in the strategic balance would make the nuclear exchange less disastrous for it than for the Soviet Union. The implication was that the United States could behave without any self-restraint and approach the brink of war to exert diplomatic pressure upon the opponent—a tactic boasted of by Dulles. The emergence of parity in the assured destruction retaliatory capabilities meant that the United States could no longer behave without restraint. For the first time, U.S. leaders had to start thinking about the need for restraint in their behavior in the international arena and to elaborate this idea publicly.[31]

The preceding discussion permits a summary of the evolution of the American interpretation of deterrence. Between the 1940s and 1980s, deterrence conveyed very diverse notions. This can be demonstrated by semantic analysis of the term's evolution. During the first brief stage of America's atomic monopoly, deterrence meant compelling or coercing the opponent—through the overt or implied threat of a preventive nuclear strike—to accept the American idea of the world order with its obvious connotation of "Pax Americana." In the second stage, deterrence acquired the meaning of "intimidating" (or, to use a term introduced by George Washington, "awing") the potential opponent from the position of superior strength.

During both stages (especially during the second when the U.S. nuclear arsenal had increased considerably and the possibilities for atomic blackmail had been more fully perceived by the American theorists) deterrence was regarded by the American leadership as the most efficient means of "containment of communism." Deterrence was not perceived as a means of keeping the Soviet Union from using its military power against the United States or its allies, but for containing social evolution and revolution all over the world. Thus, purely military and strategic capabilities were to be used to prevent social and political events that looked objectionable to the United States. To justify so preposterous a mission, the United States proclaimed any social revolution in the Third World to be the result of Moscow's interference, of direct or indirect Soviet aggression.

As the Soviet-American strategic balance approached equality, deterrence acquired its third, and its contemporary, connotation: "disinclination" of the opponent; dissuading him from attack by the threat of unacceptable retaliation. It is in this sense that the term deterrence is used in Soviet military science.[32]

BASIC PRINCIPLES OF SOVIET STRATEGY

The Soviet position toward deterrence and the present Soviet-American strategic balance has been officially and publicly expressed in many documents issued by the Soviet government. It appears in numerous statements made by Secretary-General Yuri Andropov, Minister of Defense D. F. Ustinov, and other Soviet government officials. The Soviet military doctrine is, in essence, defensive and can be expressed in the following postulates:

The Soviet Union views nuclear arms exclusively as a means of defense, a means of deterring a potential aggressor. The Soviet doctrine excludes preventive wars, concepts of a first disarming strike and a preemptive strike. Nothing but an emergency—nuclear aggression against the Soviet Union and its allies—can compel the Soviet Union to resort to this extreme means of self-defense.

Nuclear weapons are not to be used for offensive purposes but only to deliver a devastating retaliatory strike upon the aggressor that has assaulted the Soviet Union or its allies. In June 1982 the Soviet Union made a solemn pledge from the platform of the United Nations General Assembly session on disarmament renouncing unconditionally the first use of nuclear weapons—that is, their first use against any country, non-nuclear or nuclear. When adopting this decision the Soviet Union proceeded from the immutable fact, which is of a decisive significance in contemporary international situations, namely that a nuclear war, if started could well bring the destruction of human civilization and could even cause the extinction of life itself on our planet.

The Soviet Union takes exception to the callous, quantitative approach toward nuclear warfare, now popular in some quarters in the West, that sets a certain threshold of "acceptable" losses among civilian population. The aim of the Soviet Union in international affairs is to prevent mankind from slipping into war, to ensure and consolidate universal and lasting peace.

The Soviet Union does not threaten anyone and does not plan to make war on anyone. It does not have a single foreign policy objective for which a military solution might be contemplated. Specifically, the Soviet Union does not intend to assault Western Europe at all, much less with nuclear weapons. The idea of using nuclear weapons on European territory is repugnant to the Soviet people. The General Staff of the Soviet Union does not draw timetables for a "breakthrough to the English Channel."

If they want their assessment to be truly objective, the strategists and theorists in the United States and other countries who specialize in assessing the Soviet military potential have to keep in mind the peculiarities of the geographic position of the Soviet Union. Unlike the United States, the Soviet Union faces the powerful military potential of other countries and coalitions immediately across its borders in the East and in the West, as well as U.S. forward-based forces in close proximity to its frontier.[33] This environment inevitably affects the way the Soviet leadership defines levels of sufficiency for its armed forces.

Systematic threats from the United States and other NATO countries concerning "powerful destructive preemptive strikes" against the Soviet Union compel it to take certain defensive measures, specifically in the area of civil defense.

Although the Soviet Union considers nuclear weapons to be a means of deterring a possible aggressor, it does not favor peace on the basis of a "balance of terror." The Soviet Union finds it necessary to replace the balance of terror with the balance of confidence. That is why maintenance of the existing rough parity between the armed forces

of the Soviet Union and the United States or between the East and the West in Europe is not an end in itself for the Soviet Union. It supports gradual lowering of the levels of military confrontation through broad measures in the area of political and military detente, limitation and reduction of armaments. This is the way to create confidence, which can be used as a basis for more sweeping disarmament measures.

The policy based on the threat to use nuclear weapons and the actual readiness to use them becomes more and more dangerous for mankind. The monstrous arms race unfolding today is undermining world peace and security. It it is not curbed, it can put the very existence of mankind in doubt.

Certainly Soviet strategy and military doctrine were not frozen during the post-World War II years. They evolved in conjunction with the development of the material base for any doctrine—the means for waging war, military hardware, plus the realignment of political forces in the world arena, the condition of the country's economy, and the growth in capabilities of the Soviet armed forces. But whatever the stage of its evolution, the Soviet strategic doctrine has always been defensive. The Soviet Union never intended and does not now intend to threaten any state or group of states.[35]

The new strategic balance between the United States and the Soviet Union that started to emerge toward the end of the 1960s confronted American leadership with a dilemma: to accept the existing balance and to seek its conservation through negotiations or to attempt to step forward in strategic armaments to regain unilateral deterrence.

WHO IS NOT SATISFIED WITH PARITY?

A practical analysis carried out by the U.S. National Security Council and by the Pentagon under the Nixon administration demonstrated to the American leadership that a return to the situation of unilateral deterrence was unrealistic. Even if the United States managed to break away from the Soviet Union in some parameter of strategic power, this lead could not restore the military invulnerability of the United States.[36] In any situation the United States remains open to a devastating counterstrike. More specifically, a nationwide ABM system possessing considerable damage-limitation capabilities has yet to be developed, for there is no reliable defense against offensive nuclear weapons.

Under these circumstances the U.S. government decided in favor of negotiations with the Soviet Union on lowering strategic armaments levels of both nations. An attempt was made to consolidate the situation of mutual deterrence through the threat of inflicting unacceptable damage in a second (retaliatory) strike.

Naturally, the Soviet Union faced a similar problem—whether to agree to strategic parity with the United States or to try to overtake it and gain strategic superiority. The deliberate choice of the Soviet leadership was first to preserve strategic parity through negotiations with the United States and, second, to try to maintain parity on lower levels of strategic armaments in the future by taking coordinated measures toward their limitation and reduction.

Soviet leaders have more than once unequivocally and officially stressed that the Soviet Union does not aim at military superiority over the United States—in particular, it does not aim at acquiring a first-strike potential. The Soviet Union is satisfied with the existing balance of forces between the USSR and the United States, Warsaw Treaty and NATO. It considers the existing equilibrium sufficient to safeguard its security and the security of its allies. The Soviet Union is ready and willing to seal by contract the existing USSR–United States strategic parity and to do so at lower levels of armaments than the present ones.

In this connection a question can be raised: Is there a conflict between this Soviet position of restraint and the official Soviet premise that only the changed correlation of forces in the world in favor of socialism forced the United States to opt for détente with the Soviet Union and for agreements on strategic arms limitation? This alleged contradiction is being played up by such American theorists as T. Draper, R. Pipes, P. Nitze, G. Keegan, E. Zumwalt, and others. They argue that because the Soviet Union considers the change in the correlation of forces to be the key factor that impelled the United States toward détente and negotiations with the Soviet Union, the Soviet Union will not be content with its present achievements and will strive to attain superiority in strategic weapons in order to deal with the United States from a position of strength.

This line of reasoning proves convincing to many Americans; the logic seems self-evident, because that is precisely the way the United States has acted in the past. The cold war first and foremost an attempt by the United States to thrust American conditions and solutions upon the Soviet Union from a position of superior strength.

Hence under the new circumstances, when the correlation of forces favors the Soviet Union, it will start the cold war in reverse, (i.e., a Soviet cold war against the United States). Why should it be otherwise? Such is the rationale of the aforementioned American theorists who, in the past, worked to develop various plans to pressure the Soviet Union.

But the logic based on American stereotypes, on the American dream of omnipotence, is by no means a universal one. The negative outcome of the cold war made even the American leadership of the 1970s question the rationality of that logic and introduce some realistic readjustments into the nation's foreign policy. Why, then, should the Soviet Union follow American stereotypes in its planning?

It is true that the Soviet Union believes the shift in the world correlation of forces—not only military forces but also economic forces—in the Soviet favor was the main factor that urged Western nations, including the United States, to take the path of détente. What is détente, after all? It is the readiness expressed by the parties concerned to solve their contradictions and arguments not by force or by threats of using force but through peaceful means, at the negotiating table. It is the readiness of nations to develop their relations on the basis of a code that sets honest and just rules for every party in international life, with the main feature of this code being the principle of peaceful coexistence. It is the acceptance by two great powers—the Soviet Union and the United States—of the principle of equality and equal security and the readiness they proclaimed to exercise maximum efforts to prevent nuclear war and to find solutions to the problem of disarmament. The Soviet Union has always expressed readiness to subscribe to all these principles; moreover, it contributed a lot to their conceptual development.

However, the United States did not agree to principles of equality while it thought it was still able to dictate to the Soviet Union from a position of superior strength, or, to put it in terms of the concept of deterrence, while the United States aspired to use its strategic potential for coercion or intimidation of the potential opponent. Washington started a constructive dialogue with Moscow on equal terms only after U.S. leaders percieved the shift in the correlation of forces—not only between the United States and the Soviet Union but also within the world at large, including Western nations—and concluded that it was pointless to hope to press the Soviet Union into accepting purely American solutions in a situation where it is impossible to solve a number of international problems without Soviet participation.

This unsuccessful American effort to corner another great power is in itself sufficient warning of the futility of such a course. To frustrate American blackmail, to foil the plans for atomic blitzkrieg against the Soviet Union, the Soviet Union was compelled to catch up with the United States in strategic potential. But we in the Soviet Union were well aware that if we attempted to outstrip the United States in strategic arms, it would not bring any positive results because of inevitable U.S. countermeasures (and this is true for either country).

To sum up, the Soviet Union opposes attempts to start a cold war in reverse on pragmatic and economic grounds, as well as on political principle. Pragmatically, every new thrust forward in the strategic arms race, although bringing little shift in the balance (due to the inevitability of the other side's response), would increase mutual suspicion, poison the atmosphere, and bring the danger of war closer, thus inhancing and not diminishing the threat to national security. Economically, it is better to use extra resources to improve the living standard and increase the production of consumer goods, than to throw them in the bottomless pit of the arms race, especially since the situation of parity assures the security of the Soviet Union and its allies. With respect to political principle, the Soviet Union, although possessing the capacity to develop advanced weapons systems, would not wish to take the path of competition in military technology because that kind of competition destabilizes the strategic balance. The Soviet Union considers the main road toward security to be stabilization of the military balance by limiting and discontinuing the arms race through international agreements, keeping in sight the ultimate goal of banning all means of mass annihilation and eliminating all atomic weapons from national arsenals.

Naturally the Soviet Union cannot accept a situation in which the other side gains an advantage by violating the balance. That is why it and other countries of the Warsaw Treaty Organization, when confronted with military preparations of the United States and other NATO nations, are compelled to take corresponding measures to protect their interests and to safeguard their security.

The Soviet Union reacted with understanding and approval when, in the late 1960s and early 1970s, Washington expressed willingness to defuse the confrontation, to stabilize the situation of strategic parity by negotiations. As a result it became possible to conclude the well-known 1972 agreements on the limitation of strategic arms. Of paramount importance among these was the Treaty on the Limitation of AntiBallistic Missile Systems limiting ABM systems to two (later one) deployment sites for each country. This treaty consolidated the situation of mutual deterrence in conceptual and material ways.

It must be stressed that to decide in favor of détente the U.S. leadership had to overcome the opposition of the military-industrial complex. For the first time since World War II, political considerations were put above considerations of purely military strategy. However, the American military establishment consented to this step only after it was given three so-called assurances, including "aggressive improvements and modernization programs."[37] Because the administration agreed to its conditions, the military establishment was able to push its foot in the door of détente and thus to have a say on acceptable limits in the sphere of military détente. That is why the limits turned out to be rather narrow.

The U.S. military leadership and military theorists, forced by circumstances in the 1970s to resign themselves to certain steps toward military détente and to some reassessment of budgetary priorities in favor of nonmilitary programs, evidently had no wish to accept Soviet-American strategic parity as permanent. The century-old idea of American supremacy, of Pax Americana, continued to dominate their thinking. This attitude sought support in the nationalism that developed in the wake of defeat in Vietnam and other slips in chauvinistic hegemonic positions, like the treaty placing the Panama Canal under Panamanian sovereignty at the end of this century.

U.S. military theorists elaborated concepts and programs designed (a) to provide the United States with an opportunity to obtain some material advantages over the Soviet Union in strategic arms—either within the constraints of the agreed-upon parity (i.e., without formal violation of the letter of arms limitation agreements) or, if necessary, by breaking through these constraints—and (b) to permit translating such marginal military advantages into political ones in the diplomatic bargaining over problems of further arms reduction. In other words, the Pentagon has been striving to introduce certain material and conceptual amendments into the situation of mutual deterrence—without visibly disturbing the balance—that would make U.S. deterrence of the Soviet Union "more efficient" than Soviet deterrence of the United States. That would give the United States the opportunity to increase political pressure and would open up the prospect of using military force with impunity at the lower rungs of the escalation ladder.

The American military seems to have discerned such opportunities in various counterforce concepts, judging by its planned objective to maintain preponderance over the Soviet Union in counterforce—or countersilo—capabilities within the context of general countervalue parity throughout the 1980s. The existence of this objective is obvious not only from certain steps the Department of Defense has taken in developing arms, but also from long-term models of strategic balance developed in the United States during the 1960s and early 1970s. These models rather accurately predicted—if not prompted—the main tendency in U.S. strategic planning.[38]

In January 1974 Secretary of Defense Schlesinger proclaimed a doctrine of retargeting. This was the first official public confirmation that U.S. strageic planning aimed at achieving counterforce preponderance. The Schlesinger doctrine postulated the option of selective or even massive high-precision strikes against the opponent's missile silos and bombers or, in keeping with a variant of the same option, using U.S. strategic forces not against the territory of the main opponent but in the theater action (e.g., in Europe).[39] The Pentagon tried to convince the

U.S. public and Congress of the reliability of the Schlesinger doctrine premises in a rather peculiar way—by ascribing counterforce concepts to the Soviet Union and publicly describing scenarios where the Soviet Union was the assailant initiating a "selective counterforce strike" upon American territory.

Attributing doctrines to the Soviet Union to which it does not subscribe is dishonest at the least. Furthermore, it turns out that the Pentagon estimates submitted to Congress, avowedly containing the proof of a counterforce exchange causing but minimum damage, were trumped up. The Pentagon authors of the report were exposed by well-known American experts who showed the inadequacy of the limited war scenarios that formed the report's backbone.[40]

For purposes of theoretical analysis, two important points must be made. The Schlesinger doctrine was a variation of offensive counterforce tactics for the use of strategic systems that only makes sense in the first strike, when the opponent's weapon systems are still in place and can be knocked out. The Schlesinger doctrine was also an attempt to utilize and maximize those particular features of the U.S. strategic offensive forces in which the U.S. considers itself ahead of the Soviet Union.

WAR-FIGHTING VERSUS DETERRENCE

In light of the above, it is truly perplexing that U.S. politicians and military theorists get so excited about Soviet military doctrine being what they consider offensive. American doctrine, on the contrary, is purported to be defensive because the Soviet military is said to be preparing for war-fighting, while their American counterparts seek only deterrence. These assertions widely circulate in the United States in scholarly journals and the mass media and constitute and attempt to distort the facts of life and deliberately deceive the public.

One has to acknowledge that the military in the United States and the Soviet Union must be ready for war-fighting; that is required by their professional duty. "Combat in every sphere (on land, in the air, and at sea) is conducted through joint efforts of all the armed services in the interests of a single goal—defeating a possible opponent," writes Marshal of the Soviet Union and Chief of the General Staff of the Soviet Armed Forces, N. Ogarkov.[41]

The American military also prepares to fight efficiently. It is certainly not getting ready to capitulate and surrender to the enemy. And if one leaves out differing war goals for different states, then technically the military in every country has one and the same mission: to do its utmost in case of war, to ensure its country the favorable outcome of every battle and of the war. In this sense, trying to attribute some objectives other than efficient war-fighting to the American military is pure demagoguery. One can only express amazement at what is now written on the subject in the United States.

But if the mission of the military is to fight successfully and to win wars, then the mission of contemporary politicians is to prevent a nuclear war that can result in disaster for mankind. That is precisely the way Soviet political leaders interpret their task, and that is why the Soviet Union has been persistently striving toward nuclear disarmament, toward limitation and reduction of strategic arms.

During the Kennedy administration, the American leadership became aware that nuclear war had turned from a unilateral into a bilateral eventuality. From this point on, it began advocating nuclear war prevention measures.

The congeniality of Soviet and American stands on that matter found final expression in the period of détente, when top leaders of both countries signed a series of documents unequivocally stating their willingness and desire to prevent nuclear war.[42] Signing these documents, however, does not prevent U.S. political leaders from simultaneously proclaiming doctrines (comparable to the Schlesinger doctrine) that envisage *initiation* of a nuclear war, or from developing weapon systems (like the neutron bomb) that promote obliteration of the threshold between conventional and nuclear war, thus increasing the possibility of nuclear war.

It is hardly possible to reproach the professional military in any country for carrying out professional duties, but politicians' activities can and must be evaluated: Do they stabilize mutual deterrence, decrease military confrontation, and promote peace and disarmament; or do they aggravate military rivalry and lay the groundwork for a preemptive strike to achieve "victory" in a nuclear war? If one applies this criterion to the activity of political leadership in the United States and the Soviet Union, respectively, including political supervision of military complexes, one sees widely divergent attitudes. The Soviet leadership explicitly pledges adherence to the concepts of stability, peace, maintenance of existing parity in strategic armaments, and gradual decrease in the level of the latter, whereas U.S. politicians continue flirting with nuclear war concepts, including an aggressive counterforce strike. The above is corroborated not only by divergence in respective official statements but also by contrasting attitudes toward building up armed forces and armaments.

The American military doctrines and postures have always been permeated by a striving toward absolute security or, in other words, unquestionable superiority.

Let us take up the fate of the SALT II Treaty. Why was it rejected by Washington? Nowadays it is fashionable in the U.S. strategic community to invent various artificial justifications for this rejection, for instance, the assertion that the Soviet Union was overtaking the United States in strategic power under the cover of SALT, or that the SALT II Treaty was biased towards the Soviet Union; or it is said that the treaty was not ratified because the USSR behaved somewhere in the world not to the liking of the United States. But all of these explanations are pretexts, not reasons. The real reason is that the idea of contractually sealing the situation of U.S.–USSR parity in strategic armaments became abhorrent to an influential segment of the American leadership class (including top military leadership) after overcoming the Vietnam syndrome.

None other than General Alexander Haig, after he relinquished the post of Supreme Allied Commander, Europe, and before he was appointed secretary of state, spoke quite frankly as a private citizen. He spelled out the real reason for Washington's rejection of SALT II in absolutely unambiguous terms. Speaking before the Senate Armed Services Committee on July 26, 1979, during the hearings on military implications of the SALT II Treaty, Haig said that his "most significant concern about this treaty" was that "the treaty seems to reflect a tendency to drift from what was originally insistence on American superiority to what more recently has become acceptance of equality and parity . . . ." And why is parity so loathsome to him and his influential friends? Because, explained Haig, "in my past experience in uniform and out and in my participation in crises with the Soviet Union . . . our American President was always reassured by a backdrop of strategic superiority vis-à-vis the Soviet Union."[43] And that is the gist of the matter.

I noted earlier that for a great number of years the United States considered "deterrence" to actually mean first compellence of the other side and later intimidation of it. That goes for the political aspect of American deterrence. As to its military aspect, Washington's practical interpretation of the notion of deterrence reserved, naturally, for internal use among "those in the know" was war-fighting up until the mid 1970s. Who would dare to fight against the United States—reasoned top brass in the Pentagon and selling this reasoning to the political leadership—when the United States possessed unquestionable escalation dominance and would unhesitatingly go up the escalation ladder without blinking an eye? The American nuclear posture, though it was billed for the world public as retaliatory, in fact envisaged—in case of need—first preventive or preemptive nuclear strike, disarming counterforce or countervalue, depending on the circumstances. And almost no one in the Pentagon doubted that victory would be on the U.S. side.

So under the guise of the mutual assured vulnerability model of deterrence (the model developed by American civilian strategists and for almost twenty years described by them as applicable to both sides), the United States actually implemented not this retaliatory posture (otherwise described as MAD—mutual assured destruction—posture) but a one-sided extended deterrence, i.e., the deterrence of an offensive, war-fighting variety.[44]

This fact is acknowledged even by those American analysts who tirelessly look for any pretext to put the blame for destabilization of the strategic balance upon the Soviet Union and groundlessly accuse it of not going along with the MAD strategic philosophy. For instance, Colin Gray, in his book on MX missiles, says, "Through most of the 1950s and 1960s, U.S. strategic nuclear forces would have denied victory to the U.S.S.R. and, most probably, have limited damage to the U.S. homeland to such a degree that the concept of victory in World War III would have had some meaning".[45] In other words, the demands of the U.S. Air Force for the posture of supremacy (as quoted in the above-mentioned interview of Robert McNamara with Robert Scheer) were implemented in the U.S. strategy and strategic force posture.

But because of the change in the correlation of forces to the attainment by the Soviet Union of strategic parity with the United States—not only quantitative parity (i.e., in the number of launchers of strategic weapons), but also qualitative parity (i.e., in the actual capabilities of strategic forces)—the American deterrence/war-fighting had of necessity to become deterrence/dissuasion (or, in other terms, "pure counterdeterrence," "attack prevention," or, as Eugene Rostow would say, "equal deterrence"). Then the bulk of American military and some quarters of political leadership went into revolt. They said they wanted superiority and would be satisfied with nothing else because only superiority could give to the United States strategic forces the extended deterrence (that is, intimidatory and war-fighting) functions. To quote Colin Gray again: "Overprovision of strategic nuclear muscle at least should ensure that the United States would always have the not incredible option of attempting to escalate its way out of a local defeat".[46]

The dash toward such an "overprovision of strategic muscle" is, one might say, the raison d'être of the Reagan administration. It came to power on the pledge to "build toward a sustained defense expenditure sufficient to ... ultimately reach the position of military superiority that the American people demand".[47] And it continues and develops (on a wider financial and resource base) the program for the attainment of superiority via the counterforce route that was laid down by President Carter in his PD 59 and is further elaborated in such well-publicized documents of the Reagan administration as the Pentagon's Defense Guidance Statement and the "strategic master plan to give the United States the capability of winning a protracted nuclear war with the Soviet Union".[48]

If such is the aim of the U.S. administration, one can confidently predict that it is unattainable. The Soviet Union will certainly not allow the United States to achieve a strategic superiority transferable into a nuclear war-winning capability. And to deny it by the defensive buildup is evidently a simpler and cheaper task than creating such a capability.

While embarking on a course of confrontation with the Soviet Union, the Reagan administration is at the same time trying to justify it by putting the blame for such a turn on the Soviet Union. At one time the White House went so far as to accuse the Soviet leaders of considering "among themselves" a first strike against the United States. When asked by the *Pravda* correspondent to comment on Ronald Reagan's statement that the Soviet leaders think a nuclear war might be winnable, Leonid Brezhnev, then General Secretary of the Soviet Communist Party, replied that "to hope to win a nuclear war is dangerous madness."[49]

"Military rivalry is not our choice," says current General Secretary Andropov. "The ideal of socialism is a world without arms . . . . As to the nuclear strategic arms possessed by the USSR and the U.S.A., the Soviet Union, as is known, agrees that the two sides should, as the first step on the way to a future agreement, freeze their arsenals and thus create more favorable conditions for the continuation of talks on the mutual reduction of these weapons."[50] The Soviet Union, after it achieved strategic parity with the United States, has done nothing to change it in its favor. That the U.S. administrations, despite all the hue and cry about the so-called shortcomings of the SALT agreements, de facto observe these agreements (including SALT II Treaty) indisputably shows they are satisfied that the Soviet Union is not overstepping the agreed bounds.[51]

The Soviet strategic posture has always been and still is defensive or dissuading, especially if one turns toward the politico-military or grand strategy aspect of it. All systems of strategic arms suited for *counter-force options* were adopted by the Soviet Union only after the United States had produced and deployed them. The Soviet missiles that are now the subject of so much concern in the West were built *in reaction* to another U.S. thrust forward in the arms race.[52]

The present U.S. drive to achieve considerable advantages in strategic armaments may undermine the stabilizing principle of mutual deterrence/dissuasion without replacing it with anything more stabilizing. Such a situation will definitely increase the danger of nuclear war because any augmentation of one party's capacity to make a counter-force—disarming—strike automatically raises the tension of nuclear confrontation and makes immediate response by the other side imperative even though the action that triggered the response may not be quite clear.

TECHNOLOGICAL ARMS RACE—
NO WAY TO ENHANCE STABILITY

In a 1973 article in *Foreign Affairs*, Fred Iklé raised the question of whether nuclear deterrence could last the century. His own answer to the question was largely in the affirmative. If both sides deploy invulnerable strategic systems that guarantee retaliation rather than instant response, Iklé argued, there is nothing to undermine the system of deterrence by the threat of a devastating second strike.[53] Iklé's logic is acceptable in principle if the concept of deterrence is viewed as exclusively bilateral. One can also agree with his suggestion for solving the problem of stability of deterrence—i.e., increase the invulnerability of second-strike systems.

Iklé proposed a specific method of increasing U.S. ICBM invulnerability by locating the missiles deep underground in bedrock, so no preventive strike could eliminate any of the second-strike systems. Many other methods exist for improving the stability of mutual deterrence including increasing the survivability of the sea component of the strategic forces, simultaneous improvement in reliability of command and control systems, and preservation of the triad composition of the strategic forces. All these are unilateral actions aimed at making second-strike forces more invulnerable.

It is, however, obvious that not every way of decreasing a country's strategic force vulnerability can contribute to the stability of deterrence. In theory, a very radical and comprehensive increase in the survivability of the forces of one side is tantamount to an increase in exposure of the other side's forces. The party that feels it has been "left behind" would have to take urgent steps to catch up in second-strike force survivability or revert to other measures designed to restore the mutuality of deterrence. Certain ways of misleading the opponent as to the real balance of forces also belong to these methods of ensuring stability while, in fact, undermining it. For instance, this is true of the concept of the multiple protective structure (MPS) basing mode that was for a time adopted for a new American mobile intercontinental ballistic missile—the MX. The plan consisted of building 200 mobile MX ICBMs and 4600 hardened missile launching sites among which the missiles were to be periodically rotated at random. Conceptually MPS is a system of deception similar to installing dummy planes or tanks to confuse the enemy.

But such an approach is not an American monopoly and the other side can also resort to a strategic ruse—pretending to build more offensive systems that it actually does. To simulate a launching site is much easier than to build a genuine one. What would happen if both parties decided to take such a path? At best it would mean transporting the strategic arms race onto the plane of irrationality in which the actual forces of both sides would increase much less than the simulated show of their build-up suggested. At worst the action—reaction process would add thousands of nuclear weapons on both sides with the definite result of decreasing the stability of deterrence and impairing the security of either country.

As is known, President Reagan cancelled the MPS basing mode, and it is beyond the scope of this chapter to speculate on reasons for his decision. Evidently there were many factors against the MPS option, which was nevertheless chosen by President Carter in order to show his nerve on the eve of the 1980 election campaign.[54] On November 22, 1982, the Republican administration announced that it had decided to deploy the MX missile in the so-called Dense Pack basing mode, whereby the 100 missiles would be placed in superhard silos in an area only 20 miles square in Wyoming. Such deployment would allegedly utilize the protective phenomenon known as "fractricide" which occurs when heat and radiation released by the explosions of the first attacking nuclear warheads either melt or deflect the warheads just beyond them. But viewed from the other side, this kind of deployment is sure to look like a "trigger-happy" one, especially geared for a first-strike or a launch-on-warning tactic, which seems again to have become fashionable among the Pentagon strategists judging by the amount of space devoted to the discussion in specialized United States publications.

From the above it follows that even the manipulations with modes of deployment of strategic armaments could cause serious disturbances of the balance unless both sides tackle the problem of stability in a responsible way. Other situations could be listed in which a radical decrease of strategic systems vulnerability, rather than consolidating mutual deterrence, would actually upset the existing equilibrium and would raise the suspicions of one party as to the capabilities and genuine intentions of the other, destabilizing the balance and increasing the danger of pressing the nuclear trigger.

In these circumstances there is only one realistic way to retain the stability of nuclear balance and, at the same time, reduce the danger of war. It is not the introduction of one-sided alterations in the balance, but mutual efforts to limit and reduce strategic arms on the basis of mutually acceptable compromises, first between the Soviet Union and the United States, later drawing in other nuclear states.

A general discussion of the SALT[56] or START problems is beyond the scope of this chapter but it is clear that any limitations must not set greater constraints on one side than on the other and must not create discrepancies of any significance in the overall equation. That is why the approach adopted by the U.S. President in his proposals of May 9, 1982, concerning limitation and reduction of strategic armaments, which is aimed to restrict the advantages of the other side while leaving one's own intact, can hardly be called realistic.[57]

What factors and events can destabilize the existing global military balance and what are the ways to preserve and consolidate global stability in these conditions? The problem is very large, so it seems appropriate to select three sets of problems that have immediate bearing on the evolution of global military balance: problems related to military technology; problems of multipolar nuclear balance; problems of regional balances.

Problems of Technological Breakthroughs

None of the global projections of military technology predict any extraordinary breakthroughs in the coming years, but such breakthroughs are possible, in fact, inevitable, over the long term. It seems clear that neither the United States nor the Soviet Union is likely to make qualitative improvements in existing systems sufficient to change the condition of approximate parity between their strategic forces. Because modernization requires a long time, each side would be able to offset the disparity resulting from the opponent's improvements in strategic systems.

Only radical breakthroughs can be truly destabilizing. Most experts point first to the possibility of a qualitative leap in defensive strategic systems, the development of which has long lagged behind that of offensive systems. In particular, they foresee conceptually new systems of antisubmarine warfare (ASW) and antiballistic missile defense (ABM). The most destabilizing effect would be produced by the development of an ABM system that would preclude mass penetration of intact enemy nuclear warheads into the national boundaries. Should such an ABM be deployed by one side, it would undoubtedly radically upset the existing bilateral balance. However, the probability of the creation of such a superefficient ABM system within the next ten to fifteen years is not high.[57] Even if a certain technological concept of it should begin to take shape, its realization, at this stage, would be beyond reach economically.

Only approximate full damage limitation by active defense could provide a country with a considerable degree of confidence in being able to make a first strike with impunity. Since this kind of damage limitation is not feasible today, the warnings of American theorists about the possibility of one side carrying out a preventive counterforce strike in the foreseeable future are untenable. As noted above, although the United States emphasizes the increase in the counterforce potential of its strategic forces, for propaganda purposes this approach is groundlessly attributed to the Soviet Union. However, U.S. civilian and military leaders have more than once acknowledged that each side's possession of a triad of strategic arms make any conceivable counterforce strike a failure since even after the strike the attacked country would have enough deliverable strategic nuclear warheads to inflict unacceptable damage on the aggressor.

Allegations by American hawks of Soviet capability to make a preventive counterforce strike against the U.S. ICBM in the mid-1980s are no more than demagoguery designed to whip up the arms race in the United States and expand the political decisionmaking role of the U.S. military-industrial complex.[59]

The U.S. ICBMs carry about 9 percent of the total throw-weight of the U.S. strategic forces and slightly more than 20 percent of the total number of targetable strategic nuclear warheads.[60] Thus, even hypothetical elimination of all U.S. ICBMs would leave the bulk of strategic forces intact, a significant component of which (Trident missiles, air-based cruise missiles) possesses counterforce capabilities, to say nothing of countervalue ones. Even viewed from this purely technical angle, insinuations about the Soviet Union getting ready for a first strike against the United States do not hold water,[61] to say nothing of the fact that the Soviet Union does not subscribe politically to the first-strike doctrine.

According to Dr. William J. Perry, who was Undersecretary of Defense for Research and Engineering in the Carter administration, the Soviet threat to various components of the American strategic triad does not come simultaneously. American ICBMs are said to become vulnerable first; then the U.S. bombers will be challenged by some sort of a new Soviet capability after the mid-1980s; finally, the survivability of the sea-based leg of the triad, submarine-launched ballistic missiles, will come into question "in the early 1990s."[62] If one accepts Dr. Perry's logic, one is immediately confronted with a puzzle: Why was modernization of ICBMs, which he depicted as the weakest leg of the triad, posted as the least priority on the list of measures to counter the Soviet threat? For, according to Dr. Perry, the Department of Defense first tackled the problem of survivability of SLBMs and developed the Trident system, which is now being deployed; then the performance of air-breathing force was radically improved through development and impending development of strategic cruise missiles; also a new strategic bomber— the B-1—was built, and its modification—the B-1B—will soon be going into full-scale production. Only after that did U.S. military planners start worrying about "the most endangered leg," the ICBMs. Evidently, the Pentagon does not consider them to be that weak, despite the present hullabaloo around the subject, or the order of modernization priorities would have been different.

More than that, the Reagan administration that went out of its way to scare the public with the imminent "windows of vulnerability" of the U.S. ICBMs was evidently in no hurry at all about finalizing the method of MX ICBM deployment—the very ICBM that was supposed "to close the window." The Reagan administration first cancelled Carter's MPS mobile basing mode (though mobility was allegedly the only remedy that could ensure the survival of MX missiles), then decided to put some MXs into the old Minuteman silos, then invented the "Dense Pack." How can this absolutely leisurely attitude to the problem of new land-based missiles be reconciled with the yarn about the "window"? At the same time I can imagine what the reaction of the Republican zealots would have been if somebody had told them in 1980 that the Democrats on the SALT negotiating team had agreed to abandon the multiple protective shelters basing mode.

As for the opportunities presented by ASW systems, the growing range of submarine-based strategic systems and the corresponding expansion of the world ocean area from which submarine-launched missile strikes can be made lead to the conclusion that even the most far-flung ASW system cannot be especially efficient at the current stage or in the near future.

Development of offensive strategic systems until the end of the century will evidently evolve along the lines already determined by contemporary technological achievements. One of the main trends in improving existing missile systems is increasing their accuracy, which in principle makes it unnecessary to significantly enlarge the yield of nuclear warheads available at present. Some of the new systems will be largely based on well-proven technological principles. For instance, a miniaturized cruise missile designed to be carred by a ballistic missile is actually a maneuverable reentry vehicle (MARV). This will undoubtedly constitute a new weapon system, though based on familiar technological principles. Deploying this kind of system would destabilize the present bilateral strategic balance. Should this occur, either the Soviet Union or the United States could maintain the stability of mutual deterrence through unilateral compensatory measures, but it is obvious that the most effective way to preserve the existing balance is by international treaties committing the participants to limitation and special coordination aimed at preventing radical technological breakthroughs from upsetting the balance. This is especially true since the United States and the Soviet Union agreed in 1973 upon one of the basic principles of negotiations on the further limitation of strategic offensive arms: "The modernization and replacement of strategic offensive arms would be permitted under conditions, which will be formulated in agreements to be concluded."[63]

The most radical step in this direction could be made by accepting the Soviet proposal to conclude an agreement that would ban development and production of new types and systems for mass annihilation.[64] This would certainly contribute to the stability of mutual deterrence. However, although American experts discuss this proposal with their Soviet colleagues, the American side is apparently not yet prepared to take a far-reaching step of this kind, hoping to be able to retain and further U.S. advantages in military technology. The United States evidently aims to preserve and consolidate through agreements an approximate parity in areas where this parity exists and where technological breakthroughs are not in sight. At the same time, the United States strives to keep open and free from any limitations areas of new weapon systems development where it expects to gain preponderance. It should be obvious that such a policy cannot ensure the stablity of the balance because it compels the other side to adopt a similar approach.

The 1972 ABM Treaty (supplemented by the 1974 Protocol) has made a significant contribution to stabilizing the U.S.-Soviet strategic balance contractually sealing at last the situation of mutual vulnerability for both sides. The unlimited duration of this treaty increases the stability of the existing balance. Also of importance is the treaty's agreed interpretation in which the parties state their intent to enter consultations to agree on specific limitations if ABM systems based on other physical principles are created in the future.[65] The cause of global strategic stability could be further promoted by applying the principle stated in Article IX of the ABM Treaty (in accord with which each party undertakes not to transfer ABM systems to other states and not to deploy them outside its national territory) to other strategic weapon systems.

However, the U.S. administration now seems to be interested not in strengthening the minimum ABM regime, but in attempts to restore the United States' invulnerability by any means possible, including withdrawing from the ABM Treaty. If this path were taken by the U.S. government, it would definitely be a very serious blow to the stability of mutual deterrence. This step would tremendously increase international tensions, while hardly giving to the American generals the situation of impunity (invulnerability) they dream of. I tend to agree with Hans Bethe that at the current state of the art there is no defense against missiles.[66]

There is also a continuing debate in the American press about the influence that could be exerted on today's strategic balance by civil defense measures carried on by the United States and the Soviet Union. An extreme viewpoint is expressed by Eugene Wigner who argues that an energetic civil defense program will bring "assured survival" of 95 percent of the U.S. population and more than 50 percent of America's industrial capacity, even if the retaliatory strikes were made against American cities and industry rather than against the U.S. military complex.[67] Similarly, Nitze's one-time adviser T.K. Jones suggests that Soviet civil defense a priori dooms the United States to failure in any nuclear conflict.[68]

Understandably, efficient civil defense measures can reduce the number of casualties among the civilian population in a nuclear conflict. That is the point made in Soviet civil defense manuals. This opinion seems to be shared by the U.S. administration. But to insist that civil defense is currently the main method to ensure victory in a central nuclear conflict, as some American authors contend, is to adopt a paranoid attitude.[69]

No civil defense program can counteract the disastrous nature of a nuclear war between the United States and the Soviet Union in contemporary circumstances. To argue the contrary is deliberately to provoke nuclear war by alleging its "acceptability" because civil defense could reduce by several million the number of casualties that would, in fact, run into hundreds of millions. Evidently all recent U.S. administrations have appreciated this point, since their dollar allotments for civil defense can be expressed in tenths of a billion while their expenditure for producing and deploying strategic offensive arms amounts to tens of billions of dollars.

Problems of Multipolar Nuclear Balance

Another significant factor can upset the existing global stability if the situation is evaluated in terms of overall global nuclear balance, rather than from the perspective of possible local crises. This aspect concerns possible changes within the existing nuclear pentagonal structure due to the growth of nuclear potentials of powers other than the Soviet Union and the United States or to alterations in their doctrines.

However remote the possibility of joint Western European nuclear forces may seem, it cannot be rejected out of hand, considering past attempts in this direction. Some time ago the United States gave an impulse to West European theoretical thinking along these lines, by introducing the idea of the multilateral nuclear force. Naturally, Washington always visualized such a force under the immediate control and command of the United States. The Western Europeans, however, envisioned such forces differently. If they did not see them as a means "to spite" the United States, they at least intended to use them as a substitute for the U.S. "nuclear umbrella," whose reality they regard as more and more doubtful. Actually, the acquisition of nuclear weapons by Great Britain and France was, to a great extent, the result of their leaderships' awareness that their national interests did not always coincide with those of the United States. Certainly the NATO mechanism is more or less reliably under U.S. control at the moment. But how long will this kind of control prevail? What will finally remain under its jurisdiction and what will elude it? One must not forget that some time ago the French military doctrine envisaged targeting the national nuclear forces "à tous azimuths." True, it was but a theoretical statement divorced from actual material capabilities. But capabilities are increasing; who knows what the 1980s and the 1990s will bring.[70] I use this illustration to show that introducing a single new element of uncertainty into the global strategic equation greatly complicates the calculus of strategic stability and the very definition of deterrence.

But Western Europe is only one side of the existing nuclear polygon. There is also the Chinese side. Current Chinese nuclear arms policy ensures that the Chinese factor will, in the course of time, assume growing importance in the global strategic equation. One obviously has to agree with American projections showing that China will not acquire a first-strike capability against either the United States or the Soviet Union until the end of the century. However, both countries will have to take the Chinese nuclear factor into consideration—not only Chinese capability but also Beijing's strategy for its implementation.

Some precocious American strategists rather rashly include the Chinese nuclear factor, as well as the whole of the Chinese military potential, among U.S. assets. There are even studies developing the concept of trilateral nuclear exchanges in which the United States is supposed to strike Soviet forces located at the Soviet–Chinese border in order to "open up" the Soviet Union to China.[71]

However, such strategies of a provocative and instigative nature are based on an unstable foundation—a precarious supposition postulating that a great country like China can be manipulated to achieve goals set by certain aggressive U.S. circles vis-à-vis the Soviet Union.

The problem of deterrence, still more the problem of deterrence within the equilateral nuclear triangle, is exceedingly complex and not yet fully analyzed. This is one more reason to be skeptical about various presumptuous scenarios of triangular nuclear exchanges developed by some U.S. strategists in the naive hope that Beijing, as well as Moscow, will follow the script.

It is not accidental that a widely read study of the long-term worldwide effects of multiple nuclear explosions—prepared by the U.S. National Academy of Sciences under contract with the Arms Control and Disarmament Agency—stated as one of its main conclusions: "The Governments of the United States and of other major nuclear powers should be alert to the possibility that a geographically distant, populous other nation might determine that the degree of short-term damage to itself . . . would be 'acceptable' and that, since long-term recovery would be highly likely, might conclude that its own self-interest is compatible with a major nuclear exchange between other powers."[72]

The global nuclear balance can be influenced not only by qualitative and quantitative changes in the nuclear arsenals of nations belonging to today's "nuclear club" but also by acquisition of nuclear weapons by other states. Nuclear weapons proliferation is dangerous not only because nuclear potentials there may spring up comparable with those already in existence (as in Britain and France), but also because the emergence of more nuclear powers, some of which might try to use nuclear weapons in local conflicts, would make the task of preserving global stability virtually impossible. Due to the worldwide ramifications of their foreign policy interests, the great nuclear powers would face the permanent risk of getting involved in these local collisions (nuclear ones, at that), risking escalation of any peripheral conflict to the level of a central war. This is precisely why the problem of nuclear nonproliferation is one cornerstone of interational security.

National military potentials are meaningfully comparable only if taken in their totality. Many authors stress that to correlate actual national power of different states, it is not enough to compare respective military potentials; more factors must be considered.[73] However, should one deliberately narrow the approach and confine it to a comparison of military potentials, it becomes obvious that comparing isolated components especially without regard for the geopolitical situations of the parties is inadequate and artificial, and does not convey the actual capabilities of a state. To limit nuclear armaments, the strategic nuclear potentials of the Soviet Union and the United States were somewhat artificially disconnected from their total military complexes and were covered by corresponding agreements. This solution is easier because each side's strategic weapon system represents the main threat to the opponent in contemporary circumstances. If U.S. troops were not stationed in Europe, Soviet and U.S. land forces would not come in contact at all. The adopted approach of stabilizing the strategic arms of two countries on the principle of equality and equal security is both correct and efficient. At the same time, one cannot fail to notice that regulating the strategic arms balance on a bilateral basis does not eliminate the problems of analysis and stabilization of the general military equation in the sum of all components, especially when one deals with issues of global stability.

The Problem of Regional Balances

It is no secret that the emergence of parity in strategic armaments between the United States and the Soviet Union motivated some U.S. military theorists and also national leaders, to try to correct the existing military balance, making it more favorable to the United States through military preponderance in regional balances. What American theorists have in mind is absolutely clear. Strategic parity virtually prevents the United States from rationally using strategic nuclear weapons against the Soviet Union (for one cannot meaningfully win in such an exchange). Stress then must be shifted to local balances of power, which permit limited, relatively nondangerous (i.e., devoid of a strong escalatory impulse) trials of strength due to the existing nuclear stalemate. In these conditions, American theorists reason, creation of local military preponderance may be decisive. Evidently, that was the main consideration that motivated such Washington moves as creating the Rapid Deployment Corps, acquiring new military bases and facilities in the Middle East and elsewhere, increasing the capacity of the U.S. Navy to strike at in-shore objectives, as well as attempting to change in NATO's favor the military balance between the Atlantic Alliance and the Warsaw Treaty Organization.

In Europe, the NATO military build-up has assumed the features of a long-term campaign based on widely known decisions of the two NATO summit conferences in London in May 1977 and in Washington in May 1978. This campaign is not confined to the build-up of conventional armaments and armed forces; to greater integration of NATO national components; or to improvements in combat readiness and mobility of NATO forces stationed on the continental United States. It also comprises qualitative upgrading of NATO nuclear weapons located in Europe, including extended-range types, thus creating a radical new threat to the forces of the Warsaw Treaty Organization.

This is exactly how the Soviet Union views the decision to deploy 572 American Pershing II and cruise missiles in Western Europe. In the words of the Soviet Defense Minister, this is a step "to change Europe's strategic situation in NATO's favor."[74]

As usual, the Western bloc's attempt to gain one-sided advantage is being camouflaged as a "reply to growing Soviet threat," especially the threat from the Soviet SS-20 medium range missiles. But the Soviet medium-range land based missiles have been part and parcel of the general NATO–Warsaw Treaty military equation for the past twenty years. The Soviet Union's recent modernization of medium-range missiles was preceded on the Western side by the modernization of the British and French nuclear forces as well as by the total renewal of the U.S. nuclear-capable aviation in Europe, both land-based and carrier-based. As a result the overall European balance between the military, including nuclear, forces of the two blocs remained even. An opportunity, therefore, exists to consolidate this balance for years to come by an international agreement based on the principle of undiminished security for all the countries concerned; and there is also an opportunity not only to consolidate but to stabilize the balance at lower levels of armaments and armed forces.

Europe faces a clear-cut alternative: contractual confirmation of the existing military parity between Eastern and Western Europe and as a result reinforcement of not only political détente, brought about by the Helsinki Final Act, but also military détente; or a new arms race with all the ensuing dangers for European and global peace. The Soviet Union and other Warsaw Pact countries are ready to stabilize the existing equilibrium and to considerably reduce the present levels of armaments and armed forces on the basis of reciprocity, which is evident in the far-reaching compromise proposals made by the Soviet Union at the Geneva USSR–U.S. talks on the medium-range nuclear weapons in Europe and from the proposals of socialist states participating in the Vienna talks on the reduction of arms and armed forces in Central Europe.

At the Geneva talks the Soviet Union proposed to create a wide European zone of reduction and limitation of nuclear weapons reaching from the Arctic Ocean to Africa and from the mid-Atlantic to the Ural mountains. In this zone the Soviet Union proposed to reduce the existing medium-range nuclear weapons (starting from the range of 1000 kilometers and greater, but excluding intercontinental weapons) in such a way that in five years after the arrangement is made the USSR on the one hand and the NATO countries on the other will have no more than 300 weapons of this class. All types of medium-range nuclear weapons, both missiles and planes, ought to be included in the proposed reductions. No new nuclear weapons could be deployed in the zone. At the same time the Soviet Union proposed that the medium-range nuclear weapons outside the zone in question would be deployed in such a way as to prevent the weapons of one side from covering (reaching) the objectives of the other side within the zone.

At the same time the Soviet Union firmly opposes the American "zero option" suggestion, which requires the complete dismantling of all the Soviet medium-range missiles in exchange for non-deployment of the U.S. Pershing II's and cruise missiles in Europe. In Moscow this proposal is viewed as an attempt to unilaterally disarm the Soviet Union, because, were the "zero option" implemented, NATO would gain nearly a 50-percent advantage over the Warsaw Treaty countries in the number of medium-range delivery vehicles and would end up with three times the number of nuclear warheads on those delivery vehicles than would the other side.[75] The Soviet leadership stated many times that the Soviet Union would welcome the attainment of a real zero solution in Europe by agreeing to eliminate on a reciprocal basis all the medium-range and short-range (tactical) nuclear weapons on European soil. But NATO leadership evidently is not ready for such a radical step. At the same time, it is obvious that the Soviet Union will not allow any radical shift of the European military balance in favor of NATO.

The Americans must consider the deep and genuine anxiety felt in the Soviet Union and Eastern Europe about the military preparations carried on in Western Europe—anxiety with roots in the tragic experience of two world wars. One could not agree more with Tom Braden of the *Washington Post* who wrote:

> The one thing we must not do is try to scare hell out of the Russians by embarking on an effort to be stronger than they are along their borders.
>
> The peace of mutual terror requires care, wariness, restraint and vigilance. But the one thing that might destroy it is a chauvinistic determination to be No. 1.[76]

The same could be said about the regional balance in the East. In the Soviet–American–Chinese triangle, the balance of power between the United States and China, and between the United States and the Soviet Union, is largely determined by the balance between the nuclear components of respective military potentials, whereas the USSR–PRC power balance depends on aggregate military potentials due to the long, common land border. Thus, U.S. attempts to adjust the balance of power in the East in its favor through augmentation of the Japanese military potential, through increased projection of U.S. naval power toward the Northwestern Pacific, or through encouragement of the Chinese military build-up are regarded in the Soviet Union as destabilizing the global strategic equation, not to mention the regional one. This, in turn, can bring about corresponding military and political measures designed to compensate the Soviet Union for any unfavorable alteration in the global balance. Such measures may be taken in a different region or in a different sphere—not where the opponent's build-up occurred—that promises a better prospect of rectifying the balance.

AMBIGUITIES OF DETERRENCE IN
A MULTINUCLEAR WORLD

Apparently the concept of deterrence is hardly applicable to conditions of multilateral, rathar than bilateral, military confrontation, including challenges on the nuclear level. The term deterrence, in the interpretation it has had until now, deals with varieties of a bilateral equation only. Third parties, whenever they come into the picture, are generally treated as passive, not active, participants or allies of this or that side. At the same time, it may be assumed that various kinds of counterforce subtleties in scenarios for trilateral or quadrilateral nuclear balances will prove too much even for contemporary computers.

If one selects the criterion of covering the opponent's territory by a country's nuclear weapons, obviously the most effective and more or less calculable type of deterrence can be defined as "minimal deterrence," i.e., the assured capability, in a retaliatory strike, of country A to deliver on targets in countries B, C, or D a certain number of large strategic nuclear warheads sufficient to cause considerable damage to the population and industry of each country. This kind of threat may be considered an efficient means of deterrence in view of the price any country mentioned would have to pay should it attempt to destroy A's deterrent by making, for instance, a preventive strike against A's missiles. The concept of minimal deterrence is, in fact, the basis for the development of the nuclear strike forces of Great Britain and France.

But the multifarious interactions of all sides in a pentagonal nuclear world cannot be adequately described by the concept of deterrence, unless one postulates coalitional confrontation instead of political equidistance of all sides. Coalition diplomacy can restore the concept of deterrence somewhat, but even so the latter can hardly be applied in its original formulation, because each participant of a coalition will strive to minimize his own damage by every means, including actions that may contradict the interests of his partners. General Charles de Gaulle was the first among the leaders of the U.S. allies to conclude that, in a matter of nuclear war, one must chiefly rely on one's own forces and judgment.

If we add the effect of other factors, such as geographical location, population density, quantity and quality of conventional armaments, and size of armed forces, there can be but one conclusion: the concept of deterrence is of little relevance in a multipolar situation. The very principle of ensuring security through the build-up of strength becomes hardly justifiable in a world of several nuclear powers capable of maiming one another.

No doubt some lunatic mathematician can create a "credible" computerized scenario of a multilateral nuclear exchange favoring country A—

if the country's leadership strictly adheres to his plan. But if it is difficult—next to impossible—for politicians to depend upon computerized recommendations even when dealing with a more or less simple bilateral balance, what must be said of immensely more complex situations where every premise is highly conjectural? The result may be similar to Herman Kahn's scenarios of the future, where all alternatives are possible with almost identical probabilities of realization and the author does not take responsibility for any course of events; he only lists all conceivable options. This is one more reason to stress that the main powers must seek their security in a cooperative endeavor toward peace, starting with codification of the rules of foreign policy restraint and ending with specific commitments in the realm of military détente— tangible disarmament. What was long ago predicted by the genius of Immanuel Kant—world peace not as the wishful thinking of liberal and human rules, but as the prime necessity of life for mankind facing the dilemma of peace through international agreement or peace of the vast global graveyard—has surely become imperative in our age.

"We are doomed to coexist" with the Soviet Union, said Henry Kissinger[77] when he was viewing the world as a statesman not as a scheming politician. This phrase reflects the naked truth about the relationship between the two countries as well as the general principle of contemporary international relations, which allows no alternative to peaceful coexistence. This dictum must be comprehended by leaders of all nations—such is the gist of the problem of security at the close of the twentieth century.

THE POLITICAL DIMENSIONS OF STRATEGY

It must be understood that the risk to national security inherent in the arms race exceeds any risk involved in possible cheating while implementing arms limitation and disarmament measures. For instance, if one state, under conditions of a complete ban on all nuclear weapons testing, carries out a secret unobserved mini-explosion, are the consequences of this violation realistically comparable to those of a growing number of nuclear states mutilating our planet with numerous nuclear detonations and seeking new instruments and methods of mass annihilation?

In my opinion, strategic theory in its postwar American interpretation has arrived at a blind alley. Thus, it has become semantically possible to describe virtually any situation as favoring one side and disadvantaging the other.

On paper, one can play through any scenario, including completely absurd ones depicting a limited counterforce Soviet strike against several U.S. air bases with marginal population damage. But it is not war, it is playing with tin soldiers. One is bound to ask, what will the Soviet Union practically gain from such an attack? U.S. analysts do not give answers to down-to-earth questions like this. Instead, they juggle figures proving to their own satisfaction that it is possible to launch X missiles against Y targets in the Soviet Union or the United States with Z probability of target destruction. For them, this is an end in itself. But such theoretical ruminations are completely divorced from truly strategic, i.e., chiefly political, problems.

U.S. strategic thinking in recent years has focused on the problems of nuclear arms, of megatonnage and throw-weight, of bilateral strategic balance (specifically on the more narrow problem of correlation between the ICBMs of the United States and the Soviet Union, rather than the whole of bilateral balance). It does not take into account that, in the contemporary world, global stability also depends on many nonmilitary factors. It does not consider that, in the nuclear age, many traditional strategic categories like time, space, and demographic potential acquire new meaning and interpretation, which differ from one country to another in accordance with the geopolitical situation and socioeconomic level of development. The above categories are superimposed on global—potentially even cosmic—capacities of contemporary and prospective strategic weapons. This makes the task of achieving political aims through military means insoluble in rational terms because all these global weapon systems are systems of mass annihilation and will so remain for the forseeable future despite attempts at counterforce finesse.

If one overlooks the uses to which "strategy" has been put for the sake of alarmist propaganda, it is possible to explain the leaning of U.S. strategic thinking toward tactical problems as technological fetishism. This is corroborated by Herbert York, who was active in U.S. weapon system development. Writing on the subject of MIRV, he stated: "Almost all the important decisions were technologically determined ... . More general strategic thinking and political considerations did not enter into the process until it was too late for them to have any effect."[78]

A characteristic feature of U.S. strategic doctrine inspired by the emergence of nuclear weapons is its origin in a priori reasoning and not in the generalization of past experience. The only tangible and known element of the new atomic strategy resulting from a qualitative transformation of the means of armed struggle developed in such a way that U.S. strategic doctrine became a prisoner of military technology, the latter being the only certainty among a number of ambiguities due to entirely hypothetical conceptions of the consequences of using atomic weapons. In 1968, Bernard Brodie expressed the opinion that in the future "strategic thought will be much less concerned with technological developments than in the score of years following World War II." He wrote: "We may therefore expect, in any strategic analysis, a heightening of the importance of the political environment."[78] However, this prediction from an outstanding U.S. strategist has not yet come true, because U.S. strategic thinking persists in giving priority to military and technical factors over political ones.

The breach between narrow military "wisdom" and the real state of affairs in the world, the lack of progress in checking the momentum generated by military complexes of big states, the interpretation of the historic competition between the two social systems as exclusively military rivalry, the analysis of the evolution of international relations entirely in terms of deterrence seem to be serious enough obstacles to the cause of global stability.

But it is the unending U.S. search for purely American solutions to world problems—be it the Law of the Sea or the Middle East settlement—in short, the U.S. drive for world preeminence, for absolute security, that remains the main stumbling block on the road to stable peace.

In our age continued search for the absolute security for one country through military means can but lead to insecurity for all others and drag the world into an unprecedented catastrophe that may end human civilization on this small and still young planet of ours.

NOTES

1. According to Alexander George and Richard Smoke, "In its most general form deterrence is simply the persuasion of one's opponent that the costs and/or risks of a given course of action he might make outweigh its benefits." A. L. George and R. Smoke, *Deterrence in American Foreign Policy: Theory and Practice.* (New York: Columbia University Press, 1974), p. 11.
2. The relationship between deterrence and coercion is extensively treated in Thomas C. Schelling's *Arms and Influence* (New Haven, Conn.: Yale University Press, 1966). Schelling uses the term "compellence" while admitting that the same meaning is conveyed by the term "coercion." Incidentally, the latter term was used by Thomas Jefferson when he spoke of "peaceable coercions" that the United States could develop and use. Quoted in G. F. Kennan, *Realities of American Foreign Policy* (London: Oxford University Press, 1954), p. 59.
3. James B. Pritchard, ed., *Ancient Near Eastern Texts*, 2nd ed. (Princeton, N.J.: Princeton University Press, 1955), pp. 14-18. For a broad treatment of deterrence in the preatomic age, see George Quester, *Deterrence before Hiroshima* (New York: John Wiley, 1966).

4. Colin Gray is right when he points out that contemporary American theorists underrate the significance of past experience: "Nuclear age strategic theory has suffered severely from shallowness of its empirical base." C. Gray, "Across the Nuclear Divide: Strategic Studies," *International Security*, Summer 1977, p. 24.
5. Neither the principle of deterrence nor the word itself was really new. The word was borrowed from Latin *de terreo*, which had almost the same meaning as its contemporary English equivalent and was used by Roman politicians and authors with identical strategic connotation. Still, as far as I can judge, the term was not used in American strategic theory before the arrival of the atomic age. When George Washington in his day practiced deterrence vis-à-vis Indian tribes in North America and other opponents, he used the verb "to awe" to describe his approach.
6. G. Douhet, *The Command of the Air* (New York: Coward McCann, 1942). For detailed comment upon this theory, see B. Brodie, *Strategy in the Missile Age* (Princeton, N.J.: Princeton University Press, 1959), pp. 71-106.
7. The air war that Germany waged against Great Britain in 1940-1941 as well as the use of V-1 and V-2 missiles against the same country are pure translations of Douhet's concept of reality. Both had rather limited material and moral effect.
8. "Deterrence theory," notes Robert Jervis, " . . . is abstract and deals with states A and B, and it does not matter what national names fill these blanks." But he agrees that the theory is ethnocentric: "Like most theories of international relations developed by Americans and West Europeans, it is grounded in the experience, culture and values of the West . . . ." From this, Jervis draws that conclusion the "people from other cultures might develop quite different analyses." Robert Jervis, "Deterrence Theory Revisited," *World Politics*, 31, 2, January 1979, p. 296.
   The above is an entirely logical deduction. But I wish to stress a different point, which is that original American ethnocentrism of this theory was almost inseparable from its abstract core. Hence, when other countries—other cultures—started using it they had difficulty adding their own interpretations because of the built-in American coloration of the terminology, the America-centered orientation.
9. I realize this statement sounds unusual. However, one can speak of the general parity between the military forces of the United States and the Soviet Union in the immediate postwar period (and also when both countries completed demobilization) if one discounts the atomic monopoly enjoyed by the United States at that moment and takes into consideration a wide range of parameters of the armed forces of the two countries, including their different technical compositon and different war-fighting experiences.
10. The basic document outlining the postwar U.S. strategy and approved by the Joint Chiefs of Staff on September 19, 1945, advanced the objective of maintaining armed forces that would "make it unwise for any major aggressor nation to initiate a major war against the opposition of the United States" (not *against the United States* but *"against their opposition"*). At that, American military leadership realized that creation of military potential sufficient to satisfy this goal presented the maximum problem from a military point of view. Another JCS document dated March 29, 1946, prescribed the creation of "the absolute military security of the United States" [see United Nations, *Foreign Relations of the United States (FRUS) 1946*, Vol. I: General. (Washington, D.C.: Government Printing Office, 1972), pp. 1161-1162, 1166]. Thus, the aim was not to maintain military parity with the Soviet Union or certain limited superiority, but to create military potential that would surpass by at least one order of magnitude the military potential of any other state or even a coalition of states— there is no other way to interpret the aim of gaining "the absolute security."
11. The doctrine of containment was developed by George Kennan, who at the time headed the Policy Planning Staff of the U.S. State Department, in his famous "X" article in *Foreign Affairs* (July 1947). The same journal commemorated the thirtieth

anniversary of Kennan's article by publishing polemics of great interest. See J. Gaddis, "Containment: A Reassessment," *Foreign Affairs*, July 1977, p. 873-887; E. Mark, "The Question of Containment: A Reply to John Lewis Gaddis," *Foreign Affairs*, January 1978, pp. 430-441 (including reply of Gaddis); finally, Kennan's reply—*Foreign Affairs*, April 1978, pp. 643-645. As Henry Kissinger once observed, "The original purpose of containment was, after all, to bring about the domestic transformation of the USSR." H. A. Kissinger, "Central Issues of American Foreign Policy" in K. Gordon, ed., *Agenda for the Nation* (Washington, D.C.: The Brookings Institution, 1968), p. 607. In other words, though labeled containment, it was in fact offensive, aggressive policy.

12. The two books considered the classical exposition of the deterrence theory are B. Brodie's *Strategy in the Missile Age* (Princeton, N.J.: Princeton University Press, 1959) and H. Kahn's *On Thermonuclear War* (Princeton, N.J.: Princeton University Press, 1960). Two other books that influenced the development of contemporary strategic thinking, though tackling deterrence in a more traditional way, were H. Kissinger's *Nuclear Weapons and Foreign Policy* (New York: Harper and Brothers, 1957) and General M. Taylor's *The Uncertain Trumpet* (New York: Harper and Brothers, 1960).

   For Soviet analyses of the U.S. deterrent theories, see H. Trofimenko, *Strategia Globalnoi Voiny* (*Strategy of Global Warfare*) (Moscow: Mezhdunarodnie Otnoshenia Publ., 1968); H. Trofimenko, *SShA: Politika, Voina, Ideologia* (*USA: Politics, War, Ideology*) (Moscow: Mysl Publ., 1976); and "Voennaya Sila i Mezhdunarodnie Otnoshenia" ("Military Force and International Relations"), in V. M. Kulish, ed. (Moscow: Mezhdunarodnie Otnoshenia Publ., 1972); A. E. Efremov, *Evropa i Yadernoe Oruzhie* (*Europe and Nuclear Weapons*) (Moscow: Mezhdunarodnie Otnoshenia Publ., 1972).

13. Incidentally, this fact was recognized in various American plans for preparing war against the Soviet Union that were elaborated by the JCS and different armed services since the end of the war against Japan. "The Soviet leaders will probably appreciate that direct military invasion of the U.S.A. is an almost impossible task," stated a secret plan called Fleetwood prepared by the Joint Intelligence Committee. This was but one of at least a dozen plans for war against the Soviet Union prepared by various American political, military, and intelligence bodies during the first four years after the end of World War II. These included a plan for war against the Soviet Union in Europe called Totality and produced at the end of 1945 by General Eisenhower, then Commander-in-Chief of U.S. forces in Europe; a study entitled *Strategic Vulnerability of Russia to a Limited Air Attack* ordered by the Pentagon and compiled by its Joint Intelligence Staff. There were other offensive plans bearing code names of Charioteer, Gunpowder, Doublestar, AEC-IOI, Dualism, and at last Dropshot, which has now been published as a book. All these plans were primarily based on the U.S. atomic capability which was defined by Major General Curtis LeMay—future Commander of the U.S. Strategic Air Command—as the means to "depopulate vast areas of the earth's surface leaving only vestigial remnants of man's material work." For greater detail see Anthony Cave Brown, ed., *Dropshot: The United States Plan for War with the Soviet Union in 1957* (New York: The Dial Press, 1978), pp. I-II.

14. Robert Jervis defines deterrence theory as a "theory about the ways in which an actor manipulates threats to harm others *in order to coerce them into doing what he desires*" (emphasis added) (*World Politics*, January 1979, p. 292). In other words, an American author even now still sees deterrence only in its ultimate form—as a means to coerce, to compel the opponent. This attitude was still more widespread in the 1950s, when the United States viewed itself as a sort of monopolist on effective means of deterrence.

15. "The objectives of the United States and other free countries in negotiations with the Soviet Union ... are to record, in a formal fashion which will facilitate the consolidation and further advance of our position, the process of Soviet accommodation to the new political, psychological, and economic conditions in the world .... In short, *our objectives are to record, where desirable, the gradual withdrawal of the Soviet Union ...* ." (emphasis added) *FRUS 1950*, Vol. I: National Security Affairs, Foreign Economic Policy (Washington, D.C.: Government Printing Office, 1977), p. 274.
16. Kahn, *On Thermonuclear War*, 2nd ed. (Princeton, N.J.: Princeton University Press, 1961), p. 126.
17. Ibid., pp. 138-144. According to Kahn, "It is widely believed that if the United States were directly attacked, its response would be automatic and unthnking" (p. 126).
18. As times—and balances—change, Dr. Kahn now, in 1982, would prefer by way of nuance, or litotes as William Safire would say, the term "not incredible first-strike capability." " ... There is a distinct difference," he says. "You really can't achieve a capability which looks like it would be used, but you can achieve a capability which the other side cannot feel will not be used ...." Quoted in Safire's column in *International Herald Tribune*, August 23, 1982.
19. H. Trofimenko, *SShA: Politika, Voina, Ideologia*, p. 225.
20. Wohlstetter suggested that deployment of invulnerable nuclear forces capable of surviving enemy attacks, of penetrating enemy defenses in a retaliatory strike, and inflicting upon him unacceptable damage would decrease the tensions of the U.S.-USSR nuclear confrontation and enhance the stability of deterrence. See Albert Wohlstetter, "The Delicate Balance of Terror," *Foreign Affairs*, January 1959, pp. 211–234, and an earlier version of this study, Rand Corporation publication P-1472, December 1958.
21. The first outline of the strategy of controlled or flexible response appeared in President J. F. Kennedy's Special Message to the Congress on the Defense Budget of March 28, 1961 [John F. Kennedy, *To Turn the Tide* (New York: Harper and Brothers, 1962), pp. 55-61]. Subsequently the concept was developed in Secretary McNamara's addresses and his posture statements to Congress. The main ideas of the new U.S. nuclear posture were later summarized in Robert S. McNamara, *The Essence of Security: Reflections in Office* (New York: Harper & Row, 1968). "The Soviet Union and the United States," McNamara wrote, "can mutually destroy one another regardless of who strikes first" (p. 59).
22. See Alain C. Enthoven and K. Wayne Smith, *How Much Is Enough? Shaping the Defense Program 1961-1969* (New York: Harper & Row, 1972).
23. "We have arrived at the current size and mix of our strategic offensive forces not only because we want the ultimate threat of massive destruction to be really assured, but also because for more than a decade we have thought it advisable to test the force against the higher-than-expected threat. Given the built-in surplus of warheads generated by this force-sizing calculation, we could allocate additional weapons to non-urban targets and thereby acquire a limited set of options, including the option to attack some hard targets." (In other words, to acquire not the second-strike capability that the United States already possessed but to build up forces required for a counterforce, that is first, offensive strike). U.S., Congress, *Report of the Secretary of Defense James R. Schlesinger to the Congress on the FY 1975 Defense Budget and FY 1975-1979 Defense Program*, March 4, 1974 (Washington, D.C.: Government Printing Office), p. 35.
24. *The Los Angeles Times*, April 8, 1982.
25. A Soviet visitor to the United States is often struck by the frequency of seeing "S" (shelter) signs on various buildings in all parts of the country.

26. This decision was announced by McNamara in a speech in San Francisco on September 18, 1967, before the UPI editors (The New York Times, September 19, 1967).

27. McNamara, *The Essence of Security*, p. 64.

28. McGeorge Bundy, George F. Kennan, Robert S. McNamara, and Gerard Smith, "Nuclear Weapons and the Atlantic Alliance," *Foreign Affairs*, Spring 1982, p. 756.

29. "If I had been the Soviet secretary of defense," muses Mr. McNamara now over those times, "I'd been worried as hell about the imbalance of force. And I would have been concerned that the United States was trying to build a first-strike capability." *The Los Angeles Times*, April 8, 1982.

30. In the five years from 1960 to 1965, the United States increased the number of its intercontinental land-based ballistic missiles (ICBMs) forty-six-fold and that of submarine-launched ballistic missiles (SLBMs) fifteen-fold. *The Military Balance 1969-1970* (London: Institute for Strategic Studies, 1969), p. 55.

31. The notion of counterinsurgence—that is, quiet, special warfare in distant lands involving small forces and without particular publicity—was a by-product of the U.S. leadership's new perception of the necessity for restraint in the contemporary world. And even later, Johnson's gradual escalation of hostilities in Indochina (which afterward was subjected to acute, though demagogical, Republican criticism) was also the fruit of awareness of the need to stop the test of strength at the lower rungs of the escalation ladder.

32. It probably reflects on national character that different countries, while adopting the term "deterrence" in their own usage, furnish it with varying shades of meaning. The German equivalent for "deterrence" is usually *Abschrekung*, i.e., intimidation. The standard Japanese term is *yokushiryoku*, which conveys the connotations of more or less passive checkmating. The French translate it as "dissuasion." The Russian language comes up with two corresponding terms—"keeping out" (*zderzhivanie*) and "intimidation" (*ustrashenie*), although the latter term was more often used in the 1950s and 1960s. When used in Soviet military vocabulary, and not as a Russian equivalent for the American term, the word is invariably *zderzhivanie*, "keeping out", "dissuasion." For the American reader of Soviet literature on the subject, matters are made worse because two widely different English words—"containment" and "deterrence"—are usually translated into Russian by the same word, *zderzhivanie*, i.e., "keeping out," "not letting go," "restraining"—evidently due to some unfortunate initial slip. Even some Soviet theorists who do not read English are confused, as they study translations of U.S. writing on post–World War II strategy, because one Russian word is used to denote the diverse concepts of containment and deterrence.

33. The Soviet Union at the moment faces at least four kinds of threats, each formidable in itself: the threat coming from the NATO forces in Europe, including the nuclear forces of Britain and France and the U.S. forward-based forces in Europe; the threat from the U.S. strategic offensive potential; the threat from the PRC military complex with its huge reservoir of manpower; and the threat from large U.S. naval units in forward deployment. The United States has to worry only about the opposing Soviet strategic forces—no other genuine threat confronts the United States on land or on sea. One must do justice to President Carter in that he proved to be the first U.S. leader to admit publicly the existence of large asymmetries between the Soviet Union and the United States regarding potential military threats. See President Carter's interview with Bill Moyers of the Public Broadcasting System on November 13, 1978 (*Weekly Compilation of Presidential Documents*, November 22, 1978, vol. 14, no. 46, p. 2018).

34. For a more detailed discussion of civil defense measures in the United States and the Soviet Union in the context of action-reaction phenomena and damage-limitation

concepts, see my article "The Theology of Strategy," *Orbis*, Fall 1977, especially pp. 507-511.

35. To understand better the evolution of Soviet strategy and development of Soviet military thought after World War II, see Marshal of the Soviet Union V. D. Sokolovsky, ed., *Voennaya Strategia (Military Strategy)*, 3rd ed. (Moscow: Voenizdat, 1968); Marshal of the Soviet Union A. Grechko, *Vooruzhennie Sily Sovetskogo Gosudarstva (Military Forces of Soviet State)*, 2nd ed. (Moscow: Voenizdat, 1975); Admiral of the Fleet of the Soviet Union S. Gorshkov, *Morskaya Mosch Gosudarstva (Sea Power of a State)*, 2nd ed. (Moscow: Voenizdat, 1979); D. F. Ustinov, *Izbrannye Rechi i Statii (Selected Speeches and Articles)* (Moscow: Politizdat, 1979); Marshall of the Soviet Union N. V. Ogarkov, "Strategia Voennaya" ("Military Strategy"), in *Sovetskaya Voennaya Enciklopedia (Soviet Military Encyclopedia)*, vol. 7 (Moscow: Voenizdat, 1979), pp. 555-565.

36. Soon after his inauguration, President Nixon made a realistic assessment of the strategic arsenals of the United States and the Soviet Union: "That gap has been closed. We shall never have it again." (*The New York Times*, April 19, 1969). Similar estimates were made by leaders of the Carter administration. For instance, on April 5, 1979, in his address before a joint meeting of the Council on Foreign Relations and the Foreign Policy Association, Secretary of Defense Harold Brown said, "The potential futility of any quest for superiority derives, I believe, from the realities of nuclear weaponry and bilateral superpower relations. Modern nuclear weapons technology is such that while equivalence is a realistic goal, superiority is not, providing that the other side is determined to prevent it. Each superpower can, by actions that are well within its technical and economic capability, prevent the other from gaining an over-all advantage, much less supremacy" (DOD press release).

37. Two other assurances were "a broad range of intelligence capabilities and operations" and "vigorous research and development programs" to secure a technological lead in arms development. See U.S., Congress, Senate, Committee on Armed Services, *Military Implications of the Treaty on the Limitation of Anti-Ballistic Missile Systems and the Interim Agreement on Limitation of Strategic Offensive Arms*, 92nd Cong., 2nd sess., 1972, p. 146. "We speeded up our /military/ programs after the SALT agreement in 1972," declared Henry Kissinger later. "We stopped no program; we accelerated several: the Trident submarine and the B-1, for example. And we started the cruise missile and MX. If there had been no agreement, we could have done no more." *Public Opinion*, May/June 1978, p. 58; *The Economist*, February 3, 1979, p. 18.

38. Presumably the number of classified models of strategic balance and nuclear exchange between the United States and the Soviet Union developed in various American "think tanks" under contract with the Pentagon exceeds by 50—if not by 100—times the number of similar models in open publications. Thus, one has to judge such projects from those tidbits that get published and that understandably stress arms control and not the prerequisites for assurance of American preponderance. See, e.g., models produced by D. Ellsberg, J. Lambelet, M. D. Intriligator, and D. L Brito in D. Ellsberg, *The Crude Analysis of Strategic Choices* (Santa Monica, Calif.: Rand Corporation, 1960), p. 2183; J. Lambelet, "Towards a Dynamic Two-Theatre Model of the East-West Arms Race," *Journal of Peace Science*, no. I, 1973; M. D. Intriligator and D. L. Brito, *Formal Models of Arms Races* (ACIS Working Paper no. 2, University of California, Los Angeles, May 1976).

39. This alternative was designed primarily to boost the morale of U.S. allies in Western Europe who had come to realize the ephemeral nature of the American nuclear umbrella under conditions of Soviet-American strategic parity and elimination by the treaty of ABM systems in both countries.

The Schlesinger doctrine can be viewed in retrospect as the final attempt of the United States to doctrinally couple the U.S. strategic deterrent with Western Europe. Because the West European members of NATO did not accept this attempt, Washington evidently came to realize that it is better to decouple openly and officially than to try to sustain the myth of continued coupling. This is what underlies recent U.S. moves to sell Eurostrategic weapons to the NATO allies. "With these weapons," the American message to the European partners seems to read "you will no longer need the U.S. strategic nuclear umbrella, which you don't believe in, anyway!" This kind of reasoning has been later confirmed by no less an authority than President Reagan. Speaking to American newspaper editors in October 1981, the President said, "I could see where you could have the exchange of tactical weapons against troops in the field without its bringing either one of the major powers to pushing the button." *Time*, November 2, 1981, p. 34.

40. "Several years ago, for instance," remarked Frank Church, then Chairman of the Senate Foreign Relations Committee, "the Pentagon floated a story that the Soviets could so confine an attack on our land-based missiles as to kill only 800,000 people. A follow-up study conducted at the request of the [Senate] committee resulted in revised estimates showing that up to 22 million could be killed, even if the Soviets attacked our Minuteman bases alone." U.S., Congress, Senate, Committee on Foreign Relations, *Strategic Arms Limitation Talks and Comprehensive Test Ban Negotiations* (made public September 1978) (Washington, D.C.: Government Printing Office, 1978), p. 11.

41. *Communist*, no. 7, May 1978, p. 116.

42. "The United States and the Soviet Union agree that an objective of their policies is to remove the danger of nuclear war and the use of nuclear weapons," states Article I of the Soviet-American treaty on the prevention of nuclear war of 1973. *Department of State Bulletin*, July 23, 1978, p. 160.

43. *Military Implications of the Treaty on the Limitation of Strategic Offensive Arms and Protocol Thereto (SALT II Treaty)*. Hearings before the Committee on Armed Services, U.S. Senate, 96th Cong., 1st Sess., Part I (Washington, D.C.: Government Printing Office, 1979), p. 359.

44. For a detailed argumentation of this statement, see Henry A. Trofimenko, "Counterforce: Illusion of a Panacea," *International Security*, Spring 1981, pp. 28-48.

45. Colin S. Gray, *The MX ICBM and National Security* (New York: Praeger, 1981), p. 19.

46. Ibid., p. 20.

47. As stated in the Republican party platform adopted at the Republican National Convention in Detroit in July 1980. *Congressional Record*, July 31, 1980, p. S10394.

48. *International Herald Tribune*, August 16, 1982.

49. *Pravda*, October 21, 1981.

50. Ibid., November 23, 1982.

51. One cannot help but join Henry Kissinger in his puzzlement when he observes, "I have great difficulty understanding why it is safe to adhere to a nonratified agreement while it is unsafe formally to ratify what one is already observing." *Time*, May 24, 1982, p. 28.

52 . One of the most brilliant American strategic analysts, Bernard Brodie, wrote, when discussing various fantastic conjectures of R. Pipes, G. Keegan, and others regarding the motive forces of the Soviet strategic build-up: "Since we are looking so hard for the reasons for the Soviet Union build-up, one possibility that ought to be considered is that it was simply triggered by ours, and that it contines to be stimulated by a desire to catch up." B. Brodie, *The Development of Nuclear Strategy* (ACIS Working Paper no. 11, University of California, Los Angeles, February 1978), pp. 15-16.

53. Fred Charles Iklé, "Can Nuclear Deterrence Last out the Century?" *Foreign Affairs*, January 1973, pp. 267-285.
54. According to the U.S. Office of Technology Assessment, in view of the Soviet countermeasures designed to neutralize any advantages that the United States might hope to gain from MPS basing mode "to ensure the survival of 100 MX missiles, 360 missiles hidden in 8,250 shelters could be required by 1990, and 550 missiles in 12,500 shelters by 1995." *The Christian Science Monitor*, September 29, 1981.
55. This viewpoint seems to be shared by a number of prominent Western scholars. Alton Frye, for instance, points out that one of the strategic realities of today is that "the attempt by either side to alter the stability of deterrence by overcoming its own vulnerabilities is bound to be dangerous." A. Frye, "Strategic Restraint, Mutual and Assured." *Foreign Policy* 27, 1977, p. 11.
56. For my assessment of SALT II, see H. Trofimenko, "SALT II: A Fair Bargain," *The Bulletin of the Atomic Scientists*, June 1979, pp. 30-34.
57. The President's plan calls for a common ceiling of 850 intercontinental nuclear missiles (land-based and sea-based) with no more than 5,000 warheads on them. No more than 2,500 warheads may be installed on land-based ICBMs.

   Considering that the Soviet land-based ICBMs carry 70 percent of the total number of strategic warheads, while the U.S. land-based ICBMs only 20 percent and that strategic bombers and cruise missiles are excluded from the count in the Reagan plan, it is fair to say that the plan is flagrantly biased in favor of the United States. In comparison with this one-sideness all the so-called tilts in Soviet favor, discovered by the American hawks in the SALT II Treaty under an electronic microscope, fade into nothing.

   "The so-called radical cuts, advocated by the U.S. President, would be those for the Soviet side only," wrote *Pravda* in the editorial comment on Mr. Reagan's plan. "In Washington they would like to dismantle more than half of the Soviet ICBMs, while conceding practically nothing on their own part .... It is sufficient to say that if the U.S. administration plan were realized the Soviet strategic nuclear potential (measured in the number of warheads) would become one third of the U.S. one. And to this American potential one should add several thousands of sea-based and land-based cruise missiles which the United States intends to deploy on top of that." (*Pravda*, June 4, 1982). "I don't think the Soviets will unilaterally disarm," said former Secretary of State Edmund Muskie commenting on the President's plan. (*The Oregonian*, May 11, 1982).
58. Development of a point ABM defense is another matter. A system of this kind might be designed in the near future for protecting objects of special importance. However, nationwide deployment of such an ABM system involves an enormous expenditure, which cannot be justified from the cost/effectiveness viewpoint. Apart from that, even if the system were deployed, it would be saturated—that is, neutralized by directing a very large number of warheads against a protected point. All that such an ABM system can do is raise the cost of attacking the target for the other side.
59. Quite often the issue is stated in absolutely odius terms, inadmissible in any serious analysis. I quote: "Washington—The Soviet strategic forces in the mid-1980s will have a 10% greater capability to attack hard targets in the U.S. than the hard-target capability of U.S. forces in striking a retaliatory blow, Arms Control and Disarmament Agency said here last week." *Aviation Week and Space Technology*, September 4, 1978, p. 24.

   But if the U.S. hard-target capability in the *second retaliatory strike* is only 10 percent less than the similar Soviet capability *in the first strike*, that can only mean the counterforce capability of U.S. strategic forces in the first strike (i.e., before they are crippled by the alleged Soviet first strike) greatly exceeds that of the Soviet Union. One has every right to ask what kind of readers the authors of these so-called arguments have in mind, especially since the journal that carries them is intended for experts.

59. My estimation of the ICBM share in the total throw-weight of the U.S. strategic forces is based on official U.S. data. For detailed exposition of the estimate see my article in *Blätter für deutsche und internationale Politik* (Cologne, September 1976), pp. 1008-1018. The ICBM share in the total number of targetable strategic nuclear warheads has been derived from the table in *The New York Times*, March 21, 1982 (to be exact, the share is 22.8 percent).

60. This was confirmed by Carter's Secretary of Defense, Harold Brown: "Even without Minuteman, our surviving second-strike capability would remain large—in the thousands of warheads . . . . It is difficult, in the circumstances, to see how the Soviets could expect to gain any meaningful advantage from starting such a mortal exchange." U.S., Congress, *Report of Secretary of Defense Harold Brown to the Congress on the FY 1980 Budget, FY 1981 Authorization Request and FY 1980-1984 Defense Program*, January 25, 1979 (Washington, D.C.: Government Printing Office, 1979), p. 15.

As to the American threat to the Soviet ICBMs, Nobel Prize-winning physicist Hans A. Bethe, who has been continuously involved with the U.S. nuclear weapons programs since their beginning in 1940s, says the following "The Russians have their forces mostly in ICBMs (intercontinental ballistic missiles), a type of weapon that is becoming more and more vulnerable. I think our military people know this, but they always talk about those of the Soviets. The Russians are much more exposed to a possible first strike from us then we are to one from them." *The Los Angeles Times*, April 11, 1982.

62. See the statement of Hon. William J. Perry before the Committee on Foreign Relations, U.S. Senate, during the SALT II hearings. *The SALT II Treaty. Hearings . . . Part 4*, pp. 438-479.

63. *The Department of State Bulletin*, July 23, 1973, p. 158.

64. The Soviet Union submitted the draft of a corresponding agreement to the U.N. General Assembly (see "Sovetski Soyuz v borbe za razoruzhenie" "Soviet Union in Struggle for Disarmament: A Compilation of Documents") (Moscow: *Politizdat*, 1977), pp. 233-237. For several years this issue has been under consideration in the Committee on Disarmament in Geneva and in bilateral Soviet-American consultations.

65. See *Arms Control and Disarmament Agreements: Texts and History of Negotiations*. (Washington, D.C.: ACDA, February 1975), p. 143.

66. "Against missiles there is no defense," says Prof. Bethe. "This is a subject on which I worked quite carefully and industriously for many years before '68, looking at many ways how to tell decoys from missiles, and so on. Whatever you did, the offense could always fool the defense and could do it better." *The Los Angeles Times*, April 11, 1982.

67. See Conrad V. Chester and Eugene P. Wigner, "Population Vulnerability: The Neglected Issue in Arms Limitation and the Strategic Balance," *Orbis*, Fall 1974, pp. 764-765.

68. See T. K. Jones and W. Scott Thompson, "Central War and Civil Defense," *Orbis*, Fall 1978, pp. 681-712. i

69. This is my impression of the line of reasoning pursued by T. K. Jones and W. Scott Thompson in their article. They seem quite logical within their own "system of coordinates." However, the data the authors use are so mendacious and their premises so crazy that arguing with them with common sense is hopeless. Every assertion in the article juggles figures and "reasons" to fit the predetermined answer. One finds

an inane idea that destruction of a plant (or even of all buildings in a city) is not tantamount to destruction of all machinery and equipment, so the latter can be quickly salvaged (from the debris of Chicago or Kiev?) and used for military production. Here, again, the Soviet Union is charged with the intention of making the first strike against the United States and there is the postulate of "three waves" of blows: the Soviet Union attacks, the United States responds, the Soviet Union delivers the coup de grace. One also finds a surreptitiously introduced assumption that grossly exaggerates the actual share of ICBMs in the U.S. strategic forces; the allegation that the survivability of strategic weapon systems will be endangered by a failure in the general electric power network; and the contention that air-borne cruise missiles have almost unlimited range unless restricted by international treaties. All of this is compiled to lead the reader to the "deduction" the authors want him to make— that "to overpower the Soviet population defenses would require a five- to tenfold increase in the U.S. strategic arsenal" (p. 711). To me this looks exactly like the "solution" needed by the Boeing Aerospace Company, which is generously financing the "impartial scientific enquiry" of T. K. Jones.

70. Walter Schutze of the Centre d'Études de Politique Étrangères in Paris suggests that a "tous azimuths" strategy may be adopted by newcomers to the "nuclear club" and thus will tend to fragment, even in peace time, the present structure of interstate relationships. W. Schutze, "A World of Many Nuclear Powers," in Franklyn Griffiths and John C. Polanyi, eds., *The Dangers of Nuclear War* (Toronto: Toronto University Press, 1979), p. 91.

71. See, for example, Bruce M. Russett, "Counter-Combatant Deterrence: A Proposal," *Survival*, May/June 1974, pp. 135-140 (initially this article appeared in *Public Policy*, 22, no. 2, 1974).

72. "Long-term Worldwide Effects of Multiple Nuclear-Weapons Detonations: National Academy of Science," Letter of Ph. Handler, President, to Dr. Fred Iklé, Director, Arms Control and Disarmament Agency, Washington, D.C., 1975, p. 6.

73. One innovative approach to measuring the power of nations in the international arena is demonstrated in Ray S. Cline, *World Power Trends and U.S. Foreign Policy for the 1980s* (Boulder, Colo.: Westview Press, 1980).

74. D. Ustinov, "Military Détente—The Imperative of Our Time," *Pravda*, October 25, 1979.

75. For a detailed exposition of the official Soviet view regarding the military balance in Europe and the ways to stabilize it at lower levels of armaments and armed forces, see *The Threat to Europe* (Moscow: Progress Publishers, 1982), and *Whence the Threat to Peace*, 2nd ed. (Moscow: Military Publishing House, 1982), esp. pp. 72-90.

76. *Washington Post*, August 19, 1978.

77. *International Herald Tribune*, April 12, 1976.

78. Herbert F. York, "The Origins of MIRV," in D. Carlton and C. Schaerf, eds., *Dynamics of the Arms Race* (London: Croom Helm, 1975), p. 35.

79. Bernard Brodie, "Strategy," *International Encyclopedia of the Social Sciences*, vol. 15 (New York: Macmillan, 1968), p. 287.

Chapter 6

The Operational Level of War

Edward N. Luttwak

It is a peculiarity of Anglo-Saxon military terminology that it knows of *tactics* (unit, branch, and mixed) and of *theater strategy* as well as of *grand strategy*, but includes no adequate term for the operational level of warfare—precisely the level that is most salient in the modern tradition of military thought in continental Europe. The gap has not gone unnoticed, and Basil Liddell-Hart for example attempted to give currency to the term "grand tactics" as a substitute (already by his day the specialized usage of the directly translated term "operational-functioning machine/unit," was too well established to be redeemed.)

The operational level of war, as opposed to the tactical and strategic levels, is or ought to be of greatest concern to the analyst. In theater strategy, political goals and constraints on one hand and available resources on the other determine projected outcomes. At a much lower level, tactics deal with specific techniques. In the operational dimension, by contrast, schemes of warfare such as blitzkrieg or defense in depth evolve or are exploited. Such schemes seek to attain the goals set by

---

I am greatly indebted to my partner, Steven L. Canby, for many key ideas developed in this essay.

theater strategy through suitable combinations of tactics. It is not surprising that the major works of military literature tend to focus on the operational level, as evidenced by the writings of Clausewitz.

What makes this gap in Anglo-Saxon military terminology important for practical purposes is that the absence of the term referring to the operational level reflects an inadvertence towards the whole conception of war associated with it, and this in turn reflects a major eccentricity in the modern Anglo-Saxon experience of war. It is not merely that officers do not *speak* the word but rather that they do not *think* or practice war in operational terms, or do so only in vague or ephemeral ways. The causes of this state of affairs are to be found in the historic circumstances of Anglo-Saxon warfare during this century. In the First World War, American troops were only employed late, and then under French direction; their sphere of planning and action was essentially limited to the tactical level. As for the British, who did have to endure the full five years and more of that conflict, they mostly did not transcend their pre-1914 experience, characterized by battalion fights in the colonies.

It was precisely the failure of the British Army to extend its mental horizons that the "English" school of post-World War I military thinkers so greatly deplored, and which it set out to correct. The advocacy of large-unit armored warfare in depth by Fuller, Liddell Hart, etc. was aimed at expanding operations to transcend the tactical battlefield—and was not simply inspired by the need to find employment for the newly invented tank. In other words, their ideas were not tank *driven* but merely tank *using*. The motivating factor was not the attraction of the technology, but rather the powerful urge to escape the bloody stalemate of the tactical battlefields of World War I.

Nor did the radically different character of the World War II suffice to establish the operational level in the conduct, planning, and analysis of Anglo-Saxon warfare. To be sure, there were isolated examples of generalship at the operational level, and indeed very fine examples, but they, and all that they implied, never became organic to the national tradition of warfare. Instead such operational approaches remained the trade secrets and personal attributes of men such as Douglas MacArthur, Patton, and the British General O'Connor, victor of the first North African campaign.

Otherwise, in World War II as in Korea and of necessity in Vietnam, American ground warfare was conducted almost exclusively at the tactical level, and then at the level of theater strategy above that, with almost no operational dimension in between. Thus the theater strategy of 1944 in France (as earlier in Italy) was characterized by the broad-front advance of units which engaged in tactical combat *seriatim*.

Above the purely tactical level, the important decisions were primarily of a logistic character. The overall supply dictated the rate of advance, while its distribution would set the vectors of the advancing front. And these were of course the key decisions at the level of theater strategy. Soon after the end of World War II it became fashionable to criticize the broad-front theater strategy pursued after D-Day. But such criticisms overlooked the central fact that the American comparative advantage was in sheer material resources while U.S. (and British) middle-echelon staff and command skills were of a low order. The overly personalized criticism of Eisenhower's strategy that characterized this literature certainly did not result in the popularization of any "operational" concepts of war.

In Korea once again, the predominant pattern of warfare was set by a front-wide advance theater strategy, which practically left no scope for anything more ambitious than tactical actions. The brilliant exception was of course the Inchon landing, but characteristically this experience was assimilated as the virtuoso performance of Douglas MacArthur, instead of being recognized as a particular manifestation of a general phenomenon, i.e., the concerted use of tactical means to achieve operational-level results that are much more than the sum of the (tactical) parts.

Since the Korean War, as before it, American ground forces have continued to absorb new generations of weapons, their mobility in and between theaters has continued to improve, logistic systems have been computerized and much attention has been devoted to the management of resources at all levels. Nevertheless the entire organism continues to function only at the lowest and the highest military levels, while the operational level in between remains undeveloped. This is not due to any lack of military knowledge as such. Rather, it reflects the limitations of an attrition style of war, where there is an exaggerated dependence on firepower as such to the detriment of maneuver and flexibility. In the extreme case of pure attrition, there are only techniques and tactics, and there is no action at all at the operational level. All that remains are routinized techniques of reconnaissance, movement, resupply, etc. to bring firepower-producing forces within range of the most conveniently targetable aggregations of enemy forces and supporting structures. Each set of targets is then to be destroyed by the cumulative effect of firepower, victory being achieved when the proportion destroyed suffices to induce retreat or surrender, or, theoretically, when the full inventory of enemy forces is destroyed.

It is understood of course that in deliberately seeking to engage the largest aggregations of enemy forces, their reciprocal attrition will also have to be absorbed, so that there can be no victory in this style of war without an overall superiority in net attritive capacity. But aside from that, attrition-style warfare has the great attractions of predictability and functional simplicity, since efficiency is identical to effectiveness, and since the whole is (if no more) no less than the sum of the parts. Hence the optimization of *all* military activities in peace as in war, whether research and development, procurement, manpower-acquisition, training, staff work, or command can all be pursued in a systematic fashion—the goal being of course to improve the techniques (target acquisition, force-movement, re-supply, etc.) whose combined effect determines the overall efficiency of attritive action. Thus in seeking to enhance overall capabilities, each resource increment can be unfailingly allocated into the right sub-activity, merely by establishing which of them yields the highest marginal return: manpower or equipment, numbers or quality, fire-control or ammunition enhancements, and so on. Under a pure attrition style, all the functions of war and war preparation are therefore governed by a logic analogous to that of microeconomics, and the conduct of warfare at all levels is analogous to the management of a profit-maximizing industrial enterprise. This in turn renders possible the overall management of defense by the use of marginalist analytical techniques, with uncertainties being confined to technical unknowns. Only structural obstacles (e.g. self-serving bureaucracies, or local political pressures) remain to interfere with the pursuit of efficiency.

Thus in the whole complex of war preparation and action, uncertainties are confined to a few irreducibles. Otherwise everything can be routinized on the basis of efficiency-maximizing managerial procedures with the lowly exception of the command of men in direct contact with the enemy, in which non-managerial methods of combat leadership remain necessary.

The other main phenomenon of war, which stands in counterpoint to attrition along the spectrum that makes up the overall style of war of nations and armed services is *relational-maneuver*. In the case of relational-maneuver the goal of incapacitating enemy forces or structures—and indeed the whole enemy entity—is pursued in a radically different way. Instead of cumulative destruction, the desired process is systemic disruption—where the "system" may be the whole array of armed forces, some fraction thereof, or indeed technical systems pure and simple.

In general terms, attrition requires that strength be applied against strength. The enemy too must be strong when and where he comes under attack, since a concentration of targets is required to ensure efficiency in the application of effort. By contrast, the starting point of relational-maneuver is precisely the *avoidance* of the enemy's strength, to be followed by the application of some selective strength against a known dimension (physical or psychological) of enemy weakness. While attrition is a quasi-physical process so that fixed proportionalities will govern the relationship between the effort expended and the results achieved, relational-maneuver by contrast does not guarantee any level of results (being capable of failing totally). But neither is it constrained by any proportional ceiling between the effort made and the maximal results that may be achieved. It is because of this nonproportionality that relational-maneuver methods are compulsory for the side weaker in resources, which simply cannot prevail by attrition. But if relational-maneuver methods offer the possibility of much higher payoffs than those of attrition they do so at a correspondingly higher risk of failure. And relational-maneuver solutions are apt to fail catastrophically—unlike attrition solutions which normally fail "gracefully," that is to say gradually.

The vulnerability of relational-maneuver methods to catastrophic failure reflects their dependence on the *precise* application of effort against correctly identified points of weakness. This in turn requires a close understanding of the inner workings of the "system" that is to be disrupted, whether the "system" is, say, a missile, in which case the knowledge needed has an exact technical character, or an entire army, where an understanding of its command ethos and operational propensities will be necessary. Somewhat loosely, one may characterize attrition methods as resource-based and relational-maneuver methods as knowledge-dependent. Both the high potential payoff of the latter, and also their vulnerability to catastrophic failure, derive from this same quality.

Since in any real-life warfare, both pure attrition and pure relational-maneuver are very rare phenomena, what matters is the content of each phenomenon in the overall action, whether that is as narrow as a single tactical episode, or as broad as national style of warfare or some war preparation activity, such as the development of weapons.

Both attrition and relational-maneuver are still perhaps most familiar in the form of ground warfare. Certainly the most vivid comparison is provided by the contrasting images of the trench battles of World War I on the one hand—symmetrical brute force engagements not far removed from pure attrition—and the great encirclement battles of the 1939-1942 Blitzkrieg period on the other, warfare characterized by low-casualty, high-risk actions. Or to show equal contrast in one national army, in one war and in a single theater of operations, the theater-scale disruptive maneuver of MacArthur's Inchon landing may be compared with the cumulative firepower engagements of General Ridgeway's offensives.

It is to be recognized, however, that both attrition and relational-maneuver are universal phenomena, which pervade all aspects and all forms of war and war preparation. This can be illustrated by a number of direct comparisons, a sample of which are shown in Table 6.1.

Both attrition and relational-maneuver will be present in all real-life contexts, such that different national (or service) styles of warfare will be distinguished by the proportion of each mode in the overall spectrum, rather than by the theoretical alternatives in pure form.

Having thus suggested the universality of the phenomenon, one may focus on the attrition/maneuver spectrum in ground warfare without fear that relational-maneuver will be confused with mere movement, or indeed that attrition itself will be understood only in its narrowest tactical form of a straight exchange of firepower.

One may usefully begin to give concrete definition to the concepts here defined by way of two examples, one well-worn and the other somewhat less familiar, one offensive in strategic orientation and the other defensive, but both examples of *operational* schemes of warfare with low attrition content: The deep-penetration armor-driven offensive of the classic German Blitzkrieg, and the contemporary Finnish defense-in-depth for Lappland.

THE BLITZKRIEG EXAMPLE

The classic German Blitzkrieg of 1939-1942 was an operational scheme designed to exploit the potential of armored fighting vehicles, motor transport and tactical airpower against front-wide linear defenses. Three phases of the overall actions can be distinguished: the initial breakthrough, the penetrations, and the "exploitation."

In the breakthrough stage, axes of passage were opened through the (linear) defenses of the enemy by fairly conventional frontal attacks (and the Germans did so in World War II largely with foot infantry and horse-drawn artillery), but these attacks were focused on enemy forces holding selected, and narrow, segments of the front. The "relational" element of this stage was visible only at the theater level, insofar as soft points could freely be selected for attack (since the immediate areas behind the breakthrough points were of no particular significance in themselves).

The tactical battles fought at the front were not an end in themselves but merely a pre-condition for the next phase. Hence, neither the planning effort nor high value forces were at all focused on this stage. So long as the mobile columns spearheaded by the (scarce) tank forces could gain entry into the depth behind the front, it hardly mattered

Table 6.1
Attrition vs. Relational-Maneuver

	Attrition	Relational-Maneuver
Methods of Target Planning in Strategic Nuclear Warfare	Incapacitate enemy society by destroying high percentage of all industry and all population by the least variable of kill effects (e.g., blast rather than weather-dependent heat).	Incapacitate enemy political-military system by destroying political and military command centers and organizational headquarters; destroy selected critical war-fighting and recovery facilities (e.g., industrial bottlenecks *viz.* straight floorspace). Rely on fine-tuned kill effects.
Deployments of Ground Forces at the Theater Level	Deploy standard-format general-purpose forces to match total computed enemy capability. Freely rotate command, staff, and formations between different theaters.	Deploy theater - specialized formations configured especially to exploit the weaknesses of the particular enemy forces in each theater on a long-term basis, with in-theater promotion.
Methods of War Preparation, Research and Development Goals	Develop "best possible" systems to maximize all-round capabilities; hence develop systems *ab initio* to minimize design constraints. Hence long time-lags between generations, and broad changes needed in supporting maintenance structures upon introduction. Thus, only *major* advances can justify development efforts; hence the state of the art must be advanced. Because of long time lags between design and introduction, there will be only a coincidental correspondence between the systems so acquired and the specific configuration of combat needs upon deployment. Engineering priorities lead to revolutionary innovation, from time to time. Final design determined by limits of engineering feasibility and costs.	Examine in detail the relevant enemy forces and weapons. Identify specific limitations and weaknesses. Develop or modify equipment to obtain fine-tuning of capabilities against those forces and weapons. Modify and develop incrementally to maintain a "good fit" as enemy forces also evolve. Since new items are introduced at short intervals, accept design constraints to ensure compatibility (inter-equipment and also with supporting structures). No need to force advances on the state of the art. Create a continuum between in-theater modifications and the central development process.

what happened in the frontal area itself. This in turn allowed the command to choose the break-in points opportunistically, thus already achieving an advantage over a defender whose command remained focused on the tactical battles at the front. The eventual reward of successful defense against any one breakthrough attempt would be encirclement and capture once the next phase was executed anyway, through some other breakthrough points.

In the penetration phase, the goal of each mobile column was to advance as fast as possible, eventually to intersect at nodal points deep behind the front, there to cut off the corresponding sections of the frontal defenses.

In a tactical view, the long thin columns of vehicles penetrating through hostile territory were very weak, seemingly highly vulnerable to attacks on their flanks. Tactically, the columns were of course all flank and no "front." But in an operational view, the mobile columns of penetration were very strong, because their whole orientation and their method of warfare gave them a great advantage in tempo and reaction time. Most important, the columns were able to maintain a ceaseless forward movement since they could proceed opportunistically, moving down whatever roads offered least resistance. By contrast, such forces of the defense more capable of organized movement would have to find and intercept the invasion columns, and would thus need to go in specific directions along particular routes, failing in their mission if delayed by the frictions of war or by enemy flank-guard forces that cut across their path.

This strictly mechanical advantage was usually dominated by a command advantage. While the invasion forces did not need detailed instructions—being sufficiently guided by General Mission Orders and by tactical opportunism along the axes of advance—the action of the mobile forces of the defense depended on a command adequately informed of the shape of the unfolding battle. But this was a thing most difficult to achieve; the advance of the invasion columns would in itself generate much more "noise" than signals. Typically, the victims of the Bitzkrieg were left only with the choice of paralysis or potential gross error in "reading" the battle. Flooded with reports of enemy sightings across the entire width of the front and in considerable depth as well, the defending commanders either chose to wait for "the dust to settle" (i.e., paralysis) or else they sent off their mobile forces in chase of the sightings that seemed most credible and whose direction seemed most dangerous. In a situation characterized by the multiplicity of signals thrown out by the high tempo of armor-driven invasion columns, the chances of sorting out the data from the confusion were small indeed.

Moreover, the offense had the advantage of moving vertically across a front organized horizontally, and its advance would therefore cut lines of communication (LOCs), occupy successive nodal points in the road network, and not infrequently overrun command centers, thus further immobilizing the defenders.

These three factors in combination resulted in a net advantage for the offense in the intelligence decision-action cycle, the decisive factor in all forms of *reciprocal* maneuver.[1] So long as the invasion columns kept up a high tempo of operations, their apparent tactical vulnerability was dominated by their operational advantage since the defender's intercepting and blocking actions would always be one step behind.

A closer look at the process reveals that it was deception that provided security for the main thrusts of penetration, which were hidden in the multiplicity of movements generated by flank-guard columns, side-rails, and "abandoned spurs" in the opportunistic flow of the advance. Actually, deception was inherent to the mode of operations. A successful resistance at any one roadblock would be reported as a victory by the defense and indeed it was, but only at the *tactical* level. Operationally, resistance was made irrelevant, as the invasion columns ultimately bypassed such points.

In the "exploitation" phase, effects purely physical were compounded (and usually dominated) by the psychological effects of the penetrations, and the resulting envelopments. The bulk of the defending forces still holding the front in between the narrow axes of penetration would begin to receive reports of LOCs cut, rear headquarters fallen and famous towns to their rear overrun. At the command level, this precipitated attempts to carry out remedial actions still within the initial conceptual framework of the defense, i.e. attempts to execute "orderly withdrawals" in order to reconstitute a linear front beyond the maximum depth of enemy penetration. But that line of frontal reconstitution receded ever deeper as the invasion columns continued on their way. "Orderly withdrawal" soon acquired the character of a rearward race (with the abandonment of heavy weapons etc.). Since in 1939—1942 large, infantry-heavy forces were trying to race against small armor mobile forces, the defense, Polish, French, or Russian, could not win the race. This in turn demoralized the commanders, since even "correct" action was soon shown to be futile. And of course among the troops the abandonment of frontal defenses still intact and often entirely unattacked, news of well-known places behind the front already fallen to the enemy, and finally the actual mechanics of the rearward race (including logistic insufficiency) easily had catastrophic morale effects—not uncommonly leading to the outright disintegration of units.[2]

The exploitation phase culminated in double envelopments with a final stage of annihilation—when the foot infantry, now advancing across the abandoned frontage, finally came to grips with the fragmented forces of the defense trapped within the encirclements.

Since the attrition content of the entire action was low (and indeed almost entirely limited to the breakthrough phase) the decisive level was the *operational*. The power of the Blitzkrieg was not conditioned by the weight of resources employed, and not at all by the firepower of the forces involved; it derived rather from the method of command, from the all mobile organization of some formations, and from the training, all of which endowed the offense with a systematic advantage in the observation-decision-action cycle. Had the Germans encountered a defender itself superior in the tempo of operations, the tactical weakness of their advancing columns would then have become an operational weakness also, with fatal consequences since: 1) the defending forces on either side of the breakthrough sectors could have "flowed" sideways to close off breakthroughs faster than the enemy could act to keep them open, and 2) the mobile forces of the defense could have intercepted or actually ambushed the invasion columns, thus capitalizing on the inherent tactical weakness of forces which are all flank and no front.[3]

The Elements of the Blitzkrieg Style

Though the following analysis is confined to the operational level,[4] it suffices to illustrate the essential principles involved in the relational-maneuver method of warfare that distinguished the Blitzkrieg:

The Main Strength of the Enemy is Avoided as Much as Possible.   In the breakthrough phase, avoidance is manifest at the theater level in the fact that only a small fraction of the total frontage is attacked in serious fashion, to break open gaps through which the penetration columns can pass. Hence the overall numerical relationship between the total force of the offense employed in the breakthrough attempt, and the total defending force holding the full frontage, is irrelevant to the outcome. Avoidance is mainfest at the operational level in the fact that recognized "strategic" locations are not attacked, the selected points of attempted breakthrough being rather those which happen to be least well-defended (with the proviso that subsequent deep penetrations should be possible from those points). Avoidance is manifest at the tactical level, in the use of "rolling out" tactics to minimize frontal engagements as much as possible. In the penetration phase on the other hand, the salient form of avoidance is tactical: cross-country movement and all the flexibility of opportunism in the detailed routing are exploited to avoid islands of resistance, which are to be by-passed rather than reduced or even encircled.

Deception Is of Central Importance at every Phase. The breakthrough phase presumes successful deception. While the wedging and "rolling out" attacks are launched against selected narrow segments of the frontage, the bulk of the defensive forces along the unattacked frontage must be prevented from moving towards the intended breakthrough axes by feints and demonstrations all along the front, to mask the real foci of attack. Alternatively, where multiple breakthroughs are attempted, deception can be retroactive insofar as costly persistence is avoided, and whichever breakthroughs are successful are then exploited. Either way, success absolutely requires that the defending command remain in a state of uncertainty. This cannot be achieved by mere secrecy since the maximum period of immunity (even assuming perfect security) could not then extend beyond the outbreak of hostilities. In practice, this elevates the deception plan to full equality with the battle plan; certainly deception planning cannot remain a mere afterthought.

In the penetration phase, deception is inherent in the mode of operation. Unless the advancing columns of penetration move with sufficient speed and directional unpredictability to be masked by confusion, they must be highly vulnerable to attacks on their flanks. While it must be assumed that the progressive advance of the invasion columns will be reported, such "signals" will be masked by the "noise" of the multiplicity of sightings mentioned above. If the signal-to-noise ratio is high, and the defenders can therefore develop a more or less coherent picture of the situation (and do not lose their nerve) then the thin columns of penetration will be as vulnerable operationally as they are tactically.

In the exploitation phase, deception is embodied in the process whereby the columns of penetration cut off and encircle enemy forces that can be much larger than themselves; by then the enemy must be reduced to an incoherent mass (cf. the 1941 battles of encirclement in the Ukraine). The most complete achievement of *systemic disruption* is manifest in the final round-up stage of such battles of encirclement, when the ratio of prisoners of war to captors may be very high indeed. By that stage conventional Order of Battle comparisons between the two sides have lost all meaning. It is obvious that such successes cannot be achieved against an undeceived enemy. Even at a fairly late stage of disintegration, the victim forces could regroup in improvised fashion to defeat the encirclement if they had certain knowledge of a highly favorable force ratio.

The Intangibles Dominate. Momentum dominates other priorities (e.g. firepower capacity and lethality). Even in the breakthrough stage, the "rolling out" must quickly follow the "wedging," for otherwise the forces engaged in the latter become vulnerable to flank attacks. In fact, the breakthrough as a whole must be accomplished rapidly, because otherwise the defense will have the opportunity to redeploy its forces to secure the segments of the frontage under attack—or at least to hold the shoulders firmly. The columns of penetration in turn must pass through as soon as their way is open in order to begin their disruptive process before the defense can react. In fact, the whole operation obviously rests on the ceaseless maintenance of momentum. Organizationally, this implies a very restricted deployment of heavier/slower elements and especially artillery. Even with self-propelled artillery, the need to keep the supply tail light and fast moving will restrict the amount that can usefully be deployed. Tactically, the imperative of momentum will downgrade the importance of accuracy (for lethality) in such firepower as is employed. With the artillery, it is suppressive rather than physically destructive firepower that is wanted. And the same applies to the small-arms firepower of the infantry, the troops being trained for suppressive fire with automatic weapons, rather than for the slow-paced delivery of aimed shots. Technically, this in turn results in a requirement for combat vehicles from which infantry can fire on the move.

It is in the exploitation phase that the importance of force-ratios as such declines to its lowest point, while the importance of sheer momentum is supreme. Accordingly, a progressive thinning down of the advancing columns is preferable to the more deliberate pace that full sustainability across the geographic depth would require. It is not uncommon for the battle to end with the victors depleted and exhausted, their strength reduced to very little at the culminating moment, and in the climactic place of the battle, i.e., where the encirclement pincers close. At that time, in that place, the forces of the offense are quite likely to amount to a congerie of improvised battle groups and assorted subunits that happen to have reached that far. The implied renunciation of full-force sustainability and formation integrity stands in sharp contrast to the principles of war upheld by attrition-oriented armies (cf. "unity of command" in the U.S. Army).

It is clear that the three operational principles here discussed (avoidance, deception, and the dominance of the intangible momentum) are all interrelated, and indeed their connection is the true essence of all offensive operational methods of warfare that have a high relational-maneuver content. First, the ability to apply "localized or specialized" strengths against the enemy's array of forces implies reciprocally that the enemy's own strength is successfully avoided. That in turn can only be done by deception, since it is only a barrier of ignorance that can prevent the enemy from coming to grips with the attacking forces. Deception in turn can only be sustained if the whole operation has a momentum that exceeds the speed of the intelligence-decision-action cycle of the defending forces. Any one deception scheme must be highly perishable, so that the barrier of ignorance can only be preserved if rapid-paced operations generate deceptive impulses faster than they are exposed as such. It is because of this interrelationship that the decisive level of warfare in the relational-maneuver manner is the operational, that being the lowest level at which avoidance, deception, and the dominance of momentum can be brought together within an integrated scheme of warfare.

THE FINNISH EXAMPLE

The Blitzkrieg was offensive strategically, as well as during most tactical phases. It was dependent on the use of armor (even if not at all on any superiority in armor capabilities as such). And of course it was an historical episode repeatable only in special circumstances (e.g. the Sinai fighting of 1967). The Finnish operational method for the defense of the Lappland is by contrast strategically defensive, and tactically defensive also in most respects. It is based on the assumption that no armor at all will be available to the defense. Finally, it is a contemporary scheme theoretically reproducible in a wide variety of circumstances, subject only to availability of expendable space. These dramatic contrasts make the parallelism of operational principles between the Finnish method and the Blitzkrieg all the more persuasive evidence of their universality.

Avoidance of the Enemy's Main Strength

At the level of national strategy, this principle is manifest in the whole conduct of Finnish external policy. Soviet power is deflected by a conciliatory foreign policy. But to set limits on the degree of obedience that Moscow can exact, Finnish policy exploits the "Nordic Balance" in which Soviet pressure on Finland is inhibited by the expectation that it would evoke an increased level of NATO activity in Norway, and a proportionate adjustment in the Swedish alignment towards NATO. It follows at the level of theater strategy that the Finnish contribution to the Nordic Balance by the defense of the invasion corridors to Norway and Sweden is more important than the defense of the major Finnish population centers in the southern part of the country. Hence the most reliably powerful of Soviet capabilities, i.e., to invade the well-roaded south and to bomb Finnish cities, are virtually unopposed. It is the Nordic equilibrium that would deny to the Soviet Union the full strategic advantage of an invasion. Even with Finland conquered, Sweden's adherence to NATO would weaken the overall Baltic position of the Soviet Union. On the other hand, Finnish compliance with Soviet foreign policy desiderata pre-empts intimidation based on the capability of destroying Finnish cities. This then leaves Finnish theater strategy with a task that is much more manageable than either a defense of the south against invasion, or of the cities against air attack—that is resistance against an invasion across the largely uninhabited and mostly roadless Lappland. Even there, the task is not really to *deny* passage to Soviet forces but merely to *delay* them up to a point, and weaken them as much as possible, in order to enhance correspondingly the defensive potential of the Norwegian and Swedish forces in the North.

At the operational level, avoidance is manifest in the form of deployment of the defense, and in its mode of action. Far from trying to set up anti-invasion barriers near the border to intercept Soviet invasion columns as soon as they cross, no firm barriers are to be set up at all on the invasion routes leading to Norway and Sweden. Instead Finnish forces are to operate on either side of the invasion routes, to attack advancing Soviet columns on their flanks after side-stepping their frontal thrusts. Since the Finns can have neither effective air cover from their small air force, nor ground-based anti-aircraft defenses of great value, their protection against air attack must come from dispersal and camouflage. Dispersed Finnish forces arrayed in depth from the Soviet border across the full width of the country are to attack Soviet columns by a variety of hit and run methods, including a multiplicity of raids mounted from whatever cover is available, ambushes where practical, non-persistent mortar and artillery fires, and so on.

At the tactical level, avoidance is manifest in the fact that the tank and mechanized elements of Soviet invasion columns will not be the main target of Finnish attacks. The major efforts of the defenders will instead be concentrated against supply trucks, artillery trains, and support units—all of which can be attacked effectively without need of ATGMs, or other high-grade anti-armor weapons. In this way, even if Soviet tank and mechanized elements can reach the Norwegian and/or Swedish borders intact, they will do so with their combat-support elements weakened and their supply columns depleted.

Deception

At the operational level, deception is inherent in the structure of the Finnish forces to be deployed in the North. Large and highly visible formations of brigade and divisional size will only be deployed on the southern fringe of the trans-Lappland invasion routes, ostensibly to provide a local defense for the small towns in the area, and chiefly Rovaniemi. The main effort on the other hand, will be mounted by far less visible company sized and smaller units detached from the larger formations, and also by *Sissi* raiding teams (trained by the Frontier Guards) which may operate beyond the Soviet border. The more visible formations of the Finnish deployment will not therefore seem threatening or indeed relevant to the Soviet forces, for which any operation mounted southwards from the invasion routes would be a diversion of effort without strategic meaning.

At the tactical level also, deception will be a necessary part of each combat action. Since Soviet invasion columns will routinely provide flank guards for the "soft" elements following in the van of each armored/mechanized contingent, each Finnish tactical action must be based on two separate elements: a diversionary move, to distract the relevant flank-guard elements, and the attack proper. In a company-sized action for example, one platoon might open fire from a safe distance on the soft elements of a Soviet invasion column to attract the attention of the corresponding flank-guard forces. As soon as the latter move towards the scene, the diversionary platoon will retreat to evade their counterattack while the rest of the Finnish force attacks the now unguarded "soft" elements. Finnish forces will then break off the engagement as soon as possible, to seek safety in dispersal and any cover before regrouping to launch the next action. Similarly, the Finns cannot just mount ambushes against the invasion columns, for any ambush astride the main invasion routes would quickly be defeated by the intervention of Soviet armed helicopter elements and/or artillery fires along with direct attacks. Ambushing actions therefore require that lesser Soviet contingents (and chiefly flank-guard units) be lured into prepared killing grounds by some prior attack against the main columns, followed by a deliberate, enticing retreat. In a battalion-level action for example, a Finnish company may attack the soft elements of a Soviet invasion column, wait until flank-guard detachments arrive on the scene and then retreat from the invasion axis, allowing the Soviet detachments to pursue it until the place of ambush is reached, where the rest of the battalion intervenes.

Dominance of the Intangibles

At the level of theater strategy, the Finnish purpose is to weaken as much as possible the Soviet invasion forces without, however, engaging in costly battles against an enemy so vastly superior in heavy weapons. Hence the imperative of elusiveness. This, incidentally, explains the Finns' lack of interest in the acquisition of modern armor (which the Soviet Union offers to Finland at very reasonable prices) or much modern artillery (Tampella itself produces an excellent 155mm gun-howitzer—mainly for export), or even anti-tank missiles. Only less visible and fully portable weapons (small arms, rocket launchers and light mortars) are compatible with the principle of elusiveness that runs through the theater strategy, the operational method and the tactics. (Even TOW, the principal U.S. anti-tank weapon, presumes motor or helicopter transport; it is not truly man-portable.) Thus the solitary Finnish armored brigade (equipped with Soviet tanks and BTR-50 and BTR-60 combat carriers) is not the nucleus of an armored force eventually to be acquired, nor the tool of a quixotic intent to fight armor with armor, but rather a *training* unit that mimics the potential adversary's war-fighting behavior, used very much in the manner of the USAF's "aggressor" squadrons.

At the tactical level, the small but important *Sissi* elements would fight as outright guerillas with a special emphasis on offensive demolitions while the rest of the Finnish forces would fight as light infantry, using strike/withdraw routines with a heavy emphasis on the tactical use of expedient minefields, to the extent that mines remain available.

CONCLUSION

So very different in all other respects, the two examples here reviewed share one fundamental thing in common. In both cases, the genesis of the military ideas involved was a recognition that material weakness would ensure the defeat of any symmetrical application of forces. In the German case, the front-piercing Blitzkrieg was the alternative to the *materialschlacht* on elongated fronts that Germany could not win, if only because blockade would progressively erode the industrial strength of a Germany poorly endowed with raw materials. In the Finnish case, the gross imbalance in military power is such that Finnish forces can only provide a limited war-fighting capacity, in a limited part of the national territory, even when the methods used entail a degree of avoidance which approaches that of outright guerilla warfare. (In normal guerilla conflict, however, war protracted in time substitutes for depth, whereas in the Finnish case the operational dimension is still geographic depth.)

A sense of material superiority by contrast inspires quite other military ideas and allows other priorities to surface. In the American case historically the goal has been to accelerate the evolution of any conflict with maximal mobilization of the economy for the fastest possible build-up of forces sustainable against the largest concentrations of enemy forces possible, to maximize the overall rate of attrition. A broad-front advance theater strategy directly followed from this, if only because the broader the advance, the greater is the usable transport capacity on the ground. Therefore the larger the force that is deployable, the greater its attritive capacity. At the operational level—a level not at all important in this style of warfare—little more was needed than to coordinate the tactical actions which in turn were simple in nature, consisting mainly of frontal attacks.

The principles of avoidance and deception have not been absent in this style of warfare historically, but they were largely confined to the level of theater strategy. For example, the selection of Normandy for the opening of a second front was of course a most notable example of avoidance and deception. But the selection of Northwest France itself contradicted the principle of avoidance—which would have favored other places offering greater outflanking opportunities, e.g. southern France or, better still, the Balkans. At the operational and tactical levels on the other hand, avoidance and deception have been little used, since they stand in direct conflict with the imperative of maximizing the application of force upon the enemy's array. The aim was not to obtain high payoffs at low cost, but rather to obtain *reliable* payoffs on the largest possible scale.

The principle of momentum was manifest only at the highest level of all, the level of grand strategy, whence came insistent pressures for quick results. It was certainly incompatible with broad-front advance theater strategies, which of necessity result in a gradual progression, rather than in rapid penetrations. Nor was momentum compatible with operational methods that amounted to little more than the alignment of tactical actions—or with the tactics. A pattern of schematically predictable frontal attacks would naturally result in gradual step-by-step sequence of forward movement, sustained attack, regroupment, resupply and reinforcement, and then more forward movement, and so on. At both the operational and tactical levels, the goal of maximizing attritive results stands in direct contradiction with the maintenance of momentum; if the integrity of formations must be preserved to maximize the efficiency of firepower production, the speed of the action cannot exceed the rate of forward movement which the artillery and its ammunition supply can sustain. By contrast, in rapid-paced actions, opportunistic routing is *de rigueur* and the breakdown of formations into *ad hoc* battle groups is virtually routine, so that a progressive decline in the volume of sustainable firepower must be accepted. This is a natural consequence of rapid penetrations in depth, if only because "soft" supply vehicles cannot follow in large numbers until enemy resistance ends.

Of late, as a result of the experiences of Korea and Vietnam, a "short-war" imperative has emerged as far as Third World involvements are concerned, on the presumption that the contemporary American political system cannot sustain prolonged conflict. To the extent that the short-war imperative is accepted, a serious problem emerges, for it conflicts with a military style that precludes the very methods that can produce quick results. In this regard, the American military mindset, still firmly rooted in attrition methods, is *not* congruent with what has become an accepted political imperative. Nevertheless, far from inspiring any structural change, the poor fit between the political imperatives and the military style of preference has not even been recognized.

Worse, it also appears that the American military mindset is not congruent with the European military balance either. In the Central European theater of NATO, U.S. ground forces are still deployed to implement pure attrition tactics which presume a net material superiority (or more precisely, a net superiority in firepower production). The expected enemy, however, is in fact superior in firepower capacity overall, and would most likely achieve even greater superiorities at the actual points of contact, where its column thrusts would collide with the elongated NATO frontage. Current tactics must virtually guarantee defeat against a materially superior enemy, since strength is to be applied against strength in a direct attritive exchange.

Given the defensive orientation imposed by the grand strategy of the NATO alliance, only some relational-maneuver operational method based on the principles of avoidance (to side-step the major Soviet thrusts), deception (to mask the defenses), elusiveness (in small scale counterattacks) and momentum (on the counterstroke) would offer some hope of victory, although with considerable risks. On the other hand, it is also true that the politically-imposed theater strategy of Forward Defense precludes the adoption of the only operational methods that would offer some opportunity to prevail over a materially more powerful enemy.

NOTES

1. Parade ground infantry drill (right-turn/left-turn) preserves in symbolic form what was once a crucial attainment in the maneuver of foot forces.
2. In the German Blitzkrieg of 1939-1942, the particular form of the employment of the

Luftwaffe had its own powerful morale effects. Since the air-to-ground potential was used selectively in great concentration (*viz.* diffuse interdiction efforts) troops witnessing the intensive dive bombing of scattered points would form a grossly inflated conception of the power of the *Luftwaffe*.

3. That is indeed what happened in the Golan Heights during the 1973 war from the fourth day of the war, when the Israelis were able to outmaneuver the powerful but slower Syrian tank columns and—in more spectacular fashion—were later able to ambush the second Iraqi division sent into combat.

4. The two most important tactics involved in the Blitzkrieg operational method were: at the breakthrough stage, wedging and "rolling out," where concentric attacks by infantry-artillery forces open the way for shallow penetrations by more agile infantry which then widens the initial passage by attacks on the flanks; and, in the penetration phase, the use of light-armor and motorized (including motorcycle) elements as "precursors," to trigger ambushes and to "develop" islands of resistance, so that the tank units can directly by-pass them without delay.

Chapter 7

Deterrence and Perception

Robert Jervis

INTRODUCTION

In the most elemental sense, deterrence depends on perceptions. But unless people are totally blind, we need not be concerned with the logical point that if one actor's behavior is to influence another, it must be perceived. Rather what is important is that actors' perceptions often diverge both from "objective reality" (or later scholars' perceptions of it, which is as good a measure as we can have) and from the perceptions of other actors. These differences, furthermore, both randomly and systematically influence deterrence. Unless statesmen understand the ways in which their opposite numbers see the world, their deterrence policies are likely to misfire; unless scholars understand the patterns of perceptions involved, they will misinterpret the behavior.

A nice example shows that the problem extends both to perceptions of third parties as well as to main adversaries and underlines the way in which attempts at deterrence can not only fail but backfire if assumptions about others' perceptions are incorrect. In order to mobilize British assistance in the American-Japanese political conflict of 1907-1908, President Theodore Roosevelt sought to portray the situation as quite tense. He expected that Britain would then aid him by restraining

Japan. Unfortunately, and contrary to the President's assumption, the British perceptions of both him and the Japanese differed from his. "The British felt it was Washington, not Tokyo, which stood in need of a warning." As George William Hardinge, the permanent Under-Secretary at the Foreign Office, put it: "The President is playing a very dangerous game, and it is fortunate that he has such cool-headed people as the Japanese to deal with."[1] Thus rather than moving Britain closer to the United States, as Roosevelt expected, his actions made that country less willing to cooperate in opposing Japan.

In light of this, one might expect that statesmen would pay careful attention to how others perceive them. In fact, this usually is not the case. While they are aware that determining others' intentions and predicting others' behavior is difficult, they generally believe that their own intentions—especially when they are not expansionist—are clear. As a result, they rarely try to see the world and their own actions through their adversary's eyes,[2] although doing so would be to their advantage. If a policy is to have the desired impact on its target, it must be perceived as it is intended;[3] if the other's behavior is to be anticipated and the state's policy is a major influence on it, then the state must try to determine how its actions are being perceived. One would think, therefore, that every government would establish an office responsible for reconstructing the other's view of the world and that every policy paper would have a section that analyzed how the alternative policies would be seen by significant audiences. One theme of this essay is that the failure to undertake this task—and I do not mean to imply that it would be easy to accomplish—explains many cases of policy failure. It is hard to find cases of even mild international conflict in which both sides fully grasp the other's views. Yet all too often statesmen assume that their opposite numbers see the world as they see it, fail to devote sufficient resources to determining whether this is actually true, and have much more confidence in their beliefs about the other's perceptions than the evidence warrants.

One actor deters another by convincing him that the expected value of a certain action is outweighed by the expected punishment. The latter is composed of two elements: the perceived cost of the punishments that the actor can inflict and the perceived probabilities that he will inflict them. Deterrence can misfire if the two sides have different beliefs about either factor.

WHAT CONSTITUTES HARM?

Judging what constitutes harm is generally easier to do than estimating whether threats will be carried out, but even here there is room for differences that can undermine deterrence. On occasion, what one person thinks is a punishment, another may consider a reward. The model is Br'er Rabbit. While few cases in international politics are as clear as this, Teddy Roosevelt's threat to intervene in the Cuban internal conflict of 1903 comes close. He declared that if American property was raided in the course of the fightng, he would have to send in troops. Unfortunately, both factions believed that American intervention would work in their favor and busily set to work harassing Americans and their property.[4]

One could not have coerced Pol Pot by threatening to destroy his cities, and a similar, if less extreme, point lies behind some of current U.S. strategic policy. As Secretary of Defense Brown argued, the U.S. must "take full account of the fact [sic] that the things highly valued by the Soviet leadership appear to include not only the lives and prosperity of the peoples of the Soviet Union, but the military, industrial and political sources of power of the regime itself."[5] This requires targeting the army, internal security forces, and the Communist Party. A related argument is that the Soviet leaders are ethnic Russians who care about maintaining the dominance of Great Russia and who would be deterred by the threat to attack it but spare other areas of the USSR, thereby enabling the other nationalities to rise up and either gain their independence or dominate the post-war state. Without endorsing the answers he provides, one can completely agree with Brown's argument that "our strategy has to be aimed at what the Soviets think is important to them, not just what we might think would be important to them."[6] But this kind of analysis must be carried all the way, not stopped at a point convenient to the analyst's political predilections. To argue that the Russians could be deterred by threatening to destroy the party and internal security forces implies not only that these instruments are needed to maintain Communist rule, but also that the Soviet leaders realize this. This may be correct, but if they believe what they say, they will think the regime enjoys the support of the population and so might conclude that the party would regenerate after the war. American leaders do not think that the destruction of the state apparatus in a war would permanently end democracy; would the Soviets have so little faith in their regime that they would lack comparable beliefs?

As we have seen, threats of coercive war can misfire if the state does not understand what the other values. Threats to use brute force do not involve this pitfall, but they require the state to determine how its adversary evaluates the military balance—how it estimates who would win a war. This issue arose in the 1930s as British leaders debated how to deter Hitler. Some felt that "economic stability"—which required that military spending be kept relatively low—contributed to this goal. "The maintenance of our economic stability . . . [could] be described as an essential element in our defence system . . . without which purely military effort would be of no avail . . . . Nothing operates more strongly to deter a potential aggressor from attacking this country than our stability . . . . This reputation stands us in good stead, and causes other countries to rate our power of resistance at something far more formidable than is implied merely by the number of men of war, aeroplanes and battalions which we should have at our disposal immediately on the outbreak of war. But were other countries to detect in us signs of strain, this deterrent would at once be lost."[7] On the other hand, Churchill stressed the need for larger military forces. "An immense British army cast into the scales" was a great deterrent "and one of the surest bulwarks of peace," he said.[8] Neither side in the argument, however, tried as hard as it might have to learn exactly how Hitler saw the world and what sort of configuration of forces might have deterred him.

Deterrence can also be undercut if the aggressor does not understand the kind of war which the status quo state is threatening to wage. Japan had no doubt that the United States would fight if it attacked Pearl Harbor. But many Japanese leaders thought that the stakes for the United States were not sufficiently high to justify an all-out effort and that the United States would instead fight a limited war and, being unable to prevail at that level of violence, would agree to a settlement giving Japan control of East Asia. Similarly, Hitler expected Britain and France to fight in September 1939 but doubted that they would continue to do so after Poland was defeated. Britain especially, he believed, had sufficient common interest with Germany to conclude a peace treaty after limited hostilities. In neither case did either side understand the other's beliefs or values. Indeed the German and Japanese perceptions of their opponents would have seemed to the latter so out of touch with reality as to hardly deserve consideration. British and American statesmen knew their own outlooks so well that they thought it obvious that others knew them also. To have recognized that alternative views were possible would have implied that their self-images were not unambiguously correct and that their past behavior might be interpreted as indicating a willingness to sacrifice friends and agree to less than honorable settlements.

Becaues Britain, France, and the United States did not understand the other side's expectations, their deterrence strategies could not be effective. Their task was not only to convince their adversaries they would fight if pushed too far, but also that they would continue to fight even after initial reverses.[9] Doing this would have been extremely difficult since it would have involved presenting evidence and making commitments about how they would behave a few years later under grave circumstances. But had the statesmen been aware of the German and Japanese perceptions, they might have at least made some efforts.

For example, Roosevelt could have stressed the American tradition of vacillating between isolation and extreme involvement in international politics, of seeing the world in Manichean terms, of fighting only unlimited wars. Chamberlain might have done better explaining why he had abandoned appeasement, why Britain could not allow any power to dominate the continent, and why Britain would have no choice but to resist even if the military situation was bleak. Similarly, throughout the 1960s the United States misjudged how much North Vietnam valued reunification and believed that its threat to fight a prolonged war and inflict very heavy punishment on the North[10] could dissuade the North from continuing its struggle. American decisionmakers paid a great deal of attention to how to make their threats credible, but their misjudgement led them to ignore what was actually the crucial problem—the North was willing to fight the sort of war the United States was threatening rather than concede. They might not have been able to solve the problem even had they been aware of it, but as it was they never even came to grips with it.

PERCEPTIONS OF CREDIBILITY

Misperceptions of what the target state values and fears probably are less important causes of deterrence failure than misperceptions of credibility. Conclusions are difficult to draw in this area, however. Although many arguments about deterrence turn on questions involving credibility, scholars know remarkably little about how these judgments are formed and altered. For example, how context-bound are these estimates? Obviously the credibility of a threat is strongly influenced by the specific situation in which it is issued. The threat to go to war in response to a major provocation could be credible when the threat to so respond to a minor insult would not. But there also is a component of credibility that inheres in the threatener, not the situation. In the same situation, one country's threat can be credible where another's would not be. Part of this difference of course comes from the country's strength, its ability to carry out the threat, and its ability to defend against the other's response. But there's more to it than this. Some states have reputations for being bolder, more resolute, and more reckless than others. That is, states are seen to differ in the price they are willing to pay to achieve a given goal. But it is not clear how these reputations are established and maintained, or how important they are compared to the other influences on credibility; we cannot predict with great assurance how given behavior (e.g., refusing to change one's position on an issue) will influence others' expectations of how the state will act in the future.

To start with, does reputation attach to the decisionmaker, the regime, or the country? If one president acts boldly, will other states' leaders draw inferences only about him or will they expect his successors to display similar resolve? After a revolution, do others think the slate has been wiped clean or does the reputation of the earlier regime retain some life? If one kind of regime (e.g., a capitalist democracy) displays willingness to run high risks, do others draw any inferences about the resolve of similar regimes? How fast do reputations decay?

On these points we have neither theoretically-grounded expectations nor solid evidence. In another area we at least can be guided by a good theory. One of the basic findings of cognitive psychology is that images change only slowly and are maintained in the face of discrepant information. This implies that trying to change a reputation for low resolve will be especially costly because statements and symbolic actions are not likely to be taken seriously. Only running what is obviously a high risk conflict, or engaging in a costly one, will suffice. On the other hand, a state with a reputation for standing firm not only will be able to win disputes by threatening to fight, but has the freedom to avoid confrontations without damaging its image. But these propositions, although plausible, still lack empirical evidence.

The question of the relative importance of beliefs about the state's general resolve as compared to the role of other factors is also impossible to answer with any precision. How much do states make overall judgments about the prices others are willing to pay, as opposed to looking primarily at the specific situation the others are in? In other words, how context-bound are estimates of how others will behave?[11] The debate over the validity of the domino theory reminds us both of the importance of this topic and the difficulty of coming to grips with it. If others were more impressed by America's eventual defeat in Vietnam than by the fact that the United States was willing to fight for years for a country of little intrinsic value, they would adjust downward their estimate of American resolve. But by how much? If there is another Berlin crisis, will the Vietnam-influenced reputation be as significant as others' judgments of Berlin's value to the United States? When the new situation closely resembles a previous one in which the actor displayed low resolve, others are likely to expect similar retreat.[12] But when the situation is very different, it is not clear whether a judgment of the state's overall resolve has much impact on others' predictions of its behavior.

Even when these questions are not hypothetical they are usually hard to answer, as is illustrated by the ambiguous nature of the events that followed the American defeat in Indochina. Has Russia drawn far-reaching inferences from the American retreat? Have the NATO allies lowered their estimates of the probatility that the United States would respond to Soviet pressure or military moves in Europe? Have the Third World countries come to see the United States as less reliable? Since 1975, the Soviets have taken a number of actions inimical to American interests, the Europeans have voiced doubts about the credibility of the U.S. promise to protect them, and Third World states have been quite troublesome. But these problems do not present a sharp break from the pre-Vietnam era. It is easy to attribute any behavior contrary to American wishes to the lack of resolve that some observers think the United States displayed in Indochina. But it is much harder to establish that this is a better explanation than local conditions or general trends, such as the increase of Soviet power.

We can turn this example around and ask about the impact of the U.S. attempt to rescue the hostages in Iran. Others probably have raised their estimates of the likelihood that the United States would respond similarly in other cases in which American citizens were taken prisoner. But have perceptions of American resolve to run risks in other kinds of situations been altered? One of the main arguments in favor of using force was that U.S. promises and threats would be more credible. But scant evidence supports this view. The cost the United States foresaw in this case was not Soviet intervention, but adverse Third World reaction. Would others expect the United States to act strongly in later situations when the costs to be incurred were of a very different kind? Others would draw such an inference if they employed the concept of "willingness to incur costs" or "propensity to act with boldness" as a homogeneous category. They might, of course, be correct to do so. The willingness to act in the face of Third World opinion might be linked to a willingness to defy the threat of a Soviet military response. But we know little about whether such global characterizations are possible or whether statesmen make them.

One can also ask whether the inference would have been different depending on whether the rescue mission had succeeded or had resulted in the death of the hostages. Ironically, our logic dictates that the impact on U.S. credibility would have been greater in the latter case than in the former. Had the hostages been killed, observers would probably have thought that the American leaders knew the operation was terribly risky. If they projected this pattern of risk-taking on to later events, they would conclude that the United States would act even when it might not succeed. By contrast, if force had succeeded and others assumed that the U.S. had been confident that this was going to be the result, they would not see the act as so bold. I admit this argument is strained, and indeed I doubt that observers would follow the train of reasoning I have presented. But this underscores the difficulty of determining the inferences people draw in these situations.

The crucial question is the degree to which observers make general judgments about others' credibility rather than basing their predictions largely on the nature of the specific situation and, if the situation is a continuing one, on the history of the other's behavior concerning it. To a significant extent, deterrence theory rests on the assumption that such general judgments are important. It is this which makes it both possible and necessary for a state to credibly threaten to react to an attack on an unimportant third country with a response involving greater costs than the intrinsic value of that third area. Such a threat can be credible because, by not responding, the state will not only lose the third country but also its reputation for protecting its interests, a reputation more valuable than the costs of fighting. By the same logic, this response is necessary because to fail to rise to the challenge is to lead others to doubt the state's willingness to pay costs to defend the rest of the status quo. Both prongs of this reasoning depend on actors making relatively context-free judgments of credibility.

Even if they do, the way in which these judgments are made can defeat significant aspects of the theory and practice of deterrence. When an actor either carries out or reneges on a threat, observers can make either or both of two kinds of inferences that will influence his future credibility. First, they may alter their estimate of what I have elsewhere called his signaling reputation—his reputation for doing what he says he will do.[13] The bargaining tactic of commitment, so well known in the deterrence literature, is supposed to be effective because the state increases its cost of retreating by staking its reputation on standing firm. But this tactic will work (and this explanation of actors' behavior will be appropriate) only if actors try to determine how likely it is that others will live up to their promises and threats rather than predicting their behavior solely on the basis of estimates of what they value and the prices they are willing to pay to reach various objectives. This is the second kind of inference actors draw from others' past behavior. It ignores statements and other signals that can be easily manipulated and looks only at whether the other stood firm, compromised, or retreated in the past, irrespective of what he said he would do. If this kind of inference is dominant, then signals of commitment have little impact.

To use Thomas Schelling's terms, actors would be able to issue warnings, but not threats.[14] This would mean that an actor could not deter others by symbolically committing himself to a course of action and staking his reputation on living up to his pledges.

Finally, an ironic possibility should be noted. A concern for reputation can lead states to act and draw inferences in a pattern opposite from the one that we—and most other analysts—imply. This is not to dispute the common starting point; states often refuse to back down not because of the immediate and direct costs of doing so, but because of the belief that a retreat will be seen as an indication of general weakness and so will lead others to expect future retreats. But the desire to counteract such undesired consequences may lead a state that has retreated on one issue to pay especially high costs to avoid defeat on the next one. Thus the United States was not only willing but anxious to use force to free the *Mayaguez* because it wanted to show others that its evacuation of Indochina did not mean it would not defend its other interests—the very consequence which it had predicted would follow from a defeat in Vietnam and which justified its participation in the war. If others understand this logic and expect states to behave in this way—to follow retreats with displays of firmness—then reputations for carrying out threats do not influence estimates of credibility because—to compound the paradox—reputations are so important that states must rebuild them when they are damaged. If you have been caught bluffing in poker, are others likely to call you in the next round in the belief that you bluff a lot or are they unlikely to do so because they think that you know it is no longer safe to bluff? To the extent that the latter is the case, perceptions of credibility are influenced by the state's recent behavior, but in a way which produces equilibrating negative feedback rather than the positive feedback of the domino dynamics.[15]

JUDGING THE ADVERSARY'S ALTERNATIVES

Deterrence works when the expected costs of challenging the status quo are greater than those of accepting it; deterrence may fail and defenders be taken by surprise not only if their threats are insufficiently credible or directed at the wrong values, but also if they fail to grasp the expansionist's dismal evaluation of the alternatives to fighting. Although the deterring state realizes that its adversary has strong incentives to take action—or deterrence would not be necessary—it usually thinks the adversary has a wide range of choices. Furthermore, it almost always believes that the adversary is tempted to act because of the positive attraction of the gains the adversary hopes to make. In fact, the other state often feels that it has little choice but to act, because if it does not, it will not merely forego gains, but will suffer grave losses as well.[16] Status quo powers often underestimate the pressure pushing the other to act and therefore underestimate the magnitude of threat and/or the degree of credibility required to make the other refrain from moving. The pressures felt by Japan in the fall of 1941 and by China in the fall of 1950 illustrate why the target state can feel it must act even though it knows some sort of war will result. China and Japan perceived the alternative to fighting not as maintaining the status quo—which was tolerable—but as permitting a drastic erosion of the positions they had established. Because the status quo states did not understand this, they did not grasp the difficulty of the job of deterrence that the were undertaking. This is one reason they thought their superior power was clearly sufficient to keep the adversary at bay.

The case of the Chinese entry into the Korean War is especially striking since the United States did not even grasp the Chinese fear that, if the United States conquered North Korea, it would threaten China. American leaders had no such intention and thought this clear to everyone, just as they felt that their unwillingness to fight a limited war in 1941 was clear to all. Again, not only was there a major difference in perceptions, but one that both sides were unaware of. Deterrence failed; but more than this, the deterrence strategy could not be adequately crafted since it was not based on a correct assessment of the other side's values and fears. Similarly, the United States did not adequately face the basic question of whether deterrence was possible. In neither instance did the United States consider that even a well-developed deterrence policy might fail and therefore that it should balance the costs of war against the costs of making concessions. Since deterrence seemed likely to succeed, the painful alternative of sacrificing some values and abandoning some foreign policy goals was not to be take seriously.

SELF-DETERRENCE

The previous sections provide some reasons why inaccurate or conflicting perceptions can lead to failures of deterrence. Most treatments of this subject deal with cases like surprise attack, in which statesmen incorrectly believe that they have deterred others. While this problem is fascinating and important, we should not neglect the less dramatic other side of this coin: States can deter others unintentionally or unknowingly. Because actors can perceive things that are not there, they can be deterred by figments of their own imagination—self-deterrence, if you will. An example is the British fear throughout the 1930s that Germany would wipe out London at the start of a world war.[17] Although the Germans fed this fear by exaggerating their air strength, the enormity of the gap between the British beliefs and the German activities indicates that most of the explanation must lie with the former's perceptual predispositions. Ingenious deception schemes rarely work unless they fit with what the target already believes.

The British made two striking errors. First, they greatly overestimated the damage that would be caused by each ton of bombs dropped. Perhaps even more startling than the fact that their estimate was off by a factor of 25 is the low level of effort they put into developing the estimate.[18] Since British policy rested, in significant measure, on the belief that war would entail what would later be called "unacceptable damage," one would think that great care would have been devoted to estimating how much damage aerial bombardment would cause. In fact, almost all British analyses rested on a simple and badly biased extrapolation from the few raids on London during World War I. No competing studies were generated; no alternative sources of data or methods were used.

This error was compounded by a fundamental misreading of German air policy and air strength. The British belief that Hitler had the intent and the capability to make British cities the prime target was incorrect on both counts. The German air force was predominantly designed to support ground troops. Doctrine, plans, and aircraft for strategic bombardment did not exist.[19] The effort Germany mounted in the summer of 1940, under circumstances that neither side anticipated, was improvised.

Part of the explanation for these errors is that the German bombing raids of the First World War left a strong imprint on the decisionmakers. The public had demanded greater protection and panic had been a significant problem. But I do not think that purely cognitive or unmotivated factors were of primary importance. That is to say, the misperceptions and miscalculations cannot be accounted for by innocent intellectual and information processing errors—such as mislearning from history—that would have been corrected had they been pointed out to the decisionmakers. Rather, the errors served important functions and purposes for those making them. To a significant extent, the errors were motivated ones, useful to the actors, and facilitated valued actions, positions, or attitudes. We usually adduce perceptions and calculations as proximate explanations of decisions. But in this case the main causation runs the other way: the pessimistic assessments of German bombing were as much the *product* of policies as they were a *cause* of them.

This seems a particularly odd argument in this context because the decisionmakers were conjuring up mythical threats that restricted their country's freedom of action and eventually undermined its security. Nevertheless, different sectors of the British elite had different reasons for finding the fear of bombardment congenial. The Royal Air Force (RAF), which produced and analyzed much of the intelligence on which the estimates were based, was predisposed to believe in a potent German bombing threat because its identity as a separate service rested on the efficacy of strategic bombardment. To have recognized that the German air force's main mission was ground-support would have opened the question of whether Britain's air force should not be similarly employed. (For the same reason, the RAF resisted the idea that defense against bombers might be possible and insisted that counterbombardment was the only effective peacetime deterrent and wartime strategy. It was the civilian leaders, especially the Minister for Co-ordination of Defence, Sir Thomas Inskip, who saw that changing technology allowed fighters to destroy a sufficient proportion of bombers to make defense against prolonged bombing feasible.)

Proponents of both major foreign policy positions also had reasons to accept the pessimistic air estimates. For the appeasers, the estimates were useful by showing that the costs of war would be terribly high, thus indicating the need for international conciliation. England could contemplate opposing Germany only if it was sure that its vital interests were at stake. If the issue were only the British abhorrence of the German domestic regime and its uncouth behavior, or the mere possibility that German aims were unreasonable, confrontations were too costly to be justified. Furthermore, if the threat was from the air, the British response had to be in the same realm. Little money could be spared for the other services, especially the army. This fit the appeasement policy nicely because a defense posture based on air power would limit spending and facilitate a foreign policy that would remain within British control rather than requiring close cooperation with allies. Before 1914 the cabinet had become partly committed to France through joint naval planning and, when it decided for war, it found that the only war plan available subordinated the British Army to the French. In the 1930s, such cooperation would imply prewar ties which could interfere with appeasement and drag England into a dangerous anti-German stance. This danger could be avoided by a military policy that shunned a large army.

Ironically, the anti-appeasers also had reasons to overestimate German air strength. They thought Hitler was highly aggressive and therefore expected him to build what they thought would be a maximally effective air force. Failing to see the German weaknesses and inefficiencies, they expected the air fleet would be larger than it was. Being preoccupied with their own fears—they vastly underestimated the staying power of the working class—they were sure that Germany was planning to rely on weapons of terror. A month after Hitler came to power, Robert Vansittart, the permanent Under-Secretary of the Foreign Office, argued that the Germans were "likely to rely for their military power...on the mechanical weapons of the future...and *above all* [on] military aircraft.... Aviation in particular offers Germany the quickest and easiest way of making their power effective."[20] "It must ... be remembered," Churchill said in 1936, "that Germany has specialized in long-distance bombing aeroplanes."[21] This misreading also fit nicely with attempts to mobilize the British public: the greater the German air force, the greater the British air force should be. Furthermore, the high estimates implied that Germany was aggressive, since it was building more than defense required.

The British, then, did much of Hitler's work for him. While he sought to deter Britain, the British perceptions cannot be completely explained by the German behavior. British fantasies, developed by different groups for different reasons, inhibited accurate analysis of the German air threat and led decisionmakers to accept pessimistic views. As a result, the fact of deterrence far outran the German policy of deterrence.

Current American fears about Minuteman vulnerability and Soviet nuclear "superiority" may be similar examples of self-deterrence. Some argue that if the Soviet Union could destroy many of America's strategic forces by using a relatively small proportion of its missiles (an outcome made possible by MIRVs, a technology, ironically, pioneered by the United States), it might start a war either in the hope of gaining world dominance or, more likely, in a preemptive blow during a crisis in which it feared a grave political setback or even an American first strike. A related argument is that the Soviets are gaining a "war-fighting" ability that significantly exceeds America's. The Soviets, some fear, could do much better than the United States in all levels of warfare; the American knowledge of this places it in a situation not unlike that of England in the 1930s.

Rather than debating the validity of this position,[22] I want to raise the question of whether the analogy of the 1930s applies in the less obvious aspect I discussed earlier. While it is unlikely that statesmen are now repeating the error of overestimating the casualties from bombing, U.S. commentators are creating self-deterrence because the scenarios they are contemplating are probably mythical. The best example is a Soviet attack on Minuteman silos and other U.S. strategic forces. Although abstract American models may indicate that these forces are vulnerable, these calculations involve several simplifying assumptions—that the Russians could fire a carefully coordinated salvo of hundreds of missiles, that the figures for accuracies derived from firings over test ranges would hold true when the missiles were fired over different parts of the earth with different gravitational anomalies, that all systems will work as expected in the wartime environment. Since we lack experience with nuclear war, the models obviously are necessary, but it is not clear how seriously the results should be taken. At the very least, decisionmakers should know the assumptions they are accepting when they rely on them. They should also note the political questions which are begged. No decisionmaker has ever taken an action that accepted uncertainties as portentous as those which would be involved in a first strike. Would the side that was behind in the counterforce exchange continue to spare the other's cities? Even if both sides wanted to fight a limited counterforce war—and this would not be consistent with the Soviet approach to war—would the leaders be able to retain the necessary control over their emotions and their forces?

If the alarmist models are far removed from reality, the United States may deter itself by paying close attention to these calculations. It may act more hesitantly, become less confident, refuse new commitments or retract old ones, and even—although I doubt that this would occur—encourage the Soviets to believe it is safe to undertake actions they previously shunned. A narrowed and distorted focus on implausible contingencies has led to an exaggeration of Soviet strength which could restrict U.S. freedom of action to a greater degree than Soviet deterrence policy does. All other things being equal,[23] those who believe the Soviets are militarily superior to the U.S., and that this margin will give them an advantage in conflicts with the West, will be more likely to avoid confrontations with the Soviets than those who reject these views. Taken to its extreme, the result would be a form of self-fulfilling prophecy in which the United States would act as though it were weak, thus permitting the USSR to make gains which would confirm the belief that Soviet "superiority" was a potent weapon. It is sometimes argued that while nuclear "superiority" is militarily meaningless, the Soviets believe that it matters and so will be more likely to stand firm if they believe they have this "advantage." If the Soviets did think that the state of the current nuclear balance permitted them safely to embark on adventures, they would be more likely to provoke confrontations. In fact there is little evidence that this is the Soviet view,[24] but if American leaders think it is, they will give the Soviets an unnecessary bargaining advantage.

Those who argue that the Soviets have strategic superiority which can be used for political gains see themselves as Churchills, but they may be helping to produce the timidity that they decry. Their aim is to spur sufficient increases in U.S. arms to produce favorable results in the war-fighting calculations and therefore, they believe, to favorably influence U.S. and Soviet behavior. But if they succeed only partly and convince people that the calculations have real referents but do not convince them to build more missiles, they will have magnified, if not created, the danger that so worries them.

LIMITS TO RATIONALITY

Most arguments about deterrence, including those made above, assume that both sides are fairly rational. Some of the general problems raised by this claim have been treated elsewhere.[25] Here I want to focus on four barriers to accurate perception which reduce actors' sensitivity to new information and limit their ability to respond to unexpected situations. The first three barriers are cognitive; the fourth springs from emotions.

Overconfidence

First, there is solid evidence from laboratory experiments and much weaker, but still suggestive, evidence from case studies that people overestimate their cognitive abilities. For example, people's estimates of facts usually are less accurate than they think. When asked to give a spread of figures such that they are 90 percent certain that the correct answer lies somewhere between them, most people bracket the true figure only 75 percent of the time.[26] Similarly, people generally overestimate the complexity of the way they use evidence. They think they are tapping more sources of information than they are, overestimate the degree to which they combine evidence in complex ways, and flatter themselves by thinking that they search for subtle and elusive clues to others' behavior. Acting on this misleading self-portrait, people are quick to overreach themselves by trying mental operations they cannot successfully perform. Thus, when people are given a little clinical training in judging others' psychological states, they make more errors than they did previously because they incorrectly think they can now detect all sorts of peculiar conditions.[27] Overconfidence is also exhibited in the common rejection of the well-established finding that simple computer programs are superior to experts in tasks like graduate student admission and medical diagnosis which involve the combination of kinds of information amenable to fairly objective scoring.[28] People believe that, unlike a simple computer program, they can accurately detect intricate, interactive configurations of explanatory or predictive value. In fact, their abilities to do so are very limited.

Although a full explanation of this phenomenon is beyond the scope of this paper, overconfidence is probably fed by three factors. First, many of our cognitive processes are inaccessible to us. People do not know what information they use or how they use it. They think some information is crucial when it is not and report that they are not influenced at all by some data on which, in fact, they rely.[29] This makes it easier for them to overestimate the sophistication of their thought processes. Second, a specific aspect of this lack of awareness is that people often rely more than they realize on analogies with past events, especially recent events that they or their country experience firsthand. These events seem clear in retrospect and much of this certainty is transferred to the current situation. A third cause of overconfidence, also linked to the lack of self-awareness, is that people not only assimilate incoming information to their preexisting beliefs, a point to which we will return, but do not know that they are doing so. Instead, they incorrectly attribute their interpretations of events to the events themselves; they do not realize that their beliefs and expectations play a dominant role. They therefore become too confident because they see many events as providing independent confirmation of their beliefs when, in fact, the events would be seen differently by someone who started with different ideas. Thus people see evidence as less ambiguous than it is, think that their views steadily are being confirmed, and so feel justified in holding to them ever more firmly.

Some consequences of overconfidence for deterrence strategies are best seen in light of the two other cognitively-rooted perceptual handicaps and so the discussion of them should be postponed. But some effects can be noted here. First, statesmen are likely to treat opposing views quite cavalierly since they are often quite sure that their own beliefs are correct. Cognitive dissonance theory asserts that this intolerance arises only after the person has made a firm decision and has become committed to a policy, but our argument is that it occurs earlier, when even a tentative conclusion has been reached. Second, decisionmakers tend to overestimate their ability to detect subtle clues to the other's intentions. They think it is fairly easy to determine whether the other is hostile and what sorts of threats will be effective. They are not sufficiently sensitive to either the possibility that their conclusions are based on a cruder reading of the evidence or to the likelihood that highly complex explanations are beyond their diagnostic abilities. Third, because decisionmakers fail to realize the degree to which factors, other than the specific events they are facing, influence their interpretations, their consideration of the evidence will be less rational than they think it is and less rational than some deterrence strategies require. For example, while people realize that it makes no sense to believe that another country is likely to be an aggressor just because a state they recently faced was one, in fact the previous experience will greatly increase the chance that the state currently under consideration will be seen as very dangerous. Similarly, beliefs about the kinds of deterrence strategies that will be effective are also excessively affected by recent successes and failures. Extraneous considerations then influence both conclusions as to whether deterrence is necessary, and decisions as to how deterrents will be sought. Decisionmakers, furthermore, do not recognize this fact (if they did, presumably they would act to reduce its impact) and so overestimate the extent to which their policies are grounded in valid analysis.

Not Seeing Value Trade-Offs

The second important cognitive process that influences deterrence is the propensity for people to avoid seeing value trade-offs.[30] That is, people often believe the policy they favor is better than the alternatives on several logically independent value dimensions. For example, those who favored a ban on nuclear testing believed that the health hazards from testing were high, that continued testing would yield few military benefits, and that a treaty would open the door to further arms control agreements. Opponents disagreed on all three counts. This kind of cognitive consistency is irrational because there is no reason to expect the world to be arranged so neatly and helpfully that a policy will be superior on all value dimensions. I am not arguing that people never realize that a policy which gains some important values does so at the price of others, but only that these trade-offs are not perceived as frequently and as seriously as they actually occur.

This cognitive impediment has several implications for deterrence. First, it complicates the task of balancing the dangers in issuing threats with the costs of making concessions. Rather than looking carefully at this trade-off, statesmen are likely to be swayed by one set of risks and then evaluate the other costs in a way that reinforces their initial inclinations. For example, a decisionmaker who is preoccupied with what he and his state will sacrifice if he compromises on an issue is likely to convince himself that the danger of war if he stands firm is slight; the statesman who concludes that this danger is intolerably high is likely to come to see the costs of retreating as low. As long as the risk on which he focuses is, in fact, the greater one, and as long as the situation remains unchanging, this minimization of the trade-off will not lead the decisionmaker to choose a policy that differs from the one he would have adopted had he been more rational. But if either of these two conditions are not met, then the quality of the policy will suffer. Thus if the decisionmaker focuses first on the risks of war and finds that it looms large, he may incorrectly judge the costs of retreating as less than this. He could then abandon a policy of deterrence when rationality would dictate maintaining it. In other cases, a decisionmaker who has decided to stand firm may minimize the value trade-off by failing to take full account of the costs of his position. For example, he may come to believe that while conciliatory measures would lower the short-run risk, they would increase the danger over a longer period by leading the adversary to think that it was safe to trifle with the state's interests. In this arrangement of perceptions and evaluations, standing firm appears preferable to being conciliatory on both the dimension of prevailing on the issue in dispute and the dimension of avoiding war.[31]

The failure to face trade-offs also helps explain the tendency for states to become overextended, to refuse to keep ends and means in balance, and to create more enemies than they can afford. For example, in the years preceding World War I, Germany added Russia and Britain to its list of enemies. On top of the conflict with France, this burden was too great even for a state as strong as Germany. Although both international and domestic factors were also at work, the psychological difficulty of making trade-offs must not be overlooked. When the German leaders decided to drop the Reinsurance Treaty with Russia in 1890 they perceived minimum costs because they expected that ideological conflict would prevent Russia from joining forces with Germany's prime enemy, France. Similarly, the decision to build a large navy and pursue a belligerent policy toward England was based on the assumption that England's conflicts with France and Russia were so deep that eventually it would have to seek an understanding with the Triple Alliance. German statesmen did not see that their policy involved a greater risk of turning Russia and Britain into active enemies than was entailed by the rejected alternative policy of conciliation and compromise.

This failing was not peculiar to Germany. French policy between 1882 and 1898 sought both to rebuild a position of strength against Germany and to contest English dominance of Egypt. To pursue either objective meant risking war with one of these countries. This might have been within the bounds of French resources; war with both was not. So an effective policy required France to set priorities and decide whether it cared more about its position in Europe or about colonial issues. For more than ten years, however, French leaders refused to do this, instead thinking that the same policy could maximize the chances of gaining both goals. It took the shock of England's willingness to go to war in the Fashoda crisis for French statesmen to realize that they could not afford too many enemies and had to make a hard choice.

Carter's foreign policy provides a final example. To most of the goals of the Ford administration, the President added an increased concern with preventing proliferation and protecting human rights. He and his advisors did not seem to appreciate that pushing others on one front might diminish their ability to push them on others. Only when crises arose to clarify the mind did they decide to relax the more recent pressures in order to increase the chance of enlisting others' support for what were taken to be the more important national security goals. But by this time, a large price had been paid in terms of antagonizing others and appearing hypocritical; the overly ambitious initial policy jeopardized America's ability to achieve more limited goals.

Assimilation of New Information to Preexisting Beliefs

The third cognitive process I want to discuss is probably the most pervasive and significant—the tendency for people to assimilate new information to their preexisting beliefs, to see what they expect to be present. Ambiguous or even discrepant information is ignored, misperceived, or reinterpreted so it does minimum damage to what the person already believes. As I have discussed at length elsewhere,[32] this tendency is not always irrational and does not always decrease the accuracy of perception. Our environment presents us with so many conflicting and ambiguous stimuli that we could not maintain a coherent view if we did not use our concepts and beliefs to impose some order on it. Up to a point—which cannot be specified with precision—rejecting or providing a strained interpretation of discrepant evidence is the best way to account for all the available information. It is the way scientists behave in treating their data because science would be impossible if they altered their theories to take account of each bit of discrepant information. As Michael Polanyi puts it:

> The process of explaining away deviations is in fact quite indispensable to the daily routine of research. In my laboratory I find the laws of nature formally contradicted at every hour, but I explain this away by the assumption of experimental error. I know that this may cause me one day to explain away a fundamentally new phenomenon and to miss a great discovery. Such things have often happened in the history of science. Yet I shall continue to explain away my odd resslts, for if every anomaly observed in my laboratory were taken at its face value, research would instantly degenerate into a wild-goose chase after imaginary fundamental novelties.[33]

Similarly, statesmen who miss, misperceive, or disregard evidence are not necessarily protecting their egos, being blind to reality, or acting in a way that will lead to an ineffective policy. The evidence is almost always ambiguous and no view can do justice to all the facts. In retrospect, one can always find numerous instances in which decision-makers who were wrong overlooked or misunderstood evidence that now stands out as clear and important. But one can also note, first, that many facts supported the conclusion that turned out to be wrong and, second, those who were right treated the evidence in the same general way—i.e., they also ignored or misinterpreted information which conflicted with their views.

Even if the assimilation of incoming information to preexisting beliefs is not as pernicious as is often believed, it creates a variety of problems for deterrence strategies, especially since this cognitive process operates in conjunction with the other two just discussed. First, images of other states are difficult to alter. Perceptions are not responsive to new information about the other side; small changes are not likely to be detected. Once a statesman thinks he knows whether the other needs to be deterred and what kind of strategy is appropriate, only the most dramatic events will shakehim.[34] The problem is compounded by the common belief to the contrary that if the initial hunches about what the other side is up to are incorrect, the other's behavior will soon set the statesman straight. For example, those who see the other side as an aggressor usually argue that if this image is incorrect the other can easily demonstrate that its bad reputation is not warranted. In fact the ambiguity of most evidence coupled with the absorptive power of most beliefs means that an inaccurate image may not be corrected at a point when the situation can still be controlled.

A second and more general consequence of the cognitive limitations we have discussed is that political perceptions are rarely completely accurate and policies rarely work as designed. Statesmen cannot, then, afford to develop policies so fragile that they will fail very badly if others do not act exactly as expected. A large margin of error must be built in. The statesman who is sure that his beliefs and calculations are correct in all their details is likely to encounter serious trouble, just as defense strategies based on the need to receive tactical warning of when and where the other side is planning to move are unlikely to fail. For example, it was not reasonable to have expected the military commanders to have anticipated an attack on Pearl Harbor or to have kept the base on constant alert. The latter procedure would have greatly disrupted the urgent training program. Instead the decisionmakers should have sought a way to gain some measure of insurance against an attack with the lowest possible interference with training. The same principle applies to the construction of deterrence strategies. If they are based on an unrealistic assessment of our abilities to perceive our environment and choose among alternatives, they are likely to attempt too much and to fail badly.

Third, cognitive impediments place sharp limits on the degree to which deterrence strategies can be fine tuned, limits that are more severe than statesmen generally realize. For example, states commonly try to develop policies that exert just the right amount of pressure on the other—that is, enough to show the other that the state is very serious, but not enough to provoke desperate behavior. Or, they try to indicate a willingness to ease tensions with an adversary without cooperating to such an extent that third parties would feel menaced. At the tactical level, intricate bargaining maneuvers are planned and subtle messages are dispatched. For example, in the discussions within the U.S. government in early 1965 about what sort of troops to send to Vietnam, Assistant Secretary of Defense McNaughton dissented from the view that the initial deployment should be marines. The problem, he argued, was that the marines would bring with them "high profile" materiel, such as tanks, which would indicate to North Vietnam that the United States was in Vietnam to stay. It would be better to send the 173d Airborne Brigade, which lacked heavy equipment; this would signal Hanoi that the United States would withdraw if a political settlement could be reached.[35] But even if the actions are carried out as the decisionmaker wants them to be, precision is often defeated by the screen of the other side's perceptual predispositions.[36] As a result, while subtlety and sophistication in a policy are qualities which observers usually praise and statesmen seek, these attributes may lead the policy to fail because they increase the chance that it will not be perceived as it is intended. It is hard enough to communicate straightforward and gross threats; it will often be impossible to successfully apply complex bargaining tactics involving detailed and abstruse messages. Decision-makers often underestimate these difficulties and so try to develop plans too intricate to get across. Furthermore, because it is very hard to tell what others have perceived, statesmen often fail to see that they have failed to communicate.

Finally, since discrepant information is likely to be misinterpreted, deterrence strategies must be tailored to the other's preexisting beliefs and images, thus limiting the range of strategies that can succeed. Because the inferences which the other draws are largely determined by its initial beliefs, acts which will deter one decisionmaker will be ignored or interpreted differently by another. If the perceiver thinks that the state is deeply concerned about the issue and has high resolve, deterrence will be relatively easy. If he has the opposite view, it will take great efforts to make a credible threat. But unless the state's leaders know what the other side thinks, they will neither know what they have to do to deter it, nor be able to judge the chances of success. A frequent cause of deterrence failure is the state's misdesign of its actions growing out of incorrect beliefs about its adversary's perspective. For example, American leaders were taken by surprise in October 1962 because they thought it was clear to the Soviets that placing missiles in Cuba would not be tolerated. Since the Americans believed—

correctly—that the Soviets were not likely to run high risks, they found it hard to imagine the Soviets would try to establish a missile base abroad. U.S. leaders did not think that great efforts at deterrence were necessary because they did not realize that the move would not look risky to the Soviets.[37]

Just as the best way to understand the conclusions a person draws from a "fact-finding" mission is to know his initial beliefs rather than to know what evidence he was exposed to, so one can often make better predictions about how a state will interpret others' behavior by knowing the former's predispositions than by knowing what the latter actually did. Unfortunately, statesmen rarely appreciate this and, to compound the problem, usually have a much better idea of what they think they are doing and what messages they want to convey than they do of what the others' perceptual predispositions are. The difficulty is two-fold and two-sided. The fact that perceptions are strongly influenced by predispositions means it is very difficult to convey messages that are inconsistent with what the other already believes. And the fact that statesmen do not understand this influence reduces their ability to predict how others will react. Even if decisionmakers understood the problem, prediction would be difficult because it is so hard for them to grasp the way in which others see the world. But in this case they would at least realize that many of their messages would not be received as they were sent. Since this understanding is often lacking, decisionmakers' messages not only convey different meanings to each side, but each is usually unaware of the discrepancy. Statesmen are then likely to err both in their estimates of what the other side intends by its behavior and in their beliefs about how the other is reading their behavior. Severe limits are thus placed on the statesman's ability to determine whether and what kind of deterrence strategy is called for and to influence the other's perceptions in a way which will allow this strategy to succeed. A failure to understand these limitations imposed by the way people think will make it more difficult for scholars to explain state behavior and will lead a statesman to attempt overly ambitious policies that are likely to bring his country to grief.

DEFENSIVE AVOIDANCE

A final impediment to accurate perception that can complicate or defeat deterrence is affective rather than purely cognitive. In a process known as defensive avoidance, people may refuse to perceive and understand extremely threatening stimuli.[38] For example, the failure to see value trade-offs discussed above can be motivated by the need to avoid painful choices. At this point we do not know enough about the phenomenon to determine when these errors occur and how influential they are in comparison with other factors. But it seems clear that on at least some occasions powerful needs, often arising from domestic politics, can produce badly distorted perceptions of other countries. Thus Schroeder has argued that the British images of Russian in the period leading up to the Crimean War cannot be explained either by Russian behavior or by long-standing and deeply-imbeded cognitive predisposition, but rather were caused by shifting British needs to see Russia as threatening or accommodating.[39] Whether England tried to deter Russia or concilliate her then depended on internal factors that were neither rationally related to foreign policy goals nor susceptible to Russian influence. Similarly, states may come to think that it is relatively safe to challenge the adversary's deterrent commitments when a modicum of rational analysis would indicate that the risks far outweigh the slight chances of success if domestic or foreign needs for a challenge are very strong.

This is not only to argue that the costs of foregoing gains and accepting the adversary's deterrence can be so high as to rationally justify a challenge that the statesman knows is likely to fail; this may be unfortunate but it is not troublesome in terms of perceptions. Rather, the knowledge of the high costs of accepting the status quo can lead statesmen to ignore or distort information about the costs of challenging it. Thus Richard Ned Lebow shows why India in 1962, the United States in the fall of 1950, and the Soviet Union before the Cuban missile crisis were not able to see that their adversaries would inflict painful rebukes if they persisted: they were preoccupied with the costs they would pay if they did not.[40] To return to a case mentioned earlier, the American attempts to deter Japan failed because Japan thought the war would be limited. This error may have been at least in part a motivated one. The feeling that acquiescing to American demands was intolerable led the Japanese to adopt an unrealistically favorable view of the alternative— the only way they could avoid facing the need to sacrifice very deeply-held values was to believe that the United States would fight a limited war. That their conclusion was driven by this need, rather than by objective analysis, is indicated by the quality of their deliberations. "Instead of examining carefully the likelihood that the war would in fact be a short, decisive one, fought under optimum conditions for Japan, contingency plans increasingly took on a strangely irrational, desperate quality, in which the central issue, 'Can we win?' was shunted aside. Rather, it was as if Japan had painted itself into a corner."[41]

The result is that deterrence can be difficult if not impossible. Threats that should be credible and effective, even when the cognitive impediments discussed above are not operating, may be missed or misread. It

154 / National Security and International Stability

usually will be hard for the deterrer to realize that it is facing this danger, and even an understanding of the situation will not easily yield an effective policy since the other's perceptual screens are often opaque.

NOTES

1. Charles Neu, *An Uncertain Friendship* (Cambridge, Mass.: Harvard University Press, 1967), p. 199.
2. The British tried to do this, with some success, during World War II. See Donald McLachlan, *Room 39* (New York: Atheneum, 1968), pp. 252-258.
3. Of course accidents can lead to desired ends in ways decisionmakers had not intended, but I do not think this is common. One example may be the U.S. Navy's unauthorized harassment of Soviet submarines in the Cuban missile crisis, which probably helped convince the Soviet leaders that the confrontation was too dangerous to be permitted to continue. See Alexander George, David Hall, and William Simons, *The Limits of Coercive Diplomacy* (Boston: Little, Brown, 1971), pp. 112-114.
4. Allan Millet, *The Politics of Intervention* (Columbus: Ohio State University Press, 1968). The point is nicely made in an anecdote about a British general made by Liddell Hart:

   Jack Dill was a delightful man for any enthusiast to meet òr serve. But he was quite unable to understand that the average officer did not share his burning ardour for professional study and tactical exercises. An illuminating example of that incomprehension occurred in his way of dealing with the major commanding a battery attached to his brigade who had failed to show the keenness Dill expected. To emphasize his dissatisfaction Dill told this officer that he would not be allowed to take part in the remaining exercies—a punishment, drastic in Dill's view, which was a great relief to the delinquent, who had been counting the days until he could get away to join a grouse-shooting party in Scotland.

   The Liddell Hart Memoirs, 1895-1938 (New York: Putnam's, 1965), p. 72.
5. Department of Defense, *Annual Report, FY 1981* (Washington, D.C.: Government Printing Office, 1980), p. 67. It should also be noted that if these arguments are correct, the threat to carry out these attacks would be no more credible than the threat to attack Soviet cities because there would be no reason for the Soviet response of retaliating against American cities to be different.
6. U.S. Senate Committee on Foreign Relations, *Hearings on Nuclear War Strategy*, 96th Congress, 2nd Session, September 16, 1980 (printed on 18 February 1981), p. 10.
7. Sir Thomas Inskip, minister for coordination of defense, quoted in Martin Gilbert, *Winston Churchill, Vol. 5 1922-1939* (London: Heinemann, 1976), p. 891.
8. Quoted in ibid., p. 945.
9. Churchill had a better understanding of the problem. In 1938 he stressed to a German diplomat that "a war, once started,would be fought out like the last to the bitter end, and one must consider not what might happen in the first few months, but where we should all be at the end of the fourth year." (Quoted in Gilbert, *Winston S. Churchill*, p. 964.) For related argument, see Alan Alexandroff and Richard Rosecrance, "Deterrence in 1939," *World Politics*, vol. 29, April 1977, pp. 404-424.
10. As Walt Rostow put it, "Ho has an industrial complex to protect; he is no longer a guerilla fighter with nothing to lose." [Quoted in Department of Defense, *Pentagon Papers*, Senator Gravel Edition (Boston: Beacon Press, 1971), vol. 3, p. 153.] That North Vietnam absorbed almost unprecedented punishment is shown by John Muel-

ler, "The search for the Single 'Breaking Point' in Vietnam: The Statistics of a Deadly Quarrel," *International Studies Quarterly*, vol. 24, December 1980, pp. 497-519.

11. This question can be linked to the levels of analysis problem in international politics— i.e., the question of whether the main causes of a state's behavior are to be found in its internal characteristics or its external environment—but a full discussion would take us far afield.

12. For a paradoxical exception to this generalization, see p. 13-9.

13. Robert Jervis, *The Logic of Images in International Relations* (Princeton, N.J.: Princeton University Press, 1970), pp. 20-26, 66-112.

14. Thomas Schelling, *The Strategy of Conflict* (New York: Oxford University Press, 1963), pp. 123-124.

15. It is possible, of course, that under some circumstances a retreat leads statesmen to expect other retreats and that under other conditions they draw the opposite inference, but we do not know enough to specify the conditions.

16. Ole Holsti, "The 1914 Case," *American Political Science Review*, vol. 59, June 1965, pp. 365-378; Richard Ned Lebow, *Between Peace and War: The Nature of International Conflict* (Baltimore: Johns Hopkins University Press, 1981).

17. The most thorough treatment is Uri Bialer, *The Shadow of the Bomber: The Fear of Air Attack and British Politics, 1932-1939* (London: Royal Historical Society, 1980).

18. For a good discussion, see Paul Bracken, "The Unintended Consequences of Strategic Gaming," *Simulation and Games*, vol. 8, September 1977, pp. 300-315.

19. Even during the first years of the war, Hitler did not pay careful attention to the bombing campaign against Britain. See R. J. Overy, "Hitler and Air Strategy," *Journal of Contemporary History*, vol. 15, July 1980, pp. 410-412. Later Hitler placed great faith in the new terror weapons, the V-1 and the V-2, but he never analyzed the probable effect of these weapons with any care.

   For an argument that takes partial exception to the view expressed here, see Williamson Murray, "The Luftwaffe Before the Second World War: A Mission, A Strategy?" *Journal of Strategic Studies*, vol. 4, September 1981, pp. 261-270.

20. Quoted in D. C. Watt, "British Intelligence and the Coming of the Second World War in Europe: The Assessment of the Enemy," Ernest May, ed., *Knowing One's Enemies: Intelligence Assessment Before the Two World Wars*, forthcoming.

21. Quoted in Gilbert, *Winston S. Churchill*, p. 797.

22. I have done so in "Why Nuclear Superiority Doesn't Matter," *Political Science Quarterly*, vol. 95, Winter 1979-1980, pp. 617-633.

23. Often they are not: those who think that the Soviets are militarily strong also tend to believe that they are very aggressive and so see retreating as extremely costly.

24. As George Quester notes, it is "remarkable . . . that the overwhelming bulk of the discussions . . . of growing Soviet relative power and of possible threats come from the west." See "Defining Strategic Issues: How to Avoid Isometric Exercises," in Robert Harkavy and Edward Kalodziej, eds., *American Security Policy and Policy-Making* (Lexington, Mass.: D. C. Heath, 1980), p. 204. For an evaluation of the Soviet view, see Karl Spielman, *The Political Utility of Strategic Superiority: A Preliminary Investigation Into the Soviet View* (Arlington, Va.: Institute for Defense Analysis, May 1979). For the general Soviet view of the current situaton, see Severn Bialer, "The Harsh Decade: Soviet Policies in the 1980s," *Foreign Affairs*, vol. 59, Summer 1981, pp. 999-1020.

25. See, for example, Philip Green, *Deadly Logic* (Columbus: Ohio State University Press, 1966); Patrick Morgan, *Deterrence* (Beverly Hills, Calif.: Sage, 1977); Robert Jervis, "Deterrence Theory Revisited," *World Politics*, vol. 31, January 1979, pp. 299-301, 310-312.

26. Baruch Fischhoff, Paul Slovic, and Sara Lichtenstein, "Knowing with Certainty: The

Appropriateness of Extreme Confidence," *Journal of Experimental Psychology*: Human Perception and Performance, vol. 3, 1977, pp. 552-564.

27. Stuart Oskamp, "Overconfidence in Case-Study Judgments," *Journal of Consulting Psychology*, vol. 29, 1965, pp. 261-265.

28. For a review of this literature, see Lewis Goldberg, "Simple Models or Simple Processes? Some Research on Clinical Judgments," *American Psychologist*, vol. 23, July 1968, pp. 483-496.

29. Richard Nisbett and Timothy Wilson, "Telling More Than We Can Know: Verbal Reports on Mental Processes," *Psychological Review*, vol. 84, 1977, pp. 231-257.

30. For a further discussion of this, see Robert Jervis, *Perception and Misperception in International Politics* (Princeton, N.J.: Princeton University Press, 1976), pp. 128-142.

31. Jack Snyder, "Rationality at the Brink," *World Politics*, vol. 30, April 1978, pp. 345-365. But for the phenomenon to fit the analysis here, the value dimensions must be logically independent. This will not be true if both the perceptions of the need to stand firm and evaluations of the costs of not doing so are produced by a coherent image of the adversary.

32. Jervis, *Perception and Misperception*, pp. 143-172.

33. Michael Polanyi, "The Unaccountable Element in Science," in *Knowing and Being, Essays by Michael Polanyi*, Marjorie Grene, ed. (London: Routledge and Kegan Paul, 1969), p. 114.

34. Glenn Snyder and Paul Diesing, *Conflict Among Nations* (Princeton, N.J.: Princeton University Press, 1977), pp. 389-404.

35. *Pentagon Papers*, p. 421.

36. Most studies of policy implementation reveal that this rarely happens. For a thorough analysis that combines bureaucratic and perceptual factors that complicate attempts at coercion see Wallace Theis, *When Governments Collide* (Berkeley: University of California Press, 1980).

37. Klaus Knorr, "Failures in National Intelligence Estimates: The Case of the Cuban Missiles," *World Politics*, vol. 16, April 1964, pp. 455-467. For an alternative argument, see Richard Ned Lebow, "Soviet Risk Taking: What are the Lessons from cuba?" *Political Science Quarterly*, fourthcoming.

38. The fullest discussion is in Irving Janis and Leon Mann, *Decision Making* (New York: Free Press, 1977).

39. Paul Schroeder, *Austria, Great Britain, and the Crimean War* (Ithaca, N.Y.: Cornell University Press, 1972).

40. See Lebow, *Between Peace and War*; also Lebow, "Soviet Risk Taking." Also see Richard Cottman, *Foreign Policy Motivation* (Pittsburgh: University of Pittsburgh Press, 1977), and Alexander George and Richard Smoke, *Deterrence in American Foreign Policy* (New York: Columbia University Press, 1974), and Jack Snyder, *Defending the Offensive: Biases in French, German, and Russian War Planning, 1870-1914* (Ithaca, N.Y.: Cornell University Press, forthcoming), which does a particularly fine job of separating motivated from unmotivated errors. Sharp-eyed readers will note a shift from some of my earlier views on this point. For further discussion, see Robert Jervis, "Political Decisionmaking: Recent Contributions," *Political Psychology*, vol. II (Summer 1980, pp. 89-96).

41. Robert Scalapino, "Introduction" in James Morley, ed., *The Fateful Choice: Japan's Advance Into Southeast Asia, 1939-1941* (New York: Columbia University Press, 1980), p. 119. Also see Gordon Prange, *At Dawn We Slept* (N.Y.: McGraw Hill, 1981), pp. 16, 21.

Chapter 8

Revolutions in Warfare: An Earlier Generation of Interpreters

Peter Paret

Like all of history, the history of war and of men thinking about war is one of slow, often imperceptible change. Genuine turning points are rare; even when they do occur they are not sudden but gradual, long in coming. The new reality, once it has emerged, requires years and sometimes decades before society adapts to it and masters it intellectually. A century-and-a-half before nuclear weapons appeared, the French Revolution marked such a turning point in the history of war. The revolution altered the practice of war in fundamental respects, and as soldiers and governments began to use the new means available to them, theorists and commentators began to interpret these forces and speculate on their further development. The subject of the following pages is the intellectual situation of the men who experienced and tried to understand the military effects of the French Revolution, Napoleonic policies, and nationalism. Space does not permit a systematic comparison of the generation of the 1770s and 1780s with analysts who reached maturity in the 1930s and during and after World War II, but the reader may want to draw certain parallels and identify some differences between the earlier and the later period himself. I shall, however, conclude with a few comments on the more significant distinctions between the two groups, as I see them. Some years ago Klaus Knorr wrote an essay entitled "Threat Perception," in which he discussed the intellectual and predispositional difficulties in which governments find themselves when they try to interpret each other's signals and intentions.[1] This paper addresses not the reciprocal evaluations of governments, but the problems of cognition faced by the international community when a significant change in politico-military potential and methods is taking place.

THE EIGHTEENTH CENTURY

The revolution in war that occurred at the end of the eighteenth century was, of course, not brought about by technological innovation and did not involve the employment of new weapons systems. Instead it was caused by political developments in France from the end of the 1780s to the execution of Louis XVI and by a specific political decision responding to military needs and arrived at with great misgivings: on February 24, 1793, the convention declared all males between their eighteenth and forty-first birthdays, who were unmarried or widowers without children, to be liable for military service. Because conscription went against the intellectual and social values of the politicians who issued the decree, they surrounded the new policy with important limitations; it was to remain in effect only until 300,000 men had been raised; certain occupations were exempt; and it allowed substitutions—anyone selected for service had the right to hire a replacement if he could find one. All of these modifications at least initially tended to obscure the revolutionary nature of the measure, both to French society and to foreign observers—a matter to which I shall return. The decree, supplemented by the *levée en masse* of August 1793 and by subsequent laws, formed the bases of the vastly expanded armies of the later Revolution, the Directory, and the Empire. In 1789 the French army had 150,000 effectives. Five years later its size had more than tripled, and between 1806 and 1812 as many as 1,300,000 men were called up—a total almost inconceivable to Europeans at the time, but still no more than 40 percent of all Frenchmen liable for service.[2]

Forces of this magnitude could never have been raised by the corporative societies of the *ancien régime*, in which a few privileged groups filled nearly all officer positions, peasants and foreign mercenaries provided the rank and file, and the bourgeoisie as well as certain other groups, defined by residence status or occupation, remained legally exempt from service. Not only was the new conscript army larger; even if the heaviest burden continued to weigh on the poor, the army was becoming the military expression of society as a whole and, incidentally, provided an important means for reshaping this society by creating a consciousness of nationhood in illiterate peasants and laborers, a process that had military as well as political implications. Eighteenth century mercenaries and forcibly enrolled peasants might be motivated by esprit de corps and occasionally by local or provincial loyalties; the soldiers of the Revolution and Empire no longer felt isolated in the larger society, but regarded themselves as its armed representatives. Their government and commanders could appeal to their enthusiasm, ambition, and patriotism. And even if reality rarely matched the political rhetoric, the very fact that this rhetoric was used—which would have been out of the question ten years earlier—indicates that a change of great practical significance had taken place. The soldier felt differently about himself, he was treated differently, consequently he could be expected to behave differently on campaign and in battle. A political decision made possible by the breakup of the corporative structure of mutually exclusive social groups, and its replacement by a legally more uniform society, had created very large armed forces, composed of soldiers whose attitudes had changed. These two developments radically altered the nature of warfare.

Eighteenth-century wars are often described as limited wars in contrast to the unlimited or less limited wars waged between the 1790s and the fall of Napoleon. As far as purpose and means employed are concerned, the contrast is an oversimplification. Still, any comparison between wars in the earlier and the later period will indicate the enormous release of military energies, the increase in mobility, the geographic and political expansion of war that had occurred. Let me briefly outline the more significant innovations and the manner in which they were related, before turning to the intellectual reactions to them.[3]

The army of the *ancien régime* tended to be a cumbersome unitary force, its men concentrated in tight formations for purposes of discipline and control as much as for tactical reasons, lacking in reconnaissance and intelligence capabilities, hampered further by vast wagon trains, and dependent on a network of fixed depots and magazines beyond which troops could move six to eight days' marches at most. The far larger post-revolutionary army was articulated in increasingly permanent sub-units combining the three arms, which could operate independently almost as well as together. Its train had been reduced to one-fifth or even one-tenth of its former size, and its supply system—with its heavier reliance on requisitioning—was now far more flexible. In the old army, the main function of subordinate generals was to transmit the orders of the commander-in-chief to regiments and battalions, assure tactical alignment and cohesion, and set an example of courage to their troops. The division- and corps-commanders of the new age were expected to make independent decisions. The command and staff system of the *ancien régime* rarely consisted of more than a few adjutants, engineers, and messengers; in the new army it was considerably expanded, although only Prussia fully responded to the new challenges by developing the prototype of the modern general staff, which gradually acquired very far-reaching command authority.

Eighteenth-century infantry tactics were essentially linear, which meant that troops could attack most effectively over level, open terrain. The new tactical system combined skirmishing to initiate the action, with lines to carry on the firefight, defensive squares, and maneuver- and attack-columns—one result being that troops could now fight effectively on all types of ground. The eighteenth-century commander tried to plan his battle in advance and in considerable detail; he sought to exclude the unforeseen because by attitude and training his men were incapable of reacting quickly to new developments. The commander of the new army engaged the enemy so as to start a more or less predictable train of events, and in the course of the battle shifted and committed his forces as the occasion demanded. He was far better equipped than his predecessor to counter or exploit the unexpected. In that sense the modern battle was more natural, less artificial than the old. Frederick the Great and his opponents held back few reserves because they relied on an extensive linear front, and their first attack, when their units were still at their most mobile, tended to be the strongest. The Napoleonic commander kept numerous reserves and saved them to make his last attack decisive.

Eighteenth-century strategy sought control of territory or occupation of key points, which either compelled the opponent to withdraw or expose himself by attacking superior positions. Troops were dispersed on defensive missions, and their limited numbers and lack of mobility restricted their operational reach. With the turn of the century, the opponent's forces became the main object of operations. Large armies permitted an expansion of the theater of war and yet made concentration of effort possible. Because trained men were no longer as difficult to replace as they had been a generation earlier, the campaign year could be extended and more engagements could be fought, some of which were decisive in a new sense of the term. We should take note of the fact that, in the many wars of the eighteenth century, victories rarely did more than bring the defeated army's operations to a halt and gain time for the victor to reorganize his own forces or carry on diplomatic negotiations. Not a single battle led to the destruction of the enemy's army, because the victor could not risk the confusion, breakdown of supply, and mass desertion that would accompany an immediate pursuit.[4] Under the new system tactical success could be fully exploited, and as soon as the destruction of the enemy became a genuine possibility, the political purposes of war could be realistically expanded.

OUTSIDE FACTORS AND INNOVATION

The changes I have outlined, and the extent of which, in one or two cases, I may have exaggerated to emphasize their salient differences, did not occur at once. They evolved gradually in the course of the 1790s, and even in the heyday of Napoleonic warfare a good measure of the old and traditional continued to be mixed in with the new. But in the aggregate the changes added up to a new kind of war. The question we must now ask is how did observers—whether French or foreign—respond to the new phenomena? Obviously their reactions were affected by elements beyond their intellectual and psychological ability to recognize and understand the new, and it will be useful to take account of the most significant of these external influences.

First, with hardly an exception, the student of war did not enjoy the luxury or comfort of being able to stand back from his subject. Between 1792 and 1815 there were scarcely four years of relative peace in Europe. During this period, French analysts tried to improve the working of their military machine; foreign ones defended themselves against that machine in order not to become its next target. Analysts' interpretations were developed in wartime or under the threat of war.

Because analysts were motivated less by the wish to understand in the abstract than by the need to perfect, counter, or attempt to introduce innovations into their own military system, their particular social and political environment often warped their interpretations. An example is afforded by the foreign reaction to skirmishing, which during the second half of the 1790s became an integral part of French infantry tactics.

The ferocious discipline imposed on the rank-and-file in such services as the Russian, British, or Prussian, and the reliance these armies placed on linear formations, whose effectiveness depended on the soldier's automatic response to orders, rendered skirmishing by more than a few specially trained men out of the question. Skirmishing demanded at least a degree of independence and initiative, which could not be combined easily with physical punishment, insistence on unthinking obedience, and trust in the supreme value of close tactical cohesion. Not surprisingly, it was difficult for observers to reach an accurate appraisal of skirmishing if its adoption by their own forces would have meant fundamental changes in their recruiting system and in the relationship between officers and men, as well as a complete recasting of tactical doctrine—to say nothing of its impact on the character of their society. Many commentators, therefore, were tempted to dismiss skirmishing as the unwanted result of the French fighting with half-trained men— which had, indeed, been a factor in its early history—and to argue that skirmishing should be avoided because it encouraged cowardice by stressing the value of concealment and made the soldier unfit for fighting in line.

The accurate recognition of innovation was further blurred by the fact that the changes did not emerge full-blown, but were gradual and ongoing. The development and institutionalization of the reformed French supply system, for example, could be misinterpreted as the outcome of unsettled conditions, which would eventually be replaced by a return to order and traditional routine.

Even more important, the continued success of traditional methods impeded the clear understanding of the new. It was not the case, after all, that innovations triumphed everywhere or easily. The most influential instance of the persistent vigor of the old system was provided by the British army. Michael Howard writes that throughout the Napoleonic wars this army "remained an eighteenth century force, faithfully reflecting the stable class-structure of its society. Officiers were largely drawn from the lesser aristocracy and gentry, barely at all from the professional and mercantile middle classes. Other ranks were recruited by bounty from the marginal elements in society, and the two existed side by side in different worlds, communicating only through non-commissioned officers." Wellington, the army's dominant figure in the second half of our period, saw not need for change. Again quoting Howard: "He was a consummate master of 18th-century warfare, and the limited nature of the campaigns he was required to fight made it unnecessary to for him to comtemplate any other. If the British had had to create an army on a continental scale, they would have had to take the continental model very much more seriously; which would, in its turn have had far-reaching implications for the structure of their own society."[5] But the special circumstances of the British war effort were not so clear at the time, and the spectacle of eighteenth-century organization and drill defeating skirmishers and attack columns provided a powerful argument to those who condemned the new as an aberration.

Finally, the newness of each change outlined above could be obscured by the fact that each had roots in the past. To return to the example of skirmishing: since the middle of the eighteenth century, all major European armies included units or specialists within units trained to fight on their own, to fire individually aimed shots rather than by volley, to use concealment and cover, and so on. This common tradition made it easy for some observers to miss what was really new and important in the French development: skirmishing was no longer the exclusive practice of specialists but a method with which most soldiers were familiar, and that was no longer an ancillary but a major element in the overall tactical pattern.

Of course, if the analysts could be confused because, in rudimentary form, every innovation was already present in the old system, the same fact might benefit the reformer. Repeatedly a revolutionary change was pressed on conservatives with the assurance that nothing more was involved than the adaptation of a traditional, familiar practice to the conditions of the day. It was in this manner, for instance, that Scharnhorst, the leader of military reform in Prussia, succeeded in making conscription palatable to the king. He presented it as the logical extension of the old Prussian policy of assigning a district to each regiment from which it drew a given number of peasants for life-long service in the ranks. The revolutionary features of conscription—that it would raise a very large number of men, that it would encompass all groups in society, that its ethical justification lay in the loyalty a man owed his country as much as in the obedience he owed his ruler—these Scharnhorst did not emphasize.

To conclude this survey of the influence that outside factors could exert on the study of innovation: just because analysis and the immediate needs of policy were so closely linked, those men trying to modernize their military institutions on the whole reached a better understanding of the new warfare, and reached it sooner, than did defenders of the status quo. Throughout Europe, the politics of the radical reformers enhanced their ability to recognize and interpret the radical characteristics and implications of the changes.

If we now look at the intellectual posture of military Europe as a whole, we will find that both in France and elsewhere the separate elements of the revolution in warfare were identified and understood reasonably quickly by enough people to enable us to speak of a consensus of the modern in opposition to an increasingly defensive traditionalist point of view. Inevitably some commentators exaggerated the significance of one or another element—for example, writers identified skirmishing, or the massing of artillery to prepare a breakthrough, as the key to success in modern war. But at least the various components of the new system were recognized by many. Far less common was the ability to see how the parts were related and to understand the dynamic created by their interaction. Typical of the entire period is the attitude of one of the senior Prussian generals in 1806. He correctly foretold Napoleon's unorthodox strategy of not advancing on the main Prussian armies from the west, but of moving instead past them from the south and east, at the risk of uncovering his lines of communication, until he had interposed himself between the Prussians and their base of operations around Berlin. But this accurate prediction led to the conclusion that the purpose of Napoleon's tremendous sweep through Germany was merely to dislodge the Prussians from their strong defensive position. The analyst could not connect a new element he had come to recognize to another—the search for a decisive battle under favorable strategic conditions.

The French were less hampered than others by this piecemeal recognition of the new reality; but anyone familiar with the very extensive military literature of Napoleonic France will be struck by the almost total absence of analyses that seek the larger picture. Instead, the literature is dominated by the practitioner with an intense concern for specifics. In part, the impact Napoleon had on French military thought may have been responsible. He certainly understood the new system, some of whose components he had pushed to their full potential; but his personality loomed so large that it inhibited understanding of the manner in which these components might fit together in other hands. And, of course, the emperor's personality and psychological needs weakened the French synthesis in practice—his increasing faith in numbers and massive shock, for instance, or his refusal to yield some authority to a staff that could direct large forces deployed over vast areas.

Only rarely does the literature, French and non-French, move beyond the study of relatively unconnected or badly connected particulars toward a true synthesis. Probably the most significant example is a long essay that Scharnhorst, soon to become Clausewitz's teacher, published in 1797, while still an officer in the Hanoverian army.[6] An analysis as precise and subtle as Scharnhorst's must be the work of an exceptional mind and cannot be explained by outside circumstances; but it may be worth noting that he was ideally situated to see his subject clearly. He had served against the French both as a troop commander and a staff officer, he was a prolific writer on war with a strong interest in theory, and as the son of well-to-do peasants, who had made his way only with difficulty in a particularly elitist army, he was more sensitive than most of his peers to the social side of the revolution. It was a measure of this genius that he was by no means an uncritical admirer of everything new and French. He did not overlook the advantages France enjoyed over the Allies in the revolutionary war that had little or nothing to do with new techniques: France's more favorable strategic position; greater population and wealth; a unified political and military command; and greater incentive. But he also accurately delineated the superiority of

French organization and tactics; and beyond the military instrument, he pointed to the greater strength generated by a freer society, an element on which he thought all depended in the end.

Scharnhorst's essay was widely read, and its impact on reform-minded officers in Germany cannot be doubted. But it failed to change the character of the literature. His analytic description of the new French system in its opening phases did not lead to further broad syntheses as the system matured under and against Napoleon. It remained for Clausewitz two decades later to continue and expand on Scharnhorst's pioneering work.

An entirely different approach—Antoine-Henri Jomini's—found a wider public and numerous imitators. Jomini extracted an operational doctrine from Napoleonic practice while disregarding the social and political forces that had brought about the new warfare and now formed its context. In part he owed his popularity to the fact that he addressed himself to those very numerous soldiers whose view of their calling was limited to technical issues and the mysteries of leadership. Unfortunately the principles and laws that, he claimed, comprised the science of war, were not logically developed from a study of war in all its forms, but were part of an arbitrary checklist derived from Jomini's limited personal experiences and observations.[7]

Clausewitz, in contrast, aimed for a comprehensive analysis, moving beyond Scharnhorst's interpretation of particular campaigns and Jomini's operational recipes toward a general theory of organized violence. He tried to conceptualize the universals, the constants in war, and trace their dynamics and interactions, thus constructing an analytic framework that would encompass all varieties of war, not just the war of major forces seeking a battlefield decision.

This is not the place for a discussion of Clausewitz's theories, but it is worth noting how little effect he had on the thought of his contemporaries and of the succeeding generation. His collected works, of which 1500 sets were printed in the early 1830s, were not sold out for more than twenty years—a minor indicator that accurately reflects the limits of his influence not only on military policy but also, at first, on the study of war.

Eventually, after the storms emanating from France had blown themselves out, how accurately did the men born in the 1770s and 1780s understand the changes that had taken place? How extensive and how firm was the intellectual mastery of the new war in post-Napoleonic Europe? Again one would have to say that the theoretical and practical understanding of techniques and procedures was considerable. And as it became obvious that, although the military methods of the Revolution required some social adjustments, they did not really demand a revolutionary society, the inhibiting effects of politics on interpretation largely faded. For instance, patriotism was a possible sentiment in an absolute monarchy as well as in a republic and could be as effective a spur on individual initiative. Far less complete, however, was the understanding of such larger issues as the relationship between political purpose and strategic aims, the function politics during the fighting, or the impact of war on social development. Military analysts tended to follow the pattern that Jacob Burckhardt, one of the originators of modern cultural history, thought he could identify in nineteenth century Europe: a shift from thinking man—*homo sapiens*—to technological man—*homo faber*. Another way of putting it might be that, except for someone like Clausewitz, students of war did not rise above their time, a time marked by very rapid population growth, industrialization, and the spread of the new secular religion of nationalism. In the end, like the societies of which they were a part, the analysts lost control of the military instruments.

CURRENT PROBLEMS

I should like to conclude by taking note of a few of the more obvious differences that distinguish the situation of military analysts in the late twentieth century from that of the Napoleonic generation.

The problem that preoccupies us today—how military power can assure national security and support national policy short of major war—did not loom large at the end of the eighteenth century. Certainly the deterrent function of armies and navies was fully recognized; but essentially technological, organizational, and operational aspects of war were studied in order to improve the performance of armed forces in anticipated future conflicts. The only potentially serious dangers that a weapons system posed to its own society were its costs and its impact on the political and social structure of the country. Men sought the greatest measure of military effectiveness consonant with their economy and the character of their society. Throughout the nineteenth century, at least for major powers, the avoidance of war was not the issue of life and death it has since become.

Not only is the analyst's task very different today, his place in society has changed, and society itself—even before the advent of the nuclear age—has entered into a new relationship with war and consequently with its armed forces.

The concurrent and linked developments of mass societies and industrialization affected not only how soldiers fight but also the control that government could exert on military policy. At least in countries whose peoples acquired a role in the political process, it became increasingly difficult to conduct wars according to the dictates of *raison d'état* as defined by small political elites. Public opinion, once mobilized to support the fighting, could not easily be ignored in the conduct of overall policy. The German governments during the First and Second World Wars might certainly have made peace at any time without taking the feelings of their people into account, which would, in any case, have favored such moves. But that was not true of the Allies between 1914 and 1918, nor of England and the United States during the Second World War. Governments whose policies were in part determined by moral judgments would have found it exceedingly difficult to negotiate for peace on the basis of reciprocal concessions. But, as Felix Gilbert has recently pointed out, in democratic or ideological wars, military calculations in the service of ideological insistence on total victory may prevail over political considerations. To an extent rarely known in the eighteenth and nineteenth century, the military then become the decision-makers.

Popular opinion not only may lack political perspective—as may governments—it undoubtedly is mystified by the new weapons and their implications. War has always been an arcane art, but never more so than today. The technological and strategic issues that confront the modern soldier are far less comprehensible to most of us than were their Napoleonic antecedents to our ancestors. From a scientific and technological point of view, armed forces today are again isolated in the larger world, as they were for social reasons in the eighteenth century—an isolation, we know, that the revolution in warfare had for a time reduced. But, ironically, the growing significance of technology has led to a contrary change in the social characteristics of military analysts. In the 1790s and the Napoleonic era, the study of military affairs was almost exclusively an occupation for soldiers and former soldiers. In the course of the nineteenth century this remained generally true, although a few civilians—Friedrich Engels, Herbert Spencer, or Ivan Bloch, for example—wrote important analyses of specific wars, of the role of the military in the modern world, and even of the impact that technological development might exert on future wars. In the twentieth century, as the interaction of science, industry, and military establishments has grown very close, civilians have come to assume a leading role in the study of military problems, and a new type of analyst has emerged, who combines technological understanding with expertise in such disciplines as sociology, political science, and economics. So far as their primary mission is concerned, armed forces have become more isolated from the bulk of the population, but at the same time they are more intensely connected with particular groups within that population.

Consequently, students of the problems of war in the nuclear age find themselves in a more ambiguous, in some respects more hostile, intellectual environment than did the generation of Scharnhorst, Clausewitz, and Jomini. The Enlightenment certainly regarded war as a monstrous evil, the result of passion and ignorance, which mankind would gradually overcome. We need only recall *Candide* for an expression of this attitude, which was held not only by philosophers but also by many serving soldiers. But Voltaire not only ridiculed and condemned war, in such works as *The Age of Louis XIV* he glorified war as the expression of national energy and cultural ideals. Educated opinion in the eighteenth and early nineteenth centuries regarded military institutions and war as subjects for reform not for abolition. Except for members of a few religious sects, practically every literate person from Rousseau on accepted the validity of wars of self-defense and accepted as well the balance of power as the regulative system of international relations, a system that sought not peace at any cost but the independence of the various states and of the community of states as a whole, which often could be assured only by the threat or the use of force. Today far less unanimity exists on these matters, and at least in the West a significant body of opinion continues to deny that the international situation demands the maintenance of large, up-to-date military establishments. The study of conflict has become more emotionally charged than ever before. What impact, if any, these hostile attitudes exert on the analyses themselves would be a fascinating subject for study, but it does seem clear that analysts today face a task that scarcely troubled their predecessors. Not only must they interpret the changes in war that have taken place in our lifetime, but for the sake of their ideas they must also try to bridge the gap that has opened between the study of conflict and the attitudes and fears of the larger society. Besides identifying and interpreting the significant issues, and working to get their ideas adopted, they must now educate public opinion in the continuing possibilities and new limitations of deterrence and war as instruments of national policy. The difficulties are obvious, and so is the need.

NOTES

1. Klaus Knorr, "Threat Perception," in *Historical Dimensions of National Security Problems*, ed. Klaus Knorr (Lawrence: University Press of Kansas, 1976).
2. These figures, somewhat lower for 1789 than usually given in the literature, are based on the most recent archival study of the French army during this period, Jean-Paul Bertaud, *La Révolution armée* (Paris: R. Laffont, 1979), pp. 36, 93, 137.
3. The following discussion owes much to Hans Delbrück's brilliant analysis in his *Geschichte der Kriegskunst* (*History of the Art of War*) (Berlin, 1920), vol. iv, pp. 457-484. See also Gerhard Ritter, *Frederick the Great*, ed. and transl. Peter Paret

(Berkeley and Los Angeles: University of California Press, 1968), pp. 129-148; and Peter Paret, *Yorck and the Era of Prussian Reform* (Princeton, N.J.: Princeton University Press, 1966), pp. 7-46.

4. By contrast, eighteenth-century conditions of supply and of troop mobility and discipline made it possible to maneuver entire armies into positions in which they felt compelled to surrender.

5. Michael Howard, *War in European History* (Oxford: Oxford University, 1976), pp. 88-89.

6. For the following, see Peter Paret, *Clausewitz and the State* (New York: Oxford University Press, 1976) Chap. 4, especially p. 64.

7. Ibid., pp. 204-205. See also the informative discussion in John I. Alger, *Antoine-Henri Jomini: A Bibliographical Survey* (West Point, 1975).

Chapter 9

On Strategic Surprise

Klaus Knorr

Strategic Surprise can be defined either from the viewpoint of the state that inflicts it on another or of the state that suffers it. In launching their Blitzkrieg against France in 1940, the Germans sought to inflict surprise and succeeded in doing so. The Japanese also succeeded at Pearl Harbor, as did the North Vietnamese and Vietcong in the Tet offensive. The shared objective in these cases was to gain a major military advantage by doing the unexpected. However, Prussia achieved its brilliant victories against Austria in 1866 and against France in 1870 without taking pains to do the unexpected, although she waged war in a manner that was unexpected by the Austrians and the French. Helmuth Moltke simply designed a brilliant war-winning strategy and applied it. Yet the Austrians and French were utterly surprised. Strategic surprise, then, can also be defined as suffering a major military disadvantage by *experiencing* the unexpected.

For the purpose of this essay, I will ignore the planning and execution of strategic surprise by generals in an ongoing war, such as General MacArthur's Inchon landing in Korea. This is a fairly common event once a military conflict is under way. Instead, I will focus on surprise in *grand* strategy in which government authorities play a major role. On this level, strategic surprise comes about in two principal ways, either by the unexpected initiation or extension of war or by the unexpected intervention in a conflict already under way. Thus, Stalin was surprised when the Germans invaded the Soviet Union in 1941. Britain, France, and the Scandinavian countries were surprised by the German occupation of Norway and Denmark in 1940, and the United States was surprised by the North Korean attack on South Korea in 1950. Strategic surprise, however, is not only a matter of *whether* an attack occurs but also of *where* and *how* an attack takes place. Indeed, it is this second way, involving unexpected *modes* of warfare, that figures more frequently in the annals of strategic surprise. Thus, the French and British were surprised by the mode of German attack in 1940, the Japanese by the U.S. atomic bombing of Nagasaki and Hiroshima, and the United States—though not surprised by the fact of Chinese intervention in the Korean war—was surprised by its military scope.

Clausewitz, in his classic book *On War*, observes that strategic surprise was a relatively rare event.[1] He mentions only two cases. One suspects that the slow evolution of arms technology and the ponderous movement of European armies before and during his time mainly accounted for the results he observed. However, strategic surprise has occurred with great apparent frequency since Clausewitz wrote. As defined, surprise has been present in most military conflicts over the last 150 years, and these cases have been events of serious, if often not fatal, consequence. The Egyptian armies in 1973 were eventually on the brink of defeat even though Israel had been surprised by the Arab attack. That surprise, though not fatal, caused a high level of Israeli casualties. No wonder that strategic surprise and strategic warning have become important problems in statecraft. Yet systematic study of these phenomena has begun only recently and is far from complete.

Diverse aspects of surprise call for such study; frequency, consequences, incentives, and opportunities are certainly among them. I will not expand on the questions of frequency and consequences and will touch only briefly on incentives. In this essay, I will concentrate on opportunities.

Not much needs to be said about the *incentive* structure. The advantages of achieving strategic surprise are obvious. Surprise not only allows a scheming actor to choose time, place, and mode of engagement, it also promises denial of this knowledge to the other nation. As Clausewitz put it, successful surprise is a means of gaining immediate military superiority and has the secondary effects of confusing the defender (thereby reducing his ability to adopt coherent countermeasures) and often of delivering a shock to the defender's morale.[2] In short, surprise promises a quick military victory achieved at relatively low costs in terms of forces required and casualties sustained. Indeed, strategic surprise is apt to be the only way for an actor inferior in military resources to win against a superior enemy or to stave off defeat. It is, therefore, the actor worried about his inferiority in material resources and, in particular, one who has suffered defeat in a previous war, who is alive to the possibility of doing better by means of achieving surprise. The incentive structure becomes more complicated only when an attempt at achieving surprise involves great risks or when other kinds of disincentive, such as the need to violate international law, enters the picture. The strength of incentives is, of course, related to the perception of opportunity and requisite capabilities.

It is the *opportunity* structure that is generally much more complex and interesting than the fairly obvious attractiveness of achieving strategic surprise. I am unable to deal with this structure exhaustively in one essay and therefore will focus on what seem to me the primary and usually crucial factors or clusters of factors. These are (1) the recognition of opportunity; (2) the ability of keeping the intended target from perceiving the danger of impending surprise, and (3) the ability to decide on seizing the opportunity.

The ability to identify opportunity and work out operational plans for exploiting it clearly requires searching, inventive, and innovating minds—qualities far from common on high levels of state- and military-craft. For instance, the idea of the German Blitzkrieg in the West was conceived of by a very few kindred military spirits who found the German high command highly resistant and prevailed only after Hitler personally intervened. Germany's top generals had been resigned to the necessity of once again fighting a prolonged general war, much like World War I. Like their French opponents they were sound professionals ensconced in a bureaucracy that tended to stifle imagination. The small group of German innovators saw an opportunity for a speedy armored breakthrough in a section of the front—the densely wooded mountains of the Ardennes—which the enemy expected to be safe. A capacity for discovering a strategic opportunity that no, or very few, others could identify is evidently *one* important condition for achieving surprise. This is especially true when surprise results from an unexpected mode of warfare. But, as the German example of 1940 reveals, it is not enough for a few individuals to invent and design strategic schemes aimed at providing opportunities for surprising the opponent. The critical condition is that people at the top level of governmetal and military bureaucracies adopt such schemes and prepare for their implementation.

In recent history, by far the most important opportunities for seizing surprise have been provided by two factors: advances in science and technology, and various weaknesses displayed by the victim of surprise. Examples of seizing technological opportunities are the Prussian victories of 1866 and 1870. The use of the new railroad and telegraph systems presented the specific opportunity for rapidly mobilizing and concentrating superior forces on the chosen battlefield. Gordon Craig attributes the quick and astounding defeat of Austria mainly to the Prussian development of a general staff, which exploited methods of scientific planning for innovating novel modes of warfare. In contrast, Austrian (and French) commanders disdained such staff planning, regarding it as mere paperwork.[3]

Michael Howard concluded that the equally unexpected defeat of France in 1870, until then regarded as Europe's preeminent military power, was ultimately the result not so much of incompetent generalship and differences in armament as of a "faulty military system."[4] The Prussians had succeeded in adapting the ongoing industrial revolution to the conduct of war, while the French had not even considered these larger military implications of quickening industrial development. A third example, from World War II, is the German combination of massed armor and tactical aircraft used for thrusting quickly and deeply through enemy lines and enveloping the disorganized opposing forces. It was not that the Germans had more tanks and aircraft but that they innovated a new and bold manner of their use which condemned the French and British to surprise and defeat. The American employment of atomic bombs against Japan is another obvious example of the exploitation of new science and technology.

Evidently, technological opportunities for springing surprise on an opponent depend both on the pace and breadth of scientific and technological progress and of differences in national abilities to perceive and exploit these opportunities. Not only must technological possibilities be recognized—and this requires true inventiveness—their exploitation must also be made operationally effective in terms of weapons, military forces, doctrine, strategy, and tactics. This will not happen unless the top decisionmakers are converted. Witness the long struggle of U.S. enthusiasts for the aircraft carrier against the battleship admirals before World War II.

The entire process resembles that of developing new types of civilian goods. A great deal of innovational development and investment is demanded in order to span the distance from the gleam of a new idea to successful merchandising. Because nations differ in the eagerness, skill, and risk-taking with which new applications of force are derived from scientific and technological growth, the more adept are able to surprise the laggards.

But there is a further consideration here. Throughout the ages, advances in military technology, whether slow or rapid, have exhibited a tendency to favor either defense or offense, depending upon the relative significance of the enhanced value of firepower and the shock of offensive attack. These alternative effects of the technological state of the art are relevant to our problem inasmuch as it is generally assumed that the technological superiority of offense favors surprise while its technological inferiority obstructs surprise and tends to make the outcome of conflict a matter of fairly static warfare and gradual material attrition. But the stated implications of this tendency, although correctly perceived, are being accepted with excessive finality.

To begin with, it is often unclear prior to war, especially when no major conflict has taken place for some time, what precise effects arms technology has generated in these terms. In retrospect, it is perfectly clear that defensive technology was superior to the offensive in World War I. Yet this was by no means recognized by governments and military leaders before the event. As we know, they expected a very short war rather than a stalemated one of slow attrition. Moreover, if the basic technological superiority of defense over offense is recognized by leaders, this gives the prospective attacker an additional incentive to look for a strategic surprise that would avoid the bloody stalemate of prolonged hostilities. It was precisely this incentive that led the Germans to develop the Schlieffen Plan, which might have succeeded in 1914, had this imaginative strategy not been compromised fatally by General Schlieffen's successors. Anxiety about another stalemate in the West in the second World War also prompted a few German planners—especially Generals Von Manstein and Guderian—to invent the Blitzkrieg which—as the later war in Russia suggested—exploited a special and perhaps fleeting technological opportunity to reverse the fundamental trend. Technological trends are ordinarily complex and do not uniformly favor either offensive or defensive operations. This gives room for the innovative mind to intervene and, at least temporarily, to defy an overall trend. This is how trends tend to beget countertrends.

In short, the proposition that evolving technology favors one side or the other is, after all, only a *tendency* and does not warrant flat expectations. Tendencies can be evaded or counteracted by superior innovational responses. The effect of new technology to favor fire power, and thus defense, was already present in 1866 and 1870, as it was earlier during the American Civil War—hence the bloodiness of individual battles. But Moltke found the means to counter the advantage of tactical defense by a new form of swift strategic maneuver. His ability to sidestep adverse technological conditions by preemptively exploiting recent technological progress in transportation and communications permitted him to reap the fruits of strategic surprise.[5] Israel, in the Six Day War of 1967, succeeded in reenacting Blitzkrieg against its Arab opponents not because technology favored the offense but because its preemptive attack, brilliantly executed, surprised and defeated the Arabs before their defensive capabilities could be properly brought into play. It seems to me that the defender who close-mindedly relies on a basic trend in weapons technology to make offensive operations too costly furnishes the attacker with an opportunity for staging strategic surprise. This is what happened to France in 1940. The evolution in arms technology had in fact favored the concept of the Maginot Line.[6] The Germans, however, found holes in the defensive system and punched through with one annihilating blow. The famous Maginot Line was never breached.

Technological opportunity is only one, though a major, condition allowing strategic surprise to be planned. Exploitable weaknesses in an opponent's posture for deterrence and defense represent another extremely rich source of opportunities for surprise. Indeed, it is not easy to find cases of strategic surprise that did not benefit from the involuntary cooperation of the victim, and quite often this contribution is a necessary and sufficient condition of success. The use of atom bombs on Japan is one of the few exceptions.

The kinds of vulnerabilities are many and difficult to summarize. Most are obvious enough not to require elaboration, and I will only list them in order to sufficiently dwell on those that are analytically complex and interesting. First, a relatively low level of military preparedness and particular weaknesses in force structure, weaponry, and deployment readily present opportunities. Second, and related is a persistent inclination of defenders to overestimate their own military capability—especially in their qualitative aspects, e.g., morale, generalship, strategy—relative to that of the opponent. Both Austria in 1866 and France in 1870 relied too much on what they believed to be their proven superiority in the traditional martial virtues. They both underrated Prussia'a development of a modern general staff that invented and applied a technological concept for swiftly concentrating massive forces converging from different directions on the decisive battlefield. Dash and bravery were no match for this well-functioning deployment machine.

Third, there is the standard difficulty in international threat perception of drawing correct inferences from information that is fragmentary, quickly becomes obsolescent, and is, above all, inconsistent and ambiguous. This tendency often accounts, in part, for a low level of defensive preparation and the tendency to overestimate one's own strength vis-à-vis the opponent's. As Roberta Wohlstetter put it in her trenchant case study on Pearl Harbor, this is the classic problem of disentangling "signals"—the available indicators of impending action—from the surrounding "noise", that is, all the other information that distracts attention.[7] The essential point is that it is not easy to sift the one from the other, except in retrospect when the outcome is known.

The central problem is, of course, that ambiguous information can have alternative explanations and can be usable for different forecasts. Subsidiary factors can magnify the difficulty. As was the case before the Japanese attack on Pearl Harbor, the signals may be bureaucratically dispersed. Their assembly at one point was then a prerequisite to discovering a significant pattern. In other instances, warning signals were disregarded or belittled because the source of the information was regarded as untrustworthy. The source that cries "wolf" too often is not believed when the warning happens to be valid. (Stalin discredited the warnings of a German attack from Churchill and Roosevelt because he suspected them of trying to deceive him. He assumed that they were interested in provoking war between Nazi Germany and the Soviet Union.)

The routine of threat perception also lacks alertness to anything bold and out of the ordinary the opponent might plan, especially if assessments have fixed upon another contingency. Anticipating the Japanese attack on Pearl Harbor would have taken a great deal of imagination, even though Japan had acted similarly on February 9, 1904, when its naval forces attacked Port Arthur one day before the government declared war on Russia. The French conclusion in 1940 that German armor would not attempt to lunge through the Ardennes area was far from unsound. As already mentioned, the German high command opposed the idea. It was an unexpected choice that only alertness to the unusual would have taken into account.

I want to emphasize that ambiguity of information is a very widespread factor in preventing correct and timely warning of attack. After all, opponents may undertake partial military mobilization or deploy forces on a critical boundary for backing threats rather than for preparing an attack. It was this alternative explanation that helped Stalin in 1941 to reject the warnings of an impending German invasion. Similarly, in 1967, the concentration of Warsaw Pact troops near the Czechoslovakian boundary *could* have served the exclusive purpose of pressuring the Czechoslovakian government, and this alternative interpretation misled the intelligence services of several countries. Indeed, it is quite likely that the Soviet leaders has hoped to coerce Czechoslovakia by means of a military threat and resorted to an actual invasion only when this threat was defied. As another example, the Japanese commanders who attacked Pearl Harbor were under instruction to do so only if they were virtually certain of achieving surprise.

In other words, the state initiating a threatening military action may be pursuing multiple plans and its final choice of operation depends upon unfolding circumstances. Ambiguity of the opponent's intentions is inherent in such cases. One cannot predict what an opponent will do as long as he has not decided on his future course of action. But proper threat perception should therefore include a range of contingencies. Had American intelligence conceived of a Japanese naval raid on Pearl Harbor as a possible contingency and had U.S. forces been patrolling the North Pacific approaches to the Hawaiian Islands, there would have been no attack at Pearl Harbor.

But there is a still deeper problem that militates against proper threat perception. The perceiver does not approach his task of ferreting out warning wignals from ambiguous information with an unstructured, that is, completely open, mind. He approaches the job with a set of assumptions about how the relevant outside world is constituted. He has developed a concept about the other actor's pattern of behavior and capabilities. These analytical preconceptions are often based on sound reasoning from past experience. French assumptions about the unlikely choice of the Ardennes for an armored breakthrough were professionally solid. Similarly, the British were surprised by the German occupation of Norway because they assumed that simultaneous German troop landings over a thousand-mile stretch of rugged coastline were far too risky to be considered feasible in the face of vast British naval superiority. The Norwegians were surprised because they shared the British assumption. The U.S. government was surprised by the Soviet deployment of long-range nuclear arms on Cuba because intelligence professionals had observed the Soviet Union over the decades to be extremely unadventurous in its use and deployment of force. To place nuclear missiles in Cuba seemed to these analysts extraordinarily adventurous; they concluded, therefore, that the Soviets were installing something less offensive in Cuba.

Reliance even on apparently sound assumptions about an opponent is evidently risky and may court surprise. This is so because an actor can break an established pattern of behavior, especially when he sees a strong incentive for doing so or because the actor seeking to inflict surprise scans unusual possibilities near the edge of feasibility. In the case of the deployment of missiles in Cuba, the assumptions of American intelligence were not wrong. The Soviets had not intentionally shifted to adventurist behavior. Soviet intelligence sources had apparently miscalculated likely American reactions. Acting on this premise, Soviet leaders thought that their action in Cuba carried little risk. The American reaction surprised the Soviet government.

One reason Stalin did not believe in a German attack in 1942 was because all of Hitler's previous attacks (on Austria, Czechosovakia and Poland) had been preceded by weeks of strident demands and other overt crisis behavior. Because this had not happened vis-à-vis the Soviet Union, Stalin inferred that an attack was not imminent, but this time Hitler acted outside his usual pattern. No matter how carefully forecasts of an actor's behavior are derived from a study of the past, they can prove wrong because past conduct is not necessarily indicative of future conduct. No such projections into the future should enjoy full confidence. In matters of great consequence, the possibility of future deviant behavior should never be dismissed. In an earlier paper, I called this the problem of "behavioral surprise."[8]

In addition to the often observable fact that apparently sound assumptions can mislead us, there is the still deeper problem that the choice and use of preconceptions is guided by subconscious predispositions rather than by objective analysis of past experience, and that this guidance tends to lead the perceiver astray. Any number of particular phenomena may account for predispositions that distort perceptions of the real world around us. Ideological and ethnocentric stereotypes, and emotions such as contempt, conceit, and hatred may veil reality from us. Following their glorious victory of 1967, the Israelis' conceit contributed to a discounting of Arab will and capabilities. Perhaps the most common of these underlying predispositions is wishfulness, that is, the widespread human tendency to expect what one would like to see happen. The most striking example of this in recent history was Stalin's surprise by the German attack in 1941. The Germans had gradually concentrated large forces along their boundary with the Soviet Union. The British and American governments and the Soviet intelligence services had warned Stalin of an impending German attack, as had German deserters. Yet Stalin rejected all warnings. Until the German armies actually invaded his country, he refused to believe that they would do so and preferred to interpret German troop deployment as a means of threatening the Soviet government for the purpose of wresting concessions from it. Is is generally accepted in the literature that Stalin perceived his country to be militarily unprepared for war with Germany and believed that another year was required to ready it for battle. He wanted that extra year very badly and this wishfulness distorted his perceptions.

More generally, one observes that societies reluctant to spend enough on deterrence and defense, because they wish to allocate resources to other purposes, are also inclined to lower their expectations of foreign military threats. Once these predispositions take hold, discrepant information is easily ignored or explained away because it is unpleasant to revise one's perceptions; and the inertial power of these predispositions is all the greater because they intervene subconsciously in the perceptual act, and because relevant information, including warning signals, is usually equivocal. In short, strategic warning is not easily heeded when it means accepting an unwelcome prospect.[9]

Viewing all the problems of proper threat perception and threat assessment together, one must admit that they are truly formidable. It is not a matter of stupidity. There can be no such thing as knowledge of the future. All we can do is conjecture and our guesses have a good chance of being proven wrong. But it is less than wise to set too much store by our conjectures, whatever the care we have taken in developing them. The ultimate fact of uncertainty regarding the future should always remain a part of our expectations.

One additional related problem deserves to be mentioned. Warning signals may make the intended victim of strategic surprise unsure, convinced neither that a threat is acute nor that it is absent. Of course, once the *possibility* of a threat is recognized, whatever the probability attributed to it, true suprise is excluded. Yet the attacker may still enjoy a strategic advantage either because the defender, unsure about his future security, is reluctant to embark upon full countermeasures and absorb the cost involved, or because he is afraid that such defensive action may prove provocative and increase the likelihood of attack.

Turning to some specific capabilities that help in planning and executing strategic surprise, there is, first of all, the ability to withhold or diminish warning to the intended target state. The actor planning surprise may be able to add to the victim's difficulty of receiving and correctly interpreting warning signals. Warning may be withheld or greatly reduced if a surprise attack can be launched without prior deployment or other highly visible activities indicating the possiblity of attack. Note the persistant NATO worry that, on the central front in Europe, the Soviets might be able to attack from a standing start. Of course, this ability to launch a surprise move without telltale preparations depends, in turn, on various favorable conditions, such as the achievement of complete surprise, a low state of defensive preparedness on the part of the target state, and technological factors that permit lightning offensive strikes.

The capacity for maintaining full secrecy about preparations for inflicting strategic surprise is obviously another factor that reduces the chance of warning. Before launching their surprise occupation of Norway in 1940, for instance, German troops assembled for the operation were told only at the very last moment about their destination.

Countries evidently differ appreciably in their ability to depend on discipline for preserving secrecy. Closed societies and authoritarian governments obviously enjoy an advantage in this respect. Finally, a state intent on surprising another may resort to deception in order to mask its preparations. It will then issue disinformation to make it harder for the target country to separate signals from the accompanying noise. For example, when military surprise requires the assembly of large bodies of troops and equipment, large-scale military maneuvers can be used to deceive the opponent. This is what the Egyptians did several times before they attacked Israel in 1973. The Israelis discovered that it was too costly for them to start mobilization every time Egyptian forces approached the Suez Canal in a manner which could end up in no more than a large-scale training exercise. Of course, there were other reasons—again, faulty Israeli assumptions—that allowed the Arab states to achieve strategic surprise in this case. But playing the maneuver game contributed to this effect. The Allied commanders who planned the Normandy invasion went through elaborate measures of deception in order to make the Germans expect a landing in the Pas de Calais area (although it can be argued that this was a matter of tactical rather than strategic surprise).

The ability to approximate unitary decisionmaking is a final condition that affects a state's capacity for springing strategic surprise on another. Risks, perhaps very dangerous risks, are often associated with initiating an unexpected war or an unexpected form of attack. The pros and cons, therefore, may be hotly debated and, even if caution or timidity do not prevail and a plan is not rejected outright, divided counsels may cause the plan to be compromised and weakened to such an extent that its chances of success are fatally diminished.

Thus, the famous Schlieffen Plan devised by the German general staff before World War I was so much impaired by compromise that, in 1914, though coming close to success, it eventually failed. This plan—intended to overcome technological conditions favoring defense and hence a protracted war of attrition, which Germany could not hope to win—depended on concentrating a very large proportion of German forces on the right wing in the North and luring French armies into an invasion of thinly defended southern Germany. Various objections, notably the inability to accept a French invasion into southern Germany caused this bold plan to become seriously impaired. By contrast, the German strategies of surprise in World War II would not have been adopted without Hitler's authority to make final and binding decisions nor, of course, without Hitler's penchant for performing daring and dramatic acts. In each case, there was too much opposition in the German military command structure at the time for risky strategies of surprise to have been adopted without Hitler's decisive intervention.

This does not mean that an absolute personal dictatorship is a prerequisite for choosing a strategy of surprise. The basic form of government is probably only a minor factor in this connection. The Japanese decision to attack the American fleet at Pearl Harbor was made by a tightly-knit elite group. And as the American use of atomic bombs in Japan shows, democratic societies are also able to plan and execute strategic surprise. Once a war is on and public backing is strong, such societies can adopt the necessary forms of tight decisionmaking. The qualification "once a war is on" indicates, however, a restraining factor. On the other hand, conflicts of interest over strategy are by no means impossible or unknown in authoritarian countries. Witness the compromising of the Schlieffen Plan in pre-World War I Germany. This is one of the subjects on which more systematic research is badly needed. The question ultimately focuses on the existence of a decisionmaking structure in which the representatives of conflicting interests lack a paralyzing power of veto and in which innovation and risk-taking are held in high esteem. The overwhelming influence of the military in such decisionmaking is by no means a sufficient or even a necessary condition. Many historical examples disclose that those at the top military levels are often inclined toward excessive caution—perhaps because they expect to be blamed if an unorthodox strike fails—and that it takes civilian leaders for boldness to prevail.

Decisionmaking problems regarding the planning of strategic surprise tend to be compounded when the plans involve cooperation among sovereign allies. Not only is the planning process then more cumbersome and secrecy less maintainable, allies are also apt to differ on the risks attached to a strategy of surprise. In fact, an ally may do things on his own that endanger the surprise strategy of another. In World War II, for instance, Hitler's invasion of the Soviet Union was delayed by Mussolini's illconsidered attack in the Balkans—a delay which, giving the German forces less time before winter set in, may have prevented the capture of Moscow.

This completes my analysis of past cases of strategic surprise. There is, however, the question of whether past experience is fully or for the most part indicative of future problems of this kind. Are all the determinants of strategic surprise still operative, or have some of them been overtaken by historical change that either weakened them or removed them altogether from the list of concerns? Or, alternatively, have new determinants emerged or old ones been strengthened?

I will address the impingement of only four major forms of historical change. These, I suspect, are by far the mose significant, if not the only, ones to bear on the question. They involve the kind and degree of advances in science and technology in recent decades.

The first concerns the issue of whether the most recent progress in arms technology has not, once again, come to favor military defense over offense, thereby reducing the opportunities for mounting strategic surprise. Strategic nuclear capabilities clearly lend themselvs to surprise attack. The crucial question here is whether any attack between nuclear powers of roughly the same rank is ever worthwhile. There is obviously little, if any, incentive under conditions of mutually assured destruction. Attack by surprise approaches the level of consideration only if one power can confidently disarm the other by striking preemptively, that is, by disarming either its retaliatory forces or its will to retaliate. This condition does not prevail at the present time. Whether or not it will emerge in the future depends on the development of weapons technology, the use various countries make of it, and perceptions of the retaliatory will of the target state.

On the conventional level, a great many experts have recently taken the view that, as the Yom Kippur War of 1973 is alleged to have demonstrated, the rise of precision-guided weapons has once again conceded technological superiority to the defense over the offense.[10] However, while this thesis, if valid, restricts opportunities for surprise attack as a means of achieving quick and decisive military results, this development does not, for reasons indicated earlier, eliminate the opportunity. Ingenious planning may, as happened in 1940 or in the Franco-German War of 1870, find or create special conditions that overcome the general handicap. Means may be discovered for attacking strategically while staying tactically on the defensive, and the very achievement of strategic surprise is apt to facilitate such attack.[11] Indeed, the chance of such plans being encouraged and succeeding would be enhanced if defensive states placed excessive trust in the doctrine that pronounces the technological superiority of defense. Over-confidence can breed vulnerability. Moreover, the new thesis is by no means uncontested. The results of the 1973 war are ambiguous in this respect because its course and outcome were affected by a number of other conditions—e.g., differences in military skill, morale, and leadership, and the intervention of the superpowers. Continued Soviet commitment to a strategy of swift offensive movement indicates that Soviet strategists seem unconvinced of the imputed superiority of defensive systems, or they hope that other factors will offset or overcome it. Finally, although the impact of the possible use of tactical nuclear arms is hard to foresee, on the whole they appear to favor offensive operations because these weapons are comparatively vulnerable to preemptive first strikes unless they are highly dispersed. In addition, their first use in a surprise strike may create paralyzing confusion and perhaps even defeatism in the target country. Tactical nuclear weapons might in principle help the defense, but not many may survive the onset of war to do so. It looks as if these arms favor the offensive strategically even if they disfavor it tactically. Probably not much has changed regarding the bearing of new technology on the relative effectiveness of offensive or defensive forces. These effects are never unidirectional as both offensive and defensive systems are improved; and whatever net effect in favor of defense there might be at any one time, ingenuity can divert or overcome this tendency and, as mentioned, other factors affect the consequences.

Recent technological progress has also brought immense improvements in strategic warning systems, especially the ability to monitor signal traffic from a distance and intelligence satellites which permit a close visual monitoring of foreign military activities—although adverse conditions, notably poor weather, can temporarily deny or reduce the utility of this capability. It is, however, a capability at present fully available only to the United States and the Soviet Union, and its future spread is likely to remain confined either for reasons of costs or because the technological know-how is closely held. This development no doubt impacts significantly the possibility of strategic surprise. Certain historical cases of surprise would not have occurred if these warning systems had existed. The Blitzkrieg in the West, in 1940, might not have happened or succeeded, and the Japanese attack on Pearl Harbor certainly would not have taken place. This technology definitely helps the defender who possesses it and tends to reduce the possibilities of surprise.

Yet one should not overestimate this restrictive effect. First, there are several past cases of surprise that the new warning capability would not have prevented—e.g., the German occupation of Norway (carefully planned to benefit from cloud cover), the German attack on the Soviet Union (before which all observable information was available to Soviet government), and the atomic bombing of Japan (which hardly would have yielded sufficient observable clues in advance.) Also—and this is very significant—Israel was surprised by the Arab attack in 1973 even though it had abundant photographic and other information on Syrian and Egyptian preparations.

Advance warning by signal and satellite intelligence is of limited usefulness vis-à-vis an opponent who maintains a high state of mobilization and readiness and can strike a surprising blow from deployment customary in military exercises. If this opponent knows the availability of the new warning systems to the intended target of surprise, he will design against it, for instance, by making military maneuvers look exactly like preparations for attack. The Egyptians played the maneuver game in 1973 and the Israelis, not believing in an Arab attack on other grounds, found it too costly to mobilize every time the Arab forces made threatening moves. Moreover, they wished not to provoke an attack by defensive measures which the Arab states might regard as threatening. Technologically less sophisticated means of intelligence had been good enough in 1940 to give the British the sort of information that more modern systems would provide. They knew the fleets and number of divisions the Germans had assembled for the lightning occupation of Norway. Yet, the British were completely taken by surprise because they regarded such modest forces as grossly insufficient, in the face of German naval inferiority, for the objectives the Germans had set.

Furthermore, not all components of capability that figure in an attempt at inflicting strategic surprise are physically observable, for example, generalship and troop morale; while other components, such as new tactics, may be observable only when the attack has begun. There is also the additional complication of the time lag between the procurement of masses of information for processing, the consideration of the analytical results at the top level of decisionmaking, and the launching of countermeasures. Time lags may be lengthy enough to accomodate the execution of surprise. Finally, and very importantly, the actor planning surprise will benefit greatly if the observational capacity supplied by new technology is available to him as well, for it would help him in identifying weak spots in the other side's defenses. I am inclined to conclude, therefore, that—even though new information technologies can give warning that tends to limit the infliction of strategic surprise— it leaves ample opportunities for planning and staging of surprise.

Clausewitz was intrigued by what has been called the "fog of war," that is, the ever present severe limits on the information commanders have about ongoing battles. While in this area, too, modern means of observation and communication have been vastly improved since his time, the problem remains formidable because of technological progress in weaponry. The frequency and variety with which many new arms are now developed and deployed foreshadow formidable problems in anticipating what will happen in a future war, especially after a long absence of hostilities between major powers. I have heard many a professional soldier confess that he had no idea what would happen if a war broke out in Central Europe, especially once tactical nuclear weapons come to be used, except that the result would be utter chaos. If this assumption is valid, it may point to another way in which technological advance may present new opportunities for springing surprise. At least it would seem that such opportunities would offer themselves to military planners whose guesses are a bit better than those of the opposing side and who, by achieving surprise, can give a degree of direction as to how the evolving fog might be penetrated and put to use.

Finally, and beyond the realm of technology, there is the question of whether statesmen have not learned from past experiences how to avoid or minimize the experience of strategic surprise. We have, after all, a pretty good knowledge of the factors that have contributed to its frequent occurence. To the extent that these factors are lodged in special capabilities of the country seeking to inflict surprise, one would expect statesmen to be on the lookout for, and to have searched for, observable indicators of such capabilities. Also, to the extent that the opportunities for staging surprise are offered by the intended target state, one would expect properly focused self-analysis for the purpose of preventing or minimizing the chances of becoming the victim of strategic surprise. On both scores, the developing theory of international threat perception should facilitate such learning. Some learning, no doubt, has taken place, but on the whole, I am not optmistic in this matter.

To begin with, as plenty of examples indicate, it is far from easy to derive proper lessons from history. The tendency is to oversimplify one's reading of past events and their causes and to expect history to repeat itself in a mechanical fashion. The problem is that strategic surprise can take many forms and that these are apt to capitalize on different configurations of circumstances. This difficulty is magnified in that the systematic, as distinct from the monographic, study of past cases is still in its infancy, and preliminary research results, obtained for the most part in the academic world, have not necessarily been absorbed by statecraft, or are assimilated by it only with a considerable time lag.

Second, as we know from human experience in many contexts, learning something intelligently from past experience does not necessarily ensure that this knowledge is applied in future conduct, because our preference structure may conflict with the implications of this knowledge. If we want to do something very badly, we are tempted to ignore the lessons of the past or to reinterpret them in a way that accomodates our preferences.

Finally, recalling the first part of this essay, correct perception of future contingencies is intrinsically very difficult. As in the past, the information we must rely on will often, if not usually, be fragmentary, obsolescent and ambiguous. As in the past, analytical assumptions about the behavior and resources of foreign actors may lead us astray, especially if such actors have a strong incentive and capacity to do the unexpected and to deceive us. And as in the past, various predispositions, and notably wishfulness, may make us unreceptive to incompatible signals.

There has been one further change in parameters that does not touch on the structure of opportunities for staging strategic surprise. Rather, it permits me to return briefly to the problem of incentive. The technology and production of complex modern weapons systems—such as submarines, attack aircraft and heavy tanks—have become so exacting in terms of economic as well as technological resources that only a few nations can produce them and only the two superpowers can achieve self-sufficiency over the entire range of modern systems. Even the industrial middle powers must be selective in this respect. The upshot is that nearly all countries are highly dependent on foreign arms of a complex nature even though many are able to produce simpler arms.

The resulting dependency of most states on foreign suppliers constitutes a grave vulnerability in any prolonged military conflict. Witness the tremendous daily rate at which arms and ammunition were consumed during the Yom Kippur War. The dependent states cannot be sure that resupply will be forthcoming or delivered speedily and in sufficient volume. This vulnerability clearly makes it desirable to wage war with the armament stocks on hand and to win quickly. There is nothing like striking successfully with surprise to make this possible. It seems reasonable to deduce, on the basis of this consideration, that statecraft faces an additional incentive in seeking to inflict surprise on an opponent if hostilities cannot be avoided.

I am driven to the overall conclusion, though it is based on much guesswork, that there is no reason to suppose that strategic surprise has declined as a future contingency. I know that this conclusion is distressing. It is a conclusion I wish I could have replaced with a more reassuring one because strategic surprise, more often than not, has worked in favor of the aggressor and against the defender, and also because many a war would probably not have been started without the hope for success kindled by the opportunity of seeking to profit from strategic surprise.

NOTES

1. Carl von Clausewitz, *On War*, ed. and transl. by Michael Howard and Peter Paret (Princeton, N.J.: Princeton University Press, 1976), p. 199.
2. ibid., p. 198.
3. Gordon A. Craig, *The Battle of Koniggratz* (Philadelphia: Lippincott, 1964), chap. 2.
4. Michael Howard, *The Franco-Prussian War* (New York: Macmillan, 1961), p. 1.
5. Martin van Greveld, *Military Lessons of the Yom Kippur War: Historical Perspectives*, The Washington Papers, vol. 3, (Beverly Hills, Calif.: Sage Publications, 1975), pp. 41-42.
6. Vivian Rowe, *The Great Wall of France, The Triumph of the Maginot Line* (New York: Putnam's, 1961), p. 9.
7. Roberta Wohlstetter, *Pearl Harbor: Warning and Decision* (Stanford, Calif.: Stanford University Press, 1961).
8. Klaus Knorr, "Failures in National Intelligence Estimates: The Case of the Cuban Missiles," *World Politics*, 16, April 1964, pp. 455-467.

9. See Alexander L. George and Richard Smoke, *Deterrence in American Foreign Policy: Theory and Practice* (New York: Columbia University Press, 1974), pp. 572-576.

10. Erik Klippenberg, "New Weapons Technology and the Offense/Defense Balance in New Conventional Weapons and East-West Security," pt. 2, *Adelphi Papers*, no. 145, (London: International Institute for Strategic Studies, 1977), pp. 26-32; James Digby, "New Technology and Super-Power Actions in Remote Contingencies," *Survival*, 21, March/April 1979, pp. 61-67.

11. Van Greveld, *Military Lessons*, pp. 45-46.

Chapter 10

Toward a Soviet-American Crisis Prevention Regime: History and Prospects

Alexander L. George

Contributors to strategic studies have given a great deal of attention to a variety of urgent problems that the two superpowers have had to cope with since World War II—problems of deterrence, crisis management, escalation, coercive diplomacy, arms control, war termination, and avoidance of misperceptions and miscalculations. The equally important problem of how the United States and the Soviet Union might moderate their rivalry and competition in third areas to avoid dangerous confrontations has received much less attention. Crisis prevention may well be considered the orphan of strategic studies.

Part of the explanation for the relative neglect of crisis prevention in strategic studies is that during the Cold War the highest priority had to be given to deterrence and crisis management. The great gulf that divided the United States and the Soviet Union appeared to make it futile to utilize diplomacy and negotiation to resolve or moderate the conflicts of interest between the two superpowers. This is not to say that preventing crises was not an important objective during the Cold War, but policymakers relied largely on deterrence for that purpose; deter-

---

For a fuller treatment of this subject see the author's *Managing U.S.-Soviet Rivalry: Problems of Crisis Prevention* (Westview Press, 1983).

rence was supposed to discourage encroachments on the free world that would result in crises or war. Even during the Cold War, however, the two superpowers found ways to limit their competition and rivalry in third areas to avoid potential conflict. Perhaps the most notable instance of such cooperation in crisis prevention was the Austrian State Treaty in 1955 that created a neutral buffer state and removed it from the ongoing competition between the two superpowers in Europe.

Although deterrence was an essential part of American containment policy, it soon became evident that it was an unreliable, imperfect strategy at middle and lower levels of conflict. There are several reasons for this. A state that is dissatisfied with a given situation can usually find some way of challenging the status quo, even in the face of deterrence. It is difficult for the defending power to devise a comprehensive strategy that deters all of the options available to the opponent. And even when deterrence is successful, it is often no more than a *time-buying* strategy. Successful deterrence seldom removes the underlying conflict of interest; the motivation to change the status quo usually persists and may even become stronger. The dissatisfied state may simply await more favorable circumstances to renew its challenge. But successful deterrence does at least provide time for the two sides to use, if they will, to work out ways of reducing the conflict potential of the situation. Another lesson learned from misapplications of deterrence strategy by the United States during the Cold War is that deterrence, which is only an instrument of policy, cannot compensate for a confused or mistaken foreign policy.[1]

Since deterrence did not prevent dangerous crises from erupting during the Cold War, the United States and the Soviet Union were forced to develop an understanding of the requirements and modalities of crisis management. Fortunately the two superpowers have been remarkably successful in cooperating during crises to avoid military clashes between their armed forces. But both sides recognized that skill in crisis management could not be counted upon to prevent war in the future; both sides have seen the need to move beyond reliance on deterrence and beyond cooperation in managing crises to deal more directly with the conflicts of interest that pose the danger of war. The onset of détente following the Cuban missile crisis brought new opportunities and new modalities for crisis prevention, for then there was a shared disposition to utilize negotiation and accommodation to settle some long-standing conflicts of interest that had been bones of contention during the Cold War.

In the era of détente, American and Soviet leaders rediscovered and applied some diplomatic practices for moderating conflicts that were a standard feature of classical diplomacy.[2] They negotiated settlements of many unresolved issues of the Cold War, stabilizing the status of Berlin and recognizing the existence of the two German states and the division of Europe.

However, the problem of regulating U.S.–Soviet rivalry and competition in the Third World—the Middle East, Africa, Asia, and the Caribbean—still remains. U.S.–Soviet competition in these areas is a matter of concern for several reasons. It frequently adds to regional or local instability, even when one or the other side does not intend to exploit such instability for immediate gains. It increases the likelihood of dangerous crises into which the two superpowers may be drawn, such as the Middle East War of October 1973. And last but not least, during the 1970s the inability of the two sides to moderate their competition in third areas steadily undermined U.S. support for the entire policy of détente with the Soviet Union and, in particular, for ratification of SALT II.

One proposal for moderating and controlling U.S.–Soviet rivalry in third areas that has often been advanced is that the two sides develop a set of rules for détente or a code of conduct. This paper evaluates the utility and limitations of this approach to crisis prevention.

THE U.S.–SOVIET BASIC PRINCIPLES AGREEMENT (MAY 1972)

We already have experience with efforts to devise rules of conduct for moderating American-Soviet competition. At their summit meeting in Moscow in June 1972, Nixon and Brezhnev signed the Basic Principles Agreement (BPA), which was intended as a sort of charter defining the basis for détente. Included in the BPA was a set of general principles by which the two sides ostensibly hoped to regulate their rivalry in third areas and avoid being drawn into dangerous crises not of their own making. Considerable information on the origins of the BPA and the expectations associated with it are available in public sources, which I have supplemented by interviewing a number of high-level foreign policy specialists in the Nixon administration. Only a brief account can be presented here.

During preparations for the summit, five months before it took place, the Soviets raised with Kissinger the possibility of including a Declaration of Principles on the agenda of the summit meeting. This was not unexpected; American policy-makers were aware of the Soviet leaders' predilection for formalizing the basis of their relations with other states and their success in obtaining French and Turkish leaders' approval for such declarations. They anticipated that Brezhnev would attempt to obtain Nixon's formal acceptance of peaceful coexistence as a basis for U.S.–Soviet détente.

It is interesting, therefore, that when preparations for the summit were being made Nixon instructed Kissinger to take a tough stand on the ground rules for détente. Nixon wanted Kissinger to state the American disagreement with the Soviet definition of peaceful coexistence sharply and explicitly. In his memoirs, Kissinger reports that Nixon told him "to emphasize the need for a single standard: we could not accept the proposition that the Soviet Union had the right to support liberation movements all over the world" or the right to insist on applying "the Brezhnev Doctrine inside the satellite orbit."[3]

Kissinger, however, did not follow Nixon's instructions fully. In this and other respects, as he admits in his memoirs,[4] Kissinger softened the hard position that Nixon wished him to take during his secret trip to Moscow in April 1972, when preparations for the summit were made. Evidently Kissinger did not wish to push the Soviet leaders too hard lest he lose the possibility, to which he gave the highest priority, of encouraging them to induce Hanoi to take a more accommodating posture in the Vietnam negotiations. Shortly before the April meeting, the United States, in response to a major North Vietnamese offensive in South Vietnam, had begun bombing Hanoi and Haiphong. Later, after an intensification of the North Vietnamese offensive, Nixon approved mining the Haiphong harbor. The President was so concerned that Soviet leaders might respond by canceling the summit that he seriously considered calling it off himself. By the time he arrived in Moscow in late May, the President seemed to have dismissed any thought of thrashing out his disagreement with his hosts' concept of peaceful coexistence. Presently available information indicates that this fundamental issue was not even discussed at the Moscow summit.

As a result, the Basic Principles Agreement signed by Nixon and Brezhnev ignored the long-standing disagreement between the two sides on this important matter. Instead of opposing inclusion of peaceful coexistence in the Basic Principles document, Nixon and Kissinger contented themselves with introducing into the same document their own principles of international restraint, such as those Nixon had enunciated in his address to the United Nations in October 1970 and which Kissinger had preached to the Soviets on various occasions.

Thus, the final version of the Basic Principles Agreement included each side's favored phraseology for defining the rules of the game. Article 1 contained Brezhnev's formulation that "in the nuclear age there is no alternative to conducting . . . mutual relations on the basis of peaceful coexistence." But article 2 of the document contained phrases that clearly reflected Nixon's and Kissinger's long-standing exhortation to the Soviets to forego "efforts to obtain unilateral advantage" at the expense of the West and to "exercise restraint" in their foreign policy.[5] It should be noted, however, that these phrases were considerably more vague (since their precise scope and meaning had never been specified) than the concept of peaceful coexistence, whose implications for Soviet foreign policy in third areas had been spelled out on many occasions prior to the summit meeting. Despite the effort to balance or qualify the language of article 1 with article 2, the agreement was clearly advantageous to the Soviets.

In this important respect the Basic Principles document was a pseudoagreement. It gave the erroneous impression that the United States and the Soviet Union agreed on the rules of the game and the restraints to be observed in their competition in third areas. It would have been far preferable had the two sides openly stated in the BPA text that their disagreement over peaceful coexistence remained an unresolved issue, just as the leaders of the United States and People's Republic of China had done earlier in the Shanghai communiqué dealing with Taiwan. As it was worded, the Basic Principles Agreement eventually contributed to what domestic critics of Nixon and Kissinger referred to as the "over-selling" of détente.

The Basic Principles document also included several references to the need for cooperation in crisis prevention: the two sides agreed "to do everything in their power so that conflicts or situations will not arise which would serve to increase international tensions" and to "do their utmost to avoid military confrontations and to prevent the outbreak of nuclear war."[6]

A year later, at their second summit meeting in the United States, Nixon and Brezhnev signed an Agreement on Prevention of Nuclear War (APNW) that reiterated their commitment to cooperate in crisis prevention. Of particular interest is that this second agreement included a much stronger and more explicit requirement that the two powers engage in urgent consultations if situations that raised the risk of nuclear conflict developed anywhere.[7] This agreement was tested almost immediately in the events leading to the Arab states' attack on Israel in October 1973.

In his memoirs Kissinger minimizes the significance of the two agreements and the expectations he attached to them. But in press conferences[8] he held immediately after each of the two summits, Kissinger argued that the agreements were not empty declarations. He emphasized that while the two sides had acted to *manage* crises in the past, they had not until now attempted to lay down "general rules of conduct" to *prevent* them from occurring. Under sharp questioning by the press, Kissinger readily acknowledged that the agreements were not binding or self-enforcing and that there was no guarantee they would be observed; nonetheless, he stated, the agreements would or could make a positive contribution and he expressed a cautious hope that the BPA would mark "the transformation from a period of rather rigid hostility to one in which, without any illusions about the differences in social systems, we [i.e., the Soviets as well as the United States] would try to behave with restraint and with a maximum of creativity in bringing about a greater degree of stability and peace."

At the same time, Kissinger was reluctant—even when pressed by the somewhat skeptical reporters—to indicate how the principles would apply in specific situations around the world. Kissinger acknowledged the importance of implementing the principles but dealt with this problem in a perfunctory way, implying that implementation would depend on "good faith" and the "wisdom" of the two sides. Presently available information indicates that neither side attempted to engage the other in follow-up conversations to consider the operational implications of their agreements. Nor did the two sides attempt to set up institutionalized arrangements for periodic joint discussions about how the general principles would apply to countries and regions that were points of potentially dangerous crises. Kissinger evidently felt it sufficed to leave it to each side to adapt the general principles to any particular case. Each side would determine for itself how its behavior in concrete situations should be guided by the principles. No doubt Kissinger counted upon the Soviet leaders' interest in additional benefits from the détente process to restrain their foreign policy.

If the two sides were content to let the prospects for successful cooperation in crisis prevention rest with their agreement on general principles, one may ask whether the U.S. government initiated any policy planning studies to consider the implications of the agreements or to devise procedures for making effective use of them. My inquiries indicate that no such studies were undertaken.

The unresolved disagreements, the ambiguities, the hedges and escape clauses contained in the BPA,[9] and the absence of provisions for implementing these general principles became salient almost immediately. This will become evident as we discuss the failure of the crisis prevention agreements to forestall the Arab-Israeli war of October 1973, which erupted a few months after the second summit meeting.

THE FAILURE OF THE CRISIS PREVENTION AGREEMENTS TO FORESTALL THE ARAB-ISRAELI WAR OF OCTOBER 1973

This is a particularly important case to examine because it was the first test of the ability of the United States and the Soviet Union to put their crisis prevention agreements into effect. According to available information, from interviews as well as public sources, neither Soviet nor American leaders invoked the BPA or the APNW for any purpose, or with reference to any potentially troublesome situation, until after the Arab attack on Israel in October 1973.

It must be recognized that events leading to the outbreak of war severely tested the agreement to cooperate in avoiding crises. It is true that the Soviets did not go as far as they might have (or as far as they ought to have gone, according the one possible strict interpretation of their responsibilities under the agreements) to prevent the Arab attack or to adequately consult with the United States to enlist its cooperation to this end. Nonetheless, if one examines the totality of Soviet behavior—not only in the weeks and months immediately preceding the outbreak of the war but also in the several years prior to the war—and if one takes account of the difficult constraints under which the Soviet leaders had to operate, one sees evidence that Soviet leaders did operate with considerable restraint for a while in the Middle East and that they did make some effort to cooperate in crisis prevention. What is more, some aspects of U.S. policy in the Middle East in the years immediately preceding the outbreak of the October war, as well as thereafter, are difficult to reconcile with the injunction that both sides forego efforts to derive "unilateral advantage," which Nixon and Kissinger had included in the Basic Principles document.

As many specialists on Soviet policy in the Middle East have recognized, Soviet leaders tried for several years to discourage Egyptian President Anwar Sadat from resorting to force. Although important facts remain obscure and unverified, it appears that at first the Soviets did withhold military equipment and supplies deemed necessary by Sadat for a major Arab attack.[10] The Soviets also counseled Sadat to seek his objectives through diplomacy rather than force, and Kissinger was quite aware of this at the time. In fact, this pattern of Soviet restraint of Sadat, and Kissinger's expectation that the Soviets would continue this policy, contributed to the failure of American policymakers later on to become unduly alarmed at the flow of Soviet military supplies to Egypt and Syria or to take the other intelligence warnings of the forthcoming Arab attack seriously.

The Soviet policy of restraining Sadat entailed serious diplomatic and political costs for the Soviet position in the Middle East. At one point, in July 1972, Sadat became so frustrated and furious that the Soviets gave priority to détente with the United States over effective assistance to the Arab states that he expelled most of the 15,000 Soviet military advisers from Egypt. (It is quite possible that other considerations also entered into Sadat's decision.)[11]

The Soviet refusal to endorse and assist Arab military action in 1971 and 1972 may well have stemmed, as some analysts believe, from a desire not to damage the development of détente with the United States; but Moscow's restraint undoubtedly also reflected the Soviet leaders' expectation that the Arab states would suffer another quick defeat if they attacked Israel, leaving the Soviet Union faced with the difficult task of bailing the Arabs out, a move which might risk a military confrontation with Israeli forces if not also with the United States. More generally, Soviet leaders probably realized that their position in Egypt rested rather tenuously on the continuation of the Arab security dilemma vis-à-vis the Israelis. Thus, the Soviets could exert maximum influence at minimum cost and risk in a no-win, no-peace situation. But the unpredictable factor was Sadat; the Egyptian leader found the no-war, no-peace situation intolerable and maneuvered to take advantage of the rivalry and diplomatic disunity of the two superpowers.

Kissinger was well aware that the Soviet Union was experiencing serious difficulties in its relations with Egypt even before Sadat expelled the Soviet military advisers. In fact, while the Soviets were restraining Sadat, Kissinger was secretly pursuing a Machiavellian strategy to heighten the Soviet Union's diplomatic difficulties with its Arab clients. Kissinger hoped for and was working toward a reversal of alliances whereby the United States would replace the Soviet Union as Egypt's ally.[12] As part of his strategy, Kissinger manipulated the Soviet interest in furthering détente with the United States. While actually pursuing a unilateral American policy in the Arab-Israeli dispute, Kissinger pretended in private discussions with Gromyko to be willing to seek a basis for a joint U.S.-Soviet approach to a Middle East settlement. He drew the Soviet Foreign Minister into a series of private discussions ostensibly to formulate a set of principles for a Middle East settlement along the lines of U.N. Resolution 242. Actually, however, Kissinger engaged Gromyko in these discussions for tactical purposes related to his covert strategy. He notes in his memoirs, making no effort to conceal his diplomatic insincerity, that "the principles quickly found their way into the overcrowded limbo of aborted Middle East schemes—as I had intended."[13] In a surprisingly candid and self-congratulatory way, Kissinger explains that he pretended to be seeking a joint U.S.–Soviet approach in order "to give the Soviets an incentive to keep the Middle East calm . . . a strategy that would only magnify Egyptian restlessness with Soviet policy."[14] In other words, Kissinger deliberately slowed down diplomatic efforts to deal with the issues dividing the Arabs and the Israelis in order to produce a prolonged stalemate. He hoped thereby to demonstrate to Sadat the Soviet Union's impotence and inability to render any significant help to the Arab cause. "I calculated," Kissinger states in his memoirs, "that the longer the process went on, the more likely Sadat would seek to deal with us directly."[15]

At the first summit meeting in Moscow (May 1972) Kissinger managed—somewhat to his own surprise—to get Brezhnev to agree to a very bland communiqué on the Middle East situation that was certain to lead Sadat to feel the Soviets had decided to put détente with the United States above any real assistance to the Arab cause against Israel. The effect on Sadat was predictable. As Sadat records in his memoirs, the U.S.–Soviet communiqué came as a "violent shock" to Egypt.[16]

Less than two months were to pass before Sadat expelled Soviet military advisers from Egypt. In his memoirs Kissinger states that Sadat's action came "as a complete surprise."[17] However, a few months earlier Kissinger had found ways to let Sadat know that the Soviet military presence in Egypt prevented the United States from pressing the Israelis for concessions and, more generally, from playing a more active role in bringing about a settlement.[18]

Sadat's expulsion of the Soviet military advisers gave Kissinger the opportunity he had been waiting for and encouraging through his secret diplomacy. But for various reasons Kissinger moved too slowly to seize the opportunity. He was preoccupied with the Vietnam negotiations and did not feel the situation in the Middle East was ripe yet for major American diplomatic initiatives.[19] Sadat, becoming frustrated and impatient with Nixon and Kissinger, turned to the Soviets once again for military supplies. Sadat's explusion of the Soviet military advisers in July 1972 had faced Soviet leaders with the possibility of a total collapse of their remaining position in the Middle East. Given a chance to recoup their position, Soviet leaders were more forthcoming. Major Soviet military equipment began to flow to Egypt and Syria. Though Soviet leaders still hoped that Sadat would not plunge into war, this possibility could not be excluded, and at some point Soviet leaders evidently gave their reluctant approval for Egypt's use of force, if necessary, to recover its territory.[20]

The rapprochement between Egypt and the Soviets was well underway when the second summit meeting between Nixon and Brezhnev took place in June 1973, this time in Washington and San Clemente.

According to Nixon's own account, Brezhnev hammered at him about the danger of war in the Middle East and the need for American diplomatic pressure on Israel in the interest of the Middle East settlement.[21]

After the Arab–Israeli October war, Brezhnev and other Soviet spokesmen claimed that, at the summit meeting, the Soviet leader had given Nixon advance warning of the danger of war in the Middle East, as was called for by their crisis prevention agreements. Brezhnev's warnings, however, were general. He did not state that Sadat had definite, firm plans for a attack; nor did he pinpoint the specific dates of a possible attack. So the most that can be said is that Brezhnev's comments to Nixon constituted what intelligence specialists refer to as "political" rather than "tactical" warning.

To some extent, therefore, Brezhnev did fulfill his obligation to consult with the United States if a dangerous crisis threatened to erupt. But as so often happens, the recipient of the warning did not regard it as credible. American leaders dismissed Brezhnev's warnings to Nixon as scare tactics to pressure the United States to change its Middle East policy. The Nixon administration made little use of the warning. Kissinger might have used it, however equivocal it seemed, to energize his diplomatic activity in the Middle East and to give Sadat more credible assurance of support for reclaiming the Sinai. But Kissinger did nothing, so strong was the belief in Washington that an Arab attack against the much stronger Israeli forces would be irrational and, therefore, would not take place.

As a footnote to this account, one should note the intriguing possibility that Soviet leaders attempted to give the United States indirect "strategic" warning of the forthcoming Arab attack on Israel. The Soviets evidently received definite information about the coming Arab attack from Sadat only a few days, or perhaps a week, before it occurred. Three days before the war started, the Soviets began to evacuate Soviet civilian personnel from Egypt and Syria. The question arises whether Brezhnev intended this as an indirect signal to the United States about the forthcoming attack. According to presently available information, Soviet officials have never claimed that the pull-out was intended as a warning and that it therefore constituted an additional effort to honor the crisis prevention agreements.

Whether or not the Soviets intended their pull-out of Soviet civilians as a signal to the United States, such an unusual action might have been taken by U.S. intelligence as a strong indicator of the forthcoming Arab attack. For various reasons it was not. Moreover, nothing in the available record indicates that Kissinger considered asking the Soviets why they were taking their citizens out of Egypt and Syria and whether they expected war. It is perhaps unlikely that the Soviets would have revealed what they knew. They were caught in a situation in which honoring the crisis prevention principles conflicted with their responsibilities to their Arab allies. For the Soviet leaders to have given the United States unequivocal "strategic" warning of the forthcoming attack would have betrayed their Arab allies and deprived their attack of the military surprise on which its success depended. Under the circumstances, it is puzzling and surprising that the Soviets went as far as pulling their citizens out of Egypt and Syria.[22]

* * *

I have dwelt upon the origins of the October War because this dramatic and dangerous breakdown in the U.S.-Soviet crisis prevention agreement called into question the entire détente relationship. I have also suggested some of the complexities of the Middle East situation that made it a particularly severe first test of the new U.S.-Soviet crisis prevention agreement. After the failure of initial efforts to find a basis for diplomatic cooperation in dealing with the underlying conflict of interests between the Arab states and Israel, the United States and the Soviet Union pursued divergent foreign policy objectives and strategies in the Middle East that conflicted at critical junctures with crisis prevention requirements. Even while pretending to cooperate with each other, each power pursued a covert unilateral policy in the Middle East—the United States in seeking to effect a reversal of alliances that would exclude Soviet influence in the Middle East; the Soviet Union in arming Egypt and Syria for war. The diplomatic disunity of the superpowers gave Egypt, the local actor most dissatisfied with the status quo, an opportunity to maneuver and to use force for its own policy objectives.

This case is a reminder that crisis prevention is not subject to exclusive control by the two superpowers. Competition between them in third areas may allow a highly motivated local actor to play one off against the other and to pursue its own interests in ways that generate dangerous crises into which the superpowers are then drawn.

After the Arab-Israeli October War ended, it would have been desirable for Soviet and American leaders to discuss lessons that could be derived from that experience for clarifying and strengthening their crisis prevention agreements. Presently available information, from public sources and interviews, indicates that no U.S.-Soviet postmortem analysis was undertaken or even suggested by either side. Nor is there evidence that such a postmortem was conducted within the U.S. government to understand better the requirements for making more effective use of the crisis prevention agreements. The general principles agreed to by Nixon and Brezhnev at their two summit meetings seem to have played even less a role in constraining the behavior of the two sides in subsequent crises in Angola, the Horn of Africa, and Rhodesia.[23]

SOME TENTATIVE CONCLUSIONS

1. That the two superpowers might avoid dangerous forms of rivalry in third areas, if only they would accept a set of general rules or principles for mutual restraint, is a beguiling idea that oversimplifies the problem. Declarations of good intentions, such as those exemplified by the BPA and the APNW, are not without some potential value. But the history of these two agreements illustrates the practical difficulties and limitations.

As already noted, the Basic Principles Agreement was a pseudoagreement; the general principles concealed important unresolved disagreements over the forms of permissible competition in third areas. An important gap remained between the Soviet definition of peaceful coexistence and the Nixon-Kissinger view of mutual restraints. Moreover, each side appears to have viewed the Basic Principles as a vehicle for imposing constraints on foreign policy behavior of the other side, not its own.

2. Given the generality and ambiguities of crisis prevention principles and rules, and the fact that they are not self-enforcing, they are eventually likely to provoke charges of nonfulfillment and thus generate addition friction. Some high-ranking officials of the Nixon administration interviewed for this study concluded that crisis prevention agreements of the kind made at the summits of 1972 and 1973 were the cause of more trouble than they were worth.

3. It might be argued that if rules of conduct more specific than the general principles embodied in the BPA and the APNW could be agreed upon, it would have some value for crisis prevention. However, such rules would have to apply as restraints on the behavior of both sides. As Robert Legvold has observed, if we expect the Soviet Union to observe a certain "rule" or "pattern of restraint," we have to be prepared to do so also.[24] In practice, each side must be prepared to accept the outcome in a particular area—even an unfavorable outcome—should it observe the type of agreed restraint. For this and other reasons, the two superpowers are unlikely to find many specific rules or patterns of restraint to which they will subscribe. Consider, for example, how they would respond to a proposal that they forego actions of the following kind:

—use military forces (one's own or those of proxies or allies) to depose existing governments;

—sponsor and assist externally-based insurgents attempting to overthrow an existing government;

—support expansionist local powers that encroach on neighboring countries;

—give military assistance or aid to either side in a civil war.

The costs to a superpower of observing such self-denying rules of conduct may be nonexistent or acceptable in some cases, but excessive in others. Anticipating this, the superpowers are unlikely to subscribe to rules that unequivocally prohibit such behavior in all cases. Nonetheless, and even in the absence of a general agreement on rules of conduct, such patterns of restraint may be agreed to and/or observed on occasion on an ad hoc basis. That is, the two superpowers may agree to observe one or more of these restraints in one case but not in another. This suggests that the problem of limiting superpower competition in third areas resembles the problem of finding salient thresholds to keep a limited war from escalating. The two sides can arrive at a stable pattern of limitations in warfare via an explicit general agreement—for example, an agreement on no first use of nuclear weapons—but this is not always necessary. A stable set of limitations in any particular conflict can be achieved through tacit bargaining and/or mutual coordination of self-limiting behaviors. If this is possible in warfare, in keeping limited wars limited, it may also be possible in superpower competition in third (different) areas that is pursued by nonmilitary means. But such limitations probably have to be worked out on an ad hoc basis individually, rather than legislated in advance for all cases.[25]

4. It is difficult to avoid the conclusion that the search for agreement on a set of general rules of conduct has limited applicability and modest potential as a strategy for avoiding dangerous forms of competition and rivalry in third areas. It must be supplemented by other approaches and strategies. It confuses matters to think that the objective of crisis prevention can be achieved by devising a single, general purpose strategy imbedded in rules of behavior. Since the task of crisis prevention arises in many contexts and in strikingly different situations, the challenge to policymakers is to grasp the special characteristics of a given situation and design an appropriate strategy. We need a repertoire of strategies coupled with skill in diagnosing an emerging case, selecting an appropriate strategy, and tailoring it to the case's special configuration.

Special attention must be given to understanding and working with the political terrain in the locale and region in question. It is useful to compare U.S. policy in the Angolan case, which was poorly adapted to local and regional political forces, with U.S. policy in the Rhodesian case, which was skillfully adapted to the complex internal and regional political terrain.[26]

5. Progress in crisis prevention must begin with a recognition that U.S.-Soviet competition and rivalry in third areas cannot be legislated out of existence. Rather, we need a *differentiated conceptualization of U.S.-Soviet competition and rivalry.* A variety of interests involving security, ideology, economic, geopolitical, and prestige considerations enter into the general U.S.–Soviet competition. Both the nature and the magnitude of the competing interests vary greatly from one case to another. Moreover, the balance on interests that characterizes the competition between the superpowers varies in different parts of the world; this has important implications for crisis prevention. When one superpower perceives that the other side's interests are more strongly engaged in a particular situation than its own, it should restrain the policy objectives it will pursue and/or the means it will employ. Recognizing an asymmetry of interests should facilitate crisis prevention. In other situations, both the United States and the Soviet Union may have important interests at stake. Recognizing that a symmetry of important interests exists is likely to complicate efforts at crisis prevention.

The nature of the competition and the task of crisis prevention are different in situations and regions where neither side has important interests. A serious complicating factor in many situations of this kind is that the United States is not always able to anticipate or define the full extent of its interests before competition has reached a crisis stage. Often only when a situation has deteriorated to a certain point—as a result of significant escalation of Soviet involvement, either directly or via proxies—does its broader ramifications for U.S. interests become evident to American policymakers and force consideration of some response. This dilemma cannot be avoided by enjoining U.S. policymakers to define their vital interests in advance, for in many situations truly vital interests are not involved though, as a result of Soviet or other external Communist involvement, what is at stake for the United States increases to substantial proportions.

6. Another important complication for crisis prevention is introduced when the Soviet Union or the United States chooses to pursue its interests with restraint in third areas only when it believes such restraint to be necessary to avoid provoking a direct military confrontation with the other superpower. While avoidance of such war-threatening confrontations was certainly the primary objective of the two crisis prevention agreements signed in 1972 and 1973, another objective of undeniable importance should also be recognized. Even in competitve

situations in which the danger of a U.S.-Soviet military confrontation is remote, restraint is advisable because—as the years since 1972 have indicated—such efforts can result in mini-crises that can prove highly damaging to the overall détente relationship.

7. Given the variety and complexity of superpower rivalry in third areas, crisis prevention is oversimplified by thinking of a set of general rules of the game to regulate their worldwide competition. For the United States and the Soviet Union are engaged in a variety of "games."[27] In some, the conflict aspect of the relationship is dominant or particularly strong; but in others the cooperative aspect assumes greater saliency. The conflict potential is more acute when the United States and Soviet Union compete to advance their influence, control or resources at each other's expense; it is less so when they compete to advance their interests at the expense of third parties. Moreover, each type of game takes place in a variety of contexts and under conditions which vary from one case to another. These contextual factors can moderate or magnify the level of competition and facilitate or hamper efforts at crisis prevention. It would be erronious to assume that success in achieving crisis prevention invariably requires a high degree of (or even any) cooperation between the two sides or the same kind of cooperation in each case. In one situation, one side may find it prudent to adopt a unilateral pattern of restraint in deference to the strong asymmetry of interest that favors the other side. In another situation, both sides may need to adopt the same pattern of restraint. In still another situation the two sides may need to restrain themselves in different ways and in different degrees to avoid being drawn into a crisis.

8. Crisis prevention should be viewed as an integral part of overall foreign policy and as an objective that can be pursued by a variety of measures. Deterrence strategy, for example, will continue to be an important backup for efforts to induce Soviet restraint in third areas—brought into play when necessary but often only with other instruments of policy. While in some cases deterrence efforts may be required in the short run, the United States must also engage in preventive diplomacy of various kinds—as in Rhodesia and Namibia, for example—to achieve long-term, more stable conditions in third areas. United States foreign policy must continue to create "objective conditions" in third areas that eliminate or moderate local and regional instabilities that tempt Soviet probing.

9. United States and Soviet leaders should develop the practice of holding well-prepared high-level meetings where they discuss in detail specific situations and areas in which their divergent and/or parallel interests are engaged. Such discussions should clarify their common and conflicting interests and make appropriate policy adjustments. When

conflicting interests are involved in a particular area, they should invoke a broader set of parallel interests to find ways of limiting the objectives as well as the means each will pursue. In other words, they should resort to serious diplomatic conversations on a *timely* basis to develop *specific crisis prevention understandings* for each potential trouble spot in which their interests clash or may clash.

Holding such conversations before one or both sides become too involved and committed in a local situation may be of critical importance. In the Angola case, for example, Kissinger was criticized for waiting too long before taking up the situation with the Soviets. Such discussions should include the possibility of a mutual U.S.-Soviet disengagement or hands-off policy for a particular area and also the possibility of relying upon the United Nations, regional organizations, or ad hoc groups—such as the African Frontline Presidents in the Rhodesian case—to provide the framework and/or auspices for seeking a solution to local instability or civil war.

10. The United States and the Soviet Union can reduce the risk of becoming involved in some local conflicts by clarifying their intentions in a timely fashion in order to reduce the likelihood that each is drawn into the conflict in response to what it thinks the other is or will be doing. Similar efforts should be made to avoid escalation of superpower involvement in local crises. An unusual example of this kind of cooperation was Eisenhower's signal to Khrushchev in 1956 that the United States would not intervene in the Hungarian revolution. Another example was Stalin's diplomatic assurance to the United States within a few days of the North Korean attack on South Korea that the Soviet Union would not respond to U.S. military intervention on behalf of South Korea with a military intervention of its own.

There is, of course, no assurance that diplomatic signals of this kind will be received and/or believed. The danger of misperception is particularly serious when one power intervenes in a local situation cautiously or on a low level, probing to test the other side's reactions and, receiving no response, escalates its involvement. Failure to grasp that a probe is being made results in miscalculation that can result in an unnecessary escalation of the situation. An improvement in the ability of the two superpowers to send and receive diplomatic signals in situations of this kind is essential for crisis prevention.

11. The two superpowers can reduce the conflict potential in their relationship in some situations by adopting one or another of the practices employed by the great powers in the era of classical diplomacy. These include, but are not confined to, some variant of "spheres of influence." In addition there is the possibility of creating buffer states, neutralizing a small state, localizing a regional conflict between smaller

states (i.e., an agreement not to "internationalize" a local conflict), withholding offensive weapons to allies, etc.

12. Since not all crises can be avoided, the two powers should recognize that a crisis may afford them an unexpected opportunity to reach a specific crisis prevention agreement for that area. During the crisis, both sides should conduct themselves in ways that will facilitate an understanding thereafter for avoiding future crises in the same area. The terms on which a current crisis is terminated may be critical for achieving such an agreement. (The quid pro quo agreement between Kennedy and Khrushchev that ended the Cuban missile crisis—the United States agreeing not to invade Cuba in the future in return for Soviet removal of all "offensive" weapons from the island—is a positive example of this; in contrast, the October 1973 War in the Middle East ended without an agreement between the two superpowers that could help prevent new crises in that region.)

13. Finally, efforts by the two superpowers to moderate their rivalry in third areas can be expected to develop and operate with reasonable effectiveness only as part of the overall détente process. But even when that process is proceeding reasonably well, it does not guarantee that the general U.S.–Soviet crisis prevention agreement will be effective in every instance, as the origins of the October 1973 War indicate.

Some observers (and some of those interviewed for this study) believe that the Soviet leaders' incentive to operate with restraint in third areas and to cooperate in crisis prevention was weakened by their feeling that the Nixon administration backed away from its initial willingness to accord the Soviet Union equal status as a superpower. Contributing to this Soviet impression was the Nixon administration's open effort after the October War to exclude the Soviet Union from playing a role roughly equivalent to that of the United States in efforts to resolve the Arab-Israeli conflict. Soviet incentives for operating with restraint in third areas may have been further weakened by the Nixon administration's inability to deliver on its promise of granting most-favored-nation trading status to the Soviet Union without attaching conditions considered invidious by Soviet leaders. It is clear that the reconstruction of détente between the United States and the Soviet Union will have to address the whole range of their relationship. Different aspects of the relationship cannot be dealt with in isolation.[28]

NOTES

1. See Alexander L. George and Richard Smoke, *Deterrence in American Foreign Policy: Theory and Practice* (New York: Columbia University Press, 1974).
2. See Paul Gordon Lauren, "Crisis Prevention in Nineteenth Century Diplomacy," in

Alexander L. George, *Managing U.S.—Soviet Rivalry: Problems of Crisis Prevention* (*Boulder, Colorado: Westview Press, 1983*).

3. Henry Kissinger, *White House Years* (Boston: Little, Brown & Co., 1979), p. 1136.

4. Ibid., pp. 1135-1137, 1144-1148, 1150-1151, 1154-1164. Not only did Kissinger moderate the hard position Nixon wished him to take in the negotiations with the Soviets, but he put the best light possible on the Basic Principles Agreement draft in his final reporting cable from Moscow in which he assured Nixon that the agreement "includes most of our proposals and indeed involves a specific renunciation of the Brezhnev doctrine" (p. 1153). As a matter of fact, as Kissinger indicates elsewhere in his memoirs, the draft agreement contained no specific reference to the Brezhnev doctrine, only a phrase to the effect that both sides renounced any special privileges in any part of the world, which, he adds, "we, at least, interpreted as a repudiation of the Brezhnev Doctrine for Eastern Europe" (p. 1151).

5. Ibid., pp. 1131-1132, 1150-1151. Kissinger reports that Brezhnev gave him a Soviet draft of the Basic Principles document and invited him to "improve" it to make it acceptable. Kissinger and his aide, Helmut Sonnenfeldt, did redraft the document, which was then accepted by the Soviet leaders. Curiously, in describing the contents of the agreement, Kissinger mentions the principle of restraint that he included in the document but doesn't mention that it also contained the Soviet concept of peaceful coexistence. Kissinger's account also conveys the impression that he did not take exception to inclusion of peaceful coexistence in the document and did not debate the issue's implications for Soviet foreign policy. Several of my interviewees confirmed that the matter was not debated at the preparatory meeting in April or at the summit meeting in May. One interviewee observed that Kissinger and Nixon evidently believed that including their own references to "mutual restraint" and "no unilateral advantages" sufficed and that by doing so they gave peaceful coexistence a more acceptable meaning. This interviewee conceded that Soviet leaders may well have concluded that U.S. acceptance of the reference to peaceful coexistence in the document served indirectly to legitimize it. Another interviewee reflected that U.S. acceptance of the Soviet concept in the document was not in itself significant or damaging since, in actuality, Soviet behavior is subject to many constraints and potential levers.

6. The text of the Basic Principles Agreement is reproduced in U.S. Department of State *Bulletin*, June 26, 1972, pp. 898-899.

7. The text of the Agreement on Prevention of Nuclear War is reproduced by Robert J. Pranger (ed.), *Detente and Defense: A Reader* (American Enterprise Institute, 1976), pp. 145-147. The origins and development of this second agreement are alluded to by Kissinger, *White House Years*, pp. 1152, 1208, 1251.

8. See verbatim transcripts of Nixon's and Kissinger's press conferences in U.S. Department of State *Bulletin*, June 26 and July 10, 1972; July 23, 1973. Interviews with several of Kissinger's associates also established that the crisis prevention principles in the BPA and APNW were not regarded as just "windowdressing."

For a balanced evaluation of the uses and limitations of these efforts to lay down ground rules to regulate U.S.-Soviet competition, see Helmut Sonnenfeldt, "Russia, America and Détente," *Foreign Affairs*, January 1978, esp. pp. 291-294.

9. Thus, that U.S. and Soviet commitments to their allies could take precedence over the obligations assumed in the Basic Principles Agreement was implied in article 12, which stated that "the basic principles set forth in this document do not affect any obligations with respect to other countries earlier assumed by the USA and the USSR." A similar proviso was included in the Agreement on the Prevention of Nuclear War.

10. See, for example, Alvin Z. Rubinstein, *Red Star on the Nile* (Princeton, N.J.: Princeton University Press, 1977); Jon D. Glassman, *Arms for the Arabs* (Baltimore: Johns Hopkins University Press, 1975); Galia Golan, *Yom Kippur and After* (Cambridge, England: Cambridge University Press, 1977); Lawrence L. Whetton, *The Canal War* (Cambridge, Mass.: MIT Press, 1974); Robert O. Freedman, *Soviet Policy Toward the Middle East Since 1970* (New York: Praeger, 1975); William B. Quandt, *Decade of Decisions* (Berkeley: University of California Press, 1977); Nadav Safran, *Israel: The Embattled Ally* (Cambridge, Mass.: Harvard University Press, 1978). Rubinstein (*Red Star*, 192-197) also considers the alternative hypothesis that Sadat deliberately exaggerated Soviet constraints on his military plans.

11. It is also possible that Sadat believed he had to remove most of the Soviet military advisers to gain freedom of action to initiate war. Sadat might well have believed that Soviet opposition to his exercise of the Egyptian military option against Israel would have been much stronger were Soviet military advisers, some of whom were manning operational military systems, to remain, thereby raising the risk of Soviet military involvement as well as diplomatic complications.

12. Kissinger, *White House Years*, pp. 376, 379, 1247-1248, 1285-1290, 1292-1296, 1300.

13. Ibid., pp. 1294; see also pp. 1246-1248 and Quandt, *Decade of Decisions*, pp. 149-150, 158.

14. Kissinger, *White House Years*, p. 1289.

15. Ibid., p. 1290. It is possible, of course, that Kissinger presents himself in his memoirs as being more purposeful and clever in maneuvering to bring about a reversal of alliances than he actually was. But the account Kissinger gives of the unilateral policy, and of the stratagems and tactics he employed on its behalf, was confirmed in essentials in an interview with a high-ranking official of the Nixon administration.

16. Anwar Sadat, *In Search of Identity* (New York: Harper & Row, 1978), p. 229.

17. Kissinger, *White House Years*, p. 1295.

18. William Quandt, at the time a specialist on the Middle East on the staff of the National Security Council, later reported that "in June [1972] Saudi Arabia's minister of defense, Prince Sultan, reported [to Sadat] on his conversations with Nixon and Kissinger. Until the Soviet presence in Egypt was eliminated, the Americans would not press Israel for concessions." (Quandt, *Decade of Decisions*, p. 151; see also p. 158.) See also Mohamed Heikal, *The Road to Ramadan* (New York: Quadrangle, 1975), pp. 170 ff., esp. 174 and 183; and Rubenstein, *Red Star*, p. 197.

19. Following Sadat's expulsion of Soviet military advisers, Kissinger informed the Egyptian leader that the United States would not be able to take the diplomatic initiative in dealing with the Arab-Israeli dispute until after the American presidential elections in November 1972. Later, in February 1973, Kissinger told Sadat's national security adviser, Hafiz Ismail, that little could be accomplished before the Israeli elections, scheduled for late October 1973. A few weeks later Nixon approved a new arms package for Israel. (Quandt, *Decade of Decisions*, pp. 152-162.)

    The Nixon administration's failure to exploit the possibilities created by Sadat's expulsion of the Soviet military advisers is noted and criticized by Alvin Rubinstein, *Red Star*, p. 202.

20. As in the case of Soviet supplies to Egypt prior to Sadat's expulsion of Soviet military advisers, important facts remain obscure or unverified regarding the resumption and increase in Soviet military supplies in 1973 and Soviet acquiescence in and support of Sadat's war plans. See sources cited in footnote 10; also Heikal, *Road to Ramadan*, p. 181.

21. Richard M. Nixon, *Memoirs* (New York: Grosset and Dunlap, 1978), p. 885; see also p. 1031. According to Quandt, *Decade of Decisions*, pp. 159-160, "Brezhnev warned that

the Egyptians and Syrians were intent on going to war and that the Soviet Union could not stop them. Only a new American initiative and, in particular, pressure on Israel to withdraw, could prevent war."

22. It should be noted that several reports, as yet unconfirmed, allege that Soviet Ambassador Dobrynin advised Kissinger on October 5 that the Arab attack would be launched on the following day. (Tad Szulc in the *New Republic*, December 22, 1973, p. 14; Galia Golan, "The Soviet Union and the Arab-Israeli War of October 1973," *Jerusalem Papers*, The Hebrew University of Jerusalem, June 1974, p. 15.)

   The possibility that the Soviets may have intended the evacuation of their civilians as a signal to the United States is also considered by William Quandt in his *Soviet Policy in the October 1973 War* (Santa Monica: The Rand Corporation, R-1864-ISA, May 1976), pp. 11-12; see also Glassman, *Arms for Arabs*, p. 123 and Rubinstein, *Red Star*, pp. 259-262. A Soviet specialist on U.S. affairs has indicated in a private conversation that the evacuation of Soviet civilians from Cairo was done in a deliberately conspicuous manner to warn the United States of the impending attack. (Source: personal communication from Dan Caldwell.)

23. Detailed analyses of these three cases are being prepared as part of the larger project on U.S.-Soviet crisis prevention.

24. For an important statement that recognizes this necessity, see Robert Legvold, "The Super Rivals: Conflict in the Third World," *Foreign Affairs*, Spring 1979.

25. It is reported that during the Carter administration, United States and Soviet negotiators did make progress in defining general principles and for limiting conventional arms transfers to third countries. c.f. Barry Blechman, Janne Nolan, and Alan Platt, "Negotiated Limitations on Arms Transfers," in George, *Op. cit.*

26. Larry C. Napper, "The African Terrain and U.S.-Soviet Conflict in Angola and Rhodesia," in George, *op. cit.*

27. This point is made also by Stanley Hoffmann: "... the United States should seek a definition not of common rules for *the* game, but of common rules for the different games that will continue to be played." ("Muscle and Brains," *Foreign Policy*, Winter 1979-1980, p. 13.)

28. This point is persuasively argued by Legvold, "The Super Rivals."

Chapter 11

The Terrorist Use of Nuclear Weapons

Thomas C. Schelling

Sometime in the 1980s an organization that is not a national government may acquire a few nuclear weapons. If not in the 1980s then in the 1990s. The likelihood will grow as more and more national governments acquire fissionable material from their own weapon programs, research programs, reactor-fuel programs or from the waste products of their electric power reactors.

By "organization" I mean a political movement, a government in exile, a separatist or secessionist party, a military rebellion, adventurers from the underground or the underworld, or even some group of people merely bent on showing that it can be done. My list is not a definition, just a sample of the possibilities. Two decades of concern about the proliferation of weapons have generated a familiar list of national governments that may have motive and opportunity to possess weapons-grade fissionable material and some ideas about how they might behave if they had it and what they might use it for. But there is also a possiblity that somebody other than a government may possess the stuff.

Who they might be and how they might acquire it are related questions. While not impossible, it is unlikely that an entity not subject to national government regulation could independently obtain and enrich uranium for use in explosives or could produce plutonium as a reactor product and refine it for weapons use. There are undoubtedly corporations technically and financially able to do it, but not many with both the motive and the opportunity to do it without being apprehended by an adversely interested party. Access to weapons or a weapon program, or to an authorized nuclear fuel cycle, or to an official research establishment licensed and authorized by some national government, is currently the only way to do it. Identifying the opportunities and the access to those opportunities generates the answers to the question, "Who?"

Theft of weapons is an obvious possibility. As far as we know, it hasn't happened. Despite the thousands in existence, including the thousands on foreign soil, and the large numbers of people who participate in the custody, maintenance and transport of nuclear weapons, and despite earlier reports by the General Accounting Office that proper care in the transport of weapons has sometimes been lacking, I am not aware of any hint that theft has occurred in any country. And if there has been a theft, the thief certainly has not made a public announcement.

Nothing so flatly negative can be said about theft of separated plutonium or enriched uranium. An important difference between theft of the material and theft of a weapon is that nobody is likely to remove a weapon or a warhead in small pieces. A weapon, if stolen, is likely to be taken whole. Materials from some sources would have to be secreted cumulatively over a protracted period.

Gift is a possibility. There may be things a non-government organization can accomplish that a national government would prefer not, or dare not, to try. Surreptitious or anonymous activities by agents of a government we can consider part of the *national* proliferation problem; but weapons entrusted to independent or uncontrolled parties who have at least some autonomy in what to do with them should be counted part of the non-nation risk. The gift may be extorted; blackmail against a government possessing weapons or weapons material is one way of obtaining a "gift." Extortion would be especially pertinent if the recipients knew of a clandestine weapon program, and if they had a capability to hurt the government or the people concerned, but would target the nuclear capability elsewhere. In principle we should add the possibility of purchase; but in matters of corruption, "bribery and extortion" are so often together that gift, blackmail, and purchase can be thought of as unilateral intentional transfers motivated by various inducements.

Defection of civilian or military officials, or units of national military forces, is an obvious possibility once a national government has weapons, especially weapons officially available for military use. Had nuclear weapons been in the hands of French forces in Algeria in 1958, the paratroopers and Secret Army Organization that challenged the Paris government might have made threatening use of such weapons or arranged their disappearance for some later occasion. When Batista went into exile from Cuba, or Somoza from Nicaragua, or the Shah from Iran, any official holding of nuclear weapons or the materials from which they can be made could have accompanied him, left the country, or gone into hiding with other officials. The civil war that has ravaged Lebanon, the war that separated the two parts of Pakistan, the overthrow of Soekarno in Indonesia, and the turmoil in Iran from the first confrontations between officers loyal to the Shah and officers disobeying, suggest the circumstances in which something could have happened to an official arsenal of nuclear weapons. Three other NATO countries besides France—Portugal, Greece and Turkey—have undergone changes in government by violence or the threat of violence in such a way that any weapons could have reached "unauthorized hands," either at the time or on a later occasion.

It is worth speculating on what might have happened to Iranian nuclear weapons had the turmoil that began in 1978 broken out a dozen years later, when the Shah's originally planned nuclear power program would have been generating spent nuclear fuel from which plutonium could be reprocessed or weapons fabricated. The Shah or someone loyal to him might have taken weapons or material out of the country (or sent it out in advance) for the purpose of staging a comeback or defending wealth and personal security in exile. They might already have been entrusted for safekeeping to somebody abroad. Loyal troops without access to weapons might have taken steps to obtain them to keep them out of dangerous hands; disloyal troops might have sought to capture weapons for political use or, also, to keep them out of even more dangerous hands. The disintegrated regime presided over by the Ayatollah might have found it awkward and controversial to have nuclear-weapons material in the possession of some impermanent official—the President, say, who disappeared with his executioners in pursuit in July 1981. Or whoever managed to possess the material might have claimed authority under the Ayatollah to withhold it from the President or Prime Minister, without any countermand from the Ayatollah. Indeed, it isn't clear to whom it might have been entrusted by whoever might have been in a position to do the entrusting during the near-anarchy of 1979-1980. Other interested parties would undoubtedly have been willing to consider commando tactics to preempt the stuff, either because of its value in the right hands or in the wrong hands. Israel, the USSR, and the United States come to mind, as does the PLO. What would have come out of the scramble is a guess that has many answers. And as with the jewelry, the cash or the negotiable assets the Shah, or others that fled, may have taken with them, it might never have been known how much nuclear material there had been and how much was missing. A prudent royal family would have exercised the same caution with nuclear material as with gold or Panamanian bank accounts.

These different routes by which weapons or material might get out of official hands tend to compound themselves. Whatever the likelihood that, say, the government of Iran would have sold nuclear weapons or given them away, or yielded them to blackmail by the PLO, weapons in the hands of militants or disaffected naval or air forces might be less subject to inertia and inhibition, or more subject to theft or capture or plain loss in the confusion of escape and evacuation. Whoever had such weapons or material would be unlikely to hold it or transport it in labeled containers. Just what do you do with a hundred pounds of plutonium when the building is under siege and you are in a hurry to reach the airport, or you have to leave town in disguise, and you don't exactly trust the "authorized" official to whom it is supposed to be surrendered under standard operating procedures?

For now this is all just rehearsal. In ten or fifteen years it may be a live performance.

GETTING IT ALL TOGETHER

If weapons material is obtained in any of these ways from a nation with a small or clandestine weapons program, or especially from one that has no weapons program at all, the material is not likely to be obtained in the form of completed assembled bombs or warheads. For reasons of custodial security the weapons might be unassembled. If weapon development is a continuing process, a government might not commit scarce material to permanently assembled weapons of obsolescing design. A government unwilling to entrust weapons to its own armed forces might find it expedient, in dealing with senior military officials, to keep its arsenal of finished weapons in the future. A government preferring to keep a weapons option, but not to declare or leak a nuclear military capability, might reduce the lead time between weapon decision and completed weapon without marrying the fissionable material and the other components, except in laboratory rehearsal. So an organization that obtains the material may still face the task of constructing a portable explosive.

That fact makes strong demands on the organization, requiring highly qualified scientists and engineers. Some years ago Hans Bethe publicly calculated a need for a minimum of six well-trained people representing just the right specialties to do the job. Unless they already possessed weapon designs, they would need access to computers and a library. They would need the discipline and loyalty to work in secrecy and in trust. And it would take time. Recruiting the team secretly would be difficult; even clandestine advertising could give the whole thing away. Mercenary engineers might feel uneasy about an enterprise that required them to leave no trace, an enterprise premised on willingness for large scale violence and not likely to give much thought to the welfare of mercenary engineers if secrecy were at stake. If the key people were sympathizers rather than mercenaries, they would want to participate in the planning of what was to be done with the weapons. In sum, it appears to require a group of significant size, high professional quality, and excellent organization and discipline to convert unauthorized or illicitly obtained materials into a useable weapon.

A consequence is that there would be time and opportunity to make plans, to assure that the weapons or the opportunity were not wasted, and to work out the technical and tactical problems of exploiting the weapons once produced. If the material was obtained for an existing emergency there might be urgence in completing a weapon promptly and exploiting it at once. Otherwise a major consideration would be that exploiting the weapon early would eliminate secrecy, stimulate countermeasures, close the source of material if it remained open, and use up the unique occasion of "first revelation."

I conclude that people capable of all this will be able to do some pretty sophisticated planning. There will be time and motivation to think about how to use this unique capability. They may wait for the right occasion; they may patiently create the right occasion. They may be in no hurry. They could hope not to need to actually use their weapon. And they are likely, having thought long and explored alternatives in detail before embarking on their plan, to be better prepared intellectually than their adversaries.

If they decide to claim possession of a nuclear bomb and, as at Hiroshima, do not wish to deplete their supply by an innocuous demonstration or to risk failure in an open test, they will have to be prepared to prove that they have what they claim. But they will have had the time, and probably the right people, to have considered how to authenticate their claim—what technical demonstrations are feasible, even what ambassadors to appoint in presenting their claim.

If they need to preposition a few weapons and can best accomplish it before their victims have any inkling of what is up, there will be further reason to postpone revelation and more time to plan the campaign.

And a *campaign* is what they will plan, not an episode. Unlike most "terrorist" acts of recent years, the activity initiated by the announcement or demonstration of a nuclear weapon is not likely to culminate in a decisive outcome that terminates the episode. If a weapon were used to coerce, neither the success nor the failure of coercion would necessarily lead to the surrender or capture of the weapon. Even the explosion of a weapon might not be interpreted, with any confidence, as the exhaustion of the arsenal and the end of the threat. Acquisition of a nuclear-weapons capability may confer permanent status on the organization and create a permanent situation, not just initiate a finite event.

WILL THEY BE TERRORISTS?

The question is sometimes posed, will terrorists come to acquire nuclear weapons? That question starts a series of thoughts: think of all the different terrorist organizations, from Quebec to Uruguay, Ireland to the Basque country, Rhodesia to Israel. Who among them might acquire weapons material during the coming decade or two? Who would know how to produce a weapon, or even to build an organization technically and institutionally capable of bringing such an enterprise to fruition? Who among them would actually trust each other enough to want such a thing?

Those questions probably focus on the wrong issue. The proper question is not whether an organization of the kind that we think of as "terrorist" will get nuclear weapons in pursuit of its goals. It is whether any organization that acquires nuclear weapons can be anything but terrorist in the use of such weapons. Does possession of a nuclear weapon, or a few weapons, necessarily make an organization "terrorist"? Are the weapons themselves so terrorist, in any use, that they make their possessors supreme terrorists, whatever else they may or may not be?

Except for acquiring a weapon just to prove it can be done—a motive that I don't doubt appeals to some, but one that I doubt adequate to accomplish the feat—I find it hard to think of any exploitation of nuclear weapons by a *national government*, other than one with a sufficient arsenal for battlefield use, that would not be terrorist. Even the language of "mass destruction" in categorizing these weapons suggests intimidation and reprisal rather than battlefield effectiveness.

The concept of "massive retaliation" is terrorist. My dictionary defines terrorism as "the use of terror, violence, and intimidation to achieve an end." And to terrorize is "to coerce by intimidation or fear." The passive form, known as "deterrence," (using the root of the word "terror") need not connote bloodthirstiness, but there is a thirty-year tradition that the appropriate targets for nuclear forces are cities or populations, and that strategic nuclear forces induce caution and moderation in an adversary by threatening the destruction of the enemy society. I imply nothing derogatory or demeaning about strategic nuclear forces by emphasizing the traditional expectation that their primary use is to deter or to intimidate, and thereby to influence behavior, through the threat of enormous civilian damage.

It is worth remembering that on the only occasion of the hostile use of nuclear weapons they were used in a fashion that has to be considered "terrorist." There was a nation that had a very small capability to produce nuclear bombs. The need was sufficiently urgent that it was decided to go ahead with "revelation" when only two were in hand. The hope was to stun the enemy into surrender, or to create such a tremor that the government itself would change into one disposed to surrender. The possibility of a harmless detonation in an unpopulated place was considered but rejected on grounds that the demonstration might fail (possibly through incomprehension by the witnesses) and in any event would deplete the stockpile by half. The weapons couldn't be wasted on a remote battlefield; and even military destruction in the Japanese homeland would be incidental compared with the shock of an anti-population attack. With a modest pretense at military-industrial targeting, the industrial city of Hiroshima was chosen. No warning was given that might have allowed interference with the demonstration. And so much was at stake—the possibility of continued warfare and the prospective loss of more millions of lives, mostly Japanese—that the demonstration's casualties might be justified as the price of persuasively communicating the threat and precluding any militarist refusal to take the threat seriously. When the response to the first bomb was not prompt enough, the second was dropped on Nagasaki, depleting the arsenal altogether. (Whether a third was ready for delivery, the victim government could not know.)

The bombs on Hiroshima and Nagasaki remind us that, from the point of view of those who use the weapons, use favors the right side. It may even be hoped that use will minimize the ultimate violence to the enemy.

To make the comparison more contemporary, we can contemplate the kind of use that might be made by a national government with a few nuclear weapons—"few" meaning single numbers or teens, few not only by comparison with so-called nuclear powers but too few for decisive use on the battlefield. It is generally expected that population threats, verbal or communicated by detonation, would be the obvious role for such weapons, and that even nominally "battlefield" use would be intended mainly for intimidation rather than local target destruction. A national government with only a few such weapons would not have any but a "terrorist" mode in which to use them. There are many ways to differentiate a national government from a non-governmental entity, but the "terrorist" quality in any use of nuclear weapons does not seem the crucial differentiation.

If a government that exploited any genuine or pretended nuclear capability would appear to "descend" to the level of a terrorist organization by doing so, an organization other than a national government that possessed or could credibly claim to possess nuclear weapons conversely might "ascend" to the status of a government. It might seek its own permanence as a nuclear mini-state even if lacking territory. Or it might claim a territory or seek a homeland, identifying itself as the rightful claimant to legitimate authority in some existing state. Considering the status and "prestige" that are supposed to go with the fearsome accomplishment of producing or otherwise acquiring nuclear bombs, and recognizing that something as vaguely defined as a Palestine Liberation Organization can achieve diplomatic recognition, it should not tax our imaginations to suppose that an organization with the ability to acquire the wherewithal to produce nuclear weapons might proceed to set up its own foreign office and dispatch its own ambassadors to the governments with which it proposed to do business.

This idea is supported by the consideration that an organization that could have one bomb could well have more than one. So even violent use of a weapon might not exhaust the campaign. Furthermore, "successful" exploitation of a weapon, for a non-governmental entity as for a national government, would likely achieve its purpose without explosion, without destroying the weapon itself. So the organization need not contemplate its own demise, as a nuclear ministate, in the event of initial success.

MODES OF UTILIZATION

It is hard to foretell what mode of exploitation might be adopted by some organization that comes into possession of nuclear weapons. It is especially hard because the people who would decide the strategy could have had weeks or months or longer to think and argue intensely about what their "nuclear strategy" should be. Most of us have not spent weeks or months attempting to anticipate that exercise. And because we have not identified our specific candidate, we have no vivid image of either its objectives or its limitations to help sharpen our imaginaton or to screen out the implausible. We can, however, generate a menu of some possibilities with which to acquire some notion of the range of surprises to which we may be subject someday.

Not the most dramatic but an effective way that a small nuclear-weapon capability might be exploited would be to announce it—announce it non-belligerently and do nothing else. The announcement might require identifying who had it, unless the organization or its affiliation was already well known. Alternatively the information could be allowed to leak; and if there was already conjecture that the organization was acquiring a nuclear capability the "announcement" might take the form of merely not responding negatively (or convincingly) to inquires. The fact of possession could be interpreted as an implicit threat. If the object were to gain attention and status, a believable announcement ought to do the trick. The announcement could of course be secret and limited to a few addressees, perhaps the target governments toward whom the weapons represented an implicit threat, perhaps a friendly government that might or might not welcome the news of such support.

Some effort to authenticate the claim would accompany the announcement. We have fictional and journalistic accounts of how this might be done—revealing details of theft or capture that only thieves or captors could know, inviting or kidnapping witnesses for a "show and tell," delivery of a weapon facsimile or a sample of weapons-grade material, open declaration by the distinguished scientists who had designed and assembled the weapons, or of course a "test" detonation. Depending on the risk of interception, the latter could be by surprise, at an unannounced time and place, or by "invitation" or advance tip-off.

An alternative passive, but more dramatic, mode might to be eschew announcement and proceed to demonstration. If the object were to strike a little terror, an anonymous blast might do; and although minor terrorist groups might claim authorship in the usual style, the authentic perpetrator should have no difficulty proving his claim.

In case it seems that mere announcement, unaccompanied by overt threats and demands, would lack the climactic quality one expects to find associated with a non-nation nuclear capability, it helps to reflect that announcement or, alternatively, leaks and undenied conjectures, are what one usually expects of a national government. Except for the initial American revelation, mere announcement (or even letting another government do the announcing) has been the custom. Those who believe that Israel has nuclear weapons, whether in readiness or ready for quick assembly, must believe that "announcement by denial" is a believable tactic. (Whether they believe that Israel also made some explicit but discreet revelations, I don't know.) In any case, there is nothing about "mere" announcement that precludes becoming more explicit later. The way it is done would depend, too, on the manner in which some national governments might, between now and then, have conducted their own revelations or tests or first uses. An effective way to announce possession, if the most likely target government had just announced that it possessed nuclear bombs, would be "We do too."

In a more active mode, the organization could secretly or openly approach the target government, i.e., the government whose behavior it hoped to influence by formulation of demands. There are at least four combinations: open announcement coupled with secret demands, secret display or announcement associated with open demands, or both secret or both open. There might be more than one target government; the "victim" might be different from the "target," the overt threat made against one government with the intent of intimidating another. For example, a Libya that nominally threatened Israel might be aiming its terror at Americans.

A target might be a populace, not a government. Panic, evacuation, political pressure on a government, or mass civil disobedience or obstruction could be the response either to mere announcement or to a threat aimed obliquely or directly at the population. Winston Churchill was reportedly concerned, at least briefly, that the German bombing of London might cause disorderly evacuation, and those were pretty small bombs.

The most active mode of intimidation would be to detonate a weapon on a live target. Hiroshima represented intimidation: the object was not to eliminate that city; the true target was the emperor's palace in Tokyo. A weapon could disable a nation by destroying the center of the capital city; and a weapon or several might be used by surprise on a military installation or troop concentration. But even on a military target, nuclear weapons might be intended more to terrorize a populace or to intimidate a government than just to cause local blast and radiation damage. (A nuclear facility might be judged an appropriate target by an organization that wanted the drama of military use but wanted to target hearts and minds rather than bodies.) Detonation against some target is evidently more likely if there is a war on.

Not out of the question is the possibility that a weapon would be offered for sale. Whether a dedicated group of scientists and engineers would elect to turn a profit rather than perform a diplomatic miracles strains my credulity, but only somewhat; a weapon obtained opportunistically from a military arsenal seems more compatible with mercenary utilization. Putting a weapon up to public auction would be a clever bit of mischief. It might be purchased by someone desiring the weapon, or ransomed by a government that could finance preclusive purchase. There might be the usual difficulty with kidnap ransom, namely, of showing up to collect the money or giving one's mailing address; but the father of Patty Hearst was ordered to deliver ransom to a third party— food for the poor—and that strategy, if the owner isn't after the money itself, takes care of half the problem. The other half is credibly surrendering the weapon.

An outside possibility is that an organization acquiring a nuclear weapon would surrender it with ceremony, not against ransom or on any conditions or concessions. It could be an effective anti-nuclear demonstration. Such a consummation seems incompatible with the deadly serious and dangerous task of designing and constructing a weapon; but a less professional organization that obtained a military weapon by theft or hijacking might be tempted to dramatize disarmament in that fashion. (Or it might announce a contest: now that the organization has it, what should it do with it?)

STRATEGIES FOR TERRORIST USE

Nuclear weapons are enormous, discrete, unrenewable, and scarce. They are too valuable to waste or to entrust to any but the most reliable operatives. They are out of proportion to most things that terrorists demand in response to some finite threat—like something or someone held hostage. Only recently has a single finite opportunistic terrorist threat—the Americans captured with the embassy in Tehran—been parlayed into a quasi-permanent source of intimidation. Assassination of a head of state is an act to compare to a nuclear threat or nuclear test, but assassination doesn't lend itself to a protracted strategy of coercion. Few terrorist incidents of recent decades therefore contain interesting suggestions for terrorist activity on a nuclear scale.

A characteristic of nuclear weapons, unlike live hostages, occupied buildings, hijacked ships or aircraft, or stolen precious objects, is that there is no inherent limitation on how long a nuclear threat can last and no necessity for surrender of the weapon at the end of a successful negotiation. In ancient times hostages were taken in large numbers as security against the good behavior of a tribe, a town, or a nation. In recent times, with the ambiguous exception of Iran, terrorist hostages have been dynamically unstable assets, not capable of being held indefinitely in comfort and safety either for captives or captors. The ultimate mobility and security of the captors depends on release *from* as well as release *of* the hostages. We have to look back to the occupied countries of World War II, or eastward to more recent military occupations, to find instances of "steady-state" rather than "episodic" hostages.

An important distinction for the terrorist use of nuclear weapons— whether by a small nation or organization or by great nations like France, the United States, and the Soviet Union—is between deterrence and compellence. (I apologize for the *word* "compellence," which I introduced some years ago for this purpose, but not for the *distinction*, which has been understood since historical times.) By "deterrence" I mean, of course, inducing an adversary or a victim *not* to do something, to continue not doing something. The world takes the preposition "from." According to my dictionary, "to discourage or keep (a person) from doing something through fear, anxiety, doubt, etc." It is the more passive kind of coercion. By "compellence" I mean inducing a person *to do* something through fear, anxiety, doubt, etc. "Compel" takes the preposition "to." My dictionary contains no word specialized toward this more active kind of coercion, so I coined the word.

Deterrence is simpler. The command to do something requires a date or deadline; to keep on not doing something is timeless. Acquiescence to a compellent threat is visibly responsive; doing nothing in face of a deterrent threat is not so obvious. Acquiescence to a compellent threat invites another demand; complying with a deterrent leaves things unchanged and leads to no sequel. Compellent threats have to be spelled out: "go back" needs an indication of how far, "give help" an indication of what and how much; while "don't" usually takes its definition from what exists. And if a compellent threat is met by inaction, no event or initiative triggers or mandates the execution, while violation of a deterrent threat, unless softly and gradually done, initiates the action. In military affairs the deterrent threat can often target the same activity that constitutes the violation, while a compellent threat must often find a target disconnected from the desired response: "don't advance or I'll shoot" makes the connection, while "send money or..." cannot usually target the money but must find some linkage elsewhere.

I propose that terrorist nuclear threats have a comparative advantage toward deterrence. The more familiar terrorist actions of recent years had the dynamics and disconnectedness of compellence. Organizations making nuclear threats, like nuclear nations, have a credibility problem; deterrent threats are more credible. One of the great advantages of deterrent threats is that they often do not need to be articulated. They are typically addressed to some obvious overt act. If you draw a gun on somebody approaching he may stop whether or not you tell him to; if you want him to turn around, take the keys from his pocket, and throw them to you over his shoulder, you have to say something. Not only does the deterrent threat economize communication and minimize ambiguity, it permits one to create a threat without doing anything belligerent, without acknowledging, even while denying, that one is threatening.

It was easy to draw up a list of things that the U.S. government might have done but didn't do for fear of jeopardizing the hostages in Tehran. It is not so easy to draw up a convincing list of affirmative U.S. actions that were coerced through the hostages, except for the final ransom.

A second distinction for terrorist nuclear strategy is between military and civilian targets. A nuclear threat, and especially a detonation, will frighten, terrorize, and intimidate, whatever the target indicated in the threat or attacked by a bomb. But if the unofficial mini-state aspires to international diplomacy and identifies its role as taking part in international conflict, especially military conflict, it may want to legitimize its possession of weapons, its campaign of intimidation, even its use of nuclear explosives, by nominally confining its attention to military targets. It may not want to discredit the side that it favors. If the organization considers itself immune to reprisal because it has no homeland and its location is unknown, it may not wish to make its intended beneficiary a target for reprisal. As in a conflict between India and Pakistan, Argentina and Brazil, Israel and Syria, Cambodia and Vietnam, or South Africa and any black nations of the continent, terrorist organizations may not want to appear inhumane and terrorist, and may select military targets to attack or to threaten.

Similarly, the actions deterred may be military. Just as the United States would not consider nuclear threats except against some military "aggression," and all nations that make reference to nuclear weapons of their own do so in reference to self-defense or commitments in defense of allies, the terrorist organization may adopt the custom and confine its threats to the deterrence of military actions.

In doing so it need not look more terrorizing than France or the United States. By eschewing "massive retaliation" against homeland populations, and avoiding threats of destroying "enemy societies as such," it may legitimize its nuclear role and appear less inhumane or destructive than the greater nuclear powers. Whatever it achieves for the organization, striking the posture may not cost them much.

In choosing actions to deter and targets to threaten, nuclear terrorists may enjoy the advantage of multiple victims. When an action they want to deter can be obstructed by any one of several deterrable actors, they may select their victims and targets for likely compliance. Let me use an historical instance as an example, one that does not have to be wholly invented. During the October War of 1973 many European countries denied the United States the privilege of refueling aircraft carrying ammunition and equipment for Israel. No nuclear threat was needed: it was megatons of energy to be withheld, not delivered, that deterred cooperation with the United States. But Portugal, justifying two decades of pretense that it had anything to contribute to NATO, allowed use of airfields in the Azores. A pro-Arab terrorist organization, acting on its own or fronting for a government that had a few nuclear weapons, might have declared the resupply of Israel an aggressive intrusion into a military conflict, one that they would resist with their modest nuclear force. They simply could have threatened to explode their weapon near a base on which U.S. planes were refueling, unless the airlift ceased. Assuming they could have proven possession, their ability to carry through on the threat could have been credible. The United States might have been deterred. Alternatively, the Portugese government might have been deterred. Or third, civilian employees and others near the threatened site could have been motivated to strike, to obstruct, to evacuate. If the threat was not heeded, and a weapon was detonated in the vicinity, the perpetrators would at least have caused minimal civilian damage in attacking a military operation. Whatever the political and diplomatic consequences of such a stunning event—and on that I am not even going to conjecture—it at least does not appear a wholly self-defeating threat, or even a self-defeating action, from the point of view of an organization wholly sympathetic to the Syrian-Egyptian cause.

Notice that if we go back and replay the scenario, allowing some Israeli nuclear counter-threat that might entail equally imaginative targeting, we have an indeterminate situation, one in which the fact that the nuclear organization is not a recognized nation does not make much difference. I have heard comparable scenarios involving a government like Libya's, conjecturing how a government like that of Libya, if it had a few nuclear weapons, might operate through a front organization, issue a threat anonymously, or even detonate a weapon without acknowledging its role. I have heard scenarios in which some small nation's nuclear weapons are entrusted to the air force or navy and escape the control (or appear or are alleged to have escaped the control) of the national government. Whether the nuclear-armed entity in these stories is a nation or not does not make much difference.

Like governments in these scenarios, an organization that is not a government would not necessarily condition its nuclear participation on a request from the government for whose benefit it appears to be intervening. The real purpose may not even be to help the "beneficiary."

Governments are of course more susceptible to nuclear reprisal, or almost any other kind of reprisal, than an unattached or anonymous organization. Countries can be denied exports, blockaded, diplomatically ostracized, or even subjected to non-nuclear attack if they appear about to create a nuclear inferno in a population center or to rupture a moratorium on the use of nuclear weapons that has survived since V-J Day. In contrast, an organization that needs only a small boat to dock in a metropolitan harbor, with a nuclear weapon on board and some place to operate a two-way radio, can hardly be starved into second thoughts by denial of soybeans, military spare parts, or air traffic; and it evidently cannot be invaded or captured or we wouldn't have the problem in the first place.

The difference is undeniably important, but need not be decisive. Up to the point of actually exploding a weapon, a national government may be in no more danger of diplomatic or military counteraction than an organization that is not a government. Even a nation that actually used nuclear weapons against enemy troops or enemy population would not necessarily be subjected to nuclear reprisal. Fear of escalation, abhorrence of anti-population attacks, and an interest in enhancing rather than abandoning nuclear restraint, could inhibit some potential nuclear retaliators, especially if other modes of reprisal or disabling attack were available. And if the non-government organization uses its nuclear status in military support of a particular country, the country so "helped" might not escape all blame. So the difference, though important, is not decisive.

SAFEGUARDS AGAINST NON-NATIONAL WEAPONS

Eventually we may need a domain of strategy for coping with these lesser nuclear threats, coming from either national governments or non-governmental organizations. It is likely to be different from the principles and ideas developed during the past three decades for the Soviet–American or NATO–Warsaw confrontation, and at least as complicated. It will be especially complicated by the utter lack of symmetry between the United States and any such nuclear adversaries or clients as we have been talking about. I do not propose to outline any such strategy here.

But in preventing the acquisition of nuclear capabilities by non-national entities at least one principle, I think, is undeniable: the best way to keep weapons or weapons-material out of the hands of non-governmental entities is to keep it out of the hands of national governments. Saying that doesn't get us very far, but it does remind us that this is the problem we have already worried about, or a large part of it. International war—war between nations that are enemies of each other—is only one relevant occasion when possession of nuclear weapons might make a terrible difference.

The main military activity of military forces around the world is overthrowing their own government or fighting other military forces in the same country—air force against navy, officers against enlisted men, East against West Pakistan, Moslem against Christian, royalist against anti-royalist. The risks that nuclear weapons, or the material from which such weapons can be assembled, would actually play a role in hostilities seems to be enhanced by the fact that military action in much of the world is so characterized by internal disorder and loss of national control over military forces. There is just a chance, maybe only a prayer, that some governments or heads of government may appreciate the dangers—to their own country and to themselves—of acquiring a weapons capability. Aside from becoming a target of nuclear blackmail or nuclear attack by joining the ranks of declared nuclear nations, some governments might possibly recognize how divisive a small nuclear capability could be.

What should a wise head of government respond if offered immediate delivery of a few nuclear weapons? I think, "Not yet—let me think about where to put them." Just as a prudent citizen might be appalled when a truck arrived and conspicuously delivered objects of great value that he had inadvertently won in some lottery, fearing that robbers would arrive before safeguards could be erected and he would be left in worse shape than before the goods arrived, nuclear weapons could pose difficult questions for a head of state, perhaps especially for a civilian head of state.

Does he trust his senior officers sufficiently to put his weapons in military hands? Can he dare to display his distrust by keeping them from the military? Would he have to provide them to the competing military services or can he elevate one service as the sole nuclear force? Could he, as Secretary McNamara could not in the early 1960s, get enthusiastic military acquiescence in electronically safeguarded presidential control? And could he in some future war—a contingency that has to be considered possible, otherwise why nuclear weapons?—let an army be surrounded and immobilized—like the Egyptians at Suez in 1973—even captured, without authorizing some use of these supposedly awesome weapons? And what use might that be? And if he withheld the weapons, wouldn't he then regret having possessed them?

I wish there were evidence that some heads of government shared my misgivings. I have never heard representatives of Pakistan or Iraq or Argentina explain that a positive interest in nuclear weapons should never be imputed to them because the weapons are far more dangerous than they are worth. We might not believe them if we heard them say it, but it would be good to know that it had occurred to them.

There is little that can be credibly done by the United States to increase the alarm any heads of non-nuclear governments might feel at the prospect of getting close to having the weapons. We have too evident an interest of our own. It must furthermore be exceedingly difficult to get a president, defense minister, minister for nuclear power, and chief of armed forces to sit together around a table and acknowledge that they may shortly be on opposite sides of a coup or civil war, or evacuating in disorder, and that they would therefore be wise not to encumber themselves with as competitive a prize as a nuclear arsenal.[1]

NOTE

1. The work of a number of authors on this subject is collected in Augustus R. Norton and Martin H. Greenberg (eds.), *Studies in Nuclear Terrorism*, (Boston: G.K. Hall & Co., 1979). See also Lewis Dunn, "Nuclear Coup d'Etat," *The Journal of Strategic Studies*, May 1978. Other journals to watch for relevant reading are *Conflict, An International Journal*, and *Terrorism, An International Journal*.

Chapter 12

Nuclear Proliferation

George H. Quester

Nuclear proliferation may be a different problem from all the others discussed in this volume, simply because it is an issue on which the Soviet Union is not the adversary.

As someone else has drifted into the role of adversary in this area of arms management, the difference is not trivial. Whatever we identify as Soviet operating behavior shifts substantially in relevance, for we now have the Soviets again as "allies." The relevance of our normal confrontation approach to "a superpower" may decline drastically in significance; instead, we are confronting aspiring nuclear-weapons states, i.e., *erstwhile* superpowers.

A DIFFERENT ADVERSARY?

But how long has the nuclear proliferation problem been seen as changing the post-war polarization of American confrontations with the Soviet adversary? For how long has the United States indeed sensed itself to have a "proliferation problem"? The U.S. proliferation concerns have gone through a fascinating metamorphosis since 1945. On a very simple dichotomy, on whether the United States has been "opposed" to proliferation, one could identify at least three major stages, not unlinked to issues of confrontation with the Soviet Union.

A first stage emerged in the immediate aftermath of the use of nuclear weapons against Japan, when President Harry S. Truman announced that the United States intended to hold on to "the secret" of nuclear weapons, rather than sharing it with our allies as we had shared other forms of military technology during World War II. In immediate practical terms, this was reneging on earlier agreements between President Franklin D. Roosevelt and Prime Minister Winston Churchill calling for postwar British-American sharing of nuclear weapons capabilities, as the reward for Britain having pooled its nuclear research effort into that of the U.S. Manhattan Project. The Americans may have been unconscious of reneging, as President Truman seemed genuinely unaware of the promises Roosevelt had made to Churchill, and the British accepted the exclusion with reasonably good grace.[1] This first "nonproliferation policy" was thus expressed in very global terms but was typically read between the lines as based on distrust of the Soviet Union.

As the Cold War emerged, the policy goal was seen more and more as the delay of Soviet acquisition of such weapons. If Americans had been asked in 1945 to state which country they least wanted to see become the second nuclear power, many or most would have named the Soviet Union (assuming, that is, that Germany and Japan were already ruled off the list, safely under American and Allied occupation). A few Americans might have put some other powers on the list ahead of the USSR—perhaps Great Britain or France in a fear of traditional imperial tendencies, perhaps Canada or Mexico in apprehension of future border conflicts—but these responses would have been unusual; as the Cold War emerged more clearly between 1946 and 1948, such preferences would have been rare indeed.

It is interesting to speculate about American attitudes toward nuclear proliferation, and nuclear weapons strategy in general, had Britain somehow beaten the USSR to the position of being the second power to detonate and acquire nuclear weapons. Would we have had a wave of abstract strategic speculation about future nuclear wars, or about "balance of terror" deterrence, between the United States and Britain, possibly poisoning relations between two allies? Would this wave have been an immunization of sorts against the speculation that later followed the Soviet bomb? By letting the Soviets go first in challenging the American monopoly, the British did important things to American attitudes on nuclear proliferation, letting these generally become aligned with attitudes on the cold war.

A second major stage of broad American attitudes toward nuclear proliferation thus came in the wake of the 1949 detection of a Soviet nuclear weapons test detonation. In the years that followed, the American public and government seemed less and less concerned about general nuclear weapons spread as, in effect, "the worst had already happened." The British explosion of a nuclear weapon in 1952 thus produced no evocation of American concern. Tactical nuclear weapons were deployed to Europe as part of Eisenhower's greater reliance on nuclear weapons to avoid the costs of conventional arms preparations, and the issue of Allied access to such weapons was opened on many fronts, generally in an approving way. Where any resistance persisted to the sharing of nuclear information, as for example in the French nuclear program, it was typically expressed in cold war terms of fear of the USSR, i.e., on worries that the Communist sympathies of some prominent French nuclear physicists might lead to shared American information being passed along to the Soviet Union.[2]

The first stage of American nuclear proliferation attitudes had, as mentioned, shown some aspects of treating all the world as adversaries—opposing the spread of nuclear weapons to *anyone*. But, in a matter of a few years, this became fixated on the cold war confrontation with the USSR. The second round of attitudes on nuclear weapons then was focused entirely on the cold war. Where sharing nuclear information might hurt the United States and the western alliance in a confrontation with the Soviet bloc, it would be opposed. Where such sharing would strengthen the western alliance, however, it would be tolerated, or indeed even encouraged. The American attitude toward Canadian access to nuclear weapons, for example, was virtually to press them on the Canadians, even when they were reluctant to have them.[3]

Some attitudes of the Eisenhower administration can easily be painted as foolish here, too generally tolerating access to American nuclear weapons by the forces of countries like Belgium and West Germany, Greece and Turkey, Taiwan and South Korea. On the supposedly civilian side, these were also the years of "Atoms for Peace," the first major American program for sharing broad-ranging nuclear technology, research reactors, and information about plutonium, seen by many as the seeds of today's nuclear proliferation problem.[4]

Yet one can present an interesting rebuttal to such an indictment of the Eisenhower approach; namely it was good service for important alliance considerations and, in the process, was not bad service for the anti-proliferation concern. The Eisenhower approach was quite simply to avoid and discourage discussion of the abstract proliferation question, for if American alliance commitments were kept as solid and credible as Eisenhower intended them to be, there might be no need for Frenchmen or Germans or South Koreans to want such weapons for themselves.

The mass of Americans and the U.S. government, were thus probably not concerned about nuclear proliferation before 1960 as they were about containing and frustrating Soviet expansionism. Yet it is possible (if not so easy to prove) that the government was more concerned with proliferation but was working under the theory that the most productive policy was to avoid showing concern. To publicize that one did not trust an ally with nuclear weapons might have been the first important step in getting him to reexamine *his* trust of the alliance.

The third stage emerged in 1960 with the election of the Kennedy administration, the entry of France into the nuclear weapons club, and signs that China was moving to do so as well. The beginnings of a more general worldwide concern about halting nuclear proliferation had shown up from 1958 to 1960 in a series of United Nations General Assembly resolutions by the Irish calling on states lacking such weapons to forego them and, in effect, to form and take pride in membership in a "non-nuclear club."[5]

For a host of reasons, this third attitude finally settled in as dominant in the United States. While the Nixon administration clearly did not share it as much as Kennedy and Johnson had, Nixon could not feel free to return to the simple tolerance and ambivalent attitudes of the Eisenhower years. We will return a little later to sort out the importance of the differences in approach among Johnson, Nixon, Ford, and Carter, but the broad answer to our basic question has been settled. Since 1961, the U.S. government and people have become clearly *opposed* to nuclear proliferation, just as they were opposed before 1949, but with the important difference that we now have had to become resigned to full Soviet membership in the nuclear weapons club; this rank of possible adversaries to whom we are opposed does not, for the moment, include Moscow, and on this question we may even now hope to treat the USSR as a semi-ally.

How total could such a supersession of cold war attitudes by anti-proliferation ones be? To what extent could we be choosing to sacrifice the interest and security of our allies in Europe, Japan and elsewhere, simply to pursue the goal of reducing the risks of the spread of nuclear weapons?

No one ever maximizes a single goal to the exclusion of considerations of all others—not in foreign policy, not in any aspect of human life. Soviet-American negotiations in the middle 1960s on the Nuclear NonProliferation Treaty (NPT) sometimes raised suspicions, for example, that the USSR was treating the issue mostly as an opportunity for propaganda against West Germany. Under such circumstances, it was obviously likely that the United States would, at points, put security and political interests of the Bonn regime ahead of simple accommodation of the USSR in getting an agreed treaty. The German roadblock was then effectively dissolved in a more general détente between Bonn and Moscow, whereupon the Soviet propaganda depictions of West Germany as the major object of proliferation fears ended.

Failure of the two superpowers to coordinate effective pressure to keep India from detonating a nuclear explosive similarly showed an instance where traditional competitive "cold war" considerations took priority over jointly held Soviet-American concerns about nuclear weapons spread. India was simply too big and important a country for either side to be sure that the other would not, at the last moment, pull some double-cross by welcoming India into the nuclear weapons club; whichever side had held the line in denouncing the move might then have suffered too great a loss of prestige and support in India.

Yet, leaving these examples aside, it is indeed remarkable how much coordination and cooperation there has been between Moscow and Washington in trying to halt the spread of nuclear weapons, a kind of cooperation which has found each side ready to pay some costs as part of the joint effort and ready to forego some opportunities.

At virtually all international negotiations on the subject of nuclear proliferation, the pattern has been the same. Soviet and American delegations stay in close consultation, comparing parliamentary strategy on how to rebut moves that might upset the anti-proliferation regime. Their statements on the proliferation problem are virtually identical, expressing great concern about the worldwide costs and disutility of further nuclear weapons spread, and voicing full support for the inspection and verification provided by IAEA (International Atomic Energy Agency) safeguards. Soviet-American coordination has often left such close U.S. allies as Britain or West Germany feeling irritatingly left out. Delegates from non-English speaking countries, who have to listen to both superpowers' speeches in translation, complain that they have difficulty remembering which one is speaking, since they come through exactly alike.

This kind of cooperation has shown up at conferences of nuclear supplier nations in London, at meetings of the IAEA Board of Governors in Vienna, at all the international negotiations about the Non-Proliferation Treaty, and at sessions of the United Nations General Assembly. It can indeed be argued that there is no topic on which Soviet-American cooperation has been as close or reliable as on nuclear proliferation. If either superpower's delegation had not had time to read a new Brazilian motion, for example, it would not be above asking the other how it should vote. Members of the two delegations came to know each other well over time and became very accustomed to the cooperative, and almost conspiratorial, atmosphere on the proliferation issue.

The strong Soviet support for IAEA inspection might surprise some who remember how other Soviet-American negotiations on disarmament have so often tended to get hung up on the issue of verification; the United States has classically argued that unverified disarmament agreements would never be executed, while the Soviets have claimed that inspection was unnecessary among nations of goodwill and was an insulting intrusion into a sovereign realm, tantamount to espionage. Even the first years of Soviet-American convergence about the risks of nuclear proliferation saw some continuation of the back-and-forth on inspection here—early drafts of the Soviet proposal for an NPT made no reference to safeguards, and Soviet delegates sometimes were tempted to endorse Indian objections to IAEA inspection.

Some of the earlier disagreement was of course based on an assumption by both sides that the west would be inherently open (i.e., prone to give away any of its attempts to cheat on a disarmament agreement, even if there was no formal inspection process), while the Soviet bloc would be closed, quite able to carry off weapons preparations in secret. What changed the attitudes on both sides, all for the better, may simply have been that some of this apparent asymmetry disappeared. The Soviets at a certain point had to reconcile propaganda about fears of a German nuclear weapons program with their earlier propaganda about an inherent lack of need for inspection. By 1967 therefore the Soviets had suddenly become "more Catholic than the Pope," endorsing and demanding IAEA inspection for all non-weapons states, even where the proposed American draft of the treaty would have been content with "IAEA or equivalent" safeguards (i.e., Euratom safeguards instead of IAEA in the West German case).

Soviet propaganda had thus painted a portion of the west (specifically West Germany) as being just as unreliable for an unverified disarmament agreement as the west had previously painted the Soviets. As the Soviets came to believe their own new propaganda, they had to become more realistic and open-minded about the plausible need for inspection (while Americans, in defending the Germans, paradoxically started echoing some earlier Soviet comments about how a certain amount of trust is needed if disarmament schemes are not to be killed off by excessive vigilance).

We can leave outside of our discussion whether later disclosures of secret U.S. government armed operations in the Johnson and Nixon administrations might not have also had some of the same impact on the Soviets who, given that the free press operations of any open society could no longer be counted upon to provide reliable verification here, decided that they might indeed also need verification for any disarmament agreement involving the United States.

Our earlier visions of inspection behind the Iron Curtain always had assumed that the Communist authorities would do everything they could to hem in and hamstring the investigating authority because they had secret weapons programs to hide or because they feared that the presence and example of an inspector from the outside would be destabilizing and upsetting for Communist domestic order. The record to date of IAEA inspection in Communist countries has been quite the opposite. To be sure, there are no IAEA safeguards within the Soviet Union, since the NPT does not require nuclear-weapons states to submit to any such inspection of their peaceful facilities (such inspection would be rather pointless in any event, since additional bombs here can be run off far more easily in the military facilities). Yet there are such safeguards in each satellite of Moscow which installs nuclear reactors to produce electricity. The reception of IAEA inspectors in places like East Germany has apparently been the model of cooperation, a model which the Vienna Agency would very much like to see matched in western countries, where it more often has to overcome hurdles erected by grudging and complaining businessmen.

The United States and USSR reached agreement on the inspection question by 1968, in the drafting of an NPT. By 1978 the form of inspection—IAEA safeguards for all parties to the treaty—was no longer a major issue anywhere. The convergence of the two powers on the issue was an important illustration of how the new shape of the nuclear proliferation problem has unfrozen some old attitudes both sides had inherited from the more confrontational days of the Cold War.

The proliferation problem is a very serious danger to the world, posing threats of death and destruction that cannot be ignored. With particular reference to the Soviet-American rivalry persisting since the Cold War, however, it could also be seen as something useful, a "common enemy" drawing Moscow and Washington into some patterns of cooperation, establishing conduits for communication, opening new lines of thinking, setting precedents. One can always speculate that the Cold War would have been ended quickly if only Hitler had been discovered alive in Argentina, secretly equipped with a new military force to reopen World War II. "The enemy of my enemy is my friend" is an old adage, and the proliferation of nuclear weapons into the hands of a possibly hostile, irresponsible, or crazy regime constitutes such an enemy.

While the earliest Soviet propaganda seemed to simply use the proliferation issue to depict the politically democratic and pro-American West German government as a new version of Naziism, this shifted in time, as noted, to a more serious Soviet consideration of the risks of nuclear weapons spread anywhere. Genuine cooperation then got underway.

How much the nonproliferation goal can outweigh other goals will always be somewhat up in the air, on both sides. When the temptations of an operation in Angola or South Yemen or Afghanistan are too great, the Soviet will lapse into adversary behavior, even at the cost of undermining established precedents and cooperation on the anti-proliferation front. However, when the risk becomes serious, with another power reaching for nuclear weapons, the more cooperative mode of behavior may return.

THEORIES OF DÉTENTE AND THEORIES OF PROLIFERATION

It would be clearly wrong to assume that the nuclear proliferation problem has been at the center of Soviet-American relations over the past decade, for other explanations and worries need to be introduced. The decade saw an apparent replacement of the "Cold War" with a new period of "détente," but not without some serious second thoughts and disquiet as to where the change was leading. If the Soviet Union has seemed to have adopted more cooperative and realistic approaches to the world due to the nuclear proliferation issue, not everyone would accept such an explanation for the broader picture of the lessening of tension between east and west. The end of the Cold War cannot be attributed simply to changes or moderations in Soviet behavior, for there are at least two strong alternative theories to also be considered.

A first alternative theory would explain the emergence of détente as the result of the strengthening of other power centers around the world besides those of Washington and Moscow, new power centers which no longer need to cling to a superpower for alliance and protection, but rather can reactivate the old multipolar balance-of-power game in playing everyone off against everyone else. After World War II, when Europe, Africa, and Asia were generally a series of power vacuums open to whomever first raced to move into them, the result was predictably a bipolar world or preemption and confrontation, resulting in what we call the Cold War. When the countries of Western Europe and Japan recovered their political and economic viability, a very different pattern might have ensued, with happier results for all.

This theory would thus suggest that the Cold War ended because those very problems ended which had first stampeded the two sides into it. This theory does not presume any Soviet meekness or mending of ways, but rather that both sides no longer encountered the kinds of temptations and worries that a game theorist would recognize as part of prisoners' dilemma.

But a second alternative theory would present a quite different view of détente, without any great deal of optimism behind it. Not a few commentators on these developments have now expressed fears that the "détente" has simply stemmed from a new American weakness, as the American people and government, in the wake of the Vietnam defeat, have lost their willingness to make sacrifices to protect political democracy around the globe. Perhaps this is because the costs in the war proved far greater than most Americans had anticipated. Perhaps it is also because there has been a drastic reexamination of American power, suggesting that this was indeed not slated to be "the American Century," that our ability to influence others was less than we thought. Such a loss of American resolve could also be appearing because a significant fraction of Americans have moved leftward in their value preferences—no longer rooting against the Ho Chi Minh's of this world, but openly cheering for them; no longer hoping for free press and free elections and political democracy in the states of Africa and Asia, but rather rooting for Marxist dictatorships, in the belief that these can more rapidly achieve an "economic democracy," with a fairer sharing of material wealth, and quicker relief of poverty and starvation.

All of the above are thus part of an explanation that would view "détente" as part of a new American meekness about international events. This is an explanation which would not find hope that the Soviets are becoming so much more reasonable, or that tensions and disputes around the world are solving themselves.

Without thus attempting to evaluate the merits of such alternative theories, I'll say a few words about how the nuclear proliferation possibility relates to them. I will first consider whether nuclear proliferation is necessary or important to the emergence of the national strengths around the globe which may have reduced the *needs* for Moscow or Washington to intervene. I will then look at the impact of proliferation on any possible American *desires* for isolation, as opposed to intervention.

Nuclear weapons are sometimes given too much credit for setting up the multipolarity that may lie behind part of détente. China and France assuredly provide some of the best examples of how alliance partners which once seemed so monolithically aligned to Washington and Moscow now take delight in playing each off against the other, attacking the two superpowers in turn. Since China and France are each nuclear weapons states, the fourth and fifth "proliferators," the quick deduction might be drawn that their move for nuclear weapons was crucial to setting up their independence.

Yet countries like Germany and Japan show just as much independence of Washington as does Rumania of the USSR, such that nuclear weapons proliferation is not so demonstrably indispensable in this case. The argument thus can be made that the first two nuclear powers already checked each other and cancelled each other out; as the armed struggle between Washington and Hanoi very much demonstrated, neither could then force its will on any other state by nuclear arms. If only one country had nuclear weapons, it might have been willing to use them quickly enough to force another state to surrender. This was true of the United States against Japan and might have been true against the Hanoi regime. It also might have been true of the USSR against China, or against the United States, as well as Britain against Iceland. But with two nuclear powers on the scene, caution replaced arrogance.

Additional nuclear weapons capabilities beyond the first two thus may be neither necessary nor sufficient to establish military and political independence. The resurgences of local conventional military strength, economic strength, and political viability would have made countries feel secure enough to relinquish alliance coverage, to stand up to and defy former patrons.

The argument that local nuclear forces discourage war and reinforce independence is an old one, quite familiar to anyone who has read the writings of Pierre Gallois.[6] Yet, except for special cases, it is probably a wrong argument, for it very much understates the coverage of nuclear umbrellas and the strength of local defenses. Does Australia need its own bomb to be secure? No, because American bombs very likely would be used if any other nuclear power were to menace the government in Canberra. Do the Philippines need their own bomb to be secure? No, because the waters around the islands and the existence of an American fleet make an invasion decidedly impracticable.

Therefore, if the Philippines and Australia and other states these days find it less necessary to toe the line of one of the superpowers, it is not because of nuclear proliferation. Acquisition of such weapons would be redundant and would not be as effective as the other sources of independence and strength which have now spread to such countries.

Is nuclear proliferation thus redundant everywhere? Are the arguments of Gallois irrelevant generally? Not quite, for we must turn to a series of special cases, the so-called "pariah states" of the world, states whose survival is continually threatened by their immediate neighbors, while the outside world chooses to resign itself morally to the attack.[7] States in this category might include Israel, South Africa, Taiwan, South Korea, and perhaps someday Pakistan and Yugoslavia. Since the processes of détente and the new balance-of-power have not worked out so well for them, these are states which may consider nuclear weapons as a necessary and effective solution for their special national security problems.

Of the countries that have established themselves to date as having nuclear explosives, Britain, India, and France (despite Gallois) do not really fit this pattern. China perhaps did when—exposed to the risk of a Soviet overthrow of Mao and unable to invoke American help—it turned to an independent nuclear capability as the means of ensuring national independence. If Israel and Taiwan were to reach for nuclear warheads, it would be for similar reasons. If Argentina or Brazil did so, however, it would be (like Britain, France, and India) for reasons of prestige rather than security.

We will thus have to concede a few cases where nuclear weapons may not be redundant to the insurance of a country against armed attack. Yet the peace-minded outsider can hardly view this with equanimity, as the net contribution of such nuclear proliferation to peace will always be a little tentative and shaky. Most "nth" nuclear forces for the foreseeable future are likely to come in a form extremely vulnerable to preemptive attack. When two sides invest in nuclear forces coupled to delivery systems inviting preemption, the result might someday be a "war nobody wanted," arising simply because each side did not dare to wait to see whether the other was restraining itself, each striking because attacking was better than being attacked.

Countries around the world are now generally more independent and seem more able to stand up for themselves, thereby perhaps freeing Americans to relax about issues of intervention and mutual security. If any of the causal background for this were by any stretch of the imagination to be nuclear proliferation, however, the inclination to "leave well enough alone" might not last very long.

It is thus appropriate to move our second alternative theory and its ties to nuclear weapons spread. Will further proliferation finally turn around what might have been an American retreat from the world?

Whatever the impact on the *likelihood* of war, nuclear proliferation may eventually make Americans more world-minded and interventionist again, because potential wars would be much more damaging for the peoples caught in them and the United States itself might suffer in the fallout and misfires of a nuclear war anywhere on the globe.

The Indian nuclear detonation very clearly had an opposite impact on American attitudes from the fall of Vietnam. The Vietnam war seemed to teach Americans that we tend to back the wrong side in Asian and other foreign conflicts, or that (if backing the right side) we tend to be unproductive when intervening in such conflicts and bear costs that are too high. The Indian detonation conversely served as a reminder that there are still events in faraway places that should be headed off, events that have little to do with capitalism and Marxism, but hinge simply on an enormous gimmick of technology, the explosive capacity of uranium and plutonium. When nuclear proliferation replaces the spread of Communism as the fear, the plausible damage to the United States at once becomes more tangible and clear again. Lyndon Johnson could not get Americans worried about a wave of Communist guerrilla insurgencies continuously encroaching upon us all the way back to Malibu Beach, but a plausible result of nuclear weapons spreading to a regime like Khaddafy's might indeed be a nuclear warhead dropped on Los Angeles. If the morality of balancing political democracy vs. economic democracy was becoming more debatable, the morality of keeping wars non-nuclear between India and Pakistan, or between Israel and Egypt, or between Argentina and Brazil, or between Iraq and Iran, remains clearer.

We might shift then from perceptions of morality to the American sense of capability (though here the bases for American reasoning may turn out to be less well-taken). An American public that, on capability terms alone, has despaired of beating Asian guerrillas in Asian jungles, or of beating the Cuban Army in African jungles, has still not lost faith in its capability to slow down someone else's acquisition of the advanced technology for peaceful or military nuclear protests.

A similarity in lines of reasoning can be shown as a "domino theory" applied to nuclear proliferation, much like the one that used to lie at the heart of fears about counterinsurgency and the containment of the Communist world. Why were the dominoes expected to topple each other in such an endless chain in the old worries? If country A went Communist, it might lead to the same in the contiguous country B, simply because their common frontier produced interactions by which the guerrilla movement could spread itself. Or the fall of country A could produce a similar fall in non-contiguous country J, because of the precedent set, simply because the resolve of the United States and its partners had been called into question in country A.

The same linkages emerge on proliferation. The bomb in India can induce a bomb in Pakistan, simply because of the border they share, or it can produce a bomb in Brazil, because of the precedent. (The prevention of nuclear proliferation might also have been labelled the "containment of nuclear weapons possession.")

The spotting of analogies has its limitations, of course. If the logic of the resistance is the same, one need not infer that the logic is wrongheaded on the proliferation problem just because so many concluded that it was wrong on insurgency and the spread of Communism. Above all, to repeat, it may this time entail a different set of adversaries.

REALPOLITICIANS, DOVES, AND
HAWKS

The novelty of the nuclear proliferation issue at times has driven analysts back to some sort of "basic principles" on what international competitions are all about. This has led to some substantial distortions and oversimplifications based on a crude and basic *Realpolitik*.

Americans explaining to themselves why they, in conjuction with the Soviets, should oppose nuclear proliferation sometimes lapse into as simple a formula as "of course everyone wants to have the best in weapons; we were just lucky enough to have gotten them first, leaving us free to keep others from getting them." This picture of course would instantly be endorsed by Indian or French or Brazilian opponents of the NPT and of any effort to prevent the spread of nuclear weapons. While this interpretation may satisfy the more "tough-minded" American students of international politics, it will also of course upset those who aspire to a less selfish and more world-oriented foreign policy for America.

Parallel to the view that this is all simply a power contest are some observations, from "realpoliticians" and moralists alike, that the resistance to the spread of nuclear weapons is somewhere unrealistic or hypocritical as long as the superpowers themselves do not abandon their own enormous nuclear weapons stockpiles. Again this is a view that some Americans and others can jump to easily enough, but it is one that may be quite fundamentally mistaken.

The reality of the nuclear proliferation issue is considerably different. It is simply not the case that the issue only pits the "haves" against the "have-nots." Many important states lacking nuclear weapons will be just as opposed to nuclear proliferation as are existing nuclear-weapon states—opposed even to getting nuclear weapons for themselves. The costs and benefits of this issue involve more than the increments that might be generated for power positions of countries around the world; they involve calculating what the further spread of such weapons can do to the cost and likelihood of war.

As suggested above, the ideal number of nuclear weapons states for the maintenance of peace and political stability in the world may be two. Any number above two may be redundant, simply because the basic two check each other. To have just one nuclear power, by comparison, might be unbearable because that one would be tempted to dictate political decisions to the world. To have "none" might strike many as the best goal of all, but the difficulties of merely establishing adequate "nonproliferation" safeguards to prevent anyone from becoming the seventh or eighth suggests how burdensome it would be to prevent someone from sneaking into the much more exploitable position of the "first and only." The reduction of the world nuclear weapons club to zero would be the central part of a general and complete disarmament (GCD) scheme, but the difficulties of inspection and verification would probably make such a scheme impossible forever.

What role does the overarching balance of nuclear forces thus play on the nuclear proliferation problem? This is the same question we have been asking from issue to issue throughout this volume.

The argument will be presented here that the assured second strike retaliatory forces of the United States and USSR are altogether helpful—not an obstacle—for the stand against nuclear proliferation. While diplomats and propagandists for the erstwhile "nth" countries sometimes pretend to believe the opposite, this is largely a window-dressing for other arguments. Would Brazil, or Israel, or Yugoslavia, or South Korea be less likely to make nuclear weapons if the Soviets and Americans threw all of theirs into the ocean? Most probably not.

What then is the link between the Soviet-American Strategic Arms Limitation (SALT) talks and the campaign against nuclear proliferation? Despite the working of Artile VI of the NPT, which calls for "negotiations in good faith ... on a treaty on general and complete disarmament under strict and effective international control"[8] there is in reality very little substantive connection. In the unlikely event that either of the two superpowers was to devise some new first-strike counterforce capabilities which could actually prevent retaliation by the other, then the fundamental balance insuring peace would be upset and so would the belief that further spread of nuclear weapons to additional nations is redundant and counterproductive. But this remains an improbable outcome, even if SALT failed entirely.

The link between SALT and the nuclear proliferation question is thus mostly cosmetic. If the United States and the USSR insist on wasting money on redundant strategic nuclear systems, this "vertical proliferation" will tend to give naive laymen the impression that nuclear weapons are gaining in political and military significance everywhere, thus strengthening the political parties and factions from country to country that favor national nuclear weapons programs. If superpower negotiations, whatever the substance, could conversely produce the image of superpower restraint and agreement, the opposite political effect could be achieved in some potential "nth" countries.

The changed alignments of the nuclear proliferation question thus catch off-guard some of the more polarized segments of the American spectrum of political analysts and advocates. At one extreme is the "dovish" arms-controller approach, which has long seen all forms of disarmament as worth greater consideration and has long looked forward to greater détente with the Soviet Union, as well as elimination of international suspicions generally.

While this school of thought certainly opposes the further spread of nuclear weapons to additional countries, in its heart of hearts it is reluctant to see such a partial form of arms restraint without parallel restraints on the superpowers too. All well and good so far. This viewpoint makes a most serious mistake, however, when it becomes tempted almost to mortgage or hold hostage the anti-proliferation effort in an attempt to extract greater arms concessions from Moscow and Washington. To applaud a Yugoslav, Brazilian, or Indian statement that "small nations cannot renounce nuclear weapons, unless the great powers do so as well," is to make the fundamental error of assuming that all good things in life must come along together.[9] The "nth" diplomats issuing such statements are hardly typically "dovish" themselves, but eagerly seek an excuse, any excuse, to get their own countries into the nuclear weapons club.

The halting of the superpower arms competition would be a good thing. The prevention of further nuclear weapons proliferation would be a good thing. But the two are not tied together nearly as closely as some statements would have it. For an American liberal to cheer that they might be tied together in some "iron law" which forces fairness all around is to throw the baby out with the bathwater.

If the dovish end of the spectrum finds it difficult to see the separability of the issues here, the hawkish end is also not so comfortable with the form of the proliferation question.

Advocates of confronting the Soviet Union are of course quite aware that the appearance of nuclear weapons in the arsenals of additional countries will not be without importance. Writers of this school can provide learned and coherent discussions of how the likelihood of war, and the cost of war, may be raised if Libya, or Israel, or Argentina, or Japan get nuclear weapons. Yet one senses, with a few very important exceptions, that their hearts are not in it, that—at the end of the article or the conference—they will come out with "open-minded" suggestions that nuclear proliferation will perhaps be stabilizing anyway, instead of destabilizing or that it will perhaps be inevitable, as "no one has even been able to kill off a weapon in the past."

At the risk of doing an injustice to some other defense analysts, i cite Albert Wohlstetter[10] and the late Donald Brennan as two prominent analysts who showed an ability to worry simultaneously about Soviet missile capabilities and nuclear proliferation. For the bulk of the rest of this end of the spectrum, I have the strong suspicion that sleep may be lost about the Soviet Navy or Soviet multiple-warhead missiles, but that it was never lost about nuclear weapons spreading to additional countries.

Why this seeming reluctance to get genuinely concerned about nuclear proliferation, among these Americans who are more skeptical about whether the Cold War is really over, who are more worried about Finlandization and Soviet defense procurements?

Some of this is a carefully thought out distrust of the Soviet commitment to any joint effort like the resistance to nuclear proliferation, as we must fear a Soviet opportunism, aggressiveness, and hostility that will hurt the United States sooner or later. Some of it is instead simply a skepticism about whether nuclear weapons can ever be constrained, on the horizontal or vertical proliferation front. At this "gut-reaction" level, a few of these analysts might even be accused of liking nuclear proliferation, just as they like weapons in general, having quite the opposite of the dovish arms-controllers' aversion to all things military.

At times, the argument has been made that most of the suspect "nth" nations will be anti-Soviet in their political orientation, such that we can look forward to a harvest of increased Soviet discomfort and handicap if proliferation rolls on, and hence should not be concerned about stopping it. Where one is moreover particularly concerned for the survival of a special "pariah state," (e.g., Israel, South Korea, or Taiwan), one might of course welcome the hints of nuclear weapons spreading to these countries, since the hints work to force the neighbors and the world to acknowledge that the "pariah" cannot be "pushed into the sea," or "liberated," or wiped out.

Not all such "hawkish" unconcern about the priority of halting nuclear proliferation is so badly taken; as noted throughout this chapter, there will always be conflicting considerations that have to be given weight as well. One nonetheless runs into a serious tendency to error here, if the "proliferation is inevitable" line is given too much lip service. For this is as yet hardly proven and often amounts to nothing more than a rationalization for always putting other priorities first. (It would also be a gross error, of course, to forget how much more horrible any war between two states will be in the future if it is fought with nuclear, rather than conventional, weapons.)

Some mistakes Americans will make about nuclear proliferation policy stem from misleading carryovers from older dovish or hawkish attitudes about the confrontation with the USSR. Other errors, however, will emerge from a different kind of carryover from the past.

Whatever their political persuasion, the evidence suggests that the bulk of Americans exaggerate the extent to which the United States is still the supplier of nuclear technology to the world. There are numerous suggestions of this in the attitudes of the U.S. Congress. One can similarly argue that some executive branch policies put forward under the Carter administration were based on such a misperception. A very clear illustration of such attitudes can be found in polls of American public opinion, where the man on the street shows a great unawareness about how many cats have already been let out of the bag, of how many countries have already received American equipment and/or have been manufacturing their own.

Would you approve of the U.S. giving nuclear reactors and nuclear development assistance to (read list) or would you disapprove?[11]

	Approve	*Disapprove*	*Not Sure*
Australia	24%	58%	18%
Japan	15	68	17
Brazil	11	71	18
Argentina	10	72	18
Taiwan	9	73	18
Iran	7	74	19

THE ROLE OF PRESIDENTS

On something as important as controlling the spread of nuclear weapons, no one could claim that the attitudes of the American President were not of central significance. An attempt will be made here to sketch the attitudes from one presidential administration to another on this question, beginning with a quick return to the contrast between Truman and Eisenhower.

As noted earlier, President Truman had outlined what could have been labelled as a very tough and hard anti-proliferation position. Drawing substantial support from the public and Congress, the administration's position in the years before the Soviet detonation was that the United States would keep the secrets of the atomic bomb and indeed would hold all nuclear energy technology quite closely. The United States generally adhered to the policy, although there were a few information releases that might not seem so consistent with this, in part because the public's thirst for information about such an amazing new area of technology was in tension with its support for secrecy. The publication of the Smythe Report in 1945, for example, made details public that would help save time and energy for any other country seeking to make nuclear weapons.[12]

In the Acheson–Lilienthal Report forwarded to the United Nations as the Baruch Plan, the United States offered to submit all its own nuclear capability to international control and ownership. Whatever the merits and seriousness of this proposal, the Soviets rejected it. The Baruch Plan might, in some views, have ruled out any future "proliferation problem" by reducing the number of nuclear weapons states from one to zero, under rigorous international controls assuring that no one would ever again become the "first" nuclear weapons state. By a different interpretation, the plan simply—by design or inadvertently—would have made the American monopoly permanent.

The entire Truman policy, including the Baruch Plan, might thus be attacked for its straightforward explication, and open-and-above-board approach that would be typical of Democratic Presidents on this question. If the American policy of "calling a spade a spade" on limiting access to nuclear secrets had the advantage of honesty, it nonetheless might be blamed with making states like the USSR and Britain more determined to break the American monopoly.

The Eisenhower policy, as noted, was instead to reduce the explication and abstraction of such issues. It fuzzed over the issue of whether the United States was disinclined to share nuclear information, by sharing at least some kinds. It fuzzed over whether any U.S. ally would need nuclear weapons of its own, by asserting that massive retaliation by the United States was of course likely if the Soviets were to attack a U.S. ally. Congress, in the powerful Joint Committee on Atomic Energy, sometimes balked at the extent of nuclear information sharing the Eisenhower administration was inclined to tolerate; yet these years nonetheless saw a sharing of weapons technology with Britain, a great opening of general (hopefully peaceful) technology under the "Atoms for Peace" program, and a forward deployment of American "tactical" nuclear weapons into Europe in close proximity to the forces of various NATO allies, including those of West Germany.

As on the question of limited war, the Eisenhower analysis seemed to be that one made the nuclear proliferation issue worse by bringing it out into the open, by discussing it publicly in any precise and clear terms. If one refused to display an understanding of the limited war problems in public, the Soviets might stay deterred (despite the American writers on limited war breaking into print in the 1950s), and American allies (despite Gallois) might remain content with the American nuclear umbrella. During the Eisenhower administration, France indeed chose to acquire its own nuclear weapons, but the rest of the problem had not come into full force as Eisenhower left office.

As on many other questions, the Kennedy administration then behaved quite differently on the nuclear proliferation issue, speaking openly of "putting the nuclear genie back into the bottle." Kennedy meant this to include a halt to further nuclear weapons spread and a deemphasis on American nuclear weapons as the deterrent to attacks on Europe or elsewhere (with perhaps even a total withdrawal of such nuclear weapons from the NATO zone, as conventional ground forces were instead to be expanded to provide a more graduated deterrent).

With the Irish Resolutions of 1958, 1959, and 1960 setting the stage (the Eisenhower administration had even abstained on the 1958 and 1960 resolutions), the Kennedy administration launched a number of trial balloons about a non-proliferation treaty. In the aftermath of the Cuban Missile Crisis, with the agreement on a partial nuclear test-ban and the general détente with the Soviet Union in 1963, a serious mutual exploration of the nuclear proliferation issue was begun with the Soviets.

These efforts had of course not yet culminated when Lyndon Johnson succeeded Kennedy in office. The expansion of the Vietnam War in many ways set back such efforts, in that it pitted the United States against the Soviet Union in another military conflict. Yet, the negotiations went ahead, as noted, with the Soviets making a major concession by adopting a more realistic attitude on the question of IAEA safeguards.

By 1967, the administration thus had an additional reason to second the efforts of the people in the Arms Control and Disarmament Agency (ACDA) who had been advocating such a treaty ever since the Kennedy years. The conclusion of such an agreement might sooth critics of the Johnson administration who had been charging that all prospects for détente were being thrown away in the Vietnam War fighting.

The Nuclear Non-Proliferation Treaty was thus signed by the United States immediately upon its presentation in July 1968, as the United States and Soviet Union at last agreed on a final text of Article III, spelling out provisions for inspection.

Richard Nixon defeated Hubert Humphrey in the election of 1968, again producing a major shift in policy on the nuclear proliferation question. At earlier stages Nixon occasionally had been critical of the treaty and of any emphasis on nuclear proliferation which would come ahead of maintaining close relations with U.S. allies. Such sentiments had been voiced just as often by his new director of the National

Security Council, Henry Kissinger. At a time when the USSR was still directing much of its nuclear proliferation propaganda specifically at West Germany—while the Bonn regime was still taking its time about agreeing to sign the treaty—this was not altogether surprising. Given the earlier Eisenhower tendency to avoid open discussions of the proliferation issue and possible conflict of interests it might produce among Allies, this was again to be expected.

With the treaty already negotiated and signed by the U.S. government, Nixon and Kissinger admitted that the U.S. had no choice except to continue to support it; but pressures to achieve signature and ratification, in Bonn and elsewhere, were almost totally lifted. This may have been a policy of "benign neglect," as the West German and the governments were more likely to accept this restriction on their future military options if they were not being openly pressured on it. Yet at many points, the policy of the Nixon-Kissinger administration from 1969 to 1974 seemed to be more simply "neglect," rather than "benign neglect," as the government seemed too distracted by other issues to assign any attention to the nuclear proliferation problem.

There were thus a number of occasions where the United States government could have exerted influence to achieve an earlier signature or ratification of the NPT, or a more general submission to IAEA safeguards, and where nothing along such lines was done. To pick just one example, many issues were bandied back and forth in the American retrocession of Okinowa to Japan, but one sees no evidence that the United States ever offered to give up any of its demands in exchange for a speedier Japanese NPT ratification.

Part of the difficulty came from Nixon's and Kissinger's genuine skepticism about the urgency of the nuclear proliferation problem, compared with other considerations. Part of it stemmed also from Kissinger's desire to control most of the operations of U.S. foreign policy himself; the price was that the agenda for attention was limited by his capacities, and other topics denied him the time to concentrate very much on the question.

Much of this changed in 1974 as the entry of the Ford administration closely followed the Indian detonation of a "peaceful nuclear explosive." There was assuredly no connection between the Indian detonation and Nixon's being driven from office; one has little evidence that Gerald Ford held very different views on nuclear proliferation from Nixon's. What most likely happened was that the Indian detonation convinced Henry Kissinger, continuing as Secretary of State under Ford, that the prevention of nuclear weapons spread should henceforth draw much more of his own attention and more backing from the U.S. government resources.

The Indian detonation, followed soon after by announcements of a nuclear sale from West Germany to Brazil, indeed also galvanized the American public and Congress to demand much more effort to contain nuclear weapons spread. In the face of congressional demands that something be done, Kissinger and Ford clearly did not have the option to continue neglecting the problem.

The result in these last two years of Republican rule may have come close to an optimal mix of activity, blending the Kissinger penchant for low-key and somewhat concealed diplomacy (which we have noted characterized the Eisenhower years on this issue as well) with a real sense of need for action. Since the United States had become only one of many suppliers of advanced nuclear technology, the Nuclear Suppliers Conferences convened in London might seem the model for coordination and cooperation among countries sharing an aversion to further nuclear proliferation. The conferences produced extremely cooperative behavior from the Soviet Union—adhering to the pattern we have described—from Britain and Canada, and after a time from France and West Germany as well.

Discussion of the significance of presidential style brings us to President Carter, elected in 1976 over President Ford. A number of factors almost foreordained that Carter would come into office demanding a more explicit and extensive policy again on nuclear proliferation. Some of these might seem to be the source of possible policy mistakes.

To begin, Carter portrayed himself in the campaign as possessing expertise on nuclear matters, having served in the Navy under Admiral Rickover and knowing about nuclear propulsion reactors. At a point where the American public was becoming concerned about both the proliferation and pollution risks connected with nuclear energy, Carter's past career fortuitously gave him some good issue identification. Second, as the candidate running against an incumbent, Carter was naturally tempted to favor a change in policy. His general approach moreover bore some of the same "rational activism" that had accompanied Kennedy into office after Eisenhower in 1961, showing a desire for clarity, rationality, and the "best" solution to problems. Finally, to the extent that a new Democratic regime was likely to bring back into government some people and ideas from earlier Democratic regimes, the return of this team was likely to renew and expand the commitment of the executive branch to the halting of proliferation.

In the wake of the Indian detonation and the Brazilian deal, the U.S. Congress was of course very committed to demanding action. Yet, for the reasons cited above, it would be fair to describe the Carter administration as less resistant to congressional pressures than a returned Ford administration would have been.

Ronald Reagan's defeat of Jimmy Carter's bid for reelection in 1980 brought in one more shift in presidential stance, back toward the lowered visible alarm about nuclear proliferation of previous Republican administrations. It was announced that the prevention of further proliferation was still regarded as important but that this would have to come "in the context of the entirety of American foreign policy." This is a formula with which hardly anyone could disagree but which, at the least, suggests a more subtle approach and, at the worst, a substantial reduction of attention and priority for this question.

THE ROLE OF CONGRESS

The role of Congress has not been unimportant on nuclear policy since 1945. In a way, this shows how unusually significant Americans have thought the nuclear question to be, ever since they were so suddenly filled in on it at the end of World War II. The Joint Committee on Atomic Energy thus began with some very special prerogatives and, over the years, captured a reputation for special strength and competence, as it periodically forced changes in the policies of the executive branch.[13]

The joint committee, throughout the Eisenhower administration, showed itself more concerned about nuclear weapons spread than was the President himself, although often still expressing such fears in terms of possible leaks to the Soviets (the original "proliferation problem"). At the same time, it strongly supported the development of peaceful uses of nuclear energy, for a portion of its original mandate under the MacMahon Act stemmed from a fear among scientists and the general public that military secrets would be held too tightly, frustrating the exploitation of this new form of science for good civilian purposes.

The 1974 Indian detonation turned many people against the status quo, whatever the status quo was. One casualty outside the Congress was the Atomic Energy Commission, divided into the Nuclear Regulatory Commission (NRC) and the Energy Research and Development Agency (ERDA). The congressional casualty was the Joint Committee on Atomic Energy, whose functions were divided among several committees as part of a general committee realignment.

What had seemed strong and competent policy was, in retrospect, painted as complacent and excessively permissive. Whatever the policy balance among considerations of military strength, civilian energy development and non-proliferation had been, the demand now was for "new policy," with the implication that most or all previous policy had been inadequate.

U.S. Congressmen generally tend to wander between the roles of being patrons of special constituencies and being broad critics of policy. In the nuclear field, this has translated into being patrons of the development of a peaceful nuclear industry or being critically suspicious of whether American security was compromised by insufficient vigilance against Communist acquisition of additional nuclear weapons (or perhaps compromised by nuclear proliferation in general). The Indian detonation of a nuclear explosive, and the threat that Brazil was moving in the same direction, thus served to shift Congress quite pronouncedly from the first role to the second, bringing substantial loss of influence for those congressmen who had looked too engrossed with the first role.

As the executive branch turned toward a less openly vigilant antiproliferation stance under President Reagan, the Congress continued to be a source of demands that nuclear technology be restricted or that it be shared only under quite stringent safeguards.

THE ROLE OF BUREAUCRACY

Moving away from the Presidency and the Congress, one must (as on each arms issue being examined) also consider the interests and influences of the lower level bureaucracy and the private industry with which it deals.

It is a useful starting point to assume that most such bureaus and firms tend to convince themselves that the national interest is best served when the country buys as much of their product as possible. "Where you stand depends on where you sit" is the traditional cliché, and it rings true often enough.

The Atomic Energy Commission and private firms involved in the nuclear industry have thus consistently favored full development and exploitation of nuclear power production within the United States and abroad. Critics would charge that such exploitation of nuclear power has been premature; its defenders, especially after the enormous rise in oil prices, could point to it instead as a wise use of resources. Whoever has been right about the facts, it is not startling to discover that those government officials and private firms whose careers and profits will benefit from successful development of nuclear power have radiated optimism about it.

However, the AEC also has had a different product to sell, a product potentially very useful for halting proliferation, namely the techniques used in safeguards inspection. Such inspection is almost certainly necessary to prevent the spread of nuclear weapons; one hopes that it will also be sufficient.

One has typically seen AEC officials and executives of private firms like Westinghouse part company somewhat on the safeguards question, with the private firms echoing some of their potential foreign customers in voicing skepticism about whether such safeguards are really so necessary. Getting the U.S. government to be less strict about safeguards over the years has suggested an increased chance of foreign sales, with predictable consequences in corporate attitudes.

One might now shift to a different set of bureaucratic vested interests, those of the various desks of the State Department and the Arms Control and Disarmament Agency (ACDA). It is no surprise, from all we have said, that ACDA favors disarmament, perhaps because disarmament is a good product, perhaps simply because disarmament is ACDA's product. From the Kennedy administration to those of Johnson, Nixon, Ford and Carter, until the substantial purge at the outset of the Reagan administration, ACDA thus kept the faith on the American interest in nonproliferation, at times amounting to a relatively weak lobby on the Washington scene, at other times not so weak.

Turning to the rest of the State Department, however, one encounters some contrary vested interests. The embassies to each foreign country and the desk covering that country in Washington have tended to advocate good relations with that country (just as predictably as in the cases cited above). Where a firmer nonproliferation policy is consistent with this, no problem of conflict emerges, but where the country in question is showing signs of resenting the NPT or other barriers against proliferation, the result has been to add one more voice in Washington in favor of going slower on this front, of putting other priorities ahead of the halting of nuclear weapons spread, of trusting allies rather than showing distrust for them.

Congressional dissatisfaction with the alleged complacency of the past led to the demise of the Joint Committee on Atomic Energy and (as noted) the breakup of the Atomic Energy Commission. In an almost direct acceptance of the theories of bureacratic politics portrayed above, the charge was made that AEC's promotion of nuclear energy had kept it from giving much priority or attention to its regulatory duties over that technology; the AEC was accused of being too eager to license new construction and sales, or too tolerant of industry practices risking pollution and proliferation.

The solution adopted was twofold. The regulatory and licensing function was shifted to a new Nuclear Regulatory Commission (NRC) which would have no management responsibilities and thus hopefully would develop no new vested interest in "as much use of nuclear energy as possible." The management functions of the AEC were embodied in a new Energy Research and Development Agency, which (as its title clearly suggests) was meant to develop a vested interest in *all* forms of energy—not excluding wind power and solar heating, examples with no pollution or proliferation problems at all. With the coming to power of the Carter administration, ERDA was absorbed into a new Department of Energy with still broader powers and mandates, but again hopefully balanced to avoid becoming overly attached to the promotion of nuclear facilities at home and abroad.

Consistent with its swing back in the opposite direction, the Reagan administration has moved to abolish the Department of Energy and reduce the authority and power of the Nuclear Regulatory Commission, while again encouraging the development of nuclear power.

There is of course more than a little truth to the bureaucratic politics theories; the theories suggest that every government agency has special interests just as does every private firm, so that we should all be on our guard against what organizations try to sell us. Yet it would be a mistake to blame what we buy from decade to decade simply on the salesmanship and machinations of the suppliers, for Congress and the public come to the scene with some consumer opinions and preferences of their own. It is quite ironic that the post-Hiroshima legislation establishing a civilian Atomic Energy Commission and the matching congressional Joint Committee on Atomic Energy were based on the fear that the bureaucratic self-interest of the military would lead to too little development of civilian uses of nuclear energy, while the congressional reaction after 1974 was that we had too much. If the U.S. military had wanted to kill off civilian use of nuclear energy in 1946, this would simply have been because it feared that too many military secrets would leak out in the process of civilian use. But that is of course what our nuclear proliferation problem of today is all about.

The mistakes in the handling of nuclear energy may thus not turn out to be so much the machinations of selfish bureaucrats, but rather the inherent difficulties of prediction on scientific and political variables.[14] Scientists around the world in 1946, or in 1976, had difficulty assessing the pollution hazards connected with the use of nuclear reactors to generate electricity. Scientists in 1946 had great difficulty predicting how long it would take for the USSR or Britain to develop their own nuclear weapons. Scientists today genuinely disagree among themselves about how easy it will be for some suspect "nth" country to divert plutonium or enriched uranium from a peaceful nuclear facility to the production of nuclear explosives.

The entire country may have erred on the side of complacency in the period before 1974 (although the complacency and alleged inactivity of this period is very easily overstated), but it may have erred in other directions since. Above all, however, one is tempted to conclude that the major problem comes with the decisions and perceptions of President and Congress, and with the inherent unpredictability of events, rather than with selfishness of bureaus, for the bureaucrats can be found on either side of an issue.

SOME LESSONS

What can one put forward, therefore, as tentative lessons? We can begin by repeating a point already made several times, that "proliferation" is in many ways a new issue for Americans, having only a superficial resemblance to the original anti-Soviet proliferation issue after Hiroshima. There were moments when commentators on the 1967-1968 NPT negotiations spoke of a "diplomatic revolution" with Germany, Japan, Italy, Brazil, France, India, Sweden, and Rumania being pitted against the United States, Soviet Union, Britain, Canada, etc. The "revolution" phrase was obviously too strong, since so many real issues still continue to divide Moscow and Washington, and since countries like Sweden, Japan, West Germany, and France hardly have turned out to favor worldwide nuclear proliferation when the chips are down. Yet the partial realignment of conflict and the new complication of issues indeed can make some old attitudes about "disarmament" and "the Cold War" very misleading for sound decisionmaking.

And an equal and matching error can come from a different direction. A few analysts, in discovering the "newness" of the nuclear proliferation problem, will leap to the conclusion that "nothing has been done" to try to head off this problem, that the "barn door must be shut as soon as possible, lest any more horses get out." To discover a problem that earlier had not been so widely perceived is sometimes to conclude that urgent solutions and immediate action are required. The "new" problem quite naturally is seen as an "additional" problem, with an "additional solution" needed very quickly.

This kind of response, of which one could accuse the Congress and perhaps also the Carter administration, may stem from an incomplete perception of what exactly is so "new" about nuclear proliferation as a problem. One part of the newness is the confusion of alliances, as we obviously have resigned ourselves to the USSR, Britain, France, and Communist China remaining nuclear weapons states, but are trying to head off any additional states joining the club. Another part of the newness, however, is simply that many more states are now privy to the technology and professional competence needed for nuclear ventures. They are capable of selling such materials or equipment, even if the U.S. government were to disapprove, and are capable of producing such materials and equipment for themselves. Given the widespread public exaggeration of American special competence in this area, it would be a mistake for the Congress and Presidency not to compensate against such exaggerations. This is, of course, a point that executives of the American nuclear industry never tire of making.

If one had a sudden all-in-òne solution to the nuclear proliferation risk, perhaps based on cutoffs of American assistance, perhaps based on something else, it might be well to apply it. If one does not have such a solution, however, it may be wise to sift through the various half-measures, put into place under Eisenhower and Kennedy and ever since, to see whether the array of such measures might not yet be managed into an effective barrier, stopping the further spread of nuclear weapons, or at least slowing it down to a very manageable pace.

The response to nuclear weapons spread may thus show that Americans did not draw a general lesson of weakness from the failures of Vietnam, but only a very specialized sense of limitation. We are perhaps resigned to being unsuccessful as jungle infantry, an inhibition which many Americans had already accepted back in the Truman and Eisenhower days, only to overcome it under Kennedy in the spirit of the Green Berets, but then to return to it as Vietnam turned sour. Where the field is that of advanced reactor design and uranium enrichment, however, Americans may still trust their superior competence and want to apply it for decisive results.

It is hardly proven yet that such superiority cannot be successfully applied, but the application may require more patience. For many decades, the United States will be seen as an important source of all that is advanced and conducive to material well-being around the world. The threat that this may be cut off, as the price of an "nth" national decision to invest in nuclear weapons, is not such an unreal or weak threat. Countries will have their own capability to make nuclear weapons without the United States helping them; this is a fact to which Americans must adjust. But they will still need United States cooperation if they wish to have rapid economic growth.

In light of earlier and more recent policy, we need to guard against being misled by the bureaucratic special interests of government agencies; yet, as noted, it is a mistake to assume that this has been the source of all our problems or that simple vigilance against this would guide us to wise policy.

A more important lesson may come on the role of self-confirming hypotheses about the proliferation risk. In the case of our Cold War confrontations with the Communists world, we now often ask ourselves whether the conflict was real from the start, or whether it ensued from some sort of mirror-image misunderstanding, whereby each side became

254 / *National Security and International Stability*

prematurely worried about the other, took a few precautionary steps, and then seemed to confirm the worries of the other side, leading to a few more precautionary steps, arms races, and wars. Was such the nature of the beginnings of the Cold War, of the U.S.-Chinese conflict, of the war in Vietnam?

A similar possibility of course applies to the nuclear proliferation issue. Can we at times be premature in our suspicions, producing a tension and hostility in our relations with some particular country in a way which then strengthens the domestic political clout within that country of the very factions which favor a nuclear weapons program? Or was the lust for such weapons there all the time, such that we were wise in starting as early as possible to do all we could to prevent such a move? Who was wiser on nuclear proliferation policy, Eisenhower or Kennedy, Kissinger or Carter? The answer must vary from case to case.

The American economic and political leverage is there, but it will typically have to be used subtly and indirectly. The payoff of an assurance that more countries will not acquire nuclear weapons may not come on a nicely packaged once-and-for-all basis, but rather as an ongoing year-by-year pattern of behavior, where proliferation is postponed, and postponed, and postponed.

NOTES

1. For good accounts of the emergence of the British nuclear program, see Margaret M. Gowing, *Britain and Atomic Energy* (London: Macmillan, 1964); and *Independence and Deterrence* (New York: St. Martin's, 1974); and Richard Rosecrance, *Defense of the Realm* (New York: Columbia University Press, 1968).
2. Joel Larus, *Nuclear Weapons Safety and the Common Defense* (Columbus: Ohio State University Press, 1967); and H. L. Nieburg, *Nuclear Secrecy and Foreign Policy* (Washington, D.C.: Public Affairs Press, 1964).
3. For the tensions between the United States government and the Diefenbaker administration in Canada, see Peter C. Newman, *Renegade in Power* (Toronto: McClelland and Stewart, 1973).
4. A good overview of the "Atoms for Peace" program can be found in Arnold Kramish, *The Peaceful Atom and Foreign Policy* (New York: Harper and Row, 1963).
5. The emergence of the U.N. General Assembly resolution by Ireland for a "non-nuclear club" is discussed in William B. Bader, *The United States and the Spread of Nuclear Weapons* (New York: Pegasus, 1968), p. 36-51.
6. Pierre Gallois, *The Balance of Terror* (Boston: Houghton Mifflin, 1961).
7. For a good analysis of the issues of the "pariah states" see Robert E. Harkavy, "The Pariah State Syndrome," *Orbis*, vol. 23, no. 3 (Fall 1977), pp. 623-650.
8. The text of the NPT can be found in United States Arms Control and Disarmament Agency *Documents on Disarmament, 1968* (Washington, D.C.: U.S. Government Printing Office, 1969), pp. 461-465.
9. For example, see William Epstein, *The Last Chance: Nuclear Proliferation and Arms Control* (New York: Free Press, 1976).

10. For example, see Albert Wohlstetter, *Swords from Plowshares* (Chicago: University of Chicago Press, 1978).
11. Polls cited in *Current Opinion*, vol. 5, issue 4 (April, 1977), p. 40.
12. Henry DeWolf Smyth, *Atomic Energy for Military Purposes* (Princeton, NJ.: Princeton University Press, 1945).
13. A useful account of the emergence of the MacMahon Act and the post-war arrangements for the management of the uses of nuclear technology can be found in Thomas Morgan, *Atomic Energy and Congress* (Ann Arbor: University of Michigan Press, 1956).
14. The standard presentation of the bureacratic politics view here is to be found in Graham Allison, "Conceptual Models and the Cuban Missile Crisis," *American Political Science Review*, vol. 63, no. 3 (September 1969), pp. 689-718. For an important counter, see Stephen D. Krasner, "Are Bureacracies Important? (Or Allison Wonderland)," *Foreign Policy*, no. 7 (Summer 1972), pp. 159-179.

Chapter 13

Nuclear Proliferation and the Probability of Nuclear War

Michael D. Intriligator and Dagobert L. Brito

INTRODUCTION

This paper studies the effects of nuclear proliferation—the acquisition of nuclear weapons by additional nation states—on the probability of nuclear war. There are of course multiple interrelated effects of nuclear proliferation in addition to its effect on the probability of nuclear war, such as economic effects on the global distribution of wealth, political effects on the structure of alliances and alliance relationships, and military effects on the nature of war.[1] All of these effects are, however, arguably less important than the question of nuclear war outbreak itself. Thus the focus of this paper is the influence of additional nuclear weapons states on the probability of nuclear war.

The principal analytic conclusion of this paper is that there may be different qualitative effects of proliferation on the probability of nuclear war, depending on the number of existing nuclear nations, and that in

The authors wish to acknowledge support of the National Science Foundation under their collaborative grants on "Behavioral and Economic Foundations of Arms Races." They also wish to acknowledge the support and assistance of the Center for International and Strategic Affairs at UCLA and the Murphy Institute for the Study of Political Economy at Tulane. Finally, they wish to acknowledge the helpful suggestions of William Kelley, Steven J. Brams, Thomas Saaty, and Gordon Tullock.

certain instances proliferation may *reduce*, rather than increase, the probability of nuclear war.[2] The principal policy conclusion of this paper is that where there are adverse effects on world stability from an additional nuclear nation, these effects may be partly offset by policies and programs which have the effect of reducing the probability of accidental or irrational war.

Related arguments on the effects of nuclear proliferation have been presented by Gallois, Wentz, and Tullock. Gallois argued that additional nuclear weapons states, such as France, would so raise the stakes of a potential conflict that such proliferation would make nations more cautious and thus reduce the probability of nuclear war.[3] Wentz argued that it might be in U.S. interests to promote selective nuclear proliferation.[4] Tullock treated multicountry situations and argued that the existence of nuclear non-belligerents could reduce the probability of nuclear war.[5]

The effect of nuclear proliferation on the probability of nuclear war depends, among other things, on the nature of the new nuclear nation, its regional situation, its specific new capabilities, delivery vehicles, political stability, alliance relationships, and many other factors. A major point that will be made here, however, is that it also depends to a significant degree on the *number* of existing nuclear nations. The acquisition of nuclear weapons generally has qualitatively different effects on the probability of nuclear war by an additional nuclear nation, depending on the existing number of nuclear nations. The different qualitative effects of the number of nuclear nations on stability against war outbreak is somewhat similar to the different qualitative effects of the number of contending nations on the stability of the international system. The latter issue was considered at first in the context of the question of whether a bipolar or a multipolar world would be more stable. Kenneth Waltz argued that added nations would be destabilizing because of loss of predictability, while Deutsch and Singer argued that added nations are stabilizing because of the greater possibilities for stabilizing interactions.[6] Later authors have attempted to reconcile these disparate views by noting that there may, in fact, be different qualitative effects depending on the number of nations.[7] Similarly, effects of nuclear proliferation on the probability of war may depend on the number of nuclear nations.

SOME SPECIFIC SITUATIONS

Specific situations can be used to illustrate the different qualitative effects of proliferation on the probability of nuclear war. The next section presents a more formal model of this.

Consider first the case of the initial nuclear nation. If this nation is engaged in a war, it can use its nuclear weapons without fear of retaliation in kind, leading to a high probability of their use. In fact, the only time nuclear weapons have been used has been in precisely this situation, by the United States against Japan in 1945.

Next consider the case in which there is a nuclear power and a newly emerging nuclear power. The probability of use would also be high in this case, since the existing nuclear power may feel that it has the capability of eliminating a potential rival without fear of retaliation. In fact, during the period of nuclear monopoly by the United States from 1945 to 1949, serious suggestions were made that it use atomic weapons against the Soviet Union to eliminate it as a rival for global power. In 1948, for example, Bertrand Russell argued for such a preventive war against the Soviet Union in view of the U.S. nuclear monopoly at that time.[8]

The relatively high probability of war of both the one-nuclear-nation case and the case of one nuclear nation and an emerging nuclear nation is reduced as the new nuclear nation acquires sufficient nuclear weapons to deter the major nuclear power. With enough nuclear weapons on each side, the bipolar world is one of great stability against war outbreak, since each nuclear nation then has enough weapons to inflict unacceptable damage on the other on a retaliatory second strike.[9]

Consider then the situation of two major nuclear powers and one newly emerging nuclear power. There is still the danger of a "surgical strike;" however, it is less than in the previous case since the existing powers must either act together—which is a difficult achievement—or run the risk of retaliation by the other or being weakened vis-à-vis the other in the case of a unilateral action. The uncertainty over the reaction of the other nuclear power will make each hesitant to strike at the newly emerging power.

After the third nuclear power has acquired sufficient weapons to deter a strike by one of the first two powers, the probability of war is even further reduced since its presence and capabilities restrain the major powers from initiating a war either against it or against each other. Each power is uncertain of the response of the other, which can either assist the attacked nation or not participate and become the dominant power in the postwar world.

As additional nations acquire nuclear weapons there is even greater uncertainty over the reaction of other nuclear powers to the initiation of a nuclear war, further reinforcing general deterrence and enhancing stability against war outbreak. The probability of a deliberate initiation of a war decreases as the acquisition of nuclear weapons restrains the existing nuclear nations. A key factor in the decision to initiate a nuclear war is the postwar distribution of power. Increasing the number of nuclear nations implies that a nation which initiates a war would be relatively worse off in the postwar environment, both in the case where the other nuclear nations are belligerents and in the case where they remain neutral. Increasing the number of nuclear nations also increases the uncertainty as to how other nuclear powers will react during and after a war. As the number of nuclear nations rises above three or four, both the relatively more disadvantageous postwar situation and the uncertainty over the behavior of other nations become more important and outweigh the presence of an additional candidate for initiating a war. With these numbers of nuclear nations there is a rapid increase in the number of potential nations or coalitions with which any initiating nuclear power would have to contend both during and after a war.[10]

While the probability of a calculated attack may fall to near zero, there remains the probability of an accidental or irrational war via either technical mishap or irrational action. For several reasons, this factor plays a relatively more important role as the number of nuclear powers increases. First, with greater numbers of nuclear weapons and nuclear nations there is a greater chance of such an accident. Second, the new nuclear powers are likely to be less sophisticated technically and less able to develop adequate safeguards. Third, these nations may have less stable political institutions. Thus, the probability of war eventually increases because of a greater chance of accidental or irrational war.

Consideration of specific situations suggests that there may be different qualitative effects of a new nuclear nation on the probability of war, depending on the number of nuclear nations. These different effects may be considered the resolution of three influences stemming from the acquisition of nuclear weapons by an additional nation: The *first effect* is that of a new nuclear nation being an additional potential initiator of a war and a potential target. This effect *increases* the probability of war, and it is the dominant effect in the case of one or two nuclear nations since the new nuclear nation will have a minimal stockpile with no retaliatory capability. The *second effect* is that of a new nuclear nation being an additional potential retaliator and/or a nation that could become a dominant power after a war in which it was not a belligerent. Uncertainty over the possible reaction of a new nuclear nation will restrain the existing nuclear nations. This effect *decreases* the probability of war, and it is likely to offset the first effect for a "small" number of nuclear nations. The *third effect* is that of a new nuclear nation increasing the chance of accidental or irrational war. This effect *increases* the probability of war, and it is likely to become the dominant factor in the case of a "large" number of nuclear nations, particularly if the probability of war among them by calculation has been reduced to virtually zero because of uncertainty over the response of other nuclear nations.[11] The chance of war by accident or irrational action is further augmented by the possible acquisition of nuclear weapons by non-industrialized states without effective delivery systems or by subnational groups.

The major policy implication of this analysis is that of reorienting policy away from non-proliferation per se and toward control over accidental or irrational war. While nuclear weapons proliferation may either increase or decrease the probability of war, control over accidental or irrational war must reduce the chances of war. In fact, many problems associated with nuclear proliferation could be overcome by policies and actions, both technical and political, that would reduce the chance of accidental or irrational war. The nuclear nations as a group should probably be more concerned over accidental or irrational war than over nuclear proliferation. This policy conclusion is even further strengthened when considering the relative numbers of weapons involved. There can be considerably more value in controlling the accidental or irrational detonation of one of the thousands of warheads in all the current nuclear nations than in preventing the acquisition of a small number of weapons in a new nuclear nation. There may, for example, be merit in the superpowers sharing their technology to control nuclear weapons with the other nuclear nations, or even in all existing nuclear nations sharing this technology with all potential nuclear weapons nations. Such policies, which have the effect of lowering the probability of accidental war, can significantly offset the potentially destabilizing effects of nuclear proliferation.

A FORMAL MODEL

The specific situations mentioned earlier suggest the different qualitative effects of nuclear proliferation shown in Figure 13.1. In this figure the probability of nuclear war, W, is shown as a function of nations, n. Starting from a disarmed world of no nuclear nations, adding one nuclear nation increases the probability of nuclear war since the single nuclear nation may use its power against other nations. The probability also increases with a single existing nuclear nation and a newly emerging nuclear nation. In this situation an added nuclear nation represents an added candidate to initiate a nuclear war, and in acquiring nuclear capabilities, the new nuclear nation typically will not be capable of deterring a rival nation. In such a situation nuclear proliferation could lead to a "surgical strike" and thus a relatively high probability of nuclear war.

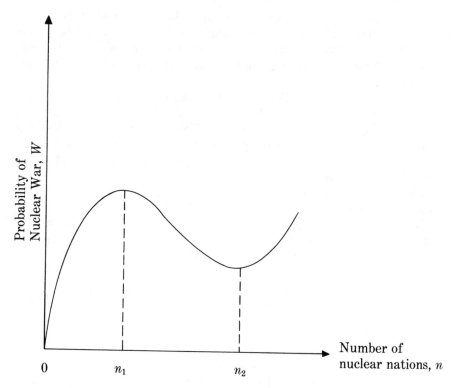

Figure 13.1. Probability of nuclear war as a function of the number of nuclear nations.

Beyond a certain critical number of nations, however, shown as n_1 in Figure 13.1, there may be a qualitatively different effect of nuclear proliferation on the probability of nuclear war. With sufficient numbers of nuclear nations, an added one could *reduce* the chance of nuclear war. The rationale behind this reduction is that, while an added nuclear nation would represent one more nation that might initiate a war, it also represents one more power with which all existing nuclear nations must reckon. Its nuclear weapons acquisition would restrain the existing nuclear nations, since each would be uncertain of the new nuclear nation's reaction to a nuclear war, particularly a calculated attack. Each could not be sure whether the new nuclear nation would enter a nuclear war on its side or against it, or whether it would simply wait on the sidelines and dominate the postwar situation. Eventually, however, when there is a sufficiently large number of nuclear nations, the added stability engendered by reductions in the probability of a calculated nuclear war is exhausted as this probability becomes vanishingly small. What remains is the probability of accidental or irrational nuclear war, which increases with the number of nuclear nations and which eventually, at n_2, causes the curve in Figure 13.1 to rise once more.

These different qualitative effects of proliferation on the probability of nuclear war can be explained in terms of a more formal model. Consider a world of n nuclear nations. Let p_j be the probability that nation j will initiate a nuclear war, where p_j depends on the number of nuclear nations

$$p_j = p_j(n) \qquad j = 1, 2, \ldots, n \tag{1}$$

As n increases, each existing nuclear power will find that the payoff for initiating a nuclear war decreases. If the new nuclear power is an ally, it will have a share in the payoff from a nuclear war. If it is an opponent or an ally of an opponent, it will present an additional deterrent threat. If it is neutral it can exploit postwar weaknesses. Thus, the probability of any one nation initiating a nuclear war does not increase and eventually falls as more nations acquire nuclear weapons. Eventually, for large enough n,

$$p_j(n + 1) < p_j(n) \qquad j = 1, 2, \ldots, n \tag{2}$$

Approximating finite changes in n by derivatives with respect to n,

$$\frac{dp_j}{dn} < 0 \text{ for large enough } n \tag{3}$$

A more complete discussion of this point appears in the Appendix.

The probability of nuclear war, assuming that each nuclear nation can act independently in initiating such a war, is then W where $1 - W$, the probability of no war is

$$1 - W = (1 - p_1)(1 - p_2) \cdots (1 - p_n) = \prod_{j=1}^{n} (1 - p_j) \tag{4}$$

Taking logarithms,

$$\ln(1 - W) = \sum_{j=1}^{n} \ln(1 - p_j) \tag{5}$$

$$\frac{\ln(1 - W)}{dn} = \frac{-1}{1 - W} \frac{dW}{dn} = \ln(1 - p_n) - \Sigma \left(\frac{1}{1 - p_j} \right) \frac{dp_j}{dn} \tag{6}$$

The change in the probabilty of nuclear war as the number of nuclear nations changes can thus be written[12]

$$\frac{dW}{dn} = (1 - W) \left[\ln \left(\frac{1}{1 - p_n} \right) + \sum_{j=1}^{n} \left(\frac{1}{1 - p_j} \right) \frac{dp_j}{dn} \right] \tag{7}$$

According to this expression, the change in the probability of nuclear war as nation n acquires nuclear weapons can be decomposed analytically into the sum of two separate factors. The first factor in (7) is

$$(1 - W)\ln \frac{1}{1 - p_n} > 0 \qquad (8)$$

which represents the direct effect on the probability of nuclear war of the acquisition of nuclear weapons by the nth nation. This factor is always positive, raising the probability of war. The second factor in (7) is

$$\sum_{j=1}^{n} \left(\frac{1 - W}{1 - p_j} \frac{dp_j}{dn} \right) < 0 \qquad (9)$$

which represents the indirect effect on the existing n nuclear nations initiating a nuclear war as a result of the acquisition of nuclear weapons by an additional nation. From (3) this factor is negative for large enough n and never positive, with the advent of nation n as a nuclear power generally lowering the weighted sum of the derivatives dp_j/dn. For small n, however, this factor can be positive. At some point beyond the $n = 2$ case, however, the presence of a new nuclear power should lower the probability of nuclear war. For example, if this applies to the $n = 3$ case

$$\left(\frac{1 - W}{1 - p_1} \right) \frac{dp_1}{dn} + \left(\frac{1 - W}{1 - p_2} \right) \frac{dp_2}{dn} < 0 \qquad \text{for } n = 3 \qquad (10)$$

In this case the probability is lowered since: if the third nuclear power is allied with one of the two existing nuclear nations it adds to their deterrent capability, lowering the probability that either would initiate a nuclear war; while if the third nuclear power is not allied with either, each of the two nuclear nations will fear that in intitiating a nuclear war the third nation will dominate the postwar situation. Similar reasoning applies for $n = 4, 5, \ldots$, as added nuclear nations restrain the existing ones from initiating a nuclear war by either adding to deterrent capabilities or threatening to dominate the postwar situation.

The overall effect of added nuclear nations on the probability of nuclear war is thus given as the sum of two factors, as given in (7). The overall effect can be positive or negative, depending on the relative magnitudes of the two factors. It is reasonable to conclude, however, that initial increases in n raise the probability of nuclear war because of the first factor, which is always positive. The second set of increases in n then lower the probability because of the second factor. Beyond some point, however, the p_n probabilities may be so close to zero that their derivatives become vanishingly small. At this point, the second factor vanishes, so the probability is again rising. Thus the qualitative behavior of Figure 13.1 can be explained in terms of the decomposition of the effect of proliferation into the two terms in (7) and a consideration of their signs and relative magnitudes.

Consider how the symmetric case in which the n probabilities of each nation initiating a nuclear war are all equal

$$p_1 = p_2 = \cdots = p_n = p = p(n) \tag{11}$$

where $p(n)$ is the probability that any nation will initiate a war, given the presence of n nuclear nations. In this case the probability of war is

$$W = 1 - (1 - p)^n \tag{12}$$

so (5) can be written

$$\ln(1 - W) = n \ln(1 - p) \tag{13}$$

and (7) can be written

$$\frac{dW}{dn} = (1 - W)\left[\ln\left(\frac{1}{1-p}\right) + \left(\frac{n}{1-p}\right)\frac{dp}{dn}\right] \tag{14}$$

where the first term is positive and the second term is initially positive, then negative, and finally zero, leading to the different qualitative behavior shown in Figure 13.1. In the figure there are two points at which the derivative in (14) vanishes—the maximum point at n_1 and the minimum point at n_2. Setting the derivative equal to zero in (14) leads to the condition

$$\frac{dp}{dn} = \frac{1}{n}(1 - p)\ln(1 - p) = \frac{1}{n}H(1 - p) \tag{15}$$

which can hold only when dp/dn is negative (since $\ln(1 - p)$ must be negative) and which involves, on the right, the entropy function

$$H(1 - p) = -(1 - p)\ln(1 - p) \tag{16}$$

The condition in (15) is met at two points, the first being where $p(n)$ is falling and the second derivative is negative and the second being where $p(n)$ is falling but the second derivative is positive.

Consider now the fact that the probability of any nation initiating a nuclear war, $p(n)$ in (11), can be based on either a deliberate or calculated attack or an accident. Assuming these are independent and additive possibilities

$$p(n) = q(n) + r \tag{17}$$

where $q(n)$ is the probability of a calculated attack, dependent on the number of nuclear nations, and r is the probability of an accident or irrational action, which is assumed independent of n. Then (14) can be written

$$\frac{dW}{dn} = (1 - W)\left[\ln\left(\frac{1}{1 - q(n) - r}\right) + \left(\frac{n}{1 - q(n) - r}\right)\frac{dq}{dr}\right] \quad (18)$$

The first term is always positive while the second term is initially positive, then negative. As n becomes large, $q(n)$ falls to zero, so eventually, for large n

$$q(n) \approx 0, \frac{dq}{dn}(n) \approx 0. \quad (19)$$

In this case, therefore, for large enough n

$$\frac{dW}{dn} = (1 - W)\ln\left(\frac{1}{1 - r}\right) > 0 \quad (20)$$

so the probability of accidental war, r, leads to the eventually rising probability of war, as indicated in the final rising section of the curve in Figure 13.1.

SUBSTANTIVE IMPLICATIONS AND OVERALL CONCLUSIONS

We have argued that when there are very few nuclear nations, an added nuclear nation would most likely *increase* the probability of nuclear war by providing both an additional nation to initiate such a war and an additional target. The new nation may be particularly important as a target to the extent that it has a minimal stockpile with no retaliatory capability. An existing nuclear nation might then be tempted to take out this minimal stockpile by a "surgical strike."

With more nuclear nations, an added one would most likely *reduce* the probability of nuclear war by providing an additional restraining force for all the existing nuclear nations. In particular, uncertainty over the possible reaction of the new nuclear nation may restrain the existing ones, more than offsetting the presence of an additional potential initiator and an additional target.

Eventually, with a large number of nuclear nations the probability of nuclear war among them by calculation may be reduced to virtually zero since any one nuclear nation would fear the response by the others to its initiating a nuclear war. The probability of accidental or irrational nuclear war remains, however, and it can account for the probability of nuclear war ultimately rising with more nuclear nations, particularly if they are newcomers to nuclear technology and/or headed by irrational leaders. On a relative basis, the probability of an accidental or irrational nuclear war becomes more and more important relative to the probability of a deliberate nuclear war as the number of nuclear nations increases beyond the first few.

The acquisition of nuclear weapons by non-industrialized states without an effective delivery system probably has little influence on the probability of nuclear war, although it may involve changes in the global distribution of wealth due to direct or indirect threats to the preeminent position of the nuclear powers. Perhaps the greatest impact of such proliferation of nuclear weapons on the probability of nuclear war is due to an increased chance of war by accident or irrational action. There may, however, be important *regional* effects of proliferation of nuclear weapons in non-industrialized countries. In fact, the same type of initially positive and then negative effects probably hold in the regional context for precisely the same reasons as developed in the global context. A single bomber capable of penetrating the air defenses of an adversary may be all that is needed for a non-industrialized nuclear power to have a credible threat. All of the probabilities in the regional context are, however, probably considerably reduced due to the presence of large industrialized nuclear nations that could intervene in a regional nuclear confrontation. For this reason it is important that regional nuclear arms races not be decoupled from the global arena since, when they are, they involve great potential instability, including limited deterrence at best and a relatively high probability of accidental or irrational nuclear war.

It should not be inferred from our analysis that we are suggesting that proliferation is harmless or even desirable. An analysis such as ours must, of necessity, abstract from reality. As a result, some implications of the model can be misleading if naively applied to policy formulation.

Our model does suggest a major change of thrust in policy, however. It suggests that there is a trade-off between slowing the proliferation of nuclear weapons and reducing the probability of accidental or irrational nuclear war. We would argue that now or at some future time the nuclear nations should reorient their policy away from non-proliferation per se and toward control over accidental or irrational nuclear war. While proliferation of nuclear weapons has possibly negative, as well as possibly positive, effects on the probability of nuclear war, control over accidental war *must* reduce the chances of nuclear war. We would further argue that the major nuclear nations as a group should now be relatively more concerned than they have appeared to be over the possibility of accidental or irrational nuclear war, and that they should take both technical and political steps to reduce the chance of such a war.

APPENDIX

Let $E[n,i,a,b]$ be the expected return to the ith country of initiating a belligerent action against the countries in b while allied with the countries in a, where a and b represent possible coalitions of the N existing countries and where there are n nuclear nations. Let $E^c[n,i,a,b]$ be the expected return of not initiating that action. If

$$\frac{\partial}{\partial n} \sum_a \sum_b E^c[n,i,a,b] - E[n,i,a,b] > 0 \qquad \text{(a)}$$

it would follow that increasing n lowers the probability of nuclear war p_j.

Consider the nth new nuclear nation. If n is in coalition b, then

$$\frac{\partial E}{\partial n}[n,i,a,b] < 0 \qquad \text{(b)}$$

since a nuclear opponent is unambiguously more threatening than a non-nuclear opponent. If n is not in a or b, however, then

$$\frac{\partial E}{\partial n}[n,i,a,b] \leq 0 \qquad \text{(c)}$$

since, at best, the new nuclear power will not exploit any past war weakness. Finally, if n is in a,

$$\frac{\partial E}{\partial n}[n,i,a,b] \leq 0 \qquad \text{(d)}$$

which follows from the assumption that any existing nuclear power can duplicate the military strength of a new nuclear power and not have to share in the payoff from a war. This assumption is warranted since nuclear weapons entail very high fixed costs but low marginal costs.

From the above inequalities it follows that

$$\frac{\partial}{\partial n} \sum_a \sum_b E[n,i,a,b] < 0 \qquad \text{(e)}$$

The sign of the term $(\partial/\partial n) \sum_a \sum_b E^{c(n,i,a,b)}$ is more difficult to determine since for small n it has been argued that it is large and negative.[13] As n increases, however, the effectiveness of nuclear weapons in extracting concessions from other countries becomes negligible. Thus it can be argued that for n larger than a critical number

$$\frac{\partial}{\partial n} \sum_a \sum_b E[n,i,a,b] - E^c[n,i,a,b] < 0 \qquad \text{(f)}$$

which implies that

$$\frac{dp_j}{dn} < 0 \text{ for large enough } n \qquad (g)$$

as assumed above in equation (3).

NOTES

1. See Brito and Intriligator (1977a) for a discussion of the economic effects of strategic weapons, particularly nuclear weapons, on the allocation of international rights, including rights to resources, commodities, and global wealth. See Brito, Buoncristiani, and Intriligator (1977) for a discussion of the political effects of changes in the threat point of the bargaining game and Brito and Intriligator (1977b) for a discussion of changes in an alliance. See Intriligator (1967, 1968, 1975), Brito and Intriligator (1973, 1974), and Intriligator and Brito (1976, 1977) for discussions of the military effects of strategic weapons, including the choices of targets and rates of fire.
2. See Intriligator and Brito (1978) for a preliminary and informal discussion of this conclusion. The present paper provides a formal treatment of the effects of proliferation on the probability of nuclear war.
3. See Gallois (1961), originally published in French in 1960. See also Subrahmanyam (1975) for a related discussion from an Indian perspective, including a critique of the logic of the position of the nuclear nations on proliferation.
4. See Wentz (1968), who suggested that U.S. assistance in helping Japan acquire nuclear weapons could help stabilize the Far Eastern situation, by establishing Japan as a serious counterthreat to China.
5. See Tullock (1974), who argued that since nuclear weapons are exhausted in a nuclear war, a nuclear-armed non-participant would be likely to dominate the postwar world, inhibiting the initial outbreak of war. His analysis of nuclear proliferation is in the context of a discussion of the balance of power.
6. See Waltz (1964) and Deutsch and Singer (1964).
7. See Kaplan (1966), Rosecrance (1966), and Morgenthau (1975).
8. See Kann (1962), p. 235.
9. See Intriligator (1975), where it is shown that there exists a cone of mutual deterrence in the weapons plane of alternative pairs of numbers of weapons held by each nuclear nation. For all weapons configurations in this cone, each country holds sufficient numbers of weapons to deter the other from initiating a war, so such points are ones of stability against premeditated attack.
10. If n is the number of nuclear nations, the number of potential opposing nations or coalitions is given as the combinations of $n - 1$ nations taken one at a time $\binom{n-1}{1}$ single opposing nations, $\binom{n-1}{2}$ opposing pairs of nations, $\binom{n-1}{3}$ triples, ..., to $\binom{n-1}{n-1}$ or 1 grand coalition. The total number of possible opposing nations or coalitions is thus

$$s^{n-1} - 1 = \binom{n-1}{n} + \binom{n-2}{n} + \cdots + \binom{n-1}{n-1}$$

For example, when $n = 4$—say, A, B, C, D—the seven opposing nations or coalitions for nation A are B, C, D, BC, BD, CD, BCD. See also the next note.
11. In the last note the second effect, which decreases the probability of nuclear war, was related to the number of potential opposing nations or coalitions, $2^{n-1} - 1$. The first effect, that of a new initiator or target, which increases the probability of nuclear war,

can be similarly related to the number of pairs of nations, since a war would start between two nations. If n is the number of nuclear nations, then this number of pairs of nations is given as the number of combinations of n nations taken two at a time:

$$\binom{n}{2} = \frac{n!}{2!\,(n-2)!} = \frac{n(n-1)}{2}$$

Similarly, the third effect, increasing the probability of nuclear war due to accident or irrational action, is related to the number of nuclear nations n, since increases in n will generally increase the probability of accidental or irrational nuclear war. All three effects operate at all n, but the "pairs effect" tends to dominate initially; the "opposing nations or coalitions effect" tends to dominate next, since $2^{n-1} - 1$ increases much faster than $n(n-1)/2$; and the "accident or irrational action effect" tends to dominate ultimately, since the overwhelming number of opposing nations or coalitions has driven the probability of calculated nuclear war down to zero but has not eliminated the probability of accidental or irrational nuclear war.

12. Of course n is an integer, so this derivative is an approximation to the finite change, $W_{n+1} - W_n$.

13. See Intriligator (1975).

REFERENCES

Brito, D. L., A. M. Buoncristiani, and M. D. Intriligator (1977). "A New Approach to the Nash Bargaining Problem," *Econometrica*, 45: 1163-1172.

Brito, D. L., and M. D. Intriligator (1973). "Some Applications of the Maximum Principle to the Problem of an Armaments Race," *Modeling and Simulation*, 4: 140-144.

———(1974). "Uncertainty and the Stability of the Armaments Race," *Annals of Economic and Social Measurement*, 3: 279-292.

———(1977a). "Strategic Weapons and the Allocation of International Rights," in Gillespie and Zinnes (1977).

———(1977b). "Nuclear Proliferation and the Armaments Race," *Journal of Peace Science*, 2: 321-328.

Deutsch, K. W., and J. D. Singer (1964). "Multipolar Power systems and International Stability," *World Politics*, 16: 390-406.

Gallois, P. (1961). *The Balance of Terror*. Boston: Houghton Mifflin Company.

Gillespie, J. V., and D. A. Zinnes, eds. (1977). *Mathematical Systems in International Relations Research*. New York: Praeger Publishers.

Intriligator, M. D. (1967). *Strategy in a Missile War: Targets and Rates of Fire*. Los Angeles: Security Studies Project, UCLA.

———(1968). "The Debate over Missile Strategy," *Orbis*, 11: 1138-1159.

———(1975). "Strategic Considerations in the Richardson Model of Arms Races," *Journal of Political Economy*, 83: 339-353.

Intriligator, M. D., and D. L. Brito (1976). "Formal Models of Arms Races," *Journal of Peace Science*, 2: 77-88.

———(1977). "Strategy, Arms Races, and Arms Control," in Gillespie and Zinnes (1977).

———(1978). "Nuclear Proliferation and Stability," *Journal of Peace Science*, 3: 173-183.

Kahn, H. (1962). *Thinking about the Unthinkable.* New York: Horizon Books.

Kaplan, M. A. (1966). "Some Problems of International Systems Research," in *International Political Communities: An Anthology.* New York: Doubleday.

Morgenthau, H. J. (1975). *Politics among Nations,* 5th ed. New York: Alfred A. Knopf.

Rosecrance, R. (1966). "Bipolarity, Multipolarity, and the Future," *Journal of Conflict Resolution,* 10: 314-322.

Subrahmanyam, K. (1975). "India's Nuclear Policy," in O. Marwah and A. Schulz, eds., *Nuclear Proliferation and the Near-Nuclear Countries.* Cambridge, Mass.: Ballinger Publishing Company.

Tullock, G. (1974). *The Social Dilemma.* Blacksburg, Va.: University Publications.

Waltz, K. N. (1964). "The Stability of a Bipolar World," *Daedalus,* 93: 881-909.

Wentz, W. B. (1968). *Nuclear Proliferation.* Washington, D. C.: Public Affairs Press.

Chapter 14

Military Strategy and Political Interests: The Soviet Union and the United States

Roman Kolkowicz

INTRODUCTION: SOVIET AND AMERICAN STRATEGIC PARADIGMS AND TRADITIONS

Soviet and American approaches to strategic problems in the nuclear era may appear to be similar: their military technologies are similar; the qualitative and quantitative aspects of their respective weapon systems are generally understood by both sides; they have both been engaged in protracted diplomatic and technical negotiations on strategic arms limitations with certain mutually acceptable results. And yet the two countries diverge sharply on many fundamental issues regarding the uses, limitations, and purposes of military power and the rules of the game that are to govern it. This divergence, often disregarded by Western technical experts, is of vital importance to our understanding of the profound misperceptions in the whole range of strategic and political issues inherent in the superpower relationship.

I want to thank Donna Beltz for invaluable research assistance in the preparation of this paper.

There are several fundamental disparities in traditional Soviet and American approaches to the use of military force in the pursuit of national objectives. These attitudes may be described as lying at two ends of a spectrum, polarized between the instrumental, strategic, and highly politicized Soviet approach and the more emotional, apolitical, and moralizing American approach. One might suggest that Machiavelli and Clausewitz are the intellectual and spiritual models of the Soviets, while the American tradition has its roots in its early Puritanism and more recent democratic liberalism.

The roots of modern American strategic theory and doctrine lie in the scientific spirit of the Enlightenment and in the optimistic tradition of democratic liberalism, which envisaged man's ability to control, manage, and order conflict by rational scientific and technological means. The earlier tradition was reflected in the words of the English theorist W. Lloyd: "The general who knows these things can direct war enterprises with geometrical precision and lead to a continual war without ever getting into the necessity of giving battle."[1] More recent aspects of this tradition are embodied in the positive and optimistic premises of systems analysis, crisis management, and vast literature on deterrence.

The traditional American approach to the use of military force has been pugnacious, but not "cunning and premeditated; rather it is a romantic impulse that erects boldness and initiative into patriotic tenets, but only in response to provocation."[2] George Kennan saw this American trait as wrathful righteousness:

> Democracy fights in anger—it fights for the very reason that it was forced to go to war. It fights to punish the power that was rash enough to provoke it—to teach that power a lesson it will not forget.[3]

Until very recently, American policy makers,

> [have] looked on war and peace as two distinctly separate states. War has been viewed not as a continuation of policy but as a failure of diploma-cy.... The American response to war has been to view it as the use of force in a great moral crusade in which there is no room for the deliberate hobbling of American power.[4]

This American tradition was challenged by events in the post-World War II period, particularly by the dismal war in Korea. It was further challenged by the rise of modern deterrence strategists, who rarely if ever asked questions about ethical or normative values but became preoccupied with problems of efficiency and economy in the application of force toward a given end. Modern American strategists began to aspire to *realpolitik*, asserting the "principle that military power should be subordinated to national policy, and that the only legitimate purpose of military force is to serve the nation's political objectives."[5]

The challenge and eventual rejection of earlier American tradition was considered necessary because although "the practical necessity of military power [is] obvious to Americans today," it is not sufficiently obvious because "military power does not automatically translate into national security."[6] And when military policy and strategy lack limited and attainable objectives and become, in effect, ends in themselves, they cease to be controllable and predictable instruments of national policy.

These challenges to the uses of military power eventually resulted in a new American "tradition," a radically different approach to the uses of military power. The evolution of various theories, doctrines, methods, and models of conflict and warfare under the general heading "deterrence" emptied American strategic thought of much of its political and ethical content and yielded abstract metaphors, deductive theories, conflict management techniques—a veritable science of warfare. However, much of this activity was focused on one type of war (and methods for its avoidance), namely, an all-out nuclear war between the two superpowers and their alliance systems.

Western perceptions of Soviet approaches to the use of force for political purposes are usually couched in terms of opportunism, deception, and flexibility: "The Kremlin has no compunction about retreating in the face of a superior force. . . . Its main concern is to make sure that it has filled every nook and cranny available to it in the basin of world power."[7] William Kaufmann saw the Soviet Union and its allies as "notorious practitioners of violence," and unlike in the United States, military means in Soviet hands "have been a highly flexible instrument of policy."[8] Robert Osgood maintains that the "communist approach to war and the use of military power is as notable for its fusing of power and policy as the American approach is notable for its dissociation of power and policy."[9]

If, on the American side, we witness a rejection of certain political and moral traditions assumed unsuitable for this sinful world, or at least improper for a superpower, this is not the case on the Soviet side. In the Soviet Union there exists a straight, doctrinal, and political tradition that goes back to Clausewitz, via Engels and Lenin, and reaches into the present via Stalin and his successors.

The Soviet tradition has different origins: one of its key progenitors is von Clausewitz, who "rejected both the optimism and dogmatism of the eighteenth century theory"[10] and who held that war was neither a scientific game nor an international sport, but an act of violence: "We do not like to hear of generals who are victorious without the shedding of blood" because this leads to an underappreciation of the terrible nature of war and might lead to a condition where "we allow our swords to grow blunt . . . until someone steps in with a sharp sword and cuts our arms off our body."[11] Clausewitz was known, with good reason, as one of the "Mahdis of Mass" who gave theoretical justification to the "rage of numbers" and identified the "idea of war with that of utmost violence."[12]

The spirit of Clausewitz remains alive in the Soviet Union. His ideas permeate contemporary Soviet military theories and defense policies. Party leaders find the Clausewitz dictum that "war has its grammar but not its own logic"[13] most useful in legitimating political primacy over military professionalism, since the logic of politics also governs war. The other famous Clausewitz dictum—that war is merely a continuation of politics by other means—has regained full acceptance after two decades of debate and vacillation, and has again made war rational, thinkable, and winnable. Even some of Clausewitz' earlier works on military art have been rediscovered by the Soviet military in recent years and used to rationalize and justify proposals for the offensive, mobile type of theater warfare, with or without the use of nuclear weapons.[14] In short, current Soviet military doctrine has fully regained its "object":

> Since war has its origins in a political object, we see that this first motive, which called it into existence, naturally remains the first and highest consideration to be regarded in its conduct. . . . Policy will therefore permeate the whole action of war and exercise a continuous influence upon it . . . for the political design is the object, while war is the means, and the means can never be thought apart from the object.[15]

Accordingly, Clausewitz maintained that war can never be separated from politics and that, should such a separation "occur anywhere, all the threads of the different relations become in a certain sense broken and we have before us a senseless thing without an object."[16]

Clausewitz found avid readers and attentive students among the Marxists and the Bolsheviks. Engels, probably the most sophisticated student of military affairs among them, wrote to Karl Marx that "I am now reading Clausewitz *On War*." Engels found it to be "a strange way of philosophizing, but very good on the subject." He went on to define the essential Marxist (and Soviet) approach to military power and war, as distilled from Clausewitz:

> Fighting is to war what cash payment is to trade, for however rarely it may be necessary for it actually to occur, everything is directed towards it, and eventually it must take place all the same, and must be decisive.[17]

A recent Soviet volume on military strategy brought this tradition into the contemporary realm: "In his remarks on Clausewitz' book *Vom Kriege*, V. I. Lenin stressed that 'politics is the guiding force, and war is only the tool and not vice versa.'"[18]

Another Soviet and Russian tradition is reflected by Prince Andrey in Tolstoy's *War and Peace* on the eve of the Battle of Borodino:

> War is not a courtesy but the most terrible thing in life; and we ought to understand that and not play at war. We ought to accept this terrible necessity sternly and seriously. It all lies in that: get rid of falsehood and let war be war, and not a game.[19]

Leon Trotsky, the founder of the Red Army, aptly expressed another Soviet view on war: war "bases itself on many sciences, but war itself is no science, it is a practical art, a skill, a savage and bloody art."[20] He would approvingly quote the Clausewitz maxim: "in practical arts one should not drive the flowers and foliage of theory too high, one should rather keep them close to the soil of experience."[21] This sobering admonition by the great philosopher of war is particularly relevant to our study.

PROBLEMS OF CONCEPTUAL DEFINITION

To the Western strategic analyst, Soviet writers on strategic and military problems behave like scholastics, adhering to obscure formulations of questionable relevance to the serious study of war and strategy. To Western deterrence theorists, the public formulations of Soviet strategic and limited warfare concepts and doctrines appear peculiarly simplistic, anecdotal, tautological, and "soft" in relation to the impeccably logical, tightly reasoned Western theories of deterrence and limited war. They find Soviet military writings to be excessively politicized and historical and subordinated to the given values and whims of political elites; their primitive and "unsophisticated" approaches exasperate Western analysts. Such exasperation is reflected in the remarks of the American editors of *Soviet Military Strategy* by Marshal V. D. Sokolovskii: "Nowhere in this book, as in most Soviet literature as well, are there to be found signs of serious professional interests in concepts like controlled response and restrained nuclear targeting, which have been widely discussed in the West." The Americans appear discouraged by a persistent "theme of automacity of global nuclear war" and interpret this as serving to reinforce the credibility of Soviet nuclear retaliation "but also to discourage the United States and its allies from entertaining ideas that ground rules of some sort might be adapted for limiting the destructiveness of a war, should one occur."[22]

This Western exasperation with Soviet strategic analysts is reciprocated with equal force: Soviet military and political analysts dismiss much of Western strategic and limited war theory as pretentious, pseudoscientific, and even metaphysical:

> The idea of introducing rules and games and artificial restrictions by agreement seems illusory and untenable. It is difficult to visualize that a nuclear war, if unleashed, could be kept within the framework of rules and would not develop into an all out war. In fact, such proposals are a demagogic trick designed to reassure public opinion.[23]

The authoritative volume *Marxism-Leninism on War and Army* vigorously rejected as "a cynical and deliberate falsehood" the idea that "the prudence of the opponents will make it possible to coordinate their nuclear targets against which these weapons would be aimed."[24] A distinguished Soviet military strategist, General N. Talenskii, expressed the Soviet position clearly:

> When the security of a state is based on mutual deterrence with the aid of powerful nuclear weapons rockets, it is directly dependent on the goodwill and designs of the other side, which is a highly subjective and indefinite factor.[25]

Soviet analysts find Western strategic sophistries objectionable and unacceptable on several grounds:

1. The apolitical nature of Western military doctrines, which in effect subordinates politics to the more narrow technological and bureaucratic imperatives and to the abstract notions of game theory and formal logic. A recent Rand Corporation study assessed this problem quite realistically:

> American strategic thinking—born predominantly of civilian defense specialists bearing legal, technical and distinctly non-military intellectual outlooks—is deeply rooted in the proposition that nuclear war is unwinnable in any practical sense . . . it has also produced an increasingly predominant belief that deterrence stability (hence U.S. security) is best served

by a strategic environment of mutual vulnerability. The Soviets reject "mutual vulnerability" out of hand as an abdication of political responsibility.[26]

The study goes on to describe insistent Soviet disavowals of such Western strategic ideas as demonstration attacks, limited nuclear operations, and slow motion counterforce duels, treating such American conceptualizations of strategic issues "with alternating bemusement, perplexity and sarcasm."[27] Marshal Grechko reflects this Soviet view of "bourgeois military theorists who propagate quite a different viewpoint" from that of communist military analysts, and is troubled by the fact that Western military theorists "regard war as a mere armed clash between the two sides . . . in other words, they emasculate the political content of the concept of war."[28]

2. The status-quo supportive nature of deterrence and limited war theory and its corollaries: A recent Western critical study of deterrence observed that "deterrence is a policy which, if it succeeds, can only frustrate an opponent who aspires to changing the international status quo." The study concluded that although the consequences of continuous frustration of expansionist and anti-status quo aspirations are not easily predictable, they are nevertheless "not necessarily benign."[29]

Soviet analysts frequently attack what they perceive as this pernicious Western attempt to impose Western rules of the game of politics and strategy upon socialist countries and on countries in the Third World that are trying to emancipate and liberate themselves from colonial or imperialistic shackles:

> The development of a new international situation more favorable to the cause of peace in no way signifies an interruption of the strenuous and sharp struggle which Soviet policy is waging. There are no pauses in international relations just as there is no rest in the struggle which accompanies their development.[30]

N. I. Krylov, Marshal of the Soviet Union, claimed that "the imperialists are trying to lull the vigilance of the world's peoples by having recourse to propaganda devices to the effect that there will be no victors in a future nuclear war. These false affirmations contradict the objective laws of history."[31] General Bochkarev asserted that "Marxist-Leninists are not panicked in the face of the terrifying danger created by imperialism nor do they depict it as a prelude to the end of the world."[32] And General Zhilin stated that détente and deterrence, implicit in peaceful coexistence, do not rule out war, nor do they imply stable peace: "That is why all the talk about an end of the era of wars and the arrival of an era of universal peace is premature and dangerous."[33]

A recent Rand Corporation study asserted that "the center of gravity of Soviet doctrinal discussions is decidedly hostile to this way of thinking" and that the Soviets pay "no homage whatsoever to the abstract concept of stability" assumed in the West under the concept of a *"mutual* assured destruction relationship."[34] And generally speaking, to the Soviets the concepts of "equivalence" and "balance" are found to be "unnatural" because they imply "the enshrinement of the status quo, something alien to every known tenet of Soviet political, ideological and historical doctrine."[35]

3. The interdependent, controllable, mutually balanced, and self-constrained nature of Western doctrines of war: Soviet analysts are particularly skeptical of those claims by Western strategic analysts regarding the ability to control, limit, and fine tune the applications of force and coercion in war. They question Western claims to omniscience, omnipotence, and ubiquity of cool reason and rationality, which are implicit or explicit in many Western studies on limited war. As the Rand Corporation study indicated, "If there is little convergence in Soviet and American writing on deterrence, there is even less complementarity in their statements on limited strategic war."[36]

Soviet analysts are particularly vehement in questioning and rejecting the sweeping claims on limited war: "To lull the vigilance of the peoples, the U.S. militarists are discussing the possibility of limiting nuclear war." The prudence of the opponents, they say, will make it possible to coordinate their nuclear strikes and thus limit the targets. According "to Western military theoreticians, such limitations will reduce the destruction of material values and the privations of the people to a minimum."[37] The Soviets find this idea not overly credible, because they would have to "rely on the chance that the aggressors will be prudent and will impose certain limits on the use of nuclear weapons."[38]

In Western parlance, limited war presupposes certain kinds of cooperation, coordination, constraint, and self-denial by the belligerents. The United States has evolved several military doctrines premised in such cooperative and interdependent constraints among the belligerents, while the Soviet Union remains adamant in resisting such notions and prefers unilateral and independent modes of military initiatives. The Soviets find curious and unrealistic the notion that limited war would remain contained, would resist escalatory pressures, and would terminate through "intra-war bargaining." A survey of Soviet writings on the controllability of escalation and the possibility of limitation in nuclear conflict indicates "no Soviet acceptance of restraint once that threshold has been crossed."[39] In that sense, they have not come far from their earlier rather dogmatic assertions, as expressed by their then Defense Minister Marshal Malinovskii, that "no matter where a tactical atomic weapon might be used against us, it would trigger a crushing counter-blow."[40]

In the past the Soviets have found it particularly difficult to formally accept the idea of limited warfare, especially limited warfare with the use of nuclear weapons. Soviet political leaders have gone on record as opposing this idea because of the escalatory pressures and generally unpredictable consequences. Khrushchev, Brezhnev, and others have at various times reiterated the proposition that "global wars are known to have started from local wars" and that because of "rapid development of military technology, it will be even more difficult to put any limits on armed conflict if this conflict starts in any single region."[41]

The unorthodox character of limited war is complicated by its implicit logic and rules of the game:

> While the enemy must be fixed and hit hard on the battlefield, and if possible deterred from expanding the scope and intensity of the conflict, he must also be allowed to extricate himself from his adventure without a serious loss of prestige or substance. The conditions of limited war require the maintenance of a delicate balance between firmness and tolerance.[42]

This unorthodoxy and its peculiar characteristics have troubled Soviet military and political leaders, particularly in the event of the use of nuclear weapons. Stressing certain inherent contradictions in the asserted logic and rules of limited war as depicted in Western strategic literature, the Soviet author of the authoritative study *Soviet Military Strategy* asserts:

> By its character, a limited war contains two problems: on the one hand such a war must be conducted decisively and with the best methods using the necessary forces and means to achieve the set political and military goals; on the other hand, in a limited war, the armed forces must be used in such a way as to reduce the risk of a limited armed conflict escalating into a general war to a minimum.[43]

Soviet strategists raised questions about the fundamental Western assumptions concerning the conduct of limited war because "little is known about the effectiveness of this (nuclear) weapon on the battlefield, of the possible political, military and psychological consequences of its use." The Soviets also maintained that Western assertions about control, effect, and consequences of battlefield use of tactical nuclear weapons were based on questionable assumptions: "It is extremely difficult to foresee how an enemy will react to the very fact of the use of a tactical nuclear weapon, even on a limited scale." And the reactive options available to the other side are many, ranging from refraining to employ a retaliatory limited strike, to responding with a nuclear retaliatory strike of limited scale; or even, through miscalculation, responding on a much greater scale by means of "strategic and operations tactical means, thus unleashing an all-out nuclear war."[44]

Soviet strategists also stressed the great difficulty in distinguishing between a tactical and strategic weapon merely from its operational use, and the possible false signals of miscalculations in response. The problem of means of delivery for tactical nuclear weapons complicates the limited war calculus even further. The Sokolovskii volume concluded with a rather skeptical assessment of keeping limited war really limited and not having it explode into an all-out nuclear holocaust:

> In spite of all these theories and concepts, one can state with assurance that the strategy of limited warfare based on the use of only tactical nuclear weapons will involve the dangers analogous to those connected with the strategy of "massive retaliation."[45]

This Soviet concern with keeping limited war limited was also shared by many in the West. The problems of escalation control and thresholds observance were widely discussed in the professional literature without quite resolving the issues or allaying the concerns. Thomas Schelling reflected a consensus when he described the Korean War as having set "patterns and precedents that have affected, and will affect the conduct of limited war and the planning for it."[46] But, he warned, it "may be only one possibility, one pattern, one species of a variegated genus of warlike reactions," and this no more a model "of what limited war really is than the first animal the Pilgrims saw reflected the wildlife of North America."[47] He urged the consideration of certain restraints and thresholds that would provide limits in warfare. Among the limits and thresholds he discussed were "no nuclears," which is "simple and unambiguous," while "some nuclears would be more complicated." He said there is "a simplicity, a kind of virginity, about all-or-none distinctions that differences of degree do not have."[48] Among the other ultimate thresholds he described were a direct confrontation between Soviet and American troops in battle and observance of the national boundaries of the United States and the Soviet Union, thus keeping "the homelands of the two major adversaries inviolate."[49] He saw these thresholds as finite steps in the enlargement of war or a change in participation: "They are conventional stopping places or dividing lines. They have a legalistic quality, and they depend on precedents and analogy."[50] Some of these thresholds have made a claim to being the "ultimate limit," the last stopping place before all-out war, yet Schelling considered none of them the be "sacrosanct."[51]

The idea of limited war in the nuclear context began to gain acceptance and support in the West in the 1950s. Its proponents had to overcome the resistance of the "don't rock the delicate-balance-of-terror-nuclear-deterrence boat" thinking of that period. War, even little limited war, in the shadow of the bomb, under assumed conditions of a very unstable balance of terror, was considered unthinkable, particularly if it were to involve a confrontation between the two major nuclear powers. The critics of limited war marshaled many strong arguments against it: It was likely to undermine the strategy of deterrence because making the use of force, particularly nuclear force, "thinkable" and acceptable would weaken the necessary self-restraints implicit in deterrence. Moreover, if it were assumed that force could be applied in controlled, managed, and revocable ways, leaders would be tempted to use it at an assumed low cost and risk. The critics argued that endowing the use of military force in the nuclear era with political utilities would undermine deterrence and motivate certain leaders to exploit it for specific and instrumental purposes. They asserted that the calculus of limited war and its assumed logic presupposed rational and reasonable decisionmakers on both sides. The assumption was considered to be not only highly questionable but also particularly dangerous in the event of escalatory pressures during hostilities, which could very well lead to a catastrophic "explosion" rather than the desirable "expansion." In general, limited war was fraught with too many uncertainties and risks to be a viable policy premise.[52]

However, several developments of the 1950s indicated the possible merits and utilities of limited war. First, the rigidities and low credibility of massive retaliation doctrine created an enormous disparity between ends and means that would very likely paralyze the political will to act. This argued for greater flexibility and closer congruence between the perceived threats and the applied or implied use of retaliatory force. Second, the lessons of Korea were driven home, reinforcing the first argument in favor of flexibility to avoid getting bogged down in ground warfare in remote and disadvantageous areas of the world. Third, it was argued that the availability of more flexible options would relax the tense either/or deterrence confrontation in crisis and in effect enhance the stability of deterrence.

From the ensuing strategic debates in the United States emerged a sense of the implications of limited war, with or without the use of nuclear weapons, and its then rudimentary conceptual and theoretical aspects. The term "limited war" has become identified with several kinds of restraints and limitations upon the conduct of hostilities. Robert Osgood defined it in general terms as:

A war fought for ends far short of the complete subordination of one state's will to another's and by means involving far less than the total military resources of the belligerents, leaving the civilian life and the armed forces of the belligerents largely intact and leading to a bargained termination.[53]

It became apparent that unlike the sharp and satisfying definitions of strategic deterrence, limited war theory remained difficult to define precisely because its limitations are contingent upon judgments, defined by degrees, and perceived from different perspectives. However there is a general agreement in Western thought that the following constitute the parameters of limited war:

1. Wars that are limited in geographic scale rather than "world wars" that span the globe. (The Korean, Vietnam, and Middle East wars would fit this category.) The problem becomes a bit complicated when it involves "coalition wars," which may remain limited in one sense but be geographically dispersed.
2. Wars that are limited in their *objectives*, which could be territorial or political, but fairly specific and perceived by all sides to be so.
3. Wars fought with *limited means*—in effect, where the belligerents are deliberately "hobbling" themselves by the quantity and quality of weapons and technology employed. The Korean War may be used as an example; both sides had access to nuclear weapons but practiced restraint, thus shackling their military force.
4. Wars in which the belligerents limit themselves to *certain targets* and deliberately avoid other available targets.

This description of limited war and its parameters is more of a normative model—an ideal type, what it ought to be—than a reflection of historical reality. While some conflicts of recent decades reflected these parameters, others did not, and still others fit different conceptual or analytic rubrics. And the Soviet and other communist typologies and categorizations of war do not quite conform to those of the West.

The official Soviet position on types of warfare has not changed much in recent decades (although informally there have been certain significant changes to be described in subsequent sections of this paper). Their formal view, reflected in a variety of authoritative statements and studies, may be summarized as follows:

a. *Categories of war according to their sociopolitical character*:
   Wars between states of opposing social systems
   Wars between imperialist and former colonial systems
   Civil wars between the proletarian masses and the bourgeoisie
   Wars between capitalist states

b. *Categories of wars according to their scale*:
   World wars between two opposing systems
   Local wars confined to two or more countries
   Wars of national liberation[54]

In practice, the Soviets distinguish between three types of wars: (1) *world war* between the two superpowers and their coalitions, with massive employment of nuclear weapons that would devastate both countries in massive salvos of strategic weapons in counterforce and countervalue targeting modes; (2) *limited wars* that would not involve the superpowers but would be fought with their direct or indirect involvement, with or without nuclear weapons; and (3) *local wars*, or wars of national liberation in the Third World, which would remain nonnuclear, conventional, and contained in scope, targets, weapons, and objectives.

It is clear by now that there are several fundamental disparities in Soviet and American approaches to strategy, foreign policy, and the uses of force in the pursuit of national interests. The main reason for the persistence of these conceptual, perceptual, doctrinal disparities lies in the asymmetrical nature of the two belief systems and in certain cultural, historical, and political conditions of these two countries. We are dealing with two orthodoxies—mutually exclusive by their nature— each claiming a monopoly of a "scientific" truth.

At the root of the problem lie different perceptions of deterrence and uses of force in the nuclear context. Deterrence theory is a uniquely American construct, shaped by certain historical, political, institutional, and idiosyncratic influences and circumstances in the post-World War II period. Deterrence was conceived in its modern sense when it became possible to threaten vast damage and pain while leaving opposing forces intact. The atomic bomb that ended World War II and the bipolar international system that emerged from it provided the conditions for modern deterrence theory: "the former made deterrence necessary and the latter made it possible."[55]

The problem with deterrence theory in the United States has been an excessive reliance on deterrence threats and alliance commitments as the primary tool of foreign policy vis-à-vis the Soviet Union, a tool that by the mid-1950s had become an inflexible response to almost any perceived communist encroachment in the world. In effect, the specific American nature of deterrence tended to "reinforce policymakers' tendency to rely too heavily on deterrence strategy and deterrence threats in lieu of the more flexible instruments of inter-nation influence associated with classical diplomacy."[56]

A fundamental flaw of deterrence was that it became theoretically most-developed and practically best-applied to acute bipolar conflicts where great values were at stake and where the potential for great violence was high. At the same time, this led to a poverty of theoretical and doctrinal development of conflicts below the strategic and bipolar level, resulting in the forced use and application of strategic deterrence doctrine to conflicts at lower levels of the threat spectrum:

> This attempt to extend the applications of flexible response into the lower portion of the spectrum is exactly analogous to the earlier attempt to extend, through massive retaliation, the applications of strategic deterrent forces into the next lower portion of the spectrum, to try to deter limited war.[57]

Military theory and doctrine remained rooted in the American tradition, that is, as if trying to bend the laws of warfare in the nuclear era to conform to traditional American *preferences*, which are assumed to include:

—the massive use of strategic rather than conventional or tactical forces;
—the substitution of technology for manpower because of the assumed high valuation of human lives;
—the unhobbled use of military force in war;
—punitive warfare against a despised enemy with unconditional "surrender";
—primacy of military consideration once warfare begins;
—clear resolution and conclusion of war;
—avoidance of entangling ground warfare in "remote areas" of the world.[58]

Since World War II (and to a lesser extent World War I) reinforced these American preferences (not necessarily realities), it was thought rational to extend them into the postwar period, specifically to relations with the communist world. Thus the classic American model of war and the strategies for dealing with it may be characterized as a direct confrontation between the two superpowers and their respective alliances, along a central confrontational axis in Europe, across NATO/

Warsaw Pact territories, with clearly demarcated rules of the game, and with the communication and signaling characteristics so highly regarded by deterrence purists. This was perceived as a bipolar, either/or confrontation which, by the very nature of its terrible threat and terrifying consequences, would mitigate against a suicidal initiation of hostilities by the Communists and validate the logical and theoretical content and political utility of deterrence strategy. This might be called a "cowboy strategy," reflecting American preferences, styles, and values. It also reflected a set of very practical concerns and preferences, since this ur-scenario was premised in American advantage and Soviet disadvantage: We had the strategic and nuclear high cards and the Soviets did not.

The Soviets, however, did not comply with American deterrence theories, preferences, or even fantasies. Instead of confronting the United States and NATO directly and frontally in the European NATO/Warsaw Pact theater, the Soviets chose to probe, feign, and challenge the United States and its allies in areas remote from Europe. Moreover, the Soviets' challenge was undertaken indirectly by proxies and allies. One might say that Soviet military and political behavior reflects a "commissar strategy," which is essentially nonconfrontational, or more properly, confrontation-avoiding under conditions of low Soviet advantage and control. This strategy is largely manipulative, deceptive, theoretically inelegant, methodologically "unsophisticated," and shrouded in ambiguities. It is a strategy of confrontations *and* negotiations, one that rejects the stark American deterrence alternatives of either/or (either stable peace or nuclear incineration) for the Soviets' own neither/nor deliberativeness (accepting neither the imperatives of perfectly stable peace and atrophied international political process nor the alternative of nuclear mutual suicide). The Soviets view strategic doctrine as a highly politicized means-ends *process* rather than the American ends-means *teleology* of Armageddon-avoidance.

Ultimately, deterrence strategy is logically and politically suitable to a conservative status quo, balance of power state with no territorial but widespread and vital international economic interests; a power possessing strategic superiority with traditional values that favor minimal involvement in remote areas; a power that has historically relied on technological and economic means for implementing its foreign policy. It is a policy for dealing with a troublesome, dangerous but weaker adversary by launching terrible threats of punishment to appeal to the bully's sense of survival.

Soviet strategy is suited to a quasirevolutionary, expansionistic power interested in changing the international status quo. It is appropriate for a power that emerged on the international scene after World War II as a strategic inferior and whose traditions rely on the brute force of mass armies, guided primarily by defensive continental strategies and with defensive coastal navies—a country that has had little experience with massive projection of its forces beyond the Eurasian mass. It is the strategy of a country with global and universal ideological and political interests and claims, but one that is not in a hurry, believing that history and time are on its side.

Deterrence may have been a logical and suitable strategic theory and doctrine for the United States during its period of ascendance in international affairs. America enjoyed clear strategic superiority with a supportive society whose internal goals were in harmony with its external policy goals. I confronted a Soviet Union whose leadership was divided, whose allies were restless and unreliable, and whose military capabilities were inadequate and inferior to those of the West.

However, the times have changed. The Soviet Union has become a military power at least equal to that of the United States and has moved from its continental, defensive military position toward a global super-power. In the final analysis, Soviet strategic doctrines have shown themselves to be more flexible and adaptable than those of the West. While the United States has remained largely committed to deterrence strategy and some of its variations, despite the profound changes in international and regional politics, the Soviets have shown an interest in experimenting with various strategic formulations to fit strategy to policy and to the ever-changing political and technological circumstances. At present, Soviet strategy consists of a strategic nuclear shield—for the primary purpose of deterring and thus neutralizing the threat from the West—and a flexible and powerful strategy of engagement in the vulnerable and vital areas of the Third World by the Soviet Union's conventional sword, its general purpose forces.

The United States remains rooted in a deterrence fixation under various assured destruction scenarios. Some recent efforts to provide more flexible, rapid deployment forces deployable across pressure points of Soviet southward expansionistic trajectory are too new and incomplete for a proper evaluation. American positions on theater nuclear forces and doctrines in Europe are causing its NATO allies much discomfort.[59] The much-vaunted flexible options policy (which rests on such notions as: the control of escalation through recognition of thresholds and target distinctions; the willingness to compete in pain endurance and risk-taking; and war-termination by intrawar bargaining) is not much of an improvement and lacks certain kinds of political credibility.[60] (The recent P.D. 59 represents a shift from the MAD doctrine of "city-busting." It nonetheless limits itself to a central war context, i.e., that in the event of a central war, rather than targeting cities the United States would concentrate on "hard" targets—countervalue versus counterforce. This does not bear on limited war as seen in the Soviet context and to be discussed in this paper. P.D. 59 deals essentially with collateral damage limitation in a central war context: a concept still roundly rejected in Soviet military literature.)

Recent Soviet public interest in the feasibility of limited and local war and systematic preparations for such contingencies may reflect strategic-doctrinal maturity. The Soviets clearly understand that, in the nuclear era, major powers need the security of a credible nuclear strategic deterrent force before they can safely adopt limited war doctrines and policies. The reason for this lies in the logic of deterrence and limited war: to remain limited, wars directly or indirectly involving the major powers need credible fallback reserves of a strategic (assured destruction) retaliatory threat that would act as a decelerator of escalatory pressures and provide boundaries. The espousal of limited war without a credible deterrent retaliatory threat potential would leave a state open to manipulation and blackmail, a situation analogous to a strategic context in which one side lacks a credible survivable second-strike capability. In recent years the Soviets have fulfilled these necessary criteria—they have built a powerful and credible nuclear deterrent and a vast modernized general purpose force.[61]

CONTINUITY AND CHANGE IN SOVIET APPROACHES TO THE USES OF FORCE

In a 1970 submission to the U.S. Senate Committee on Foreign Relations, this author stated the following:

We would want first to examine certain entrenched Western beliefs and misapprehensions about the Soviet Union and U.S.—Soviet relations. Among these beliefs are:

—that we can bleed them to death economically, by forcing them to keep up with us in an intensive arms race
—that we can still attain meaningful strategic superiority
—that we can expect an internal political and social upheaval in the Soviet Union or in the communist bloc.

I would suggest that such beliefs are unrealistic and to some extent wishful thinking. It may be more realistic to assume that:

—the Soviet Union is going to continue its arms program, if necessary to ensure strategic equality
—the Soviet Union is not seriously interested in first strike or surprise attacks on the United States

—the Soviet Union is interested in stabilizing the expensive arms race and would seek to avoid confrontations with the United States in areas of vital interests

—*but that, the Soviet Union is also going to selectively probe in the soft areas of the world for opportunities and expansion, regardless of the SALT outcomes.*

Thus, while SALT is a desirable Soviet objective, it is not the one-and-all objective of Soviet policy. As a matter of fact, one would argue, that Soviet interests in SALT, while presumably realistic and serious, are part of a larger policy for the seventies. The postulated objectives of the Soviet policy are:

—*hold* and stabilize their Western flank (NATO, U.S.) through SALT, European Security Conference, etc.

—obtain greater freedom to deal with China (and also prevent a two-front confrontation)

—*explore* opportunities south of Russia, via a capillary expansion in the regions of Middle East, Mediterranean, and North Africa.

Such a policy is seen by many Soviets as one of low risks, low costs, and potential high payoffs; while a continued confrontation and arms race with the West is seen as one of high costs, high risks and low payoffs.[62]

Nothing that has ensued would motivate me to change that assessment of the Soviet military and political calculus. In fact, the Soviets seem to have closely followed that projection. And there is little reason to assume they will depart from that policy line significantly in the coming decade, since the "alignment of political forces around the world" reflects current Soviet perceptions and assessments.

The late Soviet Minister of Defense Marshal Grechko stated: "We have never concealed the basis of Soviet military doctrine." He went on to say that "the principles and details of the doctrine are clearly expressed in the policies of the Communist Party and the Soviet Government and in the state of our Armed Forces." In fact, he continued, they are "fully reflected in our manuals and regulations." Marshal Grechko also stressed the fact that Soviet doctrine "particularly its military art, adapts itself to the times" and it becomes "amended and developed according to the alignment of political forces in the world and the policy pursued by the State."[63]

There is little reason to disagree with Marshal Grechko's statements, even though they are somewhat self-serving. We will therefore examine the current realignment of political forces, the derivative opportunities and challenges to the Soviet state and interests, and the adaptation of

Soviet military doctrine to these changes. In brief, we shall explore the implications of Soviet achievement of strategic parity; the subsequent relaxation of strictures against the feasibility and utility of limited and local war, particularly in the regions south of Russia; and the modernization and changes in Soviet doctrines on limited war.

In the mid-1960s Thomas Wolfe observed that "the relatively meager treatment customarily given in Soviet literature to the question of conducting limited warfare is in marked contrast to the attention bestowed on general nuclear war."[64] Wolfe believed that until the mid-1960s this reflected the major Soviet concern for the contingency they feared most (massive nuclear attack) and for the rapid or even automatic escalatory possibilities inherent in local or limited war. He found, however, that there were already signs that the Soviet doctrinal position on local and limited war was undergoing some change. Although there was still ambiguity and inconsistency in Soviet treatment of the subject, and no unifying doctrine of limited war evolved, there was less rigidity on the problem of escalation in local conflict.

Since the mid-1960s the Soviet position has undergone some substantial changes in doctrine, capability, and perceived utility. Although still formally adhering to the earlier, ideologically correct position, which rejects callous and deliberate use of military power (except in "just" wars), the Soviets have appraised the implications of the changed correlation of power in the 1970s and 1980s. By the late 1960s and in the 1970s Soviet analysts began to publicly consider implications of the coming Soviet achievement of nuclear parity with the United States. A debate ensued in open and classified Soviet literature (recalling the earlier strategic debates of the 1950s and 1960s) that focused on the proper roles of nuclear and conventional forces in war. Although the voice of the more conservative advocacy was heard, the authoritative and sophisticated position of the realists appears to have prevailed and set out the new Soviet position:

> In our times conditions may arise when in individual instances combat operations may be carried out using conventional weapons. Under these conditions the role of the conventional means and the traditional services of the armed forces are greatly enhanced. It becomes necessary to train troops for various kinds of warfare.[65]

The author, a well-known Soviet military analyst, then proceeds to argue against those who would interpret such renewed emphasis on conventional forces and limited warfare as a "negation of the contemporary revolution in military affairs," that is, negating or reducing the role of tactical or even strategic nuclear weapons. He dismisses those backward views because "one cannot agree with this opinion," and then lectures his more obtuse colleagues:

> The point is that the new possibilities of waging armed struggle have arisen *not in spite of, but because of the nuclear missile weapons*. They do not diminish their combat effectiveness, and the main thing, they do not preclude the possible use of such weapons.[66]

The point is well taken. Soviet doctrine and policy in the past decade have closely followed this reasoning. In effect it meant a loosening of the strictures against theater warfare, with or without nuclear weapons, and the endowment of conventional forces with vital military and political roles in consonance with the alignment of political forces in the world.

This new emphasis on the vital role of conventional forces and the possibility of limited and local war with conventional forces is also evident in the Soviet defense minister's recent statement: "There has been a great improvement in the fire, shock and maneuver capabilities of troops," which makes it possible to "assign them very decisive missions on the battlefield which they are capable of accomplishing without resorting to nuclear weapons."[67]

In the past decade the Soviets have been realigning their foreign policy and military doctrines in the triadic mode described above: Their massive nuclear capabilities are to neutralize and stabilize their relations with the West; their theater forces, both nuclear and conventional, are to enhance deterrence but also to serve as a war-fighting capability in Europe and Asia in the event deterrence fails; their conventional forces are to serve as the vital military and political element in Moscow's new expansionistic policies in the Third World. This Soviet appreciation of realistic targets of opportunity in the Third World is reflected in numerous statements, including the following:

> ... the outcome of the historic battle between socialism and capitalism largely depends on how the revolutionary movement will develop in the non-socialist world and what path the nations liberated from colonial oppression will follow.[68]

The new opportunities for Soviet exploitation in the Third World endow the conventional forces with several important roles, including the possibility of fighting local wars. The central role of these forces is evidenced in the admission of the American author of a recent Pentagon study on Soviet theater nuclear warfare. The author states that although

> this study began as an analysis of the Soviet nuclear threat to NATO . . . during the course of this study it became apparent, however, that the real heart of the Soviet threat has been and still is, the ground forces, particularly the tank armies and combined arms armies.[69]

Thus, even though in the European context Soviet doctrine envisages the use of nuclear weapons in theater warfare, "the heart of the Soviet concept is in reality not the initial nuclear barrage, but rather what might be called the exploitation forces." These are essentially conventional forces, trained and equipped to operate in a nuclear environment, but with increasing concern "to maintain their capability to fight and not become excessively dependent on nuclear weapons."[70]

When we turn to the Third World we find that conventional forces and weapons and their modes of employment in "local wars appear to be regarded as a principal mechanism to be exploited by the Soviet Union in expanding their influence and hegemony."[71] Since these areas appear to hold the greatest promise of Soviet exploitation, and since the Western strategic deterrence forces play a marginal role in such areas, the Soviets feel that their military doctrine for these areas is correct.

The use of conventional forces in support of Soviet expansionistic pressure in the Third World makes sense. Soviet exploratory policies and tactics remain essentially prudent and cautious and rather non-provocative or provocation-avoiding. The various roles of their conventional forces, as seen by the Soviets, include protector and patron of anti-Western regimes (Afghanistan, Syria, South Yemen, Ethiopia, Iraq, Angola and Libya) as a factor in influence-building in those regions; and as a supplier of expertise, training, weapons, and intelligence to their clients and proxies. As the head of the political organs of the Soviet military indicated, "the Soviet Union's ability to give assistance to the working people waging a revolutionary, liberation struggle and the volume of this assistance have become greater still in the present conditions."[72]

In sum, Soviet doctrines of limited and local war, based on achieving parity in strategic nuclear capabilities, reflect current and foreseeable Soviet political and military interests. This also suggests that the Soviets will continue to improve, modernize, and enhance their strategic, theater, and local warfare capabilities.

The new global mission of the Soviet military, which is premised in the massive strategic nuclear shield of deterrence forces and the more flexible and politically viable sword of their conventional and theater nuclear forces, was asserted by Marshal Grechko:

> At the present stage, the historic mission of the Soviet Armed Forces is not restricted to their function in defending our Motherland... but to support the national liberation struggle in whatever distant region of the planet it may appear.[73]

CONCLUSIONS AND PROJECTIONS

Soviet foreign policy objectives and military doctrine became congruent in the 1980s. Since the mid-1960s, Soviet foreign policy has pursued triadic primary goals (stabilized relations with the West; containment and isolation of China; exploration and expansion in the Third World, generally in the areas south of Russia), and Soviet military doctrine has become congruent with these foreign policy objectives. The Soviets' massive strategic nuclear shield is to provide a stable deterrence basis with the West; limited war doctrines and forces, with or without nuclear weapons, are to provide additional deterrent and war-fighting capabilities on the primary, contiguous flanks of the Soviet Union (Europe and Asia); while the conventional projective capabilities are to provide the cutting edge and the persuasive presence in support of expanding and exploratory policies in the Third World. This triadic orientation of Soviet foreign and military policy makes large claims on Soviet resources, manpower, and managerial/political talents; however, the Soviets seem persuaded that their time has come and the costs and risks are tolerable measured against prospective gains. Contemporary Soviet military thinking can be seen as based on a parry-and-thrust concept. Their vast nuclear forces serve as the deterrent shield against Western nuclear strategic forces; their general purpose forces serve as a flexible sword probing and thrusting into the vulnerable and soft regions of the world south of Russia, whose strategic, political, and economic values are of overriding importance to the Soviet leaders.

To enable them to explore the Third World for targets of opportunity, the Soviets had to neutralize American strategic preponderance and create credible deterrence and war-fighting forces on their two most exposed and dangerous flanks: NATO/Europe and China/Asia. The Soviets have achieved these objectives at great costs of manpower and weaponry, and in the process stirred up deep suspicions in the West and

China. However, the primary Soviet expansionary trajectory lies neither in Europe nor China but in the direction south of Russia, particularly in the Gulf region, the Middle East, and Africa.

The Soviets are generally convinced that political payoff lies in a prudent and preferably indirect use of their conventional forces in the Third World rather than in the politically inert strategic nuclear deterrent. This view has been expressed by one of the most influential Soviet analysts: "It has become clear that this [nuclear] might is becoming progressively less usable as a political weapon" and therefore the "sphere of applicability" of such weapons "for rational political ends is inexorably shrinking."[74] Of course, this is not to denigrate the crucial and decisive dissuasive and "holding back" functions of the vast strategic nuclear capabilities, without which the conventional and theater forces would become meaningless. But having obtained the strategic deterrence forces frees the Soviets to press on with the risky—albeit tempting—game of expansion southward. After all, the Soviets have turned out to be adept students of Western deterrence strategists, who have been asserting that the more stable the strategic deterrence the greater the willingness and freedom to risk the use of lower-spectrum forces for political ends.

The Soviets have rediscovered the wisdom and relevance of their long-dead revolutionary strategists, Marshals Tukhachevskii and Frunze, who preached a gospel of revolutionary warfare that included concepts of highly mobile, offensive, deep-thrust, airborne military operations, not along a wide straight-line front (á la Stalin) but along selective points of the enemy lines; the use of surprise, secrecy, deception and pre-emption; the vital role of armor, artillery, and mechanized infantry that are indispensable for high mobility, surprise, troop dispersal, and target-denial (these being particularly relevant in a nuclear battlefield environment). These aspects of revolutionary warfare are being updated and used as Soviet training and doctrinal modifications for their forces.[75]

The dominant motive force of Soviet political and military action is dialectical: the compelling "push to the utmost" derived from Clausewitz is moderated by the restraining Leninist *caveat* regarding the avoidance of "adventurism." This Bolshevik *yin-yang* combination provided the parameters for their inherently aggressive and expansionistic tendencies during the long formative period of Soviet Russia, which was marked by a perception of threat from the outside and by military inferiority and insecurity. However, the powerful restraints of the Leninist admonition (and the risk of losing it all through high risk and foolish gambles) are eroding: The Soviets feel less threatened, more secure and powerful, and they sense that the Western capitalist countries are less than monolithically unified.

There is little doubt that the Soviets are committed to gradual, nonprovocative but sustained exploration of vulnerable regions of the Third World as targets of opportunity. They are building the requisite forces, weapons, and technologies to project Soviet influence and power into these regions during this decade. Their doctrines and operational and tactical guidelines, and their training programs are congruent with these objectives.

The Soviets have practiced confrontation-avoidance whenever a direct clash with the other superpower seemed unavoidable. In the 1980s the situation will have changed drastically, since the Soviets are at least as powerful as the United States and the theaters of most likely confrontations are logistically accessible. Given the American traditions described above and the newly gained Soviet might, a confrontation between the two superpowers in Asia, the Persian Gulf, the Middle East, or Africa would have very ominous implications. The Soviets are not likely to blink first in an eyeball-to-eyeball confrontation. Given the current trend of events, it is not unreasonable to say that the superpowers are on a potential collision course in the 1980s.

NOTES

1. H. Rothfels, "Clausewitz," in Edward Mead Earle, ed., *Makers of Modern Strategy* (New York: Atheneum, 1966), pp. 99-100.
2. Robert E. Osgood, *Limited War: The Challenge to American Strategy* (Chicago: Chicago University Press, 1957), p. 34.
3. George Kennan, *American Diplomacy, 1900-1950* (New York: Mentor Books, 1951), p. 59.
4. Morton H. Halperin, *Limited War in the Nuclear Age* (New York: John Wiley and Sons, 1963), p. 19.
5. Osgood, *Limited War*, p. 46.
6. Ibid., p. 14.
7. Kennan, *American Diplomacy*, p. 53.
8. William W. Kaufmann, ed., *Military Policy and National Security* (Princeton, N.J.: Princeton University Press, 1956), p. 102.
9. Osgood, *Limited War*, p. 46.
10. Rothfels in Earle, ed., *Makers of Modern Strategy*, p. 100.
11. Ibid.
12. Ibid., p. 93.
13. Carl von Clausewitz, *On War* (Combat Forces Press, 1953), p. 16.
14. See V. Ye. Savkin, *The Basic Principles of Operational Art and Tactics*, translated and edited under the auspices of the United States Air Force (Washington, D.C.: U.S. Government Printing Office, n.d.), pp. 22-23.
15. Clausewitz, *On War*, p. 16.
16. Ibid., p. 596.
17. Cited in Earle, ed., *Makers of Modern Strategy*, p. 158.

18. Marshal of the Soviet Union, V. D. Sokolovskii, ed., *Soviet Military Strategy*, Rand Corporation edition (Santa Monica, Calif.: The Rand Corporation), p. 98.
19. Cited in Osgood, *Limited War*, p. 33.
20. In Isaac Deutscher, *The Prophet Armed* (Oxford: Oxford University Press, 1976), p. 482.
21. Ibid.
22. Sokolovskii, *Soviet Military Strategy*, Rand Corporation edition, "Introduction" by the American editors H. S. Dinerstein, Leon Goure and Thomas W. Wolfe, pp. 44-45.
23. G. D. Arbatov, *Problemy Mira i Sotsializma*, no. 2, February 1974, p. 46.
24. *Marxism-Leninism on War and Army* (Moscow: Progress Publishers, 1972), p. 100.
25. N. Talenskii, "Anti-Missile Systems and Disarmament," in John Erickson, ed., *The Military Technical Revolution: Its Impact on Strategy and Foreign Policy* (New York: Institute for the Study of the USSR, 1966), pp. 225-227.
26. Benjamin S. Lambeth, "The Political Potential of Soviet Equivalence," *International Security*, Fall 1979, p. 27.
27. Ibid., p. 31.
28. A. A. Grechko, *The Armed Forces of the Soviet Union* (Moscow: Progress Publishers, 1977).
29. Alexander L. George and Richard Smoke, *Deterrence in American Foreign Policy* (New York: Columbia University Press, 1974), p. 5.
30. *Kommunist*, June 1972, Editorial.
31. Marshal of the Soviet Union, Chief of the Strategic Missile forces, N. I. Krylov, "The Instructive Lessons of History," *Sovetskaia Rossiia*, August 30, 1969.
32. Cited in Leon Goure, et al., eds., *The Role of Nuclear Forces in Current Soviet Strategy* (Miami: Center for Advanced International Studies, 1974), p. 61.
33. General P. Zhilin, "The Military Aspects of Detente," *International Affairs* (Moscow), no. 12, 1972, p. 25.
34. Jack L. Snyder, *The Soviet Strategic Culture: Implications for Limited Nuclear Operations* (Santa Monica, Calif.: The Rand Corporation, 1977), p. 18.
35. Lambeth, "The Political Potential of Soviet Equivalence," p. 28.
36. Snyder, *The Soviet Strategic Culture*, p. 19.
37. *Marxism-Leninism on War and Army*, p. 99.
38. Ibid., p. 100.
39. Benjamin S. Lambeth, *Selective Nuclear Operations and Soviet Strategy* (Santa Monica, Calif.: The Rand Corporation, 1975).
40. Thomas W. Wolfe, *Soviet Strategy at the Crossroads* (Cambridge: Harvard University Press, 1965), p. 123.
41. *Marxism-Leninism on War and Army*, p. 98; also in Wolfe, *Soviet Strategy at the Crossroads*, Chap. 10.
42. Kaufmann, ed., *Military Policy*, p. 127.
43. V. D. Sokolovskii, ed., *Soviet Military Strategy*, 3rd ed., ed. and transl. by Harriet Fast Scott (New York: Crane, Russak & Co., 1975), p. 68.
44. Ibid.
45. Ibid., p. 69.
46. Thomas C. Schelling, *Arms and Influence* (New Haven, Conn.: Yale University Press, 1957), p. 130.
47. Ibid., p. 158.
48. Ibid., p. 158.
49. Ibid., p. 159.
50. Ibid., p. 133.
51. Ibid., p. 157.

52. Halperin, *Limited War in the Nuclear Age*, p. 64.

53. Osgood, *Limited War*, p. 47.

54. The Soviets, like other communists, also separate all wars into just and unjust wars: unjust wars are those initiated by the capitalists against progressive countries and forces in the world; just wars are those conducted by progressive forces in revolutionary, national liberating and anti-imperialist struggle. And though the Soviets have at all times been concerned with escalatory spirals and pressures in war, and have been warning of the dangers of even small and local crises getting out of control and exploding into total nuclear war, they have nevertheless retained the just/national liberation war formula for ideological and political reasons.

55. George and Smoke, *Deterrence in American Foreign Policy*, p. 20.

56. Ibid., p. 7.

57. Ibid., p. 45.

58. It is rather ironic that the American preferences remained largely unfulfilled and in effect American troops became bogged down in land wars in Asia (Korea and Vietnam), where strategic preponderance played a limited role in the conduct and outcome of the war.

59. See Uwe Nehrlich, "Theatre Nuclear Forces in Europe: Is NATO Running Out of Options?", *The Washington Quarterly*, Winter 1980.

60. Snyder, *The Soviet Strategic Culture*.

61. V. M. Bondarenko, *Kommunist Vooruzhennykh Sil*, December 1968.

62. Submission by Roman Kolkowicz to Senator Gore, Chairman of the Sub-Committee on Committee on Foreign Relations, United States Senate, April 15, 1970, pp. 593-594.

63. Grechko, *The Armed Forces of the Soviet Union*, pp. 273-274.

64. Wolfe, *Soviet Strategy at the Crossroads*, p. 118.

65. Lt.-Col. V. M. Bondarenko cited in Harriet Fast Scott and William F. Scott, eds., *The Armed Forces of the USSR* (Boulder, Colo.: Westview Press, 1979), p. 55.

66. Ibid.

67. Cited in Joseph D. Douglass, *The Soviet Theater Nuclear Offensive, Studies in Communist Affairs*, vol. 1 (prepared for the Office of Director of Defense Research and Engineering, Net Technical Assessment), p. 113.

68. Goure, et al., *The Role of Nuclear Forces in Current Soviet Strategy*, p. 62.

69. Douglass, *The Soviet Theater Nuclear Offensive*, p. 46.

70. Ibid.

71. Ibid.

72. General A. A. Epishev, *Some Aspects of Party-Political Work in the Soviet Armed Forces* (Moscow: Progress Publishers, 1975). Another view regarding the global mission of the Soviet armed forces is: "Greatest importance is being attached to Soviet military presence in various regions throughout the world, reinforced by an adequate level of strategic mobility of its armed forces ... In those cases wherein support must be furnished to those nations fighting for their freedom and independence against forces of international reaction and imperialist interventions, the Soviet Union may require mobile and well-trained and well-equipped forces ... Expanding the scale of Soviet military presence and military assistance furnished by other socialist states (i.e., proxies) is being viewed today as a very important factor in international relations." V. M. Kulish, *Voennaia Sila i Mezhdunarodnoe Otnoshenia*, 1972, cited in Scott and Scott, eds., *The Armed Forces of the USSR*, p. 57.

73. Marshal of the Soviet Union A. A. Grechko, "The leading Role of the CPSU in Building the Army of a Developed Socialist Society," *Problemy Istorii KPSS*, May 1974.

74. G. A. Arbatov, *World Marxist Review*, no. 2, February 1974, p. 56.

75. See Savkin, *The Basic Principles of Operational Art and Tactics*, pp. 22-23. It is interesting to compare contemporary Soviet views on the vital importance of nonstrategic forces with their views of the early 1960s. In announcing the new Soviet military doctrine in January 1960, Khrushchev announced proposed massive reductions of conventional forces and rationalized them as follows: "Our state has at its disposal powerful rocket equipment. The military air force and navy have lost their previous importance in view of the modern developmet of military equipment. . . . In our time the defense potential of the country is determined, not by the number of our soldiers under arms and the number of persons in naval uniform. . . . " Cited in R. Kolkowicz, *The Soviet Military and Communist Party* (Princeton, N.J.: Princeton University Press, 1967), p. 151. Note also Khrushchev's candid outburst, printed in *Pravda* on September 22, 1964, just about one week prior to his ouster from power: "When I went out onto the training field and saw the tanks attacking and how the antitank artillery hit these tanks, I became ill. After all, we are spending a lot of money to build tanks. And if—God forbid, as they say—a war breaks out, these tanks will burn before they reach the line indicated by the command."

Chapter 15

American Perceptions and Strategic Options in the Korean War

Robert R. Simmons

After World War II, the United States sought to halt the spread of communist states by a policy of containment. Its major geopolitical concern was Europe. Before 1950, American strategists had perceived Korea as not holding great military importance. But on June 25 (June 24, Korean date), 1950, with no other Communist aggression to control, Korea immediately took the role of a testing ground. Because Europe had been assumed to be the major area of contest, Korea had previously received scant attention in military planning. The war caused a 180° turn. As a result of this sharp and jagged turn around, the decisions were often made on an ad hoc basis.

The Korean War remained the sole testing ground for containment during this period. The geographical and political 'knowns' provide a general perspective to the crisis: (1) a politically weak President was about to face mid-term elections; and (2) neither Japan nor Europe was in the early stages of a Communist invasion. It is probably that Washington's response on June 25, 1950 would have been altered if there had been different resources or geographical priorities.

I would like to express my appreciation to Sylvia and Edwin Simmons of Auburn, New York; Maria Hrycaiko-Zaputovitch of the Universities of Toronto and Guelph; and George Nef of the University of Guelph, Guelph, Ontario, Canada, for their generous help.

Korea synthesized the policy of containment and a military strategy into a series of tactical responses. It bridged the conventional-strategic massive response (e.g., air superiority) and the later plans for nuclear weaponry applied to a country-sized theater. The strategy of the Korean War (sometimes referred to in Western academic studies as the Korean Civil War) was the consequence of the experiences of World War II, which were both constrained and facilitated by the new nuclear technology and the specific nuances of a localized civil war. The response to the Korean crisis, in the form of a limited war model, would in turn condition the strategic frame of reference for the United States at the time of Vietnam.

The United States emerged from World War II as a victor unconvinced that triumph meant security. The focus of anxiety reverted to the pre-World War II fear of the Soviet Union building an empire at American expense. Washington was determined to resist perceived Soviet expansion, which was analyzed in global terms. American participation in World War II had been widely supported, but shortly after 1945 the U.S. taxpayers and potential soldiers were not eager for a new series of sacrifices. The hope was that U.S. science could provide capabilities necessary to respond to anticipated crises caused by the Soviet Union.

The Berlin crisis of 1948 demonstrated that American military technology would now compensate with air power for its smaller army. This example reinforced the fact that although the Soviet Union held a marked superiority in conventional land forces, the United States possessed a monopoly on "the ultimate weapon," the atomic bomb. The paradigm for the "next conflict" was "massive retaliation." The main tenets of this posture need to be spelled out: (1) a new war which would call for the few available atomic weapons would also need only a few targets to assure a rapid successful conclusion. Unfortunately for the American planners, the Soviet Union did not supply these elements. The dramatic development which had decided the U.S. entry into World War II had been the spectacular attack on Pearl Harbor. But after 1945, the Soviet Union had not actively or suddenly used its own armed forces in a dramatic invasion. Neither Czechoslovakia nor China fit this model. Yet the political changes in these two countries symbolized the losses which were unfolding—the fear that more were to follow. (2) The coming war was envisaged as global. (3) Europe was seen as the major battlefield. (4) The Third World was considered to be of tertiary security importance.

Within the emerging U.S. perspective of this World War, in 1947 the Joint Chiefs of Staff drew up a possible future scenario for conflict in East Asia, *MOONRISE*.[1] This military sketch foresaw a rapid Soviet conquest of East Asia: Korea within twenty days, Manchuria and North China within fifty days. This plan, and others to follow, held three general premises: first the opponent's strength would be substantial in each conventional military category; second, the Soviets controlled the political decision, and armies of its satellites; and third, East Asia held the least strategic interest for the Soviet Union. Washington's apprehension centered on a general war with the Soviet Union and it perceived Moscow's main objective as the conquest of Western Europe. Consequently, the United States had not planned in detail for a limited war in East Asia. Threats in this region, including even localized conflicts coordinated by the Soviet Union, were analyzed as diversionary techniques. Possible East Asian conflicts were seen as in the "deceptive" category. Therefore plans drawn shortly after *MOONRISE* ranked—in descending order and strategic importance—Western Europe, the Middle East, and East Asia.[2]

This war scenario was predicated on the assumption that the Soviet Union was the single aggressive opponent and that it totally controlled the bellicose plans of its satellites. This mind-set hindered attempts to balance Soviet and Chinese (and Indochinese) nationalisms; the enemy was perceived as aggressive and monolithic. American strategic studies often viewed these countries as tightly bound. Only cautious recognition was given to divisions within the Communist alliance. In retrospect, however, questions arise. Was the alliance a unity of convenience held together by fear of a common enemy? Could the West have dealt with these differences profitably and avoided full-scale conflicts? The fact that these are not unique questions suggests that an answer had not been absorbed until recently.

This anxious assessment, "World War III or nothing" did, however, provide a benefit. It offered a rationale for the public programs and financial support to the machinery considered necessary to deter a Soviet global war plan. Such public support had built-in limitations: people were weary of personal, physical, and financial burdens, and this impeded putting the policy of containing Communism into effect. Nevertheless, this reticence was checked by the aggressiveness the Soviet Union seemed to be directing against the United States and its allies.

The harmonious but brittle political tie binding the Soviet Union and the United States during World War II had been rapidly frayed by fierce and hostile bargaining. It should be noted, however, that Communism did not seep inexorably into every opening. For example, and ironically, the Soviet occupation army arrived on the Korean Peninsula one month before the American forces. The Soviet forces, however, voluntarily stayed north of the previously agreed upon border; the thirty-eighth parallel. The Soviets probably felt that the Communist organization embryonically present in the south would emplace a Communist regime there without the Soviets running a risk of a direct war with the United States.

At the end of World War II, Washington did not foresee a symmetrical meshing of U.S. and Soviet interests, although it did hope for a series of general agreements. The United States could induce such agreements while it retained the monopoly on the atomic bomb, a military advantage that also had important uses in American domestic politics. The Truman administration needed this posture of external strength to balance the charge that it was "soft on Communism." Popular conservative thought, to be symbolized shortly thereafter by Senator Joseph McCarthy's anti-Communist stance and his virulent criticism of the Truman administration, was a constant reminder that the government must maintain a firm anti-Communist policy.

These domestic political constrains made it difficult for President Truman to recognize the new government in Beijing—even though the defeat of Chiang K'ai Shek in Taiwan at the time appeared imminent[3]— or to withdraw support from the French regime in Indochina. The domestic political strictures became narrower and firmer with two developments. On September 22, 1949 the Soviets exploded their own nuclear device; on October 1, 1949 the People's Republic of China was officially established. A new and pessimistic public mood swept across the United States. Within a week Congress voted in the NATO appropriation, accompanied with accelerated air power, increased funding for a more effective deterrent weapon: the Hydrogen Bomb.

The United States had pursued the policy of supporting its military forces stationed in Western Europe at the expense of decreasing its strength in East Asia. Recently released documents (although it should be noted that others may point to different inferences) suggest that the U.S. military strategists were sensitive about the risk involved in the effort to bolster Europe's defenses. For example, a memorandum for the State-Army-Navy-Air Force Coordinating Committee in June 1949 stated that it was in full agreement with the following analysis reached on September 29, 1947:

> It should be the effort of the Government through all proper means to effect a settlement of the Korean problems which would enable the U.S. to withdraw from Korea as soon as possible with the minimum of bad effects ... The United States has little strategic interest in maintaining the present troops and bases in Korea ... *The forces now deployed in Korea are sorely needed elsewhere* (emphasis added). Therefore, it would be highly desirable to withdraw our forces from Korea and to utilize them for essential and pressing needs.[4]

In addition to acknowledging American military fragility, the above assessment also recognized Soviet caution about contesting its former ally over an area that the USSR felt would become communist without involving it in a direct major war with the United States. In all likelihood, the Soviets may have had a similar paradigm. The 1947 memorandum went on to say that "in event of hostilities in the Far East, our present forces in Korea would be a liability without being strengthened, which in turn would necessitate the weakening of U.S. forces in Europe."

Global strategy for U.S. military planners with their major concern concentrated on Europe allowed some attention, but not alarm, given to Korea. A CIA report of February 28, 1949 judged that:

> Withdrawal of U.S. forces from Korea in the Spring of 1949 would probably in time be followed by an invasion, timed to coincide with Communist-led South Korean revolts, by the North Korean People's Army possibly assisted by small battle-trained units from Communist Manchuria ... Assuming that Korean Communists would make aggressive use of the opportunity presented them, U.S. troop withdrawal would probably result in a collapse of the U.S.-supported Republic of Korea, an event which would seriouly diminish U.S. prestige and adversely affect U.S. security interests in the Far East.[5]

A dissent to this assessment by the Intelligence Division, Department of the Army was more somber: " ... the continued maintenance of a small United States Army force in South Korea would be only a relatively minor psychological contribution to the stability of Korea." The report suggested that a North Korean action short of an invasion "might bring about the results desired by North Korea and, presumably, Soviet authorities, without incurring the risks involved in a military operation." This could be accomplished by infiltrated-caused subversion and riots. In 1949 General W. E. Todd, director of the Joint Chiefs of Staff Joint Intelligence Group, told the Senate Foreign Relations Committee: "We feel that if the Soviets attach any priority to areas in which they would like to move by means of armed aggression, Korea would be at the bottom of that list of priorities."[6]

This military expectation was reinforced by government specialists analyzing possibilities of where the war would occur. A convincing example of what was considered most probable is provided by leading Soviet specialist George F. Kennan in his 1967 *Memoirs*:

> At some time in late May or early June 1950, some of us who were particularly concerned with Russian affairs in the department were puzzled to note, among the vast "take" of information that flows daily into

the ample maw of that institution, data suggesting that somewhere across the broad globe the armed forces of some Communist power were expecting soon to go into action. An intensive scrutiny of the Soviet situation satisfied us that it was not Soviet forces to which these indications related. This left us with the forces of the various satellite regimes, but which? Summoning the various experts to the table, we toured the horizons of the Soviet bloc. Korea came up in due turn. For information about military matters in that country, we were dependent on a long and indirect chain of communication, passing through two military establishments, as I recall it: the one in Japan and the Pentagon in Washington. The word that reached us through this indirect route was that an inauguration of military operations from the Communist side in that country was practically out of the question: the South Korean forces were so well armed and trained that they were clearly superior to those of the Communist north; our greatest task, we were told, was to restrain the South Koreans from resorting to arms to settle their differences with the north. Having no grounds to challenge this judgment, I accepted it (I have always reproached myself for doing so) and we passed on to other things. But nowhere else understandably enough, could we see any possibility of an attack, and we came away from the exercise quite frustrated.[7]

In sum, American intelligence expected that war could affect Korea, but that possibility was analyzed as of less immediate concern than the threat to Europe.

President Truman's military posture hardened during the late 1940s with each successive contest. It was widely perceived in Washington that a major conflict was coming. General MacArthur echoed the bulk of the military advice being given to the President. In a march 1949 newspaper interview, he traced an American line of defense which left out both South Korea and Taiwan, on the assumption that in a general war (the expected type), they would be strategic deficits.

Secretary of State Dean Acheson's famous speech of January 12, 1950 (which was reported on page one of the *New York Times* of January 13, 1950) similarly omitted South Korea, Taiwan, and Indochina from the U.S. defense perimeter. This speech was more ambiguous in its strategic implications than its later critics would allow. This policy statement acknowledged the difficulty that the U.S. military faced when seeking to be the "free world's guardian." At the same time that this speech avoided mentioning military commitments, it offered economic assistance with the political-military agreements implicitly attached.

On January 5, 1950 a week before the Secretary of State's speech, President Truman declared that the United States would not protect Taiwan against an invasion from the Mainland. This statement was

publicly proclaimed with the apprehension that Beijing would successfully invade Taiwan.[8] On January 30, 1950 the interlocking and reinforcing damage being suffered by the U.S. foreign policy caused President
Truman to direct the State and Defense Departments "to make an
overall review and reassessment of American foreign and defense policy
in the light of the loss of China, the Soviet mastery of atomic energy and
the prospect of the fusion bomb." After analysis, the document was
returned from the National Security Council and proposed as NSC-68 on
April 7, 1950.[9] (Interestingly, the document was not signed until after
the Korean War began on September 30, 1950.)

The official (although not announced as such) program emphasized the
defense and protection of regions where the United States then held
political-economic-military influence. It did not call for "liberation" of
then-Communist areas, a feature which was not welcomed by the
conservatives. Yet its general idea took hold with a worried public which
wanted the Moscow-directed expansion halted. This meant a greater
military expenditure than was currently taken from the taxes of a
people who were only recently unburdened from the costs of a major
war. NSC-68 alluded to the necessity of an effort similar to the one
which had just ended in 1945. However, with the lack of general and
congressional support, the goal of a rapid increase in popular support
appeared unlikely before the events of June 1950.

President Truman understood this shaky and unbalanced support for
U.S. security policy, and he correctly perceived that NSC-68 policies
would need to be explained in terms of direct threat to American
security. He was also aware that NSC-68 meant a great military effort
in times of peace, doubling or tripling the budget, increasing taxes
heavily, and imposing various kinds of economic controls. It meant a
great change in the normal peacetime way of doing things. It was
estimated that the Soviet Union would achieve a deterrent stockpile of
nuclear weapons within four years. The U.S. monopoly of atomic bombs
would then vanish. Moreover, Soviet ground forces were superior to
American ones. U.S. intelligence sources expected that the Soviets
would probe American defense capabilities and intentions, but would
not enter a general war before 1954. Korea was considered only one of
numerous possible targets; in fact it ranked near the bottom of the list.

NSC-68 firmly summarized the immediate military dangers which the
United States faced:

> In the light of present and prospective Soviet atomic capabilities, the
> action which can be taken under present programs and plans, however,
> becomes dangerously inadequate, in both timing and scope, to accomplish
> the rapid progress toward the attainment of the United States political,
> economic, and military objectives which is now imperative.

A continuation of present trends would result in a serious decline in the strength of the free world relative to the Soviet Union and its satellites. This unfavorable trend arises from the inadequacy of current programs and plans rather than from any error in our objectives and aims. These trends lead in the direction of isolation not by deliberate decision but by lack of the necessary basis for a vigorous initiative in the conflict with the Soviet Union.

Our position as the center of power in the free world places a heavy responsibility upon the United States for leadership. We must organize and enlist the energies and resources of the free world in a positive program for peace which will frustrate the Kremlin design for world domination by creating a situation in the free world to which the Kremlin will be compelled to adjust. Without such a cooperative effort, led by the United States, we will have to make gradual withdrawals under pressure until we discover one day that we have sacrificed positions of vital interest.

It is imperative that this trend be reversed by a much more rapid and concerted build-up of the actual strength of both the United States and the other nations of the free world. The analysis shows that this will be costly and will involve significant domestic, financial and economic adjustments . . .

In summary, we must, by means of a rapid and sustained build-up of the political, economic, and military strength of the free world, and by means of an affirmative program intended to wrest the initiative from the Soviet Union, confront it with convincing evidence of the determination and ability of the free world to frustrate the Kremlin design of a world dominated by its will. Such evidence is the only means short of war which eventually may force the Kremlin to abandon its present course of action and to negotiate acceptable agreements on issues of major importance.[10]

Two months after the submission of NSC-68 to the President, the Korean War began. The defense budget was shortly tripled. It is understandable that this last development would have been expected, in the wake of fears concerning an ever-expanding and increasingly more powerful Soviet Union. The major factor in the rapid fulfillment of the financial and manpower requests of NSC-68 was the realization of what had previously been feared: a sudden and dramatic invasion by communist forces. However, this did not take place in the European theater as expected but rather in the Asian arena, a largely unanticipated development. It was taken for granted that the North Korean military was simply carrying out direct orders issued by the headquarters of a multi-armed by single-headed monolith.

Little attention was given to the idea that the individual nationalisms of the Soviet allies might exercise specific effect upon international relations. This omission continued to hamper U.S. foreign policy during much of the subsequent decade and a half. The view that Moscow had an unshakeable grip on its "puppets" also impeded a diplomatic agreement with China, and encouraged the American involvement in the Indochina war.

The view that Korea largely represented a Soviet feint in a relatively unimportant section of the globe was strengthened by a 1949 Joint Chiefs of Staff report evaluating Korean military importance. "The United States has little strategic interest in maintaining the present troops and bases in Korea ... and in the event of hostilities in the Far East they would be a liability."[11] A *Memorandum for the Chief of Staff, U.S. Army* sent to the Joint Chiefs of Staff on June 20, 1949, elaborated on the reasons by Korea was not then considered to be of vital and immediate importance:

a. From the Strategic viewpoint, the position of the Joint Chiefs of Staff regarding Korea, summarized briefly, is that Korea is of little strategic value to the United States and that any commitment to United States use of military force in Korea would be ill-advised and impracticable in view of the potentialities of the over-all world situation and of our heavy international obligations as compared with our current military strength ...

c. The Joint Chiefs of Staff desire to emphasize that, as concluded in the study, the possible courses of action listed as 5c and 5d would be militarily unsound. The first of these which envisages the introduction of a military task force into Korea composed of United States units and units of other member nations of the United Nations, would be practicable only in and when it has become possible to organize United Nations armed forces for the Security Council under the terms of Article 43 of the United Nations Charter. The second of these possible courses of action would amount to reoccupation of South Korea. This, for reasons well stated in the study, would invite serious consequences while offering no tangible advantage. Furthermore, either course of action might lead to major military involvement ...

Present information indicates that withdrawal of U.S. forces will probably result in communist domination and it is extremely doubtful if it would be possible to build up the constabulary in the time and with the facilities available which would be able to prevent Soviet encroachment. Therefore eventual domination of Korea by the U.S.S.R. will have to be accepted as a probability if U.S. troops are withdrawn. However, the presence of an augmented constabulary might be a temporary deterrent to overt acts by North Korea forces.[12]

The refrain of restraint continued in U.S. military intelligence research and advice. Contrary to popular folklore, American military strategists did not think that the defense of South Korea would be worth the expense, particularly because the priority was given to the protection of Europe.

The June 20, 1949 Joint Chiefs of Staff memorandum noting that the U.S. forces in Korea were weak was reinforced by the thought that this limited strength was needed elsewhere to face other potential crises. Throughout this period, until it formally entered the fighting, Washington issued statements that could be read as signals by the opponent. For instance, on May 2, 1950 Senator Tom Connally, Chairman of the Senate Foreign Relations Committee, publicly declared that he did not think that Korea was of "very great importance. It was testified before us that Japan, Okinawa, and the Philippines make the chain of defenses which is absolutely necessary." Washington did not refute the statement.

Paralleling this restrained concern over the military security of Korea was an awareness of the fragility of the South Korean political system. That apparent weakness was accurately seen as a temptation to North Korea. It is noteworthy that sympathetic reports from the U.S. Embassy in Seoul also commented about the vulnerability of South Korea. For example, a CIA report of April 19, 1950 indicated the severe stress placed upon the legitimacy of the Seoul government:

The general elections to Korea's National Assembly scheduled for 30 May are expected to reduce President Rhee's autocratic control of the country. There will be a substantial strengthening of the parliamentary position of the Democratic National Party, a relatively talented and well-organized group representing landed and business interests that have been critical of Rhee's corrupt and inefficient administration. Such an election result would impose the likelihood that economic policies, urged by U.S. officials, would be carried out. Also, the opposition party's greater influence would tend to reduce the serious misuse of police powers which have contributed to Rhee's unpopularity. These developments would considerably lessen the chances for Communist exploitation in Korea.[13]

This account managed to convey warmth and hope with cautious doubts about the regime's durability. (This approach was echoed in later

Asian crises when the United States backed a government that lacked popular support.)

Rhee did hold elections, rather than lose U.S. support. Just before the voting took place, however, thirty of his leading opponents were arrested in anti-Communist raids. Nonetheless, of the 168 seats in the National Assembly, his party collected only forty-eight, with the other 120 going to contending—and leftist—parties. The new Assembly immediately began to consider peaceful reunification, i.e., a willingness to compromise with the North, a move that certainly went against President Rhee's desires.

Domestically, the South Korean regime was weak. Washington, however, was quite willing to provide external support because of its strong anti-Communist stance. The American polity faced a somewhat analogous—though inverse—situation. President Truman's administration did not receive strong domestic backing and indeed it was, in this context, under heavy fire from militant conservatives. Washington's main foreign policy became centered on opposing world communism. Each anti-Communist move by the Truman administration was greeted favorably by conservative voters and congressmen. Yet aside from local crisis, no ostensible major threat to U.S. security existed.

The beginning of the Korean Civil War (albeit, an internationalized domestic war) allowed the administration to appear as the defender of freedom, thus greatly increasing domestic support. Because of this heavily moralistic stance, the programs outlined in NSC-68 which put a very heavy burden on the American public were widely accepted. Consequently, in late June 1950, American forces entered the war without much domestic protest. On the contrary, the move was widely supported by both defenders and opponents of the administration. This approval continued because the American participation in the Korean War was generally seen as necessary to stem the spread of Soviet-directed communism. However, it was not as simple as that. Professor Robert Slusser has observed that:

> Gradually as tempers have cooled and as new evidence has become available the complexity of the problem has become apparent and the outlines of a new interpretation have begun to emerge. It becomes increasingly clear that any attempt to solve the problem must take into account not only Soviet policy but also the tangled complexities of North Korean priorities and that the once dominant Western view of a war started on orders from Moscow must be drastically modified.[14]

One recently declassified document drafted as a memorandum for the Joint Chiefs of Staff emphasizes this "complexity." The United States forces were losing in the first few weeks of the war and estimates of the conflict's potential wider effect were starkly drafted:

> Estimates based on five possible situations in Korea: North Koreans prosecute war with limited Soviet aid; Chi Com troops are introduced; Soviets employ enough troops to jeopardize U.N. positions; Soviets initiate military action in other areas than Korea; present situation is first step in a planned Soviet global war. U.S. should undertake four measures consonant with NSC-68: reinforce troops in Korea; restore potential of U.S. forces worldwide; accelerate the U.S. air defense program; augment forces with a small balance expeditionary force.[15]

At first the American armed forces had a limited objective—the restoration of the boundary at the thirty-eighth parallel. The "limited war" was to be fought as a prime test of U.S. determination to contain the expansion of world Communism. Washington had been unsuccessful on the Chinese Mainland but, it had already begun providing military assistance to French Indochina and the Philippines, which faced similar threats from the Vietminh and the Huks respectively.

Initial announcements concerning the introduction of U.S. forces explicitly declared that American troops did not mean to be "liberators" of North Korea. In late July 1950, however, when Communist forces were halted at the southern tip of the peninsula, Warren Austin, the U.S. delegate to the U.N., began to allude to a change in goals; the United Nations was told that it should ensure the attainment of complete individual and political freedom for the whole Korean Peninsula. In October 1950 the U.N. General Assembly demonstrated agreement by promising to take the appropriate steps to ensure freedom throughout Korea. Shortly before that, on September 1, 1950 Austin also showed support for these ideas when he affirmed that Koreans had a right to be free, independent, and united. The war was not to be the first "liberation" of a Communist state.

The spectacular naval landing at Inchon on September 15, 1950, which allowed the rapid rout of much of the North Korean armies, prompted Washington's forces to drive toward the northern frontier. This heady victory was also compounded with American domestic support to end the "war of agression" by driving the North Korean invaders out of South Korea altogether. The fluctuation of goals in the Korean War appears to conform to William J. Fulbright's later charge of the "arrogance of power." When the United States waxed militarily strong, so did its political intent. Another illuminating example was the use of the Seventh Fleet. It's proclaimed intention was to protect each side of the Taiwan Straits from the other.

As the conflict in Korea settled into a bloody stalemate, the original and loudly proclaimed policy of constraining Chiang K'ai-shek's forces to Taiwan started to pale. Forces from Taiwan began to raid, and sometimes to occupy briefly, small areas of Mainland territory. For example, on February 29, 1951, the Joint Chiefs of Staff, with the approval of the President stated:

> In the event of clearly identified Chinese Communist air or sea attack against Formosa of the Pescadores, no objection will be interposed to the Chinese Nationalist Government retaliating immediately against targets on the Chinese mainland. This position will be conveyed to the Chinese Nationalist Government through diplomatic channels... [16]

These messages of support for limited U.S. involvement in the Chinese Civil War continued to flow. A July 1951 memorandum from the Joint Chiefs of Staff provides a typical example:

> There is no restriction on your employment of United States naval and air forces as between support of Korea operations and defense of Formosa.
>
> You will interpose no objection to the Chinese National Government retaliating immediately against targets on Chinese mainland. (This position has been conveyed to the Chinese National Government through diplomatic channels.) [17]

The fact was that Taiwan was in armed conflict with the Chinese Mainland during the Korean War and that the United States did not restrain the forces based on Taiwan. This policy sent two main messages to both foes and allies. First, the Nationalists were encouraged to hope that they would return to the Mainland with the support of the United States. Second, President Eisenhower's so called unleashing of the Chinese Nationalists in 1953 was dramatically pronounced as a new program. But it was in fact merely a rewriting of what had been going on off the Southern China coast. There well may have been sound reason for the announcement. On the one hand, it reminded the Communist adversary that Washington might indeed become more bellicose. On the other hand it reassured a tired U.S. public after two-and-a-half years of an apparently interminable war that the new U.S. government's policies under President Eisenhower might lead the adversary to put an end to the conflict.

In his book *War and Politics* (p. 105), Bernard Brodie brings back into focus the oft forgotten success of belligerent American warnings that the United States would employ nuclear weapons (although these warnings were not the sole reason for bringing the Communists back to the peace negotiating table).

> If President Eisenhower's threat really played the part that he thought it did in bringing the other side to an appropriate negotiating attitude ... willing to treat reasonably, and as eager as ourselves to bring the fighting to an end ... it casts some light again on what might have been if the United Nations Command had not prematurely stopped its swiftly-moving offensive two years earlier.[18]

The "threat" referred to the use of nuclear weapons.

Such policies, however, can and did lead to further and compounded difficulties. Pacifying an ally, by not "leashing" him presents at least potential military problems. The weaker ally might decide to set the pace unilaterally for both battle and negotiation tactics. South Korean President Rhee presented such an example. From 1951 to 1953, Washington and the Tokyo-based U.S. military command exchanged messages on how to prevent President Rhee from seizing complete control of the south's civil and military force in an attempt to attack the north.

U.S. General Mark Clark, in the summer of 1952, was worried that Syngmam Rhee would seek to take advantage of civil disorders to continue martial law in a bid to arrest political opponents and "march north." General Clark, from Tokyo, told Washington that he had formulated a plan in case Rhee took these extreme measures:

> a. President Rhee would be invited to visit in Seoul or elsewhere— anywhere to get him out of Pusan.

> b. At an appointed time the UNC commander would move into the Pusan area and seize between 5 and 10 key ROK officials who have been leaders in Rhee's dictatorial actions, protect all UNC installations deemed advisable, and take over the control of martial law through the Chief of Staff, ROK Army, until it is lifted.

> c. Rhee would then be informed of the action taken as a "fait accompli." He would be urged to sign a proclamation lifting martial law, permitting National Assembly freedom of action and establishing freedom of the press and radio without interference from his various strong armed agencies.

> d. If President Rhee would not agree to issue the proclamation, he would be held in protective custody incommunicado and a similar proclamation would be presented to Prime Minister Chiang Taek Sang.

e. It is believed that the Prime Minister would agree. However, if he does not, it would then be necessary to take further steps approaching a UNC interim government.

Political differences between Seoul and Washington continued, but the Seoul government did not independently seize a military initiative. The U.S. Command inhibited any separate move by South Korean forces. On July 15, 1952, General Clark cabled Washington:

> The use of ROK Army alone is not considered advisable since it might perpetuate a form of civil war, or if such did not result, then later, enmities caused by the ROK Army action might result in serious repercussions against individuals in the ROK Army who acted against their own countrymen. I consider it preferable to use a majority of ROK troops augmented by UN troops under UNC command.[20]

It is noteworthy that General Clark did not hesitate to use the words "civil war." Although this term was frequently used by government analysts at the time, it was even more frequently ridiculed then and later by academics. The view of the Korean War as only a Moscow-directed conflict within the larger context of the Cold War undoubtedly had some merit, but it also obscured the relevance of other contributing factors. Recent studies have begun to recognize that internal forces in Korea itself helped to "cause" the Korean War.[21]

Both PRC (People's Republic of China) and Soviet policies carried the risk of open warfare with the United States, a strategy they considered necessary for three major reasons: (1) it would avoid a setback to the morale and steady structure of the Communist camp; (2) it would keep (or at least hinder) U.S. ground forces away from their borders; (3) the PRCs entrance would prolong a drain on U.S. economic and military resources and leave open the possiblity and terms of negotiations.

These possible causes for China's intervention are at least in part a mirror-image for the reason underlying the American involvement. U.S. government declarations notwithstanding, Washington—both publicly and privately—perceived that a failure to intervene would in fact have weakened the policy of containment. It would have cast doubt on the credibility of a stable U.S. world-alliance structure. A global war was foreseen and provisions made for it. Korea, however, was perceived as the only conflict where the United States could demonstrate its firmness without risking total war, and where it could confirm that "world Communist expansion" could be checked.

The U.S. entrance taught China an abiding lesson about its "friendship" with the Soviet Union. Despite its revolutionary rhetoric, the USSR did not dispatch armies to fight alongside China's in Korea. The supplies which China received were likewise meager. As U.S. forces approached China (and the Soviet Union's border as well), Soviet arms support diminished steadily. Indeed, when two U.S planes fired upon a Soviet airdrome in early October 1950 (after the U.S. successful Inchon landing which caused the rapid North Korean retreat north), the USSR did not react by retaliating against North Korea's enemy.[22] If the United States perceived Korea as a tactic to divert attention from Europe, it is also plausible to speculate that the Soviet Union might have suspected the reverse: the United States was using Korea to distract Soviet military attention from Europe.

Both Moscow and Washington generally viewed the Korean War as an ideological and geographical test, or a drain, but not as a sole focus. They saw the war as a billiard ball in the international system. China, Taiwan, and both Koreas, however, saw it as a struggle for survival. Socialist theorists assume, underline, and sometimes overplay contradictions within the capitalist-imperialist world. But it is as possible and profitable to analyze differences between the socialist group as well. Differing needs and objectives existed in the Communist camp during the Korean War. For example, the larger state did not satisfy the material needs of the weaker. The United States, in turn, formed a view of a monolithic opponent—and willed this perspective to later Vietnam observers. Their perception prevented American policymakers from identifying, encouraging, and capitalizing on such differences.

It must be noted, however, that some analysts did not totally agree with the general assumption of an impending world war. In late June 1950, for example, the American Embassy in Moscow presented its assessment of a possible Soviet response to the North Korean invasion. Washington responded:

DEPT appreciates importance considerations set forth EMBTEL 1734, June 26, and recognizes disadvantages of involving SOV prestige more directly in Korean aggression. Our proposed approach was predicated on belief, so ably set forth in EMBTEL 1726, June 25, the SOVS not now prepared risk possibility full-scale war with West and hence will not permit themselves to become directly involved in Korean hostilities. We WLD expect them for this and other reasons, assuming that UN and U.S. reaction to Korean attack is firm as it has been, to reply to our approach by denying their responsibility for action of QTE North Korean GOVT UNQTE hence to refuse to permit themselves to be directly involved.

Our reasons for considering an approach along these lines desireable at this time were FOL: We decline to view that, as long as SOVS can utilize their satellites or stooges to take aggressive action without serious danger of becoming involved themselves, they will be likely to employ this device with increasing boldness. If, on the other hand, it can be made clear to them that aggressive action by satellites risks involving their prestige directly, they may, in light considerations set forth EMBTEL 1726, be more cautious in pushing such tactical extremes.[23]

Throughout the war, emphasis was placed upon fighting Communism, rather than on nationalism. This simplistic dismissal of the local factors tended to obscure the war's origins and how it was to be fought. For example, when United Nations forces were being driven south by China in November 1950, President Truman announced that the United States would take whatever steps were necessary to stop the aggression. Asked if this would mean the use of the atomic weapon, President Truman's reply indicated that it would include every weapon that the United States had. This left an erroneous impression because the Joint Chiefs of Staff had already recommended against the use of the nuclear bomb.

Such public statements prompted the United Kingdom Labor Prime Minister Clement Atlee to travel immediately to Washington to question the purpose and future of the war. The Prime Minister was worried about a future war in Europe and wished to counsel the President against using the atomic bomb in a conflict in Asia which would deflect military concern from Europe. Atlee suggested that underneath a "Communist you can find a nationalist." The President replied that China was a:

satellite of Russia and will continue to be satellites as long as the present Peiping regime is in power. He [the President] thought they were complete satellites. The only way to meet communism is to eliminate it. After Korea, it would be Indochina, then Hong Kong, then Malaysia... He does not want to go to war with China or anyone else, but the situation looks very dark to him.[24]

It is noteworthy that, during this December 1950 conference, U.K. and U.S. leaders voiced the same worry about the so-called fall of dominoes. President Truman's public remarks concerning his fear of the spread of Communism—which necessitated the U.S. containment policy—have been widely cited. But it should also be emphasized that Prime

Minister Atlee (who perceived "creeping communism") reinforced the President's determination to continue American defense of the free world. The President's comment was:

> We want to keep Japan and the Philippines, Indonesia, India and Pakistan and all the other Asian powers. We need to hold the line in the UN. He [the President] agreed strongly concerning the European question. The best line was to keep marching together: There was, however, a danger of a deteriorating situation in the East. He did not know enough of Japanese feeling to comment upon that. He thought, however, that the Japanese might think America's real objection to meeting with the Chinese was that China was an Asiatic power and that we were not willing to treat them as equal.[25]

The perspective that China lacked autonomy assisted the U.S. decision not to risk a war with China. The fear of the Soviet Union's armed strength served as a check on American thoughts of risking another approach to China (and Soviet) borders. China's armies had repelled successfully the American approach to its rim in November 1950. Washington was convinced by this active deterrence not to try again. Beyond this lesson, however, was the fear of Soviet military intervention. The Joint Chiefs of Staff were acutely aware of the possibility of a Soviet presence and deliberated about its responses. For example, in July 1951, a Joint Chiefs of Staff message read:

> It is agreed in principle that, in event of Soviet attack against FECOM, United States and other UN forces will be withdrawn from Korea and you should plan accordingly. Situation may require some immediate movements of your forces by air.[26]

It therefore appears that the Soviet Union would have been able to repel American forces by a concerted—although probably limited—demonstration of determined capabilities.

General Matthew Ridgway on September 19, 1951 cabled a warning from Tokyo that reinforced the worry about an unpredictable Soviet Union:

> Every authoritative U.S. Government intelligence estimate I have seen contains substantially the statement that "Soviet Armed Forces are in an advanced state of preparation for war." Current stability of their Far Eastern Forces, ground, sea and air, is such that, if exercised the adoption of a strategic defense by my forces would be the only logical and feasible

course of action in the initial stages of the war. For the same reason my present primary mission would remain the most logical and feasible primary mission.[27]

The American reaction to the Korean War has been analyzed at great length in many works. But at least three questions concerning the war's first half-year should be raised anew: (1) in what type of war was the United States involved; (2) how unique were the actions of General MacArthur; (3) who was the enemy, the Soviets, the Chinese, the North Koreans?

Was the Korean conflict a "civil war" fought between two sections of one nation . . . albeit with external help and guidance? Professor Okonogi Masao persuasively points out that 1948 witnessed the formation of *two* governments, each of which perceived itself as the only legitimate regime of the peninsula. This he calls the "maturing conditions of civil war . . . Nevertheless, although conditions for an outbreak of war had matured within Korea, the war, when it came, did not occur independently of the intentions of the great powers," Professor Okonogi continues:

> The most remarkable aspect of the entire political process leading up to the outbreak of the Korean War is that domestic Korean forces were always more inclined toward armed unification than were external forces. Therefore, the role of the international environment throughout was to deter rather than foment war, with the exception of the period just before the war's outbreak.[28]

This observation also should encourage an objective-as-possible look at available material (i.e., what Professor Okonogi calls the "domestic roots" of both halves) concerning South Korea's desire to march north. The Communist world did refer to the Korean conflict as a "civil war," which automatically prompted Washington to dismiss the categorization as Communist propaganda. Interestingly, as noted, the American Joint Chiefs of Staff also referred to the possibility of a civil war within South Korea. (In this context, it must be remembered that both North and South Korea's borders were drawn without consultation with external powers.) During this war the opponent was pictured as the Soviet Union. For example, on January 11, 1951 the chairman of the National Security Resources Board portrayed the fearsome threat posed to U.S. national survival:

> The United States and its allies of the free world are fighting a war for survival against the aggression of Soviet Russia.

The United States and its allies are losing the war, on both the political and military fronts.

How the free nations have allowed themselves to be brought within sight of defeat by the Soviets is a complex and debatable history. If there is a single reason why we are not losing, however, it is because the free nations of the world have allowed Soviet Russia to put them on the defensive everywhere.

On the military fronts in Korea and Southeast Asia the free nations are on the defensive because they are fighting the war in the Far East on a basis which most favors the Soviets and least favors the free nations. We are attempting to match men for men and tanks for tanks, instead of fighting most effectively with those elements of military supremacy we now have in the Far East—air power and naval power.

On the political front the free nations are on the defensive everywhere. This is primarily because during an era in which the naked power of aggression heeds only naked power, the free nations do not in political discussion bring up their prime power advantage, the atomic bomb and the capacity to deliver it. That advantage now gives possible superiority of power to the free world, but it is a power which every week from here on will steadily decline.

The free nations cannot hope to survive this war against Soviet aggression if it is continued on the basis of defensive containment.

The hour is late. The odds may be stacked against the free nations; but it is still possible to take the offensive in this fight for survival.[29]

Usually, it has been emphasized in the narratives of the United States engagement in Korea, particularly after China entered, that one military leader—General Douglas MacArthur—actively advocated retaliation against China's entrance. During this intensely felt period of fear, it is more accurate, however, to state that there were also others, both within the military and the general public, who wished to strike directly at China.

Before the dismissal of General MacArthur, suggestons dispatched to the U.S. forces might have motivated China's reaction on the scale of November 1950. In late February 1951, the Joint Chiefs of Staff "with the approval of the President," directed that:

In the event of Chinese Communist air or sea attack against the United States forces outside Korea, the principle of immediate retaliation against targets on Chinese mainland is approved. However, subject to right of immediate self-defense, you will inform us concerning the Chinese Communist attack and receive approval of your proposed retaliatory action prior to attacking targets on Chinese mainland.

It is not comtemplated that retaliation would follow in case of Chinese Communist attacks upon United States or Chinese Nationalist reconnaissance aircraft flying over or in immediate vicinity of Chinese territorial waters.[30]

Although American forces had enjoyed a military victory after Inchon landing in September 1950, what had appeared to be an inevitable triumph was soon followed by a series of defeats. By the winter of 1950-1951, they were eagerly searching for a magic way to recapture the prize of victory. It is understandable that General MacArthur, a World War II hero and the respected (both by the United States and much of Japan) leader of the American occupation of Japan, would rebel against a defeat in Korea. We can interpret how much he resented and resisted the order from Washington that told him not to attempt another approach near China's border.

It should be noted, however, that General MacArthur was not the rigid "hawk" usually pictured. He usually requested Joint Chiefs of Staff approval for his actions in situations that were often rapidly changing. An example of this is briefly described in a Joint Chiefs of Staff account:

The Joint Chiefs of Staff had requested the opinion of CINCFE as to the desirability of destroying by air the power installation on the Korean side of the Yalu River in the eventuality of a Chinese attack across the 38th parallel. CINCFE stated in reply that the preservation or the destruction of these power installations was predominantly a political rather than a military matter and that he had been strictly enjoined to abstain from their destruction. In view of public announcements on the matter he recommended against reversal of that decision which transcended the immediate tactical campaign in Korea.[31]

On the one hand Washington allowed U.S. and Nationalist air flights provocative to China; on the other, it told General MacArthur that he could not "march north." It is interesting and ironic to note that, shortly after General MacArthur's dismissal, a memorandum formulated by the Joint Chiefs of Staff for the Secretary of Defense on July 13, 1951 appeared to repeat most of MacArthur's themes. The Joint Chiefs were concerned that the armistice negotiations might fail, and they considered it necessary to increase military pressure on the enemy. The memorandum outlined the following provisions:

a. Continue preparations to place the Nation in the best possible position of readiness for general war on relatively short notice;

b. Direct the Commander in Chief, United Nations Command (CINUNC) to increase immediately the scale of military operations in the Korean campaign to the maximum consistent with the capabilities and security of the forces now available;

c. Remove all restrictions concerning advances into North Korea, at least to the neck of the North Korean peninsula;

d. Remove all restrictions against attacks in North Korea, including restrictions against attacks on Rashin, the Yalu River dams, and the power installations on the Korean bank of the Yalu River;

e. Extend the area for pursuit and the air-to-air action in air engagements initiated over Korea by disregarding the border between Korea and Manchuria (loosely termed "hot pursuit"), such pursuit to include destruction of enemy planes after landing, and neutralization of opposing antiaircraft fire.[32]

It should also be noted that strategy discussions between the Joint Chiefs of Staff and the political administration also were divided. For example, on November 21, 1950, Secretary of State Dean Acheson met in the Pentagon with Admiral Sherman and Air Force General Vandenberg. After an apparently free exchange of opinions, Secretary Acheson left. When he had gone, Sherman and Vandenberg (generally perceived as a moderate) agreed that the Chinese Communists must either quit or the United States would have to hit Manchuria. These were the military-political tensions in which General MacArthur was caught. It can be argued that he sought to strike a balance between priorities that to him, half-a-globe distant, appeared to be erratic.

In June 1953, while it appeared that the armistice was about to be signed, President Rhee continued his vigorous appeal for a success in the war. His case was that his country had been invaded without warning by the Communists and that the United States had promised to defend Korea. In fact, during the euphoric period after the Inchon success, the United States had firmly spoken of liberating all of the Korean peninsula. Now, in the spring and early summer of 1953, President Rhee complained bitterly about America's desertion of its promises of solidarity.

On May 25, 1953, with the armistice agreement apparently about to be signed, Washington sought to reassure President Rhee by offering promises of continued military assistance if hostilities broke out again. Large amounts of economic and military aid were also pledged. These supports were not sufficient to mollify President Rhee. He did, however, moderate the strident call of refusing to abide by any armistice settlement. This change in public pronouncements began to convince General Mark Clark that the South Korean President would cooperate with American negotiation plans.

General Clark cabled Washington:

> In summary, while Rhee shows determination to gain his objectives, and manifests unconcealed disdain for what he chooses to term appeasement, modulation of tone of his message and circumspection with which he personally has acted alleviate some of apprehension as to emotional and reckless acts. Rhee's message although premised falsely on proposition that UN started to settle the Korean problem by mil means is relatively more favorable than we had feared.[33]

On June 18, 1953, however, the public posturing of calm was shattered when 25,000 allegedly non-Communist prisoners of war were unilaterally freed by Rhee without U.S. consultation. This singular move almost wrecked the negotiations because the Communist side believed that Rhee's action had the sanction of his powerful ally. Washington was forced to pay in order to restrain Rhee from similar actions. A payment of $200 milion in economic assistance was shortly given, along with an agreement to help enlarge the South Korean army.

Washington had undervalued the nationalist fervor that prompted the South Koreans to take at least one step contrary to the wishes of their powerful ally; a move that was taken despite the overwhelming U.S. resident forces. The Communist side assumed that the United States was at least aware of what was to happen. With its strength, this Communist argument continued, the United States must be held responsible for an act which almost prolonged the war. The West held the converse view of this logic: North Korea could only have invaded the South with the active support and direction of the Soviet Union. These two hypotheses are mirror-images which reflect a perspective that the war was engineered by either the Soviet Union or the United States. The missing and vital factor in either analysis is nationalism: the leaders of both North and South Korea were nationalists although they did have strong external ties.

The American options in response to the Korean Civil War could in general have followed one of four main possibilities. The first would have been the non-involvement of U.S. military forces and finances. This would have entailed a return to the isolation existing prior to World Wars I and II. This goal was difficult to pursue after the World Wars because there was a perceived active global threat directed by the Soviet Union, combined with dramatic advances in military technology. The single such advance in World War I had been the airplane; in World War II it was the atomic bomb. These factors made it difficult for the United States to withdraw from world politics.

The second option would have been to threaten the Soviet Union with the use of nuclear weapons, which in turn might have brought pressure to withdraw support from their satellite. The danger would have meant opening the Pandora's Box of risking a two-front war: Europe as well as Asia. This direct confrontation might have led to the feared global war.

The third option would have meant giving further covert military assistance to the Syngman Rhee regime.

The final option, and the one chosen, was to demonstrate firmly the U.S. refusal to accept the destruction of an anti-Communist ally. This had far-reaching implications for U.S. foreign policy; it encouraged the support of many unpopular dictators and the refusal to begin open relations with Communist states.

The war did not result in a conclusive outcome of a military victory for either side. Each side misperceived both the interests and capabilities of the other, and the outcome, if anything, was a costly and convoluted stalemate. For the North Koreans, whose aim was to reunify the peninsula under Communist rule, the confrontation could hardly be called a success. The human and material costs of the war had been devastating. The only bright spot was that the P'yongyang regime consolidated a *de jure* recognition of the status quo which, in fact, had existed since 1945. For the USSR, besides the cost in material and wounded pride, the war provided an acid test which severely strained Soviet "fraternal relations" with would-be allies. The People's Republic of China not only suffered the same type of losses as did its two partners, but it also realized that it could not count on the complete support of the Soviet Union to "push the imperialists into the sea." On the positive side, it could be argued that the war prevented a hypothetical U.S. and Nationalist invasion of Mainland China from ever becoming a reality. The benefit then, for each Communist state, was self-preservation.

The record of the South Korea-United States alliance was not any better. The Republic of Korea survived, but at a monumental expense. However, that regime did not fulfill the domestic criteria upon which Washington had proclaimed it was depending. On the contrary, it demonstrated a fundamental tenet of American foreign policy that has endured: Washington's willingness to support any regime, no matter how repressive and anti-democratic, providing it help to maintain international stability and the encouragement of free enterprise. The massive American involvement in Korea, certainly not a military success, had far-reaching negative political implications. It did not prevent the continuation of a Communist regime in Korea, nor did it prevent the emergence of similar states in Southeast Asia. Most importantly, it failed to provide a clear warning against American intervention in analogous situations. The experiences of the Korean War have set the parameters of American strategic response to limited wars (in the Third World referred to as wars of national liberation). It is not surprising, therefore, in general terms, to find a similar response to the Indochina Crisis. One could even fear the presence of this pattern of response in such regions as Iran and Southern Africa in the not-so-distant future. (These words were written in early 1979, well before the seizure of the U.S. Embassy in Tehran.)

NOTES

1. Roger Dingman, "American Planning for War in East Asia," Paper prepared for the Conference on American Strategy in East Asia, Harvard University, 1978, p. 12.
2. Ibid. See also Thomas H. Etzold, "The Far East in American Strategy, 1948-1951," Paper prepared for the Conference on American Strategy in East Asia, Harvard University, 1978, p. 9.
3. The Central Intelligence Agency reported April 19, 1950 on " ... the forthcoming [successful] invasion of Taiwan, which they are expected to launch in the second half of 1950," *DDRS* (Declassified Documents Reference System) (Arlington, Va.: Carrollton Press, 1975), p. 283D.
4. Ibid., 75A.
5. Ibid., 10B.
6. Quoted by John Lewis Gaddis, "Korea in U.S. Politics," in Yonosuke Nagai and Akira Iriye, eds., *The Origins of the Cold War in Asia* (Tokyo: University of Tokyo Press, 1977), p. 287.
7. George F. Kennan, *Memoirs, 1925-1950* (Boston: Little, Brown, 1967), pp. 511-512.
8. The CIA advised on June 14, 1950 that "the USSR probably considers its membership in the world organization worth returning to and will resume its UN seat once communist representatives have replaced the Chinese Nationalists. In the long run, this later development appears unavoidable." *DDRS*, 1975: 284A.
9. For a brief history of the document and its relationship to the Korean War see Alexander L. George and Richard Smoke, *Deterrence in American Foreign Policy: Theory and Practice* (New York: Columbia University Press, 1974), pp. 154-155.
10. Thomas H. Etzold and John Lewis Gaddis, eds., *Containment: Documents on American Policy and Strategy, 1945-1950* (New York: Columbia University Press, 1978). For a comprehensive description of the defense budget before and during the Korean War, see Warner R. Schilling, "The Politics of National Defense: Fiscal 1950" in Warner R. Schilling, Paul Y. Hammond, and Glenn H. Snyder, *Strategy, Politics and Defense Budgets* (New York: Columbia University Press, 1962), pp. 1-266.

11. The document is reprinted in "NSC-68: The Strategic Reassessment of 1950," in Etzold and Gaddis, *Containment*, pp. 383-385, 440-442.
12. *DDRS*, 1975, p. 10B, 1B.
13. *DDRS*, 1977, p. 283E.
14. Robert M. Slusser, "Soviet Far Eastern Policy, 1945-1950: Stalin's Goals in Korea," in Nagai and Iriye, *Origins of the Cold War in Asia*, pp. 141-142.
15. *Declassified Documents Quarterly Catalogue*, vol. 4, no. 4 (Arlington, Va.: Carrollton Press, January-December 1978), p. 154.
16. *DDRS*, 1975, p. 17B.
17. Ibid.
18. Bernard Brodie, *War and Politics* (Princeton, N.J.: Princeton University Press, 1973), p. 105.
19. *DDRS*, 1975, p. 160A.
20. Ibid., p. 161C. This practice was followed in later wars.
21. Okonogi Masao, "The Domestic Roots of the Korean War," p. 311.
22. Robert R. Simmons, *The Strained Alliance: Peking, P'yongyang, Moscow and the Politics of the Korean Civil War* (New York: The Free Press, 1975), p. 177-180.
23. *DDRS*, 1975, p. 162D.
24. *DDRS*, 1977, p. 131D.
25. *DDRS*, 1975, pp. 28F-30B.
26. Ibid., p. 17C.
27. Ibid., p. 160B.
28. Masao, "The Domestic Roots of the Korean War," p. 311.
29. *DDRS*, 1978, p. 63B.
30. *DDRS*, 1975, p. 17B.
31. Ibid., p. 17A. General MacArthur's military planning and warnings echoed in May 1977 by U.S. Army General John Singlaub. Speaking from his position as Chief of Staff in South Korea, he warned that "if we withdraw our ground forces on the schedule suggested [four to five years], it will lead to war." Unlike the General MacArthur precedent, however (when that General was allowed to speak this way for a longer period during changing situations), General Singlaub was rapidly replaced. Another "lesson" learned from the U.S.-Korean experience was to reenforce the policy that the American military should not—at least publicly—deal with political decisionmaking.
32. Ibid., p. A.
33. Ibid., p. 165A.

Chapter 16

The H-Bomb Decisions:
Were They Inevitable?

Barton J. Bernstein

On January 31, 1950, after weeks of public speculation and military and congressional pressure, President Harry S. Truman announced that America would seek to build an H-bomb. Five weeks later, on March 10, after additional pressure from the Department of Defense and the Joint Chiefs of Staff, he privately ordered the Atomic Energy Commission to expand facilities in preparation for the production of the H-bomb.

Ever since these momentous decisions, memoirists and analysts[1] have disputed why Truman made these commitments and whether they were correct? Did he miss an opportunity to achieve international control of atomic energy and end the nuclear arms race, or at least to renounce American development of the H-bomb and perhaps secure forbearance from the Soviet Union? Why did he choose to accelerate the H-bomb project? Was he responding to bureaucratic pressures, a technological-

Earlier versions of this paper were presented in 1976-1978 to various seminars at Stanford University—the Values, Technology, Society Forum; the Arms Control Program, the History Department colloquium, and the Uses of Knowledge seminar—in 1979 to a Dickinson College faculty seminar, and in 1980 to a session of the organization of American Historians. I am grateful to the many members of these groups who provided criticism.

scientific imperative, congressional and domestic political pressure, his sense of international needs, or some conjunction of these pressures? Did crusading scientists, a demanding military, and their congressional supporters force him to act? Put differently, if such ardent proponents as nuclear physicists Edward Teller and Ernest O. Lawrence and AEC Commissioner Lewis Strauss had not existed, or had lacked powerful allies in Washington, would Truman have chosen differently?

I THE SOVIET BOMB AND AMERICAN RESPONSES

On September 3, 1949, an American plane over the North Pacific picked up the first tell-tale evidence that the Soviets had conducted their first atomic explosion. After about two weeks of analysis, leading American scientists concluded that the Soviets had exploded their first A-bomb.[2] Despite the scientific estimates in 1945 that the Soviets would achieve this breakthrough in 1949 or 1950, most had come to believe that the first bomb would not be developed until 1952 or later.

For policymakers in Washington, there was a sense of dismay (that the American nuclear monopoly was ended), shock (that it had happened so soon), and anxiety (that it was another Communist triumph after the "loss" of China). "This means that we are in a straight race with the Russians," concluded Under Secretary of State James Webb.[3] "The Soviet bomb changed everything," Secretary of State Dean Acheson later stated.[4] If the American nuclear monopoly had helped deter Soviet aggression in Europe, as some believed, would the Soviet bomb free the Soviets to push westward in future years?[5] At a minimum, there seemed reason for new uncertainty and additional anxiety.

Privately Truman contended that the Soviets had not created an A-bomb and his announcement on September 23, 1949, mentioned an atomic explosion (not a bomb). He decided to release the news because he believed he had no choice, for the news would soon leak out and might then create a panic.[6] The administration's carefully devised strategy was to issue calm public announcements emphasizing that the expected had occurred and that America was not imperiled.[7]

The administration made no immediate effort to seize upon the event to justify a larger military budget. However, the Soviet bomb did compel a reconsideration of American atomic energy policy and created pressures within and on the administration to expand nuclear facilities and production. Senator Brien McMahon, Democratic chairman of the Joint Committee on Atomic Energy, renewed his call for a larger atomic energy program. It was an expansion that he had been urging since mid-summer and one that a special National Security Council committee, probably spurred by the bomb, soon recommended to the President.[8] Before the discovery of the Soviet test, the Department of Defense had proposed a large expansion of the atomic program and some of the AEC commissioners were dubious. The Soviet bomb quickly dissolved their reluctance, and on October 10 the special NSC committee recommended a supplementary appropriation of $300 million.[9]

Truman was briefly reluctant to ask Congress for this supplement because he did not want to appear to be anxiously responding to this new Soviet challenge.[10] In fact, according to AEC commissioner Gordon Dean, Senator McMahon's former law partner, Truman was "mad because McMahon gave out news on the expanded program. [Truman] did not want the Russians to think we were afraid of them."[11]

In late September, when the AEC's General Advisory Committee (GAC), composed of nine prominent scientists, met, there was little impulse to act in response to the Soviet bomb. Isador I. Rabi, the Nobel physicist, wanted to advise a stepped-up program,[12] but other members, apparently led by J. Robert Oppenheimer, the GAC chairman, counseled delay and reflection. Summarizing the GAC's conclusions, Oppenheimer reported, "We felt quite strongly that the real impact of the news of Operation Joe [the Soviet bomb] lay not in the fact itself but in the response of public opinion and public policy to the fact. For this reason and because we ourselves doubted our wisdom in foreseeing this response, we wanted to postpone making any recommendations. . . . " In short, there was no need for speed, maybe even no strategic need to expand the program. The GAC's next scheduled meeting was early December, but Oppenheimer stressed, "we are . . . on call should [the AEC want our advice]."[13]

Admiral Lewis Strauss, a financier and conservative Republican on the AEC, was deeply troubled by the Soviet breakthrough and concluded that prompt, dramatic action was necessary: America should move to a "crash" effort—modeled on the wartime Manhattan Project—to build the H-bomb.[14] Conceived in 1942 and largely postponed during World War II in favor of the A-bomb (which was necessary to create the high temperature to ignite a fusion reaction), the H-bomb had received little attention in the postwar years. Shortages of skilled personnel and resources, emphasis on improving fission weapons, and doubts about feasibility all subtly coalesced to slow the project. Up to late 1949, the AEC and the GAC had unanimously endorsed work on the H-bomb, but the project had never received priority. Its most ardent supporter, Edward Teller, despairing of pushing the government into a vigorous quest for the Super, as it was called, had returned to university research and devoted only part of his time to weapons work.[15]

There was an immediate need, Strauss informed his fellow commissioners on October 5, 1949, to do more than just increase production of fissionable materials in order to "maintain our lead." The time had now come, he declared, "for a quantum jump in our planning . . . an intensive effort to get ahead with the super."[16] His message was that America needed this powerful weapon—unlimited in theory and easily available in magnitudes equivalent to millions of tons of TNT—if it could be created.

Strauss did not expect to persuade most of his fellow commissioners to push for the Super. He found commissioners Sumner Pike and Gordon Dean were open minded, but not convinced, about it, and Strauss had reason to expect that Henry D. Smyth, the only physicist in the group, and David Lilienthal, the chairman, would reject his proposal. Though it would be very difficult for a minority of one on the Commission to triumph and change national policy, Strauss knew that he had allies elsewhere: Teller, maybe Lawrence and the Berkeley group, and some scientists at Los Alamos; and McMahon and his associates on the committee, who were scratching around for ways to add to America's nuclear strength, had recently flirted with the Super. Strauss also deftly campaigned for the Super with Admiral Sidney Souers, an acquaintance from the navy during World War II who was now secretary of the NSC. Strauss' strategy presumably was to alert the President of the possibility, to plump for it through Souers, who had the President's ear, and to push the program past a recalcitrant AEC. Strauss soon learned from Souers that the President had not known about the H-bomb but, in the words of the official AEC history, "Truman wanted Strauss to force the issue up to the White House and to do it quickly."[17]

II OPPOSITION TO THE H-BOMB

In mid-October 1949, the Atomic Energy Commission, already considering further expansion,[18] asked its General Advisory Committee to review the entire AEC program. What "might well be curtailed or stopped?" it asked. Should there be more expansion and accelerated production of atomic bombs? Or possibly—either instead or in addition—speeded development of the Super? "Is it clear that the United States would use it . . . ? What would be its military value if it was used? Would it be worth 2, 5, 50 [A-bombs]? What would be the cost of the 'super' in terms of scientific effort, production facilities, dollars, and time? Since the principal alternative . . . appears to be improvements in size, weight, and manageability of present types of weapons [how] should these possibilities be evaluated in relation to the 'super'?"[18] Such questions reached far beyond a request for scientific advice, for the AEC was requesting a military assessment and even suggesting an analysis of international diplomatic advantages.[19]

The campaigning of Teller, Ernest O. Lawrence, Luis Alvarez, and their Berkeley group helped spur discussion in Washington of the Super. Lawrence and Alvarez, visiting Washington in early October, pushed for a speeded-up Super project with Senator McMahon, who was enthusiastic; with some members of the AEC staff, who endorsed it; with some of the Joint Chiefs of Staff, who liked the proposal; and with the AEC commissioners.[20] Lilienthal, the AEC chairman, was appalled by their enthusiasm for such a powerful weapon. "Lawrence and Alvarez were 'drooling' over the H-bomb," Lilienthal complained in his diary. "Is this all we have to offer?" he lamented.[21]

Lilienthal, himself, was in anguish. When he took the position as AEC chairman, he had naively expected that he could devote most of his efforts to peaceful application of the atom. Instead, he found himself presiding over a weapons-making establishment, where the military needs were never clear, relations with the other commissioners were sometimes sour, and he was frequently embattled with congressmen because of his liberal past (Tennessee Valley Authority) and the AEC's slow ways. He desperately hoped for some path out of the nuclear arms race and regretted the growing reliance on nuclear weapons as a deterrent and guarantor of victory, but he could not devise a solution. He was a man in agony, torn between his hopes for peace and his obligation to improve nuclear weapons. "More and better bombs," he lamented in his diary. "Where this will lead . . . is difficult to see. We keep saying, 'We have no other course'; what we should say is 'We are not bright enough to see any other course.'"[22] Unable to carve a path out of the arms race, he did not want to add to the moral burden and world danger by pushing for the H-bomb. Its unlimited power, if it could be built, seemed to pose new moral and international issues and to etch in bold relief the gnawing ones that he could not solve or escape.[23]

Oppenheimer, a most complicated man, shared many of Lilienthal's doubts and fears. Former head of the wartime Los Alamos laboratory which had actually produced the A-bombs for Hiroshima and Nagasaki, Oppenheimer never escaped the sense of guilt for producing those bombs. He had told Truman that he felt he had blood on his hands.[24] He had spoken publicly of the "physicists knowing sin."[25] Yet, typical of his ambivalence, he had never clearly said that the bombing of Hiroshima and Nagasaki was morally wrong or that he wished he had not helped the nation-state to deliver mass terror and kill more than 110,000 Japanese.[26] Now, confronted with the question of the H-bomb, a program that he and the GAC had long supported, he was compelled again to consider moral issues. Linked to more practical matters, these moral doubts helped shape his attitude toward the Super.

In a letter to James Conant ("Uncle Jim"), GAC member, president of Harvard, and a major architect of the Manhattan Project, Oppenheimer poured out his distress. Lawrence and Teller were, Oppenheimer derisively wrote, "two experienced promoters" exploiting fear and anxiety. He stressed that the Super was a "weapon of unknown design, cost, desirability, and military value." Unfortunately the McMahon committee, "having tried to find something tangible to chew on [since the Soviet bomb] has found its answer. We must have the 'super,' and we must have it fast." Though Oppenheimer was unsure whether the Super ("the miserable thing") "will work, [or] that it can be gotten to a target except by ox cart," it was not these technical problems that dominated his thought. He feared that emphasis on the Super as a solution would "further worsen ... the unbalance of our present war plans." He was resigned, he said, to the quest for the Super. "It would be folly to oppose the exploration of this weapon. We have always known it had to be done. ... " It was, he concluded, a distasteful matter—technically uncertain, militarily dubious, morally offensive, and certainly no answer to the Soviet bomb.[27]

Conant, also feeling guilty about Hiroshima and Nagasaki, firmly opposed the Super project. Like the others on the GAC, he had earlier endorsed the slow quest for the H-bomb, which, if it could be created, might have reached fruition in the late 1950s. But now, faced sharply with a plan for a greatly accelerated program, he too faced the moral and international political issues that the slower pursuit of this weapon had allowed him to slide past. His conclusion: Don't build it. "Over my dead body," he said, in a memorable phrase. "The real answer," Conant argued, was "to revamp our whole defense establishment," expand conscription, and re-arm Europe.[28]

The Conant position of firm opposition and the Oppenheimer statement of agonizing reluctance contrasted with the attitudes of Glenn Seaborg, a Berkeley chemist, who could not attend the GAC meeting of late October but sent Oppenheimer a letter sketching his position. Though reluctant to support the Super, Seaborg uneasily concluded: "I would have to hear some good arguments before I could take on sufficient courage to recommend not going toward such a program." He deplored having the nation put "a tremendous effort" into the Super but he did not see any alternative. His own thinking at the time was so unclear, at least as expressed in his letter, that he left unstated whether his doubts were moral or military, or whether he regretted accelerating the arms race, or whether all these themes troubled him.[29]

At the GAC meeting on the weekend of October 28-30, 1949, the eight members, often joined by the AEC commissioners, listened to George Kennan, who sketched relations with the Soviet Union and may have hinted at his belief that America should again seek international control of the atom; to Hans Bethe, a physicist who had decided not to work on the Super but confined himself to an analysis of the feasibility of the project;[30] and to General Omar Bradley, chairman of the Joint Chiefs, who said that the principal advantage of the Super would be "psychological."[31]

Lilienthal lamented that the analysis by the military was so flimsy: "It's quite evident that the full import of the Russians' success, and their prospect of a substantial stockpile in the next [few] years, hasn't yet sunk in...." Under the new conditions, with the Soviet Union possessing atomic bombs, what would America do if the Soviets attacked western Europe with conventional forces? Would the United States use atomic bombs? So far as Lilienthal could determine, the military answer was that this was "a close question—meaning, I guessed, that we wouldn't."[32]

After the Saturday afternoon session, Lilienthal summarized positions: "Conant flatly against it [the H-bomb]. Hartley Rowe, with him: 'We built one Frankenstein.' Obviously Oppenheimer inclined that way. [Oliver] Buckley sees no diff. in moral question [A-bombs as bad as H-bombs], but Conant disagreed—there are grades of morality. Rabi completely on other side. [Enrico] Fermi ... thinks one must explore it and do it and that doesn't foreclose the question: should it be made use of? Rabi says decision to go ahead will be made; only question is who will be willing to join in it. I deny that there is anything inevitable in political decisions. Lewis [Strauss] says the decision won't be made by popular vote, but in Wash. Conant replies: but whether it will stick depends on how the country views the moral issue."[33]

Conant and Cyril Smith, another GAC member, wanted a public dialogue on the issues. Strauss seemed to oppose this position. At least some of the participants were clearly troubled that the nation was not being invited to discuss the issues and that citizens, including many scientists, were barred from the dialogue. The secrecy seemed unnecessary.[34]

On Sunday, the General Advisory Committee, with Oppenheimer doing much of the drafting, put together its conclusions: an increase in production facilities; greater emphasis on creation of tactical nuclear weapons; support for the "booster" (a fission-fusion weapon of up to about 300 kilotons); and opposition to a speeded-up project for the Super. All opposed pursuing it "with high priority" even though there was, in their estimation, "a better than even chance of producing the weapon within five years." All hoped that the government would not even pursue research to determine whether the technical problems could be solved and whether the weapon was feasible. Short of an actual test, they acknowledged, many of the basic technical-scientific solutions could not be evaluated, but they were denying the scientific-technological imperative: that scientists had a duty to learn whatever could be discovered. They were arguing that a higher morality (the danger of genocide) should block the pursuit of knowledge[35] For many who had been involved in the wartime A-bomb project and carried the guilt of Hiroshima and Nagasaki, this counsel represented a transformation of stated morality about the obligation of science and the scientist.[36]

"It is clear," they wrote, "that the use of this weapon would bring about the destruction of innumerable human lives; it is not a weapon which can be used exclusively for the destruction of material installations of military or semi-military purposes. Its use therefore carries much further than the atomic bomb itself the policy of exterminating civilian populations."[37] In theory, then, the H-bomb, to use Strauss' phrase, represented a "quantum jump" in the capacity to kill. Small H-bombs were possible, the GAC acknowledged, but they would serve no useful purpose since they would not be "an economical alternative" to fission weapons. Because of vagueness about design of the H-bomb and uncertainty about its power, the GAC concluded that a cost estimate was "clearly impossible." But if one used the criteria of damage area per dollar and likely restrictions on air carrier capacity, "it appears uncertain . . . whether the super will be cheaper or more expensive than the fission bomb."[38] The loose implication: The super was an economic gamble and might well siphon off scarce resources more wisely used for fission weapons.

The six-member majority (led by Oppenheimer and Conant) sought unconditional renunciation of the H-bomb, while the minority (Rabi and Fermi) sought conditional forbearance. For the majority, the weapon was strategically unnecessary (because the Soviet Union had few large cities and the United States had enough fission bombs) and immoral (because it was potentially genocidal). They believed it would be "a threat to the future of the human race." Moreover, American development of the weapon would injure the nation's moral position and presumably weaken America in the Cold War race for allies and international support. Even if the Soviets developed the H-bomb, the United States would still have enough A-bombs for adequate deterrence or, if that failed, retaliation. "In determining not to proceed to develop the Superbomb," they concluded, "we see a unique opportunity of *providing by example* some limitation on the totality of war and thus eliminating the fear and arousing the hopes of mankind."[39]

The minority (Rabi and Fermi) offered a more sharply worded statement of moral objections but ended by proposing conditional forbearance: try to develop the bomb only if the Soviets will not pledge renunciation. Even if adequate control machinery were not established, Rabi and Fermi concluded, the pledge would probably be sufficient since a Soviet test could probably be detected and America could then jump back into the race.

The Rabi-Fermi argument implicitly undercut the majority conclusion (unilateral renunciation) by suggesting that under some conditions the H-bomb would be useful and necessary to the United States if the Soviets had it. Curiously, Rabi and Fermi never spelled out their thinking on this vital matter: Under what conditions? Would the bomb be strategically or psychologically valuable, or both? Nor, strangely, did the majority opinion draw forceful issue with this lurking set of assumptions in the Rabi-Fermi statement.[40]

The reports—taken individually or together—were defective. They were loosely written, failed to spell out critical implications, and did not make clear either their assumptions or the precise basis of their conclusions. For example, in the majority report was the argument of "no strategic necessity" for the Super sufficient to support their conclusion that the bomb should not be sought? Did the strategic argument then liberate them to stress morality? If so, what if new arguments emerged which undermined the position of "no strategic necessity"? Would the moral argument then have to yield? And what role did the concern about technical-scientific difficulties play? If the Super later looked "technically so sweet", in Oppenheimer's words, that it could not be resisted,[41] after Teller and Stansilaw Ulam proposed their configuration, why did that technical-scientific breakthrough cancel out the earlier moral or strategic arguments?

Beyond that, why did all deem the Super immoral but the "booster" (to about 300 kilotons) and tactical nuclear weapons moral? It was not simply a matter of size but of likely targeting. They were suggesting that the "booster" and tactical weapons would *probably* be used against military targets but that the H-bomb would *probably* be used against cities. The GAC was moving toward a counterforce (as opposed to a counter-city) and tactical nuclear—war strategy,[42] but the argument was murky.

There was also a major unaddressed question: Since bombing was quite inaccurate, was the greater power of the H-bomb—with its capacity to destroy a larger area—a useful or vital compensation for inaccuracy? The GAC also failed to spell out two themes that influenced the decisions of at least some members: the belief that America was well ahead in nuclear science and thus that American testing of an H-bomb might give the Soviets critical information to speed their own project;[43] and that renunciation of the Super might improve relations with the Soviets and even allow international control of atomic energy.

Such criticisms should not be understood as an indictment, only as a statement of shortcomings. Men who had long lived with the nuclear arms race and, in some cases, guilt about Hiroshima and Nagasaki were being asked to examine questions that reached near the core of their assumptions, careers, and beliefs. In a rushed weekend, even when aided by some earlier private discussions, they could not establish firm leverage on these troubling matters. They faced a formidable challenge—one they could not fully meet.

Oppenheimer later acknowledged that, given the importance of the issues, they might have spent more time on the reports. At the time, however, "most had commitments to be somewhere else and all were pressing to get done and leave. The result was a hasty job of writing. We raised our point that...still seems ambiguous." According to Oppenheimer, in the words of an interviewer, at the time of the meeting "they were rather pleased with themselves." They believed, as he put it, "they had reached a meeting of sensibilities rather than minds on the matter...." At the end, they congratulated him on successfully chairing such an important meeting and they congratulated one another.[44]

Oppenheimer, hoping to carry the GAC's campaign to the White House, decided first to discuss the report with Secretary of State Dean Acheson, with whom he had first become friendly when they labored together in 1946 on the Acheson-Lilienthal outline for international control of atomic energy. Acheson, as Oppenheimer found, "wished he could go along with [the GAC], but didn't think he would be able to...Acheson didn't see how the President could survive a policy of not making the H-bomb." Though Acheson claimed to be depressed about the matter, Oppenheimer doubted whether the Secretary of State was so deeply troubled—at least not as depressed as Oppenheimer. After that conversation, as Oppenheimer later explained, he concluded that the GAC position would fail.[45] The American quest for the Super was inevitable. Having failed with Acheson, Oppenheimer realized there was no value in seeking a meeting with the President, for Acheson probably knew Truman's inclinations and would obviously advise him to seek the bomb.

III SPLITS AMONG AEC COMMISSIONERS

The AEC members were hopelessly split. After nearly a week of discussions in early November, they recognized that they could not send Truman a unanimous recommendation on the Super.[46] The best they could do unanimously was to acknowledge the pressures on the White

House, plead for public discussion of the issues, offer an assessment of some technical matters, and suggest some questions to guide the President's inquiry.[47]

They understood, they stressed, that there were domestic pressures on him for an early decision: "Several scientists had become missionaries for the project"; others had opposing views; and Senator McMahon and his committee, after conferring with Teller and Lawrence, were pressing for the bomb. Why not, the AEC commissioners urged, invite a public dialogue on the issues, since open discussion is "inescapable, ... necessary, and ... desirable." Moreover, they noted, knowledge of the H-bomb was already so widespread that a decision by the President not to build the bomb could not be kept secret.[48]

All agreed that the Soviets could probably develop the bomb in about the same period the United States would need, that an American project, if continued, would have to be vigorous to meet the possible Soviet schedule, and that the Super "may not greatly increase our retaliatory capacity in terms of square miles of destruction by 1956, as compared with ... production [instead] of fission bombs."[49]

Among their basic questions: Could the American decison (for or against) the Super be used to break the Soviet-American stalemate on international control of atomic energy? Could the United States use the decision on the Super as a diplomatic or psychological weapon in the Cold War? "If war is inevitable or likely, is our position improved by the ... Super?"[50]

Commissioners Lilienthal, Smyth, and Pike opposed the quest for the bomb. Their arguments were similar to the GAC's. Lilienthal stressed that a decision for the bomb would set back the President's peace program, injure the nation's image abroad, "not increase our over-all strength," and promote the dangerous "misconception and illusion [that nuclear weapons are] the chief means of protecting ourselves and of following our national policy." The Super, he concluded, was not militarily necessary. It might add slightly to America's strategic power, but that small increment would not compensate for the serious psychological and political damage.[51] Smyth, generally agreeing, argued bluntly: "the military advantage of 'Supers' to us is doubtful even if the Russians do develop them ... our general standing in the world would be worsened by our development of 'Supers.'"[52] Belatedly submitting his individual statement, Pike retreated from opposing development to opposing a major effort, but his argument had the effect of objecting to any quest for the bomb: There would be few Soviet targets for a H-bomb, and, given the possibility that the bomb could not be developed and that the scarce materials and personnel would have been wasted in a fruitless effort, it was wiser to stay with A-bombs.[53]

Both Dean[54] and Strauss opposed unilateral renunciation of the H-bomb. They hoped that Truman might first privately seek Soviet agreement on banning nuclear weapons. If that approach failed or the military opposed it, then America needed the H-bomb.

Strauss presented a forceful argument for the bomb: " ... the United States must be as completely armed as any possible enemy." Probably already knowing of the espionage by Klaus Fuchs, who had access during World War II to thermonuclear research at Los Alamos, Strauss contended that the Soviets might be ahead in the race and near success. How, he argued, could the opponents of the H-bomb, including the GAC, support the "booster" and not the Super? Both were horrible, both greatly expanded the damage area, and both were necessary. The GAC was, in short, morally inconsistent. Moreover, the Soviets ("a government of atheists") was not likely to be dissuaded on moral grounds. Not forbearance, but strength, was essential to American well-being. Strauss' arguments, submitted to the President after a discussion with Senator McMahon,[55] buttressed the senator's own pleas for the H-bomb.[56]

IV TRUMAN APPOINTS ACHESON: THE KEY ADVISER

On November 18, 1949, the news broke that the administration was considering whether to build the H-bomb. Senator Edwin Johnson, in a luckless moment, had mentioned the secret issue a few weeks before. On November 18, the Washington *Post*[57] probably guided by some bureaucratic interests in the then-secret controversy, revealed Johnson's indiscretion.

With the press and the nation learning of the controversy, the earlier pressures on Truman were likely to increase as a public dialogue erupted. Upon his orders, all government officials were directed not to discuss the issues.[58] The President probably wanted to avoid a public dialogue, to reduce the pressures, and possibly to gain time for a carefully weighed decision. At minimum, his strategy seemed designed to allow him to maintain flexibility partly by controlling the flow of information to the public.

How should he go about deciding whether or not to pursue the Super—in a crash program, or at all? Clearly, he needed advice, for the issues were complicated and technical, involving military need, diplomatic power, and possible tradeoffs against fission weapons. If he relied upon men on his own staff, who might analyze the competing recommendations from the GAC, the AEC, the Joint Chiefs, and possibly others,

Truman could better retain the flexibility to accept or reject staff proposals. If he created a committee representing the bureaucratic interests, he would risk losing that flexibility.

Did Truman have his own inclinations? Certainly. He had actually given up hope for international control of atomic energy and, like Acheson, did not expect to gain improved relations with the Soviet Union.[59] Under pressures from McMahon and his committee, and with the Joint Chiefs wanting the H-bomb, Truman was being pushed by strong political and bureaucratic forces. Unless the Super proved to be too expensive (that was unlikely) or would seriously disrupt the A-bomb program and weaken America, he had no reason to resist it. It would meet needs at home and aid him abroad, creating what Acheson called "situations of strength."[60]

Yet, rather than making an abrupt decision, Truman hit upon the strategy of appointing a three-man advisory committee:[61] Lilienthal, who opposed the bomb; Secretary of Defense Louis Johnson, who was for it perhaps largely because his Joint Chiefs wanted it and it seemed cheap;[62] and Dean Acheson, the Secretary of State who, like Truman, was inclined toward it. This special NSC committee, by including key appointments from the AEC, Defense, and State, institutionalized the major bureaucratic interests to explore the issues and possibly to work out a compromise. The likely result—with one for the Super, one opposed to it, and one inclined toward it—was roughly predictable: the report would favor the bomb.

The key vote and the key person was Acheson, the member of the cabinet whom Truman most admired and most trusted, aside from Treasury Secretary John Snyder, a Missouri crony. Acheson loved and respected the President and served him loyally. Even when the secretary was embattled with the Congress and accused of "losing" China, the President was unwilling to sacrifice him to improve relations with the legislature. Mutual need and mutual loyalty bonded together the patrician Acheson and the midwestern Truman. They shared a common view of the world and especially of the Soviet Union. On those rare occasions when the two men differed and Truman decreed, the loyal secretary never even revealed to intimates at State that there had been disagreement. Acheson then made the President's policy his own. He was, in a sense, the President's "first minister." Acheson chafed only at Truman's fiscal parsimony which left the President reluctant to spend the larger sums on defense that Acheson, fearful that American power could not meet its obligations, believed were essential to win the Cold War.[63]

Acheson, though inclined toward the Super, would (as Truman knew) scrupulously investigate the issues. He had already informed the President that he had directed associates at the State Department to consider the impact of "Joe I" on foreign policy, the diplomatic advantages and liabilities of the Super, and the prospects for international control of atomic energy.[64] He had also discussed these problems with Oppenheimer and Lilienthal[65] to try to understand them and to stay in control of major policy issues. Acheson, an ambitious and arrogant man, was not reluctant to intrude into the bailiwick of arms policy. Whatever influenced diplomatic relations, he would have argued, was within his arena of obligations.

As a skilled attorney accustomed to probing all the arguments in preparation for his own case, Acheson carefully canvassed the opinions of the interested parties. Usually he probed their thinking and pushed them to analyze assumptions and conclusions without revealing his own. Lilienthal, for example, marveled at Acheson's ability and only belatedly recognized Acheson's own inclinations.[66] Oppenheimer understood earlier that the Secretary would favor the quest for the bomb.[67] Perhaps Oppenheimer recognized better than Lilienthal that Acheson did not share their hopes for improving relations with the Soviet Union by foregoing the H-bomb.

When Acheson spoke to Oppenheimer, whom he liked and admired, the secretary, according to a close associate, could not understand Oppenheimer's analysis. "You know, I listened as carefully as I knew how, but I don't understand what 'Oppie' was trying to say. How can you persuade a paranoid adversary to disarm 'by example'?"[68] For Acheson, the contrary analysis was controlling: Only a vigilant, better armed America could halt communist nibbling or massive aggression and ultimately triumph in the Cold War. Military strength, not efforts at negotiation, was essential to victory.[69]

Within the Department of State, Acheson sought competing advice from the two leading members of the Policy Planning Staff: George Kennan, the architect of containment and director of the staff; and Paul Nitze, the man scheduled to replace Kennan. Nitze, whose analysis of Soviet malevolence and American needs closely comported with Acheson's, argued that the nation must explore the feasibility of the Super: "it is essential that the U.S. not find itself in a position of technologicial inferiority in this field." His implication was that the new weapon represented valuable additional military power and important international prestige.[70]

In contrast, Kennan, originally author of the doctrine that fruitful negotiations with the Soviet Union were impossible, had reversed himself and hoped America would make a sincere effort at international control of atomic energy. Unfortunately, despite his anguish and effort, he could not formulate a plan likely to be acceptable to both the Soviet Union and the United States. The basic problem, he stressed, was that the administration did not want international control, for the atomic bomb was the keystone of America's military edifice. The administration relied on nuclear superiority to compensate for inferiority in land forces and believed that the bomb deterred Soviet aggression in Europe and promised a speeded victory if war erupted on the continent. The bomb, Kennan reluctantly acknowledged, would not be surrendered. The American offer of international control was a propaganda battle, not a sincere quest.[71]

By late December 1949 or early January 1950, it was becoming clear to Acheson that there was no compelling argument against seeking to determine the feasibility of the H-bomb and many for exploring the possibility. The bureaucratic and political pressures were great—especially from the Joint Chiefs and the McMahon committee. It would be "intolerable," the Joint Chiefs declared, if the Soviets developed the weapon and the United States lacked it. Determination of its feasibility was essential to planning for retaliation and in international affairs. The bomb could be an added deterrent to war, be used to create more flexibility in conducting war, be employed efficiently as a substitute for a greater number of A-bombs, and might well be a more efficient use of scarce materials. Such arguments, the Joint Chiefs concluded, "decisively outweigh the possible social, psychological, and moral objections. . . . "[72] Offering similar arguments, McMahon and presumably the Joint Committee were also pushing for the Super.[73]

Acheson, already under attack for "losing" China, did not want to face a domestic political battle on why he and Truman were leaving America strategically weak. Nor did he have powerful allies who might have assisted him if he had wished to oppose the H-bomb. The scientific community was split, with the bulk of influential physicists against the weapon, but they did not constitute a major bureaucratic or political force. In a national debate, the prestige of Lawrence and his Berkeley group, as well as that of Teller, would have partially offset Oppenheimer, Conant, and Bethe. The AEC was almost divided down the middle and Lilienthal, long embattled with sections of Congress and about to retire, was not a strong political ally. Put bluntly, domestic political forces seemed to dictate pursuing the H-bomb.

As importantly, Acheson's sense of the nation's military and diplomatic needs also stressed the likely value of the Super. It would be militarily and politically unacceptable, as Nitze argued, for the Soviets to develop the weapon and the United States to be without it. America's prestige might be found wanting. Its military power might be suspect.

For Acheson there was no need to choose between domestic and international consideration since, in his analysis, they comfortably coalesced. He did not have to weigh them, to decide which was primary.

Only if these purposes and pressures had conflicted, if they had been rivals and not allies, would Acheson have faced a difficult choice. How would he have decided? Probably for international power.

What arguments might have deterred Acheson from seeking the H-bomb? Not morality. He may have been uneasy about the power of the weapon, but for him it was only an extension of the capacity of the A-bomb. It was not morally different.

Had he believed that the H-bomb might defeat his hope for a larger military budget, he might have been in conflict. But while there was a danger that the Super would reduce anxieties about Soviet military power, and thus erode support for a greatly enlarged military budget, Acheson was not prepared to oppose the Super to nurture those anxieties. That would have been unfair to Truman, sure to anger Congress, certain to create a major impediment to the larger military budget, and ultimately self-defeating. Acheson did want the Super for the power it offered.[74] And how could he oppose the weapon and push for a larger military budget without seeming bizarre? He would be turning down the prospect of great military power and yet arguing for spending more to gain other kinds of military power—tactical nuclear weapons, stronger conventional forces, and the capacity to stop communist aggression in the Third World. He wanted more military strength—conventional, tactical-nuclear, and the H-bomb—and support for each might help gain him the others. Opposition to the Super could, in turn, impair his chances for the others, especially for strengthened conventional forces.[75]

It would be unwarranted to conclude that Acheson was cynically going through a ritual of meetings and deliberations to reach a predetermined conclusion. Rather, as he investigated the issues and tested ideas, his own earlier inclinations were reinforced. Put simply, through dialogue and analysis he moved from inclination to policy. It was an honest effort. Yet, his conclusions were virtually inevitable, as Truman anticipated.

V THE DECISION FOR THE H-BOMB

The six-week period, from December 22, 1949 to January 31, 1950, was the period when policy was explicitly formulated. The special NSC committee (of Acheson, Lilienthal, and Johnson) met only twice: on December 22 to explore issues, and on January 31 to agree on final recommendations. At the first meeting, Lilienthal was still hopeful; by the last meeting, he knew that he had been defeated. Between the two meetings, Lilienthal watched the chances for the Super soar, as the Joint Chiefs and the Joint Committee put on pressure and as Acheson slowly unveiled his own position. Lilienthal continued to repect and admire Acheson, delighted by his capacity to probe and question, and concluded that the military and some crusading scientists, abetted by McMahon and his committee, were the chief enemies.

At the first meeting of the special NSC committee, Lilienthal found reason to praise Acheson's openness ("a fine bit of exposition by a master of the craft"); the secretary said they were conferring this time "not . . . to reach [a] decision, but to think together." General Bradley, explaining the thinking of the Chiefs, argued that the H-bomb might be a great deterrent. It might keep the peace and push the Soviets toward international control. Johnson stated that the Department of Defense would forego the quest for the Super only if the Soviets accepted the American plan for international control. Others meeting with the committee stressed the military advantages of the H-bomb.[76]

Lilienthal, unable to control himself, poured out his dissent. He "couldn't disagree more [with these military arguments; the] purpose and course of mankind [is] wrapped up in this; that's the trouble and has been, treating this as if gadgets can be dealt with without relation to men's objectives and philosophy." "It's now clear," he lamented in his diary, "that sponsors [of the H-bomb] are scientists and military establishment active and ardent."[77]

Acheson was trying hard to make men probe their assumptions, partly because that was his way and partly because he found himself in opposition to Oppenheimer and Lilienthal, whom he liked and respected, and in line with Johnson, whom he neither liked nor respected. He told Secretary Johnson: "Now, don't come into this meeting and say the Joint Chiefs say so and so, and that's our position. Then all the President has is what the staff says; he wants us to think this through ourselves. If he wanted staff's view he would have asked for it."[78]

Under Acheson's questions, Lilienthal started to see more clearly the contradiction between America's military policy and its support for international control. "If we keep saying we want the control policy when we don't," Acheson said, "we are perhaps fooling others, but we shouldn't commit a fraud on ourselves."[79] For Lilienthal, the implication seemed clear: dramatically shift the military policy. For Acheson the implication was somewhat different: recognize the centrality of atomic weapons, and also strengthen the conventional arsenal. Acheson and Lilienthal, though inspired by different purposes, wanted a reassessment of military policy.[80]

By January 19, Acheson knew that the President was close to a decision and wanted to approve the quest for the Super. A recent report from the Joint Chiefs had confirmed Truman's thinking, and it was in line with Acheson's own analysis. Acheson informed an associate, "I had about reached the position we should advise the President to go ahead and find out about the feasibility [of the H-bomb]. But that we should be quite honest and say that in advising this action, we are going quite a long way to committing ourselves to continue down that road." The decision to produce the bomb would almost ineluctably follow if it proved feasible. What might look like a minimal decision was, as Acheson and others knew, far-reaching.[81]

Under Acheson's direction, associates in the State Department prepared his position on the Super: efforts could and should be "accelerated" (not a "crash" venture) without handicapping other programs. Sole possession of the bomb by the Soviets "would cause severe damage not only to our military posture but also to our foreign policy position." The Soviets would probably seek the weapons regardless of the American decision, and the Soviets would not accept the American plan for international control of atomic energy. By this analysis, America was not accelerating the arms race but simply acting from necessity to stay ahead of the malevolent and intransigent Soviets.[82]

Acheson sent the draft to Johnson and Lilienthal, and met with the AEC chairman on January 26 to explain his thinking. The secretary explained that the President should authorize the effort to determine feasibility (give the "green light"). It was the decision that Acheson had indicated to Oppenheimer on November 4, but this was the first time that the secretary had clearly expressed his judgment on the matter to anyone outside the State Department since the President had appointed the special committee. "I gathered," recalled Lilienthal, "that it was [Acheson's] view that without such an immediate go-ahead from the President the excited atmosphere ('row') in Congress and in the Government would make most unlikely any useful 'new look' at our military and political posture and policies."[83] To the end, even when facing defeat, Lilienthal preferred to see Acheson as being pushed by bureaucratic and political pressures and not himself as hankering for the weapon.

The three-member meeting on January 31 quickly dealt with the question of feasibility: the H-bomb project would be accelerated. The important details were left open, for the AEC and Department of Defense—according to the recommendation—would consult on scale and rate. There were two other issues. Should the committee, as Acheson and Lilienthal desired, propose a reexamination of American military policy and the role of nuclear weapons? And should they, as Acheson and

Lilienthal preferred, propose that the President defer any decision on production of the H-bomb (beyond what was required to determine feasibility) until this reexamination was completed? Secretary Johnson quickly acceded to the call for reexamination even though it could whittle away his authority, but he objected to the second. Apparently Acheson then quickly backed away from that proposal.[84] Why? He probably wanted to avoid an argument on what was, basically, a marginal matter, for Acheson recognized that there was no need for an explicit statement to protect the President's option to defer a decision on production, and also understood, as he had told an associate on January 19, an ultimate decision for production (if the bomb was feasible) would be hard to resist.[85]

The meeting was strained but never acrimonious, for it was a brief session (under two hours) designed basically to ratify decisions already reached. At the end, Secretary Johnson suggested that they go to the White House at 12:30 p.m. that day, using his appointment with the President to deliver their report. Johnson, in Lilienthal's words, said "the heat was on in the Congress and every hour counted in getting this matter disposed of."[86]

The ten-minute session at the White House was ritualistic. Acheson knew that Truman intended to go ahead with the H-bomb project, and the secretary had probably informed the President of the substance of the recommendation. Lilienthal and Johnson also expected Truman to endorse the recommendations.

According to Lilienthal, Truman "said that he had always believed that we should never use these weapons and that our whole purpose was peace; that he didn't believe we would ever use them but we had to go on and make them because of the way the Russians were behaving; we had no other course."[87]

Lilienthal, given a brief hearing, explained some of his reservations. He apparently did not discuss his belief that the H-bomb was immoral but instead dwelled upon his fear that the President's announcement would lull Americans into believing that nuclear weapons were the best defense and the H-bomb a possible panacea. In Lilienthal's view, Americans would not understand some of the military weaknesses—that nuclear weapons could not adequately defend Europe. Truman interrupted to explain that he could not delay a decision on seeking feasibility until there was a reexamination of military policy and power: "[T]here has been so much talk in Congress and everywhere and people are so excited he really hasn't any alternative but to go ahead and that was what he was going to do."[88]

Truman had made the politically popular and bureaucratically safe decision. The public, according to polls, overwhelmingly favored the effort to build the bomb. When the House learned of Truman's decision, it provoked some applause. Democratic leaders united in expressing their enthusiasm, "I think it was wise," said Senator Tom Connally, chairman of the Foreign Relations Committee, who summarized the sentiments.[89] For Truman, the dictates of politics, the expressed needs of the military, the wishes of Acheson, and the demands of international politics had comfortably coalesced. His own inclinations, his perceptions of needs, and his key adviser all pushed him in the same direction. For all these reasons, Truman's decision was virtually inevitable.

Had the project threatened to cost billions, rather than about another $100 million, he would have faced conflict. But, given the estimated costs, he could continue to aim to balance the budget and keep a tight lid on military spending while meeting what he deemed the needs of defense and his foreign policy. (" . . . we have got to have it if only for bargaining purposes with the Russians," he said.) "[T]here was actually no decision to make on the H-bomb," he told his staff. In a sense, he explained, the decision had been made in the autumn when he decided to expand the AEC budget. The action of January 31 followed comfortably from that earlier budgetary decision.[90]

VI MISSED OPPORTUNITIES

Robert Bacher, a prominent physicist, complained to Oppenheimer that it seemed to him the President could hardly have decided otherwise, given the background of public opinion. "The amount of speculation and real information on the subject as a whole is most discouraging, and this seems to preclude any sensible discussion until this situation is corrected," Bacher said.[91] Few Congressmen noted that secrecy had barred a public dialogue. Senator Arthur Watkins, a Utah Republican, was virtually alone in Congress in declaring that "the whole country ought to be consulted about a decision like this." Congress "as a whole," he lamented, had not been given enough information to intelligently assess the President's action.[92]

Twelve prominent physicists, including Hans Bethe and Victor Weisskopf, alarmed by the administration's decision, asked that the President declare a policy of "no first use" of thermonuclear weapons. "[N]o nation has the right to use such a bomb, no matter how right its cause," they asserted. "The bomb is no longer a weapon of war, but a means of extinction of whole populations. . . . " America, they argued, would be justified in using it only if the Soviets first employed it. So troubled were Bethe and others by the prospect of mass killing that they refused to work on the H-bomb.[93]

Some prominent physicists called for renewed efforts at international nuclear disarmament. Senator McMahon, who had ardently pressed for the H-bomb, abruptly shifted his emphasis and urged a program to end the arms race and establish world peace. In early February, he publicly proposed a United Nations meeting on disarmament, a leaflet barrage on the Soviet Union, and a $50 billion American budget for worldwide economic aid to be administered by the UN, if the Soviet Union would join America in giving up nuclear weapons.[94] Senator Millard Tydings, chairman of the Senate Armed Services committee, urged Truman to convoke a world conference for disarmament.[95] So great was the horror of thermonuclear war that men, long accustomed to supporting large defense budgets and even calling for more nuclear weapons, were desperately struggling to find some way out of the Soviet-American impasse and the arms race. None offered a basic examination of the Cold War or even of the Soviet-American stalemate on international control of atomic energy. Instead, they offered exhortations and hopes.

This "peace offensive," launched by such unlikely men as McMahon and Tydings and gaining popular support,[96] placed the administration on the defensive. Truman quickly responded, declaring that there was no need for a new approach to the Soviet Union and that the Baruch plan, rejected by the Soviets in 1946, was still a generous American offer.[97] Acheson, angered by McMahon and Tydings, offered what he deemed a devastating analysis of their pieties. Weakness, he argued, was an invitation to the Soviets "to fish in . . . troubled waters." A meaningful agreement with Soviet Union was impossible, and therefore, he stated, it is "our basic policy to build situations [of] strength"—a policy that "will require very strong nerves."[98]

"My constant appeal," he later wrote, was that Americans must "face the long, hard years and not distract us with the offer of short cuts and easy solutions begotten by good will out of the angels of man's better nature." In February, he said, "Until the Soviet leaders do genuinely accept a 'live and let live' philosophy, no approach from the free world . . . and no Trojan dove from the Communist movement will help to resolve our mutual problems."[99]

Was an opportunity missed in 1949-50 to achieve international control and end the nuclear arms race, as Kennan had hoped? International control was then impossible: America would not give up nuclear weapons, and the Soviets probably would not have accepted what the administration considered adequate controls. What would have happened if the United States, as Oppenheimer and others on the GAC had urged, had decided on unilateral renunciation of the H-bomb? Might the Soviets have done the same? Was a critical opportunity to stop the thermonuclear race lost?

Sketchy evidence suggests that the Soviets were already seeking the H-bomb.[100] But the extent of their effort and the magnitude of their commitment remain unclear. Probably the Soviets would not have believed an administration declaration (unless some inspection was allowed) that America was unilaterally or conditionally foregoing the Super, though many may justifiably regret that the effort was not made in 1949-50.

Had the United States chosen unilateral or conditional renunciation, would it have taken a serious military risk? No. In the short run, the stock of atomic bombs, already probably numbering over 100 and growing in size,[101] could compensate for a Soviet H-bomb, if it had been developed. And probably, as Oppenheimer then argued and Herbert York maintained in 1975, the Soviets were behind in thermonuclear research and actually speeded their project by using information they gained from American tests in the early 1950s.

Given the actual developments in the 1950s, York contends that the Soviets might not have developed the bomb, without this unintended American aid, until about 1958-1959. And if the United States had initially renounced the quest for the Super and the Soviets had not, their testing in 1953 would have informed the United States of Soviet progress, and the United States could have joined the race and developed the bomb in about 1955-1956.[102]

Such counter-factual estimates are, of course, based upon the pattern of *actual* developments in the early 1950s. Not surprisingly, no likely American administration, and certainly not the Truman-Acheson administraton, would have taken such a gamble. It was politically and militarily risky, and thus undesirable. Even the Truman-Acheson defenders today could argue that, in 1949-1950, an alternative scenario was quite possible (though not very probable): that the Soviets first made the Ulam-Teller breakthrough, and the United States was less successful and did not achieve this breakthrough until about 1954 (rather than 1951), thus greatly delaying the American program; and the Soviets, rather than developing ICBMs in 1957, were successful somewhat earlier and built them in 1955. If so, the United States, according to this "unhappy scenario," would have been years behind in the H-bomb race and, in the mid-1950s, would have faced a Soviet Union armed with thermonuclear weapons deliverable on ICBMs when America had neither. America would not have been imperiled, unless the Soviets had many missiles and warheads, but America's prestige would have been impaired and its power suspect. What would that situation have changed in the history of the 1950s? A thaw in the cold war? More bellicose Soviet behavior and greater American caution? Such speculations, though tantalizing, are beyond the scope of this paper.

VII EXPANDING THE COMMITMENT

Truman's public announcement of January 31 had spoken of "continuing"[103] the quest for the H-bomb, but actually he was authorizing acceleration of the effort, with the scale and rate to be determined by the AEC and the Department of Defense. Within six weeks, President Truman, under pressure from the Joint Chiefs and the Defense Department, agreed to the further expansion of facilities in preparation for production of the bomb if it could be built.[104] Why did he make this decision and thus virtually commit himself to production of the H-bomb?

It would have been hard for him to resist these pressures, and there is no evidence that he wanted to do so. Had he wished to keep open his options, however, he might have seized upon the "peace offensive" of early February, sought to enlist the support of McMahon and Tydings, among others, and asserted that America would make another effort to end the nuclear-arms race. For Truman and Acheson, such a venture would have been unimaginable.

In mid-February, two events had intervened to push Truman to erode his options. He received a warning that the Soviets might have many A-bombs and even the H-bomb;[105] and then a JCS request, backed by Secretary Johnson, for an "all-out program of hydrogen bomb development."[106]

Earlier, the Joint Chiefs had stated that a decision on production "in quantity" of the H-bomb could be deferred until the weapon's feasibility was established and means of delivery (presumably a plane) determined.[107] But on February 16, a new analysis (admittedly speculative) quickly changed their thinking. That day, Brig. Gen. Herbert Loper, a member of the Military Liaison Committee, reported that the Soviets might have a stockpile of A-bombs and might have even tested the H-bomb. On February 20, Robert LeBaron, Chairman of the Military Liaison Committee, concluded that this analysis might be correct "if we make certain assumptions that now seem possible in light of the [Klaus] Fuchs espionage" and in light of the fact that the CIA cannot completely cover the Soviet Union. Four days later, fueled by these reports, the Joint Chiefs and Secretary Johnson urged "an all-out program of hydrogen bomb development."

Faced with this new request, Truman again appointed a special three-man NSC committee with Acheson, Johnson, and Henry Smyth from the AEC substituting for the retired Lilienthal. Smyth said that the AEC was already "moving as fast as it could on production...." Meeting with representatives from the State and Defense Departments, Smyth proposed that they recommend that Truman order the AEC to prepare for H-bomb production. Acheson and Johnson speedily agreed, and on March 10, 1950 Truman comfortably endorsed their unanimous recommendation.[108]

In making this decision, he moved closer to committing himself to production of the H-bomb in quantity. Unlike the decision of January 31, however, this time he chose to keep the matter secret. America was speeding ahead in the quest for the H-bomb. Secrecy—as dictated by the President—barred the American public and many congressmen from knowing of the commitment.[109]

VIII CONCLUSIONS: TRUMAN'S VIRTUALLY INEVITABLE DECISIONS

Truman's decision of January 31st was virtually inevitable. He felt no reason to resist this commitment and many reasons—both domestic and international—to choose to make it. He was not compelled to do so by powerful, domestic-political and bureaucratic forces, but he would have found these strong forces hard to resist—if he had wished to. He did not. Senator McMahon, his Congressional colleagues, the Joint Chiefs, and AEC commissioner Strauss, as well as scientists like Teller and Lawrence, who were not powerful in the political community, reinforced the President's own desires and predilections for the Super. Strauss was valuable in forcing the issue to the White House, but, given the anxieties and aims of others after the Soviet explosion, his efforts were not essential to the decision. There were many who could and would have played his role. Had there been no Strauss, or no Teller and Lawrence, or no McMahon, or even none of them, the process would still have operated in approximately the same way and with the same results. However, had the Joint Chiefs, like Oppenheimer and Lilienthal, opposed the Super, then Truman might have faced serious political difficulties at home, for he would have been clashing with the Chiefs in their area of expertise. But the Joint Chiefs were strongly pushing the President for the H-bomb.

Had Truman wanted to resist domestic bureaucratic and political pressures for the H-bomb, he might have taken his case to the people. Public opinion was confused and he might have reshaped it to oppose the H-bomb. It would not have been an easy task in a nation where many condemned Truman and Acheson for "losing" China, and the quest might have injured him with the electorate. In late January and early February, Americans overwhelmingly favored (73 to 18 percent) seeking to build the H-bomb but also slightly favored (48 to 45 percent) trying negotiations with the Soviets for international control of atomic energy before the United States sought to build the H-bomb. Truman did not want to make such an effort with the Soviets, and most Americans (70 to 11 percent) believed it would fail.[110] His policy of secrecy barred dissenting scientific advisers like Oppenheimer and Conant from arguing publicly against the Super, and left some with a lingering sense that they could have persuaded the nation that an American H-bomb was unnecessary.

In March, probably under the tutelage of McMahon, Tydings, and others, public opinion swelled (69 to 23 percent) for seeking international control first, even though most (60 to 17 percent) still anticipated failure.[111] Had Truman wished, he might have successfully exploited this sentiment for international control to delay his decision of the 10th. He had no desire to do so. Instead, he and Acheson campaigned to persuade Americans that the McMahon-Tydings "peace offensive" was wrongheaded and dangerous, that America needed greater military power, and that the Soviets would not accept international control. Under such tutoring, many Americans gave up their faint hopes for avoiding the H-bomb. If there was a "missed opportunity" to avoid the Super, Truman and Acheson never rued the loss.

Ultimately, the key men were Acheson and Truman, who on the H-bomb, as with so many other issues in the Cold War, found themselves in comfortable agreement. In view of their similar suspicions of the Soviet Union and their desire for more military power, that agreement was virtually inevitable. By appointing Acheson to the three-man advisory committee, Truman created an institutional mechanism that virtually assured him that he would receive a recommendation for the Super. Acheson's endorsement and the committee's recommendations shaped the way for Truman's momentous decisions on the H-bomb. They were virtually inevitable.

NOTES

1. For major interpretations, see: Warner Schilling, "The H-Bomb Decision: How To Decide Without Actually Choosing," *Political Science Quarterly*, vol. 76 (March 1961), pp. 24-46; Richard Hewlett and Francis Duncan, *A History of the United States Atomic Energy Commission*, Vol. II, *Atomic Shield, 1947-1952* (University Park, Pa.: Pennsylvania State University Press, 1972); Herbert F. York, *The Advisors: Oppenheimer, Teller, and the Superbomb* (San Francisco: W. H. Freeman, 1975); Robert Gilpin, *American Scientists and Nuclear Weapons Policy* (Princeton: Princeton University Press, 1962), pp. 64-111; Joyce and Gabriel Kolko, *The Limits of Power* (New York: Harper, 1972), pp. 504-509; Stanley Blumberg and Gwinn Owens, *Energy and Conflict: The Life and Times of Edward Teller* (New York: Putnam's, 1976), pp. 184-298; Gaddis Smith, *Dean Acheson* (New York: Cooper Square, 1972), pp. 138-171; David McLellan, *Dean Acheson* (New York: Dodd, Mead, 1976), pp. 168-185. and David Rosenberg, "American Atomic Strategy and the Hydrogen Bomb Decision," *Journal of American History*, vol. 66 (June 1979), pp. 62-87. For major memoirs and recollections, see: Dean Acheson, *Present at The Creation* (New York: Norton, 1969), pp. 345-349; U.S. Atomic Energy Commission, *In The Matter of J. Robert Oppenheim-*

er: *Transcript of Hearing Before Personnel Security Board, Washington, D.C., April 12, 1954 through May 6, 1954* (Washington: Government Printing Office, 1954); David Lilienthal, *The Journals of David Lilienthal*, vol. 2, *The Atomic Energy Years, 1945-1950* (New York: Harper, 1964), pp. 580-634; Lewis Strauss, *Men and Decisions* (Garden City: Doubleday, 1962), pp. 208-230; R. Gordon Arneson, "The H-Bomb Decision," *Foreign Service Journal*, vol. 46 (May 1969), pp. 27-29, (June 1969), pp. 24-27, 43; Harry S. Truman, *Memoirs*, vol. II, *Years of Trial and Hope* (Garden City, N.Y.: Doubleday, 1956), pp. 296-315.

2. Gen. Hoyt Vandenberg to Secretary of Defense, September 19, 1949, President's Secretary's File (PSF), box 199, Harry S. Truman Library (HSTL).
3. Matthew Connelly, Cabinet Minutes, September 23, 1949, Connelly Papers, HSTL.
4. Interview with Dean Acheson, February 16, 1955, Post-Presidential Papers, HSTL.
5. See, for example, Walter Lippman, "Today and Tomorrow," Washington *Post*, September 27, 1949, p. 13; editorial, *The Times* (London), September 24, 1949, p. 5.
6. Eben Ayers, "Russian Atomic Bomb," n.d., Ayers Papers, HSTL; and George Elsey, handwritten notes, September 24, 1949, Elsey Papers, box 88, HSTL; and transcript of interview with Harry S. Truman (for memoirs), ca. 1953, Post-Presidential Papers, HSTL.
7. See Statements by Truman, Acheson, and Webb, September 23, 1949, in *Department of State Bulletin*, vol. 21 (Oct. 3, 1949), pp. 487-488. On reactions abroad, see "Foreign Reaction to Announcement of Atomic Explosion," n.d. (probably Oct. 1949), PSF, box 201, HSTL.
8. Sen. Brien McMahon to Truman, September 28, 1949 (two letters); and Truman to McMahon, October 11, 1949, PSF, box 112, HSTL. On the expansion, see AEC minutes, September 14, 1949, Historian's Office, Department of Energy (DOE).
9. Gordon Dean to AEC Commissioners, Historian's Office, DOE.
10. AEC minutes, October 7, 1949, Historian's Office, DOE.
11. Gordon Dean Diary, October 19, 1949, Historian's Office, DOE.
12. Warner Schilling interview with Oppenheimer, June 11, 1957, Oppenheimer Papers, Library of Congress.
13. Oppenheimer to David Lilienthal, September 26, 1949, Oppenheimer Papers, box 46; GAC minutes, September 22-23, 1949, Historian's Office, DOE.
14. Strauss, draft (ca. Sept. 29, 1949), Strauss Papers, Office of Lewis Strauss (Washington, D.C.). For influence on Strauss, see William Golden to Strauss, September 25, 1949, Strauss Papers. These papers were scheduled for the Herbert Hoover Library and may already have been shipped there.
15. AEC, "Thermonuclear Weapons Program Chronology" (1953-1955), pp. 2-17; Historian's Office, DOE; Hewlett and Duncan, *Atomic Shield*, pp. 362-364; and Teller in AEC, *In the Matter of . . . Oppenheimer*, pp. 712-714.
16. Strauss to commissioners, October 5, 1949, in AEC, "Thermonuclear . . . Chronology," p. 22.
17. Hewlett and Duncan, *Atomic Shield*, pp. 373-374.
18. AEC, "Minutes of Program Council," September 23 and 26, 1949, Historian's Office, DOE.
19. Lilienthal to Oppenheimer, October 11, 1949, Strauss Papers; and quotes from Sumner Pike to Oppenheimer, October 19, 1949, Historian's Office, DOE. On pressing for GAC meeting, Dean in AEC minutes, October 12, 1949, Historian's Office, DOE.
20. Oppenheimer to Conant, October 21, 1949, in AEC, *Matter of Oppenheimer*, p. 242; and Hewlett and Duncan, *Atomic Shield*, p. 378.
21. Lilienthal, entry of October 10, 1949, *Lilienthal Journals*, II, p. 577.
22. See, for example, Schilling interview with Oppenheimer; and *Lilienthal Journals*.
23. Lilienthal, entry of October 10, 1949, *Lilienthal Journals*, II, p. 577; "Mr. Lilienthal's Opening Remarks . . . , October 29, 1949," Historian's Office, DOE.

24. Interview with Acheson, February 17, 1955, Post-Presidential Papers, HSTL.
25. *Time* (February 23, 1948); Herbert York, "The Debate Over the Hydrogen Bomb," *Scientific American*, vol. 233 (Oct. 1975), p. 108, sees Oppenheimer in this statement as "clearly revealing [his] inner feelings."
26. See, for example, Oppenheimer in *New York Times Magazine* (August 1, 1965), p. 8.
27. Oppenheimer to Conant, October 21, 1949, AEC, *Matter of Oppenheimer*, p. 242; Lilienthal, entry of October 29, 1949, *Lilienthal Journals*, II, p. 581.
28. Quote from Teller, in AEC, *Matter of Oppenheimer*, p. 715; and Conant, *ibid.*, p. 387.
29. Seaborg to Oppenheimer, October 14, 1949, in AEC, *Matter of Oppenheimer*, p. 238.
30. GAC minutes, October 28-30, 1949, Historian's Office, DOE. On Bethe's attitudes, Teller's testimony, *Matter of Oppenheimer*, p. 715. The minutes simply say about Kennan that he "presented his views of the Russian situation and replied to a number of questions from Committee members." My inference about the content of his presentation or answers is based on knowledge of his general views at the time.
31. Lilienthal, entry of October 29, 1949, *Lilienthal Journals*, II, p. 581.
32. Ibid.
33. Ibid.
34. Ibid.
35. GAC report, October 30, 1949, AEC Doc. 349, Historian's Office, DOE, and reprinted in York, *Advisors*, 149-156. Part of what is deleted from the document seems to be summarized in Arneson, "The H-Bomb Decision," (May 1969), p. 29.
36. Cf., Oppenheimer address, Los Alamos, November 2, 1945, James Franck Papers, University of Chicago.
37. GAC report, October 30, 1949.
38. Ibid.
39. Ibid. Emphasis added.
40. York, *Advisors*, 42-56, is more impressed by the reports. Interview with Acheson, February 17, 1955, suggested that the "morality" argument was additional and probably marginal. For a different criticism, see interview with Sidney Souers, ca. 1955, Post-Presidential Papers, HSTL.
41. "Technically so sweet" is from Oppenheimer's 1954 testimony about his 1951 attitude (after the Ulam-Teller configuration was suggested), in AEC, *Matter of Oppenheimer*, p. 251.
42. See Gilpin, *American Scientists*, 89-94, 98-100.
43. York, *Advisors*, p. 100 on Oppenheimer's belief that the Soviets would derive substantial benefits from American testing. And see AEC, *Matter of Oppenheimer*, p. 248.
44. Schilling interview with Oppenheimer.
45. Schilling interview with Oppenheimer. The Oppenheimer-Acheson meeting probably took place on November 4, 1949. (Notes on Acheson's Schedule, n.d., Acheson Papers, box 63, HSTL.)
46. AEC minutes, November 4 and 7, 1949, Historian's Office, DOE; Hewlett and Duncan, *Atomic Shield*, p. 385-391.
47. AEC, Memorandum for the President, "Subject: Development of a 'Super' Bomb," November 9, 1949. "Thermonuclear Chronology," pp. 38-43.
48. Ibid., p. 39. They were more deft in characterizing McMahon's position.
49. Ibid., pp. 40-41.
50. Ibid., p. 41.
51. Ibid., App. A, pp. 44-45.
52. Ibid., pp. 46-47. Smyth acknowledged that, in the future, "failure of renewed attempts at international agreement might require an early review of our decision not to make a 'Super.'" (p. 43) Like the Fermi-Rabi (GAC minority) report, he did not suggest why a review and possible reversal (quest for feasibility) might be necessary. By late

December or early January, Smyth shifted and supported the quest for the Super. (Smyth to Strauss, September 21, 1953, Strauss Papers.)

53. Pike, memorandum to the Commission, November 28, 1949, "Thermonuclear Chronology," pp. 50-51.

54. Gordon Dean, in App. A, pp. 45-46.

55. Strauss to President, reprinted in Strauss, *Men and Decisions*, pp. 219-222. Professor Richard Pfau has suggested to me that Strauss' arguments had shifted from staying ahead (October 5, 1949 memo) to not falling behind, because he may have known about the Fuchs espionage. For suggestive support, see AEC minutes, 1949, Historian's Office, DOE.

56. Sen. McMahon to Truman, November 1, 1949, and Truman to McMahon, November 2, 1949, PSF, box 201, HSTL.

57. Washington *Post*, November 18, 1949, p. 1.

58. Hewlett and Duncan, *Atomic Shield*, p. 394.

59. For Truman's thinking, see, among other sources, Truman's comments in interview with Sidney Souers, Post-Presidential Papers, HSTL, and Arneson, "Blair House Minutes," July 14, 1949, Historian's Office, DOE.

60. Acheson, *Present at the Creation.*

61. Robert Dennision to Truman, November 18, 1949, proposed the appointment of this committee, which was the same one that Truman had appointed in the summer to make recommendations on expansion of the atomic energy program. (PSF, box 201, HSTL)

62. Technically Johnson had not taken a formal position, but some of the Joint Chiefs wanted it. (Gen. Hoyt Vandenberg in AEC, *Matter of Oppenheimer*, p. 137; and Oppenheimer to Conant, October 21, 1949, in ibid., p. 242) On delays before Defense took a clear position, AEC minutes, November 30, 1949, Historian's Office, DOE.

63. On the Acheson-Truman relationship see, for example, interviews with Acheson, February 16 and 17, 1955, Post-Presidential Papers; Acheson, *Present at the Creation*, pp. 729-730; and Truman, *Memoirs*, II, pp. 428-431.

64. Acheson, "Meeting with the President," November 7, 1949, and ibid., November 14, 1949, Policy Planning Staff Papers, Nitze Files, box 50, Department of State Records, RG 59, National Archives.

65. Notes on Acheson's Schedule, Acheson Papers, box 63.

66. See, for example, Lilienthal entries of November 1, December 25 and 30, 1949, and January 31, 1950, in *Lilienthal Journals*, II, pp. 583-584, 613-614, 615, 633.

67. Schilling interview with Oppenheimer.

68. Quoted in Arneson, "The H-Bomb Decision," May 1969, p. 29.

69. See for the development of Acheson's thought and his willingness to entertain competing notions, minutes of meeting, November 3, 1949, and Webb to Atomic Working Group, December 3, 1949, Policy Planning Staff Papers, Nitze Files, box 50. On November 3, Acheson suggested, in the words of the minutes, "perhaps the best thing is an 18-24 month moratorium on the super-bomb—bilateral if possible, unilateral if necessary—during which you do your best to ease the international situation, come to an agreement with the Russians, put your economic house in order, get your people's minds set to do whatever is necessary to do, and if no agreement is in sight at the end of that time . . . then go ahead with overall production. . . . " As late as December 3, Webb thought that Acheson had not made a decision yet on the H-bomb.

70. Nitze, draft, December 19, 1949, Policy Planning Staff Papers, Nitze Files, box 50.

71. Kennan, "International Control of Atomic Energy," January 20, 1950, Atomic Energy Files, Department of State Records, Department of State. Parts are also published in Department of State, *Foreign Relations of the United States*, 1950, vol. 1, pp. 22-44.

Earlier drafts are in these Atomic Energy Files. For critiques, see for example, Robert Hooker to Kennan, December 19, 1949, Atomic Energy Files.

72. Joint Chiefs of Staff to Secretary of Defense, November 23, 1949, PSF, box 201, HSTL. Also see Joint Chiefs of Staff to Secretary of Defense, January 13, 1950, PSF, box 114, HSTL.

73. McMahon to President, November 21, 1949, AEC Doc. 350, Historian's Office, DOE. Later, presumably to add pressure, he sent copies to Defense and the AEC. (McMahon to AEC, January 9, 1950, Historian's Office, DOE)

74. In his later notes for the Princeton seminars, Acheson wrote, "The consequences of our not pressing forward. (1) On assumption another (Russia) got it [the H-bomb]. In my view very serious." (Princeton Transcripts, HSTL)

75. See NSC-68, April 14, 1950, FRUS, 1950, I, pp. 234-292.

76. Lilienthal entry of December 25, 1949 (on December 22 meeting), *Lilienthal Journals*, II, pp. 613-614. For earlier staff work for Lilienthal, see J. H. Manley to Lilienthal, "Working Committee," December 13, 1949; Manley to Lilienthal, "Working Committee," December 16, 1949; and Manley, "Military Worth," Historian's Office, DOE.

77. Lilienthal, entry of December 25, 1949, *Lilienthal Journals*, II, pp. 613-614.

78. Lilienthal, entry of December 30, 1949, *Lilienthal Journals*, II, p. 615.

79. Ibid.

80 See, for example, Lilienthal entries of December 30, 1949 and January 31, 1950, *Lilienthal Journals*, II, pp. 615, 624-632.

81. Acheson, memorandum of telephone conversation [with Sidney Souers], January 19,1950, Acheson Papers. Also see Ayers Diary, January 21, 1950. On advance knowledge of Truman's intentions before the meeting of January 31, 1950, see also Johnson to Strauss, February 1, 1954, Strauss Papers. Truman may have been confirmed in his decision by an awareness, from briefings by Bradley, Johnson, and others, that American strategic bombing with A-bombs would leave much of Russia's strategic military and production areas relatively unimpaired. (President's Schedule, January 5 and 10, 1950, PSF.) On January 23, Truman definitely received a substantial briefing on this subject. (Philip Morse, *In At the Beginnings* (Cambridge, Mass.: Harvard University Press, 1977), pp. 258-259.) The larger report is JCS 1952/11, February 10, 1950, CCS 373, September 23, 1948, Records of the Joint Chiefs of Staff, RG 218, National Archives. For an earlier study (assuming that all planes reached their targets), see Report to the JCS, "Evaluation of Effect on Soviet War Effort Resulting From the Soviet Strategic Air Offensive," May 11, 1949, in Organization, Research, and Policy Division (OP 23), Office of Chief of Naval Operations Records, Naval Archives, Naval Historical Center, Washington, D.C. Rosenberg, "American Atomic Strategy," pp. 79-83 emphasizes the influence of these reports on the H-bomb decisions. For another view from mine on "minimal decision," see Schilling, "H-Bomb Decisions."

82. See Arneson, "H-Bomb Decision," May 1969, p. 26.

83. *Lilienthal Journals*, II, p. 620 note.

84. Lilienthal, entry of January 31, 1950, *Lilienthal Journals*, II, pp. 623-632; *Present at Creation*, p. 348.

85. Ibid.; and Acheson, memorandum of telephone conversation [with Sidney Souers], January 19, 1950, Acheson Papers. Why didn't Lilienthal refuse to sign the report? He probably thought he would have more efficacy if he signed the report and *then* presented his doubts to Truman.

86. Lilienthal, entry of January 31. 1950, *Lilienthal Journals*, II, pp. 632-633, and quote on p. 632.

87. Ibid.

88. Ibid.

89. Washington *Post*, February 1, 1950, pp. 1 (quote) and 11; New York *Times*, February 1, 1950. In a poll of January 28-February 2, a vast majority (73-18 percent) thought that the United States should try to make the H-bomb. See George Gallup, ed., *The Gallup Poll: Public Opinion* (New York: Random House, 1972), vol. 2, p. 888.

90. Ayers Diary, February 4, 1950.

91. Robert Bacher to Oppenheimer, February 4, 1950, Oppenheimer Papers, box 18.

92. Washington *Post*, February 1, 1950, p. 11.

93. *F.A.S. Newsletter*, February 14, 1950, Papers of Federation of American Scientists, University of Chicago; New York *Times*, February 5, 1950, p. 1; Bethe to Norris Bradbury, February 14, 1950, Los Alamos Laboratory Papers, Los Alamos Laboratory. Also on scientific protest, see Linus Pauling to Leo Szilard, February 1, 1950, Szilard Papers, Library of University of California, San Diego.

94. New York *Times*, February 3, 1950, p. 2.

95. *F.A.S. Newsletter*, February 14, 1950.

96. In the AIPO poll of January 28-February 2, a slim plurality of Americans (48-45 percent) thought "we should try to work out an agreement with Russia to control the atomic bomb before we try to make a hydrogen bomb." In March, the majority became overwhelming (68-23 percent). Interestingly, most thought in the first poll (70-11 percent) and in March (60-17 percent) that the effort to negotiate international control would fail. (*Gallup Poll*, II, p. 888; and *Public Opinion Quarterly*, vol. 14 [Summer 1950], p. 372.)

97. Truman news conference, February 9, 1950, in *Public Papers of the Presidents: Harry S. Truman* (Washington: Government Printing Office, 1965), pp. 152-3.

98. Acheson press conference, February 8, 1950, *Department of State Bulletin*, vol. 22 (February 20, 1950), pp. 272-274.

99. Acheson, *Present at Creation*, p. 379.

100. I.N. Golovin, *I.V. Kurchatov* (Bloomington, Ind.: Selbstverlag Press, n.d.), trans. by William Dougherty, pp. 67-72.

101. This is a conservative estimate based upon the U.S. Nuclear Weapons Stockpile Non-Nuclear Mechanical Assemblies of 680 in Fiscal 1950, 228 in 1949, and 53 in 1948. (Data in John Griffin to author, March 9, 1976.)

102. York, *Advisors*, pp. 96-103; and York, "Debate over the H-Bomb," pp. 110-113.

103. President's statement, January 31, 1950, in *Public Papers: Truman*, 1950, p. 138.

104. NSC Special Committee, "Report on Development of Thermonuclear Weapons," March 9, 1950, PSF, box 202, HSTL.

105. H.B. Loper to Robert LeBaron, "A Basis for Estimating Maximum Soviet Capabilities for Atomic Weapons," February 16, 1960, with LeBaron to Secretary of Defense, "Basis for Estimating Maximum Soviet Capabilities for Atomic Weapons," February 20, 1950, PSF, box 201.

106. Louis Johnson to President, February 24, 1950, Historian's Office, DOE.

107. Joint Chiefs of Staff to Secretary of Defense, January 13, 1950, PSF, box 114.

108. Hewlett and Duncan, *Atomic Shield*, pp. 416-417; AEC Minutes, March 1, 1950, Historian's Office, DOE.

109. For complaints about secrecy, see Oppenheimer to Hanson Baldwin, April 12, 1950, and Baldwin to Oppenheimer, April 12, 1950, Oppenheimer Papers, box 19; and Lilienthal, quoted in Strauss to Souers, February 16, 1950, Strauss Papers. For later developments see Hewlett and Duncan, *Atomic Shield*, pp. 430-432; and President's request for supplemental appropriation for AEC ($260 million), July 7, 1950, *Public Papers: Truman*, 1950, p. 519.

110. Gallup, ed., *Gallup Poll*, II. 888; and *Public Opinion Quarterly*, Vol. 14 (Summer 1950), 372.

111. Ibid.; and *Gallup Poll*, II. 888.

Chapter 17

On Memories, Interests, and Foreign Policy: The Case of Vietnam

Michael Nacht

In Graham Greene's *The Quiet American,* a fictional account of love and war in Southeast Asia, the following exchange takes place between Fowler, a skeptical, opium-smoking English war correspondent, and Pyle, a bright, young, confident American Intelligence officer:

Fowler: Sometimes Viets have a better success with a megaphone than a bazooka. I don't blame them. They don't believe in anything either. You and your like are trying to make a war with the help of people who just aren't interested.

Pyle: They don't want communism.

Fowler: They want enough rice. They don't want to be shot at. They want one day to be much the same as another. They don't want our white skins around telling them what they want.

Pyle: If Indochina goes—

Fowler: I know that record. Siam goes. Malaya goes. Indonesia goes. What does "go" mean? If I believed in your God and another life, I'd bet my future harp against your golden crown that in five hundred years there may be no New York or London, but they'll be growing paddy in the fields, they'll be carrying their produce to market on long poles, wearing their pointed hats. The small boys will be sitting on the buffaloes. I like the buffaloes, they don't like our smell, the smell of Europeans. And remember—from a buffalo's point of view you are a European too.

Pyle: They'll be forced to believe what they are told; they won't be allowed to think for themselves.

Fowler: Thought's a luxury. Do you think the peasant sits and thinks of God and democracy when he gets inside his mud hut at night?[1]

Greene's work was first published in 1955, a full ten years before the United States introduced large numbers of combat troops into South Vietnam. His words were prescient, for the conversation between Fowler and Pyle was repeated with slight variations in Vietnam and the United States for almost twenty years thereafter. What was the United States doing in Vietnam? What were American objectives? What were the aims, hopes, and aspirations of the South Vietnamese people? How did American intervention differ from french colonial rule? What was the nature of the threat—to South Vietnam, to Asia, to the United States?

Americans and others debated these questions *ad nauseum*, particularly from the time U.S. Troops assumed a major role in the war in Vietnam until the collapse of the South Vietnamese government almost a decade later. The answers differed then and differ now because our views of what is central, and what is peripheral, to American foreign policy vary, because we cannot agree on the appropriate means to achieve specific ends, and because we read the historical record differently to reinforce our notions of success and disaster.

Despite these variations, a dominant view has taken hold. It is now commonly agreed that the Vietnam War was a disaster for the South Vietnamese people and for the United States and should not be repeated. "No more Vietnams" is a sentiment most Americans can and do endorse, even if they are not able to articulate what this slogan means. What has prompted this dramatic shift from the views expressed by Pyle to the equation of Vietnam with everything that is undesirable in American foreign policy? Clearly, in the early 1960s Americans held certain views and retained certain images about international politics and about themselves that they no longer accept. The agony of the Vietnam experience produced this change.

This paper explores in a preliminary fashion the way images of international politics are formed; reviews the principal elements of the American world view that, in my judgement, led naturally and easily to the American military intervention in Vietnam; and concludes with an assessment of contemporary American images of international politics in the wake of the Vietnam experience. The central question under investigation is, what has been the effect of the Vietnam War on the American self-image and on the U.S. role in the world?

SOME THOUGHTS ON IMAGES

Because of the inherent complexity of human affairs, individuals continuously form images of the physical world that surrounds them. Such images can be defined as "mental conceptions held in common by members of a group and symbolic of a basic attitude and orientation."[2] Social scientists, however, have had great difficulty either explaining how particular images are formed or identifying the conditions that lead to their transformation. This difficulty has persisted whether one is discussing individuals, small groups, or national governments. In international relations, few scholars have been able to develop a theory or set of theories that convincingly explains behavior among states.[3]

However, it may not be necessary to formulate a theory to understand the role of images in international relations. I submit that the work of two scholars—one a philosopher of science and the other a social psychologist—provide compelling arguments that can be extremely useful in analyzing international politics, although the scholars are not specialists in this field nor have they applied their theoretical concepts to such phenomena. The philosopher of science, Thomas Kuhn, has written his views most comprehensively in a work aimed at explaining how scientific progress is made. The social psychologist, Leon Festinger, has written at length on how individuals cope with information that runs counter to their firmly held set of beliefs.[4]

A brief sketch of each theory will suffice. Kuhn argues that when someone new comes to the world of science he or she finds an existing set of rules of how to think about problems, a collection of shared assumptions, and a common belief in the location of the discipline's frontiers. Kuhn labels these rules and norms the "paradigm" that governs and dominates thinking in the discipline. According to Kuhn, at any point in time there is a paradigm that is widely, though never universally, accepted in the field. How then is scientific progress achieved? Kuhn states that a young person or someone new to the field discovers, perhaps by accident, a phenomenon that cannot be readily explained by the existing paradigm. The phenomenon is almost always characterized as an anomaly by senior people in the field and is dismissed as a trivial variation from the norm rather than a reason to doubt the universal applicability of the paradigm. But further research reveals a whole class of activities that the paradigm cannot adequately explain. Over many years, or even decades, a search for a new set of norms and guidelines that explains these recently discovered phenomena is undertaken. Eventually a competing paradigm is formulated that challenges much of the thinking of the established one. If the new paradigm cannot withstand the critical challenges of its doubters, it quickly disappears. But if it can, it polarizes the field; after some time a transfer of allegiances from the old paradigm to the new begins. Eventually, all but a few diehards have deserted the old paradigm and the new one has become the established set of rules for the discipline. This process is repeated, with another paradigm rising to replace the now established paradigm. Given the cumulative nature of scientific inquiry, this process of paradigm replacement is, according to Kuhn, how scientific progress is made.

Festinger's theory of cognitive dissonance can best be illustrated by example. Suppose a man who greatly enjoys gastronomy finds that he is grossly overweight. His physician informs him that the extra weight he is carrying is highly detrimental to his health and advises him to adopt a strict diet, eliminating virtually all his culinary delights. What choices does the man have? He may of course follow his physician's advice, stick to the diet, and lose the weight. But he has several other options. He can continue his gastronomic activities, justifying his action on several grounds. First, he could argue that eating is part of his life, that he enjoys it greatly, and that he would rather live a shorter, happier life eating what he wishes than be healthy but miserable. Second, he could cite Winston Churchill, who lived past ninety, as a counter-example to the notion that overweight necessarily shortens one's life. Third, he could argue that to follow his physician's dietary restrictions would be so stressful that he might develop ulcers or high blood presure or have to resume smoking cigarettes just to cope, each of these being equally or more detrimental to his health than being overweight. Fourth, he could say that he preferred to take his chances with his condition.: "One cannot avoid all the dangers in life anyway; you can get hit by a car crossing the street, you know."

The man is torn between doing something he wishes to do that may have unpleasant consequences or foregoing the activity. Festinger terms the unpleasant consequences "dissonance" and he asserts that the existence of dissonance, being psychologically uncomfortable, motivates the person to reduce the dissonance by avoiding situations or information that would increase it. In his own laboratory work Festinger observed several additional modes of behavior:

1. Following a decision there is an active search for information that supports the action taken ("cognitive consonant" information).
2. Following a decision there is an increase in confidence in the decision. Individuals find the chosen course of action far more attractive than the alternatives that were rejected.
3. Once the decision is made, it is very difficult to reverse it.
4. Characteristics 1-3 vary directly with the importance of the decision. The more important the decision, the more pronounced these effects.

Although it would be unjustified, even foolish, to claim a tight fit between the theories of Kuhn and Festinger and American policy in Vietnam—certainly such a fit cannot be demonstrated rigorously—a strong argument can be made that both theories enhance our understanding of how the United States could find itself in Vietnam and even shed some light on current American images derived from the Vietnam experience.

THE CONTAINMENT PARADIGM

By 1950, if not sooner, the United States had definitely adopted the containment policy as the cornerstone of its foreign policy and as the principal guideline for dealing with the Soviet Union. The containment policy had, of course, been articulated publicly by George Kennan in his famous "X" article in *Foreign Affairs*[5] and had previously been espoused by Kennan and others inside the government. Kennan argued that in the postwar period Soviet expansion was the principal threat to the Western world, and he called for a "long-term, patient but firm and vigilant containment of Russian expansive tendencies." Most often quoted was Kennan's observation that

> Soviet pressure against the free institutions of the western world is something that can be contained by the adroit and vigilant application of counterforce at a series of constantly shifting geographical and political points, corresponding to the shifts and maneuvers of Soviet policy.

Kennan argued that successful application of the containment approach would not only thwart Soviet foreign policy goals but would eventually lead to a reform of Soviet domestic political institutions; this in turn would modify the Soviet Union's expansionist tendencies.

The containment policy was appealing on several grounds. The principal lesson that American policymakers had derived from World War II was that appeasement of potential aggressors only brought on aggression. The Munich experience could never be repeated. In the aftermath of the war, with the consolidation of Soviet control over much of Eastern Europe, the threatening character of Soviet rhetoric, and the intransigence of Soviet negotiating behavior, the Soviet Union appeared as the sole threat to Western institutions. The United States had emerged from the war as the world's strongest nation, both militarily and economically. Anticipating the disintegration of the British and French colonial empires, the Truman administration assigned itself the role of leading the defense of the West.[6] It defined American national interest as anticommunism. The containment policy, though remarkably vague as stated in Kennan's *Foreign Affairs* article, was consistent with the memories and interests of American policymakers and provided a general guide for the conduct of U.S. foreign policy. Though it was criticized by Walter Lippmann and others for permitting American foreign policy to be determined by Soviet initiatives, containment provided a framework more compelling than any alternative offered by its critics.

In his published work, Kennan did not distinguish between political and military means to implement the policy, nor did he identify specific geographical regions where it was to be applied or avoided.[7] But events led successive American administrations to apply the policy with a universality that was not particularly sensitive to the idiosyncracies of geography and to rely most heavily on the military instrument for its implementation. Indeed, this sense of the global applicability of containment was in evidence by 1950 when a major review of America's national strategy made the following point:

> Our position as the center of power in the free world places a heavy responsibility upon the United States for leadership. We must organize and enlist the energies and resources of the free world in a positive program for peace which will frustrate the Kremlin design for world domination by creating a situation in the free world to which the Kremlin will be compelled to adjust. Without such a cooperative effort, led by the United States, we will have to make gradual withdrawals under pressure until we discover one day that we have sacrificed positions of vital interest.[8]

By the time John Kennedy became President in 1961, the containment policy had a proven track record. A combination of economic assistance, military presence, and alliance building by the United States in Western Europe had halted Soviet westward expansion at the frontiers of Eastern Europe. The Truman doctrine maintained the pro-Western orientation of Greece and Turkey.[9] Even the painful Korean War experience could be legitimately judged a success in that American military intervention established the *status quo ante* and maintained a non-Communist government in South Korea. Clandestine operations in Iran and Guatemala and the use of Marines in Lebanon served to thwart Communist expansion in the 1950s. Moreover, the network of bilateral and multilateral alliances established by the United States during the Eisenhower administration gave the policy international political legitimacy. Except for the triumph of Communist forces in China, which remained a highly contentious issue in American domestic politics, and the Castro victory in Cuba, which, from the Washington perspective, was not initially thought to be a Communist success but rather a nationalist success, the containment policy had an unblemished record.

Recall, then, the stirring words of John Kennedy's inaugural address:

Let every nation know, whether it wishes us well or ill, that we shall pay any price, bear any burden, meet any hardship, support any friend, oppose any foe to assure the survival and success of liberty.

In the long history of the world, only a few generations have been granted the role of defending freedom in its hour of maximum danger. I do not shrink from this responsibility—I welcome it.

To those people in the huts and villages of half the globe struggling to break the bonds of mass misery, we pledge our best efforts to help them help themselves, for whatever period is required—not because we seek their votes, but because it is right.[10]

The President's words were the quintessential endorsement of and commitment to the containment paradigm—an open-ended pledge to prevent the spread of communism anywhere. By 1961 containment was the established orthodoxy of American foreign policy with broad and deep support in the Congress, in the bureaucracy, in the business, labor, and academic communities, in journalistic circles, and throughout the body politic.[11] Given containment's entrenched position, it would take highly significant contradictory evidence to dislodge it.

PARADIGM ADJUSTMENT

Kuhn argues that most scientists spend their careers adjusting, refining, and extending the existing paradigm rather than seeking its replacement. This suggests that paradigm criticism is not the norm but the exception in scientific research. Perhaps the same can be said of political-military analyses, which argue for adopting new techniques or for reorienting priorities without challenging fundamental policy assumptions. In the 1950s, in particular, a substantial amount of creative intellectual work sought to tailor American foreign and defense policy to the changing international environment. From Kuhn's theoretical perspective, however, this work would have to be defined as a paradigm adjustment because it focused on techniques of policy implementation rather than on formal challenges to the existing containment policy. Three conceptual developments were especially relevant to the Vietnam policy adopted in the 1960s: limited war theory, theories of coercive diplomacy, and theories of counterinsurgency.

Limited war theory was an outgrowth of American experience in Korea as well as an intellectual reaction to the weakness of the massive retaliation doctrine, which had been enunciated by Secretary of State John Foster Dulles at a meeting of the Council on Foreign Relations in New York in January 1954. The Korean War had been a frustrating experience because the United States had deliberately refrained from widening the conflict to avoid a war between the United States and the Soviet Union or, at the very least, a full-scale war between the United States and the People's Republic of China on the Chinese homeland. The Korean War was a precedent-setting limited war in three respects: first, after several policy reversals, it was fought by the United States with the specifically limited objective of ensuring that South Korea was not ruled by a Communist government; second, it was waged in a geographically limited area, with the extension of the war to Chinese territory expressly forbidden by President Truman despite the protests of General Douglas MacArthur; and third, it was fought with limited use of weaponry—particularly, no nuclear weapons.

In the aftermath of the Korean War, several American civilian strategists—Bernard Brodie, William Kaufmann, Robert Osgood, Henry Kissinger—felt that future wars would be similarly limited in objectives, geography, and weaponry and were concerned when the Eisenhower administration adopted a policy of planning to use, or at least threatening to use, nuclear weapons "at a time and place of our own choosing" to counter Communist aggression in Europe or in gray areas not dominated by either the Soviet Union or the West. The civilian strategists found the policy of massive retaliation wanting because, they argued, it was not credible to our adversaries, our allies, or ourselves.[12] It was inconceivable that the United States would initiate nuclear war with the Soviet Union in response to a border incursion in Southeast Asia. The strategists emphasized the importance of credibility in making a policy of deterrence work. They stressed the need for the United States to acquire capabilities to match those of our adversaries if we wished to deter their aggressive acts or to defeat them on the battle-field, should deterrence fail.[13] Osgood in particular warned that the United States was moving into an age of limited war that would not be accepted by the American people unless American objectives were explained carefully and convincingly.

Many of these ideas were adopted and amplified by Maxwell Taylor in a book published before Kennedy took office. It sufficiently impressed the new President that he appointed Taylor his personal advisor on military affairs. In Taylor's work the term "flexible response" was coined: "the need for a capability to react across the entire spectrum of possible challenge, for coping with anything from general atomic war to infiltrations and aggressions such as threaten Laos and Berlin."[14] Thus Kennedy brought with him not only a reaffirmation of containment but an intellectual commitment to acquire the capabilities to implement the policy more effectively than had been possible previously.

Techniques of coercive diplomacy were also part of the intellectual inheritance of the Kennedy administration. Among the important con-cepts superbly articulated by strategists Thomas Schelling and Herman Kahn were: sensitivity to the importance and subtleties of signaling, to the psychology of threat, and to the significance of tacit agreements; ability to distinguish between deterrence (punish the opponent *if* he acts) and compellence (punish the opponent *until* he acts); and applica-tion of a strategy of controlled escalation to indicate to an opponent the punishment he will receive if he continues to pursue his goals.[15] Although neither Schelling nor Kahn had any direct connection to U.S. policy in Vietnam, a number of key officials in the Kennedy (and then the Johnson) administration were familiar with their ideas, and there is fragmentary evidence to suggest that some of these concepts were embraced in the formulation and execution of U.S. strategy in Viet-nam.[16] Whether it was the intention of the authors—it must be stressed that neither Schelling nor Kahn publicly advocated that their strategic theories be applied by the U.S. government in prosecuting the war—the net effect was to induce a sense of confidence among U.S. policymakers that they could manipulate the conduct of the war far more effectively than they actually could.

This sense of confidence was undoubtedly bolstered by the Cuban Missile Crisis in October 1962, which was taken by members of the Kennedy administration to be a validation of the efficacy of coercive diplomacy. It demonstrated that by using the carefully controlled threat of force, the Communists could be made to back down. It indicated that by keeping lines of communication open, by making unambiguous signals about one's intentions, and by leaving clearly labeled "outs" for the opposition, the United States could prevail. That this formula's success in a Soviet-American confrontation might not necessarily imply a similar success in Southeast Asia was not widely appreciated in Washington before 1965.

Because of the growing sense in Washington in the early 1960s that insurgent warfare was the principal act of Communist expansionism that the United States would have to confront, the Kennedy administration was able and willing to develop counterinsurgency capabilities as a principal element of U.S. military force posture. As early as January 1961, Soviet Premier Khrushchev had said that "wars of national liberation" were "just" wars that he endorsed "wholeheartedly and without reservation."[17] The impression in Washington was that "the Khrushchev speech, though sufficiently tough, confined its bellicosity in the main to the underdeveloped world; and here, as Kennedy understood, the Soviets were confronted by opportunities that they could not easily resist."[18] That the United States needed effective military forces to counter rebellion, subversion, and guerilla warfare was an unchallenged assumption in the early days of the Kennedy period, and it drew particlar support from Robert Kennedy, attorney general; Walt Rostow, deputy assistant to the President for National Security Affairs; and Roger Hilsman, director of the Bureau of Intelligence and Research in the Department of State.

The literature on counterinsurgency techniques was developed primarily by military officers and others who had had first-hand experience confronting guerilla warfare in Malaya, the Philippines, Greece, and elsewhere. Samuel Huntington, one of the few American scholars to take an interest in the subject, offered the following observations in introducing a collection of essays on guerilla warfare:

Revolutionary warfare is the struggle between a nongovernment group and a government in which the latter attempts to destroy the former by some or all of the means at its command, and the nongovernmental group attempts by all the means at its command to replace the government in some or all of its territory. The post-World War II struggles in Indochina, Malaya and Algeria were revolutionary wars. . . . Guerilla warfare is a form of warfare by which the strategically weaker side assumes the tactical offensive in selected forms, times and places. . . . To win a revolutionary war, it is necessary to carry on a prolonged campaign for the support of a crucial social group. Guerilla warfare and counterguerilla warfare must be directed to this goal. Thus, the immediate problem of the United States is to develop a doctrine of counterguerilla warfare as one element in a broader politico-military strategy of counterrevolutionary war.[19]

Huntington's plea was heeded even before his words had been published. In the first year of the Kennedy administration the Special Warfare Center at Fort Bragg, North Carolina, was charged with training Special Forces to fight in the jungles of less developed countries; additional centers were established at Camp Pendleton, California, in Panama, Okinawa, and West Germany; and a Counterinsurgency Committee directed by Maxwell Taylor was established to oversee the development of this military capability.

In the early years of the Kennedy administration, the containment paradigm was not only reaffirmed, it was adjusted to accommodate strategies of limited war, concepts of coercive diplomacy, and techniques of counterinsurgency. Each adjustment made American military intervention more likely and easier to justify. In the early 1960s it was very difficult to see, at least from Washington, that Vietnam would be anything but another successful application of the paradigm.

DEFENDING THE PARADIGM

If Kuhn tells us something about paradigm development and adjustment, Festinger provides insight into paradigm defense and the process by which allegiances are transferred from the old paradigm to the new. Those with a vested interest in the old paradigm seek information and individuals to support their view and screen out, avoid, or ridicule sources of dissonance that undermine their position. This pattern was followed with the Vietnam policy.

When President Kennedy entered office, Eisenhower warned him that Laos was in trouble and could not afford to be lost to the Communists. In talks during the transition period between their presidencies, the two did not mention Vietnam except as an area that would be threatened if Laos fell. In January 1961 the American presence in Vietnam was limited to a 685-man Military Assistance Advisory Group. But by the time of Kennedy's death in November 1963, more than 16,000 U.S. personnel were in the country, President Diem of South Vietnam had been overthrown, the political scene in Saigon was acutely unstable, and the military situation in the countryside vis-à-vis the communists was deteriorating rather than improving.

These developments may be defined in Kuhn's terms as anomalies: phenomena that were not readily explained by the existing paradigm. Some observers immediately felt that the United States was headed for trouble, that the old rules were not applicable to Vietnam, that American priorities were becoming distorted. But in Washington policy circles this was clearly a minority view that carried very little weight.

After succeeding Kennedy, Lyndon Johnson reaffirmed the American commitment to containment and its applicability in Vietnam. He approved several steps to promote American military pressure against North Vietnam and used the Gulf of Tonkin incident in August 1964 to obtain from Congress (by a vote of 88 to 2) blanket approval and support of "all necessary measures to repel any armed attack against the forces of the United States and to prevent further aggression." Johnson justified his need for the powers provided by the congressional resolution in the following terms:

> The challenge that we face in Southeast Asia today is the same challenge that we faced with courage and that we have met with strength in Greece and Turkey, in Berlin and Korea, in Lebanon and Cuba. And to any who may be tempted to support or to widen the present aggression I say this: There is no threat to any peaceful power from the United States of America. But there can be no peace by aggression and no immunity from reply. That is what we meant by the actions that we took yesterday.[20]

By this time some individuals inside and outside the government questioned the direction of U.S. policy in Vietnam, but their attitude can only be described as a mixture of hope and concern and in no way an abandonment of the containment paradigm. Perhaps the *New York Times* summed up the American mood most aptly with an editorial published the day after passage of the Gulf of Tonkin Resolution:

> President Johnson ... now has proof of a united Congress and a united nation: he has demonstrated his own capacity for toughness. And the Communists have been left in no doubt about American determination. This is a position of strength from which the Administration can and should now demonstrate that it is as resolute in seeking a peaceful settlement as it is in prosecuting the war.[21]

During the next twelve months the United States undertook extensive bombing of North Vietnam and began placing large numbers of American combat troops on the ground in the South (the number rising from 125,000 men in July 1965 to 543,000 April 1969).

During this period of escalation, spokesmen for the administration—perhaps Secretary of State Dean Rusk most frequently and most articulately—presented the case for American military involvement in Vietnam. At least eight reasons were offered to justify American actions:

—to contain communism and prevent confirmation of the domino theory, which predicted that the fall of Vietnam would lead to the sequential fall of all the independent states of Southeast Asia much like a row of falling dominoes;
—to contain Chinese expansion;
—to honor American commitments to the Southeast Asia Treaty Organization (SEATO);[22]
—to repel aggression from North Vietnam;
—to permit South Vietnam the right of self-determination;
—to demonstrate that the United States keeps its word;
—to satisfy South Vietnam's request for American assistance;
—to prove that wars of national liberation cannot succeed.

The costs, risks, and benefits of these interrelated objectives were never fully spelled out, but the American people judged them to collectively have sufficient merit to support the policy for a very long time.

In the early period of American military involvement, the only high-level official openly skeptical of the policy was George Ball.[23] He argued that the costs of a widening military involvement in Vietnam outweighed the potential benefits of retaining a non-Communist government in the South. He rejected arguments that drew an analogy between the Korean War and the Vietnam War. Ball was particularly concerned that American overinvestment in Vietnam would have deleterious effects on the U.S. position in Europe. Consequently he urged that the President seek a political solution to the conflict that would avoid deeper American military involvement.

But Ball was arguing from a position of weakness: he was a European expert, not an Asian specialist; he was alone in his opposition; and much of his case rested on unproven assertions of what would happen if the focus on American military policy were maintained. The reading of the historical record by most of his colleagues failed to support Ball's contentions. Moreover, Ball's criticisms probably served Lyndon Johnson well, because Johnson, who was committed to the policy and totally disagreed with Ball's views, could justify to himself and others that he was being exposed to the full range of policy options.[24]

THE TRANSFER OF ALLEGIANCES

No single event completely transformed American opinion about the war in Vietnam or shattered American confidence in containment. Rather, it was a slow, gradual process, an accumulation of dissonant information for almost fifteen years. Different individuals and groups, with different stakes in the policy, withdrew their allegiance from the paradigm at different times, stimulated by different events. It took many years for the paradigm's weaknesses to become widely recognized. Recall that it was not until 1968 that public opinion polls in the United States showed that more than 50 percent of the American public was opposed to military intervention in Vietnam. Until 1973 the Congress, despite its deep division over the war, remained passive and failed to adopt any measure indicating unequivocal dissatisfaction with American policy. Even the presidential election of 1972 between Nixon and McGovern—in many ways a plebiscite on U.S. policy in Vietnam—demonstrated the unwillingness of the American people to admit failure and to demand the unconditional withdrawal of all forces from the area. unconditional withdrawal of all forces from the area.

What can be noted, however, are several key developments that led to important defections from the ranks of paradigm supporters. They may be summarized as follows:

Gulf of Tonkin Revelations—Senator William Fulbright, chairman of the prestigious Senate Foreign Relations Committee, who steered the Gulf of Tonkin Resolution through the Senate, learned in 1965 that the administration had provided a highly incomplete and misleading account of the events that led to the incident. Feeling that he had been a victim of the Johnson administration's duplicity and becoming increasingly convinced of the weakness of U.S. strategy, he became an outspoken critic of American policy. His criticism was particularly important because it broke the bipartisan consensus in the Congress on U.S. foreign policy that had been in evidence since the days of Arthur Vandenburgh and the Truman administration. Fulbright's eloquent and vigorous attacks, while ridiculed by Johnson, provided a prominent Southern establishment figure as a rallying point for the developing antiwar movement.

Discriminatory Draft—It became evident by the mid-1960s that Americans doing the fighting and dying in South Vietnam came disproportionately from black and other minority groups, with large numbers of middle-class white youths able to avoid the draft through deferments. Eventually this led important members of the Civil Rights movement, including Martin Luthur King, Jr., to become vigorous opponents of the war.

Sino-Soviet Split—A few American analysts as early as the late 1950s detected that the Soviet Union and the People's Republic of China were in open disagreement because of ideological differences, boundary disputes, competition for influence in the less developed countries, personal animosity between Mao Tse-tung and Khrushchev, and other reasons. As appreciation of this split spread among American intellectuals, it undercut the argument that the United States was confronted by a monolithic Communist movement and severely weakened the strategic rationale for American intervention.

Criticism by Southeast Asian Specialists—There was little expertise on Southeast Asia in the United States. But the few notable authorities, particularly Bernard Fall and Robert Shaplen, emphasized the differences between the reality of the situation as they saw it and the premises of American policy: the heroic figure of Ho Chi Minh to the Vietnamese people; the historical animosity between the Chinese and the Vietnamese and between the Vietnamese and the other peoples of Southeast Asia; the non-democratic traditions and apolitical interests of the Vietnamese peasantry; the cleavages between the Catholic, French-speaking urban elite in Saigon and the Confucian and Buddhist peasants in the countryside; and the innate corruption of the successive Saigon regimes compared to the more effective organizational techniques of the Viet Cong. These observations tended to undermine the arguments that the war was about Chinese expansion or South Vietnamese self-determination, and served to blur the distinctions between the evils of South and North Vietnamese Communists and the evils of corrupt South Vietnamese anti-Communists.

Deleterious American Domestic Effects—The mounting criticism of the war, particularly among the young, intellectual, and minority groups, led to substantial upheaval in the form of demonstrations, sit-ins, and boycotts. Television coverage of the war brought the conflict into the homes of millions of Americans nightly. American casualties, mounting toward 50,000 became a potent issue and galvanized additional opposition to the war. Annual expenditures of $30 billion to finance the war effort began to produce inflationary effects in the economy. By 1968 social upheaval was quite widespread and had become a tangible cost of the war, leading Alastair Buchan, for example, a sage and highly respected British observer of the American scene and a specialist on European-American relations, was forced to conclude by 1968 that "the Vietnam War is the greatest tragedy that has befallen the United States since the Civil War."[25]

Defection of Kennedy Administration Officials—Key members of the Kennedy administration who stayed on to work for President Johnson became progressively disillusioned about the effectiveness and appropriateness of the policy. The disillusionment started as early as 1964 and was quite pronounced by 1966. The sense of asymmetry between the limited war waged by the United States and the total war waged by the Communists; the ability of the North Vietnamese to absorb vast amounts of punishment; and the inability of the United States to transform the South Vietnamese government into an effective, less authoritarian, and widely supported regime brought on the resignations of George Ball, Roger Hilsman, and others. Robert McNamara and John McNaughton also turned against the policy and, although they stayed on in the Johnson administration (McNaughton was killed in a plane crash in 1967), they lost much of their influence with the President. Johnson interpreted these desertions as being motivated by the animosity of members of the Eastern establishment toward a Texas-born president and their desire to see him replaced by Robert Kennedy.

Criminal Acts by the American Military—Further erosion of support for the policy was produced when it was documented that criminal acts had been committed by the American military in Vietnam, thus obscuring the previously held image of the American hero in conflict with the Communist villain. The massacre at My Lai, the bombing of hospitals in North Vietnam, the falsification of body counts to satisfy quantitative measures of effectiveness, and the subsequent cover-up of these acts by high-level U.S. military officials generated the view that there was considerable corruption in the American war effort.

Tet Offensive—Perhaps more than any single event, the Tet Offensive demonstrated a gap between the American public's perception of the war and the military reality. President Johnson and his colleagues had spent much of 1967 building the case that most hamlets and cities in South Vietnam were safe from Communist attack and that the war was being won. But on January 31, 1968, forces of the National Liberation Front attacked many towns and cities in the country as well as every significant American military base. Although Communist forces ultimately suffered great losses, American policy had been dealt a grievous political blow.

Open criticism of American policy spilled onto the pages of major American news magazines and was endorsed by leading figures in broadcast journalism. It was Tet that led many Americans to transfer their allegiance from the containment paradigm.

Lack of Allied Support—With the transfer of allegiances away from the policy quite pronounced by early 1968, Johnson replaced McNamara with Clark Clifford, who had been a strong supporter of military intervention. Clifford went on a factfinding tour of the region, expecting to be bolstered by allied support for the U.S. war effort. He found instead only the mildest expressions of support and unwillingness by the Asian Pacific nations, except for South Korea and Australia, to contribute more than a token military presence to Vietnam. This lack of enthusiasm was crucial in changing Clifford's mind about the policy, and his change of mind was perhaps the decisive event that led President Johnson to halt the escalation of the war and to decide not to run for reelection.

Widening of the War Effort—Despite the criticism of the application of containment to Vietnam, the Nixon administration sought to disengage from Vietnam only under conditions that would permit the South Vietnamese government to continue functioning for several years. This led to the decision to intensify the war effort by invading Cambodia (to rid the Communists of sanctuaries) and increasing the frequency and destructiveness of the bombing, even while reducing the total level of U.S. combat troops in the area. These actions led some to believe that American military involvement might not end without congressional action. A substantial impetus was thus provided for the passage of the War Powers Act to constrain the ability of the President to wage war without congressional authorization.

The cumulative effect of these experiences was to transfer allegiances from the containment paradigm, destroying its legitimacy. And, because of *The Pentagon Papers* and the subsequent documentation of presidential wrong-doing in several areas by Kennedy, Johnson, and Nixon, a substantial dose of skepticism now pervades American attitudes toward whatever policies the President adopts.

TOWARD A NEW PARADIGM?

In the aftermath of the Vietnam experience no new paradigm has emerged to replace containment. A transfer of allegiances away from containment has taken place without moving toward any alternative. In this sense Kuhn's description is not applicable; instead, during the years since the fall of Vietnam, we have witnessed an unsuccessful search for a new set of guidelines to govern American foreign policy. Now three schools of thought can be distinguished: paradigm defenders; paradigm adjusters; and paradigm deniers.

The paradigm defenders essentially argue that the premises of containment are correct and that the United States failed in Vietnam only because its domestic political processes prevented the policy's proper execution. According to this view, the United States made only one crucial error during the war: it abandoned South Vietnam. The United States also applied its military force in too limited and too gradual a fashion, permitting North Vietnam to adjust to the incremental changes in military pressure. Future American intervention should still be guided by the objective of containing Communism, particularly Soviet expansionism. But U.S. strategy should emphasize the rapid application of maximum military force. Adherents of this view emphasize that South Vietnam was ultimately defeated by conventional forces from North Vietnam and not through Communist victories in guerilla warfare. They note that the domino theory was proven correct—Cambodia and Laos have fallen and Thailand is now gravely threatened. The principal concern of the paradigm defenders is that, as a consequence of Vietnam, the United States has lost the will to conduct an active foreign policy. Too many lessons and the wrong lessons will have been learned.

The paradigm adjusters argue that the Vietnam experience should teach us a good deal. We should now understand that Communism is a movement that, in and of itself, does not threaten vital U.S. interests. Indeed the United States can conduct economic relations with Communist regimes and can play balance of power politics among Communist states. The Vietnam conflict was essentially a civil war in which American intervention and the containment paradigm should have played no part. The Vietnam experience should teach us that the United States cannot be the world's policeman, that it is of crucial importance to understand indigenous political, cultural, economic, and historical patterns of behavior in formulating particular regional policies, and that we must remember who our close allies are—Western Europe, Japan, Israel—and not confuse them with other nations whose importance to the United States is a second- or third-order priority. The post-Vietnam experience suggests, according to this view, that the domino theory was incorrect: the Association of Southeast Asian Nations (ASEAN), Japan, South Korea, and Taiwan are as prosperous and as stable today as at any time in the last twenty years. Moreover, the Vietnam experience demonstrated the limitations of counterinsurgency techniques, strategic bombing, and coercive diplomacy. The United States must never again become embroiled in a conflict in which there is an asymmetry of incentives, with the United States having less at stake than its opponent. The principal threat to the United States is Soviet expansion, and this threat can be checked by enlisting the support of our allies and those nations in local areas threatened directly by such expansion.

The paradigm deniers argue that nothing is needed to replace containment, that the world is simply too complex and too unpredictable to formulate any useful set of general guidelines for American foreign policy that is applicable across both functional issues and regional areas. The one lesson that should be learned from the Vietnam experience is that international politics is not science and that it is both foolish and dangerous to believe in and try to implement any general guideline—no matter what its character—to foreign policy problems. There are no universal norms in international affairs. The Vietnam war was *sui generis*, as all wars throughout human history have been. Those who seek patterns in international conflict are doomed to find them and be misled by them. The United States, instead, should be guided by specific interests in particular regions that are subject to constant reexamination and redefinition. If the Soviet Union, or any other nation, bases its foreign policy on a set of universal norms, it too will suffer a fate similar to the American experience in Vietnam.

It is likely that the American wounds from Vietnam will remain sufficiently sore to preclude adopting the thesis of the paradigm defenders. Similarly, the American penchant to address global problems and the desire to introduce theory and concept into policy make it unlikely that the paradigm deniers will have their way. Instead, containment will surely be adjusted, refined, and relabelled. In its new form it will serve as the new paradigm. The Vietnam experience will be the dominant memory shaping this paradigm—whether we wish this to be the case or not.

NOTES

1. Graham Greene, *The Quiet American* (New York: Bantam Books, 1957), pp. 86-87.
2. This is one of several definitions of the word offered in *Webster's Seventh New Collegiate Dictionary* (Springfield, Mass.: G. & C. Merriam Company, 1970), p. 415.
3. Robert Jervis has been particularly active in this field. See *The Logic of Images in International Relations* (Princeton: Princeton University Press, 1970) and *Perception and Misperception in International Politics* (Princeton: Princeton University Press, 1976). But despite his subtle use of theoretical models and historical examples, Jervis also fails to construct a conceptual framework with wide-ranging applicability.
4. See Thomas Kuhn, *The Structure of Scientific Revolutions*, 2nd ed. (Chicago: University of Chicago Press, 1970) and Leon Festinger, *The Theory of Cognitive Dissonance* (Evanston, Ill.: Row, Peterson & Co., 1957). Kuhn's work has been the subject of great debate and criticism. See particularly Imre Lakatos and Alan Musgrave, eds., *Criticism and the Growth of Knowledge* (London: Cambridge University Press, 1970). And Festinger has been criticized by several of his colleagues in social psychology. But for purposes of explaining aspects of international politics especially relevant to American policy in Vietnam, Kuhn and Festinger have far more to tell us than their critics.
5. "Mr. X," "The Sources of Soviet Conduct," *Foreign Affairs*, July 1947, pp. 566-582. At the time, Kennan was director of the Policy Planning Staff in the Department of State.
6. This abbreviated interpretation of the highly complex immediate postwar period that led to the Cold War obviously rejects revisionist interpretations of the origin of the conflict, which stress either American aggresiveness or a process of mutual misperception.
7. In recent years, Kennan has claimed that containment was misunderstood and misapplied, and a debate has arisen over whether his criticism is justified. See John Lewis Gaddis, "Containment: A Reassessment," *Foreign Affairs*, July 1977, pp. 873-887 and Eduard Mark, "The Question of Containment: A Reply to John Lewis Gaddis," *Foreign Affairs*, October 1977, pp. 430-441.

8. *A Report to the National Security Council by the Executive Secretary on United States Objectives and Programs for National Security*, April 14, 1950, p. 63. Known as "NSC 68," this important document was declassified in February 1975.

9. Truman claimed in his memoirs that this doctrine was "the turning point in America's foreign policy, which now declared that wherever aggression, direct or indirect, threatened the peace, the security of the United States was involved.... It must be the policy of the United States to support free peoples who are resisting subjugation by armed minorities or by outside pressures." See Harry S. Truman, *Years of Trial and Hope*, vol. 2, (New York: Signet Books, 1965), p. 129.

10. *Department of State Bulletin*, February 6, 1961, pp. 175-176.

11. Note, for example, that in 1963 David Halberstam, who subsequently became one of the most outspoken critics of containment and American policy in Vietnam, wrote that "Americans have given their solemn word that they will stay to win here [Vietnam]. If they fail, the word will be out that Americans are paper tigers." Quoted in Henry Fairlie, "We Knew What We Were Doing When We Went Into Vietnam," *The Washington Monthly*, May 1973, p. 21. One of the few noted scholars who argued consistently that containment could not be applied successfully in Asia was Hans Morgenthau. But his views were not taken seriously by Washington policymakers.

12. It is now clear that massive retaliation was adopted not only because it was the preference of Eisenhower and Dulles on strategic grounds, but also because it would provide a rationale for reducing the defense budget, which was in keeping with Republican Party preferences at the time.

13. Among the most important works that made these points were William Kaufmann, *The Requirements of Deterrence*, memorandum no. 7 (Princeton, N.J.: Center of International Studies, 1954) and Robert Osgood, *Limited War: The Challenge to American Strategy* (Chicago: University of Chicago Press, 1957).

14. Maxwell D. Taylor, *The Uncertain Trumpet* (New York: Harper and Brothers, 1959), p. 6. Taylor and Mathew B. Ridgeway, each a former U.S. Army Chief of Staff, as well as James N. Gavin, former U.S. Army Deputy Chief of Staff for Plans and Research, called for the acquisition of such capabilities as Kennedy took office.

15. Schelling must be credited with all of these insights except the notion of controlled escalation. His work *The Strategy of Conflict* (London: Oxford University Press, 1960), was based in part on articles published in the *Journal of Conflict Resolution* and several journals of economics between 1956 and 1959. A later work, *Arms and Influence* (New Haven, Conn.: Yale University Press, 1966), in which the distinction between deterrence and compellence was made, drew to some extent on articles published by Schelling in journals in the early 1960s. Kahn's views on controlled escalation were presented in *On Escalation: Metaphors and Scenarios* (Baltimore: Penguin Books, 1966). He offered his views to several high-level civilian and military audiences prior to the book's publication.

16. Among the officials with these concepts were McGeorge Bundy, William Bundy, Roger Hilsman, Robert Kennedy, Robert McNamara, John McNaughton, and Walt Rostow. Language and concepts strikingly familiar to those of Shelling and Kahn may be found at several points in the Pentagon Papers. Note, for example, the following items cited in *The Pentagon Papers: The Senator Gravel Edition*, vol. 3 (Boston: Beacon Press, 1971), pp. 119-120, 124, 694-702, and 632, respectively.

    a. An interagency study group under the Department of State's Vietnam Committee produced an interim report on March 1, 1964 entitled "Alternatives for the Imposition of Measured Pressure Against North Vietnam." The objectives were to force North Vietnam to cease support of the Viet Cong; to strengthen the morale of the government of South Vietnam while reducing Viet Cong morale; and to prove to the world U.S. determination to oppose Communist expansion.

b. A draft presidential memorandum was completed May 23, 1964 that spelled out a thirty day scenario of graduated political and military pressures against the North. However, it was never adopted.

c. In March 1965 John McNaughton developed an elaborate plan of controlled military escalation against North Vietnam. The purpose of the proposed escalation was to demonstrate that the U.S. has "kept promises, been tough, taken risks, gotten bloodied, and hurt the enemy very badly. We must avoid harmful appearances which will affect judgements by, and provide pretexts to, other nations regarding how the U.S. will behave in future cases of particular interest to those nations—regarding U.S. policy, power, resolve and competence to deal with their problems."

d. In a memorandum to Secretary McNamara dated November 16, 1964 on "military dispositions and political signals," Walt Rostow made the following points: "Following on our conversation of last night I am concerned that too much thought is being given to the actual damage we do in the North, not enough thought to the signal we wish to send. The signal consists of three parts: a) damage to the North is now to be inflicted because they are violating the 1954 and 1962 Accords; b) we are ready and able to go much further than our initial act of damage; c) we are ready and able to meet any level of escalation they might mount in reponse; if they are so minded."

Moreover the Rolling Thunder bombing strategy as formulated by International Security Affairs and opposed by the joint chiefs of staff was defended by using Schelling's strategy.

It cannot be stated unequivocally, however, that the writings of Schelling or Kahn or both inspired these proposals and evaluations.

17. See N. S. Khrushchev, "For New Victories for the World Communist Movement," *World Marxist Review*, January 1961, pp. 3-28.

18. Arthur Schlesinger, Jr., *A Thousand Days* (Boston: Houghton Mifflin Company, 1965), p. 304.

19. Franklin Osanka, ed., *Modern Guerilla Warfare* (New York: The Free Press of Glencoe, 1962), pp. xvi, xxi.

20. These words were part of a speech Johnson delivered at Syracuse University the day after passage of the Gulf of Tonkin Resolution. See Lyndon Baines Johnson, *The Vantage Point: Perspectives of the Presidency, 1963-1969* (New York: Holt, Rinehart and Winston, 1971), pp. 112-114.

21. *New York Times*, August 8, 1964, p. 18.

22. South Vietnam was not a party to the treaty. But a protocol to the treaty specified that the parties unanimously designated Cambodia, Laos, and "the free territory under the jurisdiction of the State of Vietnam" as states and territory to which provisions of the treaty concerning collective defense and economic assistance were applicable.

23. Ball was originally appointed undersecretary of state for economic affairs in the Kennedy administration. In late 1961 he was promoted to undersecretary of state, the number two position in the department. He held this post until 1966.

24. In his memoirs Johnson described Ball as playing the role of devil's advocate on Vietnam policy. See *The Vantage Point*, p. 147. Perhaps Johnson was unaware that the definition of the term "devil's advocate" is "a person who upholds the wrong side, perversely or for argument's sake."

25. Alastair Buchan, "Questions about Vietnam," *Encounter*, January 1968, p. 8.

Chapter 18

The ABM Debate

George Rathjens

INTRODUCTION

In September 1967 Robert McNamara, then Secretary of Defense, announced that the United States would deploy an anti-ballistic missile defense system, primarily to defend the country against missile attack by China. The announcement was remarkable in that it was a codicil to a most eloquent statement of why an attempt to defend against Soviet missiles would be a mistake, and because there was relatively little concern at that time in policy circles, or in the country at large, about a Chinese "threat."[1] The announcement followed a dozen years of intragovernmental controversy about deployment of defenses to cope with Soviet missiles.

During those years, few in the technical community questioned the feasibility of destroying a single adversary reentry vehicle with a nuclear-armed interceptor missile. There was, however, very considerable doubt, particularly during the late 1950s and early 1960s, about the feasibility of constructing a system that could track a large number of incoming objects, discriminate between warheads and decoys, and then destroy a large fraction of the former.

Depending as it did on mechanically-steered radars and relatively slow interceptor missiles, the army's state-of-the-art system of the early 1960s, Nike-Zeus, offered little hope of success. Technical performance was greatly improved, however, with the development during that period of phased-array radars and interceptor missiles capable of very high acceleration. The former, when coupled with an appropriate computer, could in principle track many objects simultaneously and, by observing the differential effects of atmospheric drag, discriminate between warhead-containing reentry vehicles and lighter decoys. Launch of the high-velocity interceptor missiles, Sprints, could be delayed until this discrimination had occurred, and still adversary warheads could be destroyed before their detonation could seriously damage ground targets.

There were, however, serious problems with Nike-X, the army's concept for an ABM defense base on these developments. First, defense of the whole country based on intercept after reentry would require a prohibitively large number of interceptors: at least tens of thousands. Alternatively, if only cities and other key targets were to be defended by Sprint interceptors, or by any other kind of local defense, it would be possible for adversary warheads to be detonated in undefended areas upwind of cities. Without a highly effective shelter program, enormous numbers of fatalities could be expected from radioactive fallout. Second, it was clear that by the time a nationwide Nike-X system could be deployed, the Soviet Union could employ multiple independently targetable reentry vehicles (MIRVs) on its missiles, thereby greatly increasing the number of warheads that would have to be intercepted. Particularly with MIRVs, it seemed very likely that the "cost exchange" ratio would continue to be highly disadvantageous for the defense, just as had been the case with Nike-Zeus: each increment of defense could be offset, at a much lesser cost, by the Soviet Union's procuring a capability to deliver more warheads. Third, it was possible that high altitude detonation of nuclear weapons, defensive or offensive, would adversely affect radar performance. Finally, there was the possibility of catastrophic failure of the defense for reasons not predictable in advance, a serious concern considering the impossibility of ever testing the system in an environment remotely like that in which it might have to perform.

McNamara found the arguments against deployment of an ABM defense persuasive, as had his predecessors. Of particular concern to him was the likelihood of a Soviet reaction. He, and many in the "arms control community," were convinced that construction of U.S. defenses would lead to a compensating improvement in Soviet offensive capabilities. Indeed, an over-reaction was possible, considering the inherent great uncertainty in defense effectiveness. Thus, an ABM deployment was seen as a major impetus to what McNamara called "the mad momentum intrinsic to the development of all new nuclear weaponry" and as an impediment to efforts at strategic arms control. Others, notably some of the joint Chiefs of Staff and members of Congress, disagreed. They favored system deployment because they were more sanguine about effectiveness, and/or skeptical that the Soviet Union would react as McNamara feared it would.

By 1966 it had become increasingly difficult to resist pressures for an ABM deployment, especially in light of Soviet efforts: Construction of a true ABM system around Moscow and of defenses elsewhere, which some interpreted as ABM-related, although the prevailing view was that they were only air defenses with little ABM capability or potential. After the Johnson-Kosygin summit meeting at Glassboro in June 1967, when McNamara failed to convince Premier Kosygin of the wisdom of mutual restraint in the deployment of defenses, some kind of ABM deployment had become a political necessity in the eyes of the President. Hence, McNamara's announcement of the decision to go ahead with the China-oriented defense, which came to be referred to as the Sentinel plan.[2]

THE SENTINEL DEBATE

Sentinel was to defend the whole country from fifteen sites, mainly with relatively slow, very long-range interceptor missiles—Spartans, a carry-over from the old Nike-Zeus program. With intercept to be accomplished well outside the atmosphere, no discrimination between warheads and decoys would be possible before launch of the Spartan interceptors, but it was argued that China—in contrast to the Soviet Union—could present at most only a very limited threat for some years: a modest number of warheads and no effective decoys. Still, some Sprints were to be included in the Sentinel system, not to defend population but, in recognition of the criticality of the radars, to defend them. Two kinds of radars were to be involved. Five north-facing Perimeter Acquisition Radars (PARs) were to be deployed to detect incoming warheads (and other objects) and to provide preliminary tracking information about them. This information was to be passed to a Missile Site Radar (MSR), one of which was to be deployed at each site to control the engagement. The MSRs, operating at higher frequencies than the PARs, would be less susceptible to radar blackout by high altitude nuclear explosions.[3]

Sentinel was not the answer to anyone's prayers. McNamara hoped it would meet the political need for some kind of affirmative deployment decision without provoking a Soviet response. Yet, what favorable reaction there was from ABM proponents was based on their seeing Sentinel as a first step toward a Soviet-oriented system. It was not surprising that they saw it that way. The components were essentially the same as would have been incorporated in a Nike-X Soviet-oriented defense. Moreover, the army decided to locate some of the sites near cities, as had been envisaged in the Nike-X plans. This was quite deliberate: such deployment would facilitate expansion to heavy defense in the event of a later decision to move in that direction and meanwhile would provide a superior defense against light attacks for at least a few cities—at no greater cost than if the sites were in remote areas.

Local opposition to Sentinal developed because of concern about land-taking and societal disruption generally associated with large construction projects, and because of the fear of the possible accidental explosion of the very high yield Spartan warheads. This opposition was largely unanticipated. Indeed, in earlier intra-governmental discussion about Nike-X there had been concern that complaints would come from those cities *not* covered by terminal defenses. As it turned out, the decision to locate the defenses at sites in close proximity to large cities was a major factor in the scale of opposition, in media coverage, and in providing opportunities for "defense intellectuals" and others from the technical community to question the plan.

There were three questions: was a Chinese "threat" an imminent possibility; would the system "work"; would its deployment contribute to escalation of the Soviet-American arms race?

At the time, China's development of an ICBM capability seemed like a second-order problem to many and—particularly to those who opposed the Sentinal decision—a distant possibility.[4] Their judgment has had some vindication: until 1980, China did not conduct a full-range test of an ICBM that could reach the forty-eight contiguous states.

Whether the system—if deployed—would have "worked," cannot be answered as definitively. Part of the problem is the question of expectations. The administration's primary rationale was that the system was needed to enhance U.S. credibility as a guarantor of the security of nations that might be threatened by China: it was needed so that the U.S. could act freely and credibly in Asia, undeterred by the prospect of Chinese retaliation with nuclear-armed ICBMs against one or more U.S. cities.[5] Clearly, that objective could be met only by a virtually leak-proof defense, considering the damage that might be inflicted by a single three-megaton Chinese warhead. Although administration spokesmen claimed a damage-denial capability for Sentinel,[6] the limited number of interceptors and radars, the possibilities of the blackout of radars, the use of decoys or other penetration aids with which a Spartan-based defense could not cope, and system failure for other reasons, all raised doubts at the time about the defense being leak-proof. Nothing has happened since that would suggest such doubts were ill-founded.

On the other hand, the system *might* have been able to cope with a very limited number of missiles launched by accident, and that was a secondary rationale for it. To do so, however, necessarily would have involved delegation of authority to launch interceptors to low command echelons—indeed, possibly to the computers—since the time available for making a launch decision would be short: less than ten minutes in some cases for submarine-launched missiles. Administration spokesmen did not respond to queries about whether they envisaged such delegation of launch authority.

Whether or not deployment of Sentinel would have fueled the Soviet-American arms race, as many opponents feared, must also remain an unanswered question. It has been suggested, however, and with some basis, that such fears were exaggerated and based on a simplistic model of the dynamics of the Soviet-American arms competition. It is very likely that the Soviets would have credited the system with some effectiveness in degrading any attack by them against the cities where defenses were to be deployed. While the Sprints were to be there ostensibly to defend the collocated radars, they could have been used to defend the cities as well, and with that possibility, Sentinel looked technically superior to the system the Soviets were deploying around Moscow at the time. Moreover, there was the possibility of upgrading the defense, as the Chinese "threat" might evolve.

It does not follow, however, that the Soviets necessarily would have responded by accelerating their build-up in offensive forces or planning to build to higher levels than in the absence of U.S. defenses. Those fears and assumptions, widely held in the arms control community, were based in large measure on a belief that, in the absence of defenses, the Soviets would build their strategic forces to a "sufficient" level and then stop. The continuing build-up in Soviet strategic forces in the late 1970s and other developments including, notably, the continuation of U.S. MIRV programs after the conclusion of the ABM treaty, have raised doubts about both the concepts of "sufficiency" and "action-reaction" as determinants of the strategic force postures of the superpowers.

The amount of weight that should be attached to these concepts is a matter of continuing importance and debate. If one believes there is very little to the "action-reaction theory of the arms race"—that the strategic offensive programs of one side will be very little influenced by "damage-limiting" programs of the other, e.g., by air, ABM, anti-submarine warfare (ASW) or civil defenses, or even counterforce capabilities—there may be a strong case for such programs, even if the cost-exchange ratio is unfavorable.[7] Belief in the "action-reaction" theory leads to quite the opposite conclusion.[8]

Returning to Sentinel, what more can appropriately be said? It was a success in meeting what was almost certainly the immediate objective for it. It looked enough like the beginnings of a serious Soviet-oriented ABM defense and was so construed by those about whom President Johnson was most concerned—the Joint Chiefs of Staff and pro-ABM factions in Congress and elsewhere, including particularly the Republican Party—that the charge of an "ABM gap" was obviated as an issue that could be used against the Democrats in the political campaign of 1968. But it was a short-lived success achieved at some price. Many thought it a nonsensical plan. The result was a large and vocal opposition and further erosion in the credibility of the defense establishment, already low at that point in time because of the Vietnam War.

The stage had been set for a congressional debate of virtually unprecented nature: a pitting of outside experts against Defense Department experts in the evaluation of a major weapons system.[9]

Could the administration have achieved its objective at a lower cost? In retrospect, it seems possible. Siting the defenses in remote areas would have produced much less opposition, both from local citizenry and the arms control community; and yet, such a program might well have been sufficient to mollify most of the proponents of ABM deployment. At the other extreme, the administration might have gone ahead with the army's proposal for a Soviet-oriented defense, and this might have been done without stimulating greater immediate domestic opposition than occurred. Very likely, such a decision could have been implemented, however, only by first replacing McNamara as Secretary of Defense; and probably that would have had to have been done prior to 1967, considering his opposition to such a deployment during that year and his effective exploitation of the country's most respected technical advisers in support of his position.[10]

As it was, the incoming Nixon administration inherited a plan for which there was little support and to which there was growing and potentially troublesome opposition. The range of options for change open to the administration was, however, severely limited. Implementation of a full-scale Soviet-oriented defense would have been exceedingly costly and hard to justify, considering that by then the technical inadequacies of the system had been widely publicized and largely accepted in the defense and arms control communities. Simple termination of Sentinel and limitation of the country's ABM effort to research and development would have provoked a confrontation with the Joint Chiefs of Staff and would have been unacceptable to many of the new administration's supporters. Such a retrogressive move would also have meant giving up what was perhaps its best "bargaining chip" for the strategic arms limitation talks with the Soviet Union.

THE SAFEGUARD DEBATE

"Safeguard" was the administration's solution to the problem. Initially, it was to involve the defense of Minuteman missiles at two of the nation's six Minuteman ICBM sites—Malmstrom Air Force Base, Montana and Grand Forks, North Dakota—essentially using the same components that had been proposed for Sentinel. The prospect was held open for a Phase II expansion to defend additional ICBM sites and SAC bomber bases—as well as Washington, D.C., as a national command center—against possible Soviet attack. Included in Phase II was also the possibility of a "light" (i.e., a Sentinel-type) defense of the whole country. The rationale was the same as adduced earlier: to cope with a possible Chinese threat or accidentally launched missiles. Significantly, however, the sites for the light area option were to be some distance from large cities, in contrast to the Sentinel plan.

Safeguard would maintain the momentum of some kind of ABM deployment while offering important advantages compared with Sentinel. Its immediate focus was on what was widely held to be a more plausible and more worrisome threat—the possibility of the Soviet Union's developing a capability for destruction of a large fraction of the U.S. ICBM force in a preemptive attack. It would get the defense away from the large cities and hence would remove the cause of much of the vocal opposition that Sentinel had engendered. And it was likely to be much less troublesome to the arms control community since, on the assumptions prevalent in that community—those relating to action-reaction and sufficiency—it would not be as great a stimulus to Soviet strategic offensive development.[11] Finally, a defense of missile silos (i.e., a "hard site" defense) would *in principle* be more feasible than defense of population.[12] This is in part because missile silos are designed to be much more resistant to the effects of nuclear explosions than cities (a point discussed later), but also because of the difference in standards of performance demanded. Leakage of a few adversary weapons through a population defense would generally have catastrophic consequences; moreover, each urban target, for many purposes—as for example in the case of the Sentinel defense—would have to be defended on the assumption that the *attacker* might preferentially attack some targets very heavily while perhaps not attacking others at all. In the case of missile silos, the loss of a substantial fraction might be quite acceptable. The *defense* might elect to defend a part of the force preferentially, not bothering to expend resources defending the rest. The attacker, however, would have to allocate his forces without knowledge of which particular silos were to be defended; hence, would likely expend more weapons on undefended targets than needed to destroy them, while perhaps attacking defended ones with insufficient force.

There were, however, two broad questions raised by the Safeguard decision, and these provided the foci for the debate that immediately followed the announcement: was it likely that U.S. strategic forces would be rendered vulnerable by Soviet developments on the time-scale envisaged by the administration; and if so, was Safeguard the best solution to the problem—could it be effective?

At the time of the decision, the Soviet Union was deploying very large ICBMs, SS-9s, that had been tested with multiple warheads. Members of the technical community disagreed on whether these were independently targettable but not on the possibility of the Soviets deploying missiles with such capabilitiis in the not-distant future. It also seemed inevitable that the accuracy of Soviet missiles would improve. Thus, there was the prospect of the Soviets obtaining a theoretical capability of destroying—in the absence of U.S. countermeasures—nearly all of the U.S. ICBM force with a fraction of their ICBMs. The critical questions were when this might occur and how much confidence the Soviets might have in their ability to execute such an attack, whatever the theoretical possibilities, given the serious operational problems involved and the impossibility of exercising such an attack with a high degree of realism.

The first question received disproportionate attention during the debate. The answer depended on assumptions about the rate of Soviet ICBM deployment; the number, yield, and accuracy of the MIRV warheads they might carry; the "hardness" of U.S. missile silos; and particularly the reliability of Soviet missiles, and whether or not failures could be compensated by more-or-less instantaneous targetting of back-up missiles. Administration witnesses and supporters suggested that, in the absence of defenses, a Soviet force of 420 to 500 SS-9 ICBMs might suffice to destroy 95% of the Minuteman force and that such a force might be deployed by 1974-1975.[13] The opponents generally argued that a much larger fraction of U.S. ICBMs would survive such an attack and also questioned whether the Soviets would build 400 to 500 SS-9s by 1974-1975. Some conceded the possibility of an effective Soviet counter-force capability in that timeframe, but asserted a larger Soviet force would be required. The prevalent opposition view, however, was that development of an effective Soviet counterforce capability would take longer. It was the right view, as is now clear: in January 1980, Secretary of Defense Brown stated:

> within a year or two we can expect them [the Soviets] to obtain the necessary combination of ICBM numbers, reliability, accuracy and warhead yield to put most of our Minuteman and Titan silos at risk from an attack with a relatively small proportion of their ICBM force.[14]

It might be argued that the seven or eight year "slippage" is a consequence of Soviet force levels having been limited by SALT, but it now seems exceedingly unlikely that the capability could have been achieved as early as the mid-1970s, even without the SALT constraints. The Soviets never deployed the SS-9 with MIRVs, and as early as mid-1971, well before the conclusion of the SALT I negotiations, it had become clear that a mid-1970s disarming strike based on by-then-demonstrated technology was not a realistic possibility. A Defense-CIA-sponsored study by Thompson-Ramo-Wooldridge which reached this conclusion was leaked to the press,[15] and although Deputy Secretary of Defense Packard was, to say the least, evasive when questioned about the study,[16] non-government witnesses with access to intelligence information confirmed the reasonableness of its findings.[17] So, too, did the air force, at least by inference, in saying that the threat to the Minuteman force was a late-1970s-1980s problem:

> . . . the Minuteman force can survive the present threat without the added protection of an active defense. However, there are threat projections for the late 1970s and early 1980s which would bring Minuteman security into question.[18]

Neither the administration nor its supporters made any serious effort to deal with the question of the confidence the Soviets might have in their ability to execute such an attack, and that remains a relevant question in current debates about the evolution of a Soviet counterforce capability.

The administration failed also to deal effectively with the opponents' claim that the Soviets could probably not destroy the U.S. submarine-based missile force (the SLBMs) and bomber forces concurrently with an attack against U.S. ICBMs.

During the Safeguard debate Secretary of Defense Laird alluded to possible serious vulnerability of U.S. submarines to Soviet ASW capability occurring as early as the mid-1970s:

> The next question: Is there any reason to believe that our Poseidon force will be vulnerable to preemptive attack during the early 1970's?

If this particular question is limited to the period through 1972-1973, I would say I believe that our force will remain very free from attack. If you go beyond that time period, I would have to question that seriously, and I would be very happy in our executive sessions to get into the possibilities of some of the new things that are taking place in this particular area.[19]

Soviet ASW capabilities have not since developed to anything like the degree of which he warned, nor was there any real basis for his allusion then.[20] The Senate Foreign Relations Committee was understandably skeptical, particularly after the expression of a contrary opinion by Rear Admiral Levering Smith, the director of the navy's Polaris-Poseidon program. It therefore held a special hearing on the subject with Harvey Brooks, probably the nation's leading non-government expert on ASW, as a witness. Brooks said he knew of no basis for Laird's remarks.[21] These observations and another Laird made before the Foreign Relations Committee—"They [the Soviets] are going for a first strike capability. There is no question about that"[22]—led to still another special hearing by that committee.[23] It was perhaps the most bizarre and frustrating episode of the ABM debate. After seventy-five pages of testimony, Secretary Laird had still not explained to the committee's satisfaction what he meant by the last remark—whether his reference to a first strike related to just the U.S. ICBM force or to the whole U.S. retaliatory capability, including SLBMs and bombers.

By the next year his comments on the ASW threat were more restrained:

. . . the Soviet Navy today might be able to localize and destroy at sea one or two POLARIS submarines. But the massive and expensive undertaking that would be required to extend such a capability using any currently known ASW techniques would take time and would certainly be evident.

However, a combination of technological developments and the decision by the Soviets to undertake a world-wide ASW effort might result in some increased degree of POLARIS/POSEIDON vulnerability beyond the mid-1970s. I would hope that POLARIS would remain invulnerable at least through the 1970s. But, as a defense planner, I would never guarantee the invulnerability of any strategic system beyond the reasonably forseeable future, say 5-7 years.[24]

Administration spokesmen and supporters also suggested that the Soviets might attack the Strategic Air Command (SAC) bomber bases with sea-launched ballistic missiles (SLBMs), and that this could be done with especially great effectiveness if those missiles were launched on depressed trajectories, in which case, the flight and warning time would be so short that few bombers would be able to escape destruction. The opposition, and later the air force,[25] pointed out that because of the roughly thirty minute flight time of ICBMs, the bombers would have adequate warning of attack if the Soviets launched their ICBMs to make impact at about the same time as their SLBMs; and that if they launched their two missile forces at the same time, there would be an interval of about twenty minutes after the bombers were destroyed during which the Minuteman force might be launched before its destruction: hence, it would seem impossible for the Soviets to execute a coordinated attack which they could be confident would destroy both the Minuteman and U.S. bomber force.

In summary, the discounting of concerns about ICBM vulnerability—because of the relative invulnerability of the SLBM force and the likelihood that a significant number of SAC bombers would survive a Soviet attack—seems to have been justified.

Probably the most authoritative statement about the "first-strike" problem—at least regarding the mid-1970s—was that of Secretary of Defense Schlesinger:

> There is just no possibility that a high confidence disarming first strike is attainable for either side even against the ICBM components of the strategic forces on both sides and certainly not against both sets of forces, SLBMs and ICBMs.[26]

But, of course, this was not the last word on the subject. The Safeguard-related debate about the vulnerability of U.S. forces to a counterforce attack, and the recent debate about Minuteman vulnerability and the need for the MX missile, remind one of how prescient P. M. S. Blackett was when he warned, after a similar debate in the late 1950s, that questions about the delicacy of the strategic balance would remain with us for many years, and that we might again be confronted with arguments—in his view false—to prove it unstable.[27] It would appear to be a cyclical problem, peaking at about ten-year intervals.

The second broad question that arose during the Safeguard debate, that of its effectiveness, proved just as troublesome to its supporters: to some, apparently more so, since they avoided talking about it, insofar as possible, preferring instead to focus attention on whether there would be a threat to Minuteman in the absence of defense.

Safeguard was vulnerable to attack by both Soviet missiles and U.S. opponents, primarily because the components, particularly the MSR, were poorly matched to the job of defending missile sites. This was hardly surprising since they had been designed to defend urban areas.

Requirements for the two missions are very different. Since cities are easily destroyed, adversary warheads in the megaton-yield range must be intercepted several miles from the city—hundreds of miles if fall-out is to be avoided—whereas missile silos are designed to withstand the effects of such weapons detonating within a fraction of a mile. For city defense, interceptors should therefore have a range in excess of 10 miles as Sprint had. For defense of hardened missiles, shorter range, less expensive interceptors may be adequate.

But the more critical difference is in radar requirements. The question arises as to whether, in attacking a defended target or group of targets, an attacker should first try to destroy the radars and the associated computers that control the defenses or should simply allocate its weapons to primary target(s).

If the objective is to destroy a city, the answer will generally be the latter: a single large weapon aimed at either a city or a radar would likely destroy either target, but the former more easily. Thus, there would be no advantage in attacking a radar unless it could control defenses of several cities or a city of such great area that several weapons might be required to destroy it.

In the case of an ICBM site, however, the situation is just the reverse. Many weapons would be required to destroy the ICBMs in their silos— at least two or three hundred in the case of a Minuteman wing—but a single weapon could destroy a radar, and if it were like the MSR for Safeguard, it could be done with a lower yield or less accurately delivered warhead than would be required for destroying ICBM silos. With the radar destroyed, the defense would be impotent.

With Safeguard, the problem could have been alleviated, in principle, by deploying a number of MSRs at each Minuteman base. This option was rejected, however, because of high cost. The MSR was, then, the Achilles' heel of the defense. It had to be assumed that, in any attack against a defended Minuteman wing, the MSR would be the first priority target.

Thus, the effectiveness of Safeguard depended on a number of interceptor missiles being sited near the MSR and allocated to its defense. That was an unattractive option, particularly since if the radar were not attacked, interceptors so sited could not—because of inadequate range—defend ICBM silos near the periphery of the Minuteman base. Most critical was the fact that the number of interceptors to be procured for Safeguard was to be small. The opponents argued that if the numbers were made public, the limited capability of Safeguard would be obvious, but the administration refused to release them. From cost figures in the public domain, however, one could estimate that the number of interceptors per site would be about one hundred. When the

ABM Treaty was concluded, it indeed allowed only one hundred interceptors per site; and when the Grand Forks site was finished, it had thirty Spartans and seventy Sprints.

Because the number of interceptors was to be so limited, and because of the problems of radar vulnerability, Safeguard could have been useful over only a very narrow range of threats at best. The administration argued that the number of surviving Minuteman missiles would be increased by a factor of two or three with a two-site Safeguard defense. What it did not willingly concede, at least in 1969, was that if the adversary "threat" was somewhat less than hypothesized, Safeguard would not be needed, or that if it increased by as little as 10 percent over its estimates, the effect of the Safeguard defense would be negated. At the rate Secretary Laird was hypothesizing in making his case for Safeguard, such an increase in the "threat" would have amounted to about a year's production of Soviet SS-9s, or a few months' production if they were deployed with more numerous, smaller warheads optimized to attack the MSRs.

Safeguard's opponents identified these problems and more. Most of those with technical backgrounds argued that if a defense was needed it should be based on a redesigned system—particularly including cheaper, harder, less capable, redundant radars—and that such a defense could be deployed in sufficient time to meet any plausible threat—perhaps, in less time than would be required for the Safeguard deployment.

They also suggested other solutions to the Minuteman vulnerability problem: increasing the "hardness" of the silos; doing nothing until there were more conclusive indicators of a threat; then, if necessary, procuring either more Minuteman missiles or more SLBMs, either of which would require less time than the Safeguard defense and would be more cost-effective.

They also claimed that bomber vulnerability could be significantly reduced by greater dispersal, particularly to bases further from the coasts.

At the time, the reactions of administration spokesmen and supporters to such suggestions were generally negative. Within a year or so, however, programs to disperse the bombers of the Strategic Air Command, to further harden the Minuteman missile silos, and to develop a hard-site missile defense system based on radar development for that purpose were all being implemented. The Low Altitude Defense System (LoADS), under consideration for the defense of MX, is a direct derivative of the last effort. If deployed it will use not only much more suitable radars than the MSR of Safeguard but also a shorter range interceptor missile about half the size of Sprint.

The 1969 debate came to a head on August 6 when an amendment to delete funds for Safeguard failed of passage in the Senate on a 50-50 vote. The narrowness of the a administration's victory and the exposure of Safeguard's limitations ensured, however, that the debate would continue.

These were also undoubtedly important factors in development of positions espoused by the administration in the 1970 debate. In 1969 it had based its position on the effectiveness and desirability of defense in the event of a failure of arms control efforts. Deputy Secretary of Defense Packard testified, "It provides a hedge against failure of arms control. If the Soviets refuse a workable agreement, then this country will be able to move to a protection of its second-strike force, if the Soviets continue to install more effective weapons."[28] John Foster, the Director of Defense Research and Engineeering said, "We think on the basis of those kinds of calculations [cost-exchange calculations] that we can on an economic and practical basis, defend the Minuteman field against anything the Soviets will throw at us."[29] In 1970, the claims for it were more modest. Secretary of Defense Laird said:

> To be perfectly candid, Mr. Chairman, it must be recognized that the threat could actually turn out to be considerably larger than the SAFEGUARD defense is designed to handle. That is one reason we have decided to pursue several courses which should lead to less expensive options for the solution to this problem than expanding SAFEGUARD to meet the highest threat level. We have further decided to continue deployment of SAFEGUARD because the additional cost needed to defend a portion of MINUTEMAN is small if the full area defense is bought. SAFEGUARD can also serve as a core for growth options in defense of MINUTEMAN if required.[30]

One of those less expensive options has been mentioned above: development of a radar specifically designed for a hard-site defense.

In addition, in 1970 the administration proposed adding more Sprint interceptors to the first two Safeguard sites and defense of a third Minuteman site at Whiteman Air Force Base, Missouri. It also asked for authorization for long lead-time work for five additional sites. One of the five would provide defense of an additional Minuteman base and another of Washington, D.C.

A rationale for all the additional sites was that they would provide a defense for some bomber bases and would be a major step toward a nationwide China-oriented defense. The penultimate sentence in Laird's statement, above, is the most explicit suggestion in the public record of a move by the Nixon administration to sell the whole Safeguard program primarily as a Chinese-oriented defense, with defense of Minuteman being a relatively low-cost marginal benefit.[31] The administration went as far as the previous one in claiming both effectiveness and need for a China-oriented defense, with the President at one time saying that such a defense would be "virtually infallible . . . and, therefore gives the U.S. a credible foreign policy in the Pacific area which it otherwise would not have."[32]

The renewed emphasis in 1970 on the China rationale was no doubt a consequence of the growing realization that, with the exposure of its technical inadequacies, it was becoming almost impossible to sell Safeguard as a defense of Minuteman. This was especially the case after a secret study, commissioned by John Foster, concluded:

> If the only purpose of Safeguard is defined to be to protect Minuteman, phase IIA as defined in March 1969 [the expansion beyond the first two sites] should not proceed. Instead a dedicated system for active defense of Minuteman should replace or, if the need for the MSR is proved, augment Phase IIA.[33]

Finally, in efforts to get support, administration spokesmen made two other arguments: they raised the specter of the necessity of an expansion of U.S. strategic offensive capabilities if Safeguard were not continued, and, indeed, expanded beyond its Phase I proposals of 1969; they claimed that its termination would weaken the U.S. negotiating position in the strategic arms limitation talks (SALT), then underway.

The Senate Armed Services Committee refused to go along with the long lead-time efforts toward a Chinese-oriented defense, but Safeguard survived debate in the Senate that year, 52-47. This was clearly because some senators, unpersuaded of its utility as a defense either for Minuteman or against China, were greatly influenced by the argument that Safeguard was needed for negotiating purposes.[34]

Thereafter, SALT dominated further consideration of ABM questions. In its budget submission in the Spring of 1971, the administration requested authorization for a fourth Safeguard installation, but asked that it be given the flexibility to decide later whether the defense should be of a fourth Minuteman field—this one at Warren Air Force Base, Wyoming—or of Washington, D.C. This was a reflection of the fact that it was not then clear what would be permitted by an ABM treaty, nor for that matter, what the administration really wanted.[35] Safeguard's utility as a defense was again questioned in congressional hearings that year, but there was no longer a prospect of congressional action preventing deployment. "Bargaining chip" arguments were more accepted than in the previous year. Who would have liked to have been charged with sabotaging SALT by denying the administration the negotiating cards it needed?

When the ABM Treaty was concluded it permitted each country two sites, one for defense of its capital and the other for defense of a missile site. There was, however, little interest in a defense of Washington, and apparently little in the Soviet Union in defense of its missiles. No work was done on these options, and in 1974 the two parties agreed to reduce the number of allowed ABM sites to one for each country.

With the conclusion of the treaty, the United States terminated work at the Malmstrom site—not much had been done anyway, in part because of strike-caused delays—but completed the installation at Grand Forks. Full capability was achieved in October 1974, but the system had perhaps the shortest operational life of any major weapon system ever procured by the United States. Within weeks, Congress acted to have the facility put in "moth balls," permitting only the Perimeter Acquisition Radar to remain operational. George Mahon, chairman of the House Appropriations Committee, and earlier a supporter of Safeguard, captured the feelings of many, declaring:

> We have spent $5.7 billion preparing to defend ourselves against the intercontinental ballistic missile. The Safeguard system has not been effective except perhaps from a cosmetic standpoint. If we had done nothing it would have been the same.[36]

This cost, which included R & D, exceeded the first Defense Department estimates for a *two-site* deployment by about 35 percent.

WAS IT ALL WORTHWHILE?

Others would argue that the $5.7 billion was well spent: that without Safeguard, it would have been impossible to conclude the ABM treaty or an agreement with the Soviet Union to limit offensive arms, and that these agreements, particularly the former, were well worth the price.

The lines so clearly drawn during the debate become blurred on these questions. Those in the arms control community who have generally attached the highest value to the SALT I agreements, particularly the ABM Treaty, were almost all opposed to both the Sentinel and the Safeguard plans. Some, but by no means all, discounted the importance of "bargaining chips" in arms control negotiations. Those who supported the ABM plans have generally believed in the importance of "bargaining chips," but have valued arms control agreements less highly and, discounting the action-reaction theory, have particularly questioned the desirability of trying to limit defensive systems. Perhaps the extreme example was Donald Brennan, a strong supporter of the ABM plans, who said, "the proposed ABM Treaty does the wrong thing well and the Interim Agreement [the agreement limiting offensive systems] does the right things badly."[37]

Would Brennan have judged the $5.7 billion well spent? Almost certainly not. Although he advocated the expenditures, the money bought neither defense nor agreements that he valued. And what of the ABM opponents? Most would doubtless say the agreements are worth $5.7 billion, but some would argue that we could have developed more useful technology while spending that amount, or less; others, that we probably could have gotten the agreements without a Safeguard program of any kind.[38]

Clearly, judging whether the Safeguard program was worthwhile is not easy, and no definitive answer is possible.

*   *   *

This becomes even more obvious when account is taken of the effects of the debate on the credibility of the defenders and managers of government programs and on the public image of the role of scientists as technical advisors on matters of public policy.

As the debate wore on it became increasingly obvious that both the Chinese threat to U.S. population and the Soviet threat to U.S. retaliatory capabilities had been exaggerated, and that the proposed ABM deployments were not reasonable responses to either. This was obvious to most of those in the defense establishment by 1971, even if it was not in 1969. One cannot help feeling empathy for them in their difficult positions. They had to carry on like good soldiers (or resign), greatly constrained in responding to technical criticism.

The question of deployment of radars designed for hard-site defense posed an especially difficult problem. If such radars had been substituted for the MSR and more interceptors had been deployed, as many critics suggested, defense capability would have been so improved that it would have been difficult to give it up or severely limit it. And, reaching agreement with the Soviet Union on a treaty that would permit such a hard-site defense, while prohibiting or limiting other kinds of ABM defense, would have been exceedingly difficult, perhaps impossible. There was therefore intragovernmental pressure to play down the option of defense designed for the purpose.[39]

Some of Safeguard's defenders and other spokesmen for the administration were caught in an especially unpleasant bind when they had to defend limiting it to one site and one hundred interceptors. They felt the wrath, particularly of Senator Henry Jackson, who had carried the ball for the administration in the Senate in 1969 and 1970, but who then obviously felt used and betrayed with the severe limitations of the ABM Treaty. Senator Jackson to Ambassador Smith and other members of the SALT delegation:

> For 3 years, the administration has argued for an ABM concept, namely, the defense of Minuteman. Now the administration has effectively abandoned it. And I want to understand why. For 3 years, this administration said that the defense of Minuteman was absolutely vital. Today, it argues that isn't the case. But the administration can't show that the threat to Minuteman—which Safeguard was designed to counter—won't exist under this agreement.
>
> I would say the delegation treated the Minuteman defense in a cavalier way. You utterly walked away from it.
>
> I just hate to dump money into a thing at Grand Forks which will not provide a credible defense. In the past, the administration's position was that an ABM site limited to 100 interceptors wouldn't be effective. So, why did we propose a limitation of 100 which we knew or should have known was inadequate to protect Minuteman?

And he was no less hard on the military. Speaking to the army general in charge of the Safeguard program and to the Chief of Staff of the air force, he said:

> I think the military is going to lose its credibility to be very candid about it. It is now throwing away the arguments it made 3 years in a row.
>
> When you people come up here wanting money and wanting programs, you had better be credible, or you won't be getting any cooperation from me. You have got to be honest. You can't come up here when you are demanding a weapons system with one line and then when you are trying to justify a treaty take an opposite line. You have a long shopping list that you want to buy, but if you use the treaty to justify the shopping list, you are going to have problems. You're going to have them from me if no one else. I am just fed up with getting one kind of an answer under one set of circumstances and exactly the reverse under another. There is too much of that going on. The credibility of the professional is on the line. We politicians put our credibility on the line every time we run for office, and

the professionals have got to stand up too. I am not referring to you specifically or personally, because I am not being personal about this. But I am addressing myself to the military professionals as a group. If you don't straighten yourselves out, we are not going to have any military system left, and we are not going to have any defense left.

If it is the view of the Joint Chiefs that there is no threat to the survivability of Minuteman, it is going to be hard for you to argue that the other elements of the Triad have to be upgraded to compensate for a threat to Minuteman. But, if it is your position that Minuteman is threatened, it's going to be hard for you to defend a SALT agreement that scraps the ABM defense of Minuteman. So which is it?[40]

Skepticism in Congress about the competence and, in some cases, the integrity of government officials was not limited to proponents of Safeguard, as a colloquy, involving Senator Fulbright, an opponent, illustrates. At issue was the aforementioned O'Neill Report. Two of its contributors, Sidney Drell and Marvin Goldberger, felt that Dr. John Foster had misrepresented its conclusions.

Dr. Drell. I want to comment specifically ... at this point because Dr. Foster's remarks indicate that we made recommendations which in fact we did not make. Dr. Foster remarked during this testimony that "the report ... said ... that this equipment will do the jobs that the Department of Defense wants to do." This is an incorrect statement. The report of the O'Neill committee contains no such far-reaching conclusion. ...

I want it to be absolutely clear that I do not intend in any way to impugn Dr. Foster's integrity by these remarks.

Senator Fulbright. Mr. Chairman, I do not understand that statement. What do you intend? You just said he is a liar. What do you intend to impugn?

Dr. Drell. Senator, Dr. Foster, as I go on in my statement to say, has very many important responsibilities and it is not at all difficult for me to imagine that after a 6-month time lapse he does not have an accurate recollection—

Senator Fulbright. Do you mean he is confused about it?

Dr. Drell. I believe so.

Senator Fulbright. That is a very charitable remark because we had him here specifically to answer these questions.

I do not know why you have to put in that statement when it denies what you have just said. It only leads to confusion in the public mind.

I can assure you that this is not the first time we have been lied to by Administration witnesses.[41]

Until the ABM debate, Congress had generally been reluctant to challenge the executive branch on technical matters, but the skepticism and distrust that developed during that debate has carried over to this day and has not been limited to defense programs. It may well be, as was suggested by some in the Senate, that the 1972 defeat of the administration's supersonic transport program was a consequence of its defense of Safeguard.

*   *   *

Within the technical community there was a debate about the debate: one of the bitterest since the Oppenheimer controversy. It was triggered by a request of the Operations Research Society of America (ORSA) from Albert Wohlstetter, a proponent of Safeguard, that it conduct an inquiry into the conduct of several witnesses who had appeared before congressional committees in opposition to Safeguard.

ORSA complied with the request and directed its attention over a period of almost two years not to the utility and appropriateness of Safeguard as a defense but rather, as suggested by Wohlstetter, to the issue of Minuteman vulnerability. It had little to say about the testimony of proponents of Safeguard except for that of Wohlstetter, for which it had high praise, but roundly condemned several opponents.[42]

The publication of its report received considerable press coverage and approbation from the White House (Donald Rumsfeld, then counselor to the President). It also caused much dissension within the Society and triggered an inquiry by Senators John Sherman Cooper, Phillip Hart, and Stuart Symington, all opponents of Safeguard, of a number of the most knowledgeable people, both pro and anti-ABM, about its appropriateness and the soundness of its conclusions.

Harold Agnew, then director of the Los Alamos Scientific Laboratory, and a pro-ABM expert, took strong exception to the report, but other ABM supporters commented favorably on the propriety of the inquiry and on its findings. For example, Edward Teller wrote that the ORSA Report was remarkable for its competence and objectivity.

All the ABM opponents were critical of the effort, most of them extremely so. Harvey Brooks said the proceeding "could be characterized as consciously or unconsciously dishonest."

And, Morton Halperin said:

> it is difficult to overestimate the triviality of the issue on which the ORSA panel focused....
>
> That the ORSA panel permitted Wohlstetter to define its agenda—and then chose to hide that fact—is inexcusable, totally unprofessional, and in complete violation of the standards it sets in the body of its report on criteria for reviewing a study. The committee failed to evaluate the statements by the administration or its supporters. It examined only a few of the issues raised by critics—those specified by Wohlstetter in his letter.
>
> The report is useless in seeking to evaluate the analysis presented by the administration, its supporters, or its critics. It is equally useless in seeking to assess, even with hindsight, whether initiating Safeguard in 1969 was indeed vital to American Security.[43]

So much for the objectivity of science.

* * *

Most of those involved in the ABM debate felt that it had significant effects on the scientific community.[44] On the negative side, there were feelings that it had resulted, or would result, in a diminution in respect for the community, in the availability of government funds for support of university research, and in the willingness of scientists to serve in government and on advisory committees. And the debate as a whole, not just the ORSA affair, had divisive effects on the scientific community. There was a feeling, especially among ABM proponents, that those on the other side of the issue were not objective. Anne Cahn reports two industrial scientists saying:

> I think anti-ABM scientists were less objective than proponents. A number of people against the ABM took [sic] the feeling that the country is spending too much on defense, that the Viet Nam war is a bad thing, that the military-industrial complex is pushing the country, ... ABM was one issue on which they could get the country and Congress to focus.... It got to be an emotional issue. They let their technical judgments be colored.

and

> I'm incensed at the dishonesty in the positions of the opponents. They represent themselves as experts. They clearly are not.[45]

Others, though, felt that the debate was important in showing that scientists cared enough to get involved. James Killian, science advisor to President Eisenhower, said:

> In a period where technology is being questioned it helped to give an indication that scientists are sensitive to the problem of making sure technology's effects are not harmful. We need to give more expression to the many strong convictions regarding the social importance of the management of technology for social benefits.[46]

ABM, TWELVE YEARS LATER

With renewed concern about the vulnerability of the Minuteman force to a disarming missile attack, there has been a renaissance of interest in the ABM question in the last several years.[47]

A substantial discussion of current issues would be out of place here, but perhaps a few brief comments may not be.

Some of those now writing on the subject appear to have rather distorted views of the positions of those who opposed ABM deployment during and prior to Safeguard debate. First, from some of these current writings one gets the impression that much of the opposition was based on a belief that a mutual hostage relationship is preferable to one where the Soviet Union and the United States would be defended more or less effectively.[48] It is unlikely that many of the ABM opponents held that view. Most would have favored defense of population and industry had they thought it could be effective. Their opposition was based on the belief that the exchange ratio greatly favored the offense and faith in the action-reaction theory: that efforts at defense would stimulate a compensating, or more-than-compensating, increase in adversary offensive capablities.

Second, some of the current writing also suggests that the opposition to Safeguard had its basis in generalized opposition to any kind of ABM defense. This may have been true of some opponents, but it was certainly not true of most of those who were most prominent in the debate. As their writings and congressional testimony make clear, their opposition was based very largely on (1) skepticism about the need for defense of the Minuteman force against a Soviet attack and of the whole country against a Chinese threat; (2) skepticism about the appropriateness of the proposed defenses, particularly considering the possibility of other options; and (3) belief that the *particular* design was likely to be interpreted by the Soviet Union as the beginnings of a nationwide population defense, an interpretation which, it was believed, would lead to greater increases in Soviet offensive capabilities than would otherwise occur.

Third, much of the current writing suggests that there have been such dramatic improvements in ABM defense technology that it is a new ballgame: that it is time to start thinking afresh about defense of both missile sites and population. In reality, no such impressive changes have occurred. Changes in terminal defense technology have been evolutionary and along the lines advocated by many involved in the Safeguard debate. It seemed then that a *properly designed* hard-site defense might be cost-effective. With LoADS, it *may* now be in sight. These writers also suggest that current proposals for area-type defenses are revolutionary compared with defenses based on PARs, MSRs, and Spartan interceptors. One might better say they are visionary, in some ways reminiscent of the more far-out proposals of the 1960s. While there has been progress in defense R & D, that is also true on the offense side; and there is little reason to believe that current prospective offensive capabilities will be more easily dealt with by area defenses than those in prospect then. On cost-exchange grounds the offense will continue to have the advantage.

Finally, there is the question of whether we are likely to see a Safeguard-like debate in the years ahead. There are reasons to believe that, if there is an ABM debate at all, it may be quite different.

In large part, the earlier debate was as confusing and acrimonious as it was for two reasons, neither of which now obtain.

First, with the country bitterly disillusioned about the war in Indochina, anti-military sentiments were very strong. Safeguard (and before it, Sentinel) provided particularly vulnerable targets for an expression of those feelings.[49]

Second, those involved treated the subject as a military problem to which technology was relevant, when in fact the motivations for ABM deployment were almost entirely political rather than military. The result was shifting rationales for systems to be built of components that were poorly matched to those rationales. In proposing such solutions, the Johnson and Nixon administrations presented opponents with opportunities that were hard to resist, and the debate began with the opponents holding very strong cards.

Now, with anti-military sentiments less prevalent, political and emotional factors *may* be less important in any future debate. There will, however, be a new factor: differences of opinion about the worth of the ABM Treaty and the feasibility of modifying it to permit some kind of defense. Argument is already surfacing, and there is some evidence that the administration is neither much committed to the treaty nor well-informed about it.[50]

It is conceivable that there could be a resurrection of interest in a defense of U.S. industry and population, and if that happens we are likely to see a debate that is qualitatively like those intra-governmental debates of the 1960s about Nike-Zeus and Nike-X, but surely with greater and better informed public involvement.

It is more likely that serious interest in ABM defense will be limited to the more feasible option of defense of ICBMs and possibly other hard targets. Arguments about whether we need be greatly concerned about attacks against U.S. ICBMs will surely continue, and just as was the case in 1968-1971, there may be debate on whether defense is desirable. But assuming LoADs or a variant of it is the defense of choice, there is likely to be less argument about whether the defense is technically matched to the problem.

NOTES

1. The announcement was made September 18, 1967, in an address in San Francisco to the United Press International Editors and Publishers. Chapter 4 of McNamara's book—*The Essence of Security* (New York: Harper & Row, 1968)—is based on the San Francisco speech and develops the case against an anti-Soviet defense. The case for an anti-Chinese defense is relegated to an appendix in the book.

2. The politics of that decision have been discussed elsewhere by Morton Halperin, "The Decision to Deploy ABM: Bureaucratic and Domestic Politics in the Johnson Administration," *World Politics*, vol. 25, p. 62, Oct. 1972; and by John Newhouse, *Cold Dawn*, pp. 77-101, (New York: Holt, Rinehart & Winston, 1973). See also, *The ABM Debate: Strategic Defense & National Security* by Edward Randolph Jayne II, (Ph.D. thesis, MIT, 1969). The latter includes much material on the earlier ABM debate as well.

   My commentary is limited to the debate that developed after the Sentinel decision was made and particularly to the debate on the Safeguard ABM plan that followed it.

   The reader should understand that I can hardly claim to be an objective observer of those events. I was active in opposition to both plans.

3. Detonation of a nuclear weapon produces ionization of the atmosphere (and the materials of which the weapon is made). Radar beams passing though such a plasma will be attenuated and/or refracted. The seriousness of the phenomenon—blackout—depends critically on the height of detonation, radar frequency, and weapon yield.

4. It is of interest that all fifty-two anti-ABM scientists surveyed by Anne Cahn, mostly in 1970, felt that the Sentinel decision could best be explained as the result of political pressure. Only six of twenty-two pro-ABM scientists believed that was the best explanation, while thirteen apparently believed the administration's rationale of a growing Chinese threat. "Eggheads and Warheads: Scientists and the ABM" (Ph.D. Thesis, MIT, 1971), p. 123.

5. See McNamara's interview with *Life* magazine, September 29, 1967, and Paul Warnke's defense of Sentinel before the Advocates' Club, Detroit, October 6, 1967.

6. John Foster, then Director of Defense Research & Engineering, Department of Defense Appropriations for 1969, U.S. Congress, House, Hearings before a Subcommittee of the Committee of Appropriations, 92nd Cong., 1st sess., pt. 2, March 13, 1968, p. 455; and Paul Nitze, then Deputy Secretary of Defense, U.S. Congress, House, "Scope, Magnitude, and Implications of the United States Antiballistic Missile Program," Hearings before the Subcommittee on Military Applications of the Joint Committee on Atomic Energy, 90th Cong., 1st sess., November 6, 1967, p. 7.

7. Albert Wohlstetter and Colin Gray, in particular, have questioned the action-reaction theory, and, the former at least, whether there is an "arms race": Wohlstetter, "Is There A Strategic Arms Race?" *Foreign Policy*, no. 15, Summer 1974, p. 3, and "Rivals, But No 'Race,'" *Foreign Policy*, no. 16, Fall 1974, p. 48; Gray, *The Soviet American Arms Race* (Lexington, Mass.: Lexington Books, 1976), and "Nuclear Strategy: A Case for a Theory of Victory," *International Security*, Summer 1979, p. 54.

8. Robert McNamara has certainly been the best known and most influential expositor of the "action-reaction" theory, *op. cit.*; Herbert York, who is responsible for the phrase "the fallacy of the last move," has been another. See *Race to Oblivion*, part 2, (New York: Simon & Schuster, 1970). I, too, have been a believer and continue to feel that American weapons development and acquisition decisions are much influenced by what the Soviet Union does and by what we believe it might do. I believe that probably the inverse is also true; in other words, that there is much to the action-reaction theory. It is, however, increasingly clear to me that other factors—e.g., bureaucratic aggrandisement and interservice rivalry, momentum, considerations of employment, industrial profits, balance of payments, prestige, and, perhaps above all, a general belief that "more is better"—may be relatively more significant as determinants of weapons decisions than some of us believed a decade and more ago.

9. In the beginning, the debate focused on the Sentinel decision. The decision also provided impetus for Senator Kennedy's call for an independent evaluation of the ABM question. His call was a significant factor in organizing the opposition to the Sentinel and the Safeguard ABM plans. It also led to the production of *ABM: An Evaluation of the Decision to Deploy an Antiballistic Missile System*, edited by Abram Chayes and Jerome Wiesner (New York: Harper & Row, 1969).

10. He arranged to have all past and present Special Assistants to the President for Science and Technology and Directors of Defense Research and Engineering meet with the President in January 1967 to discuss the ABM question. All, predictably, said they were opposed to the army's Soviet-oriented, Nike-X defense plan.

11. Henry Kissinger, then Assistant to the President for National Security Affairs, may have been misled through conversations with former Cambridge associates into believing that many in the group who were opposed to Sentinel and a full-scale Soviet-oriented defense would go along with the defense of ICBMs. This may have been a factor in the Safeguard decision. See Cahn, "Eggheads", pp. 196-197; and Lawrence Freedman, *U.S. Intelligence and the Soviet Strategic Threat*, (London: Macmillan, 1977), p. 148.

12. Anne Cahn found that among anti-ABM scientists 43 percent believed hard site defense feasible or probably feasible, while only 21 percent believed this of a light-area (i.e., Sentinel-type) defense and only 1 percent of a heavy (i.e., Soviet-oriented) urban defense. The corresponding figures among pro-ABM scientists were 97 percent, 97 percent, and 52 percent. Cahn, "Eggheads," p. 129.

13. The intelligence estimates leading to this conclusion were a matter of great controversy. Analyses by the Central Intelligence Agency did not support the administration position, nor originally did the National Intelligence Estimate (NIE) for 1969. The NIE was changed, apparently as a result of pressure on Richard Helms, the Director of Central Intelligence, from Henry Kissinger and Secretary of Defense Laird. The controversy is discussed in some detail by Freedman, *U.S. Intelligence*, especially chap. 8.

14. Harold Brown, Department of Defense, *Annual Report for Fiscal Year 1981*, p. 85. The statement is based on the assumption of use by the Soviets of SS-18, and possibly other, missiles, more advanced than the SS-9.

15. *Washington Post*, June 17, 1971.

16. U.S. Congress, Senate, Hearings on *Arms Control Implications of Current Defense Budget* before the Subcommittee on Arms Control, International Law and Organization of the Committee of Foreign Relations, United States Senate, 92nd Cong., 1st sess. on Arms Control Implications of Current U.S. Defense Budget, June and July 1971, pp. 171-175.

17. See, e.g. York, ibid., p. 100.

18. Hearings on *Fiscal Year 1972 Authorization for Military Procurement, Research and Development, Construction and Real Estate Acquisition for the Safeguard ABM, and Reserve Strengths* before the Committee on Armed Services, United States Senate, 92nd Cong., 1st sess. on S.939 (H.R. 8687), pt. 2, March-May 1971, p. 1693.

19. U.S. Congress, Senate, Hearings on *Authorization for Military Procurement, Research and Development, Fiscal Year 1970, and Reserve Strength* before the Committee on Armed Services, 91st Cong., 1st sess. on S.1192 and S.2407, pt. 1, March-Aril 1969, p. 192.

20. By reading the classified estimates of Soviet ASW capabilities, I confirmed this myself, and so testified, ibid., p. 1310-1311.

21. U.S. Congress, Senate, Hearings on *Strategic and Foregin Policy Implications of ABM Systems: Anti-Submarine Warfare, Multiple Independently Targeted Reentry Vehicles (MIRV)*, before the Subcommittee on International Organization and Disarmament Affairs of the Committee on Foreign Relations, 91st Cong., 1st sess., May and July 1969, pp. 623-643.

22. Ibid., p. 196.

23. U.S. Congress, Senate, Hearing on *Intelligence and the ABM* before the Committee on Foreign Relations, 91st Cong., 1st sess., June 23, 1969.

24. U.S. Congress, Senate, Hearings on *Authorization for Military Procurement, Research and Development, Fiscal Year 1971, and Reserve Strength*, before the Committee on Armed Services, 91st Cong., 2d sess. on S.3367 and H.R. 17123, pt. 1, February and March 1970, p. 32.

25. U.S. Congress, Senate, Hearings on *Fiscal Year 1972 Authorization for Military Procurement, Research and Development, Construction and Real Estate Acquisition for the Safeguard ABM, and Reserve Strengths* before the Committee on Armed Services, 92nd Cong., 1st sess. on S.939 (H.R. 8687), pt. 2, March-May 1971, p. 1652-1653 and U.S. Congress, House, Hearings on *Military Posture* before the Committee on Armed Services, 92nd Cong., 1st sess., May 5, 1971, p. 4523.

26. U.S. Congress, Senate, Hearing on *U.S.-USSR Strategic Policies* before the Subcommittee on Arms Control, International Law and Organization of the Committee on Foreign Relations, 93rd Cong., 2d sess. on U.s. and Soviet Strategic Doctrine and Military Policies, March 4, 1974, p. 38.

27. P.M.S. Blackett, "A Critique of Some Contemporary Defense Thinking," *Encounter*, April 1961.

28. U.S. Congress, Senate, *Strategic and Foreign Policy Implications of ABM Systems*, Hearings before the Subcommittee on International Organization and Disarmament Affairs of the Committee on Foreign Relations, 91st Cong., 1st sess., March 26, 1969, p. 263.

29. U.S. Congress, Senate, *Authorization for Military Procurement, Research and Development, Fiscal Year 1970, and Reserve Strength*. Hearings before the Committee on Armed Services, 91st Cong., 1st sess., March 20, 1969, p. 225.

30. U.S. Congress, Senate, *Hearings on Authorization for Military Procurement, Research and Development, Fiscal Year 1971, and Reserve Strength*, before the Committee on Armed Services, 91st Cong., 2d sess., February and March 1970, pp. 36-37.

31. For a discussion of this unsuccessful effort see Freedman, *U.S. Intelligence*, pp. 150-152.

32. New Conference, January 30, 1970, *Public Papers of the Presidents, Richard Nixon,* 1970, p. 20.

33. The "O'Neill Report," *The Congressional Record,* vol. 116, August 6, 1970, pp. 27723-27728.

34. John Newhouse describes an effort on July 23 by Henry Kissinger to sell the ABM to Congress using the "bargaining chip" argument in *Cold Dawn,* pp. 187-188. Gerard Smith, the head of the U.S. SALT delegation, and Henry Kissinger have reported that Smith's having made that argument may have been decisive. See Smith, *Doubletalk,* (Garden City, New York: Doubleday, 1980); and Kissinger, *White House Years* (Boston: Little, Brown, 1979), p. 551.

35. For the most concise discussion of this see Raymond Garthoff, "Negotiating with the Russians: Some Lessons from SALT," *International Security,* Spring 1977, pp. 10-13. Also Smith, *Doubletalk,* pp. 205, 255; Newhouse, in *Cold Dawn,* pp. 182-185, 217, 225-231; Kissinger, *White House Years,* pp. 539-547, 810-813.

36. *New York Times,* November 25, 1975.

37. U.S. Congress, Senate, Hearings on *Strategic Arms Limitation Agreements* before the Committee on Foreign Relations, 92nd Cong., 2d sess. on Executive L, 92D Congress, 2D Session and S.J. Res. 241 and S.J. Res. 242, June 28, 1972, p. 186.

38. My own view is as follows: "Bargaining chips" are important, and probably no significant agreement(s) could have been reached without the United States having had something it could put on the table. The ABM treaty was, and is, worth quite a bit; the offensive agreement, very little. We should have accepted the Soviet offer to conclude an ABM treaty earlier, preferably one banning defenses totally, without insisting on coupling it with the offensive agreement. We would then have invested less in Safeguard before scrapping it.

   If such an issue arose again, I would resist investing in such a "bargaining chip" as Safeguard, even at the risk of forestalling an arms limitation treaty. The whole experience, and, even more, subsequent arms control efforts, have raised grave doubts in my mind about the utility and wisdom of arms control negotiations. I have come to question whether the costs incurred in negotiations—unneeded weapons and political effects—are likely to be justified, considering the kinds of agreements that seem possible and the likelihood that in some instances no agreements may be reached even after prolonged efforts.

39. Smith, *Doubletalk,* pp. 202, 206, 209.

40. U.S., Congress, Senate, Hearings on the *Military Implications of the Treaty on the Limitations of Anti-Ballistic Missile Systems and the Interim Agreement on Limitation of Strategic Offensive Arms* before the Committee on Armed Services, 92nd Cong., 2d sess., June and July 1972, specifically pp. 351, 353, 375, 469, 470, and 472.

41. U.S. Congress, Senate, Hearings on *ABM, MIRV, SALT, and the Nuclear Arms Race* before the Subcommittee on Arms Control, International Law and Organization of the Committee on Foreign Relations, 91st Cong., 2d sess., March-June, 1970, pp. 534-535.

42. Wohlstetter and ORSA were particularly censorius of my conduct but Jerome Wiesner, Steven Weinberg, W.K.H. Panofsky and Ralph Lapp were also indicted.

43. The ORSA report, an expurgated version of the Wohlstetter instigating letter, other correspondence, and a minority comment of the ORSA Council are to be found in the Society's journal, *Operations Research,* vol. 19, no. 5, September 1971.

   Letters commenting on it and references to press stories appeared in vol. 20, no. 1, January-February 1972, pp. 205-246.

   A large part of the report and commentaries on it appeared in *Minerva,* vol 10, no. 1 and 2, January and April 1972.

   A dissenting commentary on the report by Phillip Morse, a founder of ORSA and its first president, has been reproduced in the *Congressional Record* along with comments by myself, Steven Weinberg and Jerome Wiesner, October 15, 1971, S.16332-S.16338.

A critique (that also appeared in *Minerva*) by Paul Doty is to be found in *Controversies and Decisions: The Social Sciences and Public Policy*, edited by Charles Frankel, (New York: Russel Sage, 1976).

The response to the Cooper-Hart-Symington inquiry and comments by them appear in the *Congressional Record*, February 1972, pp. S 1921-1951 and S 2839-2841.

Much of the material covered in the ORSA report is also dealt with at length in *Policy Analysis within the Anti-Ballistic Missile Debate* by Arye Ehud Levy-Pascal, (Ph.D. thesis, University of California, Berkeley, 1974), a peculiar document in that Levy-Pascal appears to have taken only selective account of the Congressional Record commentaries and others, and even more remarkably, virtually none of technical and operational developments during 1970-1973 that cast doubt on the administration's 1969 defense of Safeguard, the ORSA report and his own modeling.

44. Cahn found that a majority (59 percent) of the anti-ABM scientists she interviewed felt the effects had been, on balance, favorable; but that a majority (70 percent) of the pro-ABM scientists felt the debate had harmful effects. "Eggheads," p. 142. Her survey was conducted before the ORSA controversy developed. My guess is that had it been taken afterwards there would have been an increase in the numbers in both factions who would have judged the debate harmful.

45. Ibid., p. 150.

46. Ibid., pp. 139-141. My own view is that the debate was overwhelmingly beneficial, partly for the reasons mentioned by Cahn, but mainly because it was important in correcting a number of illusions about science and public policy: that "experts" are necessarily right or that they can even agree on technical issues; that the issues can be understandable only to experts; that there can be complete objectivity in approaches to problems of technology and public policy; and that technical issues can be easily isolated from political ones. One would hope that we can do better in dealing with the last two problems, but the Safeguard debate should have a sobering effect on expectations.

47. See especially Keith Payne, *The BMD Debate: Ten Years After* (Hudson Institute); William Schneider, Jr., Donald G. Brennan, William A. Davis, Jr., and Hans Ruhle, *U.S. Strategic-Nuclear Policy and Ballistic Missile Defense: The 1980s and Beyond*, (Institute of Foreign Policy Analysis, Inc., April 1980); Stephen Rosen "Safeguarding Deterrence," in *Foreign Policy*, no. 35, Summer 1979, p. 109; the papers in *U.S. Arms Control Objectives and the Implications for Ballistic Missile Defense*, Center for Science and International Affairs, Harvard University, November 1979; and *Ballistic Missile Defense: A quick Look Assessment*, Los Alamos Scientific Laboratory, June 1980. ABM questions are also discussed in Gray, "Strategic Stability Reconsidered," *Daedalus*, Fall, 1980, p. 135; Jan Lodal, "Deterrence and Nuclear Strategy," *Daedalus*, Fall 1980, p. 155; and William Kincade, "Over the Technological Horizon," *Daedalus*, Winter 1981, p. 105.

48. Striking examples are to be found in Kissinger, *White House Years*, pp. 208, and 216 and in remarks made by him in Brussels, August 1979. *Survival*, November/December 1979, p. 265.

49. This appears the have been the way the Nixon administration, or at least Kissinger, saw things (*White House Years*, Chap. VII).

50. In suggesting that the U.S. should consider deploying ABM defenses, Secretary of Defense Caspar Weinberger has said, wrongly, that the treaty expires in 1982. *U.S. News & World Report*, April 13, 1981, p. 45. (Article XV specifies that the Treaty shall be of *unlimited duration*. It does come up for *review* in 1982. Article XIV.)

Chapter 19

MIRV

Herbert F. York and G. Allen Greb

The multiple independently targeted reentry vehicle (MIRV), whose beginnings were relatively innocent and unpretentious, has turned out to be one of the most portentious developments of the 1960s and 1970s. "Indeed," the political scientist Ted Greenwood notes, "MIRV is probably the single most important technical innovation in the field of offensive strategic forces since the ballistic missile."[1]

In this chapter we shall outline the origins of MIRV technology and explore the strategic analyses which led to the military requirements for it. In addition to discussing the bureaucratic and political considerations that transformed these requirements into decisions to develop and deploy MIRV, we shall examine separate analyses which looked toward the future and showed that MIRV eventually would result in very severe instabilities in the superpowers' strategic relationship. Finally we shall describe the current situation in which those predicted instabilities are fast becoming stark reality and in which all suggested solutions to the problem seem to carry with them new problems which may be more serious than those they are intended to solve.

MIRV technology evolved from myriad independent sources during the late 1950s and early 1960s. In the early and mid-1960s several separate though interconnected research groups developed two lines of analysis supporting the practical application of this technology in our strategic forces. At least three political issues of the decade worked to promote MIRV and led to firm and irreversible decisions to develop and deploy it. Diverse government organizations—chief among them the air force, the navy, and the Office of the Secretary of Defense—supervised the various elements and phases of the program, and several private organizations—most importantly the Lockheed Missiles and Space Company, the Aerospace Corporation, and Thompson-Ramo-Wooldridge's Space Technology Laboratories (TRW/STL)—performed the actual research and development work. In turn a complex advisory structure very effectively interconnected these many organizations and their various responsible levels, causing a free flow of information and arguments throughout the entire structure. The result was a web of interwoven programmatic strands leading ultimately to $\overline{\text{MIRV}}$, a web so complex and so highly interconnected that the decision paths could have been cut in many different places without significantly altering the final outcome: MIRVs deployed on U.S. missiles in the early 1970s.

THE ROOTS OF MIRV TECHNOLOGY

The basic objective of MIRV is to make it possible for a single rocket to simultaneously launch several warheads either at an equal number of separate targets or at the same target but on very different trajectories. The key to its operation is the so-called Post Boost Control System (PBCS), commonly called the "bus." The bus contains its own propulsion unit, a guidance system, and several reentry vehicles as passengers. Its mode of operation is illustrated in Figure 19.1.

After the main rocket boosts it into orbit and after a brief period of coasting, the bus uses small vernier rockets to refine its trajectory until it is aimed as precisely as possible at target number one. It then gently ejects one of the warheads, which coasts inexorably to that target. Once the first warhead has been released the bus alters its course in preparation to release the second. The bus can achieve its intricate course maneuvers in several ways. If, for example, the PBCS is accelerated or decelerated along the direction of its current trajectory, the impact point of the next reentry vehicle (RV) will move downrange or uprange accordingly. Likewise, boosts directly to either side move the impact point right or left. However, a brief impulse directed along a line in the plane of the trajectory but approximately normal to it produces a result many would find surprising: the impact point does not change, but the

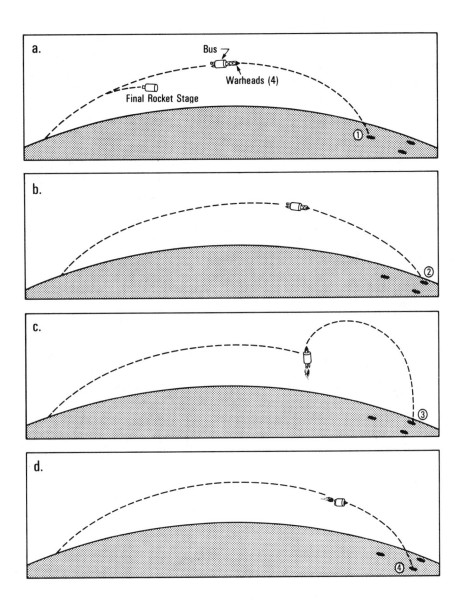

Figure 19.1. MIRV Post Boost Control System Operation.

time of arrival of the RV may be advanced or delayed by as much as several minutes. This process is repeated until all the warheads have been launched at their targets. Decoys and other "penetration aids" could be released with some or all of the warheads as well.

Two complex subsystems are critical to the proper operation of the bus: a propulsion unit with a coast and restart capability and an inertial guidance device able to modify velocity and altitude. Ironically the initial development of these and other MIRV-related technologies had no direct connection with any requirement to improve either missiles or missile warheads. They emerged instead from completely separate programs with separate goals, specifically with projects begun in the late 1950s designed to launch a number of satellites with a single booster.

Concerned about the first Soviet intercontinental ballistic missile (ICBM) launch in August 1957 and Sputnik I in October of the same year, the U.S. research and development community produced a flood of new ideas about how to make and use missiles and satellites. Prominent among these was the multiple satellite concept. The first serious proposal for such a system had missile defense as its objective. Designated the ballistic antimissile boost interceptor (BAMBI), defense analysts hoped to use it to intercept an enemy's missiles during the initial few minutes of flight while the booster motors were still operating. Two versions of BAMBI were proposed; both would have put large numbers of satellites in orbits from which missiles could be detected and destroyed during the early stages of flight. Neither was built but the Advanced Research Projects Agency (ARPA) of the Department of Defense studied the proposals extensively in cooperation with the Rand Corporation. Founded in 1958 also as a reaction to Sputnik, ARPA made a point during its early years to exchange key technical personnel with industry. This became a common practice among the various companies involved in missile and space technology in general. Consequently many of the experts who fashioned the BAMBI and other early strategic defense proposals later became members of the organizations that designed true multiple warhead hardware.

Another system whose basic technology was adapted to MIRV was the Able-Star. A second stage vehicle designed for use with a Thor booster rocket, the Able-Star was the first spacecraft to incorporate a main propulsion engine that could be shut off and restarted in space. The Able-Star also contained several subsystems—including restart, guidance, and control devices; a programmer; and an accelerometer—which are essential to the operation of MIRVs. The Able-Star made its initial test flight in April 1960, and two months later it was used to make the first U.S. multiple satellite launch. Three years later the United States used a similar but more sophisticated system, the Atlas-Agena combination, to place two so-called Vela satellites in completely different orbits. Satellites of this type have been utilized extensively to monitor compliance with various arms control treaties.[2]

The immediate technological ancestor of the air force MIRV was yet another multiple satellite launcher called Transtage, illustrated in Figure 19.2. A highly flexible PBCS using a Titan III rocket booster, Transtage had a coast and restart capability like the Able-Star and Agena, but it carried a larger payload and could execute more complex and extensive maneuvers. In June 1966 a Titan III-C/Transtage combination put eight one hundred pound defense communication satellites in eight separate equatorial orbits. The operation was comparable in nearly all respects to that of the MIRV bus. Using its ability to coast and restart, Transtage achieved the necessary circular orbit and gently nudged off one of its satellites with compressed springs. With four fifty-pound thrust vernier motors designed to control pitch and yaw, it then added a small increment of velocity and ejected the second satellite, repeating the maneuver for each of the remaining six. As a measure of the importance of Transtage to MIRV development, Director of Defense

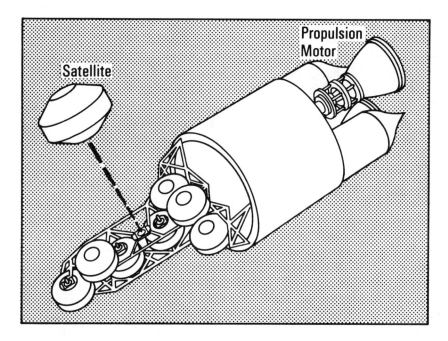

Figure 19.2. Transtage PBCS configuration.

Research and Engineering John Foster, Jr. pointed to its successful operation in 1968 to convince skeptical congressmen that all the essential engineering problems of MIRV had been solved.[3]

The close relationship between these several multiple satellite systems and later MIRV missiles also can be traced through their various industry and in-house contractors. TRW's Space Technology Laboratories, for example, which were responsible for the systems engineering and technical direction of the Air Force's Minuteman III MIRV, had been heavily involved in the BAMBI, Able-Star, and Vela programs. Similarly Lockheed, the designer of the navy's Poseidon MIRV, developed the Agena spacecraft. The Aerospace Corporation, responsible for working out various advanced reentry systems concepts for the Minuteman III, did the systems engineering for both the Titan III and Transtage. Finally, in the air force itself, the space and missile systems office (SAMSO) supervised both the Transtage project and the later MIRV program.

THE ANALYSES UNDERLYING MIRV

Two main lines of technical and strategic analysis have provided the foundation of the MIRV development and deployment program. The more important line of argument, and the one of earlier origin, was built around the idea that a U.S. MIRV system was the best and surest way to penetrate any antiballistic missile (ABM) that the Soviets might develop. The second line of reasoning involved the notion that under certain circumstances MIRV provided a way of increasing or "multiplying" the effectiveness of the U.S. ICBM force.

The roots of the first of these lines of analysis go back to the early 1950s by which time various intelligence indicators pointed unequivocally to the existence of a substantial Soviet program to develop long-range, eventually intercontinental, rockets. The United States responded to this information by reorienting and accelerating its own missile program in the first years of the Eisenhower administration. In addition, the U.S. Army initiated a program designed to develop an antiballistic missile (ABM) as a further and seemingly logical extension of the several programs it already had underway to develop and deploy antiaircraft missiles. At about the same time, evidence concerning a possible Soviet ABM began to accumulate. As usual, by a process known as mirror imaging, the fact of our own ABM program strongly reinforced the conclusions of U.S. intelligence analysts about the Soviet work in this field.

In late 1957, about a month after the Soviet Union launched Sputnik I and at least partly in response to that event, Defense Director of Guided Missiles William Holaday established an ad hoc committee called the Reentry Body Identification Group. The purpose of this committee was to determine whether the designers of U.S. offensive missiles then under development (land-based ICBMs and submarine-launched Polarises) should take seriously the possibility of defense against missiles and, if so, what they should do about it. The committee was fully informed about the U.S. ABM program (at that time the Nike-Zeus missile) and was aware that the Soviet Union had a similar program underway. In early 1958 the committee concluded that the possibility of missile defense should be taken seriously, and it described a number of countermeasures for the offense, including decoys, chaff, reduced radar cross-sections for the RV, blackout, tank fragments, and, most important in the context of this report, multiple warheads.[4] All of these "penetration aids" except the last are designed to confuse the defenses; multiple warheads penetrate defenses simply by saturating or exhausting them.

The Reentry Body Identification Group's report was unusually influential, coming as it did at a rather critical juncture in U.S.-Soviet relations. Eventually both the services and the defense establishment in general accepted most of its conclusions. The air force incorporated several of the deception devices discussed by the Reentry Group in its early penetration aids packages, and the Navy developed a multiple warhead system for the A-3 version of its Polaris missiles.

The Polaris A-3 warhead system consists of a cluster of three separate RVs, each of which contains a nuclear warhead. This type of system is called a multiple reentry vehicle or MRV (as opposed to the more sophisticated MIRV). The cluster of three warheads is launched as a unit, and the unit is aimed as accurately as possible at a particular single target. After the boosters burn out, the three RVs are separated from each other and given small additional impulses which cause them to impact in a triangular pattern centered on the target. Officials have never disclosed the actual dimensions of this triangle, but the physical situation as it was perceived in the late 1950s set obvious limits: the separation had to be more than a few tenths of a mile—otherwise all three RVs could have been destroyed simultaneously by a single nominal nuclear explosion in the atmosphere—but less then a few miles—otherwise the dimensions of the triangle would have exceeded the size of most Soviet cities. The navy deployed the first MRVs on Polaris A-3s in 1964.

But even before the navy took this action three separate developments intervened and brought about major changes in the thinking of U.S. defense analysts. The acquisition of much more detailed information about the Soviet ICBM and ABM programs, as a result of newly instituted satellite reconnaissance; the steady increase in our general knowledge about the missile/antimissile interaction as a result of our own development work in these two areas; and the growing realization that certain destructive effects of large nuclear explosions extended over much larger distances in outer space than they did within the atmosphere all led to intensive study and continuous reassessment of the twin problems of how the United States might build an ABM of its own and how U.S. missile RVs could penetrate any defensive system the Soviets might deploy. It was only the last of these three developments, however, which indicated that the deployment of simple MRVs would not provide a long-term solution to the ABM penetration problem, and which also cast doubt on at least some of the proposals for assuring penetration through the use of large numbers of lightweight decoys.

The growing awareness in the early 1960s of the great range of the destructive effects of extra-atmospheric explosions on missile RVs came from theoretical calculations by a number of analysts and information gleaned from the U.S. extra-atmospheric tests in the South Atlantic in 1958 and in the South Pacific in 1962. These experiments and calculations showed that the range of the destructive effects of multimegaton extra-atmospheric explosions—particularly those induced by X rays and neutrons—on even specially "hardened" RVs could be hundreds of kilometers. These facts in turn made it clear that if the Soviets developed an ABM based on very large explosions in outer space, the relatively very small inter-RV separation distances inherent in the MRV approach would not suffice. Moreover, deployment of such an ABM system would also greatly reduce the utility of at least some of the decoy schemes then being developed, such as those involving large numbers of metallized balloons or other very light weight objects.

The Soviets also conducted some very high yield extra-atmospheric tests in 1961 and 1962, including experiments which pointed directly to an interest in the ABM problem. All of this activity reinforced the fears of U.S. weapons experts concerning the adequacy of our plans for penetrating (hypothetical) Soviet ABMs, and even led some American analysts to conclude that the Soviets somehow had "solved" the ABM problem. In fact, Edward Teller, in testimony opposing the limited nuclear test ban treaty of 1963, suggested that the reason the Soviets were willing to have a ban on tests in the atmosphere and outer space was that they indeed "solved" this problem themselves and intended by this means to preclude the United States from doing so. "I believe that the Russians have acquired this knowledge," Teller maintained. "I believe that, because they have acquired this knowledge, they don't need any more atmospheric tests, and I believe that is why Khrushchev is willing to sign the treaty at present."[5]

MIRV provided a convenient solution to the problem posed by large extra-atmospheric explosions. MIRV solves the problem by allowing the RVs to be widely separated from each other but with each one individually aimed at a specific target as precisely as technology will allow. It is important to note that the targets themselves do not have to be widely spaced. In fact, one of the Navy's early paper studies of MIRV involved sending three RVs against a single target, but with their arrival times greatly separated. One RV would travel along a so-called minimum trajectory, a second would travel along a generally lower and therefore faster trajectory, and a third along a higher and therefore slower trajectory. Each trajectory connected the same origin and the same target, but the times of arrival were widely different, and the RVs consequently would be separated by hundreds of kilometers by the time they approached their common target.[6]

A number of individuals and groups in both the air force and the navy missile and space development networks perceived the MIRV idea (some would say "invented" it) as a solution to the ABM penetration problem.[7] This is not at all surprising since these organizations also employed the people who invented and developed the PBCS bus and other techniques for putting multiple satellites into precisely controlled orbits and for putting ICBM decoy RVs on predetermined trajectories. (The latter work was part of the Air Force Advanced Ballistic Reentry System (ABRES) program.) As we have seen, in the air force case these were SAMSO, TRW/STL, the Aerospace Corporation, the Rand Corporation, and these organizations' interlocking advisory committees. In the navy case, the Special Projects Office, the Lockheed Corporation, and their advisory groups carried out this work. Any attempt to single out separate "inventors" of MIRV, therefore, is fruitless and reveals little about the process of MIRV development as a whole.

The other line of strategic analysis which supported MIRV development during the 1960s involved its capability under certain specific circumstances to "multiply" the total effectiveness of a given ICBM force. To understand this matter, four different cases must be distinguished, each of which is discussed below. Case 1 consists of a hypothetical attack on a system of relatively soft, small targets, such as medium-sized cities and most conventional military targets. This is the simplest case to analyze. To do so we need only recall that, in the 1960s, typical single RV thermonuclear warheads yielded a major fraction of a megaton, while the "standard" nuclear warheads that destroyed Hiroshima, Nagasaki, and a small fleet of U.S. naval vessels at Bikini in the 1940s yielded twenty kilotons (kT) or less. Thus, if a single RV missile payload is replaced by an n-fold MIRV system, the number of targets of this type that can be destroyed is simply multiplied by the factor n, provided only that the yield of an individual MIRV warhead does not drop significantly below 20 kT. That was indeed the case as it was planned and realized during the decade. The Poseidon carried the smallest MIRV warhead actually deployed, and even it had approximately 40 kT.

Case 2 consists of a hypothetical attack on a number of extended, relatively soft targets, such as very large cities and widely spread-out industrial areas or military installations. To analyze this case we first note the simple physical fact that the *distance* from a nuclear explosion at which the blast overpressure reaches a given level varies as the *cube root* of the yield of the explosion over a wide range of values. This means that the *area* over which a given or greater level of overpressure will be experienced is proportional to the *two thirds* power of the yield. This in turn means that if the total yield of an *n*-fold MIRV system is precisely equal to that of the single RV system it replaces, the maximum area that will experience a given or greater level of overpressure—and hence damage—increases as the one-third power of *n*, or twice as much area when *n* equals eight. In reality, however, a MIRV system will have considerably less total yield than the single RV system it replaces if both are built to the same level of technology. There is no simple algebraic way of describing this more complicated situation, but in a typical real case it turns out that the total area destroyed is very roughly the same for either a MIRV system or the single RV system it replaces.

Case 3 consists of a hypothetical attack on relatively hard point targets using MIRV systems characterized by technical parameters—accuracy and yield in particular—*as these actually existed* in the most advanced versions of the systems available in the 1960s. At that time the combination of yields and accuracies of U.S. long-range rocket systems was such that weapons experts commonly estimated single shot kill probabilities for single RV systems in a broad middle range, roughly between 30 and 70 percent. (Good estimates of yield were readily available to the informed public, but good estimates of U.S. accuracy and Soviet target hardness were not and still are not. This was not only because the facts were secret but also because they were not sufficiently well known and understood.) In such a case, replacing a single RV by the corresponding MIRV system would result in a substantial increase in kill probability if the total yield remained the same and if no other technological penalties resulted. This in essence is what defense officials John S. Foster and Alain Enthoven claimed about the proposed MIRVed Minuteman III system in 1968.[8]

As in Case 2, however, the total yield of a real MIRV system is less, and there are other penalties (such as from fratricide and, possibly, from deficiencies in accuracy and reliability), so that the calculated total kill probability inherent in the MIRV force may be greater, the same, or smaller. Worse still, from the analysts' point of view, the benefit of MIRVing cannot really be estimated reliably in this case. This complicated and uncertain situation made it particularly easy for analysts to bend estimates to support their particular prejudices.

Case 4, the most interesting at the present time, consists of a hypothetical attack on a system of hard targets by a MIRVed force charcterized by technological parameters as *they were estimated for the late 1980s in the 1960s*. In the 1960s the combination of accuracy and yield commonly predicted for the American (and Soviet) forces of the 1980s was such that the calculated single shot kill probabilities based on these two factors alone would become virtually 100 percent. In this event, an especially significant, easily understood, and reliably estimable situation arises.

Consider first two non-MIRVed forces of equal numbers facing each other, and consider what would happen if one force made a surprise or preemptive attack on the other. In such a situation, the average readiness and reliability of the attacking force, rather than the accuracy-yield combination, would determine the result. If the combination of these factors is taken as 80 percent (a not uncommon assumption), Side A would destroy 80 percent of Side B's force, leaving 20 percent surviving. Now suppose Side A changes to a two-fold MIRV system. Given the accuracies predicted at the time, the single shot kill probability would still depend almost solely on the readiness-reliability factor. Thus the first salvo by Side A still would leave only 20 percent of Side B's ICBMs in tact, and the newly possible second salvo would leave only about 20 percent of those, or 4 percent in all, surviving. For still higher multiplicities, the single shot capability derived from yield-accuracy considerations only eventually falls well below 100 percent and the calculations become more complicated, but the predicted results follow the same theme: MIRV systems with such technological characteristics make it theoretically possible to achieve virtually total annihilation of one side's silo-based ICBMs in a surprise attack by the other. Such a possibility obviously puts great value on surprise and preemption and that, in turn, can lead to the "crisis instability" analysts frequently worry about. The degree of such instability of course hinges upon the relative importance of ICBMs in the total strategic force, but since the mid 1960s the dependence on land-based missiles has been high in both the U.S. and Soviet cases.

In summary the analyses of the 1960s demonstrated that the substitution of MIRVed systems for simple RV systems in the short run would result in the assured penetration of any ABM system then foreseen and also would result in a moderate increase in the effectiveness of strategic forces, the question of ABM penetration aside. For the long run (twenty years or more) these analyses predicted a very substantial increase in the effectiveness of MIRVed systems. In addition many officials foresaw the increased capability projected for the 1980s as creating a very undesirable situation in which surprise preemptive attack would become (or appear to become) a much more tempting option than previously. These predictions in fact were borne out, but as is nearly always the situation, the short-term rather than the long-term considerations carried very much more weight at the time. In particular weapons-oriented analysts, who stressed the short-term gains in combination with other political and strategic factors to urge the development and deployment of MIRV, easily won the day over arms control advocates who emphasized the long-term negative implications of the new technology.

MIRV IN THE BIGGER PICTURE IN THE 1960S

Each of the two major aspects of MIRV—as ABM penetrator and as force muliplier—and the various subcases of each of these entered into the decisionmaking process about whether to proceed with the system or not. The weight and role of these factors, however, depended strongly on the nature of larger and more general issues decisionmakers had to contend with at the time. A brief review of three such more general issues and how they and the MIRV question interacted follows.

Every Secretary of Defense finds himself involved in a many dimensional struggle with the services and, usually, the service secretaries and chiefs, over the nature and scope of national defense. Typically the principal focus of this struggle is the argument over how much money should be spent and by whom. On the one hand the secretary's job is to provide the best defense the nation can afford, and, as a member of the President's staff, he has to allow himself and his plans to be influenced by the overall national situation, especially including internal and external economic factors. The services and their leaders, on the other hand, being in effect insulated from these broader concerns by the office of the Secretary of Defense and the man himself, inevitably—and many would say properly—take a more parochial view. The result is that the secretary in effect fixes a more or less firm budget ceiling, and the services tend to resist it. There is typically a difference of several tens of percentage points between what the services believe is really needed and what the President and the Secretary of Defense believe can be afforded. To be sure, by the time the service secretaries prune their staff and command requests, the difference may only be 10 percent when the budget is finally honed and polished, but the sum of all the additional claims made during the course of the year—direct to the Congress, through the press, or through other third parties, as well as directly— amounts to many tens of billions of dollars. In the course of the resulting debates, specific technical or strategic arguments in support of all sorts of systems appear, and more general cries such as "don't put the budget ahead of survival" are made.[9]

During the 1960s, decisions on whether to develop or deploy MIRV interacted strongly with such general arguments over the total budget. Two aspects of MIRV played particularly important roles in this interaction. First MIRV itself was relatively inexpensive. Most of the development work had been subsumed under other projects, either as part of our space program or as part of ABRES, a program whose purpose was the general improvement of all aspects of reentry systems, including ABM penetration, as well as accuracy and other technical features. Moreover the most expensive part of the MIRV program in the deployment phase was the nuclear explosives, and these—as always since the end of World War II—were paid for out of the Atomic Energy Commission budget, not the Department of Defense budget.

Second, and even more important, the prospective deployment of MIRV provided powerful arguments against two other exceptionally expensive prospective programs: the deployment of a U.S. ABM system and a great, perhaps severalfold, expansion of the U.S. long-range strategic force. After a brief initial uncertainty, Secretary of Defense Robert McNamara and his colleagues reaffirmed the conclusion reached at the end of the Eisenhower administration that an ABM system was impractical and unnecessary. Probably the simplest argument against an ABM—any ABM whether for general area defense or point defense—was that it could be readily defeated by saturation and that MIRV provided a cost-effective way of achieving this. As pointed out above, such an idea was a major stimulus in the minds of MIRV's technical promoters, and it became an important part of the Secretary of Defense's anti-ABM arguments as well.[10]

The prospective development and deployment of MIRV played a similar role in the argument over the size of the U.S. strategic forces. The Eisenhower administration legacy included a not-quite-definitive plan for a strategic force roughly the size of its present composition: about 1,000 land-based ICBMs, about forty-five Polaris submarines, and some hundreds of long-range bombers. The air force especially disagreed with these tentative planning figures and urged numbers of ICBMs varying from 3,000 to as many as 10,000. In Novermber 1960, for example, General Curtis LeMay of air force headquarters revealed that current plans envisioned the construction of about 2,600 missiles, adding "it is possible that more than . . . 3,000 will be required, particularly should the Soviets choose to build large numbers of hardened missiles individually dispersed." A few months later, General Thomas Power, commander of the Strategic Air Command (SAC), reportedly suggested the 10,000 figure directly to Secretary McNamara and President Kennedy.[11] Such huge forces would have cost far more than Kennedy intended to spend on strategic offense. MIRV provided an alternative and much less expensive means of expanding the number of warheads (although of course not the megatons) in the force. In sum, then, MIRV was not only cheap in itself, but the prospect of its deployment became a powerful element in the arguments the secretary and his staff marshalled at budget time against two other extremely expensive programs.

Another dimension of the continuing argument in the Department of Defense over "how much is enough" involves the question of how much capability to destory and kill is needed, cost considerations aside. The Secretary almost always finds himself defending a moderate position (in effect supporting a force of about the size that has by that time accumulated) against an attack by those who always want more, no matter how much is in hand. The arguments can be cast in relatively specific terms involving number and size of targets, or in more general terms of overall balance, or in still more general terms of promoting or avoiding an arms race, but the result is always the same. In this particular case the promotion of MIRV supported the relatively moderate position (as measured from within the defense establishment) because it provided a means of expanding the number of targets the force could bring under fire without simultaneously expanding the total megatonnage in the force, as a single increase in the number of rockets would have done and as some hawks would have much preferred. Indeed MIRV was a very controversial issue within the air force for several years in the mid-1960s, for just this reason. The so-called big bomb people—and there were many—insisted that MIRVing cost too much in terms of lost explosive power per individual warhead and argued strongly against it. They correctly foresaw that the development of MIRV would swing the argument against a desired increase in total megatonnage.[12]

A third dimension of the ongoing argument and debate in the Department of Defense involves the interpretation of technical and other intelligence. The data are never complete, and even if they were, projection of future Soviet capabilities would still be uncertain. As a result there are always wide differences in the projections of Soviet forces. These differences are not only those presented in the much discussed footnotes to the National Intelligence Estimates (NIEs). Often the most extreme views are held by persons of high rank, position, or influence who may have direct access to the Secretary of Defense or the President or their immediate staffs, but who are not among those actually responsible for preparing the NIE and its footnotes. The secretary must cope with all of these views, not just the official estimates. His task is complicated, moreover, by the fact that these more extreme but less professional interpretations frequently find their way into congressional testimony and even the press.

The matter of Soviet ABMs provides one of the most flagrant examples of this process. A number of analysts, among them "think tank" staff with access to raw intelligence data, argued forcefully but incorrectly during the 1960s that several Soviet antiaircraft systems either were ABMs or had substantial present or prospective potential as ABMs, and otherwise greatly exaggerated the significance of the Soviet work in this field. They used these exaggerations to support further arguments for across-the-board defense increases, as well as for more specific increases and an acceleration of strategic defense, offense, and civil defense programs. As in the fiscal and forcesize debates, the secretary again found himself arguing as a moderate in support of more realistic intelligence analyses (again as measured in defense establishment terms). The prospective deployment of MIRV did not, of course, enter directly into such arguments, but it did render them less important and thereby helped to defuse this particular issue.

Responding to congressional pressure, Director of Defense Research and Engineering John Foster summarized the official Defense Department position on MIRV in 1969. Reflecting concern for many of the issues just discussed, Foster justified the system both in terms of its relation to the potential Soviet ABM threat and to the arms race in general. "We need a more reliable method of delivering our deception devices and our warheads," he told the House Committee on Foreign Affairs.

> We need to be able, essentially, to spread them out in space so that one Soviet defensive nuclear burst cannot destroy several American warheads or a whole cloud of decoys.
>
> We did not want to solve this problem by adding to the number of American offensive missile launchers. Increased numbers of missile launchers could, of course, insure penetration of Soviet city defenses. This solution to the problem, however, would carry an unacceptably high risk of stimulating the arms race, which we would like to avoid if at all possible.
>
> Instead, we turned to Minuteman and Polaris improvements that could give us ... MIRV ....

Technologies of this type had been considered since about 1960 for the purpose of increasing the target coverage of a single missile. However, the United States' decision to deploy this technology was based primarily upon our requirement to penetrate Soviet defenses, not upon its multiple-target capability.[13]

Conspicuously but characteristically absent in Foster's statement was any mention of cost or budget considerations.

OPPOSITION TO MIRV

The few objections to MIRV that did arise in the mid-1960s were based largely on the situation presented in Case 4. That is, when the exchange ratio—defined as the number of an opponent's missiles destroyed by the optimum firing of each MIRV missile—inevitably rose well above unity, a serious instability in the strategic relationship would result. MIRV opponents viewed this instability in two forms: a short-term crisis instability and a long-term chronically unstable condition, sometimes referred to as an arms race instability. They believed that a crisis instability would arise simply and directly because a high exchange ratio placed a high premium on striking first. The long-term arms race instability would derive from the former; that is, when it finally became evident that a crisis instability was not far off, a determined and possibly frantic effort to eliminate that potentiality would ensue.

Until 1966 the services and the Defense Department conducted the MIRV programs at a higher than normal level of secrecy. Early opposition thus remained centered almost entirely within the executive branch, mainly in the Arms Control and Disarmament Agency (ACDA) where the principal responsibility for long-range strategic and arms control considerations lay. Two ACDA officials, Herbert Scoville and George Rathjens, warned as early as 1964 about the destabilizing effect MIRV could have on the Soviet-American strategic balance. A few individuals in the office of the Secretary of Defense—in particular Martin McGuire and Ivan Selin of systems analysis and Morton Halperin of international security affairs—had parallel views, but their internal effort to achieve at least a six-month delay in MIRV testing failed to gain support.[14] Even this meager opposition was muted because, in general, the groups and individuals most concerned about this aspect of the MIRV problem also opposed the ABM and, as pointed out above, the potential deployment of MIRV was one of the most effective arguments against a defensive missile system.

Secretary of Defense McNamara removed much of the veil of secrecy surrounding MIRV in an interview published in 1966.[15] From that time on, opposition to MIRV became more widespread, but it remained thin and confused largely because of the greater attention paid to the ABM and the way the MIRV and ABM programs interacted both politically and analytically. As Greenwood says, "the MIRV controversy was never more than a minor skirmish compared to the bitter fight over ABM."[16] Individual public arms control advocates expressed interest in the problem, as did their longstanding organizations—the Federation of American Scientists (FAS), Pugwash, and the Council for a Liveable World. A few new ad hoc anti-MIRV coalitions were also created. In addition several of the senators most deeply involved in the nearly successful attempt to stop ABM became simultaneously concerned about MIRV. Senators John Sherman Cooper (R-Kentucky) and Philip Hart (D-Michigan) appealed directly to President Johnson in 1968 for a postponement of MIRV testing. The following year another group of legislators, led by Senator Edward Brooke (R-Massachusetts), called for hearings to review the MIRV programs, and Brooke himself introduced Senate Resolution 211 to suspend testing. None of these efforts to rally further anti-MIRV feeling succeeded, however.[17]

Much of the opposition to MIRV in the late 1960s focused on the possibility that some type of ban on the system might be included in the Strategic Arms Limitation Talks (SALT) initiated by the United States and Soviet Union in 1969. Originally, many hoped that the U.S. MIRV program could be halted short of actual deployment by including it in SALT I. But, as usual, arguments supporting such an action were met with counterarguments in which MIRV, in effect, played the role of a "bargaining chip." In addition some argued that the best way, perhaps the only way, to stop MIRV was to ban its testing, since MIRV testing was in principle observable and verifiable, whereas MIRV deployment was not. But others argued that MIRV testing had already gone too far for that, and still others held that, in any event, clandestine tests could carry development far enough to make deployment feasible. In the end the United States did put forth some proposals in the early phases of the SALT negotiations that would have banned or significantly inhibited MIRV, but these were accompanied by requirements for forms of inspection and verification which went well beyond anything that might have been acceptable to the Soviets (or for that matter to the U.S. military).[18]

The net result was that practical, usually technical, short-term considerations dominated the MIRV decisionmaking process—as, for example, in connection with the preparation of the budget—and the long-range, more political, and broadly strategic considerations had little impact. In

1964, McNamara authorized development of MIRV for both the Minuteman and the Poseidon. He authorized, and Congress approved, deployments the following year as part of the FY 1967 budget and the first MIRVs were actually in place on Minuteman in 1970 and Poseidon in 1971. Soviet MIRV deployments followed those of the United States by a few years. According to the best public sources, the Soviets first flight-tested MIRVs in mid-1973 and deployed them on their land-based missiles in 1975.[19]

The SALT II negotiations, completed in Spring 1979, did succeed in drawing up some limitations on MIRVs (although the resulting agreement remains unratified). Those limitations, however, are both complicated and a very far cry from the complete ban the original opponents of MIRV had wanted. In brief, the treaty limits the total number of MIRVed missiles on each side to 1,200, of which no more than 820 can be land-based missiles. In addition the number of RVs on any land-based missile of a type existing at the time of ratification can never exceed the maximum that by then had been flight-tested for each case. The one new land-based missile permitted each side by SALT II can be fitted with no more than ten warheads. In the case of submarine launched missiles, the maximum in effect is fourteen RVs, the number that long since had been deployed on the U.S. Poseidon.[20]

THE CURRENT SITUATION

By 1977-1978 and the beginning of the Carter administration, it had become widely apparent that the predictions of the MIRV opponents either had or were about to come true. In fact the discussion within the national security community, broadly defined, became centered in large measure on *when* rather than *whether* the worst would happen. The exchange ratio in the single missile sense already had passed unity, and most defense analysts believed this would occur for the overall land-based force sometime in the late 1980s. Experts of course could be much less confident about accuracies than they could about force size and loadings. But nearly everyone who had reasonably good access to the pertinent data regarded the figures—and more importantly the trends in the figures when combined with best guesses about the outcome of the coupled accuracy-yield-hardness calculations—as ominous for the strategic future.[21]

After much debate and deliberation, the Carter administration in 1979 decided to go ahead with the land mobile MX ICBM as the principal solution to the vulnerability problem. The MX (missile experimental) is planned to be a giant rocket (approximately 190,000 pounds compared to Minuteman III's 78,000 pounds) equipped with ten very accurate Mark 12A MIRV warheads. Officials considered a myriad of new basing modes for the MX, but settled finally on the so-called baseline or race track multiple protective shelter (MPS) system. The MX/MPS system in essence involves the construction of many more hardened vertical silos than there are missiles and the frequent secretive movement of the missiles from shelter to shelter.[22]

Objections to this and similar schemes came from a variety of sources, however. Many strategists noted that, in the absence of formal limits, the Soviets could defeat any MPS system simply by adding to the number of MIRV warheads (the so-called fractionation of payload). Arms control specialists were generally pessimistic about the inherent conflict between verifiability and countability on the one hand and the fundamental reliance on deception as a means of assuring survival on the other. Environmentalists opposed MX/MPS because of the large tracts of land that would be removed from the public and private domain. Finally, budget conscious critics pointed out that the price tag of such a system invariably skyrockets as new versions are introduced with more realistic design and cost estimates.[23] For all these reasons, some leading weapons analysts and designers sought and proposed alternatives to land-based ICBMs, including new ideas for air-based and sea-based systems.

In addition to these plans for new basing modes, some individuals revived a long-standing hypothetical solution to the problem of Minuteman vulnerability, one that allows virtually no room for error. This old idea, originally spoken of in the 1960s as "launch on warning" (LOW) has been rechristened "launch under attack" (LUA) by its supporters. A number of arms control advocates and other moderates in the strategic debate endorse it as a preferred alternative to MX/MPS and its relatives.[24] They foresee the operation of a near perfect command, control and communication (C^3) system which could determine if any opponent had launched a preemptive strike and respond by launching U.S. ICBMs before the incoming missiles arrived. Those who continue to oppose it point out that the ultimate decision for this LOW or LUA would have to be left either to computers or a "preprogrammed President," and that it would create nightmarish technical problems if and when other nuclear states put it into practice.[25]

The instability created by MIRV thus remains a critical concern for the Reagan administration, made even more immediate by revised intelligence estimates of SS-18 and SS-19 capability and accuracy. Consensus continues that this is a grave strategic problem, but current defense analysts are again at odds over how best to remedy it. Despite a fresh review of the issue by a special panel chaired by University of California physicist Charles Townes, and the Scowcroft commission, the best the Reagan team has offered to date are very general, stopgap measures.[26]

On October 2, 1981, the President presented his strategic package. He recommended heavy investment in C^3 and strategic defense, a multibillion dollar bomber revitalization program (to deploy first the B-1B and in the 1990s the Advanced Technology or Stealth bomber), and improvements in the sea-based force. Finally, he rejected the MX/MPS race track basing mode and called for deployment of a limited number of the new missiles in converted Minuteman or Titan silos. As described by Secretary of Defense Caspar Weinberger, this is only a "temporary measure, offering protection for a few years." The administration promises a final decision on MX basing by 1984.[27]

In summary, as of 1982, the views and predictions of those who in the 1960s focused on the long-term implications of MIRV have turned out to be particularly prescient. The system unquestionably created more and worse problems in the long run that it solved in the short run. One prominent ex-government official belatedly recognized this in 1974. "I would say in retrospect," then Secretary of State Henry Kissinger commented, "that I wish I had thought through the implications of a MIRVed world more thoughtfully in 1969 and 1970 than I did."[28] Moreover, the solutions to the new group of problems posed by MIRV now appear to be equally complex and perplexing; that is, they threaten to create more and worse problems in the long run than the immediate ones they are intended to solve.

NOTES

1. Ted Greenwood, *Making the MIRV: A Study of Defense Decision Making* (Cambridge, Mass.: Harvard University Press, 1975), p. xiii.
2. See Ted Greenwood, "Reconnaissance, Surveillance and Arms Control," Adelphi Paper no. 88 (London: International Institute for Strategic Studies, 1972).
3. U.S., Congress, Senate, Subcommittee of the Committee on Appropriations, *Department of Defense Appropriations for FY1969*, 90th Cong., 2d sess., 1968, p. 2110.
4. Fred Payne, "A Discussion of Nike-Zeus Decision," Speech at Brookings Institution, Washington, D.C., Oct. 1, 1964, as quoted in Edward Randolph Jayne II, *The ABM Debate: Strategic Defense and National Security* (Cambridge, Mass.: Harvard University Press, 1969), p. 42.
5. U.S., Congress, Senate, Committee on Foreign Relations, *Nuclear Test Ban Treaty*, 88th Cong., 1st sess., 1963, p. 423.
6. Stockholm International Peace and Research Institute, *The Origins of MIRV*, Research Report no. 9 (August 1973), p. 17.
7. Greenwood identifies five "quasi-independent inventors" of MIRV; there also were others. See Greewood, *Making the MIRV*, pp. 28-37.

8. U.S., Congress, Senate, Preparedness Investigating Subcommittee of the Committee on Armed Services, *Status of U.S. Strategic Power*, 90th Cong., 2d sess., pt. 1, 1968, p. 106.

9. For a general discussion and historical overview of how the defense budgetary process works, see Lawrence J. Korb, "The Secretary of Defense and the Joint Chiefs of Staff: The Budgetary Process," in Sam C. Sarkesian, ed., *The Military-Industrial Complex: A Reassessment* (Beverly Hills, Ca.: Sage, 1972), pp. 301-340.

10. "Secretary McNamara Comments on Risks of Anti-Ballistic-Missile System," *Department of State Bulletin*, (March 20, 1967), 56:442; Robert S. McNamara, *The Essence of Security: Reflections in Office* (New York: Harper & Row, 1968), pp. 62-66, 163-166; Alain C. Enthoven and K. Wayne Smith, *How Much is Enough? Shaping the Defense Program, 1961-1969* (New York: Harper & Row, 1961), chap. 5.

11. LeMay to General Thomas Power, Nov. 25, 1960, Mixed Files, Air Force Space and Missiles Systems Office (SAMSO), Los Angeles, Ca.; Enthoven and Smith, *How Much is Enough?*, p. 195; Jerome H. Kahan, *Security in the Nuclear Age: Developing U.S. Strategic Arms Policy* (Washington, D.C.: Brookings Institution, 1975), p. 88.

12. Among the most prominent "big bomb" air force officers were Generals Curtis LeMay and John McConnell. See Greenwood, *Making the MIRV*, p. 37-38.

13. U.S., Congress, House, Subcommittee on National Security Policy and Scientific Developments of the Committee on Foreign Affairs, *Diplomatic and Strategic Impact of Multiple Warhead Missiles*, 91st Cong., 1st sess., 1969, pp. 241-252, quote on p. 243. See also Senate Subcommittee on Arms Control, International Law and Organization of the Committee on Foreign Relations, *ABM, MIRV, SALT, and the Nuclear Arms Race*, 91st Cong., 2d sess., 1970, 424-524.

14. Greenwood, *Making the MIRV*, pp. 113, 124-126.

15. Richard B. Stolley, "Defense Fantasy Now Come True: In An Exclusive Interview, Secretary McNamara Explains in Full the Logic Behind the ABM System," *Life*, vol. 63 (Sept. 29, 1967), pp. 28A-28C.

16. Greenwood, *Making the MIRV*, p. 118.

17. Ibid., pp. 126-135. In addition, congressional opposition to MIRV was remarkable for its bipartisan nature. Together with those mentioned, Senators Clifford Case (R-New Jersey) and Edward Kennedy (D-Massachusetts) also played major roles.

18. John Newhouse, *Cold Dawn: The Story of SALT* (New York: Holt, Rinehart and Winston, 1973), pp. 123-124, 129-130, 173-174, 176-190; Alton Frye, "U.S. Decision Making for SALT," in Mason Willrich and John B. Rhinelander, eds., *SALT: The Moscow Agreements and Beyond* (New York: Free Press, 1974), pp. 78-87.

19. International Institute for Strategic Studies (IISS), *Strategic Survey 1975* (London, 1976), pp. 55, 121; IISS, *The Military Balance 1976-1977* (London, 1976), p. 3. See also Bruce M. Russett and Bruce G. Blair, *Progress in Arms Control?* (San Francisco: W.H. Freeman & Co., 1979), p. 114.

20. U.S. Department of State, Bureau of Public Affairs, *SALT II Agreement, Vienna, June 18, 1979*, Selected Docs. no. 12A (Washington, D.C., 1979), pp. 7, 17-18.

21. There were some public counterarguments. See, for example, Bernard T. Feld and Kosta Tsipis, "Land-Based Intercontinental Ballistic Missiles," *Scientific American*, 241 (Novermber 1979), pp. 51-61. William H. Kincade, "Missile Vulnerability Reconsidered," *Arms Control Today*, 11 (May 1981) and Colin S. Gray, *The Future of Land-Based Missile Forces*, Aldelphi Paper no. 140 (London, Winter 1977) outline the strategic "vulnerability" problem from different perspectives and provide good bibliographies on the subject.

22. Desmond Ball, "The MX Basing Decision," *Survival*, 22 (1980), pp. 58-65.

23. See, for example, Colin S. Gray, "The MX Debate," *Survival*, 20 (1978), pp. 105-112; Bruce A. Smith, "MX Proposed Legislation Stirs Strong Opposition," *Aviation Week and Space Technology*, 111 (Dec. 31, 1979), pp. 22-23; Richard Burt, "Fears on MX Found in Nevada and Utah," *New York Times*, Jan. 17, 1980; Christopher E. Paine, "MX: The Public Works Project of the 1980s," *Bulletin of the Atomic Scientists*, 36 (February 1980), pp. 12-16; Donald M. Snow, "MX: Maginot Line of the 1980s," *Bulletin of the Atomic Scientists*, 36 (November 1980), pp. 21-25; Herbert Scoville, Jr., *MX: Prescription for Disaster* (Cambridge, Mass.: Harvard University Press, 1981).

24. For a recent advocacy of a LUA system, see Richard L. Garwin, "Launch Under Attack to Redress Minuteman Vulnerability?" *International Security*, 4 (Winter 1979), pp. 117-139. For a general discussion of the major nuclear powers' C^3 machinery and how it works, see Vice Admiral G. E. Miller, "Existing Systems of Command and Control," in Franklyn Griffiths and John C. Polanyi, eds., *The Dangers of Nuclear War: A Pugwash Symposium* (Toronto, 1979), pp. 50-66.

25. Herbert York, *Race to Oblivion: A Participant's View of the Arms Race* (New York: Simon and Schuster, 1970), pp. 184-187, 232-234.

26. The Office of Technology Assessment (OTA) has also recently completed a book-length report on the MX. OTA, *MX Missile Basing* (Washington, D.C.: Government Printing Office, September 1981).

27. Ronald L. Tammen, "The Reagan Strategic Program," *Arms Control Today*, 11 (December 1981), pp. 1-3.

28. Press release, Dec. 3, 1974, quoted in Duncan L. Clarke, *Politics of Arms Control: The Role and Effectiveness of the U.S. Arms Control and Disarmament Agency* (New York: Free Press, 1979), p. 98; William C. Potter, "Coping with MIRV in a MAD World," *Journal of Conflict Resolution*, 22 (1978), p. 610.

Index

A

A-bomb, 329, 331, 333, 334, 337, 339, 341, 349, 350, 481, 483, 485, 486, 487, 491, 493, 496, 505, 506

Able-Star, 410, 411, 412, 590 (used with Thor booster rocket), 581, 593

Acheson, Dean, 306, 322, 329, 336, 338, 339, 340, 341, 342, 343, 344, 348, 349, 447 (Secretary of State), 469, 480, 489, 490, 493, 494, 495, 496, 497, 498, 499, 500, 504, 506

Advanced Airborne Nation0ltal Command Post (AABNCP), 56, 57, 90, 91

Aerospace Corporation, 408, 412, 415, 587, 593, 599

Afghanistan, 234, 293, 337, 428

Agnew, Harold, 398, 578 (Director, Los Alamos)

Agreement on Prevention of Nuclear War (APNW), 193, 195, 200, 282, 284, 291, 292

Airborne Brigade, 173rd, 151, 218

Air Force Satellite Communications System (AFSATCOM), 56, 90

Alvarez, Luis, 330, 483

ancien regime, 157, 158, 235, 236

Angola, 20, 29, 200, 201, 204, 234, 291, 292, 293, 297, 337, 428

Anti-armor weapons, 121, 172 (ATGMs)

Anti-ballistic missile (ABM), 11, 14, 37, 55, 59, 88, 380, 381, 382, 383, 384, 388 (ABM Treaty), 394, 395, (ABM Treaty), 396 (ABM Treaty), 397, 398, 399, 400, 401, 412, 413, 414, 415, 418, 419, 421, 422, 423, 546, 547, 548, 549, 552, 553, 554, 556, 561, 565 (ABM Treaty), 570, 571 (ABM Treaty), 572 (ABM Treaty), 573, 574 (ABM Treaty), 575, 577, 578, 579, 580, 581, 582, 583, 584, 593, 594, 596, 597, 603, 604, 606, 609, 610, 612

Anti-submarine warfare (ASW), 53, 85, 382, 388, 389, 552, 560, 561

anti-tank weapon, 121, 173 (TOW)

Arabs, 172, 175 (Six Day War, 1967), 179, 184 (1973), 194 (1973), 195 (1973),

196 (1973), 197, 198, 199, 205, 252,
257 (Six Day War, 1967), 262, 265
(1973), 270, 271, 282 (1973), 284
(1973), 285 (1973), 286 (1973), 287
(1973), 288 (1973), 289, 290, 291, 299
Ardennes, 177, 178, 260, 261
Argentina, 221, 224, 234, 237, 238, 239, 241,
242, 321, 326, 337, 342, 344, 349, 352
Arms Control and Disarmament Agency
(ACDA), 245, 250, 355, 363, 423, 612
Aron, Raymond, 20, 31
Association of Southeast Asian Nations
(ASEAN), 374, 539
Assured Destruction, 49, 50, 51, 55, 57, 77,
79, 80, 81, 83, 84, 87, 91
Atlas, 45, 69 (D missile)
Atlas-Agena system, 411, 591
Atlee, Clement, 317, 318, 462 (British
Labour Prime Minister), 463
Atomic Energy Commission, 248, 249, 250,
251, 327, 328, 329, 330, 331, 332, 338,
339, 341, 344, 346, 348, 360, 362, 363,
364, 365, 419, 479, 480, 481, 482, 483,
485, 490, 492, 493, 496, 499, 500, 502,
505, 506, 606
"Atoms for Peace", 229, 245, 330, 354
Austin, Warren, 312, 455
Australia, 236, 243, 341, 352
Austria, 171, 174, 176, 179, 189 (1955), 251
(Austro-Prussian War), 255, 258,
262, 277 (Austrian State Treaty,
1955)
Ayatollah Khomeni, the, 211, 307

B

BRT-50, 126, 173
BTR-60, 126, 173
Bacher, Robert, 346, 502
Ball, George, 369, 371, 533, 536
Ballistic antimissile boost interceptor
(BAMBI), 410, 412, 590, 593
Baruch Plan, 244, 346, 353, 503
Basic Principles Agreement (1972) (BPA),
191, 192, 193 (limitations of), 194,
195, 200, 279, 281, 282 (limitations
of), 283, 284, 285, 291, 292
Batista, 211, 306
Berkeley group, 330, 331, 332 (Seaborg),
340, 482, 483, 484 (Seaborg), 496
Berlin, 136, 164, 189 (Berlin crisis), 191
(detente), 243, 279 (detente), 302
(Berlin crisis), 365, 368, 441 (Berlin
crisis, 1948), 527, 531
Bethe, Hans, 332, 341, 346, 485, 496, 502
Blackett, P.M.S., 389, 563
Blitzkrieg, 115, 116 (classic), 118, 120, 123,
126, 162, 164 (classic German), 165,
167, 170, 171, 173, 174, 176, 184, 251,
254, 257, 270
Bloch, Ivan, 167, 248
Boeing 747, 56, 90
Bolshevism, 279, 293, 403, 431
Bomber, 11 (B-1), 16 (B-1), 42 (B-52), 49
(Reconnaissance-strike bomber), 55
(B-52), 67 (B-52), 77
(Reconnaissance-strike bomber,
RS-70), 87 (B-52), 426 (B-1 Band
Stealth), 618 (B-1 Band Stealth)
Bradley, General Omar, 333, 343, 485, 498
Brazil, 221, 232, 237, 238, 239, 240, 241,
243, 247, 249, 252, 321, 334, 342, 344,
345, 347, 349, 352, 357, 361, 366
Brennan, Donald, 241, 350, 395, 572
Brezhnev, Leonid, 191, 192 (B.D.), 193, 195,
197, 198, 200, 279, 280 (Brezhnev
Doctrine), 281, 282, 285, 286, 287,
288, 289, 291, 409
Brodie, Bernard, 3, 4, 5, 7 (*The Absolute
Weapon*), 23, 24, 27, 28, 32, 33, 37,
38, 39, 43, 45, 51, 53, 54, 60, 63, 68
(*Strategy in the Missile Age*), 96
(*Strategy in the Missile Age*), 313
(*War and Politics*), 364, 457 (*War
and Politics*)
Brooke, Edward, 423, 613 (Senator)
Brooks, Harvey, 338, 399, 560, 578
Brown, General George, 17, 27
Brown, Harold, 53, 54, 56, 83 (Secretary of
Defense), 85, 89, 133, 182, 387, 558
Brzezinski, Zbigniew, 53, 54, 84, 85
Buchan, Alastair, 372, 536
Buckley, Oliver, 333, 485
Bull, Hedley, 2
Bundy, McGeorge, 372, 536
Burckhardt, Jacob, 166, 246

C

Cahn, Anne, 399, 580
Cambodia, 221, 321, 373, 374, 537, 538
Canada, 228, 229, 247, 252, 328, 330, 358, 366

Carter, Jimmy, 31, 49, 52, 53, 54, 59, 83, 84, 85, 96, 148, 213, 230, 247, 248, 251, 252, 254, 331, 358, 359, 363, 364, 367, 369, 424, 616

Castro, Fidel, 363, 524

Center for International and Strategic Affairs (CISA), 3

Central Intelligence Agency (CIA), 11, 17, 47, 74, 305, 310, 387 (Defense-CIA-sponsored study by Thompson-Ramo-Wooldridge), 445, 453, 559 (Defense-CIA-sponsored study by Thompson-Ramo-Wooldridge)

Chamberlain, Neville, 135, 186

China (Peoples Republic), 72, 79, 196, 252 (intervention in Korean War), 282, 331, 340, 367, 369, 423, 429, 430, 442 (feared Soviet conquest of Manchuria and North China, 1947), 444, 448, 451, 456 (Civil War), 457 (Civil War), 459, 460, 461, 462, 463, 464, 465, 467, 468, 472, 479, 496, 524, 526, 532, 535, 548, 550, 551, 552, 555, 568, 569, 570, 573, 582

Churchill, Winston, 134, 143, 144, 177, 184, 202, 205, 218, 228, 259, 316, 328, 360, 521

Civil defense, 25, 42, 53, 85

Civil Rights movement, 370, 535

Civil War, American, 175, 257, 372, 536

Clark, General Mark, 314, 315, 323, 458, 459, 470

Clausewitz, Carl von, 12, 18 (*On War*), 27, 28, 29, 33, 34, 44, 45, 46, 47, 53, 54, 112, 158, 164, 165, 166, 168, 172 (*On War*), 185, 187, 243, 244, 245, 246, 248, 252 (*On War*), 253, 272, 274, 275, 276, 277, 293, 398, 401, 402, 403, 431

Clifford, Clark, 372, 537

Cold War, 189, 190, 181, 228, 229, 233, 234, 242, 253, 254, 277, 278, 315, 328, 329, 330, 332, 336, 337, 338, 339, 340, 346, 347, 350, 366, 369, 379, 459, 479, 481, 494, 503, 505, 545

Command Control and Communication (C³), 31, 38, 49, 55, 56, 57, 59, 87, 90, 91, 424, 617

Command Data Buffer System (CDBS), 54, 89

Committee on the Present Danger, 11, 13, 16, 19, 21, 27, 28, 43, 44

Communist Party of the Soviet Union (CPSU), 18, 30, 133, 182

Conant, James, 331, 332, 333, 484 ("Uncle Jim", president of Harvard), 485, 486, 487, 496

Connally, Tom, 310, 452 (Senator)

Cooper, John Sherman, 395 (Senator), 423, 577 (Senator), 613

Craig, Gorden, 174, 255

Crimean War, 153, 222

Cuba, 19 (Cuban missile crisis and JFK), 31 (Cuban missile crisis and JFK), 133, 151 (missile crisis), 153 (missile crisis), 179, 181, 220 (missile crisis), 211 (Batista), 223 (missile crisis), 238, 245 (missile crisis), 261, 262, 278 (missile crisis), 298 (missile crisis), 306 (Batista), 344, 355 (missile crisis), 363, 366 (missile crisis), 524, 528 (missile crisis) 532

Czechoslovakia, 177, 179, 260, 262, 302, 441

EC-121 (spy plane), 57, 92

D

D-Day, 113, 159

Damage Limitation, 50, 51, 77, 79, 80

Dean, Gordon, 329 (AEC Commissioner), 330, 337, 480 (AEC Commissioner), 482, 491

Defense Satellite Communications System (DSCS), 56, 90

detente, 190, 191, 192, 193, 196, 197, 205, 231, 234, 235, 279, 280, 282, 283, 285, 286, 287, 290, 298, 299, 332, 338, 339, 340.

Deutsch, Karl, 258, 375

Diem, President, 368, 531 (South Vietnam)

DoD Directive, 57, 91 (DoDD. 5100.30)

Drell, Sidney, 397, 576

Dulles, John Foster, 14, 22, 42, 43, 66, 68, 364, 526

E

Egypt, 172 (Arab-Israeli War, 1973), 181 (1973), 184, 196 (1973), 197, 198 (1973), 199 (1973), 221, 224, 238, 252 (Arab-Israeli War, 1973), 265 (1973),

270, 271, 285 (1973), 286, 287 (1973), 288 (1973), 289 (1973), 290 (1973), 322, 325, 344

Eisenhower, Dwight D., 14, 22, 41, 42, 45, 66, 69, 72, 113, 159, 204, 229, 230, 243, 244, 245, 246, 247, 248, 253, 291, 313, 314, 330, 331, 352, 353, 354, 356, 358, 359, 360, 364, 367, 368, 369, 400, 412, 419, 457, 458, 524, 527, 531, 580, 594, 606, 607

Ellsberg, Daniel, 69, 71, 72, 73

Energy Research and Development Agency (ERDA), 360, 364

Engels, Friedrich, 248, 401, 403

Enhanced radiation bomb, 26

Enthoven, Alain, 23, 69, 73, 601

Ethiopia, 428

Euratom, 335

European Security Conference, 423

F

Fall, Bernard, 535

Fermi, Enrico, 486, 487, 488

Festinger, Leon, 519, 521, 522, 530

Finland, 170 (WW II), 171 (WW II), 172, 173, 174

Fleet Satellite Communications System (FLTSATCOM), 90

Fletcher Committee, 93, 94

Ford, Gerald, 29, 213, 331, 357, 358, 363

Foreign Affairs, 46, 522, 523

Forward Defense, 176

Foster, John, 567 (Director, Defense Research and Engineering), 569, 576, 593, 601, 610

France, 166 (WW II), 174 (WW II), 184 (WW II), 185 (WW II), 212, 213, (WW II), 234, 235, 239, 240, 243, 244, 251, 255, 258, 260, 306, 328, 329, 330, 331, 340, 342, 345, 358, 366, 374, 518 (Vietnam), 523

Franco-German War, 1870, 268

Frederick the Great, 238

French Revolution, 234, 235 (the Convention and the levee en masse), 236, 245

Frunze, Marshal, 430

Fuchs, Klaus, 491, 506

Fulbright, William J., 456 (Senator), 534 (Chairman, Senate Foreign Relations Committee), 535, 576

G

Gallois, Pierrs, 341, 342, 354, 374

Garthoff, Raymond, 46

General Advisory Committee, 480, 481, 482, 495, 486, 487, 489, 491, 492, 503

Germany, 49 (WW II), 164 (WW II), 167 (WW II), 174 (WW II), 197 (WW II), 198 (WWII), 201 (WW II), 202 (WW II), 212 (WW II), 213 (WW II), 251 (WW II), 254, 257, 259, 260, 261, 262, 263, 266, 267, 270, 316, 328, 330, 332, 335, 340, 354 (West G.), 356 (WW II), 357 (WW II), 358 (WW II), 366

Gilbert, Felix, 247

Gilpatric, Roswell J., 73

Goldberger, Marvin, 576

Gordon, Kermit, 80 (Director of the Bureau of the Budget)

Gray, Colin S., 33, 39, 47, 48, 50, 52, 53

Great Britain, 13, 42, 159 (British Army), 179 (WW II), 184 (WW II), 185 (WW II), 186 (WW II), 197 (WW II), 198 (WW II), 200 (British Elite), 201 (WW II), 202 (WW II), 212 (WW II), 213 (WW II), 239, 241, 255, 261, 263, 271, 328, 342, 354, 366, 367, 523

Grechko, Marshal A.A., 406, 424, 428

Greece, 306, 330, 524, 529, 531

Greene, Graham, 517 (*The Quiet American*)

Greenwood, Ted, 586

Gromyko, Andrei, 286

Guatemala, 524

Guderian, General Heinz, 257

Gulf of Tonkin Resolution, 532, 534

H

H-bomb, 95, 97, 444, 479, 481, 482, 483, 484, 485, 487, 488, 489, 490, 491, 492, 493, 494, 495, 496, 497, 498, 499, 500, 501, 502, 503, 504, 505, 506

Halperin, Morton, 578, 612

Hardinge, Sir Charles, 179

Hart, Phillip, 577 (Senator), 613

Hilsman, Roger, 529 (director, Bureau of Intelligence and Research, Dept. of State)

Hiroshima, 40, 63, 252, 313, 317, 365, 366, 483, 484, 486, 489, 599

Hitch, Charles, 69

Hitler, Adolf, 183 (British leaders), 184, 198, 201, 202, 262, 266, 337

Holaday, William, 594 (Defense Director, Guided Missiles)

Horn of Africa, The, 291

Hound Dog (air-to-surface missile), 87

Howard, Michael, 240, 241, 255

Humphrey, Hubert, 356

Hungary, 297

Huntington, Samuel P., 84, 529, 530

I

India, 321, 332, 333, 334, 342, 343, 344, 345, 349, 357, 359, 360, 361, 366, 463

Indonesia, 306

Inskip, Sir Thomas, 200 (British Minister for Coordination of Defense)

Intercontinental Ballistic Missile (ICBM), 11, 14, 15, 16, 21, 41, 59, 69, 74, 75, 84, 85, 87, 88, 90, 96, 505, 550, 555 (at Malmstrom Air Force Base, Montana and Grand Forks, North Dakota), 556, 557 (Soviet SS-9), 558 (Soviet SS-9), 559, 560, 561, 563, 563, 564, 565, 584, 585, 590, 594, 596, 599, 603, 607, 616, 617

International Atomic Energy Agency (IAEA), 333, 334, 335, 336, 355, 357

Iran, 190 (hostage crisis), 306 (Shah), 318 (hostage crisis), 320 (hostage crisis), 344, 352, 473, 524

Iraq, 326, 344, 428

Ireland, 355 (Irish Resolutions)

Iron Curtain, 335

Israel, 252 (Arab-Israeli War, 1973), 257 (Six Day War, 1967), 262, 265 (1973), 270, 271, 282 (1973), 284 (1973), 286, 287 (1973), 288 (1973), 289 (1973), 290 (1973), 291 (1973), 299 (1973), 307, 311, 321, 322, 342, 344, 347, 349, 351, 539

Italy, 366

J

Jackson, Henry, 574 (Senator)

Japan, 45, 179 (American-Japanese conflict), 180, 184 (Pearl Harbor), 185, 196, 223, 251 (Pearl Harbor), 259, 260, 266, 270, 327, 328, 338, 340, 349, 352, 357, 366, 375, 467, 484, 539

Johnson, Senator Edwin, 492

Johnson, Louis, 493 (Secretary of Defense), 497, 498, 499, 500, 501, 505, 506

Johnson, Lyndon Baines, 80, 331, 335, 344, 355, 363, 528, 531, 533, 534, 535, 536, 537, 547, 553, 584, 613

Joint Committee on Atomic Energy, 354, 360, 363, 365, 480

Jomini, Antoine-Henri, 244, 245, 248

K

KGB, 48

Kahn, Herman, 529

K'ai Shek, Chiang, 444, 456

Kaufman, William W., 1, 69, 71, 77, 401, 526

Keegan, Major General George, 17

Kennan, George F., 399, 446, 485, 495, 503, 522 ("X" article), 523

Kennedy, John F., 22, 23, 29, 31, 42, 61, 68, 69, 70, 75, 298, 331, 354, 355, 359, 363, 368, 369, 524, 525, 527, 528, 529, 530, 531, 536, 537, 607

Kennedy, Robert F., 529, 536

Kent, General Glenn A., 77, 78, 80

Killian, James, 580

King, Martin Luther, Jr., 535 (opposition to Vietnam War)

Kissinger, Henry, 1, 49, 82, 280, 281, 282, 283, 285, 286, 287, 288, 289, 291, 297, 356, 357, 358, 369, 526, 618

Knorr, Klaus, 1, 234

Korea (South), 330, 342, 347, 351, 537, 539

Korean War, 22, 66, 159, 160, 175, 196, 251 (Inchon landing), 252, 297, 400, 411, 412, 413, 414, 440, 441, 442, 443, 445, 446, 447, 448, 450, 451, 452, 453, 454, 455, 465, 457, 458, 459, 460, 461, 464, 456, 466, 467, 468, 469 (Manchuria), 471, 472 (U.S.-South Korean alliance), 473, 524, 526, 531, 533

Kosygin, Alexsei, 547 (Premier)
Kruschev, Nikita, 75, 298, 409, 529, 535, 598
Krylov, N.I. (Marchall of the Soviet Union), 407
Kuhn, Thomas, 519, 520, 522, 525, 526, 530, 531, 538

L

Laird, Melvin A., 89, 560, 561, 566, 568
Lambeth, Benjamin, 26, 28, 31, 46, 61
Laos, 531, 538
Lappland (Finnish defense of), 167, 170, 171, 172
Lawrence, Ernest O., 479, 482, 483, 484, 490, 496
Lebanon, 306, 524, 532
LeBaron, Robert, 506 (chairman, Military Liaison Committee)
Lebow, Richard Ned, 223
Legvold, Robert, 292
LeMay, General Curtis, 607
Lenin, Vladimir, 41, 44, 401, 403, 431
Liberty (USS), 92
Libya, 316, 322, 349, 428
Liddell-Hart, Basil, 158, 159
Lilienthal, David, 482, 483, 485, 489, 491, 493, 494, 496, 497, 498, 499, 500, 501, 506
Lippman, Walter, 523
Lockheed Missiles and Space Company, 587, 593, 599
Loper, Brigadeer General Hubert, 506
Los Alamos, 482, 483, 491, 578
Low Altitude Defense System (LoADS), 567, 583, 585
Lukeman, Lt. Col. Robert P., 72

M

MX Missile, 16, 33, 84, 563, 567, 611 (MX/ MPS system), 616 (MX/MPS system), 618 (MX/MPS system)
MacArthur, Douglas, 159, 160, 162 (Inchon landing), 251, 447, 464, 466, 467, 468, 469, 526
MacMahon Act, 248, 360

Machiavelli, 196, 273, 286 (Machiavellian Strategy), 398
Maginot Line, 8, 11, 176, 258
Mahon, George, 394, 571 (Chairman, House Appropriations Committee)
Malaya, 358, 366, 529
Malinovskii, Marshal Rodion, 281, 409 (Defense Minister)
Manhattan Project, 39, 63, 228, 329, 329, 331, 481, 484
Mark 12A (warhead), 53, 55, 84, 87, 88
Marx, Karl, 276, 403
Marxism, 25, 27, 41, 43, 44, 235, 238, 276, 278, 279, 339 (Marxist dictatorships), 343, 403 (Bolsheviks), 405 (*Marxism-Leninism on War and Army*), 407
Masao, Okonagi, 319, 464, 465
Mayaguez, 139, 194
McCarthy, Joseph, 304, 444 (Senator)
McGovern, George, 370, 534 (Senator, 1972 election)
McGuire, Martin, 422, 612
McMahon, Brian (Senator), 480, 483, 484, 490, 492, 493, 495, 498, 502, 505
McNamara, Robert S., 14, 15, 18, 22, 23, 28, 43, 44, 45, 46, 47, 48, 49, 50, 51, 52, 60, 61, 68, 69, 70, 71, 73, 75, 76, 77, 78, 79, 80, 81, 82, 224, 325, 372, 379, 380, 381, 382, 384, 419, 420, 434, 424, 536, 545, 547, 548, 549, 554, 606, 607, 612, 614
McNaughton, John D., 151, 218 (Assistant Secretary of Defense), 372, 536
"Military Strategy and Force Posture Review", 53, 85
Minh, Ho Chi, 371, 535
Minuteman missile, 9, 11, 13, 16, 44, 48, 50, 52, 53, 54, 55, 56, 58, 60, 69, 70, 77, 78, 80, 84, 87, 88 (III ICBM), 89 (III), 93, 94 (II, 1A), 143, 202, 203, 385, 386, 387, 389, 390, 391, 392, 393, 396, 397, 398, 400, 412, 416, 421, 424, 425, 426, 555, 558, 559, 562, 563, 564, 565, 566, 567, 568, 569, 570, 574, 575, 577, 581, 582, 593 (Minuteman III), 601, 614, 617, 618
Missile Site Radar (MSR), 381, 389, 390, 391, 393, 395, 401, 548, 549, 563, 564, 565, 566, 567, 569, 583
MOLINK (satellite hotline), 56, 90
Moltke, Helmuth, 171, 176, 251, 257

MOONRISE, 302, 442

Multiple Independently-Targetable
    Reentry Vehicle (MIRV), 9, 10, 13,
    14, 55, 60, 87, 88, 96, 380, 383, 386,
    386, 407, 408, 409, 410, 411, 412, 413,
    415, 416, 417, 418, 419, 420, 421, 422,
    423, 424, 425, 426, 546, 552, 558, 559,
    586, 587, 588, 589, 590, 591, 593, 595,
    598, 599, 600, 601, 603, 604, 606, 607,
    608, 609, 610, 611, 612, 613, 614, 616,
    617, 618

Multiple Reentry Vehicle (MRV), 413, 414,
    595, 596

Mussolini, Benito, 182, 267

Mutual Assured Destruction (MAD), 25,
    38, 40, 60, 288, 421

N

NSC 68 (National Security Council), 41,
    65, 307, 308, 311, 312, 448, 450, 454,
    455

Nagasaki, 25, 39, 40, 63, 172, 215, 252, 312,
    313, 331, 332, 334, 335, 415, 484, 489,
    599

Napoleon, 157, 159, 160, 161, 162, 163, 164,
    165, 166, 167, 234, 236, 238
    (Napoleonic commanders), 239
    (Napoleonic warfare), 240
    (Napoleonic Wars), 242, 243, 244,
    246, 247, 248

National Command Authorities (NCA), 52,
    57, 83, 90, 91

National Security Decision Memorandum
    (NSDM), 52, 53, 54, 82 (no. 242), 83,
    84, 85

National Security Study Memorandum
    (NSSM), 52, 82 (no. 169)

National Strategic Target List (NSTL),
    45, 46, 72, 73

New York Times, 21, 33, 306, 368, 447, 532

Nicaragua, 211, 306

Nike-X, 380, 382, 402, 546, 549, 584

Nike-Zeux, 380, 381, 402, 413, 546, 548,
    584, 594

Nitze, Paul, 13, 19, 20, 28, 29, 41, 44, 47, 65,
    340, 341, 495, 496

Nixon, Richard, 10, 14, 18, 28, 52, 82, 191,
    192, 193, 195, 197, 198, 200, 205, 230,
    232, 245, 246, 250, 279, 280, 281, 282,
    285, 288, 289, 291, 292, 299, 331, 335,

356, 357, 363, 370, 373, 384, 392, 401,
    534, 537, 554, 568, 584

Nordic Balance, 123, 171

Normandy, 127, 174, 181, 265

North Atlantic Treaty Organization, 48,
    76, 123, 124, 128, 136, 171, 175, 176,
    180, 190, 211, 221, 223, 244, 264, 286,
    287, 288, 290, 293, 294, 304, 306
    (France, Portugal, Turkey, Greece),
    322, 324, 354, 418, 419, 421, 423, 427,
    430, 444

Norway, 123, 124, 171, 172, 178, 180, 184,
    185, 251, 261, 265, 270, 271

Nuclear Non-proliferation Treaty (NPT),
    230, 231, 232, 233, 239, 240, 245, 246,
    250, 252, 332, 333, 334, 336, 345, 347,
    355, 357, 363, 366

Nuclear Regulatory Commission (NRC),
    248, 250, 251, 360, 364

Nuclear Suppliers Conference, 247, 358

Nuclear Targeting Policy Review (NTAR),
    54, 57, 86, 90

O

October War, 198, 199, 205, 221, 271, 288,
    290, 281, 287, 299, 322

Office of Management and Budget (OMB),
    60, 96

Office of Technology Assessment, 31, 50

Okinawa, 367, 530

O'Neill Report, 397, 576

Operation Joe (the Soviet bomb), 329, 339,
    480, 494 ("Joe I")

"Operation Solarium" (Eisenhower), 42, 66

Operations Research Society of America
    (ORSA), 398, 399, 577, 578, 580

Oppenheimer, J. Robert, 329, 331, 332, 333,
    334, 335, 336, 340, 341, 343, 344, 346,
    347, 398, 480, 481, 483, 484, 485, 486,
    487, 489, 490, 494, 496, 498, 499, 502,
    503, 504, 577

Osgood, Robert, 275, 284, 364, 365, 401,
    413, 526, 527

P

Packard, David, 57, 91, 387, 392, 559, 567

Pakistan, 221, 223, 224, 236, 238, 318, 321,
    326, 342, 344, 345, 463

Palestinian Liberation Organization
(PLO), 211, 212, 306, 313
Patton, George, 112, 159
Pearl Harbor, 134, 150, 171, 177, 178, 182,
184 (and Japanese invasion), 217,
251, 259, 260, 261, 266, 270, 302, 441
Pentagon Papers, The, 373, 537
Perimenter Acquisition Radar (PAR), 381,
394, 401, 548, 549, 571, 583
Perry, William, 56, 57, 88, 90
Phillipines, 236, 312, 318, 334, 366, 455
(threat from Huks), 463, 529
Pike, Sumner, 330, 337, 482, 491
Pipes, Richard, 6, 8, 11, 12, 13, 17, 18, 19
Planning, Programming and Budgeting
System (PPBS), 43, 69
Poland, 119, 134, 166 (WW II), 185 (WW II)
Polanyi, Michael, 149, 215
Polaris, 8, 11 (submarine), 43, 44, 58, 69
(A1 missile), 70, 93, 388, 413, 419,
561, 594, 595 (Polaris A-3), 596
(Polaris A-3), 607
Polaris-Poseidon missile, 9, 13, 388, 560, 561
Portugal, 211, 221, 306, 322
Poseidon missile, 55, 87, 88 (Poseidon C-3),
412, 424, 593, 614, 615
Post Boost Control System (PBCS), 408,
411, 415, 587, 589, 591, 592, 599
Presidential Directive (PD), 31, 49 (PD 59),
54, 85 (PD 18), 86, 288, 421 (PD 59)
Presidential Review Memorandum 10
(PRM-10), 53, 54, 84, 85
Prussia, 163, 164, 171, 174, 176, 242 (and
conscription), 243, 251 (Austro-
Prussian War), 254, 258
Pueblo, (USS), 57, 92

R

Rabi, Isador I., 329, 334, 335, 480 (Nobel
physicist), 486, 487, 488
Rand Corporation, 2, 3, 7, 8, 9, 11, 24, 32,
38, 42, 43, 45, 51, 58, 67, 69, 71, 73,
93, 278, 280, 405, 407, 408, 410, 415,
590, 599
Rathjens, George, 422, 612
Reagan, Ronald, 248, 249, 250, 251, 359,
361, 363, 364, 425, 618
Reinsurance Treaty, 148, 212

Rhee, Syngman, 310, 311, 314, 322, 323,
324, 453 (President, South Korea),
458, 459, 469, 470, 471
Rhodesia, 200, 202, 203, 204, 214, 291, 294,
295, 297, 311
Rickover, Admiral, 247, 358
Ridgeway, General Matthew, 115, 162, 318,
464
Roosevelt, Franklin Deleanor, 135, 177,
185, 228, 259, 328
Roosevelt, Theodore, 131, 132, 133, 179,
180, 181
Rostow, Walter, 366, 529
Rowe, Hartley, 333, 485
Rowen, Henry, 43, 46, 69, 73
Rumania, 252, 366
Rumsfeld, Donald, 398, 577 (Counselor to
the President)
Rusk, Dean, 48, 76, 369, 532 (Secretary of
State)
Russell, Bertrand, 259, 375

S

Sadat, Anwar, 195, 196, 197, 198, 285 (and
Soviets, 1973), 286 (and Soviets),
287, 288, 289
"Safeguard", 10, 11, 14, 15, 385, 386, 387,
389, 390, 381, 382, 393, 394, 395, 396,
397, 398, 400, 401, 555, 557, 560, 563,
564, 565, 566, 567, 568, 569, 570, 571,
572, 573, 574, 575, 576, 577, 578, 579,
581, 582, 583
Sang, Chiang Taek, 314, 459 (Prime
Minister, South Korea)
Satellite Data System (SDS), 56, 90
Satellite and Missile Observation System
(SAMOS), 46, 74 (CIA satellites)
Scharnhorst, 163, 164, 165, 241, 242 (and
conscription), 243 (as officer in
Hanoverian army), 244, 245, 248
Schelling, Thomas C., 1, 138, 193, 282, 365,
411, 412, 528
Schlesinger, James R., 17, 18, 19, 20, 21,
26, 28, 31, 33, 52, 54, 56, 57, 82, 86,
88, 89, 90, 96, 389, 563
Sclieffen Plan, 175, 181, 182, 257
(Schleiffen Plan), 266, 267
Schroeder, Paul, 153, 222
Scoville, Herbert, 422, 612

Seaborg, Glenn, 332, 485
Selin, Ivan, 422, 612
"Sentinel", 10, 14, 381, 382, 383, 384, 385,
    394, 401, 548, 549, 551, 552, 553, 556,
    572, 583
Shaplen, Robert, 371, 535
Sherman, Admiral Forrest, 332, 469
Singer, J. David, 258, 375
Single Integrated Operational Plan
    (SIOP), 45, 46, 47, 52, 53, 54, 55, 56,
    57, 71, 72, 73, 83, 86 (SIOP-6), 87,
    88, 90
Sissi (raiding teams), 125, 126, 172, 173
Sloss, Leon, 54, 86
Slusser, Robert, 311, 454
Smith, Cyril, 333, 486
Smith, Gerard, 396, 574 (Ambassador, head
    of SALT delegation)
Smith, Rear Admiral Levering, 388, 560
    (director, Navy's Polaris-Poseidon
    program)
Smyth, Henry D., 330, 337, 349, 482, 491,
    506
Snyder, John, 339, 493 (Treasury Secretary)
Sokolovskii, Marshal V.D., 12, 18, 277, 404,
    411
Somoza, 211, 306
Souers, Admiral Sidney, 330, 482
South Africa, 221, 236, 321, 325, 342, 473
Southeast Asia Treaty Organization
    (SEATO), 369, 533
Soviet Military Strategy, 277, 281, 404, 410
Space and Missile Systems Office (SAMO),
    412, 415, 593, 599
Spartan missile, 10, 15, 381, 382, 383, 391,
    401, 548, 549, 551, 565, 583
Spencer, Herbert, 167, 248
Sprint, 381, 383, 391, 392, 548, 552, 564,
    565, 567, 568
Sputnik, 410, 413, 590 (Sputnik I), 594
    (Sputnik I)
Stalin, Josef, 30, 49, 172, 177, 179, 204, 251,
    259, 260, 262, 263, 275, 295, 297, 401,
    431
Strategic Air Command (SAC), 42, 67, 73,
    385, 388, 391, 420, 555 (bomber
    bases), 563, 567, 607
Strategic Arms Limitation Talks (SALT),
    240, 347, 348, 387, 393, 394, 396, 397,
    423, 424, 559, 572 (SALT I), 574
    (SALT I), 575, 613, 614, 615

Strategic Nuclear Delivery Vehicles
    (SNDV), 37, 45, 59, 72, 423
Strauss, Lewis, 328, 329, 330, 334, 337, 338,
    479, 481 (Admiral), 484, 486, 487,
    491, 492
Submarine-launched ballistic missile
    (SLBM), 47, 53, 55, 57, 59, 60, 69, 75,
    85 (Trident), 87, 88 (polaris B-3), 90,
    96, 387, 388, 389, 391, 560, 561, 562,
    563, 566
Suez Canal, 181, 265
Sweden, 123, 171 (WW II), 252, 366
Symington, Stuart, 398, 578 (Senator)
Syria, 184, 195, 197, 198, 221, 222, 270, 285,
    288 (1973), 289 (1973), 290 (1973),
    293, 321, 322, 428

T

Taiwan, 193, 229, 236, 242, 282, 304, 306,
    307, 313, 316, 330, 342, 351, 374, 444,
    447, 448, 456, 457 (Chinese
    Nationalists vs. Chinese Mainland),
    461, 539
Talenskii, General N., 278, 405
Taylor, General Maxwell, 43, 46, 69, 73,
    365, 367, 530 (Counterinsurgency
    committee)
Teller, Edward, 328, 329, 330, 331, 335,
    336, 341, 348, 398, 414, 479, 481, 482,
    483, 484, 488, 490, 496, 504, 578, 597,
    598
Tennessee Valley Authority, 331, 483
Thailand, 374, 538
Third World, 137, 190, 191, 279 (and
    superpower rivalry), 292, 293, 294,
    295, 296, 302, 325, 406, 426, 427, 428,
    429, 430, 442, 473
Thompson-Ramo-Woolridge's Space
    Technology Laboratories (TRW/
    STL), 387, 408, 412, 415, 559, 587,
    593, 599
Titan missile, 9, 13, 44, 69, 70, 387, 411,
    412, 559, 591 (Titan III), 593 (Titan
    III), 618
Todd, General W.E., 305, 446
Townes, Charles, 426, 618
Transtage, 411, 412, 591 (Ancestor of
    MIRV), 592, 593
Triad, 54, 85, 397, 575

Trident missile, 53, 84
Trinkl, Frank, 46, 73
Trotsky, Leon, 277, 403
Truman, Harry, 40, 64 (H-bomb), 228, 243,
  244, 253, 304, 306, 307, 311, 317, 327,
  328, 329, 336, 337, 338, 339, 341, 343,
  345, 346, 347, 348, 349, 352, 353, 362,
  363, 364, 368, 370, 444, 447, 448, 449,
  454, 462, 463, 479, 480, 482, 484, 490,
  491, 492, 493, 494, 496, 499, 500, 501,
  503, 504, 505, 506, 523, 524, 535
Tse-tung, Mao, 237, 342, 371, 535
Turkey, 211, 229, 306, 330, 363, 368, 524, 531
Tullock, Gordon, 258, 374
Tydings, Millard, 346, 347, 348, 502
  (Senator), 503, 505

U

Ulam, Stanislaw, 335, 348, 488, 504

V

Vance, Cyrus, 51, 54, 80, 85
Vandenburgh, Arthur, 370, 535
Vansittart, Robert, 142, 202
Vela satellite, 411, 591, 593
Vietnam War, 18, 19, 112, 128, 135, 136,
  137, 139, 151, 171, 192, 197, 235, 237,
  245, 253, 254, 283, 309, 325, 357, 358,
  359, 361, 365, 366, 367, 368, 369, 370,
  371, 372, 373, 374, 375, 384, 399, 401
Von Manstein, General Fritz, 175, 257

W

Waltz, Kenneth, 258, 374
War Powers Act, 373, 537
Warsaw Pact, 177, 223, 260, 324, 387, 418,
  419
Watkins, Arthur, 346, 502 (Senator)
Webb, James, 328, 479 (Under Secretary
  of State)
Weinberger, Caspar, 426, 618
Weisskopf, Victor, 346, 502
Wellington, Arthur Wellesley (Duke), 162,
  241
Wohlstetter, Albert, 8, 9, 11, 12, 42, 67,
  241, 350, 398, 399, 577, 578
Wohlstetter, Roberta, 177, 259
Wolfe, Thomas, 291, 424
World War I, 112, 115, 141, 148, 159, 159,
  162, 167, 173, 181, 182, 198, 199, 212,
  247, 254, 266, 267, 296, 324, 418, 471
World War II, 15, 23, 24, 30, 37, 49, 122,
  113, 116, 157, 159, 164, 167, 174, 181,
  182, 189, 219, 228, 234, 247, 248, 255,
  266, 267, 277, 285, 286, 287, 301, 302,
  303, 304, 319, 321, 324, 328, 329, 330,
  337, 360, 362, 416, 418, 420, 440, 441,
  443, 444, 471, 481, 482, 491, 523

Y

Yemen, South, 234, 293, 334, 428
Yom Kippur War, 1973, 183, 187, 268, 274
York, Herbert, 347, 504

Z

Zuckert, Eugene, 58, 93

About the Editors

Bernard Brodie was Professor of Political Science at UCLA until his death in 1978. His pioneering studies of world politics and military policy in the nuclear age received international recognition and established him as a founder of modern strategic theory. His books include *The Absolute Weapon* (1946), *Strategy in the Missile Age* (1959), *Escalation and the Nuclear Option* (1966), and *War on Politics* (1973).

Michael D. Intriligator is Professor of Economics and Political Science at UCLA, where he is also Director of the Center for International and Strategic Affairs. He is the author of *Strategy in a Missile War: Targets and Rates of Fire* (1967) and co-editor of *Strategies for Managing Nuclear Proliferation—Economic and Political Issues* (1983). His current research focuses on nuclear proliferation, arms races, and conflict theory.

Roman Kolkowicz is Professor of Political Science at UCLA, where he served as the founding Director of the Center for International and Strategic Affairs from 1975 to 1982. He is the author of *The Soviet Military and the Communist Party* (1967) and *The Soviet Union and Arms Control: A Superpower Dilemma* (1970). His current research focuses on Soviet strategic and foreign policy; Soviet civil-military relations; and the role and influence of defense intellectuals, scientists, and bureaucrats in national security decisionmaking.

Other Titles in the Studies in International and Strategic Affairs Series of the Center for International and Strategic Affairs, University of California, Los Angeles:

Published:

William Potter (ed.), *Verification and SALT: The Challenge of Strategic Deception* (Westview, 1980).
Bennett Ramberg, *Destruction of Nuclear Energy Facilities in War: The Problem and Implications* (Lexington Books, 1980).
Paul Jabber, *Not by War Alone: The Politics of Arms Control in the Middle East* (University of California Press, 1981).
Roman Kolkowicz and Andrzej Korbonski (eds.), *Soldiers, Peasants, and Bureaucrats: Civil-Military Relations in Communist and Modernizing Societies* (George Allen & Unwin, 1982).
William Potter, *Nuclear Power and Nonproliferation: An Interdisciplinary Perspective* (Oelgeschlager, Gunn & Hain, 1982).
Stephen L. Spiegel (ed.), *The Middle East and the Western Alliance* (George Allen & Unwin, 1982).

Forthcoming:

R.D. Tschirgi, *The Politics of Indecision: Origins and Implications of American Involvement with the Palestine Problem* (Praeger).
Jiri Valenta and William Potter (eds.) *Soviet Decisionmaking for National Security* (Allen and Unwin).
Dagobert L. Britto and Michael D. Intriligator (eds.), *Strategies for Managing the Proliferation of Nuclear Weapons* (Lexington Press).